MW00650238

# SISTERS OR STRANGERS?
# IMMIGRANT, ETHNIC, AND RACIALIZED WOMEN IN
# CANADIAN HISTORY

Spanning two hundred years of history from the nineteenth century to the 1990s, *Sisters or Strangers?* explores the complex lives of immigrant, ethnic, and racialized women in Canada. The volume deals with a cross-section of peoples – including Japanese, Chinese, Black, Aboriginal, Irish, Finnish, Ukrainian, Jewish, Mennonite, Armenian, and South Asian Hindu women – and diverse groups of women, including white settlers, refugees, domestic servants, consumer activists, nurses, wives, and mothers.

The central themes of *Sisters or Strangers?* include discourses of race in the context of nation-building, encounters with the state and public institutions, symbolic and media representations of women, familial relations, domestic violence and racism, and analyses of history and memory. In different ways, the authors question whether the historical experience of women in Canada lends itself to representations of 'sisterhood,' or if the racial, class, or marginalized identity of immigrant and minority women made them 'strangers' in a country where privilege and opportunity reflect criteria of exclusion. Using a variety of theoretical approaches, this collaborative work reminds us that victimization and agency are never mutually exclusive, and encourages us to reflect critically on the categories of race, gender, and nation.

MARLENE EPP is an associate professor in the Department of History at Conrad Grebel University College, University of Waterloo.

FRANCA IACOVETTA is a professor in the Department of History at the University of Toronto.

FRANCES SWYRIPA is a professor in the Department of History and Classics at the University of Alberta.

STUDIES IN GENDER AND HISTORY

General Editors: Franca Iacovetta and Karen Dubinsky

# *Sisters or Strangers?*

## Immigrant, Ethnic, and Racialized Women in Canadian History

EDITED BY MARLENE EPP,
FRANCA IACOVETTA, FRANCES SWYRIPA

UNIVERSITY OF TORONTO PRESS
Toronto Buffalo London

© University of Toronto Press 2004
Toronto Buffalo London
Printed in the U.S.A.

Reprinted 2005, 2007, 2011, 2012

ISBN 0-8020-8836-8 (cloth)
ISBN 0-8020-8609-8 (paper)

**National Library of Canada Cataloguing in Publication**

Sisters or strangers : immigrant, ethnic and racialized women in Canadian
   history / edited by Marlene Epp, Franca Iacovetta, Frances Swyripa.

(Studies in gender and history)
ISBN 0-8020-8836-8 (bound).      ISBN 0-8020-8609-8 (pbk.)

1. Women immigrants – Canada – History.   2. Minority women –
Canada – History.   3. Race discrimination – Canada – History.   4. Sex
discrimination against women – Canada – History.   I. Epp, Marlene,
1958– .   II. Iacovetta, Franca, 1957– .   III. Swyripa, Frances, 1951– .
IV. Series.

HQ1453.S58 2003      305.48'8'00971      C2003-903299-X

University of Toronto Press acknowledges the financial assistance to its publishing
program of the Canada Council for the Arts and the Ontario Arts Council.

University of Toronto Press acknowledges the financial support for its publishing
activities of the Government of Canada through the Book Publishing Industry
Development Program (BPIDP).

This book has been published with the help of a grant from the Canadian Federation
for the Humanities and Social Sciences, through the Aid to Scholarly Publishing
Programme, using funds provided by the Social Sciences and Humanities Research
Council of Canada.

# Contents

# Acknowledgments

A collection of feminist essays in Canadian history that seeks to centre the lives of marginalized immigrant, ethnic, and racialized women could have been undertaken only as a collaborative project involving a diverse group of scholars. We differ, sometimes markedly so, in our theoretical approaches and methodologies, but we do share a feminist commitment to illuminating the histories of women who struggled to build lives in often hostile and oppressive contexts. Without the shared commitment and cooperative effort of all the authors in this volume, this project would never have gotten off the ground. As editors, we are thus delighted to thank, first and foremost, our contributors, for their ongoing engagement with a volume that took several years to complete. From the initial letters of invitation and inquiry, to the workshop at which we presented and responded to individual research papers, to the preparation of final drafts and the myriad of details involved in bringing the volume to publication, the authors were all enthusiastic about the project and responsive to revisions that would make the book truly a collaborative venture.

Financial and institutional support was provided by several sources. We thank the History Department at University of Toronto which offered space and funding to host a two-day workshop for authors in 1999. Seed money provided by the Division of Humanities, University of Toronto at Scarborough, was also much appreciated. We also gratefully acknowledge financial support for the workshop from the Robert F. Harney Collaborative Program in Ethnic and Pluralism Studies at University of Toronto, then directed by Wsevolod Isajiw and later by Jeffrey Reitz, and from the Centre of Excellence for Research on Immigration and Settlement. The Harney Program also hosted a public seminar where the book project was introduced and at which a sample of its contents was profiled. We thank our colleagues at the Multicultural History Society of Ontario for supporting our efforts to produce a volume that followed on the 1985 conference on Canadian immigrant women's history, initiated by the late Robert F. Harney, MHSO director, and Jean Burnet, editor of the book produced from that conference.

A number of people gave their support in a variety of ways – by being enthusiastic about the book, by suggesting possible contributors, by providing intellectual input at different stages of the project. These include Bettina Bradbury, Jean Burnet, Agnes Calliste, Enrico Carlson Cumbo, Karen Dubinsky, Kate McPherson, Nakanyike Musisi, Lillian Petroff, Ian Radforth, Jane Thompson, Jane Turrittin.

At University of Toronto Press, editor Gerry Hallowell (now retired) and former editor Laura Macleod spurred us forward with their initial interest and enthusiastic support. Len Husband, Barbara Tessman, and Pamela Erlichman were also enthusiastic about the book from the beginning and patiently moved it towards production despite various delays along the way. We thank the two anonymous readers whose comments helped us to refine the overall manuscript. We acknowledge a publication subsidy from the Social Science and Humanities Research Council's (SSHRC) Aid to Scholarly Publications Program. All but one essay in this collection is original work; we are delighted to be able to include Enakshi Dua's 'Racializing Imperial Canada: Indian Women and the Making of Ethnic Communities' and extend thanks to publisher Routledge, and Antoinette Burton, editor of *Gender, Sexuality and Colonial Modernities* (1999), for permission to reprint.

As editors, we each thank our home institutions for both material and less tangible support for such time-consuming research projects. Individually, the editors offer the following acknowledgments:

Marlene thanks Paul Born, sons Lucas and Michael, and her mother, Helen L. Epp, for numerous gestures of love and support. She also thanks her sister editors, who were never strangers in giving intellectual stimulation, constant encouragement, good humour, sound ideas, and generous counsel.

Franca thanks her co-author Valerie Korinek for her intellectual generosity and for her sisterly support when death and grieving interrupted the writing on more than one occasion. Thanks also to the usual gang of colleagues, friends, and comrades who have taught her that it is possible to engage in rigorous debate within contexts of mutual respect: Cynthia Wright, Karen Dubinsky, Mariana Valverde, Donna Gabaccia, the members of the Toronto Labour Studies Group, and, as always, Ian Radforth. While this book could have been written only in a collaborative fashion, as chief editor, Marlene Epp ensured that our good intentions and early efforts actually materialized into a final product. In a personal and professional capacity, we thank her for her patience and warmth, her organizational skills, and for the confident calmness with which she gets things done.

Frances thanks her colleagues in Canadian and women's history at the University of Alberta for the community they provide, both intellectually and socially. She also thanks her mother, Audrey Swyripa, for unstinting support over the years. Finally, her essay in this volume could not have been written without the generous cooperation of the churches forming the case studies, particularly the clergy and parishioners who gave of their time and expertise.

SISTERS OR STRANGERS?
IMMIGRANT, ETHNIC, AND RACIALIZED WOMEN IN
CANADIAN HISTORY

# Introduction

MARLENE EPP, FRANCA IACOVETTA, AND
FRANCES SWYRIPA

In 1862, Mary Hodges was one of sixty working-class British women who arrived in British Columbia aboard the ship *Tynemouth*. She was part of an imperial immigration agenda to 'whiten' and 'feminize' the West Coast by importing single women as domestic servants and potential brides. Not all the women acted according to plan, however. When she admitted to having 'been around the sexual block,' Mary Hodges soon found her moral respectability under question. Her Anglo character was also undermined once she elected to reveal her Jewish identity and changed her name to Esther Hurst. Over half a century later, as the only Chinese woman in a small Ontario town, Lin Tee was similarly marginal to the ethnic, racial, and gender norms of the community in which she lived. Public opposition and hostility reached a climax in a violent riot over her alleged insanity and her own accusations of abuse against her husband. Both women – Mary/ Esther and Lin – were strangers in the new land they would call home.[1] Their stories and struggles, and those of other newcomer women in Canada for the past two hundred years, are the subject of this book.

The essays featured here explore the multifaceted ways in which immigrant, ethnic, and racialized women have interacted with each other, their own menfolk and families, their ethnic or racial communities, other women, and the various groups from the dominant majority they encountered in Canadian society. Being female and members of a specific racial, ethnic, or class group affected what women could or could not do, how they saw themselves (and others), and how others in turn saw them. Some of the women in these pages chafed against race, ethnicity, and gender as confining; some were more accepting of their limitations; others embraced the special gendered privileges and obligations they attached to their racial or ethnic identity. Motivated by recent developments in feminist scholarship and critical race studies, this volume ventures beyond the female experience itself to analyze how expectations and limitations based on gender were part of that experience. Some of the essays thus address men's experiences as well, recognizing that gender is a relational category and that definitions of women's roles inevitably also said something about the gendered attributes of men.

In important respects this book is a response to an earlier collection of essays on the history of immigrant and ethnic women in Canada, *Looking into My Sister's Eyes: An Exploration in Women's History*, published in 1986 by the Multicultural History Society of Ontario (MHSO). Edited by sociologist Jean Burnet of York University, that award-winning and pioneering volume was a significant step in chronicling the life stories of immigrant women and positioning them as important actors in Canadian history. Little had previously been published on the history of immigrant and ethnic women in Canada, so *Looking into My Sister's Eyes* was widely used, particularly in university and college courses in women's history, immigration history, and women's studies. As contributors to that original project, we concur with the statement that appeared on the back cover of the book: 'A beginning has been made; much remains to be done.'[2] That book was very much an exploration, a beginning step in the process of uncovering and recovering the stories of individuals and groups often marginalized even within Canadian women's history. The book emphasized the contributions that women from diverse national backgrounds had made to their families and ethnic communities in a Canadian setting – 'contributing to ethnic cohesion,' 'creating and sustaining an ethnocultural heritage,' and helping to form 'community consciousness.' In a sense, the essays represented the coming together of a vibrant and enthusiastic scholarship in women's history with an optimistic national ethnic revivalism, or 'multiculturalism,' to use the policy term that most left and feminist scholars, and certainly the editors of this collection, find problematic and use advisedly.[3] The Ontario focus reflected the provincial mandate of the Multicultural History Society of Ontario. On a certain level, the essays also reflected the personal identities of their authors, for the most part professional historians, who chose to write about the ethnic or racial communities to which they themselves belonged or identified with. Although differences and tensions, particularly those related to class and politics, were acknowledged in many of the essays in *Looking into My Sister's Eyes*, the diverse groups of women examined in that collection were viewed largely as 'sisters' – if not in relation to each other, then certainly with respect to the emphasis that the contributors placed on the commonalities they shared, especially with regard to their marginal positions vis-à-vis the anglo- or francophone majority. Also present, and equally unarticulated, was the notion that they were 'sisters' by virtue of their shared sex and socially prescribed gender roles, whose combined impact cut across any differences rising from ethnicity or race.

That first volume also retained an overriding Eurocentrism and reflected a lack of women from racial minorities, a shortcoming that participants in the MHSO conference that led to the book had criticized. Even as the book's publication was being celebrated, then, the feminist cohesion and bonding that the title suggested were being questioned. Ironically, the title itself was proposed by a male historian of immigration, the late Robert Harney, who, as head of the MHSO, initiated the project and hosted the original conference. It had also been Harney's idea to hand over the editorship of the book to a senior female colleague, but given that there were few established women's historians of immigration – itself a reflection of the newness of the field of immigrant women's history – Jean Burnet, a prominent social scientist of immigrant and ethnic groups in Canada, graciously accepted the role of editor. She took on the historical project with her characteristic seriousness and commitment, and generously collaborated with the junior scholars who dominated the collection.

In the years since 1986 and the publication of *Looking into My Sister's Eyes*, the topic of immigrant, ethnic, and racialized women has attracted a great deal of attention, discussion, and debate, and in the process the boundaries of the field have been widened and in some respects redefined. Most scholars of immigrant and refugee women, including left feminist historians like ourselves, remain committed to writing about still neglected female subjects and to 'mainstreaming' the history of such women into both women's and gender history, and Canadian history generally. At the same time, scholars working within other subfields of social history, and in related social science sister disciplines, including most recently, critical race studies and postcolonial studies, have not only investigated the history of minority women from a range of vantage points, but have also pushed and pulled at the boundaries defining the field, introduced new theoretical insights and paradigms, and re-articulated often taken-for-granted categories such as nation, nation-building, and borders.[4] Within the fields of women's studies and feminist anthropology, greater attention is being paid to issues of transnationalism and exile in the lives, writings, and identities of female émigrés, as well as their experiences of gendered violence in the war-torn or colonized states from which they originated.[5] For their part, theoretically and historically minded political scientists and sociologists – and more recently historians as well – have explored the relationship between Canada's status as a white settler nation and its imagined self-identity as a 'nation of immigrants,' combined with its disreputable history as a colonizer of Aboriginal peoples.[6] In the process, hitherto separate areas of investigation, such as immigration and Aboriginal history, have been brought together. In addition, recent studies of women and citizenship have raised questions regarding how immigrant and refugee women develop national identities and begin to function as citizens in their adopted country, often against a tide of racism or hostility.[7] The burgeoning field of postcolonial theory has also presented new frameworks for re-evaluating the subjectivities of white women colonizers and their complicit roles as oppressors of indigenous and other non-white women.[8] This history has ongoing implications for the creation of racialized and hierarchical relationships between immigrant women of different ethnic and racial backgrounds.

All of these fresh insights, perspectives, and commentaries have demanded that we ask new questions only hinted at in the discussions around *Looking into My Sister's Eyes*. Can one really apply notions of sisterhood between women whose dominant racial or class experiences are antithetical? Were immigrant women, or women who were 'othered' by virtue of race, ethnicity, and minority status, truly sisters? Or did their historic experience make them feel more like strangers – with each other, within the nation, within their immigrant and ethnic communities, and sometimes even within their own homes? In questioning existing assumptions about both 'natives' and 'newcomers,' the field, far from simply shifting from one phase (that of recovery) to another, has widened and changed. But if there is at present no fully agreed-upon project – other than a continuing commitment to give attention to the marginal – there is plenty of new activity, excitement, and renewed and new debate. The application of novel theoretical questions to historical research was accompanied, in the 1990s, by close scrutiny of official policies and practices of multiculturalism. In particular, they were critiqued for masking racism and an ethnic 'vertical mosaic' that perpetuated exclusionary attitudes and behaviour towards individuals and groups who exist outside an essentialist image of a Canadian as not only white but also of English or French background.[9] Not coincidentally, the critique arose initially from race studies scholars who were also feminist. They did not accept that a multicultural policy meant to show some accommodation for white ethnic groups could even begin to accommodate people of colour, including migrant women and those from not white or so-called Third World countries.

In posing the question – *Sisters or Strangers?* – as its main title, this volume recognizes that historical experience is so often characterized by dichotomies: that cohesion could be offset by alienation, that common gender can exist alongside oppression, that women could be simultaneously attracted and repelled by their ethnicity, that women's contributions might be undermined by their exclusion or marginalization, and that victimization and agency are never mutually exclusive. One woman's experience of becoming 'Canadian' might be very different from another's, and as such, questions of *difference* are as important to understanding immigrant women's lives as are questions of *commonality*.

Provocatively asking 'Whose Canada Is It?,' a 2000 special issue of the women's studies journal *Atlantis* examined the extent to which women of immigrant and minority groups share in projects of nation-building. Its contributors questioned 'liberal notions of Canada as a place where everyone can be both "different" and "equal,"' and suggested that dominant definitions of 'Canada' and 'Canadian' are 'class-based, racist, sexist, and heterosexist.'[10] Women barred from genuine power and resources by virtue of racial or ethnic identity are indeed 'strangers' in a country where privilege and opportunity fall according to racist and sexist criteria.

At the same time as dichotomies often characterize situations, we know, too, that neither life experiences nor scholarly analysis can be fully comprehended by opposing dualisms; the situation is usually more complex, the answers less clearly a matter of black and white, right or wrong. The question mark at the end of our title is thus a carefully placed one, and it is meant to signify not only that it is sometimes difficult to decide whether immigrant women are insiders or outsiders vis-à-vis the host society women, but also that the relationship itself can change and differ depending on context. At the same time, the title and question mark reveal our agreement with African-American and other feminist critiques of a women's history that stressed the commonalities that women shared while disregarding or downplaying the divisions among them.[11]

In recent years, historians of Canada have debated whether the study and teaching of Canadian history has been 'killed' by new social histories that recognize regionalism, gender, class, race, ethnicity, and sexuality, for instance, as important identity variables in shaping the Canadian experience. Although some participants in the controversy have expressed serious (and, in our view, misplaced) fears that portrayals of the Canadian past that emphasize multiple identities and particular interests will undermine a 'national' story and thus national unity, others have grappled seriously with the broader issues of how to make Canadian history matter to Canadians. Take, for example, Jack Granatstein's *Who Killed Canadian History?*, a short and ill-conceived book that has provoked much spilt ink. At the core of the book was a muddled argument that lumped together historians and others who rarely see eye-to-eye on matters of multiculturalism; for example, Granatstein's analysis betrayed ignorance of the fact that liberal pluralists and antiracist feminists and activists on the left represent very different groups of people, who cannot be collapsed into one category.[12] Increasingly polarized positions are being put forward by scholars who cling to singular and fixed categories of interpretation versus those who more and more analyze people and events within complex frameworks in which people act with multidimensional interests.[13] At the same time, the responses to Granatstein, and others who share his position, that have come from various fields within social history have largely accepted rather than critiqued the taken-for-granted categories of nation, Canadian nation, and for that matter, Canadian history. Arguments were put forward that the 'history of sexuality is Canadian history,' and that 'labour history is Canadian history,' and that 'women's history is Canadian history,' and so forth.[14] We believe that the evolution of a national story – if such indeed exists – revolves very much around the interaction between and negotiation over privilege and power among people with varied backgrounds, histories, and experiences based on group identification. Despite an increasing diversity in ethnic, racial, and national origins in Canada, especially in the country's urban areas, the 'vertical mosaic' remains entrenched: white, Anglo-European, and male identities are privileged above all others. The histories of racism and sexism that the essays in this volume reveal do not simply represent misguided aberrations in the past. They are manifestations of a deliberate colonial project creating a settler society founded on notions of inequality that persist today, despite the successes held up by advocates of liberal pluralism.

It is perhaps not surprising that as migration historians, who recognize immigrants and migrants as transnational peoples, and national borders and boundaries as fluid, we are inclined to question and unpack such categories as *nation*. Scholars of international migration and gendered nationalism propose that nationalism is often a male construct imposed on women who may well prioritize other loyalties over state or nation.[15] For international migrants, dual identities that mentally situate individuals in both their pre- and postmigration settings distort national allegiances in other ways. As well, globalization – seen in initiatives like the European Union or the North American Free Trade Agreement – blurs the significance of national borders, and thus identities, when some individuals can move freely across national boundaries, while others, such as migrant workers from Third World countries, are closely monitored and controlled. Proposed changes to Canada's Immigration Act in response to the terrorist acts of 11 September 2001 in the United States are explicit evidence of how racialized concepts of nation and citizenship truly are.

That said, this volume portrays a diverse cross-section of the many peoples who have made Canada 'a nation of immigrants': included here is research on Japanese, Chinese, Black, African, Aboriginal, British, Irish, Finnish, Ukrainian, Italian, Jewish, Mennonite, Armenian, and South Asian Hindu women. Despite the diversity depicted here, we acknowledge that many groups are under-represented, or even absent, especially those that were part of immigrant waves in the latter decades of the twentieth century – women who identify themselves as Muslim or Central American, for instance. Some of the authors have chosen not to concentrate on a single ethnic or racial group – the traditional focus in much of Canadian immigration and ethnic history – and opted instead for a more comparative or cross-cultural thematic approach. Some of the women studied here are defined primarily by their occupation as single workers; others are identified mainly as wives and mothers; some are widows or children; and a few function solely as symbols.

Although migration and settlement are in some way part of each essay's story, immigration is conceptualized from a number of different angles. In some cases, female immigrants are the active subjects; in others, they are the targets of external social, political, or legal agenda; and in at least one of the studies, the main subjects experience the impact of immigration as indigenous people. In some of the essays, immigration is a recent personal experience, while in others migration is a phenomenon felt in the lives of second- and third-generation Canadians. As well, several of the essays place significant weight on the premigration lives of their subjects and thus are transnational both in orientation and in terms of their subjects' identity. Given the two-hundred-year time span covered in the book, the context for the essays necessarily represents different eras in Canadian settlement history. Some immigrants arrive in Canada as part of British colonial efforts to populate the land. Others, in particular First Nations women (and men), experience the ideological and practical impact of colonization efforts: they are the 'colonized.' Some are immigrant adventurers, seeking opportunities – economic or marital – away from their country of origin. Others are refugees, fleeing or forcibly removed from their homes because of war or persecution, who thus maintain a strong identification with family and home left behind even while settling into Canadian society.

The volume, then, offers illuminating insights into the differences between voluntary immigrants and involuntary refugees (or political exiles), between Aboriginal Canadians and recent newcomers (all of whom identify, to a greater or a lesser degree, with 'somewhere else'), and between ethnic or racial identities that individuals and groups willingly adopt and those that are imposed on them. The implications are great for how we as historians, and we as Canadians, understand the role of ethnicity and race in our history and society. Within these parameters, the essays show immigrant, ethnic, and racialized women interacting in one way or another with Canadian (or pre-Canadian) society. These interactions take the form of encounters with state institutions, such as the courts, and government immigration and settlement officials; they also include relations with employers, charitable and religious organizations, neighbourhoods, and resident Canadians. In addition, the essays show women acting within the context and priorities of their own particular ethnic or racial groups, as members of communities and families that are self-defined and inward-looking and often maintain ties with 'their people' outside Canada. These ethnic and racial communities, we would argue, also legitimately form part of a larger Canadian society whose parameters are sufficiently inclusive to accommodate them.

The topics investigated here demonstrate the many angles from which contemporary scholars are examining the lives of immigrant, ethnic, and racialized women. We have the more traditional, and still important, focus on the contributions immigrant women have made to their families and communities, both in acculturation to Canadian society and in the preservation of ethnic distinctiveness. Midge Ayukawa, for instance, describes the role of Japanese-Canadian mothers in preserving Japanese cultural traditions among their children as a way of developing a sense of self-esteem and even superiority in the face of discrimination. As such, she argues, pioneer Japanese women were less victims of history than dynamic actors who created resources that allowed subsequent generations to thrive in Canada. The passing on of cultural traditions across generations is also the theme of Isabel Kaprielian-Churchill's study of intermarriage among Armenians in Canada and the United States. She notes the high rate of exogamy among Armenians today and offers suggestions for how the community might prevent the reality of mixed marriages leading to a complete loss of ethnic distinctiveness. She also exposes, however, the unflattering consequences that insistence on ethnic purity can have, such as the use of the term *mongrel* to refer to children of mixed marriages.

Drawing on international theories of colonialism and gender that have become increasingly popular since the appearance of *Looking into My Sister's Eyes*, several essays problematize the issue of race by describing how ideals of 'whiteness' and of white womanhood shaped the work of colonizers and the experience of immigrants. Cecilia Morgan examines the discourse of colonial missionaries working among Aboriginal women and men in Upper Canada during the four decades from the 1820s to the 1850s; the efforts to Christianize First Nations women included making them into 'good housewives' and 'fit mothers' modelled on the gender, race, and class identities of British white women. She suggests that the colonization project involved both a transformation of gender identities among Native people and also a reinforcement of those identities – and notions of Christian civilization that accompanied them – among the colonizers themselves. From the opposite vantage point, but using similar theoretical models, Adele Perry looks at the immigration to British Columbia of white women in the mid-nineteenth century. She observes how their arrival both confirmed and challenged the racial mission of reinforcing 'whiteness' in colonial BC. Perry points out the centrality of immigration to an imperialist agenda that was both racialized and gendered, demonstrating that the importation of white women immigrants – themselves both 'colonized' and 'colonizer' – served particular nation-building interests. Using a similar approach applied to Hindu women migrants from India at the beginning of the twentieth century, Enakshi Dua analyzes how the racialization of the idea and practice of Canadian citizenship developed as a way of excluding certain groups of potential immigrants who were not white. According to Dua, the debate over admitting women from India – the Hindu Woman's Question as it came to be called – also illuminates the gendered and racialized manner in which ethnic communities developed.

A number of the essays demonstrate the complexity of women's lives as illustrated in the conflicts and tensions that immigrant women experienced inside their families, within their ethnic communities, and in their relations with society at large. Immigrant families were not just cohesive bulwarks against 'Canadian' society but also sites for marital discord and generational conflict. *Looking into My Sister's Eyes* shared with other projects of recovery a decided discomfort with exposing the less than flattering aspects of their subjects – such as domestic violence – which was understandable given that a critical part of the collective project was precisely to debunk harsh and unfair stereotypes of immigrants and foreigners. This was further complicated when scholars presented their work to the particular communities they studied and to which in some cases they belonged; it is clearly different to address a large ethnic audience about the resilience of working people than to talk about domestic violence or wartime rape. That a maturing field of study is allowing for greater willingness to make 'public' topics formerly too 'private' for exposure is acutely demonstrated in Lisa Mar's examination of a 1919 anti-Chinese riot in Lindsay, Ontario, which erupted in response to alleged domestic violence within a Chinese-Canadian family. In this case, the Chinese-Canadian woman who accused her husband of abuse, and who sought support from Anglo-Celtic women, was in turn accused by her family of being insane. Mar argues that conflicting gender relations within the community of Lindsay played as significant a role as the racial conflict. Similarly, two cases of spousal murder in late-nineteenth-century Ontario provide Barrington Walker with a setting in which to analyze both the dynamics of black patriarchal power and the much more elusive nature of black womanhood. Walker demonstrates how formal legal documents make visible in great detail the bodies of murdered black women, yet the women as individual subjectivities remain invisible because of both their race and gender, and thus their minority status is reinforced. Although this collection is primarily about the female gender, racialized stereotypes of men are prominent in the essays by Mar and Walker. In both studies, non-white men happen to be perpetrators of domestic violence, and the sources depicting them reveal a deeply entrenched mythology that associates male violence with black and Asian men.[16] As groups situated at the bottom of an ethnic and racial mosaic, blacks and Asians were treated and portrayed using cultural constructions that demeaned both men and women. Gender relations within the household are also explored by Gertrude Mianda in her essay about black African francophone women in Montreal and Toronto. Her study illustrates how the cultural patterns – in this case regarding male-female conjugal roles – of an immigrant group can be at odds with those of the host society.

While essays by Ayukawa, Mar, Walker, and Mianda focus on the household and family as a site of conflict, other new research has rejected the image of the immigrant woman relegated mainly to the private sphere of home. While some of the authors discuss women as workers, Julie Guard also examines the political activism of ethnic women. Indeed, members of the Housewives Consumers Association were marginalized for their leftist political ideals and actions as much as for their ethnic or immigrant status. Yet, as Guard argues, the efforts of ethnic women to organize protests against postwar price hikes in consumer goods were suppressed by a Cold War national security state that stereotyped both their femininity as 'sisters' and their ethnicity as 'strangers.' Among the Housewives themselves, 'Anglo' and 'ethnic' women worked together on a common cause, but the efforts of the latter were often overshadowed by the former.

Ester Reiter's study links family commitments and political ideals in her examination of summer camps for children established by Jewish women on the left. These camps countered the effects of exclusion from WASP recreational programs, but, as Reiter suggests, they also provided a setting in which mothers could pass on their socialist politics. It is important to note that the leftist women whose ideological activities Guard and Reiter describe were marginalized because of their politics not only by 'mainstream' Canadian society but also by the mainstream within their particular ethnic communities. And yet, being othered did not mean that the women led only bleak lives, that they did not sometimes dream, or laugh, or derive self-satisfaction from labours well done. As Reiter's essay shows, Jews on the left were persecuted by an unfriendly state and were also defiant mothers who insisted on teaching their children revolutionary principles; but they also were mothers who wanted their children to have fun, to sing, and to swim in the outdoors. The lives of these women are reminders that struggle and joy are not necessarily mutually exclusive categories.

Some women's uneasy relationship with the Canadian state and citizenry is depicted in studies of immigration policy and analyses of civil and criminal cases involving immigrants. These essays at the same time demonstrate that immigrant women were not just 'acted upon' by the people and institutions of the host society, but were dynamic actors in the ongoing evolution of the Canadian nation and its population. Lorna R. McLean and Marilyn Barber, in their examination of Irish immigrant domestics before the courts in nineteenth-century Ontario, suggest that judgments regarding the women's behaviour – especially drunkenness – revolved around gender and ethnic stereotypes held by employers and justice officials. Here again, the nuances and complexities are especially important, as the essay both criticizes damaging stereotypes of Irish women and addresses the difficult topic of their drunkenness and criminality.[17] Immigration policy was another venue in which immigrant women encountered the state, as Dua's essay on the Hindu Woman Question and Karen Flynn's essay on black immigrant nurses from the Caribbean show. A third and very different encounter with institutions of the state is explored by Franca Iacovetta and Valerie Korinek, who focus on reception work and social service activities among immigrant and refugee women in the post–Second World War era. The topic in question here is food, and Iacovetta and Korinek find that even while the peculiar eating customs of immigrants were celebrated as part of postwar pluralism, immigrant women were encouraged by experts to 'eat Canadian.' In their analysis, food is a signifier of difference between cultures, but eating and the gendered functions surrounding it also were a site of power negotiation and encounter in which 'immigrant' and 'host' cultures were both transformed.[18]

Immigrants, in particular, carve out their Canadian experience with ongoing mindfulness of their lives in another country and continent. Canadian historians of immigration have been reluctant to fully address the premigration lives of immigrants as formative of who they are and how they negotiate their lives in Canada. And even more so, how relationships with a 'homeland' and a past lived elsewhere influence individuals, families, and communities well into the postmigration generations. Through an examination of the food shortages and later abundance experienced by Mennonite refugees prior to and following their immigration to Canada after the Second World War, Marlene Epp seeks to understand the place of food in their postmigration memories and lives. She suggests that for Mennonite refugees, narratives of food and eating helped to organize their memories into pre- and postmigration settings of deprivation and abundance. In her examination of newspaper images, Varpu Lindström demonstrates the way in which media propaganda created an idealized Finnish-Canadian woman based on the activities of women in Finland during the Winter War against Russia in 1939–40. In this analysis, events in the 'homeland' had a significant impact on how a hitherto marginalized ethnic group was perceived by Anglo-Canadians and how Finnish-Canadian women were temporarily transformed into familiar 'sisters.' As well, Paula Draper's study of Jewish Holocaust survivors in Canada demonstrates in very poignant ways how successful postmigration lives can belie ongoing struggles with the premigration tragedy experienced by their families and community. Using Edmonton as her setting, Frances Swyripa links both the pre- and postmigration experiences in analyzing the role gendered images play in the sacred space of Canadian ethnic churches. She is especially interested in how female (and male) symbols are used to situate the Canadian ethnic group within the secular history of the homeland, Canada, and the local community. In Swyripa's study, as with Epp and Lindström, symbols and representations of ethnic culture are the means through which particular gendered images and experiences are formed.

Related to the particular subjects in this volume are new theoretical and methodological approaches. Many of the scholars are challenging traditionally held notions regarding the docility and singular allegiances of immigrant women. By utilizing integrative categories of gender, race, class, and sexuality, for instance, the authors are illuminating the multivaried behaviour and perspectives of immigrant women. By viewing women not just as immigrants or minorities or 'ethnics,' scholars have been increasingly able to offer insights into women in their identities as women, as workers, as sexual beings, and as individuals of a certain social class or skin colour. Nor are women only viewed as agents within their families and communities while marginalized victims vis-à-vis Canadian society. Rather, new analyses portray immigrant women as sometimes victims within their own communities and also significant actors in the mainstream of Canadian history. In fact, scholars of immigration, race, and ethnicity in Canada – including those writing about immigrant, ethnic, and racialized women – are challenging traditional notions of what constitutes 'the mainstream of Canadian history' (and Canadian women's history), with interpretive frameworks that integrate the hitherto 'marginalized other.' Recognizing that mythologies surrounding the origins of Canada as a nation are Eurocentric, and that colonial settlement depended on the displacement of indigenous peoples and the subjugation of other non-white immigrants, any attempt to think about women as a group must also address disparities based on race and class.

Representing a richness and diversity in theoretical approach, the essays in this volume bring postmodern, social constructionist, narrative, feminist, antiracist, materialist, and postcolonial perspectives to their research. All of these are valuable in the ongoing task of uncovering the stories of these women. While some of the studies utilize discourse analysis to explain the self-identity and imposed identity of immigrant women, others adopt a more narrative approach, linking together women's life stories as an analytical framework. Attention to white women's class, racial, and gender identity is accomplished largely through their view of, and oppression of, a racialized 'other.' This volume also includes an increased interdisciplinary approach that utilizes literature from anthropology, literary studies, and political science, for instance. Several of the essays take an explicitly retrospective look at history, utilizing sources of recollection and analyzing the manner in which memories shaped interpretation. The essays further reveal a breadth of source materials used to unearth and understand the experiences of immigrant and minority women. One of the most important contributions of social history has been the creative use of non-traditional sources to investigate the lives of the hitherto 'neglected' and 'ordinary' segments of the population. The essays here demonstrate a sophisticated use of multiple sources including: oral interviews, personal memoirs, newspapers, court records, visual images and artifacts, and the documents of a range of public and private institutions and organizations. While some of the texts are in English, others are 'foreign-language' sources. Also reflected are fresh approaches to such familiar sources as diaries and travel writings. Significantly, most of the current research makes use of many different kinds of sources, thus enabling scholars to access questions and events from more than one vantage point.

The diversity of topic and theoretical approach is also present in the authors themselves. They include established scholars as well as more junior colleagues. Seven of the authors in this collection also contributed to *Looking into My Sister's Eyes*, so that in some respects their essays here reflect their personal intellectual development and evolving research interests over the intervening fifteen years.[19] Also reflective of current developments in cross-disciplinary research, the collective includes historians and historically minded social scientists. As is often the case in this field of study, most of the authors share the ethnic/immigrant background, racial identity, or political affiliation of their subjects, however distant that connection might be. As such, we are well aware of the dilemmas, opportunities, and politics of doing research and analysis, either from within, or from the outside looking in, on one's own ethnic community. We may have had particular access to knowledge of and custom in a community, but we have also had to deal with the possibility of being critiqued by that community because of the ways in which we have interpreted a collective history. We are acutely aware of the tension when one writes from such a vantage point. Still, depending on the time context, some of the essays draw on personal experience as evidence, as in Midge Ayukawa's memories of her Japanese mother, or Marlene Epp's comments on the food attitudes of her in-laws, or Ester Reiter's personal recollections of attending summer camp. By allowing ourselves into the 'centre' of the narrative, thus acknowledging the close connections that all historians have with their subjects, we are 'de-centring the (male) authorial voice' that has tended to disavow those connections.[20]

As academics who are feminists, the authors are also mindful that they are using women's lives to further academic careers. This can be discomforting when we recognize that we research, analyze and write from the vantage point of privileged positions in academe, yet our subjects are often women who, despite ability, did not have similar educational opportunities, who worked hard, endured discrimination of many varieties, and found ways to create dignity for themselves. Collections of essays come in different forms: They might be the product of a group of scholars who share the same research interests and interpretations, and want to make a collective intervention into a debate. Or there are collections that bring together in one volume a diversity of perspectives and approaches and in that way encourage readers and students to better understand a field of study that is characterized by a diverse range of questions, debates, and approaches. In bringing these essays and authors together, we set out to do the latter. Our intent is not to preach but to make a contribution to ongoing vitality and debate in the field of immigrant and minority women's history. At the same time, this volume aims to be what has been termed 'emancipatory scholarship.' By revealing historically the limitations, accomplishments, exclusions and contributions of immigrant, ethnic, and racialized women, we hope in a small way to contribute to breaking down discrimination and to enhancing recognition for the future.

NOTES

1 Stories drawn from papers in this volume by Adele Perry, 'Whose Sisters and What Eyes? White Women, Race, and Immigration to British Columbia, 1849–1871,' and Lisa R. Mar, 'The Tale of Lin Tee: Madness, Family Violence, and Lindsay's Anti-Chinese Riot of 1919.'

2 The editors of this volume wrote the following essays: Frances Swyripa, 'Outside the Bloc Settlement: Ukrainian Women in Ontario during the Formative Years of Community Consciousness'; Franca Iacovetta, 'From *Contadina* to Worker: Southern Italian Immigrant Working Women in Toronto, 1947–62'; Frank H. Epp and Marlene G. Epp, 'The Diverse Roles of Ontario Mennonite Women,' in Jean Burnet, ed., *Looking into My Sister's Eyes: An Exploration in Women's History* (Toronto: Multicultural History Society of Ontario, 1986).

3 The editors of this volume are critical of what they view as a naive liberalism that underlines much of the rhetoric, official and otherwise, celebrating a multicultural Canada but that is seemingly blind to the racial, ethnic, and class prejudices that continue to be part of the 'mosaic.' At the same time, they remain committed both to a humanist and emancipatory scholarship and to the possibilities that a reconfigured multiracial Canada might hold, especially for the country's marginalized workers, women, and racialized 'others.'

4 See, for instance, Inderpal Grewal and Caren Kaplan, *Scattered Hegemonies: Postmodernity and Transnational Feminist Practices* (Minneapolis: University of Minnesota Press, 1994); Nira Yuval-Davis, *Gender and Nation* (London: Sage Publications, 1997); Cynthia Cockburn, *The Space between Us: Negotiating Gender and National Identities in Conflict* (London: Zed Books, 1998); Rick Wilford and Robert L. Miller, eds, *Women, Ethnicity and Nationalism: The Politics of Transition* (London: Routledge, 1998); Tamar Mayer, ed., *Gender Ironies of Nationalism: Sexing the Nation* (London: Routledge, 2000). See also special issues of *Canadian Woman Studies/Les cahiers de la*

*femme,* 'Immigrant and Refugee Women,' 19, no. 3 (Fall 1999), and 'National Identity and Gender Politics,' 20, no. 2 (Summer 2000).

5 See for instance, a special issue of *Canadian Woman Studies/Les cahiers de la femme,* 'Women in Conflict Zones,' 19, no. 4 (Winter 2000).

6 See for instance, Daiva Stasiulis and Nira Yuval-Davis, eds, *Unsettling Settler Societies: Articulations of Gender, Race, Ethnicity and Class* (London: Sage, 1995); Ruth Roach Pierson and Nupur Chaudhuri, eds, *Nation, Empire, Colony: Historicizing Gender and Race* (Bloomington: Indiana University Press, 1998); Adele Perry, *On the Edge of Empire: Gender, Race, and the Making of British Columbia, 1849–1871* (Toronto: University of Toronto Press, 2001); Christine Miller and Patricia Churchryk, eds, *Women of the First Nations: Power, Wisdom, and Strength* (Winnipeg: University of Manitoba Press, 1997); Sherene H. Razack, ed., *Race, Space, and the Law: Unmapping a White Settler Society* (Toronto: Between the Lines, 2002).

7 See for instance, Himani Bannerji, *Returning the Gaze: Essays in Racism, Feminism and Politics* (Toronto: Sister Vision, 1993); Peggy Bristow et al., eds, *'We're Rooted Here and They Can't Pull Us Up': Essays in African Canadian Women's History* (Toronto: University of Toronto Press, 1994); Vijay Agnew, *Resisting Discrimination: Women from Asia, Africa, and the Caribbean and the Women's Movement in Canada* (Toronto: University of Toronto Press, 1996); Sherene Razack, *Looking White People in the Eye: Gender, Race, and Culture in Courtrooms and Classrooms* (Toronto: University of Toronto Press, 1998); Enakshi Dua and Angela Robertson, *Scratching the Surface: Canadian Anti-Racist Feminist Thought* (Toronto: Women's Press, 1999); Agnes Calliste and George J. Sefa Dei, *Anti-Racist Feminism: Critical Race and Gender Studies* (Halifax: Fernwood Publishing, 2000).

8 See, for instance, Antoinette Burton, *Burdens of History: British Feminists, Indian Women, and Imperial Culture, 1865–1915* (Chapel Hill: University of North Carolina Press, 1994); Inderpal Grewal and Caren Kaplan, eds, *Home and Harem: Nation, Gender, Empire and the Cultures of Travel* (Durham, NC: Duke University Press, 1996); Frederick Cooper and Ann Laura Stoler, eds, *Tensions of Empire: Colonial Cultures in a Bourgeois World* (Berkeley: University of California Press, 1997); Pierson and Chaudhuri, eds, *Nation, Empire, Colony.*

9 See, for instance, Vic Satzewich, ed., *Deconstructing a Nation: Immigration, Multiculturalism and Racism in 90s Canada* (Halifax: Fernwood Publishing, 1992); Bannerji, ed., *Returning the Gaze*; Veronica Strong-Boag et al., *Painting the Maple: Essays on Race, Gender and the Construction of Canada* (Vancouver: UBC Press, 1998); Carl E. James and Adrienne Shadd, eds, *Talking about Identity: Encounters in Race, Ethnicity and Language* (Toronto: Between the Lines, 2001); Himani Bannerji, *The Dark Side of the Nation: Essays on Multiculturalism, Nationalism, and Gender* (Toronto: Canadian Scholars' Press, 2000).

10   Tania Das Gupta and Franca Iacovetta, 'Whose Canada Is It? Immigrant Women, Women of Colour and Feminist Critiques of "Multiculturalism,"' in the Introduction to *Atlantis* 24, no. 2 (Spring 2000): 1–4. See related special issues of *Canadian Woman Studies / Les cahiers de la femme* 'Immigrant and Refugee Women,' 19, no. 3 (Fall 1999) and 'National Identity and Gender Politics,' 20, no. 2 (Summer 2000).

11   See, for instance, Ellen Carol DuBois and Vicki L. Ruíz, eds, *Unequal Sisters: A Multi-Cultural Reader in U.S. Women's History,* 2d ed. (London: Routledge, 1994), Angela Y. Davis, *Women, Culture, and Politics* (New York: Vintage Books, 1991); Jacqueline Jones, *Labor of Love, Labor of Sorrow: Black Women, Work, and the Family from Slavery to the Present* (New York: Basic Books, 1985).

12   See J.L. Granatstein, *Who Killed Canadian History?* (Toronto: HarperCollins, 1998); a similar perspective is presented earlier in Michael Bliss, 'Privatizing the Mind: The Sundering of Canadian History, the Sundering of Canada,' *Journal of Canadian Studies* 26 (Winter 1991–2): 5–17. Critical responses to the positions represented by Bliss and Granatstein include: Veronica Strong-Boag, 'Contested Space: The Politics of Canadian Memory,' *Journal of the Canadian Historical Association* (1994): 3–18; A.B. McKillop, 'Who Killed Canadian History? A View from the Trenches,' *Canadian Historical Review* 80, no. 2 (1999): 269–99.

13   The response to Granatstein has also largely ignored these important distinctions among the so-called multiculturalists, who do not fall into the same liberal camp. For an example of how politics divides multicultural historians, consider the political argument put forth in Franca Iacovetta, Roberto Perin, and Angelo Principe, eds, *Enemies Within: Italian and Other Wartime Internees in Canada and Beyond* (Toronto: University of Toronto Press, 2000); the editors argue that the internments of Italians are better understood as a political, not ethnic, issue, and that the Italian-Canadian redress campaign exposed the problems of the ethnicization of politics in a country with an official policy of multiculturalism – all to the detriment of the historical record.

14   To take one set of examples, from the history of sexuality, see Becki Ross, '"The Stubborn Clutter, The Undeniable Record, The Burning, Wilful Evidence": Teaching the History of Sexuality,' *Atlantis* 25, no. 1 (Fall 2000): 28–38; Steven Maynard, 'The Maple Leaf (Gardens) Forever: Sex, Canadian Historians, and National History,' paper presented to the conference What Differences Does Nation Make?, Harvard University, April 1999. In making this point, we are in no way disagreeing with the many excellent arguments made for the value of these approaches but rather for what they do not do – that is, not question the category of nation itself, and the Canadian nation in particular. For some useful thoughts about how Canadian historians might get out of the national trap, see, for example, Cynthia Wright, 'Troubling the Nation: On Teaching Canadian History in the Women's Studies Classroom,' *Atlantis* 25, no. 1 (Fall 2000): 137–9; Mona Oikawa, 'Re-Membering the Internment: Women, Memory, and Re-Constructing the Subject(s) of National Violence' (PhD diss., Ontario Institute for Studies in Education, 1999).

15  For a historical treatment of these themes, see, for example, Marlene Epp, 'Pioneers, Refugees, Exiles, and Transnationals: Gendering Diaspora in an Ethno-Religious Context,' *Journal of the Canadian Historical Association* 12 (2001): 137–53; Donna R. Gabaccia and Franca Iacovetta, eds, *Women, Gender, and Transnational Lives: Italian Workers of the World* (Toronto: University of Toronto Press, 2002).

16  See Razack, *Looking White People in the Eye.*

17  In comparison with the United States, where early and important histories of Irish women include Hasia R. Diner, *Erin's Daughters in America: Irish Immigrant Women in the Nineteenth Century* (Baltimore: Johns Hopkins University Press, 1983), Canadian scholarship on Irish immigrant women is slim, but see for instance, Sheelagh Conway, *The Faraway Hills Are Green: Voices of Irish Women in Canada* (Toronto: Women's Press, 1992).

18  In food history, too, Canadian historians lag far behind their U.S. colleagues, whose important scholarship on immigrants, racialized Americans, and food includes Harvey Levenstein, *Revolution at the Table: The Transformation of the American Diet* (New York: Oxford University Press, 1988) and *Paradox of Plenty: A Social History of Eating in Modern America* (New York: Oxford University Press, 1993); Donna Gabaccia, *We Are What We Eat: Ethnic Food and the Making of Americans* (Cambridge, MA: Harvard University Press, 1998). Preliminary Canadian contributions to the topic of food and newcomers includes, Jo Marie Powers, ed., *Buon appetito! Italian Foodways in Ontario* (Toronto: Ontario Historical Society, 2000); Franca Iacovetta, 'Recipes for Democracy? Gender, Family, and Making Female Citizens in Cold War Canada,' in Veronica Strong-Boag, Mona Gleason, and Adele Perry, eds, *Rethinking Canada: The Promise of Women's History*, 4th ed. (Toronto: Oxford University Press, 2002), 299–312. Dietary issues also arose between Aboriginal women and white colonizers: some examples of this are in Sarah Carter, 'First Nations Women and Colonization on the Canadian Prairies, 1870s–1920s,' in Strong-Boag et al., *Rethinking Canada*, 135–48.

19  In addition to the three editors, authors in this volume who contributed to *Looking into My Sister's Eyes* are Varpu Lindström, Marilyn Barber, Paula J. Draper, and Isabel Kaprielian-Churchill.

20  Franca Iacovetta, 'Post-Modern Ethnography, Historical Materialism, and Decentring the (Male) Authorial Voice: A Feminist Conversation,' *Histoire sociale/Social History* 33 (2000): 275–93.

PART 1

# *Nation-Building and Discourses of Race*

# Turning Strangers into Sisters? Missionaries and Colonization in Upper Canada

CECILIA MORGAN

## Introduction

'Having witnessed the degraded and filthy conditions of the Indians when they lived in their Weg-ke-wams,' wrote Methodist missionary Philander Smith, 'I felt a desire to examine their domestic economy in their *houses*; accompanied by Mrs. Hurlbut we visited most of the females.' Smith, who was staying at the Native community of Methodist converts on Grape Island in the Bay of Quinte, was writing to the denominational newspaper, the *Christian Guardian*, in the fall of 1830. On visiting their homes, Smith and Mrs Hurlbut viewed Native peoples engaged in a variety of activities, such as moccasin- and clothes-making and wood-working. 'In most cases the homes were cleanly, and their little stock of furniture in its proper order. Some cupboards, the make of Indian Mechanicks, were neat and handsomely set off plates, basons [*sic*], etc., in decent style. In some instances however there was the *appearance* and *smell* of the Weg-ka-wam,' but these instances were few, and belonged to those who, as the missionaries shrewdly remarked 'had *not entirely lost the shell from their heads*, alluding to the known jest that young quails will run off to the bush, while the shell is still on their heads.' Smith then was taken to the Grape Island hospital, run by the widows Peggy Mekigk and her sister, once notorious for their bad behaviour but now reformed characters. The Mekigks' 'manners a few years since were well known about Bath and Hay Bay. Their virtuous deportment, and industrious habits *now* command them to the care of the sick. There was a decency about the house, that no white woman need be ashamed of.'[1]

Smith was not exceptional in his attention to the domestic trappings of Native converts to Christianity. During the 1820s and 1830s, in the pages of the *Chris-*

*tian Guardian*, in other Upper Canadian newspapers, and in missionary reports, journals, and diaries the comfortable, clean, and tidy homes of Native families were celebrated as the measure of their acceptance of Christianity and civilization. And in these homes would be installed the reformed figures of the Native mother and father and their children, all engaged in learning the lessons of Christian marriage, parenthood, and family life as husbands and wives, mothers and fathers, daughters and sons, and brothers and sisters.

Such concerns over these gendered markers of 'progress' and 'enlightenment' were, of course, not limited to the borders of Upper Canada.[2] As many scholars of colonization have pointed out, reforming and reshaping – or disrupting and disturbing – gender relations in colonized societies was a project often dear to the hearts of imperial authorities and their supporters.[3] Work on the 'white settler' colony of Upper Canada, though, has yet to share in the conceptual frameworks and paradigms of international work on colonization and imperialism. To date we have only a rudimentary understanding of British and Anglo-American immigrants' dependence on Aboriginal peoples for legitimization and justification. By this I mean that the processes whereby the former developed their own identities and subjectivities by gazing and commenting on those of the First Nations and attempting to change them require further study. For many historians of the colony, the two groups are best treated separately – as if there was an apartheid (a harbinger, perhaps, of how many Ontarians would later perceive their relations with Aboriginals) – in discrete categories of historical inquiry: military affairs, land negotiations, and missionary work.[4] We know little of how, in Mary Louise Pratt's words, members of these communities might have met in 'contact zones,' spatially and temporally linked, how they might have been 'constituted in and by their relations to each other' that must be seen 'in terms of copresence, interaction ... often within radically asymmetrical relations of power.'[5]

It may not, of course, be possible to understand all these dimensions of colonial encounters, particularly those regarding the (re)constitution of Upper Canadian Native communities through their contacts with non-Natives. The problem of insufficient sources, particularly for Native women, is especially challenging. Furthermore, as postcolonial theorists have pointed out, and as I will address later, there are significant theoretical difficulties in simply trying to 'uncover' subaltern women's 'voices' and their subjectivities, particularly through the medium of missionary reports and writings.[6] My intent here, then, is not to prove whether or not Native women or Native men were fundamentally transformed in their encounters with non-Natives, particularly Protestant (and especially Methodist) missionaries. Instead, I consider why the forging of new gendered identities for indigenous peoples was part of the work of colonization, and why it was so important for so many observers of Native communities that Native women and men perform the rituals of bourgeois domesticity. As Ann Laura Stoler has pointed out, and as Adele Perry's paper in this volume also suggests, colonialism was not only about the importation of middle-class sensibilities to the colonies, but also about the making of them within colonial contexts: colonialism was not a secure bourgeois project.[7]

Yet, while the gendered dimensions of missionary work in Upper Canada were of course part of broader, international patterns, we also need to understand why and how these relationships were deployed in specific historical contexts and locations: why missionary work took a particular shape and had particular preoccupations in this colony, despite its similarities to work in other colonial settings.[8] Through their appearances in the pages of papers such as the *Christian Guardian*, images of the 'pious Indian woman' and the sober Native male breadwinner were held up to Upper-Canadian *white* audiences as examples for their consumption, edification, and education. It was not just Aboriginal peoples' lands that were appropriated in the process of Anglo-American and British immigration and settlement.

### Missionary Work, Native Peoples, and Upper Canada

Missionary work with Aboriginal peoples in Upper Canada was not new to the 1820s and 1830s. The arrival of already-Christianized groups, such as the Mohawks and the Delawares, in the wake of the American Revolution brought both Anglican and Moravian missionaries to the colony. However, evangelical revivals – gatherings aimed at religious renewal and conversion – in England and the United States during the late eighteenth and early nineteenth centuries were responsible for the proliferation of missionary societies. These societies set about raising funds in Britain, the United States, and in Europe for the protection and salvation of Aboriginal peoples making contact with Europeans. Historians of Upper Canadian missionary work consider the 1822 arrival of the Methodist Episcopal Church from New York State marks the beginning of large-scale conversions and sustained Protestant missionary work, particularly among the Mississaugas, a branch of the Ojibwa nation who had settled along the Credit River by the 1820s. During the 1820s the Methodists staged a number of revivals across the province, from Grand River, to Belleville and the Bay of Quinte, to Holland Landing on the shores of Lake Simcoe. By 1829 the church had established mission communities at the Credit River, Grape Island in the Bay of Quinte, Rice Lake (east of Peterborough), and at Holland Landing. These showcases of Christian conversion and civilization included, of course, chapels and schools. Along with the English language, religious lessons, and reading and writing, Native men and boys learned agriculture and trades such as shoemaking and cabinetry and Native women and girls learned knitting, sewing, and other house-hold skills. Missionary work among the Ojibwa was also marked by the participa-tion of prominent Native preachers, such as Peter Jones of the Mississaugas and George Copway, an Ojibwa from Rice Lake, who worked at Saugeen.[9]

Of course, the Methodists were not the only denomination involved in mis-sionary work during these decades. Other churches – the Baptists, Church of England, Presbyterians, and Roman Catholics – either expanded ongoing work in Native communities or set up new missionary enterprises.[10] As John Webster Grant commented: '[I]n Upper Canada most Indians were offered a choice of at least two Christian denominations, and some were actively wooed by three or more.'[11] That the majority of Native peoples in southern Ontario did choose Christianity during this period – or at least some *form* of it – seems indisputable.[12] Historians of missionary work have offered a range of explanations for these con-versions, ranging from the material benefits offered by Christian communities (education, medical care, new skills), the desperate conditions of groups such as the Mississaugas, who had lost much of their land and had been demoralized by disease and alcohol, and Native peoples' needs for a new set of spiritual beliefs to help guide them through the changes brought by increased white settlement in Upper Canada.[13]

Although such issues are important, I do not explore them in this context; nor do I wish to engage in the problematic exercise of assessing which church was successful at garnering the most souls. Instead, I seek to contribute to an analysis of the meaning of encounters between Natives and 'newcomers' by examining the missionaries' representation of the process of converting and garnering souls and subjectivities.

These encounters need not, it is true, be viewed solely through the lens of Methodist-generated sources. The records of other missionary societies, such as the Church of England, also record the reformation and regulation of Native men and women and their conduct as family members. The Methodists, though, expressed their concerns quite clearly and trumpeted their successes in the pages of the regularly published *Christian Guardian* and missionary reports. In Meth-odist histories, the conversion of 'heathens' was an important chapter in the church's narrative of progress and enlightenment. As well, the evangelical nature of Methodism meant that Aboriginal conversions, and the reformation of gender relations that accompanied them, were particularly significant events and pro-cesses. For the Methodists, conversion was an emotionally charged leap of faith that required a rupture with one's past and the sinful practices that accompanied it (although it did not hurt to prepare for conversion by renouncing these). It was a cataclysmic event preceded by simultaneously experienced agonies of pain, fear of being 'hardened of heart' to Christ, and yearning and hope for Christ's love; it was then marked by an invasion, a sense of transportation outside one's self-control, which in turn was followed by great joy and happiness (with, however, the ever-present fear of backsliding). This combination of fear, trepidation, release, and joy was often recorded in minute detail, as a means of witnessing the process and providing a roadmap to guide potential converts.[14]

Methodist attentiveness to the conversion process itself meant that detailed descriptions of those of Native peoples received more attention than, for example, in the pages of the Anglican Church's press.[15] And, given the Methodist belief that 'civilization' accompanied Christianization, narratives of Native men and women's acceptance of Christ were also narratives of their acceptance of bourgeois domestic decency.[16] Running through all these writings were the Methodist missionaries own emotions of pleasure and delight in the work of colonization – as well as their insistence that Native peoples were experiencing contact with Christ not as coercion, but as a voluntary and joyous transformation.

It is true that the missionaries' aims and goals were not always synonymous with those of the colonial state. On a number of occasions missionaries supported Aboriginal peoples in their opposition to white encroachment on their lands or worked with them in the negotiation of treaties. Methodist missionaries tried to prevent Lieutenant-Governor Francis Bond Head from removing the Ojibwa to Manitoulin Island, a move ostensibly designed to ease the last years of a 'dying people' but also, some historians suggest, meant to free up land for white settlers.[17] But to suggest that missionaries had sympathy for Aboriginal peoples, particularly the Ojibwa, and that their work was organized along humanitarian principles, does not mean that we can overlook the power relations at work when missionaries felt entitled to act as speaking subjects, both for themselves and for and about Native peoples to other colonists. As work on similar colonial encounters and abolitionism has demonstrated, humanitarianism may be embedded in the needs, desires, and fantasies of those performing the tasks of rescue and redemption but not necessarily in the goals and aspirations of those deemed worthy of such assistance.[18] Indeed, the ability to make decisions as to who would be offered Christian sympathy and who would not was in itself shaped by racially charged relations of dominance and hierarchy. In these decisions, missionaries' perceptions of how gender relations structured Native societies, their pernicious effects, and how they might be changed, played a significant role in their representations of missionary work.

### Turning Hunters into Christian Farmers: Native Men

Like many of their contemporaries, Methodist missionaries in Upper Canada saw the transition from a nomadic life of hunting and gathering to a settled life of agricultural production as central to the redemption of Native people.[19] In religious discourse, transformed gender relations were perceived to be essential to this shift. Native men were, of course, implicated in these relations, because turning men from hunters into farmers involved reshaping the meanings of men's work and manliness in general in Ojibwa society. Fatherhood, for example, was no longer synonymous with teaching children (particularly sons) the skills of hunting or trapping; indeed, such activities were not always considered proper paternal behaviour in the first place. Instead, in missionary discourse fatherhood was to be associated with areas such as agricultural cultivation (formerly the province of women).[20] George F. Playter wrote approvingly of the changes brought about in the Mississaugas, a group that had been 'wholly pagan, in all respects, and most beastly drunken, dirty natives in the country.' However, from the 'lowest of the low' they had now attained a state personified by men such as Jacob, 'a man of good disposition, and amiable manners; industrious, in farming, and comfortable in his home, and seldom allowed himself in intoxication.'[21] Such a desire to see Native men thus occupied was not confined to Methodists: J. Carruthers, a Presbyterian minister, remembered the 'industry' and 'thrift' of the Bay of Quinte Mohawk, who had been 'remarkable' for their industry and their acquisition of private property.[22]

As well, persuading Native men to swear off alcohol was an important means of reshaping Native manhood. The fact that the missionaries preached temperance to Native peoples, particularly men, during this period is not surprising.[23] Many of the reasons missionaries used in urging them to give up alcohol were similar to those used when 'white' communities were urged to embrace temperance. However, their arguments were also based on suppositions concerning the 'nature' of Native society which, when it encountered 'the white man,' made it susceptible to the worst effects of alcohol. Although it could not be said the drink 'loosened' the bonds of civilization, because it was assumed that Natives who drank were not 'civilized' in the first place, alcohol made Native men particularly vulnerable to the worst aspects of their own culture. For one, they might devalue those things that should be most precious. Writing in 1838 of the state of the Mississaugas in 1825, American Episcopal Methodist missionary Nathan Bangs described them as having been 'among the most degraded of all the Indian tribes in that country. From their habits of intercourse among the depraved whites, they had bartered away their land for intoxicating liquor, had debased themselves by intemperance, and were consequently lazy, idle, poor, and filthy to a most disgusting degree. They seemed, indeed, to be abandoned to a most cruel fate.'[24]

Moreover, in the evangelicals' eyes drink made men either neglect or beat their wives and children and, while it also had the same effects on whites, Native culture was supposedly susceptible to the abuse of these groups. Samuel Rose, a Methodist preacher who worked at the Yellowhead Indian Mission, wrote to his brother John in 1831 of 'Indian customs,' such as the treatment of an elderly wife by her polygamous husband: 'So one day the man being intoxicated he placed the poor worn out wife at a distance and told her that he was going to kill her, she said "you may" (then) wounded her with a gun and killed with a 'Tommy Hawk.'"[25] Christian Indians refuse spirits, the Canada Auxiliary Missionary Society was happy to report in 1825; instead, they have the comfort of sobriety, 'they are enabled to appear more decently, and to live in a more comfortable manner,' women are not abused by their 'drunken husbands,' nor are they 'made unhappy by excessive toil. By the industry of their husbands they are better provided for; and the cleanliness of their persons, and the neatness of their homes are a handsome comment on the change which has taken place in their husbands and fathers.'[26] Finally, alcohol might interfere with the sacred bond between mother and son. Ezra Adams reported to the *Christian Guardian* in 1835 that, among the 'pagan' Indians of Muncey Town, an 'aged and emaciated Indian woman' who had been drinking with her son began fighting with him, whereupon the son threw her on the fire and almost burnt her to death. Such an example, Adams noted sadly, was one of many.[27]

Christianity would also transform Native men's subjectivities and the way they expressed emotion, changes that would help them to be better husbands, fathers, and sons. Missionaries – like other whites – made much of the 'stoicism' of Natives: their supposed ability to endure pain and suffering without expressing fear, their so-called disdain for tears and other expressions of emotion, and their seeming impassive countenances. And at particular moments, Native men's faces and bodies might be read as dignified, commanding respect and admiration for their self-control. However, for missionaries this demeanour made it impossible to read their 'true' natures and determine if they had really embraced Christ or if they were still concealing 'pagan' beliefs and practices. At the very least, a lack of emotional expression might mean a hardness of heart that would prevent the reception of Christ's love. For evangelicals such as the Methodists, religious beliefs were expressed through emotional sensibilities written on men's and women's bodies. Honest acceptance of Christ was expressed through tears, sighs, trembling, lamentations, and the occasional fainting fit. 'True feeling,' many religious writers argued, should be manifested as both an expression of conversion and serve as the conduit whereby Christ could enter the unbeliever's spirit.[28] While emotional expression was eagerly sought from non-Native converts and at the deathbed scenes of professing Christians, it was even more highly prized when displayed by Native peoples. And it was Native *men* who, by and large, were stereotyped as undemonstrative, possibly because they were perceived as hunters and warriors who lacked a vocabulary for expressing emotion.

Thus 'The Missionary,' writing in the *Kingston Chronicle* in 1840 of 'The Mohawk Indians,' was happy to narrate the deathbed scene of a 'Mohawk friend

... a swarthy patriarch ... The Indian, whose stern nature has, in some measure, been softened by Christianity, however deeply he may feel, weeps but seldom; in his savage state, never, as it is deemed a weakness unworthy of a warrior; but on this occasion, no sooner was the tear of Christian sympathy seen to flow, than every one in the apartment yielded to the impulse. It was indeed an affecting sight, I doubt not each thought within himself, "It is good for us to be here." May God bless it to our spiritual improvement for his dear Son's sake.'[29] Emotional displays also marked the conversion of Native peoples in the Newcastle District, 31 August 1826, an event said to have started with the elderly chief's rebirth. Affected by many tears, he began to cry and then called out to Jesus:

> In less than ten minutes after tears began to fall, he began to tremble like an aspen leaf in the wind, in a moment more he fell to the ground like a corpse. One after another of these pagans fell to the ground. But the Lord passed over them and breathed upon them, they sprang to their feet giving praises to God. When the chief arose, with a heavenly smile on his countenance, he clapped his hand to his breast, saying 'O happy here! O, blessed Jesus, how I love thee! O, glory, glory!' One after another arose, until twenty of the thirty were praising God.[30]

It is true that this passage could just as easily be, and in fact was, used by Methodists to describe conversion scenes among non-natives. It is also true that terms such as *heathen* and *pagan* could be used to describe the spiritual, and sometimes cultural, state of white unbelievers. Yet the targeting of Native culture as in *itself* being essentially a state of savagery, a step removed from that of whites who had not accepted Christ, makes it difficult to see these terms as completely interchangeable and devoid of racial and gendered meanings. For the missionaries, demonstrating to Native men that they were permitted to express emotions, that it was acceptable – even desirable – to shed tears and feel empathy for other human beings, was a critical first step on the evolutionary path to Christian manhood. It signified to other Christians that 'savagery' had been abandoned and they were ready to become loving husbands, fathers, and sons, members of both earthly and spiritual families in Christ. Native men would no longer be immune to their dependants' sufferings; instead, they would now pity those over whom they wielded power. They now would understand the need for kindness and humane treatment of women and children, instead of the abuse and exploitation to which they presently subjected them. An 'Indian' who found religion, wrote Playter, stopped fighting with his community and stealing his wife's seed corn; instead, he became industrious, displaying kindness to his family and an anxiety to provide for them.[31] Rose wrote that a young Indian man who was supposed to kill his mother (presumably because of some 'custom' that Rose did not explain) but 'loved her and did not want to kill her,' was persuaded not to (much to his gratitude) upon hearing Peter Jones preach. 'Who can hear those dreadful facts and not thank God for the conversion of this people,' Rose wrote to his brother.[32]

## Uplifting the 'Degraded Indian Woman'

But what of those Native wives and mothers who were so threatened by their culture's violence and brutality? If there was one theme that connected the Native women of Upper Canada to their white counterparts in the missionaries' language, it was that of the elevated position of women under Christianity. This tenet was, of course, not unique to Upper Canadian evangelicals; for many Christians their religion was supposed to uplift women from the enslavement, degradation, and oppression of their 'heathen' sisters.[33] Explicitly or implicitly, this argument ran through the religious discourse on women and gender relations. It was made directly in a frequently quoted article entitled 'The Infidel Mother' by the French writer Chateaubriand. This piece bemoaned the unhappy lot of those who, living without religion, were forced into such practices as infanticide. These crimes arose because of their society's lack of appreciation of the bond between mother and child, one that could only be inculcated by religion. This article was often followed by 'Advice to Christian Mothers,' which both celebrated religious maternity and spoke of the need to preserve it.[34]

Some of this material was drawn from the ever-increasing body of writing on missionary work in 'faraway lands.' Articles such as 'Heathen Females – Licentiousness' and 'Missions – Paganism' can be seen as an international literary genre, one that straddled the border between fact and fiction but that was seen as crucial in garnering public support for missionary enterprises.[35] In this context, such literature reminded readers that Upper Canadian religious teachings were part of an international context of (benevolent) imperial expansion.[36] Tales of cannibalism, polygamy, suttee, infanticide, and female slavery (the latter category laden with hints that such a condition involved more than economic bondage) had many meanings and purposes. One was an attempt to make the category of sex transcend that of race for Christian womanhood, although the attempt itself revealed the racially bound nature of this image and the contradictions embedded in it. One report in the *Christian Guardian* proclaimed that 'these scenes of oppression and cruelty and death ought to excite the pity and sympathy of all Christian women and elicit their assistance.'[37]

Such tales also made the discourse of imperial expansion multifaceted and gave it a social face, one that might soften and humanize the implications of political and economic conquest. They also helped to justify and rationalize imperial expansion, arguing that 'British' or 'white' culture brought emancipation from 'barbarism' and 'savagery' for women, a group that in eighteenth-century British culture had come to symbolize those most in need of and likely to benefit from the humanitarian impulse embodied in Methodism.[38] In the colonial context of Upper Canada, the language of Christian uplift brought these issues very close to home. Although much was made of the effect of Christianity on Native men, it was the symbol of the enslaved Native woman that was used to represent the triumph of moral regeneration.[39] The York Female Missionary Society stressed this point in its 1830 report, commending 'the instrumentality of a few pious and indefatigable females who, touched with a feeling sense of the untold sufferings to which their sex are exposed in the barbarism of savage life, have spared no pains to meliorate their conditions, and open to them the door of present comfort and everlasting life.'[40]

In making the connection between themselves and Native women the primary bond, and in attempting to downplay, if not write out completely, the racial differences that separated them and that also might make the meanings of womanhood quite different for Native women, the society was contributing to the development of the category of 'Christian womanhood.' Although the sources consulted do not permit a full exploration of this issue, such statements hint that white Methodist women in Upper Canada may well have deployed representations of Native women in shaping their own racially charged and gendered subjectivities.[41] The category of 'the Christian woman' also permitted generalizations about the essential nature of familial – especially maternal – ties, while simultaneously exposing the socially and culturally constructed nature of these bonds. Such an approach was exemplified in the 1833 report of the Cramahe Female Missionary Society, which highlighted the need for missions in Upper Canada by relating the tale of a mother whose son won a prize from the missionaries. With great pathos, the mother expressed the wish that they had arrived sooner, for their coming would have prevented her from murdering her other son.[42] Tales of the transformation of Native homes and families, while to some degree resembling accounts of domestic happiness in white families after accepting Christ's love, made it clear that the journey from degradation to uplift was one of crossing the borders of both religion and race. Not only were irreligious activities and beliefs denied – Native society and culture (or what the missionaries believed Native society and culture to be), were also expected to be renounced. Native women, like white women, might be encouraged to speak out against the brutality of Native men, but – unlike white women – in doing so they were also expected to shoulder the cultural, social, and economic customs and values of a colonial power.

Turning the unnatural and dangerous mother into the model of loving, Christian maternity was not the only way in which Christianity would benefit Native people, for it was on the figure of the Native woman that many of the missionaries' hopes for an entire transformation of gender relations within the community were pinned.[43] Of course, when Native men became industrious and sober with Christianity they would be capable of supporting their wives and children and becoming the heads of stable households.[44] However, it was up to Aboriginal women as wives and mothers to provide the motive and inspiration, by their dutiful and industrious management of the home. Their hopes for the progress of Christianity and civilization did not acknowledge – and, generally, *could* not recognize – the ways in which patriarchal family relationships would undermine Native women's social, economic, and political status within their own societies and subject them to the dominance of both white society and that of their own husbands and fathers.[45]

The success of the Native women's work, missionary letters and reports insisted, was to be seen in the neatness and cleanliness of their homes. The triumph of civilization and Christian morality was represented not only by the abolition of infanticide and matricide but also by the presence of household furniture, tea-kettles, cleanliness, and, if possible, European-style clothes. Many of those who observed Native societies prior to conversion liked to dwell on their 'filth' as an important signifier of their abandoned and perilous state.[46] And it was up to Native women to remove the filth from their families' bodies and surroundings, thus helping them to embrace Christianity. Francis Hall, visiting the Credit community in August 1828, was pleased to report to the *Methodist Magazine*'s readers that Native women were busy scrubbing the chapel floor and 'we found every house perfectly clean and neat, and the persons of grown people and children a pattern for any peoples.'[47] Cleansed and clothed Natives, along with their furniture and dishes, were then placed within the four walls of a warm and sheltering home, a Western-style building that had replaced 'weg-ka-wams.'[48] D. McMullen, writing from Rice Lake to the *Christian Guardian* in March 1830, noted such 'improvements' as the habits of industry and economy and the fight against alcohol, but he was especially impressed by the homes of the Native residents: 'The furniture of their houses, consisting chiefly of bedsteads, tables, benches, etc., is principally of their own make and the females begin to keep their houses in tolerable good style.'[49]

Furthermore, Christianity would also reach the next generation of Native women, as a display of converted Native girls at the York Methodist chapel in 1828 demonstrated. The girls were brought out to sing a hymn for the audience that, not surprisingly, filled the chapel to 'overflowing.' The performance of hymns by Native converts, especially children, was a favourite sight for evangelical gazes. The girls compared their family lives and their own states both prior to and after conversion: 'In the dark wood and forest wild, My father roved, rude Nature's child,' they told the audience who had packed the chapel to overflowing, hunting bear and red deer with bow and tomahawk. 'My brother, in his bark canoe, Across the waves so gaily flew' in order to shoot wild duck or catch fish.

'My mother in the wigwam stay'd, The wampum's various hues to braid, or pound the samp, or dress the skin, or sew my father's moccasin.' Although such a description might sound suspiciously like work, with the wigwam resembling the four walls of the non-Native home, there could be no doubt about the deleterious effects on young Native girls. 'And I, a little Indian maid, with acorn cups, and wild flowers play'd, or by my mother sat all day, to weave the splinted basket gay. I could not read, I could not sew, My Saviour's name I did not know; My parents oft I disobey'd, And to the Lord I never pray'd.' However, the arrival of the 'white man' brought churches and school houses and the 'Indians' learnt Jesus' name. 'And holy hymns the dark wood cheer'd, I now can read, I now can sew, My Saviour's name I'm taught to know; And now my saviours, I implore, to bless the white man, evermore.' This exhibition of Native Christianity also included the girls' recitation of the Lord's prayer and the Ten Commandments, as well as a display of their writings, sewing, and knitting.[50]

The concern with homes and household objects that ran through the missionary and other religious writings on Native peoples should not be mistaken for support of consumerism. In the missionaries' understanding of contact between whites and Native peoples, the lure of cheap finery and trinkets had led to alcoholism and moral degradation. James Evans, a Methodist missionary from England, and one of the first missionaries to speak and preach in Ojibwa, told the readers of the *Christian Guardian* about an encounter between two Christian Native women from the Credit and the wife of the St Clair chief Joshua Wawanosh. The latter, being interested in Christianity, remarked on the women's plain style of dress. Upon being told that it was the sign of Christian women, she proceeded to take the ostrich plumes and silver bands off her hat, and, noted Evans, 'both her person and her mind are evidently brought under the sacred influence of Divine grace.'[51] That Methodists would frown upon ostrich plumes and silver bands might come as no surprise. Such objects, however, were particularly dangerous when their wearers were perceived as being untutored in Christian morality and lacking a clear sense of the dangers involved in wearing finery. By stripping herself of such symbols of luxury, this Native woman was also supposed to have renounced the trappings of 'paganism,' with its superstitious fetishizing of material objects that had no moral value. Readers of this anecdote might also see how the 'love of finery,' which Victorian middle-class social commentators often suggested was at the root of working-class women's moral degradation, could be a point of intersection for both racial and class distinctions, a place where the two supposedly separate set of relations converged in the early nineteenth century.[52]

Natives' acquisition of private property was an important objective for the missionaries, but it was to be limited to those essentials obtained through industry and thrift. Many of the items that were so admired in these homes were, it was stressed, the product of Native men's own material labour. The beds and cup-boards they had made signified their assumption of Christian manliness and their acceptance of the Western model of gender relations. For men, this labour was represented much more concretely than for women, whose conversion to Chris-tian womanhood was signified by the order of their homes. The labour that went into keeping a home neat and an engaging picture for visitors' comments was downplayed or rewritten as female piety and morality. It was the emotional bonds of gender relations and Christian transformation that a shiny tea-kettle signified, not the hard work that a woman had performed to keep it spotless. Relations of production thus became those of reproduction and, while not unimportant to the *missionaries*, were subject to the wider society's dismissal and relegation to the realm of 'unpaid women's work.'

This representation of emotional connections in material objects becomes even more intriguing when we consider that, in the religious writings of the press, such images appeared alongside homilies on femininity and womanhood that high-lighted and praised non-Native mothers' and wives' contributions to proper gen-der relations as *emotional*, not physical, 'housekeeping.' The articles and letters that make up the religious discourse on gender relations in Methodism did not single out neat-and-tidy cupboards as the primary signifier of women's contribu-tion to morality within the home. Rather, they spoke in abstract terms of female 'influence' as exercised by wives and mothers and of the delights of female piety. Native women, it seemed, represented a stage in the evolution of Christian civili-zation. Unlike some white women, they could never aspire to the status of 'ladies,' but perhaps in the future they would reach the point where social rela-tions could become more abstract and would take precedence over the material apparatus of Christian morality. Converted Native women were 'pious Indian women,' a designation that mingled both class and racial status. Even a supporter of Native women's reputation, like 'Otho,' who wrote to the *Christian Guardian* in response to Bond Head's assertion that native women in mission villages were bearing mixed-race children, did not grant them the status of ladies, although he claimed they were 'examples of chastity worthy of imitation.'[53] The term *lady*, as African-American feminist scholar Evelyn Brooks-Higginbotham has pointed out, was not coterminous with that of *woman*; instead, it was a trope in which race, class, and gender were 'discursively weld[ed].'[54] By linking progress to the symbol of the domesticated Native woman, religious discourse underscored the supposedly natural, inevitable, and desirable position of white women within Christian society. Furthermore, the images of gender and family relations that ran through the rest of religious discourse – images that were understood to apply to white women and men – provided an important subtext for any discussions of gender relations in Upper Canadian Native society.

Was there any other discourse, any other way of speaking about Native people that countered that of the missionaries? In the sources consulted, Native women's 'voices' are produced and controlled by missionary discourse, heard only through the filters of their reports and letters. In these sources, the narrative devices and tropes used by the missionaries, the discursive strategies (such as the uplifted Christian Native mother) that constructed Native women for a predominantly white audience, make it impossible to consider these women's subjectivities and agency, to uncover what sort of language they used to discuss the meaning of Christianity in their own lives.[55] However, the letters and reports of those Native men who worked as missionaries and missionaries' helpers hint at a more complex perspective on religious matters. Men such as John Sunday, chief of the Mississaugas at the Bay of Quinte and a Methodist preacher, focused on the spiritual importance of religion to his people. While Sunday saw the benefits of moral discipline as important, he did not tie morality to domestic relations but rather linked it to the abolition of alcohol and its attendant vices.[56] In contrast, Peter Jones appears to have shared his non-Native counterparts' concerns with reshaping of gender relations under Christianity; he also, though, stressed the need for spiritual regeneration as his people's first and foremost concern.[57] The Ojibwa chief and Methodist preacher George Copway, while noting the importance of his family in conversions, identified his people's need for religion as a spiritual matter and a means of giving purpose to lives that had been violently disrupted by white contact. 'King Alcohol,' in Copway's memoirs, was pinpointed as causing their problems, having been brought to them by 'those fiends in human shape,' 'merciless, heartless, and wicked white men' – men who were only interested in using Indians to snatch their hunting grounds.[58]

### Native Peoples, Gender Relations, and White Settler Identities

Why is any of this important? What did it matter if native men and women and their children were seen to be performing European rituals of domesticity, understood to be emulating the gendered roles and relations of white colonial society? For one, the material demands of a colonial economy do not seem to have played a significant part in missionary endeavours. After all, in the context of this particular settler society, the creation of either an Aboriginal workforce or a middle class that would mediate between a colonial government and an indigenous peasantry do not seem to have been important goals.[59] To be sure, missionaries believed that the Ojibwa's future lay in agriculture; however, there were precedents for Native agricultural communities in which gender relations looked rather different than Philander Smith's 'white woman's decency.'[60] Furthermore, given that distinct communities for Native peoples had been created during these decades – the Delaware settlement at Moraviantown and the Six Nations along the Grand River – could it not have been possible to simply leave the Ojibwa to carve out their own, separate existence and expend time, efforts, and money elsewhere? Why did missionaries and their lay supporters feel it necessary to display such interest and concern about the gendered division of labour, and new gendered identities, in Native communities?

An obvious answer, of course, would be the missionary or evangelical 'spirit' of the period, one that ranged across various colonial and national boundaries and took as a central and important project the redefinition of gender relations in English and American societies.[61] And evangelicals, in order to continue their work, needed to fundraise and to provide proof to supporters in both Upper Canada and abroad that souls were being saved.[62] Yet these responses still beg the questions: Why did the souls need to have plates, European women's dresses, and clean-and-tidy homes? Why was it thought that saving them in this way was proof of good work? The answers to these questions are too many and too complex to be fully explored within the confines of this paper. However, it is possible to venture a few suggestions about the relationship of Native communities to the missionary enterprise in Upper Canada.

The settlements at Rice Lake, the Credit River, and on Grape Island were presented to the readers of Upper Canada's religious press as sites of education and enlightenment, not just for their Ojibwa inhabitants but also for those non-Natives who might read about these scenes of religious and civilizing transformation for their own benefit. In reading about pious Indian mothers and thrifty, sober Indian fathers, white Upper Canadians could satisfy any number of colonial fantasies and desires about gender relations in their own society. During this period, after all, gender relations in Britain and the United States underwent a number of significant changes and redefinitions in which the middle-class home figured significantly; as I have argued elsewhere, Upper Canada was not immune from these developments.[63] Those who were anxious about the assertion of colonial power could assuage their fears with the knowledge, produced by the quoted 'voices' of Native women, that their lives had been improved immeasurably by the missionaries: indeed, Christianity and civilization had given them the status of 'human being,' formerly denied to them by their own culture. White women in particular might read such narratives as comforting proof that their own roles within the home and family were designed precisely for their uplift and elevation, not confinement and subjugation.[64] Those who felt no such compunctions and anxieties, and who believed that Upper Canada was theirs by divine and imperial right, might be assured that missionary work was 'taming savages,' turning them into men and women who would be docile and well behaved, who would bring up their children in the same manner, and who would not cause the new immigrants to fear their violence or any reprisals for encroaching on their lands.

Other, related concerns may have shaped the reports and their reception. While the Methodists would gain political and social respectability in the following decades, during the 1820s and 1830s they were not immune to charges of political radicalism, religious fanaticism, and a lack of social niceties.[65] Missionary work, while genuinely felt by Methodists and other evangelicals to be a duty, might also help them claim a particular kind of moral and cultural capital that other irreligious and unfeeling white Upper Canadians lacked, even if the latter sat on the Executive Council and were part of the York or Kingston elite. As we have seen, feeling and expressing a sensibility to the sufferings of others was an important part of evangelicals' worldview. Who might not suffer more than those bereft of Christ's word and whose own culture, as we have also seen, prevented them from attaining the emotional receptivity needed to hear it? Thus, missionary work with Native peoples was undeniable proof of the evangelicals' moral superiority and sensibility, despite the fact that their preachers might not have the social backgrounds and formal education of the Anglicans. Methodist claims to be helping and not exploiting Native peoples were made in the context of a society that did not always see *them* as moral subjects, one that suspected them of sedition, irreligion, and ignorance.

And male missionaries, who formed the majority of those guiding and writing about their work, were also carving out an identity of Christian manhood in these enterprises.[66] Through these labours, men such as William Case were able to create themselves as virtuous men, ones who protected weaker beings such as Native women and offered their own manliness as examples to Native men. In gazing upon these communities and offering their interpretations of them to a reading public, they created for themselves authoritative voices as men, ones with a moral and social authority that was at least partially reliant on their ability to speak for helpless others.[67] Furthermore, missionary enterprises, no matter how spiritually motivated and guided, were also 'work,' often laborious, tedious, and (although they did not like to admit it) at times thankless. And performing 'honest labour' – and teaching its habits to others – was increasingly becoming proof of a manly bourgeois identity in this colonial context.[68] If formal education, political connections, and social standing were of little use to the Methodists in the 1820s and 1830s, the claim that missionaries were performing 'honest hard work' and inculcating it as a value and practice (with appropriate gendered distinctions) among Native peoples could help overcome these social and cultural impediments. It also – and this was not unrelated – helped shape gendered identities for Methodist men and women, whether they were teaching Native men carpentry, Native women knitting, or collecting sewing supplies as members of Dorcas societies.

There was more, though, to the missionaries' work than merely proving their moral probity. As Catherine Hall has pointed out, missionary language during this period was riddled with uncertainties and ambivalences. Even those immigrants who believed in the universal brotherhood of 'man' also brought with them the baggage of white superiority.[69] While evangelicals perceived themselves as superior to unconverted whites, as we have seen, they also wished to claim that the general tenets of white bourgeois domesticity were best for Native peoples, thus making it clear that their program for the Ojibwa included assimilation into white culture. However, missionaries also expressed shame for the ways in which fellow Upper Canadians – Anglo-American or English – had treated Aboriginals. To be sure, secular writers were much more likely to express both guilt and the feeling that Natives would have been better off in their 'natural' state. 'Of all the people in creation, we think the North American Indians the most exalted – the most high-minded – the most eloquent – the most generous – the most humane – the most gentle, and the most virtuous,' wrote an anonymous author in the *Canadian Freeman*: 'The soul of one of these men, when not contaminated by the society of whites, spurns everything that is sordid, and he will willingly meet death rather than stoop to that which is vicious, mean, or unmanly ... Look at them, again, even after they have been corrupted by the society of our people, and see how harmless they are, and how peaceably they traverse our back settlements, with arms in their hands, without offering injury or insult to male or female.' The writer expressed 'astonishment' and 'regret' at their loss of their land at the hands of whites.[70] Another author described the state of the Indians at Midland and called for Roman Catholic clergy to attend them; the bishops of Kingston and Quebec need

> to place an active missionary amongst a people so far advanced in civilization and so ripe for further development ... as the white men have driven them from their hunting grounds, contaminated, by their intercourse, their native innocence, and stained their character with vice – we think it is high time that we should begin to make restitution by affording them the means of civilization and by teaching them religion and Christian virtue. There is something so lofty, so humane, and so generous, in the character of a North American Indian, in his rude state, uncontaminated with the vice of civilized society, that whenever we behold him we fancy that we view the noblest work of God – an honest man.[71]

The Methodist missionaries, however, generally saw pre-contact Aboriginal societies not as uncontaminated or lofty, in a natural and innocent state, but rather as enclaves of degradation and paganism that perverted relations between husbands and wives, parents and children. For them, a natural social arrangement was that which *they* brought to Native communities. However, the Methodists and other writers were well aware that whites bore some culpability for the state of affairs in Native communities prior to conversion. As we have seen, 'viciousness' might have been a problem inherent to Native culture but it had been exacerbated by those who should have known better, who played the role of Satan, offered alcohol to Aboriginals, and brought them corruption. In exchange for these 'false gifts,' Methodist missionaries and their supporters would offer the true gifts of piety and a moral way of life; in so doing they would redeem both the Ojibwa and the rest of white society – thus, once again, proving themselves both Christian and civilized. And warning the rest of colonial society about the Ojibwa's degraded (because un-Christian) state might respond to those who thought them better off without contact with whites, those who might have accused the Methodists of unwanted meddling.

Finally, missionary work provided examples for Methodist adherents. By providing explicit details of the conversion of Native peoples to Christian beliefs and ways of living, the missionaries also held up lessons of what was possible and desirable for whites. After all, evangelicals were well aware that religiosity could not be taken for granted; once converted, a Christian man or woman had to be constantly vigilant of his or her spiritual state. For many adherents of enthusiastic religion, backsliding was a dreaded reality. It was all too easy, once the fervour of a revival was over and its charismatic leaders had moved on to another community, for converts to revert to their sinful beliefs and practices. The articles, editorials, and letters to the *Christian Guardian*'s editor reminded Methodist readers that even the 'degraded' and 'heathen' Natives of the colony had been able to renounce their way of life and embrace new ways of being a Christian man or woman. As 'D' from Smithville argued in a letter to the *Christian Guardian* in 1835, 'to refute the calumnies of parsimonious professors, or to silence the cavils of infidelity, we can point to the savage man, first converted and then civilized, to the reformed profligate, to the "churlish" man who has become liberal.'[72] Such a feat should thus inspire those white men and women who already lived in the neat-and-tidy homes so venerated in missionary language, men and women who, by virtue of their racial membership and its gendered habits of 'civilization,' were already one step closer to Christian morality. How difficult, after all, was it to accept Christ under these conditions, when a far greater transformation had been made by their 'Indian' brothers and sisters? And, in turn, should not whites themselves serve as examples to Natives, who were in desperate need of models to emulate?

### 'Mimic' Women and Men

In missionary writings, Native men, women, and children became, in Homi Bhabha's words, 'mimic' people, as they embodied 'the desire for a reformed, recognizable other ... the subject of a desire that is almost the same, but not quite.' In missionary discourse, the 'reformed Indian' was the product of 'a complex strategy of reform, regulation, and discipline, which appropriate(d) the "Other" as it visualize(d) power.'[73] Power, in this case, did not pertain solely to the ability to seize Aboriginals' land or to command their labour; instead, power also meant the ability to transform Aboriginal subjectivity, to change the ways that Aboriginal men and women felt and thought about themselves as husbands and fathers, wives and mothers. And the desires that Native peoples embodied for the missionaries and their audiences were similar but not, as we have seen, *identical* to the desires they held for themselves.

### Conclusion

Thus the Ojibwa became figures that could be 'reformed, regulated, and disciplined,' processes that, it was suggested, would eventually occur by and through Native peoples' *own* desires. They also were figures appropriated for the edification and satisfaction of non-Native audiences' desires and fantasies even as, simultaneously, they served as warnings of the potentially tragic consequences of colonialism's power and embodied the missionaries' ambivalence towards colonialism. Not only were Native people in these writings made to perform the gendered work of colonial transformation for, it was suggested, their own sakes, they were also – and more to the point – made to perform this work for a non-Native audience. In doing so, the missionaries reminded their readers that, in the 'new' society of Upper Canada, particular kinds of homes and families, wives and husbands, and mothers and fathers formed the basis of both Christianity and 'civilization.'

NOTES

1  Philander Smith to the Editor, *Christian Guardian*, 27 November 1830.
2  A British colony established in 1791 in the aftermath of the American Revolution and the influx of Loyalist refugees, Upper Canada fell between the Ottawa River in the north and east, the St Clair River in the west, and Lakes Erie and Ontario in the south (approximating present-day southern and central Ontario). Its name was changed to Canada West in 1841.
3  For the sake of variety I have used the terms *imperial* and *colonial* interchangeably, while being aware that they are not synonymous to some scholars. I have also used the terms *British*, or *Anglo-American*, as well as *white* and, at times, *non-Native*, while realizing their limits in the early-nineteenth-century context. For the large and ever-increasing literature on imperial authorities' desires to reshape gender relations in colonized societies, see Jean Allman, 'Making Mothers: Missionaries, Medical Officers and

Women's Work in Colonial Asante, 1924–1945,' *History Workshop Journal* 38 (Autumn 1994): 23-47; Nancy Rose Hunt, '"Le bébé en brousse": European Women, African Birth Spacing, and Colonial Intervention in Breast Feeding in the Belgian Congo,' in Frederick Cooper and Ann Laura Stoler, eds, *Tensions of Empire: Colonial Cultures in a Bourgeois World* (Berkeley: University of California Press, 1997); Ann Laura Stoler, *Race and the Education of Desire: Foucault's* History of Sexuality *and the Colonial Order of Things* (Durham, NC: Duke University Press, 1995); Nupur Chaudhuri and Margaret Strobel, eds, *Western Women and Imperialism: Complicity and Resistance* (Bloomington: Indiana University Press, 1992); Mrinalini Sinha, *Colonial Masculinity: The 'Manly Englishman' and the 'Effeminate Bengali' in the Late Nineteenth Century* (Manchester: Manchester University Press, 1995); Ruth Roach Pierson and Nupur Chaudhuri, eds, *Nation, Empire, Colony: Historicizing Gender and Race* (Bloomington: Indiana University Press, 1998).

4   This is by no means to denigrate the work that has been done in these areas. See, for example, Anthony J. Hall, 'Native Limited Identities and Newcomer Metropolitanism in Upper Canada, 1814–1867,' in David Keane and Colin Read, eds, *Old Ontario: Essays in Honour of J.M.S. Careless* (Toronto: Dundurn Press, 1990); John Webster Grant, *Moon of Wintertime: Missionaries and the Indian of Canada in Encounter Since 1534* (Toronto: University of Toronto Press, 1987); Donald B. Smith, *Sacred Feathers: The Reverend Peter Jones (Kahkewaquonaby) and the Mississauga Indians* (Toronto: University of Toronto Press, 1987); Elizabeth Graham, *From Medicine-Man to Missionary: Missionaries as Agents of Change among the Indians of Southern Ontario* (Toronto: University of Toronto Press, 1975); Carl Benn, *The Iroquois in the War of 1812* (Toronto: University of Toronto Press, 1988); Edward S. Rogers and Donald B. Smith, eds, *Aboriginal Ontario: Historical Perspectives on the First Nations* (Toronto: Dundurn Press, 1994); Brian Osborne and Michael Ripmeester, 'The Mississaugas between Two Worlds: Strategic Adjustments to Changing Landscapes of Power,' *Canadian Journal of Native Studies* 17, no. 2 (1987): 259–91.

5   Mary Louise Pratt, *Imperial Eyes: Travel Writing and Transculturation* (London: Routledge, 1992), 7; see also Homi K. Bhabha, *The Location of Culture* (London: Routledge, 1994); Robert J.C. Young, *Colonial Desire: Hybridity in Theory, Culture, and Race* (London: Routledge, 1995); and, for a historical study of related themes, see David R. Roediger, *The Wages of Whiteness: Race and the Making of the American Working Class* (London: Verso, 1991).

6   For a discussion of these issues in the debates over Indian women and sati, see Gayatri Chakravorty Spivak, 'Can the Subaltern Speak?' in Cary Nelson and Lawrence Grossberg, eds, *Marxism and the Interpretation of Culture* (Urbana: University of Illinois Press, 1988), 271–313; for the Canadian context, see Ruth Roach Pierson, 'Experience, Difference, Dominance and Voice in the Writing of Canadian Women's History,' in Karen Offen, Ruth Pierson, and Jane Rendall, eds, *Writing Women's History: International Perspectives* (Houndmills, UK: Macmillan, 1991), 79–106.

7 Stoler, *Race and the Education of Desire*, 99. For other work that attempts to rethink the 'imperial centre/colonial margin' paradigm, see, for example, Anna Davin, 'Imperialism and Motherhood,' *History Workshop* 5 (1978): 9–65; Antoinette Burton, *Burdens of History: British Feminists, Indian Women, and Imperial Culture, 1865–1915* (Chapel Hill: University of North Carolina Press, 1994) and her 'Making a Spectacle of Empire: Indian Travellers in Fin-de-Siècle London,' *History Workshop Journal* 42 (Autumn 1996): 127–46; Billie Melman, 'Under the Western Historian's Eyes: Eileen Power and the Early Feminist Encounter with Colonialism,' *History Workshop Journal* 42 (Autumn 1996): 147–68; Catherine Hall, *White, Male and Middle Class: Explorations in Feminism and History* (New York: Routledge, 1992) and her '"From Greenland's Icy Mountains ... to Africa's Golden Sand": Ethnicity, Race and Nation in Mid-Nineteenth-Century England,' *Gender and History* 5, no. 2 (Summer 1993): 212–30; Vron Ware, *Beyond the Pale: White Women, Racism and History* (London: Verso, 1992); Pratt, *Imperial Eyes*; Anne McClintock, *Imperial Leather: Race, Gender and Sexuality in the Colonial Contest* (New York: Routledge, 1995); Susan Thorne, '"The Conversion of Englishmen and the Conversion of the World Inseparable": Missionary Imperialism and the Language of Class in Early Industrial Britain,' in Cooper and Stoler, eds, *Tensions of Empire*, 238–62.

8 See Catherine Hall, 'Missionary Stories: Gender and Ethnicity in England in the 1830s and 1840s,' in *White, Male and Middle Class*, 205–34.

9 Lengthier, more detailed discussions of missionary work in British North America can be found in Grant, 'Christianity and Civilization,' in *Moon of Wintertime*; Graham, *Medicine-Man to Missionary*; Smith, *Sacred Feathers*; and Peter Schmalz, *The Ojibwa of Southern Ontario* (Toronto: University of Toronto Press, 1991), chapters 5–7. In 1832 the colonial government invited the English-based Wesleyan Methodist Church into the province, as a means of countering the Episcopal church's American influence.

10 See Graham, *From Medicine-Man to Missionary*, chapters 2 and 3; see also Grant, *Moon of Wintertime*, 75–81.

11 Grant, *Moon of Wintertime*, 90.

12 Although the possibility of forms of syncretic religion or, in Grant's words, the 'yes that means no,' should not be overlooked (Grant, *Moon of Wintertime*, chapter 11).

13 Ibid., 91–5; Graham, *From Medicine-Man to Missionary*, chapter 7.

14 For a discussion of spirituality and gender in Upper Canada, see Marguerite Van Die, '"A Woman's Awakening": Evangelical Belief and Female Spirituality in Mid-Nineteenth-Century Canada,' in Wendy Mitchinson, Paula Bourne, Alison Prentice, Gail Cuthbert Brandt, Beth Light, and Naomi Black, eds, *Canadian Women: A Reader* (Toronto: Harcourt Brace, 1996).

15 It's not that the Church of England didn't describe the moral health of converted native communities but the reports and journals of Anglican missionaries tend not towards lengthy descriptions of native peoples' moral and subjective transformation;

rather, they are usually balance sheets of sacraments performed, accounts of the numbers of souls baptized, married, and buried within the rites of the Church. See, for example, Adam Elliott's letters in William Waddilove, ed., *The Stewart Missions: A Series of Letters and Journals, Calculated to Exhibit to British Christians, the Spiritual Destitution of the Emigrants Settled in the Remote Parts of Upper Canada* (London: J. Hatchard, 1838), 28–39.

16  Grant, *Moon of Wintertime*, 90.

17  Schmalz, *The Ojibwa*, 131–9; Smith, *Sacred Feathers*, 162–72.

18  For an analysis of race, gender, and ethnicity in English Baptist missionary work, see C. Hall, 'Missionary Stories,' also her 'White Visions, Black Lives: the Free Villages of Jamaica,' *History Workshop Journal* 36 (Autumn 1993): 100–32.

19  See Schmalz, *The Ojibwa*, 145–79, for a discussion of attempts to turn the Ojibwa into farmers.

20  I would like to thank Sylvia Van Kirk for reminding me of this point. See also Carol Devens, *Countering Colonization: Native American Women and Great Lakes Missions, 1630–1900* (Berkeley: University of California Press, 1992), 47–55; Sarah Carter, *Lost Harvests: Prairie Indian Reserve Farmers and Government Policy* (Montreal and Kingston: McGill-Queen's University Press, 1990); Robin Brownlie, 'Work Hard and Be Grateful: Native Soldier Settlers in Ontario after the First World War,' in Franca Iacovetta and Wendy Mitchinson, eds, *On the Case: Explorations in Social History* (Toronto: University of Toronto Press, 1998).

21  George F. Playter, *The History of Methodism in Canada: With an Account of the Rise and Progress of the Work of God among the Canadian Indian Tribes and Occasional Notices of the Civil Affairs of the Province* (Toronto: Anson Green, 1862), 240–50

22  J. Carruthers, *Retrospect of Thirty-Six Years' Residence in Canada West, Being a Christian Journal and Narrative* (Hamilton, ON: T.L. McIntosh, 1861), 31.

23  For a discussion of the temperance movement in Upper Canada, see Jan Noel, *Canada Dry: Temperance Crusades before Confederation* (Toronto: University of Toronto Press, 1995), chapters 8 and 9; for temperance work with Native peoples at Red River, see 187–9. However, missionaries did not appreciate the irony that 'drunken' Native men consumed liquor brought to them by European traders and 'explorers.'

24  Nathan Bangs, *A History of the Methodist Episcopal Church*, Vol. 3, *1816–1828* (New York: Carlton and Porter, 1838), 219.

25  Samuel Rose to John Rose, 24 August 1831, Rose papers, 1831–9, Archives of Ontario.

26  Playter, *The History of Methodism*, 268.

27  *Christian Guardian*, 4 February 1835. I do not want to suggest that alcohol was *not* a significant problem for Native communities during this period, particularly for the Ojibwa. It was, however, often pinpointed by whites as a central – sometimes the only – cause of Native suffering, having been inflicted on unsuspecting communities by

unscrupulous whites, and accordingly demonized. In contrast, colonial expansion itself came in for far less and much more muted critiques. For a more sustained examination of these issues, see Bonnie Duran, 'Indigenous versus Colonial Discourse: Alcohol and American Indian Identity,' in S. Elizabeth Bird, ed., *Dressing in Feathers: The Construction of the Indian in Popular Culture* (Boulder, CO: Westview Press, 1996).

28  See Cecilia Morgan, *Public Men and Virtuous Women: The Gendered Languages of Politics and Religion in Upper Canada, 1791–1850* (Toronto: University of Toronto Press, 1996), 112–20.

29  *Kingston Chronicle*, 16 December 1840.

30  John Carroll, *Case and His Contemporaries; or, the Canadian Itinerants' Memorial: Constituting a Biographical History of Methodism in Canada,* volume 3 (Toronto: Samuel Rose, 1871), 96.

31  Playter, *The History of Methodism*, 250.

32  Samuel Rose to John Rose, 24 August 1831.

33  See C. Hall, n. 11; Burton, *Burdens of History* and Ware, *Beyond the Pale*, especially Parts 2, 'An Abhorrence of Slavery: Subjection and Subjectivity in Abolitionist Politics,' and Part 3, 'Britannia's Other Daughters: Feminism in the Age of Imperialism.'

34  *Christian Guardian*, 28 May 1834.

35  These writings were, it is true, part of a tradition of missionary 'descriptions' of the mission field that stretched back to the seventeenth-century Jesuit *Relations*. However, by the early nineteenth century they were frequently shaped by the imagery and rhetoric of sentimental literature. For a discussion of such literature in the Upper-Canadian context, see Cecilia Morgan, '"Better Than Diamonds": Sentimental Strategies and Middle-Class Culture in Canada West,' *Journal of Canadian Studies* 32, no. 4 (Winter 1997–8): 125–48.

36  Ibid. These writings included 'Heathen Females – Licentiousness,' 11 May 1836; 'Missions – Paganism,' 17 January 1838; 'Missions – Paganism,' 4 April 1838.

37  'Missions – Paganism,' 17 January 1838.

38  G.J. Barker-Benfield, *The Culture of Sensibility: Sex and Society in Eighteenth-Century Britain* (Chicago: University of Chicago Press, 1992), 266–79.

39  See, for example, Playter, *The History of Methodism*, 249, 268; see also William Case's letter to Reverend Emory concerning work at the Credit Mission, reprinted in the *Colonial Advocate*, 4 January 1828.

40  *Christian Guardian*, 14 August 1830.

41  For a discussion of these issues within the context of missionary work, see Jane Haggis, 'White Women and Colonialism: Toward a Non-recuperative History,' in Clare Midgley, ed., *Gender and Imperialism* (Manchester: Manchester University Press, 1998).

42  *Christian Guardian*, 12 June 1833.

43  This situation provides an interesting contrast to that of mixed-race women married to British men in colonial Victoria. As Sylvia Van Kirk has shown, these mothers'

roles in 'socializing their children was circumscribed' and non-native fathers' prescriptions, along with those of the church and the school, were the agents of colonization (160). While the wives and mothers in these relationships also were expected to undergo gendered processes of 'civilization,' it is possible that class and denominational distinctions (and a slightly different context of contact) meant that Ojibwa women were expected to play a more pivotal role in their children's transformation – subject, of course, to the church's scrutiny and surveillance (Sylvia Van Kirk, 'Tracing the Fortunes of Five Founding Families of Victoria,' *B.C. Studies* 115/116 [1997–8]: 148–79).

44 John West, a chaplain with the Hudson's Bay Company, whose trips throughout British North America and the United States were supported by the Church Missionary Society, observed of the Mississaugas at the Credit that 'the neat apparel of some of the women affords a pleasing comment on the change which has taken place in their husbands and fathers' (*The Substance of a Journal during a Residence at the Red River Colony* [London: L.B. Seeley, 1827], 304).

45 Although we should not romanticize gender relations in Native societies as pre-lapsarian, gender differences did not automatically lead to gender inequalities. See Devens, *Countering Colonization*, 34–5 and also Kathleen M. Brown, 'The Anglo-American Gender Frontier,' in Nancy Shoemaker, ed., *Negotiators of Change: Historical Perspectives on Native American Women* (New York: Routledge, 1995). See also Joan M. Jensen, 'Native American Women and Agriculture: A Seneca Case Study,' in Vicki L. Ruíz and Ellen Carol DuBois, eds, *Unequal Sisters: A Multicultural Reader in U.S. Women's History*, 2d ed. (New York: Routledge, 1994). Gender, the state, and Native policy are discussed briefly in Lykke de la Cour, Cecilia Morgan, and Mariana Valverde, 'Gender Regulation and State Formation in Nineteenth-Century Canada,' in Allan Greer and Ian Radforth, eds, *Colonial Leviathan: State Formation in Nineteenth-Century Canada* (Toronto: University of Toronto Press, 1992), 173–5.

46 See, for example, Waddilove, *The Stewart Missions*, 15.

47 F. Hall as quoted in Playter, *The History of Methodism*, 345.

48 *Christian Guardian*, 27 November 1830. Similar comments, although not as clearly focused on women's role, were made by 'B' for the *Kingston Chronicle*, 28 November 1829.

49 *Christian Guardian*, 13 March 1830; see also the *Kingston Chronicle*, 5 March 1831.

50 Playter, *The History of Methodism*, 339.

51 *Christian Guardian*, 27 November 1830.

52 Ibid., 4 February 1835. See Smith, *Sacred Feathers*, 110, for a somewhat different, possibly second encounter between the women. See Mariana Valverde, 'The Love of Finery: Fashion and the Fallen Woman in Nineteenth-Century Social Discourse,' *Victorian Studies* 32, no. 2 (Winter 1989): 168–88.

53  *Christian Guardian*, 21 March 1838.

54  Evelyn Brooks-Higginbotham, 'African-American Women's History and the Metalan-guage of Race,' *Signs* 17, no. 2 (Winter 1992): 251–74. See also Barrington Walker's article in the present volume.

55  Devens, in *Countering Colonization*, argues that, during the nineteenth century, Ojibwa women were largely absent from missionaries' accounts of resistance and opposition to their work and that these women converted infrequently (63–4). I do not believe that the reports used in this paper can be read literally as a way of under-standing Native women's wholehearted embrace of Christianity, yet neither would I argue, as does Devens, that Ojibwa women were less important in missionary work. Moreover, Spivak's work on subaltern subjectivities should caution us, I think, against assumptions that these writings can be easily read 'against the grain' to simply 'uncover' the Native woman's 'voice.'

56  *Christian Guardian*, 21 March 1838. Of course, moral discipline could also play an important role in regulating gender relations and family matters but Sunday's writings, unlike those of non-native missionaries, did not stress this aspect of self-control.

57  Ibid., 7 October 1835.

58  George Copway, *Recollections of a Forest Life, or, the Life and Travels of Kah-ge-go-gah-bowh, or George Copway, Chief of the Ojibway Nation* (London: C. Gilpin, 1850), 32, 41. Although for a different kind of reading of native missionaries' writings, see Winona Stevenson, 'The Journals and Voices of a Church of England Native Cate-chist: Askenootow (Charles Pratt), 1851–1884,' in Jennifer S.H. Brown and Elizabeth Vibert, eds, *Reading Beyond Words: Contexts for Native Voices* (Peterborough, ON: Broadview Press, 1996), 304–29.

59  By this period, the Ojibwa in southern Ontario, for example, were not seen as part of the fur trade, nor were the missionaries trying to integrate them into resource-based industries such as lumbering.

60  See, for example, Jensen, 'Native American Women and Agriculture'; also Theda Pur-due, 'Women, Men and American Indian Policy: the Cherokee Response to "Civiliza-tion,"' in Nancy Shoemaker, ed., *Negotiators of Change* (New York: Routledge, 1995).

61  For example, see Mary P. Ryan, *Cradle of the Middle Class: The Family in Oneida County, New York, 1790–1865* (New York: Cambridge University Press, 1981); Leonore Davidoff and Catherine Hall, *Family Fortunes: Men and Women of the English Middle Class, 1780–1850* (Chicago: University of Chicago Press, 1987).

62  For discussions of fundraising in Upper Canada, see Morgan, *Public Men and Virtuous Women*, 202–7.

63  Ibid.

64  My arguments here are fairly speculative, as further research into this issue for the Upper Canadian context is needed. For the late-Victorian and Edwardian decades, see Cecilia Morgan, 'History, Nation, Empire: Gender and the Work of Southern Ontario

Historical Societies, 1890–1920s,' *Canadian Historical Review* 82, no. 3 (September 2001): 491–528.

65  Morgan, *Public Men and Virtuous Women*, 100–10.

66  This is not to suggest that no Anglo-American or British women participated in the daily round of missionary work. Missionaries' wives often played a critical, if underexplored, role in the mission settlements. As well, some female preachers, such as Eliza Barnes, were active in missionary work. However, few sources have survived that would permit an explicit exploration of how these missionary women might have crafted their sense of selves around the 'uplift' of native women. For a discussion of women's role in the Methodist church, see Elizabeth Gillian Muir, *Petticoats in the Pulpits: The Story of Early-Nineteenth-Century Methodist Women Preachers in Upper Canada* (Toronto: United Church Publishing House, 1991). For a discussion of the dominance of white women in missionary enterprises during the latter half of the nineteenth century, see Susan Thorne, *Congregational Missions and the Making of an Imperial Culture in 19th-Century England* (Stanford, CA: Stanford University Press, 1999).

67  For discussions of how middle-class manhood in England during this period was reliant on being a 'speaking subject,' see Hall, *White, Male, and Middle Class.*

68  Morgan, *Public Men*, 215–18.

69  Hall, 'Missionary Stories,' 248.

70  *Canadian Freeman*, 9 September 1830.

71  Ibid., 12 May 1831.

72  D., 'Cause of Missions,' *Christian Guardian*, 11 March 1835. The rest of the article was a defence of the importance of missions to the 'Indians.'

73  Bhabha, 'Of Mimicry and Man: The Ambivalence of Colonial Discourse,' in his *The Location of Culture*, 86.

# Whose Sisters and What Eyes?
# White Women, Race, and Immigration to British Columbia, 1849–1871

ADELE PERRY

## Introduction

White female immigration was an issue that garnered substantial popular attention in colonial British Columbia. It did so because it spoke deeply to that settler
society's concerns about race and gender. Analyzing the movement that orchestrated the immigration and the migrants it sponsored suggests that historians need
to revise the critical framework usually employed in much of the existing literature
on women's immigration to Canada. Historians especially need to recognize and
interrogate the significance of race to the lives of all female immigrants, including
white ones. Acknowledging the significance of race in turn leads to a questioning
of assumptions of female community and commonality. In these ways, the history
of white female immigration to British Columbia between 1849 and 1871 leads
us to question whose sisters and what eyes we evoke in our histories of women's
experience of immigration.

Historians of white settler colonies have found assisted female immigration a
useful way of addressing related questions about gender, race, and immigration.[1]
Assisted female immigration, Rita Kranidis has recently argued, offers a unique
glimpse into the 'unauthorized' colonial experience and into historical subjects
who were simultaneously colonizers and colonized.[2] It also allows historians of
immigration a revealing avenue into the relationship between migration and
imperialism, two related phenomena that are too rarely examined as such. White
settler colonies were defined by the simultaneous need to dispossess indigenous
societies and create a relatively homogenous, settler society in their stead.[3] Immigration was central to both processes.

## The 'Problem' of British Columbia, 1849–1871

The centrality of immigration to settler colonialism and its racialized and gendered character were made clear in mid-nineteenth-century British Columbia. This was a sorry example of settler imperialism. From the establishment of Vancouver Island as a British colony in 1849 to Canadian Confederation in 1871, the colony's settler population was small. Despite the grandiose visions of colonial promoters, it would be dominated by the Aboriginal population until late in the nineteenth century.[4] The absence of firm lines separating Native from newcomer further dogged the colony's claims to whiteness. Charles Gardiner, a visitor from Prince Edward Island, noted the hybridity that prevailed at a fur-trade ball in the late 1850s. 'There were the English, Scotch, French and Kanackas present,' he observed, 'and all so thoroughly mixed with the native Indian blood, that it would take a well-versed Zoologist to decide what class of people they were, and what relation they had to each other.'[5] The efforts to transform British Columbia from a First Nations to a British society were troubled both by the scarcity of white settlers and by their extensive contact with local peoples.

The prevailing ethnic and racial diversity of settler society further troubled those who hoped British Columbia could become a 'little England.' Chinese, African-American, Kanaka (Hawaiian), and Latin American settlers joined those from Continental Europe. A visiting missionary, Matthew Macfie, found Victoria, the capital city, an alarmingly cosmopolitan place in the early 1860s:

> Though containing at present an average of only 5,000 or 6,000 inhabitants, one cannot pass along the principal thoroughfares without meeting representatives of almost every tribe and nationality under heaven. Within a limited space may be seen – of Europeans, Russians, Austrians, Poles, Hungarians, Italians, Danes, Swedes, French, Germans, Spaniards, Swiss, Scotch, English and Irish: of Africans, Negroes from the United States and the West Indies; of Asiatics, Lascars and Chinamen; of Americans, Indians, Mexicans, Chilanoes, and citizens of the North American Republic; and of Polynesians, Malays from the Sandwich Islands [Hawaii].[6]

In British Columbia, visions of an orderly white settler colony were haunted both by the continued dominance of the First Nations population and by the plurality of settler society.

Visions of empire were thwarted by gender as well as by race. Gendered identities, behaviours and structures that were increasingly constructed as normative failed to reproduce themselves in British Columbia. Settler society was overwhelmingly male: while the female proportion ebbed and flowed over the colonial period, it never exceeded a high of 35 per cent of the white society and reached lows of

5 per cent. 'The population was of varied and mixed character,' remembered another missionary, 'consisting only of men, gathered from all parts of the world.'[7] A rough, backwoods male culture and conjugal relationships between First Nations women and settler men were two social phenomena that flowed from this demography. For many observers, they were the sharpest symbols of how gender was lived differently on this edge of empire.[8]

## White Women and the Politics of Empire

White women were routinely constructed as the penultimate solution to the supposed 'problem' of race and gender in British Columbia. White women were accorded a threefold role in the local colonial project. First, white women would compel white men to reject the rough homosocial culture of the backwoods in favour of normative standards of masculinity and respectability. A local journalist argued that 'the society here and throughout these colonies will prove *shiftless* for a long time, except Government or someone else provides wives for our young men.'[9] Second, they would both address shortages in the local labour market and relieve the 'surplus woman' problem in Britain. One local official wrote that 'while thousands of women, who could find happy homes here, either as servants or wives, are perhaps starving at home, their energies overtaxed, and their bodies wasted by too much work and too little food, and no opportunity occurs to them to reach this far off shore.'[10] While the black Caribbean servants whose immigration was abetted by the Canadian state in the twentieth century were treated as a sexual threat, British servant women were represented as a transformative moral force.[11] Third, white women would discourage mixed-race sexual, domestic, and conjugal relationships. White-Aboriginal heterosexual unions, thought another, were an 'evil' that could 'only be remedied by the introduction of fair ones of a purer caste into the Colony.'[12]

This discourse emphasized the political utility of ordinary, working-class women. We do not know very much about these imperial subjects whose history has been largely eclipsed by that of the articulate female elite of imperialism – missionaries, officers' wives, travel writers, and the like. In British Columbia, working-class white women were accorded a related but nonetheless specific role in the colonial project. Their contribution lay not in independent action, but in their familial role, and more especially in their ability to transform plebeian men, especially gold miners. This was a familial and sexual rather than reproductive role. White women's fertility would become highly politicized around the turn of the century,[13] but in the mid-nineteenth-century it was women's ability to control adult men that was emphasized. In the Australian lexicon, they were 'God's police.'[14] It was the imperial context that made them such: by actively participating in empire as immigrants, working-class women's moral status was transformed. Young, working-class women threatened society when they filled the workhouses, factories, or the streets of the metropole but bolstered society when they filled colonies. Supporting the assisted migration of women to British Columbia, the Bishop of Oxford, Samuel Wilberforce, explained that there was a special connection between metropole, colony, and poor women. God, he thought, seemed to have 'fitted one to the other.' Wilberforce seems to have suspected that his was a difficult argument, and took time to explain it at length:

> Only consider the number, for instance, of young girls brought up in the various union workhouses of this country. Every one of you knows the misery of that life – the miserable promise of it for the future. You know how from the experience of Poor Law Inspectors, and the testimony of every one connected with the system, is uniform, that these girls, having no future before them, being brought, as they pass from girlhood into early womanhood into perpetual contact with the worst of their own sex, whose miseries bring them back to the workhouse, and the worst of the other sex, whose idleness has taken them into it; that these young girls become demoralized: that there is no future before them, and that they often become again in after life the wretched inmates of the very same asylum, to hand on to the next generation of girls beyond them the taint of evil which they received on their very own day. (Hear, hear.) But then comes the question 'What can you do for them?' Now, I say, let any practical man in the House of Commons address himself to the subject, and let him consider carefully, with those who will help him in it, the way of providing that the parish shall be able to forestall the certain expenses it must be at in maintaining these girls in the workhouse. Let them, instead of that, before the time of girlhood is over, be sent to these new colonies of ours – there received and cared for by Christian people – thence passed out, first into the different services for which there is such an exceeding demand in these new settlements, and then naturally, by taking up of society, into the character of wife and mother ... you will have made homes in that distant land, you will have made the elevating influence of woman's society and of family life a healing blessing to those adventurous souls.[15]

For Wilberforce, and presumably for the audience that cheered him, imperial immigration was capable of transforming a threat to the nation into a defence of it.

### Assisted Female Immigration, 1859–1870

The discourse of imperial womanhood was sufficient to motivate four significant female immigration schemes. The first was piggy-backed on the arrival of the Royal Engineers, the soldier-settlers sent to assure British military authority over the mainland and colonize it. The initial detachment of 121 engineers was accompanied by 31 women and 34 children, and at least another 9 children were born on board the *Thames City* as it travelled via Cape Horn.[16] In 1860, Commander Richard Moody inquired about the possibility of assisting the passage of non-commissioned soldiers' wives and partners who had not joined the initial detachment, writing that his men were 'most anxious for their wives and "promissi sposi" to join them.'[17] In a fit of unusual enthusiasm that would never again be repeated, the Colonial Office immediately pledged their support.[18] Their patronage was premised on a rationale that would be evoked again and again in future discussions of immigration, colonialism, and gender: female immigration was desirable because it was both indicative and generative of respectable male behaviour, here represented most potently by permanent settlement.[19]

By the autumn of 1860, the emigration commissioner had co-ordinated the passage of the women on board the *Marcella*. Initially, all but one of the women accepted the offer of a free passage. On further rumination, three declined to go to British Columbia for a variety of reasons relating to the precarious circumstance and proud culture of working-class British women. One was seriously ill, one was insulted by the suggestion that she would be considered an 'emigrant' or an object of charity and presumably a woman of dubious moral standing, and another lacked the necessary money to reach the port. The *Marcella* ultimately carried only three women and four children, their passages sponsored by the emigration branch of the imperial state.[20]

The issues of gender, race, and immigration raised by the *Marcella* were highlighted by the assisted migrations in 1862–3 still remembered in popular British Columbia lore as the 'brideships.' These efforts were the result of the combined activity of British feminists, missionary agencies, and, to a lesser extent, British Columbia's elite. In London, a small group of well-to-do women known as the 'ladies of Langham Place' launched a multifaceted effort to broaden the acceptable sphere of activity for women, especially middle-class ones. Under the auspices of the Female Middle-Class Emigration Society (FMCES), they turned to immigration to British Columbia and other colonies as one amongst a series of means for fostering female self-sufficiency. They were joined in these efforts by the Columbia Emigration Society (CES), an off-shoot of British Columbia's missionary agency, the Anglican Columbia Mission. The CES was formed in London in early 1862 'to facilitate the Emigration of Industrious Women to the Colony of British Columbia.'[21]

The FMCES's first large-scale immigration was directed to British Columbia. Early attempts to establish a committee in Vancouver Island were thwarted by the unwillingness of local contacts to support female immigration. In 1861, Sarah Crease, wife of the attorney general, told the FMCES that 'I regret that I cannot give you any hopes of being able to benefit educated women by sending them out here.' Crease worried about their morality in the perilous, rough environs of Vancouver Island. 'The bane of the country is drink; assisted much by the removal of the pressure of that portion of public opinion consisting of social and family influence, which at home has so powerful an effect in helping to keep things straight,' she added.[22] Crease, like so many other white colonials, reversed the linkage made by metropolitan observers like Wilberforce and suggested that colonial contexts would make migrants less rather than more moral.

The establishment of the CES in the spring of 1862 provided the encouragement that correspondents like Crease had explicitly failed to. Maria Rye, the secretary of the FMCES, initially merely asked if she could attach a party of twenty women to the forty the CES had plucked from public institutions to travel on the *Tynemouth*.[23] When the CES responded by asking Rye to co-ordinate their entire female emigration effort in the spring of 1862, a productive alliance between metropolitan feminists and missionaries was formed.[24] It came as something of a shock for the local elite in Victoria. 'This London "Columbia Mission Meeting" has taken us quite by surprise,' wrote New Westminster missionary H.P. Wright in a private letter. While he had told metropolitan friends of British Columbia's desire for white female immigrants, he expected neither the pace nor the form that it took. 'The Bishop is as much puzzled as I am,' he added.[25] The confusion that characterized the administration of this immigration did not dampen the unprecedented public spectacle organized to greet the *Tynemouth* when it finally rolled into James Bay on 19 September 1862. Similar fanfare met the thirty-eight working-class women carried by the second female immigration vessel, the *Robert Lowe,* that arrived January 1863.[26]

It would be six more years before another female immigration effort was successfully launched. Endorsed by Governors Frederick Seymour and Anthony Musgrave, this immigration was effectively managed by a local board that aimed to implicate the local middle class by having them promise to employ an immigrant as a domestic servant and assume responsibility for a portion of her passage. When the colonial bourgeoisie proved less than enthusiastic about the immigration effort, the board modified their scope, reduced the amount of money both servant and employer would be compelled to contribute, and allowed servants to submit promissory notes in lieu of cash.[27] The board empowered Anglican Bishop George Hills, who was visiting England, to seek servants there and encouraged colonial bourgeois families to select their own servants or have British friends do so.[28] This scheme produced twenty-one assisted female immigrants carried on the *Alpha* in June 1870.

Each of these female immigration schemes was motivated by the conviction that white women had a special imperial mission and would save British Columbia's sorry imperial fortunes. Yet each of these immigration efforts left its supporters more ambivalent than assured. This constant dissatisfaction stemmed from the reformers' disappointment with the white female immigrants. Despite the grandiose promises of high colonial discourse, they did not behave like the beacons of Britannic civilization they were promised to be. The young women were not the dutiful domestic servants hyped by immigration promoters. Governor James Douglas's comments that 'with very few exceptions' the women of the *Tynemouth* and *Robert Lowe* had 'been comfortably provided for' rang hollow.[29] Of the four women included in the FMCES annual reports, one became a school teacher and married in two years; another, dubbed 'Not very successful,' found employment as a needle-woman; a third 'Left situation rashly, and afterwards found difficulty in obtaining employment'; while the fourth was described as having gone to her sister.[30] One observer remembered that many were 'carried off and married a few days after arrival,' and only two laboured for the duration of their indentures.[31]

The assisted female migrants became more famed for their expressive heterosexuality than their dutiful service. From the outset, the local reformers charged with the immigrants' care worked hard to limit the women's contact with men. The rough male culture of the backwoods rendered this task especially difficult. Whenever female migrants arrived, crowds of men turned their landing into a ribald spectacle. When the *Marcella* arrived with her cargo, young men attempted to infiltrate the ship in the harbour, and a crowd met the women as it docked.[32] When the *Tynemouth* was in harbour, five men tried, without success, to board the ship to 'catch a glimpse of the rosy-cheeked English beauties.'[33] The women's landing occurred 'before the admiring gaze of some 300 residents.'[34] So thick was the crowd watching the women move from the gunboat to their accommodations at the Marine Barracks that 'it required the united exertions of four policemen and the same number of stalwart marines to obtain a passage for the fair immigrants.'[35] 'Every available inch of ground from which a view could be obtained,' wrote the *British Columbian*, was 'occupied by men of all ages and colors, eagerly looking for a sight of the long looked for and much talked about cargo.'[36]

The spectacle did not end when the women came ashore. The crowd followed the women to their residence at the Marine Barracks and continued their surveillance project. The press dubbed the motley but vigilant male observers 'a large and anxious crowd of breeches-wearing bipeds.'[37] However anxious, the crowd did open a passage large enough for the women to march two-by-two to their temporary quarters.[38] A few days later, journalists remarked that the constant presence of young male eyes restricted the women's movements. The 'young women,' they wrote, 'were unable to enjoy a walk in the enclosure without being subjected to the gaze of a rabble of some forty persons, who hung about the premises, and leaning on the fence, scanned the inmates in a manner that was disgraceful.'[39]

The *Robert Lowe* presented a similar challenge to those charged with the responsibility of morally regulating the young women. Before its arrival, the local press admonished the receiving committee to more effectively protect the women from the diabolical attentions of aimless young working-class men. 'There is not the slightest necessity for any parade about so simple a matter as the landing of a few passengers, and we cannot conceive anything more heartless or ill considered than to have these poor young strangers, we don't care of what sex, but jeered to the rude gaze of a motley crowd of roughs who, instead of running about idle, should be engaged with the shovel or the axe earning an honest living.'[40] A special footpath between James Bay and the Immigration Barracks was created and lined by prominent bourgeois women, including the Mayor's wife, Mrs Harris, and Mrs Cridge, wife of Anglican minister Edward Cridge. Mixed-race elite women like the governor's wife, Amelia Connolly Douglas, were conspicuously absent. Despite the attempt to imbue the landing with civility and gentility, represented most notably by the conspicuous presence of elite white women, the rough, homosocial culture of colonial British Columbia again prevailed. By the time of landing, the crowd reportedly numbered one thousand. 'The girls,' condemned the *British Colonist*, 'had to run the gamut through the utterance of coarse jokes and personalities.'[41] A significant police presence did not, the newspaper thought, make sufficient use of their authority to control this rough and disorderly male crowd.[42] Despite efforts to sanitize the process, the white women's arrival again tested colonial British Columbians' claim to respectable status instead of, as was expected, ensuring it.

The ongoing and escalating efforts to monitor and protect the female migrants replicated the inevitable irony of moral regulation in a context of mandatory heterosexuality, namely, the need to simultaneously encourage and constrain, foster and monitor, male-female sexual contact. Victoria's elite was mandated with an especially contradictory task, namely to protect the women from that very thing that justified their importation – male attention and desire. A fence around the barracks ensured that the women could not leave, although 'a few straggled away, but were brought back by the vigilant police,' a committee member reported.[43] When a young woman staying at the barracks 'engaged in an animated conversation with a young man on the outside of the enclosure,' two clergyman and a naval officer quickly intervened. The *British Colonist* mocked their prudishness by suggesting that a guard of marines be placed around the barracks and that interloping men be bayoneted.[44] Instead, clergy as well as police were enlisted in the effort to shape the women's contact with the community around them. A week after their landing, Reverend Scott gave a highly publicized sermon to the women, bidding them to remember their role as colonizers and representatives of English womanhood. He told them 'always and under any circumstances to shape their conduct so that they might prove a credit to their English mothers, from whom many were now departed forever.'[45] Informal regulation continued after this initial flurry of attention. Louisa Townsend, a middle-class *Tynemouth* migrant, remembered being virtually cloistered when she first arrived on the mainland. 'I know there were a lot of soldiers and I was never allowed to go out on the street alone,' she recalled, speaking volumes to the centrality of fear to white women's experience in colonial British Columbia.[46]

These efforts aimed to ensure that the brideships would produce respectable heterosexuality, and not easy, expressive, working-class sexual contact. Yet stories of the immigrants' immorality and participation in rough, backwoods culture circulated widely. In 1863, Sophia Shaw of the *Tynemouth* married a wealthy Cariboo miner, Mr. Pioneer. Their wedding, according to Edmund Hope Verney, was a pinnacle of backwoods excess. Everything was 'carried out in tip-top style' and everyone was drunk.[47] The *British Columbian* commented that a number of women could 'fairly attribute their ruin' to the *Tynemouth*.[48] Soon after the arrival of the *Robert Lowe*, a group was charged with thieving at the Immigration Barracks and in 1864, five of the *Robert Lowe*'s passengers – Charlotte Anne Eaton *nee* Bates, Bessie Lyons, Jane Smith, Ann Fish, and Jane Atkinson – were charged with having failed to pay the balance of their passages.[49]

A trial involving a *Tynemouth* immigrant suggests some of the smaller ways that the assisted female migrants thwarted prevailing images of white women and respectability. In 1864, shopkeepers Herman Schultz and Jasper Newton Trickey were charged with raping Esther Meiss, who had immigrated on the *Tynemouth* two years before. Meiss testified that both Schultz and Trickey 'had connection with me while I was under the influence of the drink which Mr Schultz had given me.' The court testimony revealed a life that departed sharply from the images of white femininity peddled by the female immigration movement. The defence lawyer suggested Meiss had a continuing and consensual sexual relationship with various men, including Trickey. Meiss herself was willing to admit to having been 'intimate' with other men before her marriage and to patronizing a 'dancing room.' Her marriage was not a happy one. Defence witnesses testified that Meiss said her 'husband had gone away and left nothing but bread in the house' and that he would not give her 'a "bit" to buy cheese with.' In response, she reportedly threatened to leave her husband, telling him, 'You have driven it so far that I will have to turn bad.' She looked to Trickey, saying that her husband 'feeds me on nothing but dry bread and fish, but I've got a key to Mr. Trickey's room where I can get anything I want.' While Meiss denied all this, she admitted to stealing money from her husband.[50]

Meiss also suggested some of the ways that working-class women manipulated the female migration movement to their own ends. In court, she revealed that she arrived under a false name, probably in an effort to hide her Jewishness. She 'came to this country in my stepfather's name, my maiden name is Hurst; I came out in the *Tynemouth* as Mary Hodges; I was married as Esther Hurst; my sister wrote me my name, she said I was not born a christian, and I changed the name of Mary Hodges to Esther Hurst.' Yet on arrival in Victoria, Meiss seems to have joined the local Jewish community; her husband was attending synagogue when the alleged rape occurred. Meiss did not keep in touch with her shipmates, and testified to having a very limited female community.[51] Meiss hovered on the edge of operative definitions of both whiteness and respectable womanhood.

Given Meiss's difficulty in marshalling the image of a respectable white woman, it is not surprising the accused were found not guilty. The judge, who earlier banned her husband from the courtroom for prompting her, instructed the jury to find the men not guilty because of contradictory evidence. Meiss was outraged, claiming that the defence lawyer 'was a d–nation liar,' and that she'd 'like to get hold of him.'[52] This case certainly reveals some of the profound ways that white, working-class women's behaviour and identity in British Columbia departed from formal colonial discourse. Esther Meiss or Mary Hodges or Esther Hurst was not the imperial subject the FMCES had intended her to be. She does not seem to have worked as a domestic servant. Rather than reforming the disorderly, easy sociability of working-class white men in the colony, she seems to have participated in it, changing partners and attending dance halls, and, if witnesses against her are to be believed, taking cash and goods in exchange for sex. Instead of serving as a beacon for Britishness, she adopted a Jewish identity, and in doing so, revealed how she hoodwinked the do-gooders who subsidized her passage. She did not take up the role of the dutiful working-class housewife. Meiss avoided her shipmates and alienated her few female friends. She embezzled the housekeeping money, and complained bitterly and publicly when her husband failed to support her in a manner she deemed appropriate.

### Female Immigration Reconsidered

Stories like Meiss's led colonial pundits to question the merits of white female immigration. They expressed profound disappointment with the immigrants' failure to live up to the standards white women were supposed to represent. Settlers mobilized their colonial experience to portray assisted female migration as a metropolitan fantasy concocted with no knowledge or regard for the conditions of the colonies. One letter-writer claimed that immigration-supporter Angela Burdett Coutts lacked judgement in 'her consignment of girls for miners' wives.'[53] Others mocked the middle-class manners and language of those who organized the *Robert Lowe* and *Tynemouth*, damning 'the officious "meddling and muddling" of the pseudo-philanthropic semi-religious immigration societies, and their committees, agents, or friends.'[54]

Criticism of the female immigration schemes became an axis of settler-identity, a tool whereby white colonials articulated a subject-position rooted in their experience of British Columbia and explicitly differentiated from those who lacked it and implicitly from those who were native to it. English do-gooders, they suggested, possessed no genuine knowledge of colonial conditions. Rather than making working-class women more moral, backwoods life tempted them further. The white female migrants failed, explained one, because Victoria was 'crammed ... with perhaps the most dissipated and reckless set of men on earth' and presented 'no lack of temptation to the new comers.'[55] Instead of reforming them, British Columbia made working-class women even more degraded. The 'temptations of gold, rich trinkets and fine dresses,' explained another, 'is too great to be long resisted by those who have been brought up in penury and have no one man to constantly remind them how much more precious than gold and precious stones is a virtuous woman.'[56]

An 1865 visit to Australia gave Maria Rye sympathy to the settler view of assisted female immigration. In a private letter, she explained that the British underestimated the moral perils of colonies and in so doing misunderstood female immigration. Emigrants, she argued, needed to be firm, labour-loving women if they were to survive these hybrid, rough places intact:

> I think it very hard for you who are at a distance from the colonies to understand them – they are so intensely good, & so intensely bad, according to the life made of them ... I still think to the full as strongly as when I left home that women – educated or not, may come here with the very greatest possible advantages to themselves – but I see even clearer than ever that they must be broken of a certain stamp. – women who dislike work, or who are not really steady in their principles are a thousand fold better off at home – there are scores of such women in Scotland, they are not exactly idlers – not at all immoral – but they work because they *must* – & are virtuous because they are surrounded by scores of good homes & by inducements of strong every kind to go right – all this vanishes, or you waste all vanishes here – & the colonies like the testing fire of the apostle.[57]

Even Rye, who was so key in promoting white women as able to save the colonies from themselves, privately worried that women were more often corrupted by them. The difficulty of exporting adult women to colonies would lead Rye to shift her considerable energies to child migration, an enterprise that would present different, if even more daunting, political conundrums.[58]

By the close of the colonial period, the very do-gooders who nurtured these immigration efforts had come to doubt the utility of white female migration. Edmund Verney wrote to his father that the women were too obsessed with speedy marriages, easy labour, and high wages to be of much good. He preferred the young, guileless ones among the *Tynemouth's* women, who, it seems, had no personal agendas to conflict with his own. Verney deemed the entire affair 'anything but a cause for self-congratulation and pride.'[59] In 1872, Gilbert Sproat declared that his experience with three separate female immigration efforts had undermined his faith in the entire project. Sproat thought that the fundamental problem was that single female migration necessarily led to immorality. Women needed to be monitored by families to be anything other than a social threat. In general, Sproat thought, '*Unmarried female* emigration does not lead to good results.' He continued that '[n]o right thinking observant person will advocate female immigration by sea voyage from Europe to British Columbia. It is unjust to the women, and upon the whole, is disadvantageous to the province.'[60]

By the early 1870s, family migration was increasingly presented as the only way to solve the inevitable moral dilemmas presented by female immigration. The immigration board decision to shift its monies and attentions to the 'assisted passages of Families, and relatives of Farmers, Mechanics, and others settled in this Colony' suggests a profound dissatisfaction with this female immigration scheme and, indeed, the entire project of single female immigration.[61] 'The very delicate and difficult question of introducing single unmarried women into British Columbia might be partly solved by sending out a few, in charge of the heads of families – the women being from the same district as the families, and thus having an addition guard for their self-respect,' Sproat argued.[62] Assisted white female migration was problematic in large part because it suggested the possibility, and sometimes delivered the disturbing presence, of working-class female independence. Family migration, on the other hand, ensured that young women would not be allowed to run amok without adequate supervision. 'They would never leave the proper surveillance of their natural guardians,' wrote the *British Colonist* in 1869.[63] These arguments were premised on beliefs in male authority and on abiding assumptions about the nuclear family's status as the natural unit of social organization. Indeed, anything other than family groups, wrote one fan of family migration, produced an ARTIFICIAL ASSORTMENT of human beings.'[64] Just as it was difficult to square white women's lives with the grandiose promises of colonial discourse, it was difficult indeed to reconcile 'artificial assortments' with imperial visions of white womanhood.

### White Women and Colonialism

Widespread disappointment in the political effect of female migration does not, however, mean that the white female immigrants failed to serve the local colonial project. White female immigrants reinforced as well as challenged the connections between white womanhood and imperial respectability. Their lives, like those of other white women in British Columbia, were intimately shaped by the construction of white women as symbolic of empire. This could constrict the parameters of their experience, but it could also accord them levels of power and authority usually denied women on the grounds of sex. And some of the white female immigrants seem to have relished, or at least enjoyed, the power they reaped from being icons of racial separation and hierarchy in a diverse colonial society. 'Mary E.,' a *Tynemouth* emigrant and Yale school teacher, wrote that 'I am quite surrounded by Chinese and Indians.' She also spoke of the racially liminal figures of backwoods miners, likening them to disreputable working-class men in Britain. 'They are the most uncivilized-looking beings when they first come down; you would be quite frightened to be accosted by one at Brighton,' she explained. In the end, Mary found the 'others' less threatening than anticipated and enjoyed the status this racial context afforded her as a white woman. 'There are very few white women here, so they are treated with politeness by all,' she explained, adding that this status guaranteed them an audience with the local luminaries, including the 'Governor, the Bishop, the Judge, and all the great folks.'[65] Colonial life transformed Mary's class and racial status, and for that she was willing to live among Chinese, Indians, and those who would have frightened her in Brighton.

Yet, ideals of racial separation did not always define the white women's experience in uncomplicated ways. Their lives, like the men's, could be deeply intertwined with First Nations peoples, lifestyles, and customs. Susan Moir Allison's memoir of the Okanagan Valley is a telling testament to the ways that white women could be simultaneously very far from and very close to First Nations people.[66] Settler women's ability to be simultaneously racist and culturally hybrid sometimes struck metropolitan observers as ironic. Scientist Robert Brown described visiting Isabella Robb at her Comox farm in the summer of 1864. Robb, the former matron of the *Tynemouth,* apparently prided herself on being the 'first white woman' in the settlement. Yet, to Brown's metropolitan eyes, Robb seemed more Aboriginal than white. 'The old lady,' he wrote, 'apologized to me for having nothing better to offer. "Mowich" [deer], she said, was scarce just now. Formerly there was "hyou" [plenty] but now the "Siwashes" [Indians] brought in little and wanted for that little *hyou chickaman* [plenty money].' He found the juxtaposition of Robb's racism and hybridity a peculiar one. 'Mrs. Robb is an Englishwoman and of course with all a Britisher's contempt for savages, but like all others out here mixed in her conversation Indian Jargon.'[67] Robb's story suggest some of the ways that gender and class could complicate as well as reinforce racial politics. White women were summoned in the interests of empire, but they seldom served it in a straightforward manner.

### The History of Women and Immigration Reconsidered

The history of white female immigration to colonial British Columbia suggests that historians revise some of the ways in which they analyze women and immigration. It especially indicates how race is a useful analytic category to the history of immigration, including the immigration of those racialized as 'white.' The female immigrants to colonial British Columbia were highly racialized: their importation was demanded on the grounds of empire and racial mission, and to fail to analyze their history as a chapter in the history of race as well as gender is to misunderstand the female immigration movement and the women whose lives it shaped. The story of female immigration affirms what scholars like Vron Ware, David Roediger, Ruth Frankenberg, and Catherine Hall have argued: namely that whiteness, like blackness or brownness or redness, is a racial category with a history that deserves explication.[68] It also suggests that we locate Canadian history within a broader context of imperial history instead of assigning it a historical isolation not merited by its history. Doing so not only honours Canada's imperial context, but allows us to benefit from the rich secondary literatures on colonial and imperial experience.

Recognizing the significance of whiteness and empire leads feminist scholars to probe assumptions of female unity. Feminist historians need to explore more fully how race divided women from each other and structured their relationships to one another. As Australian historian Marilyn Lake argues, 'Feminism's great animating insight lies in the recognition of the systematic nature of men's power over women; its concomitant blindspot is the frequent failure to see that the sisterhood of women also involves systematic relations of domination between women.'[69] Addressing this blindspot means probing the limits as well as the possibilities of sisterhood. How did race benefit or disadvantage different groups of migrants in different ways? Were the largely Central, Eastern, and Southern European women studied by contributors to *Looking into My Sister's Eyes*, for instance, included or excluded from the category of whiteness?[70] How did their experience of racial identification shape their experience as migrants in the Canadian state's highly racialized immigration system, in Canadian society as a whole, and in relation to other women? When accessing the history of a group of female immigrants, we need to ask, in other words, when they looked into each others' eyes, did they see sisters or strangers?

White female immigrants to colonial British Columbia seem to have usually found strangers. Settler women's recollections, like those of Australian immigrants studied by A. James Hammerton,[71] contain little evidence of sustained interaction – let alone sympathy – with First Nations women, or even with non-white settler women, whether Asian, black, or Latin American. That it could be troubled by the cultural hybridity of their lifeways did not breech this palpable social distance. Nor was this distance unique. Scholars of gender and imperialism have explored how, throughout the colonial world, white women's role as 'gentle tamers' or 'mothers of the race' structured their interactions both with white men and local peoples.[72] Recognizing white women's special relationship to colonialism should not lead us to exaggerate their racism in the interests of absolving white men of their fundamental responsibility for the ravages of imperialism.[73] We can, instead explore how white women benefited from their special relationship to imperialism without exaggerating their real power within the colonial project.

Doing so will equip us to better understand immigration as well as imperialism. The two phenomena, after all, were intimately connected. The secondary literature on immigration, however, has been generally hesitant to probe the connections between empire and migration, treating the movements of European peoples as simple, apolitical movements to large, empty spaces.[74] While immigration was, without doubt, motivated primarily by straightforward social and economic needs, it was also an imperial act, part and parcel of the ongoing effort to assert white dominance and displace Aboriginal populations.[75] Exploring the relationship between empire and immigration necessitates examining the migrants sought by colonial regimes as well as those discouraged by them. British Columbia's historians have focused their attention on efforts to discourage the immigration of specific peoples, most notably East Asians and to a lesser extent, South Asians. While racist anti-immigration movements certainly deserve our historical attention, the notion that British Columbia should not accept certain peoples were premised on the firm conviction that *other* peoples were more suitable migrants. The analogous programs that fostered and supported the immigration of these peoples have gone neglected.[76] In separating the two processes, we fail to understand both, and most of all fail to understand their relationship to colony and nation-building as a whole. Reconnecting immigration with colony and nation-building means returning to a largely forgotten moment in the writing of the history of immigration to Canada, if for entirely different reasons. As Franca Iacovetta points out, earlier scholars of the Canadian nation-building school, such as Donald Creighton, acknowledged immigration 'as a key ingredient in transcontinental nation-making'[77] yet neglected the immigrant subjects. But while Creighton used this insight to celebrate nation-building and, by implication if not explication, imperialism, we can use it to critically unpack the discourse of Canadian nation and the role that immigration plays within it. Sociologists Sunera Thobani, Nandita Sharma, and Sedef Arat-Koç are doing it for the present, and historians need to do it for the past.[78]

## Conclusion

In a variety of ways, the history of assisted white-female immigration to British Columbia suggests that we question which sisters and whose eyes we refer to in our discussions of women and immigration. In the eleven years between 1859 and 1870, roughly 130 women, largely working class, mostly young and entirely white, were imported to the hybrid, unstable settler society of British Columbia. Their immigration was orchestrated because white women were accorded a special racial mission within the colonial context of mid-nineteenth-century British Columbia. Whether the experience of white women challenged or confirmed these imperial roles, it can tell us much about the connections between race, gender, and immigration, and suggest some new ways of examining the history of women and immigration in Canada. We can begin this process by acknowledging immigrant women as the divided and unstable category they were. Sometimes they were sisters, sometimes they were strangers, and sometimes, uncomfortably, they were both.

NOTES

I would like to acknowledge Marlene Epp, Franca Iacovetta, and Frances Swyripa for making *Sisters and Strangers* happen, and all of the contributors for helping me think through questions of women, race, and migration. The Social Sciences and Humanities Research Council provided funding for this project through a Doctoral and Postdoctoral fellowship. Much of this material is revised from *On the Edge of Empire: Gender, Race, and the Making of British Columbia, 1849–1871* (Toronto: University of Toronto Press, 2001).

1  A. James Hammerton, *Emigrant Gentlewomen: Genteel Poverty and Female Emigration, 1830–1914* (London: Croom Helm, 1979); Charlotte Macdonald, *A Woman of Good Character: Single Women as Immigrant Settlers in Nineteenth-Century New Zealand* (Wellington: Bridget Williams, 1990); Patricia Clark, *The Governesses: Letters from the Colonies, 1862–1882* (London: Hutchinson, 1985); Janice Gothard, '"Radically Unsound and Mischievous": Female Migration to Tasmania, 1856–1863,' *Australian Historical Studies* 23, no. 93 (October 1989): 386–404; Cecillie Swaisland, *Servants and Gentlewomen to the Golden Land: The Emigration of Single Women from Britain to Southern Africa, 1820–1939* (Oxford and Providence: Berg and the University of Natal Press, 1993); Barbara Roberts, '"A Work of Empire": Canadian Reformers and British Female Immigration,' in Linda Kealey, ed., *A Not Unreasonable Claim: Women and Reform in Canada, 1880s–1920s* (Toronto: Women's Press, 1979); Susan Jackel, ed., *A Flannel Shirt and Liberty: British Emigrant Gentlewomen in the Canadian West, 1880–1914* (Vancouver: University of British Columbia Press, 1982); Suzann Buckley, 'British Female Emigration and Imperial Development: Experiments in Canada, 1885–1931,' *Hecate* 3, no. 2 (July 1977): 26–40; Marilyn Barber, 'The Women Ontario Welcomed: Immigrant Domestics for Ontario Homes, 1870–1930,' in Jean Burnet, ed., *Looking into My Sister's Eyes: An Exploration in Women's History* (Toronto: Multicultural History Society of Ontario, 1986); Marilyn Barber, 'The Gentlewomen of Queen Mary's Coronation Hostel,' in Barbara K. Latham and Roberta J. Pazdro,

eds, *Not Just Pin Money: Selected Essays on the History of Women's Work in British Columbia* (Victoria: Camosun College, 1984); Jackie Lay, 'To Columbia on the *Tynemouth*: The Immigration of Single Women and Girls in 1862,' in Barbara Latham and Cathy Kess, eds, *In Her Own Right: Women's History in B.C.* (Victoria: Camosum College, 1980).

2 Rita S. Kranidis, 'Introduction: New Subjects, Familiar Grounds,' in Rita S. Kranidis, ed., *Imperial Objects: Essays on Victorian Women's Emigration and the Unauthorized Imperial Experience* (London: Twayne, 1998).

3 On these connections, see Daiva Staisulis and Nira Yuval-Davis, 'Introduction: Beyond Dichotomies – Gender, Race, Ethnicity and Class in Settler Societies,' in Daiva Staisulis and Nira Yuval-Davis, eds, *Unsettling Settler Societies: Articulations of Gender, Race, Ethnicity and Class* (London: Sage, 1995).

4 See Robert Galois and Cole Harris, 'Recalibrating Society: The Population Geography of British Columbia in 1881,' *Canadian Geographer* 38, no. 1 (1994): 37–53.

5 C.C. Gardiner, in Robie L. Reid, ed., 'To The Fraser River Mines in 1858,' *British Columbia Historical Quarterly* 1, no. 1 (October 1937): 248.

6 Matthew Macfie, *Vancouver Island and British Columbia: Their History, Resources and Prospects* (London: Longman, Green, Longman, Roberts & Green, 1865), 378–9.

7 A.C. Garret, 'Reminisencs, (Transcript) Anglican Church of Canada, Archives of the Diocese of New Westminster/Ecclesiastical Province of British Columbia, Vancouver School of Theology, University of British Columbia (hereafter ADNW/EPBC), PSA 52, File 57, 28.

8 On these points, see Adele Perry, *On the Edge of Empire: Gender, Race, and the Making of British Columbia, 1849–1871* (Toronto: University of Toronto Press, 2001).

9 'Inducements for Families to Settle in Victoria,' *British Colonist*, 30 November 1861 (emphasis in original).

10 Charles Good to Lord Office of the Government, 21 August 1869, British Columbia Archives (hereafter BCA), GR 1486, Great Britain, Colonial Office, British Columbia Correspondence (hereafter CO 60), CO 60/36, Mflm B-1446.

11 See Agnes Calliste, 'Race, Gender and Canadian Immigration Policy: Blacks from the Caribbean, 1900–1932,' in Joy Parr and Mark Rosenfeld, eds, *Gender and History in Canada* (Toronto: Copp Clark, 1996).

12 One of the Disappointed, untitled, *British Columbian*, 7 June 1862.

13 See, famously, Anna Davin, 'Imperialism and Motherhood,' *History Workshop* 5 (Spring 1978): 9–66. On the British Columbia context, see Margaret Hillyard Little, 'Claiming a Unique Place: The Introduction of Mothers' Pensions in British Columbia,' in Veronica Strong-Boag, Mona Gleason, and Adele Perry, eds, *Rethinking Canada: The Promise of Women's History*, 4th ed. (Toronto: Oxford University Press 2002).

14 This phrase was borrowed from Anne Summer's seminal text, *Damned Whores and God's Police: The Colonization of Women in Australia* (Victoria, AU: Penguin, 1975).

15  *Third Report of the Columbia Mission with List of Contributors, 1861* (London: Rivingtons [1862]), 52–3.

16  'British Columbia – Its Attractions As a Field for Emigration,' *British Columbian*, 30 December 1863; 'Naval and Military Intelligence,' *The Emigrant Soldier's Gazette and Cape Horn Chronicle* 1 (6 November 1858) in Charles Sinnett, ed., *The Emigrant Soldiers' Gazette, and Cape Horn Chronicle* (New Westminster, BC: The 'British Columbian,' 1863).

17  Colonel Moody to James Douglas, 29 March 1860, in James Douglas to the Duke of Newcastle, 12 May 1860, National Archives of Canada (hereafter NA), MG 11, CO 60/6, reel B-82.

18  G.C. Lewis to James Douglas, 11 August 1860, draft reply, in James Douglas to the Duke of Newcastle, 12 May 1860, NA, MG 11, CO 60/9, reel B-83.

19  G.C.L. [G.C. Lewis], in R. Moody to Under Secretary of State, 9 April 1860, NA, MG 11, CO 60/9, reel B-84.

20  T.W.C. Murdoch to Frederic Rogers, 14 November 1860, NA, MG 11, CO 60/9, reel B-84.

21  'Columbian Emigration Society,' *Victoria Press*, 8 June 1862.

22  Sarah Crease, in M.S.R. and B.R.P., 'Stray Letters on the Emigration Question,' *English Woman's Journal* 8, no. 45 (11 January 1861): 241.

23  Maria S. Rye to Bishop Hills, 16 May 1862, ADNW/EPBC, 'Bishop Hills Correspondence,' box 8 of 8, file 4.

24  Madame L.S. Bodichon to Anonymous, ND [1862]; Madame L.S. Bodichon to Lord Shaftesbury, 26 July 1862, Autograph Letter Collection, Fawcett Library (hereafter Fawcett).

25  H.P.W. to Sir, 30 April 1862, Society for the Propagation of the Gospel in Foreign Parts, 'Letters Received Columbia 1861–1867' (Transcript), BCA, Add Mss H/A/So2, vol. 2, 49–50.

26  B.R.P., 'XXVIII. – The Last News of the Emigrants,' *English Woman's Journal* 11, no. 63 (1 May 1863): 185.

27  Minutes for 20 May 1869, in Henry Mason to the Colonial Secretary, 18 September 1869, 'Colonial Correspondence,' BCA, GR 1372, reel B-1345, file 1117; Henry Mason to The Bishop, 9 July 1869, in 'Female Immigration Letter Book,' 6–9; 'Female Immigration,' *British Columbian*, 21 April 1869.

28  Henry Mason to Officer Administering the Government, 18 June 1869, 10, and Henry Mason to The Bishop, 26 June 1869, 11, in 'Female Immigration Letter Book'; George Hills, 'Hills Journal 1869' (Transcript), ADNW/EPBC, 6; Minutes for 20 April 1869, in Henry Mason to the Colonial Secretary, 18 September 1869, 'Colonial Correspondence,' BCA, GR 1372, reel B-1345, file 1117; 'Female Immigration,' *British Columbian*, 21 April 1869.

29  James Douglas to the Duke of Newcastle, 14 June 1863, NA, MG 11, Great Britain,

Colonial Office, Original Correspondence, Vancouver Island (hereafter CO 305), CO 305/20, reel B-244.

30 'Female Middle Class Emigration Society Annual Report, 1861,' Fawcett, 1/FME, box 1, file 1, 7–14.

31 S.R. Crease, 'The Bride Ships,' 'Crease Family Papers,' BCA, Add Mss 55, vol. 13, file 3, 83–5.

32 'Arrival of the "Marcella,"' *British Colonist*, 21 May 1861.

33 'Wouldn't Let Them Aboard,' *British Colonist*, 19 September 1862.

34 'Landed,' *Victoria Press*, 19 September 1862.

35 'The Female Immigrants,' *Victoria Press*, 21 September 1862.

36 'The *Tynemouth* and Her Cargo,' *British Columbian*, 24 September 1862.

37 'The "Tynemouth's" Females,' *British Colonist*, 20 September 1862.

38 'The *Tynemouth* and Her Cargo.'

39 'The Female Immigrants,' *Victoria Press*, 22 September 1862.

40 'Arrival of the Robert Lowe,' *British Colonist*, 12 January 1863.

41 'The Robert Lowe,' *British Colonist*, 13 January 1863.

42 Ibid.

43 Edmund Hope Verney to Harry Verney, 20 September 1862, in Allan Pritchard, ed., *Vancouver Island Letters of Edmund Hope Verney, 1862–1865* (Vancouver: UBC Press, 1996), 90.

44 'Shocking Depravity,' *British Colonist*, 29 September 1862.

45 'Impressive Sermon,' *British Colonist*, 22 September 1862.

46 Mrs Mallandaine (nee Townsend), quoted in N. de Bertrand Lugrin, *The Pioneer Women of Vancouver Island 1843–1866* (Victoria: Women's Canadian Club, 1928), 150.

47 Edmund Hope Verney to Harry Verney, 6 January 1863 and Edmund Hope Verney to Harry Verney, 20 April 1863, 115, 131.

48 'Female Emigration,' *British Columbian*, 3 February 1863.

49 'The Alleged Larceny,' *British Colonist*, 6 March 1863; 'Female Immigrants,' *Victoria Daily Chronicle*, 28 June 1864.

50 'Deposition' of Esther Meiss, Police Court Testimony, Victoria VI, 31 May 1864, *R. v. Schultz and Trickey*, 'Attorney General Documents,' BCA, GR 419, box 4, file 1864/38; 'Court of Assizes: Rape,' *Victoria Daily Chronicle*, 1 August 1864.

51 Police Court Testimony, Victoria VI, 31 May 1864, *R. v. Schultz and Trickey*.

52 'Profane, But Forcible,' *Victoria Daily Chronicle*, 1 August 1864.

53 Tal. O Eifion, 'A Missionary for Cariboo,' *Cariboo Sentinel*, 15 July 1867.

54 C.J.H., 'The "Female Immigration" Suits in the Summary Court,' *Victoria Daily Chronicle*, 29 June 1864.

55 Fenton Aylmer, ed., *A Cruise in the Pacific: From the Log of a Naval Officer*, vol. 2 (London: Hurst and Blackett, 1860), 295–6.

56  Monitor, 'The Vote of $3,000 in Aid of Immigration,' *Victoria Daily Chronicle*, 1 March 1864.

57  Maria Rye to Madame L.S. Bodichon, 20 September 1865, Autograph Letter Collection, Fawcett.

58  See Nupur Chaudhuri, '"Who Will Help the Girls?" Maria Rye and Victorian Juvenile Emigration to Canada, 1869–1895,' in Rita S. Kranidis, ed., *Imperial Objects: Essays on Victorian Women's Emigration and the Unauthorized Imperial Experience* (New York: Twayne, 1998).

59  Edmund Hope Verney to Harry Verney, 20 September 1862, Edmund Hope Verney to Harry Verney, 14 September 1862, Edmund Hope Verney to Harry Verney, 22 September 1862, in Pritchard, *Vancouver Island Letters*, 88, 91–2.

60  Gilbert Sproat to Lieutenant Governor, 3 November 1871, Gilbert Malcolm Sproat, 'Memo re European Immigration into B.C.,' BCA, Add Mss 257, file 3 (emphasis in original).

61  Wm. Pearse, John Robson, W.J. MacDonald to Colonial Secretary, 12 July 1870, 'Colonial Correspondence,' BCA , GR 1372, reel B-1314, file 955/23.

62  G.M. Sproat, 'Memorandum of a few Suggestions for opening the business of emigration to British Colombia, referred to as Memo C, in a letter of G.M. Sproat to the Honourable the Provincial Secretary, dated 29 August 1872,' 'Attorney General Documents,' GR 419, box 10, file 1872/1, 4–5.

63  Untitled, *British Colonist*, 17 April 1869.

64  Family Man, 'Immigration,' *British Colonist*, 26 April 1869 (emphasis in original).

65  Mary E. to Aunt, 6 November 1862, in B.R.P., 'XXVIII. – The Last News of the Emigrants,' *English Woman's Journal* 11, no. 63 (May 1863): 185.

66  See Margaret Ormsby, ed., *A Pioneer Gentlewoman in British Columbia: The Recollections of Susan Allison* (Vancouver: University of British Columbia Press, 1976) and Jean Barman, 'Lost Okanagan: In Search of the First Settler Families,' *Okanagan History* (1996): 9–20.

67  Richard Somerset Mackie, *The Wilderness Profound: Victorian Life on the Gulf of Georgia* (Victoria: Sono Nis, 1995), 65; Robert Brown, 'Journal of the Vancouver Island Exploring Expedition,' in John Hayman, ed., *Robert Brown and the Vancouver Island Exploring Expedition* (Vancouver: UBC Press, 1989), 111 (his translations).

68  Catherine Hall, *White, Male, and Middle Class: Explorations in Feminism and History* (London: Routledge, 1991); Ruth Frankenberg, *White Women, Race Matters: The Social Construction of Whiteness* (Minneapolis: University of Minnesota Press, 1993); David R. Roediger, *The Wages of Whiteness: Race and the Making of the American Working Class* (London: Verso, 1991); Vron Ware, *Beyond the Pale: White Women, Racism, and History* (London: Verso, 1992).

69  Marilyn Lake, 'Between Old World "Barbarism" and Stone Age "Primitivism": The Double Difference of the White Australian Feminist,' in Norma Grive and Alisa

Burns, eds, *Australian Women: Contemporary Feminist Thought* (Melbourne: Oxford University Press, 1994), 80. For a discussion of the implications of this argument for history, see Ruth Roach Pierson, 'Introduction,' in Ruth Roach Pierson and Nupur Chaudhuri, eds, *Nation, Empire, Colony: Historicizing Gender and Race* (Bloomington: University of Indiana Press, 1998).

70  For an example of the debate about who, exactly, was white in early twentieth-century Canada, see Constance Backhouse, 'White Female Help and Chinese-Canadian Employers: Race, Class, Gender, and Law in the Case of Yee Clun, 1924,' *Canadian Ethnic Studies* 26, no. 3 (1994): 34–52.

71  A. James Hammerton, '"Out of their Natural Station": Empire and Empowerment in the Emigration of Lower-Middle-Class Women,' in Kranidis, *Imperial Objects*, 158–9.

72  See Glenda Riley, *Women and Indians on the Frontier, 1825–1915* (Albuquerque: University of New Mexico Press, 1984); Elizabeth Jameson, 'Women as Workers, Women as Civilizers: True Womanhood in the American West,' in Susan Armitage and Elizabeth Jameson, eds, *The Women's West* (Norman: University of Oklahoma Press, 1987); Peggy Pascoe, *Relations of Rescue: The Search for Female Moral Authority in the American West, 1874–1939* (New York: Oxford University Press, 1990); Robert L. Griswold, 'Anglo Women and Domestic Ideology in the American West in the Nineteenth and Early Twentieth Centuries,' in Lillian Schlissel, Vicki L. Ruíz, and Janice Monk, eds, *Western Women: Their Land, Their Lives* (Albuquerque: University of New Mexico Press, 1988); Margaret Strobel, *European Women and the Second British Empire* (Bloomington: Indiana University Press, 1991); Nupur Chaudhuri and Margaret Strobel, eds, *Western Women and Imperialism: Complicity and Resistance* (Bloomington: Indiana University Press, 1992); Susanna Hoe, *The Private Life of Old Hong Kong: Western Women in the British Colony* (Hong Kong: Oxford University Press, 1991); Amirah Inglis, *The White Women's Protection Ordinance: Sexual Anxiety and Politics in Papua* (London: Sussex University Press, 1975); Ann Laura Stoler, *Race and the Education of Desire: Foucault's* History of Sexuality *and the Colonial Order of Things* (Durham, NC: Duke University Press, 1995); Ann Laura Stoler, 'Carnal Knowledge and Imperial Power: Gender, Race, and Morality in Colonial Asia,' in Micaela di Leonardo, ed., *Gender at the Crossroads of Knowledge: Feminist Anthropology in the Postmodern Era* (Berkeley: University of California Press, 1991).

73  See Claudia Knapman, *White Women in Fiji, 1835–1930: The Ruin of Empire?* (Sydney: Allen and Unwin, 1986); Helen Callaway, *Gender, Culture, and Empire: European Women in Colonial Nigeria* (Urbana: University of Illinois Press, 1987); Beverly Gartrell, 'Colonial Wives: Villains or Victims?' in Hilary Callan and Shirley Ardner, eds, *The Incorporated Wife* (London: Croom Helm, 1984); Strobel, *European Women*, chapter 1. For trenchant critiques, see Jane Haggis, 'Gendering Colonialism or Colonising Gender? Recent Women's Studies Approaches to White Women and the History of British Colonialism,' *Women's Studies International Forum* 13, no. 1/2 (1990):

105–15; Margaret Jolly, 'Colonizing Women: The Maternal Body and Empire,' in Sneja Gunew and Anna Yeatman, eds, *Feminism and the Politics of Difference* (Halifax: Fernwood Publishing, 1993).

74  I explore this point further in 'Hearty Backwoodsmen, Wholesome Women and Steady Families: Immigration and the Construction of a White Society in Colonial British Columbia, 1849–1871,' *Histoire sociale/Social History* special issue 'Negotiating Nations: Exclusions, Networks, Inclusions,' 33, no. 66 (November 2000): 343–60.

75  On this point in a later period, see Stephen Constantine, 'Introduction: Empire Migration and Imperial Harmony,' in Stephen Constanine, ed., *Emigrants and Empire: British Settlement in the Dominions between the Wars* (Manchester: Manchester University Press, 1990).

76  See, for instance, Patricia Roy, *A White Man's Province: Politicians and Chinese and Japanese Immigrants, 1858–1914* (Montreal and Kingston: McGill-Queen's University Press, 1989); Kay Anderson, *Vancouver's Chinatown: Racial Discourse in Canada, 1875–1980* (Montreal and Kingston: McGill-Queen's University Press, 1991).

77  Franca Iacovetta, 'Manly Militants, Cohesive Communities, and Defiant Domestics: Writing about Immigrants in Canadian Historical Scholarship,' *Labour/Le Travail* 36 (Fall 1995): 221.

78  Nandita Rani Sharma, 'Race, Class, Gender and the Making of Difference: The Social Organization of "Migrant Workers" in Canada,' and Sunera Thobani, 'Closing the Nation's Doors to Immigrant Women: The Restructuring of Canadian Immigration Policy,' both in *Atlantis* 24, no. 2 (Spring 2000); Sedef Arat-Koc, 'Gender and Race in "Non-discriminatory" Immigration Policies in Canada: 1960s to the Present,' in Enakshi Dua and Angela Robertson, eds, *Scratching the Surface: Canadian Anti-Racist Feminist Thought* (Toronto: Women's Press, 1999).

# Racializing Imperial Canada: Indian Women and the Making of Ethnic Communities

ENAKSHI DUA

## Introduction

In postcolonial formations, the existence of ethnic immigrant communities has been taken for granted. While these communities often have been portrayed as a natural response to the inclusion of 'immigrants' into Western societies, this essay illustrates that their emergence needs to be placed in the context of imperial and national struggles over the racial composition of white settler societies. In addition, I demonstrate that it has been through such struggles that female migrants from India have been racialized and gendered as creators of ethnic social spaces.

The first two women from India migrated to Canada in 1912. Although Kartar Kaur and Harman Kaur were only two of the thousands of women to migrate in that particular year, their application to enter Canada captured public attention, sparking a broad-based debate over whether women from India should be allowed to enter Canada. The debate was popularly referred to as the 'Hindu Woman's Question' (HWQ). Notably, the vast majority of those involved in the debate saw female migration from India as leading inevitably to the development of ethnic communities. While public and official opinion in Canada was divided over its desirability, there was no division among Canadians about the consequences. The inclusion of Indian female migrants meant the rise of an Indian community.[1] At the same time, Indian male migrants in Canada and leaders of the anticolonial movement in India, aware that the inclusion of these women into the Canadian nation-state would challenge the racial politics of imperialism, demanded that their wives be included in white settler societies. For these men, the presence of Indian women was necessary for the survival of their 'community' in Canada. The HWQ points to the racial and gendered politics through which ethnic communities have emerged in Canada.

Recently, postcolonial scholars have pointed out that the historical study of ethnic communities 'opens windows onto the global field of European domination and its domestic extension.'[2] This research demonstrates that these communities are the product of colonial and postcolonial policies. In the Canadian context, Kay Anderson has illustrated the ways in which all levels of Canadian government enforced racial categories through the construction of racialized spaces. Similarly, John Kelly's study points to the role of colonial administrators in the formation of Indian communities in Fiji.[3] Kelly suggests that plural societies are the outcomes of the colonial administrator's dilemma, a product of the tension between the need to find a labouring class and the civilizing project which defined this labouring class – Indian indentured workers – as dangerous to the civilizing project.

However, these authors underemphasize the ways in which struggles over women and gender played a role in the emergence of ethnic communities. In addition, the ways in which colonized peoples have shaped colonial and postcolonial policies are also downplayed. In this context, Prabhu Mohapatra's work offers a more nuanced insight into the production of ethnic communities.[4] In a study of Guyana, Mohapatra suggests that the emergence of ethnic communities was tied to a project of restoring the family among Indian indentured workers. Significantly, Mohapatra illustrates that it was not only colonial administrators who were involved in this project, but also Indian male migrants. He suggests that for Indian men, investment in the family was tied to their cultural values and ideals, as was their investment in the institutionalization of the sexual contract. While Mohapatra points to the importance of struggles over family, gender, and women in the emergence of an Indian ethnic community, what remains unclear is why Indian indentured workers were so committed to a racialized family, one that required Indian wives.

My analysis is based on an examination of a variety of official documents on male and female migration from Asia, combined with an examination of reports on the HWQ in several Canadian newspapers, both mainstream ones and those published by Indian residents.[5] As this essay illustrates, the emergence of an Indian ethnic community was the project of the actions of Canadians and Indian male migrants. For Canadians, the creation of such communities was part of the project of ensuring that Canada would remain white. For Indian male migrants, these communities were part of a struggle to make Canada multiracial. Underlying Harman and Kartar Kaur's application for entry into the country was a battle over the racial characteristics of the emerging Canadian postcolonial formation. For both groups, Indian women became the key to how these seemingly opposed goals were achieved. The project of racializing and gendering Indian female migrants was crucial for both groups.

The HWQ is rooted in the imperial and national project of making Canada a white settler formation. This project began with British colonial settlement policies, which defined Canada as an outpost of the British empire. The creation of a white settler nation involved marginalizing indigenous people from the emerging nation-state, and recruiting white settlers to occupy the lands appropriated from indigenous peoples.[6] British colonial settlement policies attempted to ensure that Canada would become an outpost of the empire by promoting emigration from the British Isles.[7] In 1869, in its first Immigration Act, the Canadian government continued to encourage immigrants from Great Britain. Despite organized efforts, however, large-scale British immigration to Canada failed to take place.[8] This, combined with the political urgency of settling the West before it was lost to American expansion, meant that by the end of the nineteenth century migrants came from throughout Europe.

During this period there was limited migration from China, Japan, and India. The Chinese were the first to enter Canada, with the first recorded migrants arriving in the mid-nineteenth century.[9] By 1867, Chinese residents made up over 40 per cent of the non-indigenous mainland population in British Columbia.[10] As Anderson notes, in the early days of Chinese migration these residents were seen as an important part of the colonial project, as their presence allowed colonial officials not only to establish their hegemony in British Columbia but also to open up new industries. However, after Confederation, the British Columbia provincial government, followed by the federal government, moved to restrict migration from China, partly by defining Chinese residents as aliens to the emerging nation-state and legally and socially ineligible for citizenship.[11] From 1885 to 1910 successive governments, through differential immigration, residency, and citizenship policies, imposed a similar legal status on Japanese and Indian migrants.[12] Successive governments also employed various means to restrict the immigration of women from China and India.[13]

By the turn of the century, Chinese, Japanese, and Indian men had begun politically and legally to challenge the politics of nation, race, and gender. Asian men filed several court challenges to immigration, naturalization, and citizenship laws.[14] In the case of Indian male residents, they organized the Ghadar Party, which advocated armed resistance to British imperialism and white settler nationalism. The Ghadars, through a variety of activities, including organizing immigration from India, attached the exclusionary racial politics of white settler nationalism.

One strategy for resisting the racial politics of Canada was to challenge the legal prohibitions against the entry of their spouses. Thus two men, Bhag Singh and Balwant Singh, who were residents of Canada, challenged the immigration restrictions imposed on the migration of their spouses with the assistance of the Indian community in Canada and the anticolonial movement throughout the empire. In 1911 they left Calcutta with their wives and children for Canada but, despite attempts in Calcutta, Rangoon, and Hong Kong, they were unable to secure passage. Finally, in Hong Kong, they were able to purchase passage for Seattle and from there they travelled to Vancouver. Since the men had previously been landed, they were allowed to re-enter Canada. However, the on-duty immigration officer detained Kartar Kaur and Harman Kaur and ordered them to be deported. Their husbands filed for an immigration hearing, challenging the validity of regulations that denied them the right to bring in their families. Their case in turn spawned the HWQ.

For Canadians, the social construction of female migrants from India as creators of ethnic communities was located in the politics of race that underlay the Canadian nationalist project. The cases of Kartar Kaur and Harman Kaur raised a thorny issue that the Canadian government had struggled with since the 1880s: whether women from Asia should be included in the Canadian body politic. Beginning in the 1880s, the unofficial policy of the Canadian government had been to ban the entry of Asian women in order to prevent the permanent settlement of Asian men. However, as the numbers of Asian men slowly increased, the presence of single men raised the spectre of interracial sexuality. As a result, by 1910, a small but vocal group of Canadians began to question the wisdom of excluding Asian women from the Canadian postcolonial formation. They suggested that the racialized nation would be better served by the inclusion of Asian women. Both policies, to exclude or include Asian women, were governed by the desire to ensure that Canada would emerge as a white settler formation. Both policies positioned female Asian migrants within ethnic communities.

Through the social construction of racial categories Canadians began to identify female migrants from Asia as different from themselves. The politics of white settler nationalism was accompanied by a discursive construction of the racial category of the 'Asiatic,' in which migrants from China, Japan, and India came to be defined as sharing membership in a common race. In order to render first Chinese, and later Japanese and Indian residents alien, Canadians argued that Asians were racially different from those seen as 'white.'

The racialization of Asian residents was crucial, for it was through this that Canadian officials could legitimize the exclusion of Asian migrants. When considering the question of prohibiting migration from China, Canadian politicians claimed they found evidence that people from Asia were of a different race to whites. As the 1885 Royal Commission on Chinese Immigration noted, 'it is a serious step to take to exclude any law-abiding workers from your country ... [though] there may be good reasons for doing so.'[15] The understanding of racial difference was organized through the trope of assimilation. According to the rhetoric of the period, not only were Asians a different and inferior race, they were a race that could neither biologically nor socially assimilate with 'whites.' For example, in arguing for the restriction of Chinese immigration, John A. Macdonald stated:

> I am sufficient of a physiologist [*sic*] to believe that the two races cannot combine, and that no great middle race can arise from the mixture of the Mongolian and the Aryan. I believe it would lend to the degradation of the people of the Pacific, and that no permanent immigration of the Chinese people into Canada is to be encouraged but under the present system there is no fear of that ... and therefore there is no fear of a permanent degradation of the country by a mongrel race.[16]

This proclaimed inability to assimilate defined Asian men and women as dangerous to the racial makeup of the nation.

According to the logic of such racial politics, the greatest danger posed to the nation was that with the entry of Asians, Canada would no longer be a 'white' nation.[17] Thus, an editorial in the *Victoria Daily Colonist* claimed that 'if they were permitted to come in unlimited numbers, they would in a short time so occupy the land that the white population would be a minority. If British Columbia is not kept "white," Canada will become Asiatic.'[18]

Protecting the racial makeup of Canada meant that the overriding concern, in both official and public domains, was to prevent Asian residents from becoming permanent members of the nation-state as citizens. Between 1880 and 1900, government policy-makers observed that while differential immigration, residency, and citizenship laws were all means of imposing an alien (and therefore temporary) status, the most effective protection was to prevent these men from sponsoring their wives and family members. As Macdonald pointed out in an parliamentary discussion on restricting the entry of spouses of Chinese male residents:

> The whole point of this measure is to restrict the immigration of the Chinese into British Columbia and into Canada. On the whole it is not considered advantageous to the country that the Chinese race should come and settle in Canada, producing a mongrel race ... the objection to the admission of the wives of Chinese immigrants. If that were allowed, not a single immigrant would come over without a wife, and the immorality existing to a very great extent along the Pacific coast would be greatly aggravated in Canada ... I do not think it would be to the advantage of Canada or any other country occupied by Aryans for members of the Mongolian race to become permanent inhabitants of the country.[19]

During this period, successive governments employed various means to restrict the immigration of women from China and India.

By mobilizing this conviction that Asians could not assimilate with the white race, Canadians began to position Asian women as creators of ethnic communities. In the debate on the HWQ, several writers and speakers argued this point. The editors of the *Victoria Daily Colonist* predicted that '[i]f they were permitted to come in limited numbers they would set up communities distinct from white communities.'[20] Significantly, these Canadians regarded the arrival of Asian women within the nation-state as the catalyst that would promote this development. They assumed that such communities were the result not of male migration but of female migration. For example, in a debate in the Victoria local branch of the National Council of Women, Mrs. Andrews is reported to have argued that 'the admission of their wives would mean a Hindu colony in British Columbia. The danger that this province, unless measures were taken to prevent it would become the home, not of British people but of Oriental was pointed out.'[21]

It is worth underscoring that because Canadians understood Asians as constituting a different race – and one that could not assimilate – it followed that Asian women would produce a different kind of nation or community from that of 'White Canada.' As the editors of the *Victoria Daily Colonist* pointed out in an editorial entitled 'A Serious Problem,' Asian women did not produce white children:

> there are considerable number of Chinese women in British Columbia, and any one can get the ocular demonstration in the streets of that city that race suicide is not popular among them. A good many Chinese boys and girls are growing up in the community ... What is the place of these people in the community?[22]

As Yuval-Davis and Anthias suggest, women also produce nations as active transmitters and producers of national culture.[23] Because Asian women were racialized as different, they were also imagined as producers of an essentially different culture. An editorial in the *Victoria Daily Colonist* pointed out the inclusion of Indian women would mean the introduction of alternative cultural practices:

> The question will arise, are the wives and families to come here under the Indian social laws ... as they exercised among various sects, or are they to come under our system? ... with the advent of family life among the Indians here how are the laws to be administered among them? Are they to have native leaders and the joint magistrate system, or will the matter be left in the hands of the police? These are all questions to be considered before Hindu women are to be allowed to come to British Columbia.[24]

Thus, both through physical and social reproduction, Asian women were positioned as producing markedly racialized communities, ethnic communities.

The tie between Asian women and ethnic communities became further entrenched as Canadians began to be concerned with the possibility of interracial sexuality. As the numbers of Asian men had slowly grown, some Canadians began to fear the presence of single Asian men. Some even began to question the exclusion of Asian women, pointing out that it raised the spectre of interracial sexuality and miscegenation. One witness warned the 1902 Royal Commission on Chinese and Japanese Immigration:

> at present the Chinese allege that they are afraid to bring their wives and children to the country ... The number of Chinese who have intermarried with whites is greater than the number of Jews who have married with Gentiles. It is possible that the coming here of Chinese in large numbers might result in bringing about conditions similar to those now prevalent in the Southern United States.[25]

Fear of interracial sexuality created some sympathy for Indian men when they pressed their cause. A small group of Canadians pointed out that the nation's interest would be best served by including Indian women. Notably, the initial response by Canadian mainstream newspapers to Kartar Kaur's and Harman Kaur's cases was positive. All the newspapers surveyed in this study initially carried editorials that argued Canada would benefit from the inclusion of Asian women. The editors of the *Globe and Mail* pointed out that 'taken from a selfish point for own moral welfare, it becomes us to let these men have their families join them.'[26] Several politicians also agreed. In parliamentary debates, these politicians began to argue for the inclusion of Asian women. In doing so, they deployed the trope of the vulnerable white women to position female Indian migrants within ethnic communities. As Lougheed argued in the Senate in 1911:

> I will put it to my hon. friend that the charge usually brought against the Chinamen, and probably which has created more indignation in the community than any other is that they have engaged, very largely, in debauching white women. How can it be expected that there is immunity from immorality of that kind so long as the Chinese women are excluded? It would be much better that they have the opportunity of debauching their own women than Europeans, particularly white women in the confines of Canada.[27]

Newspaper articles also deployed the trope of the vulnerable white woman to make the argument that Asian women were beneficial to the racialized nation. For example, an editorial in the *Victoria Daily Colonist* linked the murder of a white woman, allegedly by a Chinese man, to the HWQ. The editors suggested the entry of Indian women would protect white women from violence:

The recent murder of a Vancouver lady by a Chinamen aroused a great deal of feeling in that city against the Chinese generally ... that disposition of the body and the callousness of the murderer indicates a phase of character which is exceedingly rare among people of our own race ... In an article of our last Sunday section, the writer suggested the segregation of the Sikhs from the rest of the community ... this opinion was not suggested in a haphazard way but after a very careful study of the position occupied by Sikhs here. It is a very serious question of ultimate relations between white people and Asiatics in Canada.[28]

Ethnic communities came to be seen as a means of protecting and segregating white women from Asian men. As these Canadians pointed out, the inclusion of Asian women allowed for a new and more efficient way of regulating interracial sexuality. Rather than controlling interracial sexuality through either law or self-regulation, social regulation could take place through the formation of ethnic communities. In these spaces, Asian women would be responsible for ensuring that Asian men did not harm either white women or the racialized nation. This understanding not only integrated Asian women into the racial politics of a white settler nation, but also gendered female migrants from India as wives of Indian men.

Canadians were not alone in racializing and gendering Indian women as creators of ethnic communities, or as wives of Indian men. Indian male migrants and the Indian anticolonial movement also positioned Indian women similarly within the Canadian social formation. For Indian male migrants, the issue of including Indian women within Canadian postcolonial formation was related to a larger struggle of challenging the racial politics of the empire and white settler nationalism. However, in challenging such racial politics, they reinforced two of its central organizing discourses: male rights and racial purity. As a result, their challenges to imperialism were inherently gendered. They attempted to undermine the empire by claiming the same racial, gender, and community rights as those experienced by white settlers.

The claim of Indian male migrants for rights as British subjects was accentuated as people from India began to move throughout the empire. After slavery was abolished in 1833, colonial administrators began to look for alternative sources of labour. In 1837, colonial administrators in Australia first proposed a plan to recruit indentured labourers from India. This plan involved considerable discussion within the Colonial Office in Britain and the Indian colonial government.[29] The Colonial Office disapproved of the plan, as they pointed out that the importation of Indian indentured labour into white settler colonies could undermine white settlement policies. However, with the disruption of production by the American Civil War, several colonies – including Malaysia, South

Africa, Australia, Fiji, Trinidad, and Guyana – began after considerable discussion to recruit indentured workers from India. The intention of colonial administrators was to use the system to employ temporary workers who would, at the end of their period of indenture, return to India.[30]

From its inception, there were protests in India against the use of indentured labour. Reports of high rates of mortality and suicide, and lack of housing or medical facilities, physical abuse of workers, failure to honour indenture contracts or pay wages, denial of legal recourse made indentured labour an extremely contentious issue within India. As indentured contracts ended and workers began to take up permanent residence, the issue of residency and citizenship rights emerged. As Huttenback and Tinker demonstrate, these issues were especially pressing in Australia, South Africa, and Kenya, that is, in societies defined as white settler formations.[31] The denial of free movement and political rights on grounds of race in these societies became a symbol of the inequities of the empire.

Beginning in 1880, nationalists in India such as Tilak, Gokhale, Gandhi, Sapru, and Shastri protested against the discrimination experienced by Indians throughout the empire, pointing out that such instances stood in stark contrast to British claims that colonialism was beneficial for India and Indians. The nationalist movement in India began to demand that the British and Indian colonial governments ensure that the political rights of Indian migrants as British subjects be upheld.

In Canada, Indian male migrants identified with the broader anti-imperial struggles taking place throughout the empire. The leaders of these migrants linked the racial inequities they faced in postcolonial formations to British imperialism itself. For the Ghadars, the racism of white settler nationalism was intimately tied to the racial discrimination inherent in British colonial policies in India. Taraknath Das, one of the leaders of the movement, in an editorial entitled 'The Work Before Us' pointed to such connections:

We thoroughly realize that our fate is inseparably connected with Hindustanees at home and abroad, so our work is not limited among the handful of Hindustanees of Canada, but we have consciously and deliberately championed the cause of the Hindustanee world ... Let us get a clear picture of the situation and thorough understanding of the difficulties we have to surmount. In Hindustan, under the existing adverse conditions manhood and womanhood have degenerated, the country has become a famine land ... In the British Colonies we have not the equal status with the dogs of our European masters ... [which] can freely travel in any part of the empire with their masters, but our men, who valiantly shed their blood to cement ... can not have the privilege of bringing their wives and children in the lands of the British Colonies ... deprived of human rights, even the right of freely moving from one part of the Empire to another, and the work before us is to remedy this situation, and acquire our inalienable rights.[32]

Linked to the struggle for political rights was the struggle to reconstruct the family in colonial and postcolonial settings.[33] From the early days of migration from India, practices and policies that discouraged the movement of Indian women were a source of tension. The early movement of unfree labour was male-dominated, as plantation owners preferred male labour. Male indentured workers and the Indian nationalist press protested against this, demanding that women be included. In India, a series of commissions on indentured labour reported that the demographic imbalances raised several problems, including loneliness, suicide, promiscuity, and murder. The demand for wives was one that would be made throughout the British empire.

In the case of Canada, the Ghadars linked the inability to sponsor their wives and children to white settlement policies.[34] Their newspapers published article after article on the restrictions in sponsoring their wives, making a public demand for reform. Headlines such as 'Hindus Wives Waiting in Hong Kong,' 'British Campaigners Ask for Admission of Hindus Families' were common. These articles explicitly linked the prohibitions against sponsoring wives to the politics of race that underlay white settler nationalism. When the Canadian government denied Kartar and Harman Kaur entry, *The Aryan* ran an article entitled 'Colour Prejudice Debars Families of Sikh Settlers.'[35]

However, a masculinist and racialized project was embedded in this antiracist challenge. The main argument that the Ghadars made was that, as men, they had the male right to a wife and family. An article entitled 'The Problems of Hindu Immigration to Canada' proclaimed the loneliness brought about by the absence of Indian wives and daughters:

FOR NO WOMEN ARE ALLOWED TO ACCOMPANY THEM TO CANADA OR TO FOLLOW THEM AFTER THEY HAVE ARRIVED AND SETTLED ... YET HE IS NOT PERMITTED TO BRING HIS WIFE TO THIS COUNTRY, AND NO FEMALE CHILD OF HIS MAY COME NEAR ENOUGH TO SMILE INTO HIS EYES [capitalized in original].[36]

The demand was not just for any wife and daughter, but for those who were Indian. Through the demand for Indian wives, Indian men began to position female migrants from India as creators of ethnic communities.

In making the argument for an Indian wife, the Ghadars constantly referred to the Canadian discourse of racial purity. *The Aryan* and *The Hindustanee* regularly ran articles that referred to the fear of interracial sexuality in Canadian society.

For example, *The Aryan* quoted an editorial in the *Montreal Gazette* in an article entitled 'As Others See Us':

> In his latest book Dr. Crocier pronounces indignation on the 'mixing of antagonistic races, colours or creeds' whether by intermarriage or merely by their presence on the same soil, as the greatest political curse that can befall a nation. However smoothly things may seem to go for a while, the end is sure to be damage.[37]

Yet another article, allegedly quoting an article in the *Toronto Star*, drew on the trope of Asian male violence:

> a married Sikh with a wife and baby in his cottage will be a far better Sikh than a glowering, morose, and wronged Sikh leading a lonely life and disapproving of all he sees around him. The man should not be here if his wife is not.[38]

Another article referred to the pressure on Sikh men not to interact with white women: 'He must not be guilty of an overt look, much less an overt act lest be considered a menace to our social society. Not many Europeans could stand the strain of similar conditions.'[39]

This masculinist project tied notions of male rights to a wife to emerging notions of male citizenship rights. *The Aryan* stated:

> The cry of a 'white' Canada was raised. It was not a truth or justice-seeking Canada, but simply a 'white' Canada ... so our men cannot have home-life, which is the birth-right of every British citizen ... As it is of great importance that the Hindus who have settled here for good ought to be able to get their wives and children.[40]

The Ghadars argued that as men, and also as British subjects, they had a right to participate in patriarchal relations.

Not only did the Ghadars put forward a masculinized project, they also gendered Indian women within the context of their anti-imperial project in very specific ways. An article entitled the 'Women Problem in India' in *The Hindustanee* protested against the depiction of Indian women as subject to excessive patriarchal relations by portraying Indian women as mothers:

> As a patriarch, the male head exercised the paramount power over the family, but it was almost restricted to the question of family wealth ... The children, to the mother, however, were *ipso facto* of her bone and flesh of her flesh, that she bears them with anguish and to her supreme devotion in nursing them that the human species continue ... the mother more than the father, was looked on with a veneration in India,

which possibly no other nation of the world knows how to equal. Thus woman as mother, and not as wife, controls the social structure of Hindustanee domestic and social life.[41]

As mothers of a racialized community, the Ghadars pointed out, Indian women needed to take an active, but clearly gendered, role in the anti-imperial struggle. Both newspapers ran articles promoting female education so that women could be taught to take their gendered positions within the emerging nation. In another article, entitled 'Women Problem,' *The Hindustanee* pointed out that in India:

The ladies of the well to do leisured class Hindustanees ... are at a loss how to spend their time during the day, when their husbands are out on business and the few directions are given in the management of their households ... In America the universities have been offering many courses of study to the women, and their sisters in India would do well to emulate the ladies of the Western countries in the matter of educating themselves, whereby they will find that time will not hang heavily upon them, and at the same time, with such accomplishments in education, the once glorious womanhood of India would be restored to past fame and status.[42]

Other articles encouraged female migrants from India to take on a similar role.

Implicit in this masculinist project was the attempt to gain civil and political rights for Indian men by reproducing racialized communities in white settler formations. This practice has complicated roots. On the one hand, it is located in the Ghadars' understanding of politics of race and empire. As the strength of British imperialism was located in its ability to 'colonize' other parts of the world, the Ghadars put forward an anti-imperial strategy that employed the same process. Both *The Aryan* and *The Hindustanee* encouraged Indian male migrants to see themselves as 'colonists' involved in a larger struggle, as can be seen in the article entitled 'Hindu Colonist conference': '*The Aryan* asks the Hindu residents abroad to organize a conference where Hindu colonists in Canada, South Africa, Australia and other parts of the British Empire can meet once a year ... for the welfare of the community.'[43]

On the other hand, this strategy meant that they ended up embracing the language of colonization, albeit with a diasporic imaginary in mind. Clearly, the Ghadars engaged with the politics of race and nation in contradictory ways. They challenged the exclusionary policies of citizenship, nation, empire which denied Indians civil and political rights due to their race. Yet, in doing so they put forward a masculinist and racialized project that gendered Indian women as mothers of racialized communities. As a result, they created a set of relations with Indian women, relations in which female migrants from India became positioned as racialized markers of community, nation, and empire. Importantly, this masculinist project was tied to the Ghadars' understanding that the racial structure of the empire was maintained through communities. As a result, the demand for wives was a demand to make the post-colonial formations multiracial.

Ironically, by making this demand the Ghadars reinforced the very politics they hoped to undermine: the rigid enforcement of politics found on a commitment to racial purity. By drawing on Canadians' fear of interracial sexuality, the Ghadars suggested that the presence of 'their' women, as their wives, would protect the racialized nation. As importantly, their attempt to challenge the racism of the empire was based on extending a racialized privilege, the right to be included in white settler societies, by creating another racialized privilege: their own ethnic communities. Ironically, the Ghadar anti-imperial practice resonates with Indian nationalist discourse.[44] Like nationalism in India, the Ghadars' anti-imperial challenge remained a derivative discourse.

## Conclusion

The case of the HWQ illustrates the complex reasons why ethnic communities were promoted in Canada and the importance of female migrants from India in the creation of these communities. It demonstrates why the history of such communities in white settler societies needs to be placed in the context of struggles over the racial constitution of the Canadian nation within the British Empire. Moreover, it points to the ways anti-imperialist struggles were constituted through women, even and perhaps especially in the context of colonial modernity.

NOTES

1 In this article, the term *Canadian* refers to those who were legally defined as Canadian. This includes white immigrants and their descendants. As in this period, both Asians and indigenous peoples were denied legal rights to citizenship, this term excludes both groups. I use the term *Indian residents* or *Indian* to refer to those immigrants from India who resided in Canada but were denied citizenship.

2 K. Anderson, *Vancouver's Chinatown, Racial Discourse in Canada, 1875–1980* (Montreal: McGill-Queen's University Press, 1991), 4.

3 J. Kelly, 'Fear of Culture: British Regulation of Indian Marriage in Post-indenture Fiji' *Ethnohistory* 36, no. 4 (1989): 372–91.

4 P. Mohapatra, 'Restoring the Family: Wife Murders and the Making of a Sexual Contract for Indian Immigrant labour in the British Caribbean Colonies, 1860–1920,' *Studies in History* 11, no. 2 (1995): 227–60.

5 The newspapers that were chosen are the *Victoria Daily Colonist*, the *Globe and Mail*, the *Ottawa Citizen*, and the *Montreal Gazette*. All the newspapers are dailies. The

period covered was from 1910 to 1920. In addition, the study examined two newspapers published by Indian male migrants in Canada, *The Aryan* and *The Hindustanee*. The period covered was 1911 to 1914.

6  See R. Bourgeault, 'Race and Class Under Mercantilism: Indigenous People In Nineteenth-Century Canada,' in S. Bolaria and P. Li, eds, *Racial Oppression in Canada* (Toronto: Garamond Press, 1988); H. Dickenson, H. and T. Wotherspoon, 'From Assimilation to Self-Government: Towards a Political Economy of Canada's Aboriginal Policies,' in Vic Satzewich, ed., *Deconstructing a Nation: Immigration, Multiculturalism and Racism in 90's Canada* (Halifax: Fernwood Publishing, 1992); and D. Stasiulis and R. Jhappan, 'The Fractious Politics of a Settler Society: Canada' in D. Stasiulis and N. Yuval-Davis, eds, *Unsettling Settler Societies* (London: Sage, 1995).

7  See B. Roberts, '"A Work of Empire": Canadian Reformers and British Female Immigration,' in L. Kealey, ed., *A Not Unreasonable Claim: Women and Reform in Canada, 1880–1920* (Toronto: Women's Press, 1979); V. Knowles, *Strangers at Our Gates* (Toronto: Dundurn Press, 1997).

8  Roberts, '"A Work of Empire,"' and Knowles, *Strangers*.

9  See Bolaria and Li, *Racial Oppression in Canada*; Anderson, *Vancouver's Chinatown*.

10  Anderson, *Vancouver's Chinatown*.

11  Ibid.

12  In 1908, the Canadian government negotiated an agreement with the Japanese government which ensured that the Japanese government would take on the responsibility of restricting Japanese emigration to Canada to an annual maximum of four hundred. It was more difficult to regulate migration from India, as the issue was complicated by India's presence in the British Empire. The British government had proclaimed that imperial policies made no racial distinction between British subjects. As white British subjects had the right to migrate throughout the Empire, exclusion of Indian subjects on the basis of race exacerbated political tensions within the Empire. In 1908 the Canadian government enacted the Continuous Journey Stipulation. According to this regulation, immigrants who came to Canada other than through a continuous journey from the country in which they were 'native' were denied entry.

13  Different means were employed to restrict the migration of Asian women. In the case of Chinese female migrants, in certain periods a tax was applied to discourage their entry and in other periods outright prohibitions against the entry of women were enforced. In the case of Japanese female migrants, the treaty with the Japanese government stipulated that each year a small number of women would be allowed to enter Canada. In the case of Indian female migrants, the continuous journey stipulation, combined with a requirement that Indian migrants possess $200 was employed to prevent entry. For more details, see Bolaria and Li, *Racial Oppression in Canada*.

14  See J. Walker, *'Race,' Rights, and the Law in the Supreme Court of Canada* (Waterloo, ON: Wilfrid Laurier University Press, 1997).

15  Canada, *Report*, 1885: xiii.
16  Canada, Parliament, House of Commons, *Debates*, 1883: 905.
17  See Anderson, *Vancouver's Chinatown*.
18  *Victoria Daily Colonist*, 9 March 1912.
19  Canada, Parliament, House of Commons, *Debates*, 1887: 642–3.
20  *Victoria Daily Colonist*, 9 March 1912.
21  Ibid., 23 January 1912.
22  Ibid., 18 April 1914.
23  Nira Yuval-Davis and Floya Anthias, eds, *Women-Nation-State* (London: Macmillan, 1989).
24  *Victoria Daily Colonist*, 9 February 1912.
25  Canada, *Report*, 1902, 31–2.
26  *Victoria Daily Colonist*, 7 February 1912.
27  Canada, Parliament, Senate, *Debates*, 11 March 1911: 328–32.
28  *Victoria Daily Colonist*, 18 April 1914.
29  See R. Huttenback, *Racism and Empire* (Ithaca, NY: Cornell University Press, 1976); H. Tinker, *Separate and Unequal* (Vancouver: University of British Columbia Press, 1976).
30  Ibid.
31  Ibid.
32  *The Hindustanee*, 1 April 1914.
33  See also Kelly, 'Fear of Culture'; Mohapatra, 'Restoring the Family.'
34  The following analysis is based on an investigation of the HWQ in two newspapers, *The Aryan* and *The Hindustanee*, published by the Khalsa Divan Society. The leaders of this society, particularly Bhagwan Singh, Teja Singh, and Tarakanath Dath, were active in the Ghadar movement. As the Ghadars promoted violent opposition to British colonialism, membership in this organization was restricted to a select few. In Canada, the Khalsa Divan Society provided a forum for more open membership. For more details of the relationship between the two organizations, see H. Puri, *Ghadar Movement: Ideology, Organization, Strategy* (Amritsar: Guru Nanak Dev University, 1993).
35  *The Aryan*, 1 May 1912.
36  Ibid., 1 September 1911.
37  Ibid., 1 December 1911.
38  Ibid., 1 January 1912.
39  Ibid., 1 September 1911.
40  Ibid., 1 November 1911.
41  *The Hindustanee*, 1 April 1914.
42  Ibid., 1 May 1914.
43  Ibid., 1 August 1911.
44  See P. Chatterjee, *Nationalist Thought and the Colonial World* (London: Zed Books, 1986).

PART 2

# *Gender, Race, and Justice*

# Killing the Black Female Body: Black Womanhood, Black Patriarchy, and Spousal Murder in Two Ontario Criminal Trials, 1892–1894

BARRINGTON WALKER

## Introduction

In recent years much has been written about family violence in Ontario,[1] though few, if any, of the critical insights born out of this body of work have been applied to the writing of the history of domestic, familial, and gender relations among African Canadians. In an effort to contribute to African-Canadian feminist historiography, and to the writing of gender and the law into the history of 'blackness' in Canada and, more broadly speaking, in the Black Atlantic world,[2] this article examines black womanhood and its relationship to the 'residual patriarchy'[3] enjoyed and exercised by black men in Ontario. The issues are viewed through the lens of two late-nineteenth-century cases of spousal murders – of Martha Veney in Essex County (1892–3) and of Hannah Richardson in neighbouring Kent County (1894).[4] While, sadly, these women's stories come to our attention only because of the violence they suffered at the hands of their black male spouses, it is nonetheless evident that these cases constitute dramas in which the unstable masculine privilege enjoyed by black men became enmeshed with the lives of black women.

This chapter suggests that the reading of juridical and extrajuridical texts can deepen our knowledge of black women's history in Ontario. The lives and work of more prominent and public black women are relatively well known in contrast to their more anonymous 'sisters.'[5] Yet, the important work of black Canadian feminist scholars has shed light on the social and economic contexts that shaped the lives of more obscure figures. The existing literature on black women in mid-nineteenth-century Ontario, for example, points to their relatively high labour-force participation and the range of paid work they performed – as domestics, seamstresses, and farm labourers, for instance – and also documents the critical contributions that women based in homes made to the family economies through domestic work, childrearing, and farming. Economic activities such as taking in washing, sewing, and growing small gardens also provided some income to supplement the work of black men, which was often seasonal in nature.[6]

Recent social history scholarship using legal records and case files has well illustrated that much can be learned about marginal populations, alerted us to the value of debate and theory in historical research, and cautioned against ahistorical readings of historical texts and or other potential pitfalls.[7] The criminal cases under review here provide a window on these women's encounters with the law which have heretofore been largely ignored.[8] These black women – in particular, their black female bodies – are situated at the centre of these cases. Indeed, the black female body constitutes the terrain or the site of struggle upon which the two murder trials played out.[9] Yet, at the same time, it is precisely the way in which the discourses that constitute these trials move in and through the very bodies of these women that makes it difficult for us to unearth their stories and subjectivities (or identities). In this sense, the black body is simultaneously at the centre and periphery of these trials. Of course, in a murder trial the victim's body, female or male, inevitably becomes the subject/object of closer scrutiny; in this case, the black female bodies offer the opportunity to explore whether and in what ways blackness intersected with gender, patriarchy, and the law.

Like recent work in critical legal studies, this essay underscores the need to pay careful attention to ways in which the 'textual artifacts' – or, the formal legal documents – are comprised, organized, and structured.[10] Indeed, the stories and struggles of these women lay enmeshed within a white male legal apparatus which, in turn, privileged the men who murdered them. As we shall see, competing truth claims around the nature of black masculinity became inscribed on the bodies of these women – namely, whether the violence inflicted on them represented the fiendish behaviour of black men or, by contrast, the result of 'mad acts.' Thus, these trials centred on the motives and illnesses, that lay at the heart of the actions of these black men. And in so doing, they revealed the symbiotic but also tension-filled nature of the relationship between black patriarchy and black womanhood.[11] While remaining conscious of the perils of reconstructing black womanhood in Ontario, I also demonstrate the potential these records hold for illuminating the central themes of this essay.

### Killing the Black Female Body

During the years 1892–4, residents of southwestern Ontario and beyond were privy to two highly publicized and rather unsavory glimpses of black domestic life.

The first was the case of Martha and Anderson Veney, the commencement of which was emblazoned across newspaper headlines as far away as Toronto. The lead headline, trumpeted in bold print on the front page of the *Toronto Daily Mail*, declared, 'Murdered His Wife: The Brutal Act of a Jealous Husband.'[12] The tale of the Veneys was recounted in grim detail in both the press and the trial transcripts. One of the key witnesses at the trial, Hattie Primeaux, recounted the murder of Martha Veney in graphic fashion. From the relatively privileged vantage point of her home, located across a vacant lot some 75 to 80 feet from the Veney family home, Hattie Primeaux said she saw Martha Veney between five and six o'clock in the evening on the Sunday she was murdered.[13] Standing on the step of the Veneys' side door, Hattie had watched Martha 'humming a hymn ... [with a] dish cloth in her hand.' This moment of domestic tranquillity and piety, however, was abruptly disrupted, as Primeaux's grizzly account of what next transpired indicates. According to her testimony, Primeaux was in her house when she heard Martha scream. When she ran to the door, Martha called her twice, saying 'for God's sake Hattie.' Primeaux described what she saw next:

> Mr Veney then was holding her with her left side of the face towards me; all the left side from her mouth down her was all blood, and I says 'for God sake, Mr Veney stop,' and I called twice that way and when he heard me – I suppose he heard me holloa – he through [*sic*] her down to the ground and on her he fell. By that I ran to the corner of the house, that would be on the street, and as I looked out I saw Mr Johnson, and I says, 'for God's sake run, Mr Johnson and Mr Veney is killing Mrs Veney.' I grabbed my little boy and ran into the house and ran out again, and as I looked over that way, he was standing looking at his wife and Mr Johnson was standing just turning to go back again when he killed her.[14]

The testimony of others mirrored Primeaux's story. Weadon Johnson, to whom Primeaux turned for help, told the court that earlier that evening he had tended to his geese while engaging in a brief conversation with Anderson Veney.[15] Shortly after their conversation ended, added Johnson, he 'heard a scream' and 'supposed it was a fight scream, I supposed it was boys in the street.'[16] But when Johnson reached the street he found Primeaux instead. As he ran to get her help, he spotted Mrs Veney leaning over the gate and then headed to the back part of the house. When he got to that north side of the house, he found her lying down with 'the blood pouring from her neck about that length, a great stream of blood coming from her neck.' 'That horrified me, of course,' he added, 'I saw her gape three times.'[17] In a similar vein, the *Telegram* reported that a neighbour, George Street, on his way home 'heard screams from neighbour Veney's house' and running to the back door, witnessed a 'frightful scene': Martha Veney 'lay on the kitchen floor, her throat cut from ear to ear' while [Anderson] Veney was walking up and down the room covered with blood with an open penknife in his hand.[18] Veney suffered cuts to his neck – apparently the results of a failed suicide attempt – that were later described as severe but likely not fatal.[19] Just a few minutes after he committed the murder, Veney was arrested by Lewis Lemay, Amherstburgh's chief constable, who said he arrived at the Veneys home to find Anderson Veney 'up on a night stand with a looking glass.' Lemay grabbed Veney, 'took his knife away,' and 'took him outside.' With a handkerchief, he 'plugged the hole [in Veney's neck] so that it would not bleed too much and took him to the doctor's.' Sometime later, Lemay picked up Martha Veney's battered body from a doorway and placed it on a table in her home.[20]

A postmortem examination of Martha Veney – a five-foot-four-inch, forty-five-year-old woman who, according to the doctors who had performed the post-mortem examination, had been well developed, healthy, and well nourished – was conducted that evening in Amherstburgh town hall, and soon afterwards came the coroner's inquiry.[21] This 'inquest on the body of Martha Veney' is a graphic and unsettling illustration of how black masculinist privilege could literally be inscribed upon the black female body. In the end, Martha's body was examined by Essex County Coroner Forest T. Bell, by a twelve-member jury comprising 'good and lawful men of the said County, duly chosen,' and by two expert medical witnesses – Dr J. Proudfoot and Dr Parks. In his deposition, Dr Parks attributed Martha Veney's death to a 'hemorrhage from [the] carotid artery and jugular vein.' According to Parks, 'she could not have resisted or [fought] after such a wound ... she would probably [have] taken a step and fallen after receiving such a wound ... [in] probably 3 or 4 seconds.'[22] Dr Proudfoot, who had participated in the postmortem examination of Martha's body, corroborated Smith's testimony, saying he 'would give [the] same answers.'[23] The coroner thus concluded, 'there was reason to believe that the deceased died from violence or unfair means, or by culpable negligent misconduct.'[24]

A little over a year later, a similar tale of spousal murder unfolded in Dresden, a small town in neighboring Kent County. Hannah Richardson suffered a violent death at the hands of her husband, Hiram Richardson – dubbed the 'Dresden Fiend' in nearby Chatham newspapers.[25] On the morning of 6 November 1894, Hannah Richardson, dissatisfied with her marriage and probably fearing for her life, decided to leave her husband. Hiram accosted her in the street as she tried to move some of her belongings out of the home and into a wagon with the aid of her friend and neighbour Daphne Warren, and William H. Harris, a local 'carter and peddler.' This act of resistance clearly enraged her husband. Angered by the spectacle Hannah created by such a public show of her insubordination, Hiram reportedly said, 'if [Hannah] went on moving she'd move away a corpse.'[26] As

Hannah was 'fetching something up near the wagon,' Hiram 'punch[ed] her and knocked her down, and said I don't give a damn I am going to kill her.'[27] He then boldly proclaimed that he did not care whether they sent him to prison or to hell for killing her. As Hannah tried to run to Daphne Warren's House – she and her daughter had sought and received sanctuary there the night before – her husband 'caught her by the back of her dress [and] turned her around.' He then 'struck her on the jaw with his fist and she fell on her side by the wagon and he put his foot on her neck.'[28] Daughter Mary had witnessed her mother's murder. At one point, she told the court, she had tried to defend her mother by striking her father with a stick but he 'knocked me down twice and then went back to mother.' He 'kicked [mother] in the side and on the head and ... mashed her forehead with his heel.'[29]

While her daughter ran off to 'fetch Uncle Ross,'[30] Hannah Richardson somehow mustered the strength to crawl over to Daphne Warren's house. Having run off to get help for her friend, Warren returned home to witness the ignoble sight of Hannah Richardson, a huge gash on her neck, 'crouching up by the house with the blood running from her mouth into her lap.' Hannah's final request was for a drink of water, which Warren quickly granted. Warren later recalled that Hannah's injuries had been so severe that as she drank, 'blood was coming from her mouth in a stringy manner.' Warren helped to carry Hannah inside the house and onto a bed where she died approximately five minutes later.[31]

Hours after the murder, a postmortem examination was conducted by two Chatham medical practitioners – Dr Daniel Gailbraith and Dr Irvine Wiley – which took stock of the violence inflicted on Hannah Richardson's battered black female body. Similar to the earlier inquiry on the death of Martha Veney, the postmortem gave a graphic and telling bodily itemization of black male patriarchal power's heavy investiture in the violent suppression of black female subjectivity. Put another way, the brutal nature of this murder was reflected in the severity of the injuries Hannah Richardson sustained, which in turn gives an indication (albeit quite harsh) of the power some black men exerted over their wives. According to Gailbraith's testimony, the postmortem examination, conducted shortly after Hannah had died, showed that her 'head and neck were terribly swollen and covered with blood and the tongue protruding.'[32] He continued: 'when we first examined the chest and found the breast bone quite broken recently, this injury must have been caused by a very severe blow from some blunt instrument but there was no external injury as the clothes protected the body and neck. [The injury] was quite recently caused, [approximately] within a few hours [of the examination].' Dr Gailbraith also noted the 'deceased had evidently had a goiter – pretty large on each side of the neck,' and that 'immediately behind the fracture of the breast bone' they had found 'considerable effusion of blood and a bruise on the middle of the right lung.' The rest of the organs of the chest and stomach were all healthy, as was the brain, but the skull, though not fractured, was 'very much bruised.'[33]

The doctor discovered 'similar bruises' on the neck and head, as well as 'a rupture of the right [lobe] of the thyroid gland about 2 inches long' that, Gailbraith surmised, likely 'caused such a severe hemorrhage that the pressure of the blood on the trachea produced suffocation' and caused death. Noting that 'the lumps indicated death by suffocation as did also the protruded tongue and the venous state of the blood,' he concluded that the rupture was caused by 'a severe blow or blows.'[34]

Doctor Wiley's statement mirrored Gailbraith's: Hannah Richardson's body was that of a 'healthy quadroon woman[35]... well nourished [with] a body [that] appeared badly bruised particularly on the right side of the body [including the] right arm and right side of the head and neck.'[36] Wiley also noted that an examination of the chest 'found a fracture of the breast bone evidently quite recent [as] the bruises were ... as if received only a few hours before examination.' Wiley also told the court that his examination of 'the organs of the chest and abdomen and also the brain ... found a slight contusion on the front part of the middle lobe of the right lung caused by a recent blow,' and in addition, that 'nothing in any of these organs [was found] that would cause immediate death.' Hannah also had 'extensive swelling across the neck, particularly on the right side.' When they opened it, the doctors found the neck tissues 'filled with blood, and extensive rupture of the right thyroid gland ... sufficient to insert four fingers.'[37] Like Gailbraith, Wiley attributed Hannah Richardson's death to 'this rupture [which] fill[ed] all the tissues with blood produc[ing] pressure on the trachea thereby causing sufficient suffocation.' 'This rupture,' concluded Gailbraith, 'was caused by some severe blow on the right side of neck [and] the deceased evidently had a goiter which would render the thyroid gland more liable to rupture from a blow. I have no doubt that the rupture as stated above was the immediate cause of death.'[38]

### Fiendish Behaviour or Mad Acts?

Although the powerful, almost dramaturgical or theatrical[39] stories recounted in the narratives of the murders and the postmortem examinations placed the black female body at the centre, the trials simultaneously became preoccupied with the supposed nature of black masculinity and its association with violence – either in 'fiendish behaviour' or 'mad acts.' Stereotypes of black men as petty patriarchs within their own households drew on age-old views of black men as men who, victimized by the wider society, could turn nasty towards their own women. Although black men and women both had to endure racism, black men enjoyed relative privilege compared with black women and they could exercise patriarchal violence against 'their' women. The search for fiendish or mad acts could thus be construed as an effort to understand the very nature of black masculinity and manhood. This preoccupation with codes of black masculinity meant that the black female body came to occupy an unstable space, resting at the interstice of hypervisibility and invisibility, the centre and periphery. The victims' black female bodies became subsumed beneath and marginalized by a set of rhetorical strategies, tropes, and imagery that centred on the issues of black male subjectivity, masculinity, and madness.

Certainly, tropes and codes of black masculinity dominated the Veney trial. Predictably, the prosecution, led by R.C. Clute and Clarke, Q.C., sought to establish – by tacitly drawing on dominant tropes of black male violence – that Anderson Veney was not a respectable man and had a long history of cruelty towards his wife. The defence, by contrast, argued that this history of cruelty was the mark of an irrational mind, an outward manifestation of mental illness. For both sides then, as the case progressed, Anderson Veney came to occupy centre-stage while glimpses of Martha Veney became increasingly fleeting.

The prosecution, which argued that Veney's motive was that of 'determined jealousy,'[40] sought to establish that Veney's cruelty, jealousy, and bouts of anger were so well entrenched that even a hardworking and respectable black woman like Martha Veney was not exempt from his rage. When Hattie Primeaux was asked to comment on the state of the relationship between Veney and his wife prior to the crime,[41] she informed the court that Martha was 'always a lady' but nonetheless had been constantly subjected to a litany of verbal abuses – including accusations of 'imputed indecency' and infidelity.[42] Primeaux had also heard Anderson Veney frequently making death threats to his wife, and said he also engaged in a campaign of physical abuse against his wife. On several occasions, Hattie had seen Martha in various states of physical distress; about eight years earlier, in a fit of jealous rage Anderson Veney had thrown Martha down a flight of stairs.[43] Others corroborated Hattie Primeaux's testimony, surmising that Veney's motive was jealousy. One witness told the court that Veney boldly admitted to this after killing his wife.[44]

Veney's defence was conducted by two attorneys: Malcolm Cowan of Belleville, and most notably, Rogest Delos Davis, a well-known and well-respected black Amherstburgh solicitor.[45] Anderson Veney's access to this black male trailblazer surely must have lent him an air of masculinist respectability. Davis's distinguished career as one of the first black practising lawyers in Canada in turn lent credibility to the accused in a trial so imbued with negative images of black men. Still, the large number of first-hand witnesses meant that the defence's only credible strategy was an insanity plea, and to that end, Cowan and Davis shifted the focus from Martha to her husband. The defence counsel's cross-examination of Chief Constable Lewis Lemay sheds light on this rhetorical strategy:

Q: Had you known the prisoner long?

A: Since we were little boys.

Q: What kind of character did he have?

A: I cannot put a straw in either one of their roads.

Q: Neither he nor his wife?

A: No, sir.

Q: *We have no desire to so far as she was concerned* [emphasis added]. He had always been that kind of a gentleman?

A: As far as I can [tell] a gentleman in manners.

Q: A sociable fellow?

A: Yes.

Q: Was he inclined to be of a quiet disposition or rather the reverse?

A: Jolly.

Q: Always jolly, a good-hearted fellow?

A: Yes, sir.[46]

This represents the critical moment when the subject/object of the discourse in the Veney trial was effectively shifted from Martha Veney's body, to the black male body and psyche. More specifically, the question of how it was that such a 'sociable,' 'good-hearted,' 'jovial,' and respectable 'gentleman' could have fallen into such disrepute became a central question. Many defence witnesses – nineteen in all – were called forth in support of Veney's defence and similar themes characterize their testimony – all part of a plan to construct a [meta]narrative of Veney's insanity. Both non-medical and 'expert' medical testimony were deployed to delineate the contours of Anderson Veney's descent into madness.

The bulk of the testimony came from those who had known the accused for some time and could thus comment on his apparent descent into abnormal behaviour. Roman Smith, a man who worked with Veney as a 'steward on the lakes' testified that in recent years Anderson Veney had often looked 'wild and starey ... like a man who was going insane,' and that their relationship began to sour when Veney began acting 'very queer and entirely different to his old-time actions with me,' which included accusing Smith of having kissed his wife.[47] Another witness testified that although she and Veney generally maintained a cordial and social relationship, he had passed by her house several times recently without so much as a nod in her direction. On the fateful day, he had a 'wild distressful look.'[48] Another woman who claimed to have known Anderson Veney for about twenty-five years said he was usually 'gentlemanly' and 'polite' in nature, but that on one occasion he had looked 'strange and simply spoke to me and did not shake hands.'[49] Similarly, William H. Brown, an African-American minister of Amherstburgh's African Methodist Episcopal Church, told the court of an instance when Anderson Veney was to be 'received' into the church. The custom was for members of the congregation to extend a hand to the minister, a ritual that was tantamount to accepting the church's 'invitation' that then led to being received and registered into the church membership. Veney, however, had made a curious spectacle of himself. 'Instead of joining or giving his hand or anything of that kind,' testified Pastor Brown, 'he knelt at the pew with his back to me ... and there was not much expression on the part of myself or anyone and in a few moments he rose up and said to me, "happy"; that was of his own accord and that was about all that transpired at that time.'[50] Veney's despondent and lethargic state in prison – he had little appetite and often spent hours resting his head against the cold concrete walls – was also cited as evidence of his mental illness.

The medical experts also delivered important testimony. Dr Thomas Hobley, an Amherstburgh physician, had examined Anderson Veney a few weeks before the murder and treated him for insomnia and what Veney described as a great deal of 'misery in the head.' Hobley attributed these symptoms to 'congestion of the brain,' saying that Veney's 'intellect was weak.'[51] Dr James Samson, a medical practitioner from Windsor who visited Veney in prison a week before the trial, noted that the prisoner would not answer any questions and 'assumed a very unnatural and feeble attitude, looked exceedingly stupid and absolutely unintellectual.'[52] The prosecution tried to challenge the testimony of the medical expert, as indicated by the cross-examination of Dr Samson. As the following excerpt suggests, ironically, the prosecution drew on white supremacist tropes regarding blackness in an effort to disprove the doctor's claim of Veney's insanity.

Q: What do you say in regard to the odour of the breath or skin of insane persons?

A: There is an insane odour not easily mistaken for any other, not always easily discovered on one single patient, [but] easily discovered on a group of patients.

Q: I am instructed that the breath and odour was entirely sweet, that his peculiar odour is entirely absent?

A: All the time or now?

Q: When he was examined. Have you any knowledge you can impart to us with reference to that point?

A: I have a very fair nose and I do not want to swear to its entire absence nor that I discovered a marked absence. His race are subject to a peculiar odour ...

Q: You say that an insane man patient has a certain distinct odour that [can] be recognized by an expert. You are familiar with that odour, at least you have discovered it at times?

A: Yes, but you understand that a man in his ordinary practice is brought in contact with that very seldom.

Q: Would you expect to find the odour in one prisoner in the cell among a lot of other prisoners, a ventilated cell, a coloured man, would you be astonished if you did not find the odour there?

A:  No, I would not be astonished if I did not.[53]

This passage graphically illustrates how white supremacist imagery lurked just beneath the surface of the terms of black masculinity that came to dominate this trial. The prosecution sought to undermine the testimony of the defence's expert witnesses by raising the issue of whether the odour given off by a black male body could be readily distinguished from the odours emanating from the diseased bodies of the mentally enfeebled.

The effectiveness of the prosecution's cross-examination of Dr Samson was augmented by the testimony of more medical experts. Dr Richard Morris Bucke, superintendent of the London Ontario Asylum, stated that four examinations (consisting of physical examinations and a series of questions about Veney's personal history and the murder) had convinced Bucke that Veney was sane. Two of these examinations were even conducted in the company of Dr Samson. Dr Remi Casgrain, Amherstburgh's jail surgeon, concurred. He, like Dr Bucke, could find no compelling evidence of Veney's insanity. Under examination, Casgrain conceded that Veney may have suffered from 'simple melancholy,' but insisted that Veney's despondent and morose conduct was a sign, not of madness, but of a man in a deeply repentant state. Veney's demeanour, argued Casgrain, was 'attributable to ... [his] brooding over what he had done and the enormity of it. I asked him why he did it and he said, well, because I was bad; the devil got hold of him and made him do it and that he was sorry for it.'[54] At the close of the trial, the jury sided with the prosecution and was unmoved by the defence's insanity argument. Anderson Veney was sentenced to death, with a jury recommendation for mercy.

The Hiram Richardson murder trial followed a similar trajectory. The graphic nature of the testimony from the large number of eyewitnesses, and the postmortem examination of Hannah Richardson's body, was all the prosecution felt it needed to secure a conviction. As occurred in the Veney case, Crown counsel M.G. Cameron shifted the focus from the terrain of Hannah Richardson's battered black female body to the 'fiendish behaviour and/or mad acts' committed by Richardson. Under cross-examination by defence counsel W.J. Elliot, Mary Richardson testified to her father's inexplicable and erratic behaviour. She recounted the following incident: '[He] took all the furniture and clothing; he was in a passion the night before and threatened mother; he killed our pig and threw it in the river and wrung the chickens' necks and threw [them] in the river and the corn and the meat in the house.' She also testified that her father would routinely destroy the family's possessions, and on one occasion had even 'split up the bedstead and burned it.' Enmeshed in a peculiarly destructive cycle of behaviour,

Hiram Richardson evidently spent brief stints in Michigan, only to return home to 'buy new things and then after a while ... destroy them and go away again.'[55]

Hiram Richardson also testified at his trial, and corroborated his daughter's testimony. Though he knew he often had destroyed his family possessions, he claimed he could not remember any specific incidents. Richardson also offered his own theory regarding the roots of his proclaimed madness: he traced it back to a specific episode twelve years earlier when he 'was thrown from a wagon.' Before that, he and his wife 'were always peaceable but for the last five years we were not so.' Richardson stated that he 'felt different after the accident and sometimes felt myself dangerous.'[56]

Several witnesses testified to having seen Richardson exhibiting signs of madness. An older brother James also pointed to Richardson's wagon accident as the beginning of a pattern of odd behaviour: 'after the accident he appeared to act like a crazy man – his temper seemed worse. He used to go away for half a day and come back at night; he used to appear to be talking to himself at times and throwing his arms about. He used to get angry at times ... I don't think my brother has been sane since the accident.'[57] Similar tales of Hiram Richardson's strange behaviour were told by Richardson's employees, co-workers, and long-time acquaintances. Some of them recalled that a few years before the murder Richardson would at times begin talking to himself while doing field work, exhibiting uncontrollable bouts of temper.[58]

There was, however, little medical testimony in support of Hiram Richardson's insanity plea. One doctor was willing to say only that 'a severe injury to a head would weaken the man mentally,' but then under cross-examination, he made it clear that 'from his observation in the jail and the conduct of the prisoner in court he would believe him to be sane.'[59] Two other doctors testified at the trial. One testified that while Richardson's actions might be classified as a kind of 'impulsive insanity' or a manifestation of an 'ungovernable impulse,' his conversations with Richardson in the jail, coupled with general observations of the accused convinced him that the defendant was 'perfectly sane.' And Dr R.J. Bray, jail physician and coroner, stated bluntly, 'I haven't seen or heard anything to lead me to the belief that [Hiram Richardson] is not sane.'[60]

Richardson's claim to madness was also undermined by his very own words. At his preliminary hearing in front of Justice of the Peace Robert P. Wright approximately six months prior to the trial, Richardson was asked if he wished to say anything on his own behalf. In response, he attributed 'all the trouble' to his wife's association with the Warrens and others 'who wanted [us] to go to Detroit and spend [my] money as [I] earned it.'[61] At trial, Richardson similarly told the court that having 'found Warren in the house and heard her proposing to my wife to go to Detroit and make money easy,' he had 'forbade her [his wife] to have anything to do with them again.' But Richardson's efforts to explain his crime as that committed by a man driven by a kind of impulsive insanity[62] did not convince the court.[63] He was found guilty of manslaughter and sentenced to life in the Kingston Penitentiary.

We might view Hiram Richardson's sentence of manslaughter instead of murder as a subtle articulation of his black male privilege. The jury, while unswayed by Richardson's insanity plea, was ultimately unwilling to sentence him to death for taking the life of a black woman. For his part, Anderson Veney, guilty of the same crime but having a relatively elevated status in the community, faced a death sentence. A critical factor was the presiding judge. Justice Malcolm Street, when instructing the jury, expressed his opinion that 'a great deal of the evidence was given on the part of the defence, which you have heard, but which did not seem to me to bear very materially upon the real question.' Indeed, Justice Street bluntly expressed his view that '[t]here is no evidence ... to show that [Veney] was ignorant of what he had done, or that he was ignorant of it being a matter for which he was subject to punishment. He knew that he was arrested for having killed his wife, he knew that he killed her, and he appears to have regretted that he minded, as he said, outside talk and letters.'[64] Anderson Veney's death sentence was, however, soon overturned. Three petitions, 'signed by the residents of Amherstburgh,' and 'contain[ing] the names of the leading officials of the Town'[65] were submitted to the minister of justice on Veney's behalf. Also, medical evidence of Anderson Veney's rapid physical and mental dissipation led to the commutation of his sentence to life in prison at the Kingston Penitentiary.[66]

## Conclusion

These stories of spousal murder, the textual artifacts through which they are represented, and the case files into which they are organized, suggest the challenges involved when trying to reconstruct black female subjectivity of victims of male crime – in this instance, murder. While the outcomes of these murder trials were not necessarily determined by race, there was a heavily racialized context that shaped in significant ways the discourse of the trials themselves. This discourse highlighted the invisibility of the murdered women's identities, even while the frank commentary on their multilated bodies rendered them hypervisible.

Finally the criminal cases give us brief and veiled glimpses of the lives of these women – for example, Hannah's defiance of her husband – that deepen our understanding of the domestic lives of some nineteenth-century Ontario black women. Their identities, however, are obscured by and inextricably wrapped up with a white patriarchal legal apparatus that was most concerned with the men who murdered them. By the same token, the black men enjoyed a partial or residual patriarchal power, but in the view of the elite white males passing judgement on them, they could never fully measure up to dominant notions of masculinity.

NOTES

1 There is now an extensive body of literature on this subject that has made an important contribution to Canadian historiography. See, for example, Annalee Golz, 'If a Man's Wife Does Not Obey Him What Can He Do? Marital Breakdown and Wife Abuse in Late Nineteenth- and Early Twentieth-Century Ontario,' in Susan Binnie and Louis Knafla, eds, *Law, State and Society: Essays in Modern Legal History* (Toronto: University of Toronto Press, 1995), 323–50; Golz, 'Uncovering and Reconstructing Family Violence In Ontario,' in Franca Iacovetta and Wendy Mitchinson, eds, *On The Case: Explorations in Canadian Social History* (Toronto: University of Toronto Press, 1998), 290–311; Karen Dubinsky, *Improper Advances: Rape and Heterosexual Conflict in Ontario, 1880–1929* (Chicago: University of Chicago Press, 1993); Carolyn Stange, 'Historical Perspectives on Wife Assault,' in Mariana Valverde, Linda MacLeod, and Kirsten Johnson, eds, *Wife Assault and the Canadian Criminal Justice System* (Toronto: Centre for Criminology, University of Toronto 1995), 293–304. For an excellent treatment of a single case of spousal murder, see Karen Dubinsky and Franca Iacovetta, 'Murder, Womanly Virtue, and Motherhood: The Case of Angela Napolitano, 1911–1922,' *Canadian Historical Review* 72, no. 4 (1991): 505–31.
2 Black gay critic Michael Awkward has written eloquently on the possibilities and the pitfalls of black male commitment to 'black feminist discourse.' This commitment eschews notions of black heterosexuality in which 'notions of the female' are grounded in 'an emphasis on the achievement of black manhood at the expense of black female subjectivity.' See Michael Awkward, 'A Black Man's Place(s) in Black Feminist Criticism,' in Marcellous Blount and George P. Cunningham, eds, *Representing Black Men* (New York: Routledge, 1996).
3 I first introduced this concept in a 1998 Canadian Historical Association conference paper titled 'Sexual Conflict, Black Patriarchy, and the Law: Reading the Story of George and Eliza Ross in Ontario's Criminal Case Files, Essex County Ontario, 1882.' See also my forthcoming PhD dissertation, 'The Gavel and the Veil: "Blackness" in Ontario's Criminal Courts, 1858–1953,' especially chapter 4, 'Residual Patriarchy.'
4 Aside from a passing reference in Clayton Mosher's *Discrimination and Denial: Systemic Racism in Ontario's Legal and Criminal Justice Systems, 1892–1961* (Toronto: University of Toronto Press, 1998), I was able to uncover only one other account of the Anderson Veney trial: see Patrick Brode, 'Veney, Anderson,' *Dictionary of Canadian Biography*, vol. 13, *1891–1900* Toronto: (University of Toronto Press, 1996), 1073–4.
5 Excellent work has been done on exemplary African-Canadian women. See, for exam-

ple, Jane Rhodes, *Mary Ann Shadd: The Black Press and Protest in the Nineteenth Century* (Bloomington: Indiana University Press, 1988); Afua P. Cooper, 'Black Women and Work in Nineteenth Century Canada West: Black Woman Teacher Mary Bibb,' in Peggy Bristow et al., *'We're Rooted Here and They Can't Pull Us Up': Essays in African Canadian Women's History* (Toronto: University of Toronto Press, 1994). An example of such scholarship dealing with the twentieth century is Agnes Calliste, 'Canada's Immigration Policy and Domestics from the Caribbean: The Second Domestic Scheme,' in Vorst et al., eds, *Race, Class, Gender: Bonds and Barriers* (Toronto: Garamond Press, 1991), 133–65.

6  The lives of these less well-known women are explored in such works as Peggy Bristow, '"Whatever You Can Raise in the Ground You Can Sell It in Chatham": Black Women in Buxtom and Chatham, 1850–1865,' in *'We're Rooted Here and They Can't Pull Us Up'*; Shirley Yee, 'Gender Ideology and Black Women as Community Builders,' *Canadian Historical Review* 75 (March 1994): 53–73. For work in an earlier era dealing with the issue of black women under slavery in Canada, see Maureen Elgersman, *Unyielding Spirits: Black Women and Slavery in Early Canada and Jamaica* (New York: Garland, 1999).

7  See Franca Iacovetta and Wendy Mitchinson, eds, *On the Case: Explorations in Social History* (Toronto: University of Toronto Press, 1998).

8  For a notable exception see, Carolyn Strange, 'Wounded Womanhood and Dead Men: Chivalry and the Trials of Clara Ford and Carrie Davies,' in Franca Iacovetta and Mariana Valverde, eds, *Gender Conflicts: New Essays in Women's History* (Toronto: University of Toronto Press, 1992), 149–88.

9  The black female body has elsewhere been considered an important prism through which to examine black social history, legal history, and public policy. See for example Hazel Carby, 'Policing the Black Woman's Body in an Urban Context,' *Critical Inquiry* 18 (Summer 1992): 738–55; and Dorothy Roberts, *Killing the Black Body* (New York: Pantheon, 1997).

10  Critical legal studies (CLS) refer to a body of legal scholarship critical of more traditionalist and liberalist approaches to the study of the law. Critical legal scholars reject liberalist notions of neutrality, legal formalism and individual rights. One important subfield of CLS is critical race theory. CLS is a body of literature that endeavours to show how systems of racial oppression are maintained through laws and legal institutions that claim to be value-free, neutral, and objective. See, for example Richard Delgado's *Critical Race Theory: The Cutting Edge* (Philadelphia: Temple University Press, 1995). A Canadian example of this kind of work is Carol Aylward's *Canadian Critical Race Theory: Racism and the Law* (Halifax: Fernwood Publishing, 1999).

11  See, for example, National Archives of Canada (hereafter NA), *The Queen v. Fred Fountain*, RG 13 CC 108 Vol. 1501 and *The Queen v. Harry Lee*, RG 13 CC 753 vol. 1711, both of which are explored in chapter 6 of my dissertation 'The Gavel and the Veil.' By contrast, the historical record suggests that the dominant culture's anxieties

around the issue of race and sex meant that the kind of 'privilege' afforded the black men in these cases not as easily afforded to black men who committed similar crimes against white female lovers or spouses.

12  *Toronto Daily Mail*, 23 September 1892.

13  NA, *The Queen v. Anderson Veney*, RG 13, box 1, 1428, file 2206, Trial Transcripts (hereafter Transcripts), Testimony of Hattie Primeaux.

14  Transcripts.

15  During this conversation, Weadon Johnson extended his encouragement and support to Anderson Veney for having found religious faith. Johnson testified that he congratulated Veney, telling him, 'I am glad to understand that you have found Christ.' To which Veney was to have responded, 'It is a good thing to try and live a Christian [life].' Transcripts, 15.

16  Transcripts.

17  Transcripts, Testimony of Weadon Johnson, 16–17.

18  *Toronto Telegram*, 23 September 1892.

19  Ibid.

20  Archives of Ontario (hereafter AO), RG 22-392-0-2793, Criminal Assize Indictments (hereafter CA1), Essex County, Inquest on the Body of Martha Veney, Testimony of Constable Lawrence LeMay.

21  *London Free Press*, 14 September 1892.

22  Inquest on the Body of Martha Veney, Testimony of Dr T. James Park.

23  Ibid., Testimony of Dr J. Proudfoot.

24  Ibid., Testimony of Forest T. Bell, Coroner, County of Essex.

25  The *Chatham Daily Planet* carried the headline: 'At the Spring Assizes Trial of Two Murder Cases Crowds the Court: Richardson, the Dresden Fiend Who Deliberately Kicked His Wife to Death on the Street,' 11 April 1894.

26  AO, RG 22-487-1-12, box 1, Benchbooks of Justice William Purvis Street, Testimony of Mary Richardson.

27  Ibid.

28  AO, CAI, Kent County, RG 22-342-0-2793, Testimony of Daphne Warren.

29  Benchbooks of Justice Street, Testimony of Mary Richardson. This graphic testimony was corroborated by a man named William Fritz who also witnessed the murder. His testimony, represented as a disquieting and grotesque moment of levity in the newspaper coverage, only serves to amplify the horror of the violence committed upon Hannah Richardson's body. William Fritz: 'He was kicking his wife at the time [I] called him to desist but he did not.' Cross-examined: 'How near were you to them?' 'About fifteen feet.' 'And you stood there and saw him beat his wife and never interfered? Is that the man you are?' 'Well, sir, if you'd been there, you'd have done the same thing.' (Laughter) *Chatham Daily Planet*, 11 April 1894.

30  Ibid.

31  CAI, Kent County, Testimony of Daphne Warren.

32  Ibid., Testimony of Dr Daniel Gailbraith.

33  Ibid.

34  Ibid.

35  A 'quadroon' is generally referred to as a person of African descent who has approxi-
    mately one-fourth 'African blood' in his or her ancestral lineage or phenotypic
    makeup. This kind of racial categorization is most often called the 'one-drop rule,' a
    modality of racial categorization based on a notion of 'blood admixture' which con-
    ceptualizes African blood as a contagion, and thus even the most diffuse traces of it in
    a body renders that body 'black.' A mainstay of white supremacy in pre- and poste-
    mancipatory black life in the New World, it is interesting to note that this mode of
    racial classification was (and is) an organizing principle in the United States and also
    Canada. Other New World slavery and postslavery societies tended to favour a system
    of racial/corporeal hierarchy that made room for an 'intermediary class' of people who
    were 'neither white nor black,' also called a 'colored' or 'mestesos' caste. For an excel-
    lent discussion of the one-drop rule in Canada and the United States, and its virtual
    non-existence elsewhere in the New World see, Carl M. Degler, *Neither Black Nor
    White: Slavery and Race Relations in Brazil and the United States* (New York: Mac-
    millan, 1971).

36  CAI, Kent County, Testimony of Dr Irvine Wiley.

37  Ibid.

38  Ibid.

39  Though I have chosen not to explicitly pursue this method here, for an excellent dis-
    cussion on dramaturgy as an historical methodology that gives us insights from review-
    ing the interaction of past people as though the episodes considered were displayed in
    a theatre, see Rhys Isaac, *The Transformation of Virginia, 1740–1790* (Chapel Hill:
    University of North Carolina Press, 1982).

40  Transcripts, Testimony of Hattie Primeaux, 14.

41  Ibid., 10–13.

42  Ibid.

43  Ibid.

44  Trial Transcripts, Testimony of Lewis Lemay and James Lushington. Lemay, Amherst-
    burgh's Chief Constable, recalled he heard Veney remark that he 'killed [Martha
    Veney] in a fit of passion,' and moreover, that 'if [I] had not minded the outside talk
    and outside letters [I] would be a free man today.' Similarly, James Lushington, who
    accompanied Anderson to see Dr Proudfoot, told the court of Veney's confession as
    well as the motives behind his crime. When Lushington apparently asked Veney what
    had possessed him to commit such a crime, Veney replied, 'my wife has been unfaith-
    ful to me.' And later on, as Veney stood in his cell, Lemay asked Veney whether he had
    secured legal representation. To this Veney responded, '[N]o, I have not, it is not nec-
    essary that I should do so ... I committed the deed, and ... there is no use of my spend-

ing all the money I have got and the little piece of property I have; I would only be doing it and deprive my children of it ... I am satisfied that I will get the rope.'

45  Attorney Rogest Delos Davis was the son of an escaped Maryland slave. After a rather circuitous route that saw him work a variety of jobs, he began to study law in 1871 under the tutelage of two sympathetic whites – a county judge and an attorney. Barriers created by white supremacist opposition in the legal profession to Davis ambitions meant that no attorney was willing to allow him to pursue the crucial step of articling. Two petitions to the Ontario legislature, in 1884 and 1886, resulted in two special acts enabling him to work as an attorney and be called to the bar, provided he pass a 'requisite examination.' Interestingly, though Davis served as counsel on six important murder cases, his specialty was 'drainage litigation.' See Owen Thomas, 'Davis, Delos Rogest,' *Dictionary of Canadian Biography*, vol. 14, *1911–1920* (Toronto: University of Toronto Press, 1996), 274–75.

46  Transcripts, Testimony of Lewis Lemay, 30–1.

47  The duties of a steward on the lake included 'buy[ing] stores, look[ing] after [ones] boat and keep[ing] everything in proper order.' See, Transcripts, Testimony of Roman Smith.

48  Transcripts, Testimony of Annie Foster.

49  Ibid., Testimony of Mrs John Leslie.

50  Ibid., Testimony of William H. Brown.

51  Ibid., Testimony of Dr Thomas Hobley.

52  Ibid., Testimony of Dr James Samson.

53  Ibid.

54  Ibid., Testimony of Dr Remi Casgrain.

55  Benchbooks of Justice Street, Testimony of Mary Richardson.

56  *Chatham Daily Planet*, 11 April 1894.

57  Benchbooks of Justice Street, Testimony of James Richardson.

58  Ibid., Testimony of Richard Lucas, Richard Morton, James Langstaff, Joseph Jones. Brief synopses of witness testimony also appears in the *Chatham Daily Planet*, 11 April 1894.

59  *Chatham Daily Planet*, 11 April 1894.

60  Benchbooks of Justice Street, Testimony of Dr McKeough and Dr J.R. Bray.

61  AO, CAI Kent County, RG 22-342-0-2793, Testimony of Hiram Richardson.

62  *Chatham Daily Planet*, 11 April 1894.

63  The following entry appears in Justice Street's benchbook. This was likely read aloud to the court during sentencing: 'The crime was most brutal and the woman was killed by repeated kicks with the head by her husband the prisoner – the provocation if any was very slight. A verdict of murder would have been well justified by the evidence.'

64  Transcripts, Justice Malcolm Street's charge to the jury. Street's trial report to the Secretary of State in Ottawa, which was composed the same day as the trial, was a little

more nuanced. The trial over, the justice could now step outside of the strict confines of rather narrowly proscribed legal sentencing procedure. Street's report alluded to the fact that 'while the evidence left no doubt open as to the fact that the prisoner killed his wife, and knew at the time he did so that he was committing a murder, there was some evidence which may have led the jury to believe that at the present time, at all events, was not perfectly sound in mind.'

65   Carolyn Strange has observed that these kinds of 'post-commutation deliberations' are a regular fixture in capital case files, and can often be read as 'counternarratives' to narratives created in other texts in the file. The petition was signed on Veney's behalf by many of Amherstburgh's elite, including the mayor, an ex-mayor, a banker, a broker, and a bailiff. These petitions represented an effort to re-articulate the defence's contention that Veney was essentially a 'quiet, peaceable, industrious, law-abiding citizen [who] enjoyed the respect and esteem of all classes of our population as a man who faithfully discharged all of the duties of his station in life.' The petition goes on to state that '[o]f late years an impression has prevailed in our community that his mind had failed and that he was subject to periods of mental aberration of what was supposed to be a harmless character. On the day when the homicide was committed we believe that he was suffering from one of these attacks which for the first time assumed a violent phase and irresistibly hurried him into his fatal crime. The realization of that crime may have corrected in great measure the uncontrollable murderous impulse and restored in degree his mental equilibrium, so that a medical examination made after several months would fail to show his true condition at the time of the homicide.'

The petition concludes: 'We feel from our previous knowledge of his character, so wholly inconsistent with that one act of his life, that he must have been insane on that occasion and we respectfully submit that in any view the case is one of such reasonable doubt that the extreme penalty of the law should not be exacted.' Transcripts, Petitions to the Governor General of Canada. See Carolyn Strange, 'The Historian and the Capital Case File,' *On the Case: Explorations in Social History*, 26–48.

66   Shortly after the close of the trial, Dr Samson, a key defence witness, wrote a letter to defence counsel Malcolm Cowan informing him that he was still completely convinced of Veney's insanity and of the fact that Veney was the 'victim of some mysterious brain disease [who] presents himself as a pitiful picture of mental instability.' Samson went on to add that hanging Veney would constitute as ghastly a spectacle as was ever witnessed at the gallows and in view of all the recent utterances in the public press may even become a scandal. In the face of mounting and compelling evidence of Veney's madness, Joseph-Alderic Oiumet, the acting Minister of Justice, requested that Remi Casgrain, Amherstburgh's jail surgeon, re-examine Veney. Casgrain, however, only partially rescinded his trial testimony, stubbornly reporting in a telegram to the deputy minister of justice that, indeed, while Veney's physical condition was not so good since the trial, his mental condition was the same, sane and conscious. However,

prior to this, Dr Chamberlain, the government inspector of prisons and police institutions also examined Veney at the (rather unusual) request of the deputy attorney general of Ontario, John Robinson Cartwright. Chamberlain claimed that though Veney was sane when he killed his wife, 'brooding over his crime and confinement in prison have brought about a change. I am convinced now that he has a softening of the brain, and whether kept in prison or an asylum, he will not live over two months.' The commutation of Veney's sentence mattered little, as he died in the prison hospital before a year had passed. NA, *The Queen v. Anderson Veney*, RG 13, box 1, 1428, file 259, Trial Transcripts. Brode, 'Veney, Anderson.'

# The Tale of Lin Tee:
# Madness, Family Violence, and Lindsay's
# Anti-Chinese Riot of 1919

LISA R. MAR

## Introduction

On 31 January 1919, Lin Tee's attempts to escape an abusive marriage so divided
the town of Lindsay, Ontario, that residents took justice into their own hands in
a violent night of racial terror. A lynch mob of five hundred white men and boys
targeted Lin's husband, Lee Ten Yun, a Chinese immigrant laundry worker. The
rioters knew Lee confined his wife at home. They often had heard her screams
and many believed that Lee prostituted his insane wife out to other Chinese men
against her will. That morning a neighbour claimed to have seen her standing on
a bed wielding a stick to fend off advances of her husband and two other Chinese
men. Shortly afterward, Lin attempted to escape by leaping through the front
window of the Lee living quarters in the Chuong Sun Laundry.

An earlier escape attempt had resulted in Lin's imprisonment by her husband
at home. For months prior to the riot, townspeople, hearing Lin's screams and
concerned for her well-being, had urged authorities and politicians to intervene
in the family's apparent problems. On the night of the 31st, long simmering tensions came to a raging boil as citizens decided that if the police would not act,
then the people would.[1] Around 7 P.M., small crowds of men collected on corners, huddled in nearby doorways, and paraded in front of the Chuong Sun
Laundry, protesting Lee's cruelty and demanding that the police act. The demonstrators' bad mood created a nerve-wracking evening for the Lee family. At
9:30 P.M., Police Chief John Short arrived and arrested Lin Tee for insanity. Protesters angrily shouted to Short that he should instead arrest all Chinese men.
Short replied that no one had given him enough evidence to lay a charge.[2]

At 11 P.M., a tide of several hundred Lindsay hockey fans, rejoicing in victory over the rival Peterborough team, bolstered the angry crowd. Shouting racial taunts, five hundred men and boys shattered the windows of the Chuong Sun Laundry with a barrage of bricks, stones and ice. They demanded that Lee come out so the crowd could rough him up. Meanwhile, a fearful Lee hid in the apartment above the laundry. Soon afterward, the rioters charged the Chuong Sun Laundry with 'catcalls and yells' and wrecked it with a fury, sending a 'shower of laundry' out the window. When the rioters heard that Lee had escaped, about four hundred went home, satisfied that their message was heard. The remaining seventy-five to one hundred rioters avenged their loss by attacking two other Chinese businesses, starting with a café where Lee's co-workers from the laundry had taken refuge. The rioters smashed fixtures, looted, and threw Chinese personal possessions into the street. At daybreak Lindsay newspapers evoked images of war-torn Belgium to describe property damage.[3]

At first glance, the Lindsay riot seems part of a well-documented pattern of gender-based racism in early-twentieth-century Canada.[4] During that time, law, popular belief, and policing practices often singled out Chinese immigrant men as moral threats, especially to white women. Upon closer examination, the usual explanation of racial hatred as the only motivation for the riot did not apply. In court, Lin Tee's tale unfolded as a drama of competing gender claims set against an inescapable backdrop of race. As witnesses offered their differing reactions to Lin's case, they recounted an explosive conflict over defining and enforcing community standards. Above all, Lindsay residents debated over who should judge whether Lin's case merited police 'interference' within the sacred bounds of a 'man's family.' Their debates centred on gender claims, but in their arguments they evoked explosive claims about racial difference.

Though a single case study, Lin's tale helps chart how isolated immigrant women negotiated minefields of race, gender, and class tensions in ways that significantly differed from immigrant men. In early-twentieth-century Canada, gender-specific notions about the family helped determine when Chinese immigrants became sisters or strangers, brothers or undesirable foreigners. Historians have most often written about Chinese immigrant women as community builders, but stories of the abused are equally important in assessing how race, gender, and class impinged on immigrant women's lives.[5] While the immigrant family could be a place of refuge from a hostile society and a source of ethnic pride, as Midge Ayukawa's essay on the Japanese in this volume suggests, it could also be a site of conflict and danger.

Lin's drama played out against the background of gender and racial contests with national resonance. In her time, gender claims inflated popular fears of the 'yellow peril' of Asian immigration. Social reformers often denounced Chinese men as moral perils to women in the 1910s, and related anti-Chinese racism erupted across five of nine Canadian provinces. Though miniscule numbers of Chinese lived east of the Rockies, three anti-Chinese riots occurred there between 1918 and 1919. Popular white beliefs about inferior gender relations among other ethnic groups buttressed notions of white Anglo-Celtic supremacy, as Cecilia Morgan's analysis in this volume of native–white relations in nineteenth-century Ontario indicates. Large numbers of whites believed that both Chinese immigrants and Native peoples practised deviant gender relations. These beliefs influenced discriminatory policies from Chinese immigration barriers to forced assimilation of Native children in residential schools. Furthermore, many Anglo-Celtic Canadians viewed Asian (as well as Aboriginal and black) men as inherent perpetrators of sexual violence.

Many whites did not consider racial minority households as consisting of normal families or homes, a situation that justified drastic intervention by the state. In Ontario, provincial and municipal policies targeted Chinese men on moral grounds. For example, regulations prohibited Chinese from employing white women, and banned Chinese from living, eating, or sleeping in the business areas of their laundries and cafés. They also enabled frequent surprise inspections of Chinese residences. From Chinese viewpoints, privacy protections applied to Anglo-Celtic residents' homes frequently did not seem to apply to Chinese immigrants' predominantly male households.[6]

Given the race relations backdrop of the time, one would expect Lindsay authorities to side with Lin against her abusive husband. Why did they not believe her when single Chinese men were so readily suspect? Lin's trail has long gone cold, so we will sift meanings of Lin's family power struggle through the testimony of others.

### Lin's Sanity on Trial

On 8 February 1919, one week after the riot, Lin Tee went on trial for criminal insanity.[7] At the trial, Police Court Magistrate Jesse Bradford considered the charge that Lin was a dangerous 'lunatic' who should be confined under warrant in an asylum without her or her family's consent. The process of judgment necessarily involved contextual criteria. The law required that the Crown attorney prove two facts: first, that the accused was dangerous to herself or others; second, that the accused behaved in a manner contrary to the ordinary custom of the community in which she lived. In short, could Lin's behaviour be understood as normal under the circumstances? A third factor commonly influenced police court judgements about female insanity: If Lin was insane, could her family properly care for her?[8] Popular opinion already prior to the trial, backed by the judge, Crown attorney, police and other leading citizens, held that Lin was not sane.

Thus, the main question posed to the court was whether to send Lin back to her husband or to an insane asylum?[9]

What makes this case remarkable is the detailed testimony of neighbours, friends, and experts. Their responses to the family chronicled the integration of a Chinese immigrant couple in a relatively welcoming, small-town community. They also delineated sharp divisions in perceptions that shaped clashing gender claims about Lin's case. From morning until midnight, witnesses testified about their views of her case, while spectators crowded Lindsay's police court and heard many versions of her tale. Like many trials, hers involved competing narratives about truth and culpability.[10] Though witnesses often disagreed with each other, a story of Lin's initiative did emerge. At the trial that would decide her fate, she was apparently a silent object of judgment, but in her own view, she had tried to protect herself and her daughter from circumstances she felt she had reason to fear.[11]

**A Family in Distress**

Even before their family fell apart, the Lees stood out in Lindsay as the only Chinese immigrant family in a town largely untouched by early twentieth-century waves of immigration from outside of the British Isles. The census records only a handful of foreign immigrants living in the southeastern Ontario town. Native-born English, Irish, and Scotch Canadians made up the bulk of Lindsay's population. Except for French Canadians, others were neither recorded in the annals of the town, nor was their presence remembered.[12]

Lee, in his mid-forties, and Lin, much younger in her mid-twenties, had moved to Lindsay in 1914. They established themselves as hand-laundry workers in a small shop and Lee also worked at the nearby Chuong Sun Laundry. Lee, also called 'Willie' Lee, had lived in Canada for fifteen years, whereas Lin had immigrated more recently. In Lindsay, their employers and co-workers were all fellow Lees who probably came from the same village in China. Similarly, other groups of men with common surnames operated the five other Chinese laundries and two Chinese cafés in town. Lindsay directories show a Chinese immigrant population of about one dozen, all male except for Lin. Among Chinese immigrant men, Lee was exceptionally fortunate since few Chinese immigrants had enough funds to bring over a wife from China.[13] While in Lindsay, Lin and Lee celebrated the birth of two sons and a daughter.[14]

The Lee family settlement coincided with the migration of several thousand Chinese from British Columbia to Ontario. According to the 1921 census, the number of Chinese in Ontario was 5,625, less than 1 per cent of the total provincial population. Like Lee, Chinese workers in Ontario were concentrated in service industries. The 1921 census recorded that Chinese immigrant men comprised 40 per cent of laundry and restaurant operators in the province. Many Lindsay residents viewed households of Chinese men as foreign 'colonies' in their midst, unrestrained by the civilizing bonds of familial domesticity.[15] Canadian newspapers often portrayed Chinese men as criminals, drug addicts, and devious 'white slavers' intent on capturing white women to sell into prostitution.[16]

When eighteen-year-old Lin arrived in Lindsay in 1914, local Anglo-Celtic women befriended her. She attended the nearby St Paul's Anglican Church, and friends often visited her at home. At Lin's trial, Mrs George Mills stated, 'I visited this woman and at first found her to be a smart woman. I learned her to sew, knit, etc.' Similarly, Mrs Charles Hughes testified, 'I visited her four years ago, last August, for the first time and quite frequently since. I just opened the door and went in. The woman lived in a poor condition but what she was used to.' Though Lin was an immigrant, Hughes found communication was possible. 'She could understand me fairly well.'

In the spring of 1918, Lin Tee found an enthusiastic and devoted friend in Dr Olive Ray. Ray had just returned from China and set up a medical practice in the neighbouring village of Cambray. Lin was the only other woman in the Lindsay area who spoke Chinese, so Ray frequently travelled the twenty-kilometre distance from Cambray to Lindsay by horse and buggy. At first, '[Lin] did not receive me friendly nor did the men,' said Ray. She persisted, helping Lin with English and teaching her sewing. Eventually, Lin 'grew to love my friendship,' Ray said. To her pleasure, Ray discovered Lin to be 'quite clear, bright and intelligent.'[17] According to Ray, in August 1918, Lin turned to her friend for help with family problems: 'She cried and used shocking English words and suggested some ill treatment to the child or herself.' As the court weighed Lee's fitness to care for his wife, Ray also claimed Lin had confided in English that 'this man had a wife and two children in China.' Her husband's polygamy, Ray suggested, made him only a 'so-called' husband, erasing his legal control over his wife. Ray also intimated that Lee's abuse may have contributed to Lin's mental distress because 'she was quite clear mentally then.'[18]

Soon after Lin confided in Ray, the Lees' outwardly peaceful family life in Lindsay fell apart. Friends claimed to have found Lin in bed crying, and on Sundays she seemed extremely distressed in church. They visited more often to try to help. Hughes, who was Lin's friend for four years, reported that 'last August she would take bad crying fits, tell me that Lee was no good and that she wanted the baby to be an angel. I saw no evidence, but she told me Lee beat the baby girl.' Neighbours testified that they could hear Lin continually screaming, crying, and yelling; the sound set them on edge. Her visible and audible distress inspired many townspeople to help the family, if only to quell the noise. Based on court testimony, we can only speculate about Lin's situation, although both spousal abuse and depression seem likely possibilities. Given the widely shared belief that Lin was demented, her friends found it difficult to assess her accusations against her husband without 'proof.' Neighbours also had difficulty evaluating Lee's care of his wife until his efforts to cope clearly crossed the line of acceptable behaviour. Like many cases of alleged abuse within the family, issues of determining what was happening devolved to ambiguous questions of one person's word against another.[19] Perceptions of the family were undoubtedly complicated by racialized notions of sexual violence applied to Asian men.

Lee evidently responded to the increasing pressures of his wife's mental distress by cutting her off from her friends and community and becoming very controlling, in a pattern suggestive of an abusive husband. He also seemed at his wits' end as Lin's mental distress likely put him under great strain. Besides attending to his wife, Lee had to work exhausting days in the laundry and care for three young children, including the baby Suey Lan. Without Lin's labour, the family finances probably worsened rapidly. Lee responded to increased public scrutiny of his home with explanations that his wife was 'insane.' To the horror of his neighbours, he boarded up the windows of his house so that Lin could not escape. Her prison was a twelve- by fourteen-foot room with door locks on the outside. Neighbours could hear Lin screaming, crying, and yelling.[20]

Lee felt that he had few alternatives, since he could not work, watch his children, and monitor his distressed wife as well. In locking up his wife, Lee was following a practice from his home village in China: lock up the insane at home. In September 1919, Lee felt overwhelmed and needed help caring for the baby. The family doctor, Dr Fabian Blanchard, contacted Mrs E.E. (Eleanor Earle) Sharpe, secretary of the Children's Aid Society. Sharpe visited the home to make arrangements to take the child, with Dr Olive Ray coming along as an interpreter.[21] Lin's distraught and dishevelled condition shocked Ray and Sharpe. The two women asked if they could take Lin out for a drive, but Lee refused because 'she will get away from us.' Meanwhile, without her baby daughter, Lin became melancholy and so Blanchard treated her with sedatives. Lee had also apparently tried to medicate Lin with opium, and she had developed an addiction to the drug. Ray and Sharpe then began a campaign to place Lin in an insane asylum, where they believed she would be better cared for than by her husband. By taking this initiative, these well-meaning women soon became embroiled in conflicts over the Lee family that divided the town.[22]

**Attempts at Rescue**

At the trial, Ray and Sharpe made their case that Lin should be removed from her husband's care. They had instigated her arrest for insanity, so they took the stand first. With the help of an attorney, Mr L.R. Knight, they also defended themselves from accusations that their meddling had caused the riot.[23] Knight hammered home the point that Lee had not properly cared for his wife. Lin's accusations of abuse and her expressed desire to escape confinement prompted Ray's and Sharpe's efforts to intervene on her behalf. Nevertheless, their attempts to remove Lin from her home by committing her to an asylum without asking her consent showed a paternalism common among middle-class social reformers. Though the women probably did not start the rumours about Lee prostituting his insane wife, the rumours referred to images of Chinese gender deviance common in reform rhetoric. These critiques referred to beliefs in the authoritarian nature of Chinese husbands, the subordination of women in Chinese families, the tendency of Chinese men towards miscegenation with white women, which was often supposedly accomplished through trickery, coercion, or exchange of money, and fears that Asian male 'others' were prone to sexual violence.

Even at the height of early Canadian feminists' influence in the 1920s, critics saw feminists' racial agenda as their ideological Achilles heel. In the Lindsay Police Court, both town authorities and Chinese men alleged that the women had been motivated by racial prejudice. Indeed, Ray's and Sharpe's profile matches family-oriented reformers of their age. Ray was a Christian missionary, while Sharpe was a local feminist crusader for the vote, an ardent imperialist member of the Imperial Order Daughters of the Empire (IODE), and an avid social reformer. As a local Children's Aid Society worker, Sharpe advocated that the state should intervene within the family to protect children from abuse. Lin's case would extend the argument to include women. Sharpe was a controversial, albeit respected figure in Lindsay, a place, like the rest of Canada, that had not yet fully accepted the retreat from patriarchal privilege that child protection laws implied.[24] Historians have termed women like Ray and Sharpe 'maternal feminists' because they saw distinctive roles for women in public life, owing to their mothering characteristics. In Canada, maternal feminists often devoted special political attention to issues involving women, children, and the family. In the 1920s, their agenda included related reproductive issues facing the 'white race' in Canada, such as preventing miscegenation by regulating contact between Chinese men and white women.[25] Consequently, in Lindsay, a rhetoric of racial tolerance could support a backlash against feminist gender politics.

In response, the women's attorney L.R. Knight defended the feminists' actions as civic-minded. They should not be blamed for the riot because '[t]he action of the ladies was exactly what any right-thinking person would do.' If Lin had been sent to an asylum, or if police had acted on complaints of abuse, then the riot would have been avoided. Ultimately, he blamed Lee: 'A whole lot of responsibility rests with the husband and he is not a fit and proper person to take her to Toronto or China.' Throughout the fall of 1918, Ray and Sharpe pressed for Lin to be committed to an insane asylum. The committal required consent of two male physicians and Lin's family.[26] With Lee opposed and other male doctors in disagreement, the committal process went nowhere. Blanchard, the family doctor, testified that he had made fifty visits to the house. 'I only saw her cry once,' he reported, 'There was not the faintest evidence of ill-treatment.' He diagnosed Lin as 'suffering from nervous excitement.' Accusations of abuse had no substance because he said, 'Relationship between husband and wife were very normal and happy.'[27]

In late September 1918, Lin broke the stalemate by running away. At two in the morning, she knocked on Ray's door, her baby in her arms. Standing in the doorway, Lin said that Lee was 'no good' and that she would not go back. Ray invited Lin and the baby to stay for a while. Ray testified that Lin seemed cheerful the next morning, but by the following day she became depressed, and started to sing abnormally. While Lin stayed with Ray, Lee visited every day and, according to Ray, 'he seemed attentive.' Meanwhile, Lin's mental state deteriorated. Ray testified that Lin 'imagined she saw people in the air' and 'gradually passed into a state of moping and depression.' After a few weeks, Lin returned to her husband.[28] Events worsened, however, when baby Suey Lan fell ill and died in the global influenza epidemic in October. Ray said Lin appeared to be in a 'wild' state on the day of the funeral. As Lin's distress deepened, the sound of her screams gave credence to community beliefs that horrific abuse was occurring.

Then, late in the fall, Lee decided to move his family into the Chuong Sun Laundry, where his employers and relatives lived, so he could more easily care for Lin while he worked. They were all Chinese men at the laundry, a fact that would have significance for Lindsay residents concerned about abuse. After the move, Lee kept his wife Lin locked up in her quarters behind the laundry and did not permit her to go out. His perceived abuse aroused community ire: boys pounded on the windows and door of the laundry until they broke the glass. In December, Ray and Sharpe resolved that Lin would be better off in an insane asylum, with or without her husband's consent. They went to the police and swore out a deposition that Lin Tee was insane. Police Chief John Short then accompanied them to arrest Lin Tee so that doctors could investigate her mental condition. Ray testified that when they arrived, Lin was sitting in a chair with her hair tidy and in a condition of sanity. When Ray informed her that she would leave her husband's home, she went willingly, suggesting that she welcomed what she perceived as her friend's efforts to gain her freedom.[29]

Ray and Short took Lin to Police Magistrate Jesse Bradford's office at the Lindsay Police Court. Terrified of the legal process that she neither wished for, nor understood, Lin became very agitated. Using a Chinese boy as interpreter,

Bradford asked her whether there been any cruelty? Lin replied no, that other men did not use her, and that her husband was not cruel to her, but her problem was her baby. Given that the reputation of Chinese men in Lindsay was at stake, it is possible that the boy's translation was not accurate and thus, the question whether abuse occurred remains unclear. Lin may have feared the consequences of admitting the abuse to authorities. According to literature about familial abuse, a reluctance to involve the police and courts is characteristic of many abused women because they fear their husband's retaliation. The white community's suspicions may have also scared her into silence for the sake of her family.[30] Medical opinions of Lin's mental condition, including that of her family doctor, did not favour removing her from the home. When Lee refused again to commit his wife to an asylum, Bradford jailed Lin for one day, then returned her to the custody of her husband.[31]

Once again, Ray and Sharpe found criminal insanity law an awkward tool for rescue. Both the police and the courts applied criminal insanity charges within social contexts that were highly influenced by understandings of gender. Early twentieth-century authorities usually deferred decisions about care of insane women to male relatives. Their actions conformed to normative views of gender in marriage, in which allegedly less rational, more emotional women followed the direction of allegedly more rational, stable men. If the family could control their insane member and the community's peace was not unduly disturbed, husbands' authority in the home remained intact. As long as Lin did not pose a danger to herself and there was no irrefutable proof of abuse in the home, the police and magistrate saw no justification to interfere in the couple's domestic quarrels. Their response conformed to a common pattern in the history of policing domestic abuse: reluctance by authorities to intervene in family conflicts between husbands and wives.[32]

At home, Lee again made Lin a prisoner. He did not let her go out, nor did he allow her to see anyone except Mrs George Mills, a friend of the Chinese community of Lindsay for twenty years, who visited and brought food for Lin. In her testimony, Mills said she believed that Lee locked up Lin because she was deranged, that she did not hear about any abuse from Lin, nor did she see any evidence of ill treatment. Aside from Lin's insanity, she felt that the household conformed to prevailing domestic norms. Mills said she always found the Lee home 'clean and comfortable as a foreigner usually makes his home' and the children were 'smart and well looked after.' During her six weeks of imprisonment at home, Lin's mental state deteriorated and her desperate screams disturbed the neighbours more frequently. Once again they turned to local officials and immigration authorities for help.[33]

## The Police, Officials, and 'A Good Family Man'

Lindsay police had investigated charges of cruelty against Lee, but because no one came forward with corroborating evidence, Police Chief John Short felt the privacy of Lee's home had to be respected. From Short's standpoint, an insane woman's attempt to escape from her husband could not necessarily be interpreted as evidence of abuse. Likewise, the sound of Lin's screams did not outweigh the family's right to privacy. Town authorities claimed that a man's home could simply not be entered without specific evidence of a crime. To do otherwise would set a precedent allowing police to breech the privacy of the home. Crown attorney T.H. Stinson explained, 'It is our claim in this country that our liberty is not highly interfered with and our property is protected.' To make an exception for a Chinese family would constitute illegal discrimination because in this case, 'The law pertaining to foreigners applies to the average citizen.'[34]

Yet in response to rumours and public pressure, in early September 1918, Short investigated allegations of abuse. He described his cursory inquiry and his resulting conclusions to the Police Court:

> I investigated, and saw the China man, I saw him nursing one of the children in the hallway. His wife was on the inside, I told him the complaints and he denied them. I was satisfied there was nothing to the rumours. I went back again twice and found conditions the same. I saw the woman on both occasions. She did not look like a person who was abused. I learned from inquiries that Lee was not a man like that. I could find nothing to warrant interference. No one came to me with a specific charge. All that was brought to me were rumours. I was satisfied there was nothing in the ill treatment charge to justify police acting.

The basis of Short's good impression of Lee was his identification with him as a fellow family man. As Short testified, 'On my first visit to the home, I saw the father nursing his child. He was as fatherly as I was myself and I have nursed ten of my own. He impressed me as being a kindly man. There was no evidence of fear on the woman's part.' Short apparently did not question Lin at length. From start to finish, despite community pressure, Short held his position that Lee had done nothing wrong.[35] In January 1919, Mayor McLean, and former mayor W.M. Kylie visited the Lee family. They shared Short's feelings of gender solidarity with the beleaguered Lee: 'We were both of the opinion that rumours of abuse were absolutely unfounded. We could not realize how a man so affectionate towards a child could ill-treat his wife.'[36]

By the end of January 1919, Lin Tee's attempts to escape became more desperate. Hughes testified that 'she screamed in her efforts to get away and smashed windows to get out.' According to witness John McCrae, neighbour William Warrian 'couldn't put up with the noise.' McCrae stated that Warrian burst into the laundry where he saw 'two Chinamen on the floor and the woman standing in bed with a stick.' In court, Warrian denied the story, claiming all he saw was Lee, another Chinese man, and two boys. Yet Warrian's original story of abuse had spread like wildfire throughout the day of the riot, especially after Lin's dramatic front-window escape appeared to support his tale.[37] Minutes after Lin's escape attempt, according to *The Watchman-Warder*, a number of citizens urged that 'the parties guilty of the cruelties inflicted on the Chinese woman who had been attacked from time to time, should be put out of business and advocated strong arm methods if necessary.' Regardless of whether Lee prostituted his wife to other Chinese men, as many Lindsay residents believed, or whether he cruelly imprisoned his insane wife, his actions violated community standards. Until the morning of the riot, community leaders had upheld Lee's patriarchal privilege to protect and care for his wife, but new proof of abuse seemed to appear. One faction of elite men, frustrated with police inaction, called for the men of the town to take matters into their own hands.[38]

On the evening of 31 January, protestors demonstrated in front of the Chuong Sun Laundry. Meanwhile, Ray and Sharpe again swore out a deposition that Lin was insane and Short arrived and arrested Lin for insanity. Recalling her previous arrest, she refused to dress herself and had to be forcibly taken to jail.[39] That night, medical assessments agreed that Lin was insane: she was reportedly hysterical, 'wandering, singing, crying and laughing.' Lin was later moved to the Children's Shelter, where, in despair, she tried to kill herself by putting a nail through her arm and tying a towel around her neck.[40]

During Lin's arrest, the crowd of men outside the laundry became outraged that Short had arrested a helpless woman instead of the man they believed had abused her. Short claimed that no one had provided him with enough evidence to lay a charge. The dark temper of the men in the mob turned stormy. If the police would not act, then the people would. In the name of maintaining community standards, a night of terror ensued.[41] Gender concerns catalyzed the first part of the riot, which newspapers claimed was led by established community leaders. Five hundred men defended community standards, but they did not breech law and order beyond destroying the property of their targets, though they clamoured for violence against 'John Chinaman' (Lee), so they could run him out of town. For this group, racial hatred was a terror tactic. The crowd targeted only those Chinese men whom they believed were complicit in Lin's abuse – Lee and his co-workers at Chuong Sun Laundry. The crowd did not harm Lindsay's two-man police force, nor were neighbouring premises disturbed. Once the Chuong Sun

Laundry had been reduced to ruins, the majority of rioters peacefully dispersed.[42]

The second part of the riot involved uncontrolled looting, indignation and opportunistic racial violence. Seventy-five to one hundred rioters pursued Lee's co-workers to Charlie Ling's Dominion Café where the latter had taken refuge. There the rioters again demanded that 'John Chinaman' [Lee] be given to the crowd, but all Chinese had fled or hid before the mob arrived. These rioters were mainly younger men and boys, 'thirsting for excitement and revenge on some person.' Police were unable to restrain the unruly mob, which included the Peterborough hockey team and fans as well as Lindsay residents. A flying brick hit Police Chief Short, knocking him unconscious. Police Constable Parkes, the remainder of Lindsay's two-man police force, fled to seek help. At the third target, the Lee Chong Brothers Laundry, the mob stole laundry parcelled for delivery that belonged to their neighbours.[43] Summing up the evening, the *Peterboro Review* commented, 'Hockey success evidently drove Lindsay wild.'[44]

**Denying Discrimination**

After the riot, many Lindsay residents disavowed racial prejudice. They claimed that competing gender claims led to the riot because the authorities had not addressed Lee's wife abuse. Most of the rioters focused their anger only on Lee and his workplace, expressing racial hatred to punish him for public abuse of his wife. While wife abuse did occur in both Chinese- and European-Canadian communities, as long as it did not unduly disturb the neighbours or create a public horror, private conduct could deviate from public postures of masculinity as chivalrous protection of women.[45] In a Freudian sense, the men of Lindsay may have displaced their own collective anger and guilt over spousal abuse on the least threatening target – a Chinese immigrant man.[46] Because a minority of the mob had looted the property of innocent Chinese victims, newspapers called the event 'an anti-Chinese riot,' though they claimed conflicts over the Lee family had caused the violence. To redeem the town's good name, the *Lindsay Post* encouraged city organizations to pass 'strong resolutions denouncing the incident.'[47] An editorial on 7 February 1919, criticized vigilantism as unworthy of British liberty and manhood: 'To resort to terrorism is to deny the existence of a liberty which has been at stake in the great struggle overseas for which many thousands of Canadians have laid down their lives.' A local newspaper also editorialized that it was unfortunate that Chinese were treated so wrongly, when Canada spent thousands of dollars each year to send missionaries to China.[48]

To disavow the 'disgraceful incident,' Lindsay's Crown attorney T.H. Stinson called for charges to be laid against riot organizers. But in response, townspeople closed ranks. Police inquiries led nowhere, and although five hundred people participated, no one could be identified, no one was ever arrested, and no one was ever charged.[49] Perhaps people regretted the riot, but they did not view it as serious enough to merit turning in a neighbour. The Lindsay press joined the conspiracy of silence, identifying only members of the losing Peterborough hockey team as rioters. Eventually, the event slipped from public memory into historical oblivion. When I visited Lindsay in 1995, no one had heard about the event.

## We Are All Family: Defending Chinese Men in Lindsay

From the Chinese standpoint, the connection between the riot and discriminatory images of Chinese men demanded a response. Chinese immigrants wanted redress for the riot, that, whatever its causes, had expressed racial hatred. They complained to the Chinese consul, raising the stakes by turning the riot into a potential international incident. In addition, pro-Chinese witnesses vociferously defended Chinese immigrant men's masculine privileges against racist notions that impugned their manhood.[50] We know Chinese community viewpoints only from English newspapers because no local Chinese newspapers were available, nor were Canadian diplomatic records preserved, nor were descendants of early Chinese immigrants still living in the community.[51]

After Lee fled to Toronto, he contacted the Lee Association to assist with his defence. Prominent Toronto Chinese leader Rev. Ma T.K. Wou (Ma Jinghu) immediately travelled to Lindsay to investigate allegations that Lee prostituted his wife to other Chinese men. Accompanied by a female cousin of Lin, Ma interviewed Lin and declared that rumours of abuse were false. Like the English community, the Chinese immigrant community tolerated a degree of private domestic abuse, so Ma's findings do not erase the validity of Lin's earlier accusations. Nevertheless, the charges that inflamed the riot were most likely false. While Chinese immigrant men condoned affairs and recourse to prostitution because laws hindered them from bringing their wives, they expected husbands to cherish their wives' sexual virtue. If other Chinese discovered that Lee prostituted his wife out to other Chinese men, they would brand him as cruel and immoral, which would bring him great shame. When working-class Chinese men broke moral obligations, other Chinese immigrants blacklisted them, denying them access to Chinese networks that provided necessary credit, employment, mutual aid, accommodation, and supplies. Even Lee's employers depended on the goodwill of Chinese laundry suppliers. In general, Chinese immigrants tried to avoid behaviour that would add to racial prejudice. When a Chinese immigrant became mentally ill and disruptive to white society, fellow Chinese usually pressured the person to return to China. Family members and mutual aid organizations provided funds when needed because the collective image of Chinese immigrants was at stake.[52]

The audience at Lin's trial reflected Chinese immigrants' anxiety over the case. Ma, a Presbyterian minister and secretary of the Chinese department of the YMCA, observed as an official representative of the Chinese consul. Lindsay and Toronto Chinese also came out in force. Lee had fled to Toronto, so twenty-four-year-old Lee Ling, a Toronto police court interpreter, joined with Lindsay attorney L.V. O'Connor to organize Lee's defence.

In the end, Lee Ling and O'Connor mounted an impressive defence that successfully refuted rumours of immorality. With the help of many witnesses, they suggested Ray's and Sharpe's unwanted interference had been guided by prejudice. Borrowing a page from racist ideology, Lee's defence team argued that Lin would be better off among other Chinese than in an asylum. They claimed her innate racial difference trumped any gender claims Lin might make about the merits of escaping alleged abuse. The team's strategy complemented town authorities' preference to preserve the privacy of the family home, while deflecting accusations of spousal abuse as potentially prejudiced. Systematically, witnesses for Lee defended his marriage, cast the Chuong Sun Laundry community as a family, and portrayed the women as misguided meddlers.[53]

Lee Ling started Lee's defence by dramatically discrediting Ray's assertion that Lin's and Lee's marriage was not a true marriage worthy of the authorities' respect. Lee Ling explained that the couple were married in China by Confucian rites, and then remarried in Victoria, BC, by a Methodist clergyman in accordance with Canadian law. Furthermore, he refuted Ray's charges related to Chinese practices of polygamy and the sale of women. Most significantly, Lee Ling also reframed the court spectators' understandings of gender and family relationships among Chinese immigrants. He argued that the people living at the Chuong Sun Laundry – Lee, his wife, his children, his nephew, and others – constituted a family. 'The Lees are all cousins and belong to the Lee clan,' he said. Lee Chuong, proprietor of the laundry, added that the family had separate quarters from the Chinese men. No immorality occurred, because according to Lee Chuong, 'Lee treated his wife and children the very best.' He described Lee as a caring husband, stating, 'My uncle did not do any work for [the] past six weeks, but attended to his wife.'[54] Moreover, Lee Ling emphasized that in Lindsay Chinese immigrants' behaviour conformed to standard Anglo-Celtic morals, according to which deviant sexual practices were unthinkable. Lee Ling said, 'I investigated the rumours current about town and the local Chinamen denied them.'

Reverend Robert Brown, pastor of the Chinese Church in Toronto, added his support to Lee Ling's assertions that Ray and Sharpe did not understand Chinese immigrants. Brown had started a mission to Chinese in Toronto in 1893. Since he was familiar with Chinese immigrant men's struggles against discrimination, he sympathized with Lee. He informed the court that Lee and his clan had wealthy cousins in Vancouver. Brown's claim of respectable class connections distanced Lee from the poverty associated with laundry work, subtly attacking the race and class prejudices that informed rumours of immorality. Further, Brown defended Lee's patriarchal imperative, then asserted his own paternalism over Lin. He stated that he could better arrange to care for Lin in Toronto than Mimico Asylum. He also harshly criticized Ray and Sharpe for harming Lin through their unwanted interference and for spreading rumours. He claimed that Lin's innate weakness as a Chinese woman made her exceptionally vulnerable: 'Chinese women are sensitive and hysterical. I have had funerals where we have had to carry a Chinese woman into the church and to the grave. This woman has been persecuted, I could see today,' he said.

In his closing statement, O'Connor continued Brown's argument and accused the women and the rioters of racial prejudice. Referring to claims that Lee prostituted out his insane wife, O'Connor said, 'I heard the rumours and I could not believe them.' Sadly, those rumours 'made an impression on the women' Ray and Sharpe. Like the women, O'Connor wanted the best for Lin, but he hoped that Chinese men in Lindsay would be cleared from scurrilous accusations. 'You can come to no other finding, your Worship, than the Chinese residents are nothing but the best, and that the family life of the Lee family was above reproach. I hope you will free these Chinese citizens from the odium cast upon them.'

## Making Judgments

At midnight on the day of the trial, Police Court Magistrate Jesse Bradford announced that he found Lin insane and dangerous to herself. Bradford then attempted to reconcile divisions over competing gender claims to define and enforce community standards with a compromise. He recognized the legitimacy of the women's authority to intervene, while downplaying the possibility of spousal abuse. He had judged that Lee could no longer manage his insane wife, but he found no evidence to support charges of abuse. His finding upheld male authority in the home and it cleared town officials from responsibility to intervene more forcefully earlier in the crisis. The police chief 'could not enter the Chinese home any more than he could enter your home unless a crime had actually been committed and he was armed with a warrant, and a suspicion reasonably well-founded. The Magistrate, too, would be open to prosecution. No blame is attached to the Police or the C.A.S. [Children's Aid Society],' he said. 'It is possible that a mistake has been made in this case, but I am convinced that the women acted in the best interests of humanity. I do not hold the women responsible. They are to be commended.'

The official conclusions of the trial, embraced by the press and the court, refuted popular white beliefs about Chinese men's race and gender behaviour. In one blow, they celebrated the town's victory over racial prejudice and they defended the Christian family from future scrutiny. The *Lindsay Post* trumpeted the court's racially tolerant conclusions:

> There was not a tittle of evidence produced that anything irregular had ever taken place in the Chinese quarter: the unfortunate Chinese woman (adjudged insane by the court) had never been ill-treated, the evidence went to show, nor had she been used for an illicit purpose. She had been married by a qualified Methodist minister to her husband at Victoria, B.C., and their family life and associations were shown to have been all that really could be desired.[55]

The judgment of the court nevertheless turned a blind eye to Lin's wishes. She did not wish to return to China, her inevitable fate as a Chinese immigrant mental patient. She was not present at the trial, nor did she have a lawyer to represent her interests. At twenty-two, she was separated from her children and committed to an insane asylum where her culture and language would further isolate her. The women who interested themselves in her case undoubtedly had the best intentions, but the results for Lin were tragic.[56]

After her trial, Lin departs from public view. Privacy law prevents exploration of her medical records and thus her fate must be left to speculation. When a minority community deals with pervasive racist claims, as in the Lindsay riot, power struggles between immigrant women and men can become perilously entangled with collective struggles against racism. The Chinese community defence team sided with Lee because they felt it was necessary to refute gendered notions of white supremacy that denigrated Chinese manhood. Thus, racism's danger to Chinese men ensured that Lin's personal interests were not represented.

### Conclusion

In particular, Lin Tee's tragic tale helps limn the contours of immigrant experiences in isolated settlements remote from centres of ethnic community support. Few scholars have explored the histories of these immigrants despite their significant numbers. Their distinctive histories of race relations nevertheless merit investigation. During the First World War, thousands of Chinese immigrants moved to cities, small towns, villages, and native reserves east of the Rockies. This mobile population passed through urban Chinatowns on their way to smaller centres where entrepreneurial opportunities for laundries, restaurants, stores, and other businesses beckoned. The intimate scale of Lindsay's dozen-member Chinese community in an overall population of 6,352 encouraged daily interactions with their European-Canadian friends and neighbours.[57] When Lin Tee became distressed, many community members became involved in the family's problems.

These reactions to spousal abuse inherently involved community 'politics' because individual family members' actions in power struggles at home contributed to broader community patterns of gender and race relations. Similarly, definitions of 'madness' hinged to a degree upon historical definitions of acceptable social behaviour.[58] In Lindsay, enforcing community standards was as much an issue as definition. During the conflicts leading to the riot, Lin's female advocates asserted their moral 'right' to bring public resources of the state into the family, which maternal feminists considered their realm. These women challenged exclusively male assumptions of privilege that supported a range of paternalistic male ideologies. These male ideologies upheld a wide range of male behaviour that included protection of the vulnerable, the necessity of female dependence, and a paternalistic vision of male privilege that could at times support an abusive husband's 'right' to protect 'his' woman and manage 'his' family without public interference. As Lin's escape attempts became more desperate, paternalistic assumptions of masculinity clashed with each other and with the women's attempts to protect Lin from abuse. As such, conflicting beliefs about gender played as large a role as race in the Lindsay riot. What this particular case reveals overall is the complex manner in which gender and racial constructions interacted in community reaction and response to Lee and Lin as individuals.

NOTES

I would like to thank Franca Iacovetta, Tim Brook, Frederick Ho, Troy S. Goodfellow, Michèle Lacombe, and A.E. (Kay) Hick. An Andrew W. Mellon Fellowship, the Social Science and Humanities Research Council of Canada, and the University of Toronto supported this article.

1 'Citizens Take Law into Their Own Hands in Dealing with Chinese Residents Said to Have Abused One of Their Women,' *Watchman-Warder*, 6 February 1919; 'Mob Rule Prevailed Friday Night: Chinese Business Places Were Wrecked,' *Lindsay Post*, 7 February 1919; 'Excitement in Chinese Colony: Demented Woman Gives Trouble,' *Lindsay Post*, 7 February 1919; 'Mrs. Lee Ten Was Adjudged Insane,' *Lindsay Post*, 10 February 1919. The figure of 500 rioters and 'if the police would not act then the people would' is from the Archives of Ontario, RG 23, Series E-83, File 1.3 'Anti-Chinese Riots,' John Miller to Joseph Rogers, 11 March 1919 and John Miller, Report, 'Re Riots at Lindsay Victoria County,' Toronto, 25 March 1919.
2 'Citizens Take Law into Their Own Hands'; 'Mrs. Lee Ten Was Adjudged Insane.'

3 'Mob Rule Prevailed Friday Night'; 'Citizens Take Law into Their Own Hands'; 'The Lindsay Riots,' *Lindsay Post*, 7 February 1919; 'Lindsay's Chinatown Wrecked by Mob,' *Evening Examiner* (Peterborough, ON) 1 February 1919.

4 Much has been written about Chinese immigrants and gendered racism, including: Constance Backhouse, 'White Female Help and Chinese-Canadian Employers: Race, Class, Gender and Law in the Case of Yee Clun, 1924,' *Canadian Ethnic Studies* 26, no. 3 (1994): 24–52; Constance Backhouse, 'The White Women's Labor Laws: Anti-Chinese Racism in Early Twentieth Century Canada,' *Law and History Review* 14 (Fall 1996): 315–68; Michael Scott Kerwin, 'Re/producing a "White British Columbia": The Meanings of the Janet Smith Bill' (MA thesis, University of British Columbia, 1996); James W. St. G. Walker, 'A Case for Morality: The Quong Wing Files' in Franca Iacovetta and Wendy Mitchinson, eds, *On the Case: Explorations in Social History* (Toronto: University of Toronto Press, 1998), 204–33; Madge Pon, 'Like a Chinese Puzzle: The Construction of Chinese Masculinity in *Jack Canuck*' in Mark Rosenfeld and Joy Parr, eds, *Gender and History in Canada* (Toronto: Copp Clark, 1996), 88–100. For an extended analysis of race, gender, and changing popular images of Chinese immigrants in Ontario, see also Lisa R. Mar, 'The Politics of Yellow Peril: Images of Chinese Men with White Women in Toronto, 1900–1928' (draft article, 1994).

5 The single, book-length, oral history of Chinese-Canadian women, the Women's Committee of the Chinese Canadian National Council's *Jin Guo: Voices of Chinese Canadian Women* (Toronto: Women's Press, 1992), focuses primarily on community-building roles, as do general histories of Chinese in Canada such as Dora Nipp, '"But Women Did Come": Working Chinese Women in the Interwar Years,' in Jean Burnet, ed., *Looking into My Sister's Eyes: An Exploration in Women's History* (Toronto: Multicultural History Society of Ontario, 1986), 179–94; Harry Con et al., eds, *From China to Canada: A History of the Chinese Communities in Canada* (Toronto: McClelland and Stewart, 1982).

6 Mar, 'The Politics of Yellow Peril.'

7 The Victorian police court criminal insanity trial was a predecessor of Canada's contemporary legislation allowing involuntary confinement of the mentally ill.

8 'Mrs. Lee Ten Was Adjudged Insane'; 'Crown Attorney Acting in Connection with Recent Riot,' *Lindsay Post*, 7 February 1919. The Ontario Lunacy Act outlined the criteria for confining dangerous lunatics in an asylum under warrant and the procedure by which a judge called experts and witnesses to testify about the accused's sanity in court. C.E.T. Fitzgerald, A.H. O'Brien, J.T. Harris, and F. Flynn, eds, *Canadian Consolidated Ten Year Law Digest: 1911–1920*, vol. 1 (Toronto: Canada Law Book, 1920), 2339–42. There is considerable literature on how notions of gender, race, and class influenced committals of women to asylums, notably Carolyn Strange, *'Toronto's Girl Problem': The Perils and Pleasures of the City, 1880–1930* (Toronto: University of Toronto Press,

1995); and Wendy Mitchinson, *The Nature of Their Bodies: Women and Their Doctors in Victorian Canada* (Toronto: University of Toronto Press, 1991), who connects historical understandings of mental illness in women with prevailing gender ideologies.

9  'Special Meeting of the Town Council: Citizens Blamed for Inciting the Riots,' *Watchman-Warder*, 6 February 1919; 'Mrs. Lee Ten Was Adjudged Insane.'

10  Timothy Brook, 'The Tokyo Judgement and the Rape of Nanking,' *Journal of Asian Studies* 60, no. 3 (August 2001): 675.

11  'Mrs. Lee Ten Was Adjudged Insane.'

12  *Census of Canada*, 1911 (Ottawa: C.H. Parmlee) vol. 1, 93; vol. 2, 248–49, vol. 2, 404, *Census of Canada*, 1921 (Ottawa: F.A. Acland 1924) vol. 1, 85, 375, 486–97, 548; 'Mrs. Lee Ten Was Adjudged Insane.'

13  'Suey Lan Lee'; 'The Flu and Funerals,' *Watchman-Warder*, 31 October 1918; 'The Flu in Other Towns and Cities,' *Watchman-Warder*, 24 October 1918; 'Mrs. Lee Ten Was Adjudged Insane'; *Vernon's Lindsay Directory 1925–26* (Lindsay, ON: Henry Vernon and Son); *Census of Canada*, 1911, 1921.

14  'Mrs. Lee Ten Was Adjudged Insane.'

15  Con et al., *From China to Canada*, 301; *Census of Canada*, 1921, vol. 4, 752–3. On Anglo perceptions of foreign men, see Karen Dubinsky and Franca Iacovetta, 'Murder, Womanly Virtue, and Motherhood: The Case of Angela Napolitano, 1911–1972,' *Canadian Historical Review* 72, no. 4 (1991): 505–31; Mar, 'The Politics of Yellow Peril.'

16  See examples such as the *Lindsay Post*'s serialized story by popular British anti-Asian writer, Sax Rohmer, 'The Yellow Claw,' 8, 15, 22 March 1919; 'Orillia Celestial Heavily Fined,' *Lindsay Post*, 28 February 1919; 'Alarming Increase in Drug Traffic,' *Lindsay Post*, 24 January 1919; 'Was Epidemic Brought by Chinese Coolies?' *Lindsay Post*, 1 November 1918; 'Inspectors Raid Chinese Club,' *Lindsay Post*, 25 October 1918.

17  Ibid.

18  Ibid.

19  Regarding opinions of Lin Tee, see 'Excitement in Chinese Colony: Demented Woman Gives Trouble,' and 'Mrs. Lee Ten Was Adjudged Insane.' For literature on perceptions of family abuse, see Linda Gordon, *Heroes of Their Own Lives: The Politics and History of Family Violence* (New York: Penguin Books, 1988); Franca Iacovetta, 'Making "New Canadians": Social, Workers, Women, and the Reshaping of Immigrant Families,' in Franca Iacovetta and Mariana Valverde, eds, *Gender Conflicts: New Essays in Women's History* (Toronto: University of Toronto Press, 1992), 261–303.

20  'Mrs. Lee Ten Was Adjudged Insane.'

21  Ibid. Anecdotal accounts of mental illness in pre-1949 modern China suggest similar patterns of family responsibility. Loretta Mar described how her family cared for a 'crazy uncle' by locking him up at home. This situation resembled that of Canadians

in rural areas before asylum care for the mentally ill was widely available. Loretta Mar, interview with Jack, Arleen, and Linda Mar, recorded by Jerry Mar, 22 April 1974. Jerry Mar Collection.

22 'Mrs. Lee Ten Was Adjudged Insane'; 'Citizens Take Law into Their Own Hands'; 'Mob Rule Prevailed Friday Night'; 'Excitement in Chinese Colony.'

23 This and all subsequent trial coverage is from 'Mrs. Lee Ten Was Adjudged Insane.'

24 Interview with Mrs Grace Bright, 1 March 1995. The Children's Aid Society (CAS) in Lindsay was founded in 1895 after the inauguration of a provincial policy for aiding and protecting neglected and dependent children. It gradually expanded the scope of its activities to include providing social services to the family. Thus, CAS intervention in family power struggles was a relatively new phenomenon. Reg A. Cozens, ed., *Lindsay and Victoria Old Home Week 1–10 July, 1948 Souvenir Booklet* (Lindsay, ON: Old Home Week Committee, 1948). Linda Gordon examines how child protection advocates became drawn into wife-beating cases in this era in *Heroes of Their Own Lives.*

25 These issues also included eugenics, juvenile delinquency, and immigration restriction. See Strange, *Toronto's Girl Problem,* and Kerwin, 'Re/producing a "White British Columbia."'

26 'Mrs. Lee Ten Was Adjudged Insane.'

27 Ibid.; 'Excitement in Chinese Colony.'

28 'Mrs. Lee Ten Was Adjudged Insane.'

29 Ibid.; 'Excitement in Chinese Colony'; 'Citizens Take Law into Their Own Hands'; 'Mob Rule Prevailed Friday Night.'

30 'Mrs. Lee Ten Was Adjudged Insane.' According to Gordon, abused women felt reluctant to involve the courts, because many viewed a degree of male violence as inevitable and they and their children needed their husbands' wages to survive (Gordon, *Heroes of Their Own Lives,* 255–6, 271–5).

31 'Mrs. Lee Ten Was Adjudged Insane.'

32 Gordon, *Heroes of Their Own Lives,* 280–1.

33 'Mrs. Lee Ten Was Adjudged Insane'; 'Excitement in Chinese Colony'; 'Citizens Take Law into Their Own Hands'; 'Mob Rule Prevailed Friday Night.'

34 'County Crown Attorney Issues Statement Relating to Friday Night's Disgraceful Incident,' *Lindsay Post,* 7 February 1919; 'Mrs. Lee Ten Was Adjudged Insane.'

35 'Mrs. Lee Ten Was Adjudged Insane.'

36 Ibid.

37 Ibid.; 'Excitement in Chinese Colony.'

38 'Citizens Take Law into Their Own Hands'; 'Mob Rule Prevailed Friday Night.'

39 'Citizens Take Law into Their Own Hands'; 'Mob Rule Prevailed Friday Night.'

40 'Mrs. Lee Ten Was Adjudged Insane.'

41 Ibid., 'Mob Rule Prevailed Friday Night'; 'Citizens Take Law into Their Own Hands'; Miller, Report, 'Lindsay's Chinatown Wrecked by Mob.'

42  'Mob Rule Prevailed Friday Night'; 'Citizens Take Law into Their Own Hands';
    'Lindsay's Chinatown Wrecked by Mob.' Dominic Capeci's and Martha Wilkerson's
    concept of 'layered violence' can explain the variance in the rioters' behaviour. They
    argue that different segments of a riot can have different sets of motivations, causes,
    and organization. The first part of the riot involved protest against Lee, which was in
    part organized at the hockey game and involved community leaders. The second part
    of the riot involved a minority of less restrained young men, who continued to seek to
    harm Lee and who took advantage of their overwhelming numbers to loot Chinese
    premises. Why call this event a riot? In the scholarly literature, 'riot' connotes many
    meanings of mob violence not fomented by the state, from a spontaneous unruly
    crowd to organized acts of terror. The Lindsay riot was a night of racial terror, but
    there is ambiguity about whether the majority of rioters used racism as a terror tactic
    in a gender conflict, or whether racial terror was its ultimate aim, given the majority's
    restraint. There is less ambiguity about the actions of young men in the extreme splin-
    ter of the crowd who continued attacking Chinese property and seeking to harm Chi-
    nese men involved in Lee's abuse after the majority went home. One could argue that
    their racist and opportunistic violence against Chinese men in the second part of the
    riot belonged to patterns of violent hatred like 'gay bashing.' According to *Chinese
    Times* (*Da Han Gong Bao*), random, at times fatal, beatings of Chinese men by white
    men were common in early-twentieth-century British Columbia. Dominic J. Capeci
    and Martha Wilkerson, *Layered Violence: The Detroit Riots of 1943* (Jackson: Univer-
    sity of Mississippi Press, 1991); 'Mob Rule Prevailed Friday Night.'

43  The *Watchman-Warder* described looting as partly an attempt to make up for clothing
    lost earlier in the evening. It described the looting at the Lee Chong Brother Laundry
    as a clothing free-for-all: 'Some of the young fellows walked in an endeavour to pick
    out their own laundry and failing to get their own took some other person's to make up
    for their own loss at least that was the plan.' See 'Citizens Take Law into Their Own
    Hands'; 'Mob Rule Prevailed Friday Night'; 'Lindsay's Chinatown Wrecked by Mob.'

44  'Mob Rule Prevailed Friday Night'; 'Citizens Take Law into Their Own Hands'; 'The
    Lindsay Riots,' *Lindsay Post*, 7 February 1919; 'No Trouble at Peterboro,' *Lindsay Post*,
    7 February 1919.

45  For a discussion of chivalry, see Carolyn Strange, 'Wounded Womanhood and Dead
    Men: Chivalry and the Trials of Clara Ford and Carrie Davies,' in Iacovetta and Val-
    verde, eds, *Gender Conflicts*, 149–88.

46  For a definition of the Freudian concept of guilt displacement, see Dr C. George
    Boeree, 'Sigmund Freud 1856–1939,' www.ship.edu/~cgboeree/freud.html, 2 Novem-
    ber 2000.

47  'Regret Expressed by Public Over Friday Night's Incident,' *Lindsay Post*, 7 February
    1919.

48  'Law or Lawlessness,' *Lindsay Post*, 7 February 1919; 'The Alien Within Our Gates,'
    *Lindsay Post*, 14 February 1919 also noted that Chinese immigrants' property rights

had to be respected because of treaty obligations for China and Canada to respect each other's visiting nationals. 'County Crown Attorney Issues Statement Relating to Friday Night's Disgraceful Incident,' *Lindsay Post*, 7 February 1919; 'Special Meeting of Town Council: Citizens Blamed for Inciting Riots,' *Watchman-Warder*, 6 February 1919; 'Mob Rule Prevailed Friday Night.'

49 As a consequence, Lindsay newspapers did not report that the police charged anyone. A subsequent Ontario Provincial Police investigation found that no one was willing to talk, so no charges could be laid. Archives of Ontario, 'Anti-Chinese Riot'; John Miller to J.E. Rogers, 14 March 1919; 'County Crown Attorney Issues Statement.'

50 'Mrs. Lee Ten Was Adjudged Insane'; 'Sending Report to Chinese Consul-General,' *Lindsay Post*, 7 February 1919 (reprinted from the *Peterboro Examiner*); 'Chinese Woman Was Remanded: Case Comes Up Saturday,' *Lindsay Post*, 7 February 1919.

51 The Ontario Chinese newspaper *Shing Wah Daily News* was not available at the time of this paper's research, despite an extensive search by the author.

52 'Sending Report to Chinese Consul-General'; 'Chinese Woman Was Remanded.' Lisa R. Mar, recollections of family lore about Chinese immigrants, 27 August 1999; 'Mrs. Lee Ten Was Adjudged Insane.'

53 'Mrs. Lee Ten Was Adjudged Insane.'

54 Trial coverage for the rest of this article is from 'Mrs. Lee Ten Was Adjudged Insane.'

55 Ibid.

56 'Mrs. Lee Ten Was Adjudged Insane,' 'Mrs. Lee Removed to Asylum,' *Watchman-Warder*, 13 February 1919. According to the *Chinese Times (Da Han Gong Bao)*, Canadian immigration law required insane Chinese to be deported. UBC Library Archives and Special Collections. Chinese Canadian Research Collection, box 4, file 'Chinese Times Index 1918' states that on 23 March 1918, the *Chinese Times* published an article stating that Chinese mental patients in Canada would be deported.

57 Population of Lindsay in 1918 from Cozens, ed., *Lindsay and Victoria County Old Home Week*, 55.

58 For more elaborate interpretations of how reactions to family violence and madness involved community politics, see Linda Gordon's *Heroes of Their Own Lives* and Michel Foucault, *Madness and Civilization: A History of Insanity in the Age of Reason* (New York: Vintage, 1988).

PART 3

# *Immigrant Working-Class Women Encounter the State*

# In Search of Comfort and Independence: Irish Immigrant Domestic Servants Encounter the Courts, Jails, and Asylums in Nineteenth-Century Ontario

LORNA R. McLEAN AND MARILYN BARBER

## Introduction

In nineteenth-century Ontario, domestic servants were predominantly Irish, but most Irish women who worked as servants have remained anonymous shadowy figures in the historical record. One notable exception is Grace Marks, the subject of Margaret Atwood's prize-winning novel *Alias Grace*.[1] Previously, historian Susan Houston also used Grace Marks as a case study in an article examining how gender affected the construction of youthful criminal behaviour in the mid-nineteenth century.[2] Not only has Grace Marks received recent literary and historical attention, but she was even better known to Canadians in the mid-nineteenth century, being extensively reported in newspapers and written about by Susanna Moodie in *Life in the Clearings*.[3] A youthful Irish immigrant, one of thousands to come to North America in search of better conditions, Grace Marks achieved notoriety because, at the age of sixteen, she was convicted of the murder of her employer. Her fellow Irish servant, James McDermott, who was similarly found guilty of the crime, was hanged, but Grace had her sentence commuted to life in prison because of her 'feeble sex' and 'extreme youth.' The sensational case, involving sex, violence, and insubordination carried to an extreme, portrayed in stark relief the gender, class, and ethnic tensions in the master/mistress – servant relationship. It also revealed the complex and gendered public response to Irish immigrants. Although murder was an exceptional charge, the fate of Grace Marks exemplified the hazards encountered by some Irish immigrant women seeking comfort and independence in the new world.

While Grace Marks's Irish immigrant identity has been noted in the literature, most attention has been focused on the significance of her gender and her youth.

Susan Houston assesses how notions of femininity and masculinity influenced the evaluation of youthful criminal behaviour, thus allowing the defence for Grace Marks to call upon conventional gender stereotypes of the naive vulnerable female acceptable in mid-nineteenth-century Canada. While she links Grace Marks's love of clothes and her supposed lack of 'strength of mind' to stock qualities attributed to young Irish servant girls, she does not develop the significance of the ethnic immigrant dimension in her analysis. Similarly, Margaret Atwood, writing an historical novel rather than a documentary, tells a compelling story of Grace's harsh emigrant experience, but does not explicitly link the Irish emigrant background to Grace's own sense of her identity and her treatment. Both individual and collective memory are, as Atwood emphasizes, mutable and selective.[4] Our chapter highlights the bonding of ethnicity with gender and class in the lives of Irish female domestic servants such as Grace Marks.

Whereas most transatlantic migrations of people to North America were dominated by men, for significant periods of time women formed the majority of Irish migrants.[5] The importance of this unusual migration pattern for understanding the lives of Irish female migrants to the United States was emphasized in two American studies published in the 1980s. Both Hasia Diner and Janet Nolan attributed the preponderance of young single women among Irish migrants to economic and social conditions in postfamine Ireland.[6] The urgent need to stop the subdivision of the land meant that marriage became increasingly an economic arrangement whereby only one son inherited the family property and his wife required a dowry. As a result, by the 1880s, the Irish married at the latest age in Europe, and the custom of providing a dowry for only one daughter meant that many young women had difficulty achieving adult status through marriage. At the same time, the opportunities for women to earn a living outside the family were constrained by the lack of both industrialization and of a bourgeoning middle class that demanded domestic servants. By contrast, Irish women could readily find work as domestic servants in America and, unlike much of the work available for men, domestic service was not seasonal or sporadic. Domestic service in America was attractive as both an individual and a family strategy for betterment: it seemed to guarantee that Irish immigrant women could save money for their own future and/or send money home to aid their families. Consequently, a high percentage of Irish-born women in America worked as domestic servants.

The studies by Diner and Nolan, however, raise as many questions as they answer, especially since the authors disagree about the specific motives and goals that brought Irish emigrant women to America. While Diner and Nolan recognize that Irish women came to America to better themselves, they diverge in their interpretation of betterment. Nolan argues that women emigrated primarily to recover traditional opportunities for marriage and the adult status of wife lost to them in Ireland. By contrast, Diner takes a much dimmer view of the Irish male and hence of marriage, claiming that the women sought economic independence through waged labour and were willing to work as domestic servants in part because they were not eagerly seeking marriage as their primary goal. As Kerby Miller recently observed, neither author provides sufficient evidence to prove her assertions, and more work needs to be done in what he terms 'still a novel field of study.'[7] Importantly, though, he also suggests that the divergence of interpretation is not necessarily contradictory. Irish female emigrants were not a homogeneous group and it is highly probable that 'women from different class, regional and cultural backgrounds in Ireland had significantly different patterns of and motives for emigration.'[8]

Canadian historians have convincingly demonstrated that the pattern of Irish migration to Ontario was quite distinct from the United States. For instance, more Protestants than Catholics arrived in Ontario during the nineteenth century and the majority settled in rural rather than urban areas. In addition, the famine did not initiate mass Irish migration to Canada as it did to the United States, but instead was an aberration within a voluntary economic migration movement from traditional source areas that early established close links with Canada.[9] But these interpretations have done little to help us better understand Irish female migrants. We need also to explore the gendered features of this distinctive Irish migration movement to Canada. Preliminary research seems to indicate that, unlike the United States, women did not outnumber men among Irish migrants to Canada throughout the latter nineteenth century. Canada did not offer as many attractive female employment opportunities in either home or factory as did the United States with its larger urban centres near the Eastern Seaboard and its more mature industrial economy. In addition, postfamine chain migration to the United States helped to reinforce women's migration through family and female networks. For a brief period during the 1850s, however, women did form the majority of the Irish migrants to British North America.[10]

## Patterns of Female Migration

The predominance of female emigration occurred at a time when the source areas for Irish migration to Canada had expanded from the traditional regions of Ulster, Cork, and Dublin into the more impoverished western districts as a result of the economic problems surrounding the famine. It also coincided with the shift from Australia to Canada as the main destination for large parties of women sent from the Irish workhouses.[11] Irish women arriving in the 1840s and 1850s formed part of an immigrant group that as a whole was more destitute and had fewer skills and resources than earlier or later nineteenth-century migrants to Ontario. A larger

proportion of the famine-era migrants also were Roman Catholic and hence outsiders in the dominant Protestant culture of mid-nineteenth-century Ontario.
Those coming from beyond the traditional source areas were additionally handicapped by the lack of kinship or community networks that were so important in
offering aid and security to newcomers. The sheer number of immigrants arriving
in the late 1840s also created more problems for that group and their immediate
successors. The brief period when women seemed to outnumber men among Irish
migrants to Canada thus coincided with a time when integration into Canadian
society might prove particularly difficult.

In Canada, domestic service was the main paid employment for Irish female
emigrants. Women (like Grace Marks) who came as part of a family migration
often entered domestic service because the lack of family resources forced daughters, and sometimes wives, to seek work outside the home. The scarcity of domestic servants in Canada also enabled women to emigrate on their own from at least
the 1830s. Included among these migrants were the parties of workhouse women
whom government agents placed in domestic positions. In addition, after Confederation, the Ontario and Canadian governments explicitly recruited female
domestic servants in Ireland, providing bonuses and reduced passage fares as an
inducement to emigration. They had limited success primarily in northern Ireland because agents reported that the lack of direct connections from southern
ports to Canada made recruitment difficult in the south.[12] These 'women alone'
sometimes lacked kin or friendship networks for advice and aid and hence were
more vulnerable, but it must be remembered as well that the family was not always
a supportive institution for women.

Partly because of the predominance of Irish migration to Ontario in the early
and mid-nineteenth century, the majority of domestic servants in the province
for most of the century were Irish. Similarly, a high proportion of Irish women,
and especially Irish Catholic women, worked in service at some point in their
lives. Indeed, in his study of Hamilton in the mid-nineteenth century, Katz concluded that almost every Irish Catholic woman in the city spent part of her life as
a resident servant.[13] Likewise, Claudette Lacelle showed that Irish women dominated domestic service in Toronto.[14] Hence, domestic servants in nineteenth-
century Ontario, and especially immigrant domestic servants, became identified
with the Irish.

Employment of an Irish servant, particularly an Irish Catholic servant, did not
necessarily indicate racial tolerance on the part of a non-Irish or Protestant
employer. Instead racial and religious divisions exacerbated the class tensions in the
employer-servant relationship. Stereotypes of the 'Irish Biddy' or 'Bridget'
abounded. Frequently Biddy was portrayed as good-hearted and willing, but dim,
inept, untidy, and careless. At times, though, her seeming lack of understanding of

the mistress's instructions could also be interpreted as an assertive refusal to recognize her subordinate place in the household. For example, as depicted in the *Canadian Illustrated News*, when told by her mistress that she could no longer receive her sweetheart in the kitchen, Bridget replied, 'Thank you kindly, Mum, but he's too bashful for the Parlour.'[15] Susanna Moodie, in *Life in the Clearings*, showed some understanding of how the poverty of an Irish background ill prepared many Irish servants to meet their mistress's expectations for care of material possessions. '"Shure, Ma'am, it can be used," said an Irish girl to me, after breaking the spout out of an expensive china jug. "It is not a hair the worse!" She could not imagine that a mutilated object could occasion the least discomfort to those accustomed to order and neatness in their household arrangements.'[16] Others expressed more alarm regarding the possible risks of allowing unknown immigrants into the private sanctum of the home. Because of their supposed love of finery, Irish domestics were frequently suspected of trying on their mistress's clothes in her absence. The fear existed that such relatively harmless acts of insubordination could mirror more serious crimes such as theft from their employers or, at an extreme as in the case of Grace Marks, even murder. At the time of Marks's trial, the *Examiner* commented on the danger of hiring servants without adequate character references, especially at a time when crowds of immigrants were arriving, and the *Bathurst Courier* similarly referred to the occasionally 'polluted' nature of the incoming stream of population.[17] Doubts were particularly cast upon parties of female workhouse migrants who bore the stigma of 'pauper' and attracted newspaper attention by arriving in sizeable groups. In their public flaunting of codes of proper feminine behaviour, some of these women seemed to confirm the worst suspicions of Irish women as being drunk and immoral and lacking respectability as well as skill.[18]

Suspicions surrounding the Irish, heightened by famine-era and workhouse migration in the mid-nineteenth century, could make life more difficult for Irish women seeking work as domestic servants. Irish female emigrants generally preferred urban placements where they had more chance of establishing social contacts and associating with friends. Authorities, however, tried to direct migrants to work in rural areas because of the difficulty of filling the demand for servants outside the urban areas. As the Kingston agent reported in 1868, 'Servant girls are much enquired for, particularly from the country parts and if girls willing to work at farm houses and accustomed to milk cows and wash and iron clothes could be induced to immigrate to this part of the country, employment could be found in every township for from 20 to 50 of them at fair wages.'[19] In spite of Victorian imagery, neither the home nor rural society was necessarily safe territory for women. Although domestic service offered an opportunity for Irish women to save for a better life, it also led to downward mobility for the unfortunate. Isolation and loneliness in both rural and urban work increased the vulnera-

## ONE FOR MISSUS.

*Mistress.*—BRIDGET, I REALLY CAN'T ALLOW YOU TO RECEIVE YOUR SWEETHEART IN THE KITCHEN ANY LONGER.

*Bridget.*—THANK YOU KINDLY, MUM, BUT HE'S TOO BASHFUL FOR THE PARLOUR.

From *Canadian Illustrated News*, 7 January 1882.

bility to conflict with employers or to sexual exploitation. And a live-in domestic servant who left her work or was dismissed lost her place of residence as well as her employment.

## Irish Domestics and the Courts

In this chapter, we seek to construct a gendered analysis of Irish immigrants by exploring a particular neglected aspect: Irish domestics in courts, jails, and asylums.[20] Court records tell us about immigrant Irish servants and their work, about relationships with their employers, and about the nature of their interaction with the judicial system. Unfortunately, the records do not allow us to link directly the Canadian experience with the regional or family background of the migrant. The following sampling of cases from four Ontario communities also offers hints as to the experience of immigration for female domestics who arrived in Canada from mid- to late nineteenth century. The limitations of these documents, however, allow us to see only those who were committed to jail, as recorded in the registers, and/or trial reports. Domestics who were dismissed or left of their own accord because of disagreements with, or accusations by, their employers, do not appear. A careful reading of the cases, however, does suggest ways in which servants negotiated the imbalance of social and economic relationships in the workplace. Moreover, these records allow us to profile the women and the typology of crimes that brought them into contact with the law, and to identify how the gendered nature of public morality, as in the case of drunkenness, impacted on their lives. At the same time, we note how some female domestics may have used the jails as a refuge between periods of employment. Finally, we can observe the ways in which the legal process intersected with expanding mental illness and reform asylums.

To profile the type of criminal act that brought Irish servants into contact with the law, four counties were selected (see Table 1). These counties, York, Leeds/ Grenville, Perth, and Grey, represent a cross-section of urban and rural communities across Ontario. Taken together, these counties encompass a range of the social and economic diversity in Ontario during the Victorian era. Of a total of 1,481 women sampled from the jail registers between 1841 and 1881, 584 listed paid employment.[21] Given the large number of women who worked as servants during this period, it is perhaps not surprising that almost half the women in jail who listed occupations were servants or housekeepers. Similarly, the ethnic composition of the inmates also reflected immigrant trends during this period. Among the 239 jailed servants, the largest immigrant population was from Ireland (29 per cent or 68 women). Because the records do not list ethnic affiliation among the native-born domestics (54 per cent), we cannot determine with certainty how many were second-generation Irish.

TABLE 1
Summary of Committals for Women and Servants, 1841–1881

| Charges | All Women | | Irish Women* | | All Servants* | | Irish Servants* | |
|---|---|---|---|---|---|---|---|---|
| | Freq. | (%) | Freq. | (%) | Freq. | (%) | Freq. | (%) |
| Drunkenness | 481 | 32.5 | 248 | 43.9 | 57 | 23.9 | 30 | 44.1 |
| Vagrancy | 305 | 20.6 | 106 | 18.8 | 75 | 31.4 | 19 | 27.9 |
| Larceny | 181 | 12.2 | 58 | 10.3 | 42 | 17.6 | 5 | 7.4 |
| Insanity | 131 | 8.8 | 40 | 7.1 | 42 | 17.6 | 4 | 5.9 |
| Total | 1,481 | 100 | 475 | 100 | 239 | 100 | 68 | 100 |

* The number of Irish women and servants is underrepresented in the data. In Toronto, occupation first appears as a category in 1854 and between January 1860 and February 1864, only summary registers exist. Summary registers list only name, sex, charge, and other information related to incarceration. In addition, Toronto registers are missing between January 1874 and September 1876. In Leeds/Grenville and Grey County, occupation is not listed until 1865, and in Perth County, it appears as late as 1869.
Source: Archives of Ontario, RG 20, R-6, Brockville Jail Registers, 1848–81; RG 20, F-28, Owen Sound Jail Registers 1857–81; RG 20, F-40, Stratford Calendar of Prisoners, 1853–64 and Stratford Jail Registers 1865–81; RG 22, F-43, Toronto Jail Registers 1841–53, 1860–73, October 1876 to December 1881 and RG, F-20, F-4, Brampton Jail Registers 1854–59.[22]

The following sections outline the four most frequent reasons that led women to being committed to jail: drunkenness, vagrancy, larceny, and insanity. While insanity was not a crime per se, as we shall see, the jail served as one of several routes for individuals, including Irish servants, into asylums for the mentally ill. As well, until 1850 when the first mental asylum was built in Toronto, local jails housed many of those deemed 'insane.' The types of offences for which servants were committed are significant because they relate to the nature of the domestics' work and to the specific circumstances of female immigration and Irish ethnicity. Overall the most common reason for women and for servants to be in jail was for drunkenness and alcohol-related charges.

*Drunkenness*

While studies of nineteenth-century Ontario temperance societies identified excessive drinking as a male problem,[23] little is known of the public or private drinking habits of women,[24] particularly among specific cultural groups. Overall, public peace offences such as drunkenness formed the majority of committals in Ontario jails. For some contemporary observers, excessive drinking and the apparent rise of crime in urban areas stemmed, in part, from the recent influx of immigrants. In the minds of a particularly influential and vocal constituency, drink, immorality, and crime were intertwined, and law could play a central role in policing and punishing the offenders. A study of Toronto where half the jailed Irish servants resided allows us to see how Irish culture affected the way drunkenness was interpreted within a large urban centre.

Charges for drunkenness among Toronto women rose dramatically between 1856 and 1859 (see Figure 1). The records for 1860 to 1864 are incomplete for ethnicity and occupation; however, the data for sex and charges demonstrate that although the number of women on the register declined after 1860, most committals were for drunkenness. As well, between January 1874 and October 1876 no registers exist. A number of factors contributed to an increase in the incarceration of women in Toronto. Gender had a profound influence. Convictions for drunkenness, as with other public peace offences, carried a specific stigma for women.[25] The 'ideology of femininity, so important in defining middle class women's ideal conduct' in Victorian society, concludes English historian Lucia Zedner, 'was no less important in responding to their worst.'[26] Moreover, gendered perceptions towards drinking meant that while 'intemperance could be a manly flaw ... a woman's drunkenness was an almost unspeakable corruption of the purity essential' to motherly and societal responsibilities.[27] The rhetoric of domesticity that relegated women to the moral and domestic sphere meant harsh penalties for those who abandoned their true womanhood for the streets and bars of Toronto.[28] Notably, over several years between 1856 and 1865, an increase in the number of arrests of Irish servants for drunkenness contributed to a higher total number of female than male committals in the Toronto jail.

Further evidence suggests that the public presence and the very independence of women on the streets, contributed to their incarceration.[29] Although the vast majority of Victorian women worked in the home, the jail population overrepresents the minority of women who worked outside the domestic sphere. Among committals for drunkenness, for example, servants followed a close second to the number of women who worked in the sex trade. During their leisure hours servants undoubtedly sought pleasure in places beyond their workplace, some of which brought them into contact with the law. The high incarceration rates for the mostly single, employed working women suggest an earlier date than 1880 for the socially problematic, independent woman, and highlight the gendered nature of public peace and prosecution charges in large urban centres in the mid- to late nineteenth century.[30]

Local structural, cultural and economic factors also contributed to the rise in jailed Irish women and servants in mid-century Toronto/York. Increased incarcerations coincided with the particularly zealous efforts of Toronto officials to define

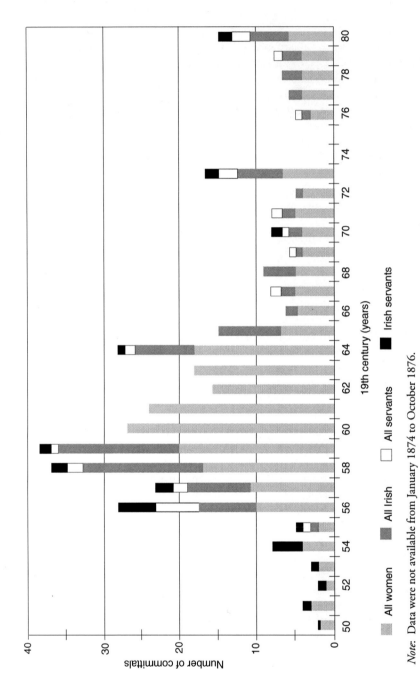

*Note:* Data were not available from January 1874 to October 1876.

Figure 1  Irish Servants and All Women Committed to the Toronto Jail for Drunkenness

and regulate behaviour on the streets and other public places within this prosperous, industrializing provincial capital.[31] The chief of police's letter to council in 1856 – written following a period of extensive Irish settlement – hinted at the potential criminality of the new immigrant population when he requested more constables to guard against the 'great many suspicious persons [who] frequent our city.'[32] Between 1852 and 1859 the number of constables almost doubled to sixty patrolling the streets and arresting disruptive drunkards.[33] The degree to which the size of police units influenced the number of committals is further supported by the rapid decline in arrests in the early 1860s when the number of police was reduced to thirty-eight men.[34] The rise of committals in the 1870s again paralleled a resurgence in the size of the force.

Given the desperate economic circumstances in the aftermath of the 1857 depression, there might also have been a greater population of displaced Irish servants. As Michael Katz points out in his study of Hamilton, Ontario, domestic servants, many of whom were Irish, faced a declining number of jobs during this period.[35] High unemployment and despair may have driven some to bars or to private indulgences.[36] Moreover, periods of high unemployment probably forced some women to seek alternative, temporary employment as prostitutes working in local taverns.

While a rowdy working-class culture might help explain the high number of women charged with drunkenness, other cultural factors might explain why the majority of women and servants in Toronto charged with that offence were Irish immigrants.[37] As American historian Hasia Diner has written, drinking was part of an Irish female domestic culture that was integral to leisure activities and celebrations. Although women were held in the jail throughout the year, celebrations involving alcohol frequently occurred during festival times or holidays when servants, like others, indulged privately and/or among friends. Eliza McClelland, a twenty-seven-year-old Irish immigrant servant, for example, was picked up for being drunk and disorderly on the eve of Hallowe'en. A clustering of committals also appears in the spring and summer months when women sought outside cool retreats, on the street, or in nearby public places. For instance, Catherine Irwin, an Irish-born housekeeper, spent several weeks at hard labour in the Toronto jail in the summer of 1859. In May 1865 she was sentenced to a month in jail after being 'found in a vacant lot on Stanley Street drunk.'[38]

Cultural stereotypes of Irish drinking, as depicted in the local media, cast a shadow of suspicion over Irish servants along with other Irish immigrants. An 1865 reprint of an article from a Montreal newspaper appeared without comment in the Toronto media. 'Those Emigrants' it noted, with particular reference to the young women who were sent out from the workhouses in Ireland, 'turn out to be thoroughly disgraceful characters.' As proof of the Irish women's undesirable traits, the paper recounted how some were 'provided with situations but in a day or two they returned drunk.' Worse still, these immigrants lacked the moral character to conduct themselves in a seemingly proper womanly fashion. 'In one respectable tavern ... their conduct was so bad they had to be expelled, and nobody who had heard of them would take them in.'[39] Other critics had their own interpretation of the instrumental role of particular media in contributing to hard times. The Irish Catholic press blamed the coverage of events in the 'anti-Catholic' newspapers. One report concluded that the 'dismissal of Irish servant girls from even their humble occupations was blamed on the influence of the Protestant press in disseminating calumnies against the Irish character.'[40]

Additional evidence also suggests that religious friction may have played a part in the large number of Roman Catholic women in jail. Across the spectrum of four counties the percentage of Irish-Catholic women charged with drunkenness exceeded that of all other ethnic groups in jail. The large proportion of jailed women in rural areas was most pronounced among Irish Catholic women, although they also represented a large proportion of the committals in the Toronto jail. Of the twenty-five servants arrested for drunkenness in Toronto, almost two-thirds were Roman Catholic and by far the largest group were Irish. As Michael Cottrell and others have written, by the 1860s many, if not the majority, of Toronto constables and municipal politicians were members or supporters of the Protestant Orange Order and displayed their partisanship on several occasions during this period of religious as well as ethnic tensions that originated from the late 1850s. Historians have recounted the consequences of the religious tensions among men representing religious organizations, such as the tragedy in 1858 when Orange members attempted to disrupt a St Patrick's Day parade and a Catholic man was fatally stabbed with a pitchfork. This incident was seen as symptomatic of the growing hostility experienced by Irish Catholics in Toronto.[41] As well, according to historian Murray Nicolson, in the 1860s Toronto policemen were 'accused of arresting Catholics while Protestants might be warned for the same offence.'[42] The findings of our research suggest that women were not isolated from the effects of religious conflict. Meanwhile, another religious leader of the day identified other influences on female incarceration. Bishop Lynch of Toronto attributed the high number of Irish Catholic women in jail to the vulnerability of many women who arrived in cities with limited financial or family resources. His letter of 1864 to the four archbishops of Ireland lamented the problems and moral delinquencies that befell unfortunate Irish migrants who resided in large cities in Canada and the United States: 'In visiting the [Toronto] jail,' he remarked, 'we found that two thirds of the bad women confined there were Catholic.'[43]

Statistics tell us about the patterns of incarceration and the typology of the Irish servants in jail. But we are left wondering about the motivation for drinking, and the impact of incarceration on servants' lives. Undoubtedly, servants drank to ameliorate periods of illness or chronic pain, to dull feelings of loneliness, and to lessen the stresses and strains of a long work day.[44] Even favourable situations did not compensate for a lack of companionship, especially among immigrant women living in Canada without friends or family. As Anne Slattery, an Irish servant from Kingston, Ontario, wrote in 1865: 'My dear Sister it is very lonesome to be here alone. You will meet many strange faces before you will friends ... Oh how happy I would be if I had a relation to spend my leisure hours with ... when my work is done I sit down and thinks [sic] of the pleasant home and loving faces I used to gaze on and tell my trouble[s] to ...'[45]

The degree to which a criminal record affected future employment opportunities remains unclear. Some sources suggest that employers regarded the 'misbehaviour' of servants, specifically their drunkenness, as distressing, but nevertheless part of the inconvenience of sharing a living space with a domestic worker.[46] Although our evidence supports this finding to a certain extent, another reading indicates that charges for drunkenness had serious implications. In our sample, many of the jailed women continued to list their occupation as 'domestic,' despite a series of arrests. Bridget McDonnell, for example, a thirty-year-old Irish Catholic servant, committed in 1857 for being drunk and disorderly, had been committed three times previously. By contrast, Irish domestic Bridget Crenan, who was charged with her first offence in 1858, listed an alias of Hickey, as did Kate Swanton who was 'otherwise' known as 'Driscoll.'[47] In addition to establishing new identities, women also escaped the stigma of arrest and/or conviction by relocating to different neighbourhoods. For those living in small towns, forging a new identity could be more difficult. If word of a miscreant servant's deeds did not travel among neighbours, the routine publication of jail statistics by name and offence in the local newspaper was readily available.[48] The case of Bridget McDonnell and others suggests that the social stigma attached to jail time and drunkenness may have restricted but did not eliminate future employment. Nevertheless, while some employers may have overlooked previous indiscretions, it is likely that jail time meant a servant lost both respectability and a reputation that would guarantee another position.

*Vagrancy*

Although jail deprived women of their liberty, incarceration could also provide shelter and food during periods of unemployment when desperate circumstances forced Irish servants, like many others, without family to seek out temporary accommodations. As was often noted in jail inspection reports, conditions were clean if spartan. Food was often adequate but rationed.[49] For some this crude form of hospitality was better than the alternative of living on the streets.[50] A careful examination of vagrancy charges highlights the particular desperation that relates directly to the nature of servants' work. Unlike most other occupations, the threat of non-residence was ever present; dismissal from employment also meant the loss of a place to live and food to eat. A striking trend emerges in the rural jails in the 1870s which highlights the impact of this occupational liability on immigrant workers.

As we have seen earlier, both servants and Irish women were among the largest percentage of committals for vagrancy. An analysis of jail registers reveals a trend in the life course of servants and immigrant women, many of whom were poor, which suggests that some entered rural facilities where limited social welfare alternatives existed during the winter months and/or periods of depression.[51] For instance, in Leeds/Grenville, Eleanor Madden, an Irish servant, and her ten-year-old daughter were convicted of vagrancy and spent a month in jail in March 1870. Similarly, Mary Cavanagh, a fifty-seven-year-old domestic worker from Ireland, was jailed for vagrancy in the winter of 1873. Among those jailed for vagrancy in Grey county the majority were either servants or labourers.

*Larceny*

While Irish servants were overrepresented among women charged with drunkenness and to a lesser extent those charged with vagrancy, few Irish servants were committed for larceny.[52] In Toronto/York, Grey, and Perth counties, almost a third of the women charged with larceny were servants, but among those only 8 percent were Irish migrants. Surprisingly, in Leeds/Grenville, with only one exception, the fifteen women charged with larceny who listed an occupation all worked as domestics. Of those, only one was Irish. Whether Irish servants were more readily dismissed than others, as suggested in the earlier remarks, is uncertain. A closer examination of several court cases allows us to explore aspects of domestic work that may have contributed to charges of larceny and/or dismissal.

Without doubt, servants had ample opportunities to steal. They were familiar with household valuables and money, information usually privy to the immediate family. Often alone and unsupervised, these women lived and worked surrounded by possessions and wealth they would never acquire. Working for and in homes of the propertied middle and upper classes, they confronted the reality of nineteenth-century economic disparity in its most transparent form. For some the temptation to steal must have been great. Despite the unbalanced nature of this relationship, both parties shared, albeit unequally, a degree of dependency and vulnerability. Given the arduous chores of nineteenth-century domestic households, many families relied on a limited pool of servants for cooking and cleaning. Servants, on the other hand, relied on a contract of employment that was at best maternalistic and at worst exploitative.[53] Furthermore, within this private household arrangement employers were vulnerable to theft by servants, and arguably servants were vulnerable to accusations of theft by employers.

Problematic aspects of the relationship between servants and employers may have also contributed to incidents of theft. Glimpses of this can be gleaned only from the testimony of witnesses, oftentimes under cross-examination by defence attorneys.[54] Details of a case in Toronto township in 1860 suggest some of the negative aspects in household working relationships. Mary Jane Borland, a servant, was charged with stealing a gold broach, locket, and purse containing $14.25. She was hired at $2.50 a month to work in a house with five related adults – grandmother, grandfather, uncle, grandson, and granddaughter. After three weeks of service, she left without payment. Under cross-examination at trial, the reportings of the granddaughter offer evocative hints about possible abuse: the granddaughter denied that her brother had abused Mary Jane by pulling her hair, and that she had never 'heard her [Mary Jane] complain of ill usage.' Furthermore, Mary Jane's employer insisted that she 'was well treated whilst there, I never quarreled with her. They quarreled on some day, I never heard what it was about. It was not more than words that I know of.'[55] The case files suggest that servants may have exacted a form of balance of payments or revenge for ill-treatment by stealing the personal possessions of their employers. Targeting a particular employer suggests that acts of aggression, indiscretion, or non-compliance with contractual agreements were the catalyst for some thefts.[56] There are certainly indications of this in the case against servant Martha Story. Martha was charged with stealing $49 from her employer, who later denied under cross-examination that there had been any 'difficulty between me and her [Martha] about money matters before that.'[57]

Questions of reputation played a critical role in defence arguments. Inherited qualities could also be an influential factor. Adeline Laraby, a young servant girl who was found guilty of larceny, had a mother who was described as 'not a good character.' Her reputation and credibility came under further disrepute when another witness testified to hearing of previous charges of theft involving Adeline. Criminologists Bruce Lenman and Geoffrey Parker remark how in recently settled communities, given the difficulties establishing guilt, 'the reputation of the suspect in the community was, at times, the only sure way to assess probable guilt.'[58] Character assessment played an important role in establishing the fundamental distinctions both in behaviour and motives. Lack of character witnesses among unemployed servants and single immigrant women offered few options for defence. Although evidence of a defendant's good character did not overturn a guilty verdict based on solid evidence, it is likely that no character witnesses or unfavourable assessments disadvantaged a defendant.

One is left wondering at the effect of silence to counter the perceptions of 'respectability' in the defence of Mary Pierce and a young girl, Sarah Jane Pierce, whom we assume was her daughter or a close relative. Mary, a housekeeper, was charged with receiving stolen goods along with fellow housekeeper and Irish immigrant, Mary Barber. Sarah Jane Pierce, age nine, was also charged with housebreaking and larceny in Brockville in 1878. According to the complainant, a local store owner, thieves had entered his house and removed food and several sundry items, including a quilt and a hat. There was no violence or property damage during the theft. Another fellow housekeeper was suspected of being an accomplice and police charged her with receiving stolen goods. Fortunately for this woman, her landlord testified to her 'good' character. This assessment proved propitious. Since police reports failed to link her directly to the theft, she was acquitted. No character witnesses, however, testified on behalf of the other two defendants. Evidence linked both Mary Pierce, who had been arrested numerous times on charges of drunkenness, and Sarah Pierce, also listed as a housekeeper, to the crime.[59] Based on hearsay it was inferred that the daughter had entered the house through a window, and then either let her mother in or passed the stolen goods through the window. Both were found guilty. The mother was convicted of receiving stolen goods and sentenced to six months in jail at hard labour, with the unusual punishment of solitary confinement for the first and last months.[60] Surprisingly, the daughter received the longest sentence of all the property cases reviewed in a sampling of crime in Ontario between 1840 and 1881 – seven years at hard labour in Kingston Penitentiary. This case, while atypical in severity of sentence and age of the criminal, alerts us to how suggestions of character and respectability might influence determinations of culpability.[61]

**From Courts to Asylum**

Although insanity was less common than drunkenness, vagrancy, or larceny as a reason for committing women to jail in the four counties sampled, the charge of insanity usually led to a much longer incarceration. From the mid-nineteenth century, persons placed in county jails because they were found to be insane and dangerous could then be transferred to an asylum for the insane by the warrant system. Warrant cases had priority over private admissions to asylums and also by-passed the requirement to have a certificate of insanity signed by three physicians. The jail route required only one doctor and the jail surgeon to sign the certificate.[62] Not surprisingly, persons admitted to provincial insane asylums, female as well as male, frequently came through local jails charged with being dangerous and likely to commit some crime. Warrant cases especially dominated admissions from the poorer or more rural parts of Ontario society, precisely the part of the population that included many of the immigrants from Ireland.

The first permanent Ontario asylum opened in Toronto in 1850 as part of a widespread movement to create specialized institutions where the insane could receive 'moral treatment' rather than simply be restrained. Prior to the building of the Provincial Lunatic Asylum, the government paid for the maintenance of lunatics in county jails where little attention was given to their health or special needs.[63] The Toronto asylum filled a major need and quickly became overcrowded. One of the early patients transferred to the Provincial Lunatic Asylum, not from a county jail but from the Kingston Penitentiary, was Grace Marks. Admitted by warrant to the asylum in May 1852,[64] she was observed there in the violent ward by Susanna Moodie who wanted to see the celebrated murderess in the asylum as well as in the penitentiary. In *Life in the Clearings*, Moodie painted a lurid picture of Grace Marks, the madwoman. 'Among these raving maniacs I recognised the singular face of Grace Marks – no longer sad and despairing, but lighted up with the fire of insanity and glowing with a hideous and fiend-like merriment. On perceiving that strangers were observing her, she fled shrieking away like a phantom into one of the side rooms.'[65] As a convicted murderer sentenced to life in the penitentiary, Grace Marks differed from the majority of women committed to asylums in Ontario in the nineteenth century. The ambiguities surrounding her committal for 'insanity,' however, were not unusual. In addition, Grace Marks was definitely not the only Irish immigrant domestic servant labelled both 'mad' and 'bad' whether because of intolerable conditions, poverty, overwork, rebellion, physical or mental illness, or mental retardation.

In 1856 the Rockwood Asylum for the criminally insane was opened in Kingston near the penitentiary. After Confederation, the federal government maintained Rockwood until the province of Ontario purchased it in 1876 and integrated it into the provincial asylum system as the Asylum of the Insane, Kingston. The Rockwood Asylum thus functioned as an institution particularly designated for the criminally insane during the first two decades of its existence and thereafter as part of the Ontario asylum system which by the 1880s included the London Asylum (opened 1870) and the Hamilton Asylum (opened 1876) in addition to Toronto and Kingston. If the Rockwood Asylum had been established four years earlier, it is the institution to which Grace Marks would have been sent. In the years from 1857 to 1885, slightly over one-quarter of the women admitted to Rockwood were identified as from Ireland (105 of 399 patients) and of these Irish women, one-third (36 or 34.4 per cent) were listed by occupation as servants. The prevalence of domestic servants among women committed to Rockwood is a clear indication of the stresses that could accompany a life in service. Significantly, servant was the occupation of over one-quarter of all women committed to Rockwood by 1875 (113 of 399 cases). As well, among the immigrant servants committed, Irish women far outnumbered all other ethnic groups combined.

As revealed by the Rockwood case files, Irish immigrant domestics admitted to the asylum were women who for a variety of reasons did not behave in a socially acceptable manner. The reasons for admission, of course, were constructed by those committing and overseeing the inmates, not by the patients themselves.[66] Hence, the majority of female Irish servants committed to Rockwood were 'said to be dangerous,' a characteristic that ensured speedy admission more than it necessarily described their behaviour. Nonetheless, the ascription could reinforce stereotypes of the unruly Irish, without distinction of gender, and arouse apprehension regarding women who were seen as deviating drastically from socially approved female behaviour.

The asylum records contain hints of the trauma that certain Irish immigrant domestics experienced in the new land, leading to the diagnosis of chronic or acute mania, or occasionally melancholia. Harriet, age twenty-three, was sent to Rockwood from the Lennox and Addington jail in 1870 suffering from chronic mania because 'being a perfect stranger ... she was arrested from her conduct as a lunatic.' Plagued by poor physical health, which undoubtedly contributed to her problems, she died of blood circulation problems ten years later.[67] Harriet's condition reflected that of other Irish domestics committed to Rockwood who suffered from isolation, poverty, or disease, but her youth was exceptional. Of the thirty-three Irish servants admitted between 1857 and 1885 for whom age is recorded, all but four were over the age of thirty, the majority being in their thirties and forties. Older age apparently made the women either less resilient or less compliant. Catherine, age thirty-four, came to the Frontenac police station in 1878 for protection because she was a stranger in the district. Arrested for vagrancy, she was transferred to Rockwood because she had delusions of being a great personage and assaulted other women in the jail.[68] Frequently the women committed were reported as having religious or other delusions. Ann, age forty, who was sent from the Carleton jail in 1869, was tormented by witches and spirits, was jealous of all women, and attempted to burn her mistress and house.[69] Margaret, age forty-five, who was also sent from Carleton county in 1880, was declared suicidal and likely to injure others. She had been hearing strange sounds that prevented her from sleeping and could not perform her household duties because she imagined that her butter-making, washing, and soap-making had been bewitched.[70] Bridget, age thirty-eight, on committal from Lennox and Addington in 1873, was one of the many Irish women who crossed the border to the United States to seek better opportunities. Obviously not happy and declared dangerous and suicidal after her return to Canada, she believed that ghosts appeared to her in Buffalo and induced her to return to Canada to commit some wicked design.[71] Grace from Lanark county, age forty at the time of her committal in 1884, was overcome by worry about money. She engaged in 'senseless incoherent talk' as well as violent conduct, imagining the government was keeping money from her that was sent by friends in Ireland.[72] Nostalgia for home disturbed Jane, age forty-four, of county Frontenac, who had visions not only of angels and devils but also of the green fields of the old sod.[73]

While some of the women, like Harriet and Catherine, were strangers and alone in the new world, others had family who were unable or unwilling to provide the considerable support needed. Pressed for survival, poorer Irish immigrant families did not have the resources to cope with women with serious problems.[74] In certain cases, other members of the family were also reported as 'insane,' but Mary, age fifty-five, from Huron County, had been deserted by her family and led a vagrant life before being committed.[75] Like Mary, four of the other Irish servants were listed as married, but the majority were single, with three widowed. Most domestic servants were not married so the predominantly single status of Irish domestics confined to Rockwood is not surprising.

Slightly over half of the Irish servants committed to Rockwood died in the institution, often after ten or more years in custody. For these women, the walls of the asylum starkly confined and buried the sad distortions of their immigrant dreams. Two who died were diagnosed with epilepsy, a disease that would later exclude immigrants from admission to Canada. One of these also had her left hand crushed in the washing machine while working in the laundry at the asylum.[76] A third woman, after twenty years in the asylum, died at a kettle while working in the kitchen as part of her asylum treatment.[77] Others were reported as succumbing to various physical problems including tuberculosis, heart disease, and breathing difficulties. Some of the Irish servants who did not die in Rockwood were transferred to another asylum, usually Toronto. Only one-quarter of the Irish servants committed by 1885 were reported as discharged, usually to family or friends.

### Refuge in Reform Asylums

Refuge in reform asylums or Magdalene asylums provided a somewhat more hopeful route from jail for Irish immigrant women down on their luck than did asylums for the insane. Reform asylums served as a type of halfway house between jail, or the street, and restoration to a respectable life in the community. For nineteenth-century Magdalene asylums, religious salvation was an integral part of the redemption process. They wished to restore unfortunate women to a respectable life of work and family and also to save them for the life to come. Because of the close connection between domesticity and respectability for mid-nineteenth-century Ontario women, Magdalene asylums prepared homeless women for domestic service. Hence, Magdalene asylums may have provided some Irish immigrant domestics with a second chance for a better life in Ontario, but only in their former occupation and only if they adapted to the discipline taught in the asylum.

Because of its importance as an immigrant-receiving city, Toronto is a good centre for examining the sanctuary offered by refuge asylums. The downward mobility of certain female migrants to Toronto aroused concern regarding unprotected women adrift in the city as early as the 1850s. Consequently, with the support of influential men and the Protestant clergy, a group of Toronto women began the Toronto Magdalene Asylum or Industrial House of Refuge in the mid-1850s.[78] The women's committee visited jails to make contact with women who were willing to come to the refuge and also admitted 'wanderers' from the streets. They aimed to 'afford the means of reformation to every fallen woman, without reference to creed or origin, who seriously desires to amend her life.'[79] The women on the streets and in the jails were portrayed not as criminals but as sinners in need of salvation.

The women's committee definitely viewed intemperance as women's problem as well as men's. As stated in the *Annual Report* for 1860, 'it is a sad truth that a very large proportion of fallen women are drunkards and that this fatal habit forms one of the chief barriers in the way of their return to the path of virtue.'[80] The same message was repeated many times, including the conclusion in 1864 that 'on searching into the cases of the inmates, we find, in almost every one, that the great cause of their wretched condition is intemperance.'[81] The literature shifted, however, from most frequently portraying the women as weak and being led into temptation by unsavoury surroundings to later portraying them as actively seeking pleasure. In 1859 the *Annual Report* stated that Canada, 'a land of strangers, presents many dangers to the young, the unprotected, and the friendless female.' For these women, the Asylum offered a refuge, 'protection from the wicked pursuer and the wily tempter.'[82] By the 1870s, the ruin of many girls was attributed more directly to their 'love of stimulants' as well as a 'love of dress and gay company.'[83] Instead of blaming an evil male seducer, the female reformers now castigated the young women themselves for their lack of restraint. An extravagant taste in dress and amusements and a willing indulgence in stimulants drew these women into debt and the downward path of sin.

The asylum sought to reform inmates through work discipline and the gospel of love. Inmates had to agree to remain at least a year, not leaving the premises or having any contact with former friends or associates. Within the refuge, they were expected to adhere to a strict daily schedule of duties, work, and worship.[84] Those who showed suitable progress after twelve months were found positions in domestic service, preferably in a country setting. The reformers urged mistresses to exercise benevolent supervision over their servants.[85] The emphasis on personal moral guidance, and the religious belief that each was placed by God in a particular social rank, however, meant that the reformers did not address the class inequities, cultural gulfs, or imbalance in sexual power that women encountered as domestic servants.

Many of the women seeking admission to the refuge would have been more aware than their benefactors of the potential hazards of domestic service. Their motives in voluntarily entering the asylum are not so clearly revealed in the records. Undoubtedly, for those leaving jail or others who had no home, the food, lodging, and clothing provided by the refuge would have seemed attractive. Irish women may already have been acquainted with Magdalene asylums. In the nineteenth century, at least twenty-three asylums or refuges were established in Ireland and these asylums seem to have been considered preferable to workhouses by at least some needy women.[86] In Canada, Irish women could turn to the asylum for short-term support even though the refuge was not intended as a temporary shelter. For example, Margaret Thurau from Ireland sought relief in the Toronto asylum after sustaining an injury while employed at Temperance House, Peterborough.[87] The annual records continually report that a number of women left after two or three months, obviously having recovered their strength and not being willing to submit to the discipline of the institution for a longer period. There also were a significant number who returned to the institution more than once, being received again in the hope that their reformation might eventually be permanent. Only a very few were dismissed on grounds of insubordination or foul language. The willingness to submit to the isolation and rigid discipline of the refuge for months or years may in part be evidence of a penitent desire for reformation but definitely reveals the harsh conditions of the city for migrant women without sufficient personal or family resources.

## Conclusion

The court and asylum records allow us to examine some of the problems encountered and even some of the strategies employed by Irish immigrant servants. Domestic service was the main paid occupation for Irish immigrant women, whether they came to Ontario with family, with friends, with a workhouse group, or on their own. The gendered nature of work, that created a continuous demand for female migrants to meet the need for servants, allowed large numbers of Irish women to join the movement across the Atlantic. The conditions of live-in domestic service, however, placed Irish women, far more than Irish men, in situations of isolation and potential loneliness. Ethnic and religious prejudice could create stressful relations with employers for Irish, and especially Irish Catholic, servants. Though Grace Marks, and women like her, were white and members of what a hundred years later would be viewed as a 'preferred' immigrant group, in the mid-nineteenth century, their working-class and ethnoreligious identity placed them near the bottom of the social ranks.

The cultural gulf between employee and employer created problems, especially for recently dislocated women with few community supports. Not surprisingly, not all Irish immigrant women were able to overcome these challenges and adapt successfully to the new society. Jail and asylum records provide a glimpse into the lives of Irish immigrant servants who were deemed a threat to public morality or the safety of society because of drunkenness, vagrancy, larceny, or insanity. In some cases, Irish servants, who were out of both work and home, actively sought admission to jail as a means of obtaining food and lodging. Undoubtedly for similar reasons, others agreed to enter the Toronto Magdalene Asylum either on leaving jail or as an alternative to jail. More often, though, Irish immigrant domestics were committed to jail or to an insane asylum such as Rockwood because they did not conform to socially approved female behaviour. A double moral standard made public drunkenness, the crime for which most Irish women were jailed, an even greater evil for women than for men. The decisions of state officials also were constructed within a context of ethnic and religious prejudgements. Stereotyped constructions of both gender and ethnicity thus conspired to limit opportunities for security and social advancement for many Irish immigrant women like Grace Marks. Immigration to Canada offered comfort and independence to many individuals, but for some hopeful women, discriminatory attitudes and unpleasant work situations made them feel like strangers, more than sisters, in the new world.

NOTES

1  Margaret Atwood, *Alias Grace* (Toronto: McClelland and Stewart, 1996). For consistency we use the term *Ontario* throughout the nineteenth century.

2  Susan E. Houston, 'The Role of the Criminal Law in Redefining "Youth" in Mid-Nineteenth-Century Upper Canada,' *Historical Studies in Education* Special Issue, 6, no. 3 (1994): 39–55.

3  Susanna Moodie, *Life in the Clearings* (Toronto: Macmillan, 1959), originally published in England in 1853 and in New York in 1854. Moodie describes Grace Marks, 'the celebrated murderess' in chapter 10, 'Grace Marks' and chapter 15, 'Lunatic Asylum.'

4  Margaret Atwood, 'In Search of Alias Grace,' Charles R. Bronfman Lecture in Canadian Studies, 21 November 1996 (Ottawa: University of Ottawa Press), 7–9.

5  Patrick O'Sullivan, 'Introduction' to *Irish Women and Irish Migration*, vol. 4, *The Irish World Wide* (London: Leicester University Press, 1997), 1, states that 'certainly for the period 1871–1971 greater female emigration is the Irish norm.'

6  Hasia Diner, *Erin's Daughters in America: Irish Immigrant Women in the Nineteenth Century* (Baltimore: Johns Hopkins University Press, 1983); Janet A. Nolan, *Ourselves Alone: Women's Emigration from Ireland, 1885–1920* (Lexington: Kentucky University Press, 1989).

7  Kerby A. Miller with David N. Doyle and Patricia Kelleher, '"For Love and Liberty": Irish Women, Migration and Domesticity in Ireland and America, 1815–1920,' in O'Sullivan, *Irish Women and Irish Migration*, 43–4.

8  Ibid., 44.

9  D.H. Akenson, 'Ontario: Whatever Happened to the Irish?' *Canadian Papers in Rural History* 3 (1982); D.H. Akenson, *The Irish in Ontario: A Study in Rural History* (Montreal and Kingston: McGill-Queen's University Press, 1984); Bruce S. Elliott, *Irish Migrants in the Canadas: A New Approach* (Montreal and Kingston: McGill-Queen's University Press, 1988); C.J. Houston and W.J. Smyth, *Irish Emigration and Canadian Settlement: Patterns, Links, and Letters* (Toronto: University of Toronto Press, 1990).

10  Susan Jenkins, 'Irish Women Immigrants in Nineteenth-Century Ontario' (honours research essay, Carleton University, Ottawa, 1989); N.H. Carrier and J.R. Jeffery, *External Migration: A Study of the Available Statistics, 1815–1950*, Studies on Medical and Population Subjects, no. 6 (London: Great Britain – General Register Office, 1953); Province of Canada, *Journals of the Legislative Assembly,* 1854–8; Province of Canada, *Sessional Papers*, 1859–65; Canada, Annual Reports of the Minister of Agriculture, *Sessional Papers*, 1868–77.

11  Dympna McLoughlin, 'Superfluous and Unwanted Deadweight: The Emigration of Nineteenth-Century Irish Pauper Women,' in O'Sullivan, *Irish Women and Irish Migration*, 66–88.

12  Ontario, 'Annual Report of the Department of Immigration,' *Sessional Papers*, 1869–89. See especially report of Sheil, agent in Southern Ireland and J. Murphy, the Cork agent.

13  Michael B. Katz, *The People of Hamilton, Canada West: Family and Class in a Mid-Nineteenth-Century City* (Cambridge, MA: Harvard University Press, 1975), 289.

14  Claudette Lacelle, *Urban Domestic Servants in 19th-Century Canada* (Ottawa: Environment Canada, Parks, 1987), 76–9.

15  *Canadian Illustrated News* 25, no. 7 (January 1882), 16.

16  Moodie, *Life in the Clearings,* 10.

17  *Examiner,* 8 November 1843, 3; *Bathurst Courier,* 22 August 1843.

18  Wesley Turner, '80 Stout and Healthy-Looking Girls,' *Canada: An Historical Magazine* 3, no. 2 (December 1975): 37–49; McLoughlin, 'Superfluous and Unwanted Deadweight.'

19  National Archives of Canada (hereafter NA), RG 17, vol. 29, file 2577.

20  For an elaboration of sources for research on Irish female domestics, see L. McLean and M. Barber, 'Making Colonial Homes: Sources on Irish, Female Domestics in

Nineteenth-Century Canada,' in Françoise Le Jeune, ed., *Contribution and Legacy of European Female Emigrants to Canada* (Nantes: Centre for Research in Canadian Studies, Université de Nantes, Peter Lang, 2003).

21  This study is based on a random sample of four jail registers, except in the case of Perth and Grey counties, where all committals were recorded because of the limited number of women. The results are accurate within a range of plus or minus 5 per cent.

22  On the use of case files for historical research see, Franca Iacovetta and Wendy Mitchinson, eds, *On the Case: Explorations in Social History* (Toronto: University of Toronto Press, 1998).

23  For the earlier period, see M.A. Garland and J.J. Talman, 'Pioneer Drinking Habits and the Rise of the Temperance Agitation in Upper Canada Prior to 1840,' in F. Armstrong, H.A. Stevenson, and J.D. Wilson, eds, *Aspects of Nineteenth-Century Ontario* (Toronto: University of Toronto Press, 1974), 171–93. On Leeds/Grenville and Lanark counties, see Glenn J. Lockwood, 'Temperance in Upper Canada as Ethnic Subterfuge,' in Cheryl Krasnick Warsh, ed., *Drink in Canada: Historical Essays* (Montreal and Kingston: McGill-Queen's University Press, 1993), 43–69. On the temperance movement in Canada prior to Confederation, see Janet Noel, *Canada Dry: Temperance Crusades before Confederation* (Toronto: University of Toronto Press, 1995). On the later women's temperance movement, see Sharon Cook, '*Through Sunshine and Shadow': The Woman's Christian Temperance Union, Evangelicalism, and Reform in Ontario, 1874–1930* (Montreal and Kingston: McGill-Queen's University Press, 1995).

24  Warsh, *Drink in Canada*.

25  Ibid.; Jim Baumohl, 'Inebriate Institutions,' 99.

26  Lucia Zedner, *Women, Crime, and Custody in Victorian England* (Oxford: Oxford University Press, 1991), 27.

27  Baumohl, 'Inebriate Institutions,' 99.

28  On the public role of women in another large city during a similar time period, see Christine Stansell, *City of Women: Sex and Class in New York, 1789–1860* (New York: Knopf, 1986). For the classic study on Victorian ideology of spatial and psychological separation, and the creation of the public world of men and the private world of women, see Barbara Welter, 'The Cult of True Womanhood, 1820–1860,' *American Quarterly* 18 (1966): 150–74.

29  Jim Phillips, 'Women, Crime, and Criminal Justice in Early Halifax,' in Jim Phillips, Tina Loo, and Susan Lewthwaite, eds, *Essays in the History of Canadian Law*, vol. 5, *Crime and Criminal Justice* (Toronto: University of Toronto Press, 1994), 185.

30  This trend resembles a national pattern of female incarceration. Studies in other parts of British North America report the highest level of committals for women between 1851 and 1861 (Hamilton) and 1865 and 1866 (Halifax). Michael Katz et al., *The Social Organization of Early Industrial Capitalism* (Cambridge, MA: Harvard Univer-

sity Press, 1982), 240; Judith Fingard, *The Dark Side of Life in Victorian Halifax* (Porters Lake, NS: Pottersfield Press, 1989), 23, Table 2, and Jane B. Price, '"Raised in Rockhead. Died in the Poor House": Female Petty Criminals in Halifax, 1864–1890,' in Philip Girard and Jim Phillips, eds, *Essays in the History of Canadian Law*, vol. 3, *Nova Scotia* (Toronto: University of Toronto Press, 1990), 205, Table 1. For the period following 1880, see Carolyn Strange, *Toronto's Girl Problem: The Perils and Pleasures of the City, 1880–1930* (Toronto: University of Toronto Press, 1995).

31 See Toronto By-law No. 322, 'By-law to Provide for the Maintenance and Care of Public Parks, Squares and Grounds': Sec. 2, 'It shall be lawful for any police officer, constable, care-taker of other person duly authorized by the Mayor or any Alderman of the said City, to exclude from the said public squares, parks and grounds all drunken or filthy persons, vagrants and notoriously bad characters, and to remove therefrom any person who is violating any By-law of the City Council, or is committing any nuisance, or is guilty of any disorderly conduct therein.' Toronto Metropolitan Archives (hereafter TMA), *By-Laws of the City of Toronto*, 30 July 1860. Again in 1868 council extended its powers over public spaces in the 'By-law for the Regulation of the Streets, Sidewalks and Thoroughfares of the City of Toronto, and for the Preservation of Order, and Suppression of Nuisances Therein.' This by-law was intended to protect city trees, limit use of fireworks and restrict bathing areas. More importantly, it included an interpretative clause that defined the word *street* to include all access routes throughout the city as part of 'public passage.' TMA, *By-Laws of the City of Toronto*, 26 October 1868.

32 *Globe*, 30 January 1856.

33 In 1859 the Police Force had one Chief, ten senior officers and sixty men. TMA, *Toronto City Council Minutes Report* No. 7, 'The Board of Commissioners of Police for the City of Toronto,' 1 February 1859. On policing in Toronto in the nineteenth century see Helen Boritch, 'Conflict, Compromise and Administrative Convenience,' *Canadian Journal of Law and Society/Revue canadienne droit et société* 3 (1988): 141–74; Helen Boritch and John Hagan, 'Crime and the Changing Forms of Class Control in "Toronto the Good,"' *Social Forces* 66 (1987): 307–35; Nicholas Rogers, 'Serving Toronto the Good,' in Victor Russell, ed., *Forging the Consensus* (Toronto: University of Toronto Press, 1984), 116–40.

34 TMA, *Toronto City Council Minutes* Appendix, 6 March 1863.

35 Katz, *The People of Hamilton*, 58.

36 In 1859, in the midst of the depression, the ratio of taverns/saloons to population in Toronto was 1 to 157, and in Stratford, an even higher 1 to 70. *Stratford Beacon*, 23 September 1859.

37 The actual number of Irish women is underestimated. The ethnicity of the 12 per cent of women who list Canada as a place of birth is unknown.

38 *Globe*, 24 May 1865.

39  *Globe*, 29 May 1865.

40  John J. Bigsby, *The Shoe and Canoe*, 2 vols. (New York: Paladin Press, 1969; originally published 1850), vol. 1, 95–6, cited in Jenkins, 'Irish Women Immigrants in Nineteenth-Century Ontario,' 73. As well, during the 1860s, when many Irish immigrants were arrested for drunkenness, the *Globe* routinely identified the birthplace of the accused.

41  Michael Cottrell, 'St. Patrick's Day Parades,' in Franca Iacovetta et al., eds, *A Nation of Immigrants* (Toronto: University of Toronto Press, 1989) and Rogers, 'Serving Toronto the Good,' 116–40.

42  Murray W. Nicolson, *Gathering Place: Peoples and Neighbourhoods of Toronto, 1834–1945* (Toronto: Multicultural History Society of Ontario, 1985), 58.

43  Cited in Houston and Smyth, *Irish Emigration and Canadian Settlement*, 74.

44  Faye E. Dudden, *Serving Women: Household Service in Nineteenth-Century America* (Middletown, CT: Wesleyan University Press, 1983), 194–201.

45  NA, CO 42/651, 182–3 cited in Turner, '80 Stout and Healthy Girls,' 48–9.

46  See Frances Hoffman and Ryan Taylor, eds, *Much to Be Done: Private Life in Ontario from Victorian Diaries* (Toronto: Natural Heritage/Natural History, 1996), 109–22.

47  Archives of Ontario (hereafter AO), RG 22, Series 392, *The Queen v. Kate Swanton*, Toronto, 1876.

48  Both urban and rural newspapers routinely published police court reports which listed both names and offences.

49  In Stratford jail, for instance, beds were without frames and mattresses rested on the floor. AO, RG 20, F-40, Copies of Council Minutes Pertaining to the Jail, 'Report of the Committee on County property and gaol management,' 7 June 1870. In Leeds/Grenville, the 'Standing Committee on County Property in Leeds/Grenville' visited the jail and 'found it in perfect order, clean and neat.' Municipal Office of the Council of Leeds/Grenville, *Minutes of the Municipal Council of the United Counties of Leeds and Grenville*, 'Standing Committee on County Property in Leeds/Grenville,' 26 February 1868.

50  Certainly some councillors felt this way. Despite sparse conditions, Perth county council was 'persuaded that many persons confined, consider it a boon to have the privilege of being so confined.' They reported on one inmate who stated that 'he was committed for ten days, and felt sorry that it was not for a month.' AO, RG 20, F-40, Copies of Council Minutes Pertaining to the Jail, 'Report of Jail Committee,' 29 January 1869.

51  For a fuller discussion on this practice, see Lorna McLean, '"Common Criminals, Simple Justice": The Social Construction of Crime in Nineteenth-Century Ontario, 1840–1881' (PhD diss., University of Ottawa, 1996), 97–136.

52  On nineteenth-century perceptions of 'the criminal servant,' see Lacelle, *Urban Domestic Servants*, 120–30.

53  Ibid., 89–104, 130–2. On the contractual obligations between master and servant, see Paul Craven, 'The Law of Master and Servant in Mid-Nineteenth-Century Ontario,'

in David Flaherty, ed., *Essays in the History of Canadian Law*, vol. 2 (Toronto: University of Toronto Press, 1983), 175–211.

54  See also Lacelle, *Urban Domestic Servants*, 130.

55  AO, RG 22, series 390, Judge Richards, York and Peel Counties, 1860, *The Queen v. Mary Jane Borland*, 227–31. Jail registers for this year are only summary and do not list the country of birth.

56  See, for example, Magdi Farni, '"Ruffled" Mistresses and "Discontented" Maids: Respectability and the Case of Domestic Service, 1880–1942,' *Labour/Le Travail* 39 (1996): 69–98 and James C. Scott, *Weapons of the Weak: Everyday Forms of Peasant Resistance* (New Haven: Yale University Press, 1985). The Master and Servant Act of 1847 was intended to deal with problems related to contractual and disciplinary problems in employment arrangements. Debates on the legislation specifically singled out household servants. Craven, 'The Law of Master and Servant,' 187–91.

57  AO, RG 22, series 390, Judge Richards, York and Peel Counties, 1860–61, *The Queen v. Martha Story*, 217–27.

58  Bruce Lenman and Geoffrey Parker, 'The State, the Community and the Criminal Law,' in V.A.C. Gatrell, Bruce Lenman and Geoffrey Parker, eds, *Crime and the Law: The Social History of Crime in Western Europe since 1500* (London: Europa Publications, 1980) 3.

59  Occupational evidence is from the jail register. AO, RG 20, Series F-6, Brockville Jail Register, 1878.

60  AO, RG 22, Leeds/Grenville, General Sessions and County Court Judges' Criminal Court, Judges' Notebook, *The Queen v. Sarah Jane Pierce, Mary Pierce, and Mary Barber*, 1878. The court sat over several days.

61  The length of the sentence might also reflect reformers' assumptions that youth were more amenable to institutional training.

62  Wendy Mitchinson, 'Gender and Insanity as Characteristics of the Insane: A Nineteenth-Century Case,' *Canadian Bulletin of Medical History/Bulletin canadien d'histoire de la médecine* 4 (1987): 102.

63  Cheryl Krasnick Warsh, '"In Charge of the Loons": A Portrait of the London, Ontario Asylum for the Insane in the Nineteenth Century,' *Ontario History* 74, no. 3 (September 1982): 140.

64  AO, RG10-20-B-1, Admission Orders Nos. 1182 and 1183, Grace Marks and Bridget Maloney.

65  Moodie, *Life in the Clearings*, 224.

66  Most literature on insane asylums focuses on the purpose of the asylums. Wendy Mitchinson, 'Reasons for Committal to a Mid-Nineteenth-Century Ontario Insane Asylum: The Case of Toronto,' in W. Mitchinson and J.D. McGinnis, eds, *Essays in the History of Canadian Medicine* (Toronto: McClelland and Stewart, 1988), 88–109 is one article that provides comparative information on reasons for committal.

67  AO, RG 10-20-F-1-1, Kingston Psychiatric Hospital, Casebook, Female, 7 May 1857–25 June 1885, 59, Registration Number 660.

68  Ibid., 176, Registration Number 1163.

69  Ibid., 28, Registration Number 455.

70  Ibid., 232, Registration Number 1287.

71  Ibid., 88, Registration Number 822.

72  Ibid., 260, Registration Number 1340.

73  Ibid., 215, Registration Number 1259.

74  Mitchinson, 'Reasons for Committal,' 94, notes that because of their poverty Irish-Canadian families could not afford to take care of their insane and sent them to the asylum.

75  AO, RG10-20-F-1-1, Casebook, Female, 1857–1885, 142, Registration Number 1055.

76  Ibid., 135, Registration Number 1035.

77  Ibid., 28, Registration Number 455.

78  AO, Toronto Industrial Refuge and Aged Men's and Women's Homes 1854–1890, *Annual Report of the Toronto Magdalene Asylum or Female House of Refuge*, 1855; 1874, 5.

79  Ibid., 1854, 6. The Matron was instructed to enter the name, date, age, religion, place of nativity, and remarks regarding the character and conduct of each inmate as well as the time and circumstances of discharge in the record book. Unfortunately, the record books have not survived but the majority of examples cited in the 1850s were Irish women.

80  Ibid., 1860.

81  Ibid., 1864.

82  Ibid., 1859. Stansell, *City of Women*, 72, explains how evangelical women's charities in New York 'embroidered a sentimentalist image of the female victim' who was a proper object of women's sympathy.

83  Ibid., 1870 and 1884.

84  Ibid., 1854, 7; 1858.

85  Ibid., 1880.

86  Maria Luddy, 'Prostitution and Rescue Work in Nineteenth-Century Ireland,' in Maria Luddy and Cliona Murphy, eds, *Women Surviving: Studies in Irish Women's History in the 19th and 20th Centuries* (Dublin: Poolbeg, 1990), 61.

87  AO, Ont. Dept. of Immigration, 1886, Lttr 975.

# Canadian Citizens or Dangerous Foreign Women? Canada's Radical Consumer Movement, 1947–1950

JULIE GUARD

## Introduction

In May 1947, the Housewives Consumers Association (HCA), a recently formed group of progressive women from differing political backgrounds, including the 'ethnic' left, caught the nation's attention when it organized a children's boycott to protest a sudden and precipitous hike in the price of candy bars. A brilliant media strategy, the children's chocolate bar boycott delivered in dramatic fashion the intended message – inflation hurt children and families. It also garnered support among a wide cross-section of Canadians for the HCA's demand that the federal Liberal government return wartime price and rent controls and enact other policies to help struggling working-class families. Like earlier rent strikes, children's brigades, bread riots, and kosher meat boycotts in Canada and elsewhere, the 1947 children's action also drew on time-honoured strategies developed by militant mothers, many of whom were ethnic women.

One of the HCA's founders, Ukrainian Canadian Mary Prokop recalled that women like herself – factory workers, mothers, the Canadian daughters of immigrant women, and female members of long-standing left-wing ethnic groups – used their networks 'to do something' about the 'rough' times caused by 'unemployment [and] prices [that] skyrocketed after the war: bread and eggs and all commodities.'[1] Although the HCA explicitly rejected a direct affiliation with any political party or organization, it came quickly under fire by keen Cold Warriors in the mainstream press, in provincial and federal cabinets, and in the community, who portrayed its membership as well-intentioned but naive women duped by Communists, including Canada's own red foreigners, into betraying their country and its values. By 1950, the organization had faded into irrelevance and lost most of its active members to a new organization, the Congress of Canadian Women, that was more closely tied to the Communist Party. When asked about the role of 'ethnic' women in the HCA, an elderly Prokop noted that the association was the product of sisterly networks of women from both the Anglo-Celtic and ethnic left, but also that such relationships could be unequal. Indeed, Prokop felt that ethnic women had played a very significant role in creating and maintaining the organization – perhaps even more crucial than that played by the Anglo-Celtic women – but that their work was never acknowledged, either by their 'Canadian' sisters, their allies in the male-dominated left, or the Canadian public.

This paper documents the rise and fall of Canada's radical consumer movement, focusing on its origins, the leaders' strategies, the role of ethnic women and their organizations, and the varied and changing responses that the group's political activities engendered.[2] As a study of a women's working-class protest movement in Cold War Canada, the essay contributes both to the already established literature on the history of ethnic women on the political left and to the developing and fast-proliferating social and gender history of the Cold War in Western capitalist countries such as Canada. The HCA offers a graphic illustration of how the Cold War national security state, supported by the mainstream media, deployed prevailing common-sense notions of femininity and ethnicity to recast this grassroots political movement in which both Anglo-Celtic and ethnic women were active as a moral contagion that required 'domestic containment.'[3]

The HCA's ethnically diverse, cross-class composition, which temporarily united women from a wide range of organizations and social positions – including professional social workers and teachers, factory workers and full-time home-makers, liberals, social democrats, and radicals, working-class and middle-class women – provides a vantage point not usual in studies of left-wing women.[4] Most studies of women on the left focus largely on the pre–Second World War era and on a small elite of writers and propagandists rather than ordinary women, and have tended to treat ethnically unmarked, normatively 'Canadian' women and groups separately from those that are identifiably 'ethnic.' By contrast, this study of the HCA, an organization that brought together women from varied backgrounds, experiences, and class positions into a post–Second World War community-based organization, provides a rare perspective on cross-ethnic relations on the front lines of radical protest in a Cold War context. With few exceptions, the important Canadian works on left ethnic women, which do indeed recognize the need to treat ethnicity and race as conceptual problems demanding analysis rather than fixed categories of identity, generally adopt the single group approach, whereas this essay deals with cross-ethnic relations among women on the left, in this instance, in a specific multiethnic lobby.[5] This study also highlights the ways that female gender and ethnicity were linked in official discourses to nativism and xenophobia, which were invoked, by both mainstream media and representatives of the state, to undermine the legitimacy of popular, grass-roots protest and destabilize dissent.

The Housewives themselves – drawing on a tradition of 'socialist maternalism' that was familiar to many left-wing and ethnic women – challenged official and popular discourses that defined postwar femininity as passive and apolitical. Evidence of this radical tradition in North America in the nineteenth and twentieth centuries and even earlier in Europe has been established by a number of studies.[6] Like anarchist, socialist, and Communist women in Canada and elsewhere, the Housewives naturalized their incursions into the normatively male domains of federal Cabinet meetings and picket lines by defining these activities as natural extensions of their roles and responsibilities as mothers. Competing and contradictory constructions of identity were the stakes in the HCA's struggle for legitimacy, a struggle expressed in the conflict between the popular and institutional discourses of anti-Communism, traitorous foreigners, and female domesticity, and the HCA's efforts to construct its own identity as class-conscious consumers, real and ordinary housewives, and militant, politically responsible citizen-mothers.

As political actors, the Housewives embodied these contradictions. Their credentials as political actors who could facilitate a diverse mass movement depended on their legitimacy as women. As mothers and homemakers, their right to speak on behalf of ordinary Canadians was incontestable. But their representation of themselves as ordinary women elided the ideological distinctions that without doubt set them apart from other 'ordinary' women. The Housewives' effectiveness as political actors rested on their conviction that ordinary people were entitled to a voice in governance and a larger share of social goods, a belief that drew directly on the political philosophy of the Communist left. Their inspiration as activists and their capacity to envision themselves as leaders in a nation-wide movement was a product of the Communist-inspired notion of social egalitarianism to which they subscribed. Many of the leading members of the organization were members of the Communist Labor Progressive Party (LPP), women's auxiliaries of Communist-led labour unions, or members of ethnic cultural organizations that were widely identified as Communist. The HCA identified themselves as part of the broad-based, left-wing movement and used many of the publicity and mobilization strategies popular with the political left, including press releases, radio broadcasts, petitions, postcards, and pickets. They expressed solidarity with the same causes that were supported by the LPP, and they recruited members and support through left-wing newspapers and community organizations. As women who were active participants in these organizations, and who were personally committed to opposing capitalism, they were ideologically distinct from most other Canadian women. As long as they were perceived as women and Canadians, the Housewives could function as the leaders of a broadly based popular movement. But as Communists or suspected Communists, and particularly as demonized foreign Communists infecting the body politic from within, the Housewives lacked credibility. Indeed, in the nativist climate of Cold War Canada, ethnic women on the left, long marginalized by their gender, class, and politics, were cast as the female carriers of infectious and noxious disease that threatened the moral health of the nation.

The strategic choice to represent themselves as 'ordinary' Canadian women was not, however, unproblematic. Like the Communist Party, which chose to portray itself as the very essence of Canadian-ness in order to avoid the added stigma attached to foreigners or those who were perceived as 'aliens' – a designation that included native-born Canadians of immigrant parents, as well as Jews of any national origin – to an already problematic political identity, the Housewives chose Anglo-Celtic women, or women who appeared to be Anglo-Celtic, almost exclusively as the public representatives of the organization. As a loosely co-ordinated network of local consumer organizations that were only episodically active, the HCA has left few records, but such evidence as exists, which includes the recollections of some of its members, makes it clear that the organization, despite its 'WASP' public face, was ethnically diverse, and indeed far more diverse than might be suggested by the names of its members, many of which had been Canadianized or anglicized. Furthermore, the organization's success, however temporary, owed much to the support of the organizations of the ethnic left in Canada. The Housewives' important links to the ethnic left were often obscured by their adoption of Canadian-sounding names, whether by changing their birth names or by adopting the Canadian-sounding names of their husbands. Prokop's name, for instance, belonged to her husband, a left-wing activist and labour organizer who had changed his name in response to persistent state harassment and the strong anti-immigrant mood of the wider public. Ann Ross, wife of Winnipeg Communist party leader Bill Ross, was a Jewish Russian immigrant whose husband was a member of the politically active Zukin family. Toronto-based HCA campaign manager Helen Weir, born Kucherian, was a Ukrainian Canadian and an active member of the Association of United Ukrainian Canadians (AUUC). Her husband, John Weir, whose family name had been Viviurski, came from a family of Communists; he wrote for several Communist newspapers, and was one of the mostly Ukrainian-Canadian Communists interned during the war.[7] The available evidence also suggests that the strategy of creating a Canadian front for the ethnically diverse HCA reinforced the marginalization of ethnic women within the organization. At least, it begs the question, did the Housewives, by cultivating a public image of themselves that conformed, in significant ways, to dominant, arguably bourgeois notions of female respectability, silence the voices of the ethnic women who, by some accounts, worked just as diligently but always in the shadow of their Anglo-Celtic sisters? Did ethnic women within the organization subscribe uncritically to the ladylike respectability of their Anglo-Celtic spokeswomen? Or did they draw on a very different tradition of female political activism that viewed bourgeois womanhood with suspicion, eschewed delicacy as a useless affectation, and prized feminine courage and strength? Did they, like the ethnic peasant and working-class women from radical European cultures described by feminist immigration historians, behave in ways that marked their distance from their Anglo-Celtic Canadian co-workers, and indeed, even from those with whom they walked picket lines and counted as allies? Drawing on the limited documentary sources available, which include police surveillance reports, newspaper coverage, and a few personal records, as well as a small number of oral histories, this study sheds light on these questions.

### Children on the Line: The Chocolate Bar Boycott, 1947

Canadians who listened to CBC Radio news on 1 May 1947 learned that children in Toronto, Montreal, and Regina had organized to protest an increase in the price of chocolate bars.[8] Many would have understood clearly the message being conveyed: inflation, and particularly the rising cost of food and everyday commodities, had become a serious problem for many families, so serious that even children were suffering from the effects of postwar economic adjustment. The children's chocolate bar boycott dramatically highlighted the growing disparity between postwar prices and postwar wages. Donning huge placards that covered them from chin to toe, these unlikely protesters provided a compelling illustration of the widening gap between family income and the price of basic commodities.[9]

The spectacle of school children organizing in cities across Canada to protest a 60 per cent increase in the price of chocolate bars, which had risen from five cents to eight cents, focused major media coverage on the Housewives Consumers Association's campaign against rising prices.[10] Militant child picketers provided good copy for radio stations and newspapers eager for entertaining, 'soft news' stories. At the same time, the construction of inflation as a matter of immediate and direct concern for children and their families conferred legitimacy on the Housewives' campaign. Protestors who might otherwise be perceived as engaging in an unseemly form of political protest reconfigured their activities as eminently respectable by invoking the moral authority of that most respectable of institutions, the family.[11]

The central plank of the Housewives' campaign was a call for an immediate change in the federal Liberal government's social and economic policies to protect the well-being of working-class families. Speaking as the ones with the primary responsibility for managing household budgets and caring for daily needs, they criticized the government for capitulating to the interests of big business, and called for sweeping reforms, and in particular, revised economic policies. Arguing that wartime price controls had come off too soon, they accused business of exploiting temporary shortages by charging exorbitant prices. They submitted a number of briefs to government committees outlining their agenda and spoke out in public meetings and in radio broadcasts, calling for a comprehensive housing policy to resolve the postwar housing crisis through rent controls and a home-building program, reforms to old age pensions, hot lunches and free milk for school children, government-sponsored child care, and a number of other social policy initiatives.[12]

Although ethnically unmarked, apparently Anglo-Celtic women were most prominent in activities such as lobbying members of Parliament; many of the Housewives' strategies, such as picketing grocery stores, organizing boycotts, and marching with babies and children down the main streets of their communities to protest the high prices of milk and bread, would have been familiar to members of Canada's ethnic communities. Community- and family-centred strategies such as these drew in part on the radical traditions of militant mothers who, in the past, had deployed public protests featuring children in ways designed to attract sympathy and attention to their cause. Ethnic militant mothers and multiethnic female communities and workforces in the United States and Canada had long been associated with defiant strategies such as these. We know, for instance, that Jewish mothers in early twentieth-century Toronto organized their children to protest the reciting of the Lord's Prayer in public schools, and that Jewish women in both Canada and the United States organized kosher food boycotts that sometimes erupted into violent clashes at the shop door. Italian-American women in New York State, like those in Italy, protected their children during violent strikes and protests by sending them to live with friends in other communities, and their aggressive behaviour on the picket-lines defies stereotyped portraits of them as cowering women. Like those in Toronto described by Ruth Frager, Communist Jewish women in early twentieth-century Winnipeg understood their activities in the politically radical secular community, like the radical education of their children, as a natural part of their roles as women. And, during the 1930s, Ukrainian, Hungarian, Jewish, Italian, and other immigrant and ethnic women in the multiethnic town of Crowland, as Carmela Patrias shows, brought their children into the streets to help them resist the police who were trying to force relief strikers back to work in a Great Depression–era strike that mobilized an entire community.[13] Similarly, left Ukrainian-Canadian women in the HCA, like Prokop, commonly brought their children to ethnic halls and political meetings; they demonstrated with babies – it was part and parcel of belonging to a politicized ethnic community. Babies and politics could go hand in hand.[14]

Stories such as that of the Housewives contribute to the growing evidence that women have long been political actors, but their activities have been overlooked in the historiography because their styles and strategies have typically differed from those of men. Politics has, according to this argument, been defined overwhelmingly as a male preserve in part because only men's political activities have been defined as political.[15] Yet a growing number of studies provide compelling evidence of women's active engagement in politics. One important study by Jennifer Guglielmo, on Italian women and labour organizing in the New York City needle trades during the late nineteenth and early twentieth centuries, offers us numerous such instances of women engaging in, and initiating, violent protest as members of a militant, multiethnic community. In 1913, for example, along with their Russian, Lithuanian, Polish, German, Greek, Irish, Spanish, and Hungarian female co-workers, an unprecedented 4,000 first- and second-generation Italian-American women rioted in protest against their employers and in defiance of their male union leaders, who had agreed with the bosses upon terms of employment that the women considered unacceptable. Like that of Franca Iacovetta, whose work reveals a similar defiance among Italian-Canadian women, Guglielmo's work challenges the conventional wisdom of historians in the United States and Canada that Italian women were docile compared to other workers. On the contrary, Italian women, like many other immigrant workers, brought with them a history of rebellion and protest nurtured in Italy, including the southern and Sicilian regions that produced many of North America's migrants. Drawing on Donna Gabaccia's work and her own, Guglielmo argues that 'women were often the more militant and outspoken activists in popular demonstrations and neighborhood movements among farm workers and urban laborers.'[16]

Like many other female militants, the Housewives defined political activism, drew on constituencies, and developed activist strategies that differed from those of labour organizations and political parties led by men. Like the Housewives, both the Canadian Congress of Labour (CCL) and the LPP called for postwar price controls, but neither organization addressed as broad a constituency as the Housewives, who reached into women's homes across the country through telephone networks and neighbourly visits. The differences in strategy are especially striking in the case of the CCL, whose leaders addressed their concerns to the federal cabinet in 1946 and 1947 through their annual 'Memorandum to the Dominion Government' in a process that brought together top union leaders and politicians but in which ordinary union members had no direct role or voice. By tying price controls to a demand for profit controls, expectations of increased productivity, and collective bargaining legislation, furthermore, the CCL's campaign focused on unionized male workers, writing women implicitly out of the negotiation.[17]

The Housewives' program, by focusing on the relations of consumption rather than production, also diverged both analytically and strategically from that of the male-dominated left. The LPP endorsed the Housewives' campaigns and urged party members and members of left-wing labour unions to participate in them, but the party had little interest in consumption.[18] Party strategy concentrated on organized labour and electoral politics, and despite the regular appearance in the Communist press of exhortations from LPP leader Tim Buck urging active support for the Prices campaign, the response from the male left appears to have been tepid. Indeed, although anti-Communists accused the Housewives Consumers Association of being nothing more than a front organization for the Communists, the evidence points to a more complex relationship. The Housewives looked to the LPP for assistance with research and publicity, and possibly for advice, but surveillance files created by the RCMP reveal that the security service could find no evidence of any more substantive connection, despite repeated instructions from senior officers to agents urging them to find such proof.[19] In contrast to the LPP, whose campaign focused on unions and their auxiliaries, the Housewives' campaigns reached out to women in traditional, family-centred roles, explaining how the conflicting interests of consumers and producers were part of the daily experience of housewives. Who knew better than the housewife, they asked, for whom purchasing was part of the job definition, that rising prices and smaller pay packets meant fewer and poorer quality groceries in the shopping basket? Pointing blame at unscrupulous corporations, whose rapacious greed for profit threatened the well-being of ordinary families, they portrayed class struggle as both reasonable and respectable, an activity well within the bounds of feminine propriety. Along with sweeping economic and social reforms, they called for a more participatory style of democracy, in which consumers would have both voice and vote in determining policy and legislation. The politicized concept of consumption implicit in these demands was animated by a conviction in the injustice of existing class relations that they shared with the Communist left. But unlike the male-dominated left, which was primarily concerned with the relations of production, their program for social justice called for a radical renegotiation of the class relations of consumption.[20] As class-conscious consumers, they expressed their demands for a radical reconceptualization of the relationship between citizens and the state in familial terms, pointing to their traditional roles and responsibilities as housewives and mothers to justify their right to demand fundamental change.

By mobilizing other women within their own communities, and including their own children as participants in political activities, the Housewives were doing what other radical women before them had done. They developed gender-specific approaches to political action that re-defined the political in ways that diverged from the strategies and perspectives of men, including those within their own organizations and cultural communities. As Guglielmo observes, while Sicilian men directed their attention on employers, Sicilian women addressed their concerns to the state, demanding protection for themselves and their children. Like other women in Italy and elsewhere, they expressed their demands for food and their opposition to government directly by destroying government offices, looting, and rioting. In common with Italian men, Italian women in Italy and the United States organized as workers and engaged in strikes and protests as members of unions where, like women from other ethnic communities, they sometimes 'distinguished themselves on picket lines, at strikers' meetings, and on organizational committees.'[21] But they also brought a feminine sensibility to their unionism, integrating family and union life by bringing children to union meetings and picket lines and identifying union activity as an important aspect of their children's education. As responsible mothers, they protected their children, not by eschewing violent confrontations with employers and police, but, as Guglielmo's example suggests, by sending their children to stay with friends and relatives. Rejecting the distinction that separated paid work from family and community, radical women in various times and places engaged in strategies such as rent strikes and boycotts and demanded education for their children and sexual freedom for themselves in terms of an integrated struggle for a more equitable world.[22] While all these demands were typically made by immigrant women in the name of the family and the community, theirs was a defiant, loud, and assertive womanhood that had little in common with the middle-class Anglo-Celtic notion of the lady.

### Radical Motherhood

The Housewives' representation of public policy as an appropriate focus of female concern and an area of public life for which women's domestic occupations provided the necessary expert knowledge, was consistent with maternalist movements elsewhere. From the late nineteenth century and into the 1930s and 1940s, European and American women had been campaigning collectively for the creation of social policies, pointing to their authority as mothers and homemakers to justify their demands. In contrast to Canada, where nineteenth- and early-twentieth-century maternal feminism was overwhelmingly middle class, European maternalism encompassed both middle- and working-class movements, although class consciousness usually varied according to class composition.[23] Within these movements, working-class consciousness informed a very different agenda for social reform than that espoused by middle-class maternalists. Social Democratic and Labour women in Australia, Sweden, and Britain, for instance, were less interested in the vote than in the creation of progressive social policy, and these working-class maternalists continued to work for change long after the suffrage was obtained.[24] Similarly, the Housewives Consumers Association, while claiming kinship with turn-of-the-century suffragists, invoked maternal authority to legitimate their demands for sweeping political reform.[25]

The radical maternalism that was implicit in the Housewives' claims to legitimacy as political actors has roots in traditions of socialist and anarchist motherhood such as those examined by Caroline Waldron in her study of turn-of-the-century anarchist Italian-American and French-speaking Belgium women whose husbands worked in the coalfields of Illinois. Like the Housewives, these women challenged the state (as well as the patriarchal relations of family and community life), demanding an enlarged role for women in the creation of a new and better world based on a re-valuation of women's domestic and familial responsibilities. As anarchists, they differed from the Communist and social democratic Housewives in their rejection of the external authority of government as inherently oppressive and their endorsement of sexual liberation in the form of free love. But like the Housewives, they claimed the right to participate in the struggle for social and political reform by pointing to their maternal responsibilities and their domestic expertise.[26] And, like the militant working-class women who joined their husbands, fathers, and brothers on picket lines in industrial towns and cities across the nation or who struck to improve their own working conditions with or without the assistance of men, they engaged in collective struggle with an enthusiasm that points to a far more combative norm of womanhood than that embraced by their middle-class sisters.[27] Women such as Mary Prokop, Lil Ilomaki (born Himmelfarb into a family of Jewish-Polish socialists in 1912 and a graduate of the Pioneers and Young Communist League), and Alice Maigis, a Lithuanian Communist, not only lived intensely political lives but their commitments and activism show that they also strongly rejected what they perceived to constitute bourgeois womanhood. Notwithstanding its hegemonic quality, not all women fell victim to its admittedly powerful influences. At the same time, the conflict between the Housewives' political activism and the demands of normative femininity was constantly at issue in the HCA's ability to retain popular support and deflect attacks on their legitimacy.

Their ability to create the large-scale social movement necessary to press such claims pivoted on their ability to reconcile the inherent conflict between promoting a radical political agenda and retaining the appearance of normative respectability. This conflict, which was becoming increasingly pronounced in the late 1940s, as Cold War sensibilities permeated cultural assumptions about behaviour and identity, was particularly problematic for women.[28] Constrained by restrictive norms of familialism and domesticity, women hovered uneasily on the margins of political legitimacy. The Housewives' attempts to mobilize women obliged them to establish beyond a doubt that womanly respectability would not be compromised by engagement in the public world of politics. In the increasingly restrictive social context created in part by anti-Communism, respectability could also be called into question by opponents who invoked fears of foreigners to discredit the organization.

## Roll Back Prices

In February 1947, news of the Housewives Consumers Association began making headlines in the pages of both the left-wing and mainstream press, from Cape Breton Island to British Columbia. Organizing in response to the repeal of federal price ceilings and galloping inflation, Housewives announced a Roll-Back-Prices campaign. Their program called for swift and decisive government action to protect consumers by reinstituting the price controls and subsidies that had guaranteed a minimum standard of living during wartime. From the West Coast, through the Prairies, and then into central and eastern Canada, Housewives Consumers Associations and Consumers Leagues came to life and began organizing parades, picketing stores that refused to lower their prices, printing leaflets, and making radio broadcasts. Membership in Housewives and Consumers groups across the country soared; by April, the Housewives claimed a national membership of 100,000 in 100 branches in cities and towns across Canada. Although it is difficult to establish the exact number of members and supporters of an organization such as the Housewives, which kept few records and has left only skimpy documentary evidence, it is certain, however, that people across Canada would have known about the Housewives and their campaigns.[29]

Loosely affiliated Housewives Consumers Associations, Housewives Leagues, and Consumers Associations in almost every province began working together to create a movement, using strategies that moved them out of the women's sections and onto the national pages of the daily newspapers. Women in major cities across Canada responded by signing petitions and postcards calling for a return to price controls and boycotting designated foods and clothing.

By early March, the western associations had banded together as the Western Housewives Consumers Associations, and with the help of economists provided by the research departments of sympathetic labour unions, produced a nine-point brief detailing their grievances and outlining proposals for change. Delegates, including a Saskatchewan provincial Cabinet minister, were nominated to take it to Ottawa.[30] Framing their demands in familial terms, the Housewives requested and got an audience with federal Finance Minister Douglas Abbott. Twelve women, representing Housewives in Manitoba, Saskatchewan, Alberta, and British Columbia journeyed to Ottawa for their meeting on 31 March. The news coverage of their lobby was sympathetic, reiterating the maternal language with which they expressed their demands, describing the Housewives as 'not interested in the new Spring hats displayed in Ottawa's store windows, but rather in milk for our babies [and] control of goods and services essential to the health and welfare of the Canadian people.'[31]

Finance Minister Abbott listened politely to their appeals for the reinstatement of price controls, and promised to take their views under consideration. Having been forewarned of their political sympathies, however, he could be confident that their demands could be safely disregarded. Early in the following week, he announced not the reinstitution of price controls, but rather their further removal.[32]

Less than a month later, the Housewives' campaign suffered another, much larger setback. On 23 April, the *Edmonton Journal* and the *Winnipeg Free Press* broke the startling news that at least four members of the delegation, as well as a number of the association's officers, were card-carrying Communists or the wives of provincial Labor Progressive Party leaders. The news was picked up by papers across the country, who ran inflammatory headlines announcing, 'Hundreds of Unwary Women Duped,' 'Communist Strategy Is Exposed,' and 'Winnipeg Central Headquarters for Communist-Led Housewives.'[33] With the publication of these articles, what had appeared to be a straightforward expression of frustration by ordinary women trying to keep house on dwindling family incomes was recast as a subversive activity.

These revelations were also a serendipity for the federal government, which could now ignore the Housewives' demands with impunity. Virtually overnight, the Housewives' challenge to Liberal policy, rooted in claims of motherhood and reflecting the interests of a large majority of Canadians, had been utterly neutralized. Even better, from the government's point of view, these revelations turned the tables, making the Housewives the target of an outraged public debate.

Newspapers across Canada filled their pages with articles and editorials expressing a range of viewpoints, but weighted heavily towards the side that saw Communist housewives as shabby fraud, a clever trap set by unscrupulous Communists, who were 'not genuinely concerned about prices, but wanted only to spread discontent ... for their own selfish and dangerous ends.'[34]

The dismal failure of the western delegation was a setback for the Housewives, but it was not yet the end. Learning quickly from their mistakes, the Housewives stepped up their campaign and attempted to reconfigure their public image. Renewing their efforts in May in preparation for another delegation in June, Housewives organized publicity events designed to highlight their connections to the family and distance themselves from the negative connotations of Communism.

In the first week of the campaign, eight hundred children paraded in Regina to protest the price of chocolate bars. The following week, twenty mothers and babies staged another parade to protest butter and milk prices. Ottawa Housewives spread the word by telephone, encouraging women to call their neighbours and urge them not to buy expensive cuts of meat. In Toronto, the Housewives set up tables on busy street corners on Saturdays, asking shoppers to sign postcards protesting high prices and making sure these were sent directly to the prime minister. And in June, Housewives across the country began a series of escalating boycotts to draw media attention to their campaign in preparation for their trek to Ottawa at the end of the month.[35]

## An Orchestrated Campaign

The Housewives denied the accusations against them, insisting that they welcomed members of all political stripes, but it appears that damage control had become a compelling concern. Distancing themselves from the discredited western delegation, Housewives spokesperson Mrs Lily Phelps made it clear that this second lobbying expedition would be very different from the first. 'This protest has been coined on a broader basis and broader representation,' she explained to reporters, 'and thus anticipates better results.'[36] Meanwhile, the politically tainted members of the previous lobby quietly announced that they would not be able to attend the June lobby, citing a lack of funds.[37]

The choice of Lily Phelps to lead the delegation also suggests the Housewives' enhanced awareness that it was important to create the correct political appearance, which meant erasing any obvious links to the LPP as well as any evidence of ethnicity. Phelps, who was president of the Toronto Housewives Consumers Association, was also a member of the Co-operative Commonwealth Federation (CCF), and neither the RCMP, the *Financial Post* or the Toronto *Globe and Mail* could accuse her of being a Communist. She was backed up by Mrs Rae Luckock, who was also a card-carrying social democrat who had won elections to both the Toronto Board of Education and the Ontario Legislature as a CCF candidate.[38] Twelve-year-old Shirley Endicott, representing the chocolate bar faction, provided additional support.[39] Although many of the activists in the HCA were members of various ethnic communities, none of these women were prominent among the delegates. Their absence in the context of the Housewives' strategic sensitivity to the ways that self-presentation was crucial to maintaining popular support adds credibility to Mary Prokop's assertion that the organization deployed its Anglo-Celtic members strategically as part of its public campaign.

The Housewives' adoption of the rolling pin as the symbol of their campaign also suggests a conscious effort to direct media attention away from their troublesome political affiliations. Deploying miniature wooden rolling-pins, made by themselves and inscribed with the words 'Roll Back Prices,' the Housewives provided the reporters covering their campaign with a catchy headline that invoked images of respectable domesticity. The newspapers obliged, running headlines such as 'Women Attack Prices – With Rolling Pins,' 'Rolling Pin Brigade Opens Local Campaign,' and 'Women Wield Rolling-Pins to Help Roll Back Prices.'[40]

No doubt hoping that the identity associated with housewifery would override that suggested by Communism, the Housewives made rolling pins the defining symbol of their campaign. To reinforce that metaphor, the two hundred delegates who arrived in Ottawa on 23 June to begin three days of lobbying gave handmade rolling-pin lapel pins to every MP in the House. Phelps herself brandished a full-size wooden rolling pin festooned with a blue ribbon during meetings with MPs and members of the Cabinet. While evidently intended to reinforce the House-wives' presentation of themselves as ordinary homemakers, the rolling pin has also typically been depicted as a weapon used by women in domestic disputes, thus invoking both female domesticity and resistance. In the real world, women some-times do deploy rolling pins as weapons, as did, for example, Guiseppina Bambace in turn-of-the-century New York City, who accompanied her grown socialist seamstress daughters to union meetings armed with a protective rolling pin tucked under her arm.[41] Indeed, a cartoon in the *Winnipeg Free Press* depicting a House-wife brandishing a rolling pin while she chased a greased pig labelled 'Prices' sug-gests that the dual meaning of the rolling pin as both a symbol of domesticity and a weapon was apparent to the HCA's supporters.[42]

The care that seems to have been taken to present a favourable image suggests that the Housewives' second trip to Ottawa was a carefully stage managed event designed to counter some of the bad publicity created by the first. And indeed, while newspaper accounts sometimes acknowledged their leftist political tenden-cies, the Housewives appear to have emerged from their second Ottawa trek with their reputations intact. Yet the media coverage of the event suggests an inverse relationship between respectability and political relevance.

Accounts of the Housewives' audience with the finance minister and two of his Cabinet colleagues in the Toronto, Montreal, and Ottawa newspapers reiterate their carefully constructed self-representations as harmless housewives, but in doing so, depict them in terms that are at once slightly ridiculous and sexually suggestive. A number of the reports focused on the assumed disruption to the normal gender and social order posed by a group of ordinary women attempting to dictate economic policy to a government minister. Evidently, this inversion seemed to some to be patently ridiculous. At least one newspaper sternly rebuked the Housewives and their supporters for daring to consider that ordinary citizens, and women at that, had the knowledge or the capacity to understand, much less contribute to, government policy. But the overwhelming response of the press was to treat the entire event as a joke.[43]

Although the Housewives purported to speak with authority, the description of Mrs Phelps wielding her rolling pin like a mace, while Mrs Beveridge explained the 'housewifely facts of life' to the finance minister suggested a parody of a real political encounter. The abundant description provided by the feature writers enabled readers to picture clearly the events: the Housewives, 'dark-haired matrons or motherly-looking, in their robin's egg blue crepe suits, chic print dresses and black net picture hats'; the finance minister, 'utterly charming, [and] wearing his friendliest smile,' equally well turned out in a ' neat brown double-breasted tropical worsted with a brown and white check cravat.'[44]

Already steeped in the restrictive idiom of postwar gender definitions, this depiction became almost salacious in its account of Finance Minister Douglas Abbott's departure from the room. Although anxious to leave, he was prevented from doing so by the Housewives, who felt that their concerns had not been adequately addressed. He finally managed to escape by squeezing through a doorway blocked by the ample figure of the 'buxom Mrs. Florence Flowerdale,' thus demonstrating 'the agility of an adagio dancer.'[45] One report, describing the event in terms that made it appear more like a slapstick comedy than a political lobby, described Abbott running down the hall of the East Block, followed by the cries of the women, 'sounding like 100-odd soprano Lou Costellos calling, "Mr Abbott! Mr Abbott!"'[46]

Overwhelmed with descriptive detail and obsessed with the gender dynamics of the encounter, these accounts deflect readers' attention from the political content of the interchange and from the minister's response to the Housewives' astute and pointed questions. A critical reader might wonder whether the women's readiness to challenge the minister on statements he had made in his budget speech and to dispute his Cabinet colleagues' claims that high food prices actually meant higher incomes for farmers wasn't the reason he was so anxious to escape.

The Housewives left Ottawa declaring themselves unsatisfied with the response of the government and promising to continue their campaign. Announcing that their campaign had only begun, Housewives endeavoured to keep the issue in the news and the pressure on government by speaking at public meetings, circulating pamphlets, and joining the picket lines of striking workers, where they gave speeches about the relationship between wage demands and price controls. In the fall, Roll-Back-Prices conferences were held in Toronto, Montreal, and Ottawa, and in December, seventy-five delegates met with the finance minister to urge him to reconsider price controls. Predictably, Abbott refused to discuss any change in policy, but the Housewives' relentless agitation kept the issue of prices in the news. Editorials decrying the inadequacy of the government's response to high prices and urging price controls appeared in both the *Ottawa Journal* and the *Toronto Daily Star*, while Abbott himself was portrayed as evasive and high-handed.[47]

## The March of a Million Names

In January 1948, the Dominion Bureau of Statistics announced that the cost of living had reached an all-time high, and the Housewives responded with calls for a new wave of buyers' strikes.[48] Only days after the publication of a report in the

*Toronto Daily Star* that boycotts were having a significant impact on sales, the Housewives launched their new campaign, the March of a Million Names. Stressing the breadth of popular support for their proposals, the Housewives announced their plans to collect a million endorsements by circulating petitions and presenting them to the finance minister.

The Housewives embarked on another round of leafleting, radio broadcasts, conferences, and public meetings, taking special care to point out the diversity of the groups and individuals who supported their cause. Members of the clergy, trade unionists, and child-care activists participated in public meetings calling for government controls on runaway prices and pointing to big business as the sole beneficiary of current policies. In particular, the Housewives accused the major bakeries of meeting in secret to illegally fix prices. They sent telegrams to Prime Minister Mackenzie King and to Paul Martin, chair of the Special Parliamentary Committee on Prices, alerting them to this activity and urging prosecution of the bakers under both the Combines Investigation Act and the Criminal Code.[49]

In preparation for yet another lobbying trip to Ottawa, during which they also planned to establish a national consumers' organization, Housewives' Associations from Cape Breton Island to Vancouver organized a variety of activities designed to reach broadly across the community. Radio broadcasts aired in Cape Breton, Regina, Montreal, Edmonton, Medicine Hat, and Timmins, in English and French, urging people to support the campaign in the interests of securing a better life for themselves and their children. Provincial prices conferences were organized in Edmonton, Vancouver, and Regina. In Toronto, Housewives canvassed door to door; in Winnipeg and Vancouver, they set up tables in shops and department stores to gather signatures on petitions supporting their call for the reinstatement of price controls. Articles endorsing the Housewives' campaign and eliciting support in the left-wing ethnic press, such as *Ukrainske Zhitya* (Ukrainian Life), the Finnish language *Varpaus*, and the *Canadian Jewish Weekly*, and their successful elicitation of support from the left-wing Association of United Ukrainian Canadians (AUUC), suggest the extent to which the organization depended on women in ethnic communities. On this point, RCMP reports confirm the oral testimonies of HCA activists, particularly with regard to the very active role of left-wing Ukrainians, who helped fill the halls in meetings in Winnipeg and various locales in the West. The AUUC also contributed much-needed funds and helped gather signatures on petitions, passed out pamphlets, and organized rallies.[50]

For their part, English-language Communist newspapers the *Canadian Tribune*, the *Westerner*, and the *Pacific Tribune* also endorsed the Housewives' campaign, as did municipal councils, labour organizations, churches, home and school associations, Catholic Women's Leagues, veterans' associations, pensioners' groups, religious leaders, teachers, doctors, town councillors, and other prominent citizens. Much of their support came from labour organizations, including trades and labour councils and a number of labour unions, but also from the Alberta Farmers Union, a number of prominent CCFers, including national CCF leader M.J. Coldwell and Saskatchewan premier T.C. Douglas.[51]

Their projected goal of a million endorsements for their program would, they asserted, constitute the largest such petition to government in Canadian history. Such a great number and variety of supporters, the Housewives pointed out, represented significant electoral strength, which could be used to replace the current government if its members persisted in their current policies. Citing broad popular support for price controls and general dissatisfaction with the government's response to what they identified as a crisis, they reminded King that a previous prime minister, R.B. Bennett, had ignored similar calls by large numbers of citizens for radical policy change to his peril. Contending that the government was seriously underestimating Canadians if they thought only Communists were concerned about the high cost of living, they threatened to work hard to bring down the Liberals in the election if their demands were not heard.[52]

Speaking in the name of thousands of citizens from all walks of life, the Housewives declared themselves unimpressed with the government's arguments against price controls and with its evasion of its responsibility to protect the health and welfare of Canadian citizens, significant numbers of whom, they stated, were already suffering from malnutrition as a result of high commodity prices. Calling for the restoration of price and rent controls and a lifting of the ban on imported fruit and vegetables, as well as significant improvements in existing social programs, the Housewives blamed the government for bowing to 'the monied interests of this country,' and recommended that they redress this injustice by reimposing the excess profits tax.

The finance minister, who had accused Canadians of living beyond their means, came in for particular criticism by the Housewives, who dubbed him, 'Eat Less Abbott.' 'Mr Abbott has dared to say that our children and families should do with less food, less clothing, less medical care, less education, less of the necessities of life. We are of a different notion,' they stated. 'If the government made proper use of social resources in the interests of the majority,' they suggested, there would be more than enough for all.[53] Hoping, perhaps, to shift individual members of Parliament, if not the government, they also petitioned the prime minister and the MPs to permit a free vote on the issue of price controls.[54]

The Housewives' efforts to establish broad popular support for their campaign were hampered by an increasingly vitriolic anti-Communism in the mainstream media, of which the Housewives were a regular target. Editorials published in the *Hamilton Spectator*, the *Windsor Star*, and the *Halifax Herald* accused the Housewives of being a particularly pernicious kind of fifth column, whose sole objective was to undermine freedom and democracy and deliver unsuspecting Canadians to their evil masters in Russia. Although they claimed to be housewives, one such article asserted, they were really a Communist front, 'organized for the violent seizure of Canada's material and human resources to enrich the world's most tyrannical dictatorship.' Don Cameron, Ronald Williams, and the other authors of these articles suggested that ordinary, decent women who were taken in by the Housewives' apparent sincerity, and who supported their campaigns, were taking a huge risk. Not only were they in danger of becoming part of an 'involuntary fifth column,' but they were almost sure to lose their good reputations as respectable women into the bargain. In addition to being publicly vilified, the Housewives were under constant surveillance by the RCMP's Special Branch, which sent regular memoranda to J.L. Ilsley, federal justice minister, detailing their activities and speculating on their intentions.[55]

In April, when the Housewives again attempted to meet with the Cabinet, having gathered over seven hundred thousand of their projected million endorsements, their requests for an audience were refused. Calling the Housewives nothing but a Communist front, whose object was to 'foster Communist propaganda,' Abbott contended that the government would not be justified in 'facilitating movements of that kind.' Indeed, when Mrs Rae Luckock, who had succeeded Mrs Phelps as president of the Housewives, attempted to enter the House of Commons bearing an armload of petitions, she was intercepted by two large RCMP officers.[56]

The finance minister's decision was applauded in the House of Commons, and even the CCF leader, M.J. Coldwell, made only a token objection. It was pointed out that refusal to see the Housewives would leave the government open to accusations of disregarding the most elementary rights of citizenship, and that most of the five hundred delegates, and most of the organizations they represented, had no connection to Communism. Abbott acknowledged both of these arguments, yet defended his decision on the grounds that those who had joined the movement were duped, and had inadvertently become propagandists for Communist dogma. His accusations were bolstered by the simultaneous disclosure in the *Montreal Gazette* that Housewives' literature had been found in a police raid on the Montreal French-language Communist newspaper *Combat*.[57]

## Dupes of Communism

Politicians and the press publicly dismissed the Housewives as a political force, either by taking them at their word and treating them as merely women, and thus not worthy of serious consideration, or by identifying them as Communists, and thus not entitled to the normal rights of citizenship.[58] Yet it was clear that they were articulating demands that a large number of Canadians found relevant. Early in 1948, the *Toronto Daily Star* reported that shopping boycotts were not only well supported by consumers, they were having a significant impact on merchants. Sales were down between 10 and 50 per cent, and it was generally agreed that prices had reached the 'supersaturation point.'[59] Moreover, although there was little doubt that many of the Housewives were, in fact, Communists, many ordinary Canadians supported their campaigns.

Women had to consider, however, whether being part of this movement was worth the cost. Between 1947 and 1950, a steady stream of articles appeared in newspapers and in magazines as diverse as *Chatelaine* and the *Financial Post*, portraying women who joined the organization or endorsed their campaigns as impressionable fools who had been duped by Communists into betraying their country and undermining all the values for which Canadians had so recently fought.[60] Even worse, close contact with Communists put women at risk of moral contagion. The overlapping membership of the Housewives Consumers Association with left-wing ethnic organizations, such as the Association of United Ukrainian Canadians, the United Jewish People's Order (UJPO), the Finnish Organization of Canada, the United Farm Labour Temple (UFLT), and the Russian Canadian Organization created further opportunities for red-baiting. While the members of the Housewives Consumers Association may look like housewives, these writers suggested, they weren't housewives at all. On the contrary, as Communists and members of non-Anglo ethnic communities, they were 'foreigners,' an identity which, they implied, was incompatible with the identity of housewife. The message to women was clear: The feminine respectability inherent in the identity of housewife was inelastic, contingent on the maintenance of a safe distance from suspicious ethnicities and political beliefs.

While media coverage steadily undermined the Housewives' claims to respectability, an alternative consumer organization emerged. In September of 1947, before the Housewives had acted on their proposal to establish a national federation of consumer leagues, the Liberals quietly sponsored one of its own. This new entity, the Canadian Association of Consumers (CAC), proved to be an elite organization that captured little popular support. Yet the favourable publicity the formation of the CAC attracted made it appear, for a time, as a more respectable alternative to the Housewives Consumers.[61]

From its inception, the CAC claimed to represent 'hundreds of thousands' of women through the 'more than 20 national women's organizations and major French-speaking groups whose leaders were part of the organizing committee.' The CAC represented itself as financially independent and self-funded, stressing that it was 'an independent, democratic, non-political organization to be completely controlled by the women who are and become members of it,' despite the fact that its set-up costs were covered by a $15,000 grant from the federal government. In contrast to the Housewives, who had been organizing home-cooking sales and bazaars to raise operating funds, most of the CAC's operating costs were also government-funded.[62]

Public statements by Mrs Blanche Marshall, President of the National Council of Women and chair of the CAC's interim committee, suggest that the primary drawing card of the CAC was its distinction from the Housewives Consumers Association. Specifically disassociating itself from any groups advocating the reimposition of price controls, despite the enormous popularity of this demand, the CAC outlined its objectives as pluralist. The new organization, Marshall explained, 'supports a policy of reasonable prices and a square deal for business and producer groups in the community [and] believes the intelligent way of working is through giving consideration in all interests in the economy as they affect the consumer.' Sidestepping the question of advocacy, she asserted that the 'policy of the CAC is to do a thorough fact-finding job before making recommendations.' Its first priority was keeping Canadian women well informed on matters of consumer interest; 'expressing opinions to government, manufacturers, and producers, and concerning itself with quality standards' were additional, but secondary, objectives.[63]

The neutral wording and non-interventionist strategy of the CAC was the antithesis of the program proposed at the founding convention of the Housewives and Consumers Federation of Canada. Over five hundred delegates representing housewives' organizations and labour unions from every province, and at least two police informers, gathered in Ottawa in April 1948 to outline an ambitious plan for sweeping social and economic change. Despite the active participation of a number of trade union men, their program reflected a kind of socialist maternalism, calling for free maternity care before and after birth, including an allowance for newborns; federal, provincial, and municipal aid to establish and maintain new child-care centres and nurseries for working mothers; low cost or free hot lunches for school children including one free glass of milk a day; university scholarships; reform of old age pensions to reduce the age limit and eliminate means tests; federal and provincial responsibility for social services, including mothers' and widows' allowances, and a universal hospitalization plan. In addition to these demands, some of which were part of a general call for social reform emanating from the Communist and social democratic left, they called for special government services for married working mothers. These more radical demands included setting up public laundry depots, home cleaning services and hot food centres providing food for home use.[64]

The CAC made no effort to compete with the Housewives' program, but focused instead on creating a more favourable public image. This consisted primarily of reminding people of the Housewives' Communist connections. Describing itself as 'non-political,' the CAC actively distanced itself from consumer groups that, it charged, had been 'infiltrated by Communists.' Marshall pointed out that the provisional National Committee of the Housewives and Consumers Federation, for example, was headed by Mrs Ann Ross of Winnipeg, whom she accused of being 'an avowed member of the Labor Progressive Party,' although, in fact, Ross, unlike her husband, was not a Communist and never joined the party.[65] Trading heavily on the white, middle-class respectability of its own executive, the CAC sent out a warning to housewives to beware of alleged consumer organizations which did not contain 'Canadian' in the name. The implications of this distinction would have been clear to people accustomed to anti-Communist rhetoric that linked foreign-ness to Communists; with its ethnically diverse composition and class-conscious politics, the Housewives and Consumers Federation was not quite respectable.[66]

In contrast to the Housewives, the CAC mounted no campaigns and attracted very little popular support. Until the 1960s, the CAC attracted only a small number of members, depending for over half of its costs on government funding. The strongest support for the CAC came from elite women, who served as the organization's officers. Many of them began their terms on the CAC executive with high social status and good political connections and they often landed well-paid positions in government and industry when they left.[67] The CAC never became the basis for a popular consumer movement, nor, in all likelihood, was it intended to; rather, it was put in place specifically to forestall the growth of the radical consumer movement that had already formed.

### Conclusion

The Housewives and Consumers Federation of Canada, which had hoped to mobilize Canadian women into a politically effective consumer movement and promote an expansion of democratic rights, was stillborn. By 1950, the Housewives Consumers Association had faded into irrelevance and lost most of its active members to a new organization, the Congress of Canadian Women, an organization that followed closely the Communist Party line.[68] In the triumph of respectability over relevance, Canadian consumers had lost an opportunity to expand their political influence and speak directly to the shaping of government policy.

Yet, although the Housewives ultimately failed to achieve their objectives, their achievements are nonetheless important. During a time when prescriptive definitions of respectability were gaining widespread acceptance, laying the foundation for the political restraint that characterized the 1950s, the Housewives were remarkably successful in mobilizing large numbers of Canadian women and men, despite their well-known Communist connections. In addition, their remarkable success in mobilizing women, who supported the Housewives' campaigns in huge numbers, constituted a challenge to restrictive postwar norms of politically passive femininity. They achieved this, not by rejecting contemporary common-sense notions linking femininity and domesticity, but rather by embracing existing cultural assumptions about female identity and redefining them. In other words, they expressed political entitlement in terms that were consistent with their experiences as women. Political activism, so defined, was compatible with their identities as mothers and housewives, identities that were both culturally recognized and endorsed, and personally authenticating. Finally, by suggesting that consumers, like producers, made a vital contribution to the economy, and thus were entitled to exercise their rights as citizens by participating in governance, the Housewives argued for a broader understanding of citizenship itself, a notion that placed at its centre the conviction that politics was not rightly the exclusive domain of elites, but a right and a duty of ordinary people.

In centring the activist role of ethnic women on the left during the Cold War, this essay joins the important literature in feminist labour and left history that has de-centred the 'white woman worker' as a central female subject and that recognizes a working-class women's history of 'unequal sisters.'[69] In so doing, this study enlarges and even redefines the political from the vantage point of marginalized and red-baited female consumer citizens in a context in which the state challenged their right to participate as full citizens.

NOTES

While any shortcomings in this essay are mine, the paper benefited from the suggestions of the volume's editors, Marlene Epp, Franca Iacovetta, and Frances Swyripa. Financial support was provided by the Social Sciences and Humanities Research Council of Canada and the University of Manitoba.

1   Interview by the author with Mary Prokop, Toronto, 15 December 1998. On earlier periods, see, for example, José Moya, 'Italians in Buenos Aire's Anarchist Movement: Gender Ideology and Women's Participation, 1890–1910,' and Jennifer Guglielmo, 'Italian Women's Proletarian Feminism in the New York City Garment Trades, 1890s–1940s,' in Donna Gabaccia and Franca Iacovetta, eds, *Women, Gender and Transnational Lives: Italian Workers of the World* (Toronto: University of Toronto Press, 2002), 189–216 and 247–298; Dana Frank, *Purchasing Power: Consumer Organizing, Gender, and the Seattle Labor Movement, 1919–1929* (New York: Cambridge University Press, 1994); Dana Frank, 'Gender, Consumer Organizing, and the Seattle Labor Move-

ment, 1919–1929,' in Ava Baron, ed., *Work Engendered: Toward a New History of American Labor* (Ithaca: Cornell University Press, 1991), 273–95.

2  Other studies that document the Housewives Consumers Association include Dan Azoulay, '"Ruthless in a Ladylike Way": CCF Women Confront the Postwar "Communist Menace,"' *Ontario History* 89, no. 1 (March 1997): 23–44 ; Joy Parr, *Domestic Goods: The Material, the Moral, and the Economic in the Postwar Years* (Toronto: University of Toronto Press, 1999), esp. chapter 4; and Joan Sangster, *Dreams of Equality: Women on the Canadian Left, 1920–1950* (Toronto: McClelland and Stewart, 1989), esp. 165–92.

3  On metaphors of Communists as moral threats and the concept of domestic containment, see, for example, Elaine Tyler May, *Homeward Bound: American Families in the Cold War Era* (New York: Basic Books, 1988); Reg Whitaker and Gary Marcuse, *Cold War Canada: The Making of a National Insecurity State, 1945–1957* (Toronto: University of Toronto Press, 1994); the essays by Julie Guard, Franca Iacovetta, Mercedes Steedman, and others in Gary Kinsman, Dieter Buse, and Mercedes Steedman, eds, *Whose National Security? Canadian State Surveillance and the Creation of Enemies* (Toronto: Between the Lines, 2000). For a discussion of enemy aliens and the Communist internees see various essays, including those by Reg Whitaker and Gregory S. Kealey and by Ian Radforth in Franca Iacovetta, Roberto Perin, and Angelo Principe, eds, *Enemies Within: Italian and Other Internees in Canada and Abroad* (Toronto: University of Toronto Press, 2000).

4  Studies of Anglo-Celtic and immigrant women that take up the problem of respectability include Joy Parr, *The Gender of Breadwinners* (Toronto: University of Toronto Press, 1991); Joan Sangster, *Earning Respect: The Lives of Working Women In Small-Town Ontario, 1920–1960* (Toronto: University of Toronto Press, 1995). Some studies of immigrant women suggest that respectability on these terms was not a concern for them. See Ardis Cameron, *Radicals of the Worst Sort: Laboring Women in Lawrence, Massachusetts, 1890–1912* (Urbana and Chicago: University of Illinois Press, 1993); Ruth Frager, *Sweatshop Strife: Class, Ethnicity, and Gender in the Jewish Labour Movement of Toronto, 1900–1939* (Toronto: University of Toronto Press, 1992); Franca Iacovetta, *Such Hard-Working People: Italian Immigrants in Postwar Toronto* (Montreal and Kingston: McGill-Queen's University Press, 1992); Franca Iacovetta, 'From Contadina to Worker: Southern Italian Immigrant Working Women in Toronto, 1947–1962,' in Jean Burnett, ed., *Looking into My Sister's Eyes: An Exploration in Women's History* (Toronto: Multicultural History Society of Ontario, 1986); Mercedes Steedman, *Angels of the Workplace: Women and the Construction of Gender Relations in the Canadian Clothing Industry, 1890–1940* (Toronto: Oxford University Press, 1997); Robert Ventresca, '"Cowering Women, Combative Men?" Femininity, Masculinity, and Ethnicity on Strike in Two Southern Ontario Towns, 1964–1966,' *Labour/Le Travail* 39 (Spring 1996): 125–58.

5  For example, Varpu Lindström, *Defiant Sisters: A Social History of Finnish Immigrant Women in Canada,* 2d ed. (Toronto: Multicultural History Society of Ontario, 1992); Frances Swyripa, *Wedded to the Cause: Ukrainian-Canadian Women and Ethnic Identity, 1891–1991* (Toronto: University of Toronto Press, 1993); Frager, *Sweatshop Strife.* For an attempt at a more comparative approach, see Linda Kealey, *Enlisting Women for the Cause: Women, Labour, and the Left in Canada, 1890–1920* (Toronto: University of Toronto Press, 1998).

6  See, for example, the essays in Burnet, *Looking into My Sister's Eyes* and in Seth Kovan and Sonya Michel, eds, *Mothers of a New World: Maternalist Politics and the Origins of Welfare States* (New York: Routledge, 1993).

7  I provide a much more detailed treatment of this issue in a forthcoming article that profiles both the Anglo-Celtic and ethnic women within the HCA. In addition to the ethnic examples in the text, other ethnic women included Ukrainian Canadians Mary Kardash and Sinefta Kozema, Finnish Canadians Taimi (Pitkanen) Davis and Mary Dennis (evidently of Russian background), as well as Lil Ilomaki, of Jewish-Polish background. Much of the information comes from interviews with former members of the HCA.

8  CBC Archives Radio News, 1 May 1947; RCMP case file, Housewives Consumers Association, Saskatoon, Saskatchewan, 24 April 1947, Cst. J.A. MacKenzie, National Archives of Canada (hereafter NA), Housewives and Consumers Federation of Canada, RG 146, vol. 3353, pt 1.

9  *Canadian Political Facts, 1945–1976* (Toronto: Methuen, 1977), 128.

10  'Bacon Hits 90 Cents Toronto Housewives Suggest Buying Strike,' *Toronto Daily Star,* 5 January 1948; 'Housewives' Agitation,' editorial, *Ottawa Citizen,* 26 April 1947; 'Buyers Strike in B.C. by Housewives,' *Montreal Standard,* 10 May 1947; *Winnipeg Free Press,* 12 May 1947; *Montreal Gazette,* 12 May 1947; *Ottawa Journal,* 13 May 1947, RCMP clipping file, Housewives Consumers Association Toronto, NA, RG 146, vol. 3440, pt 1.

11  On related struggles in other contexts, see Frager, *Sweatshop Strife;* Frank, *Purchasing Power.*

12  Untitled text of radio broadcasts, 25 and 27 March 1947, attached to RCMP case file, C.P. Activity in Labor-Progressive Party, Saskatoon, Saskatchewan, Cst. J.A. MacKenzie, NA, RG 146, vol. 3353, pt 1; 'Build More Homes Restore Price Controls Women's Meet Asks,' *Daily Tribune,* 18 October 1947, RCMP clipping file, RG 146, vol. 3353, pt 1; 'Meeting Here of Housewives,' *Ottawa Citizen,* 9 February 1948, RCMP clipping file, RG 146, vol. 3440, pt 1.

13  Frager, *Sweatshop Strife;* Carmela Patrias, 'Relief Strike: Immigrant Workers and the Great Depression in Crowland, Ontario, 1930–1935,' in Franca Iacovetta with Paula Draper and Robert Ventresca, eds, *A Nation of Immigrants: Women, Workers and Communities in Canadian History, 1840s–1960s* (Toronto: University of Toronto Press,

1998), 322–358; Paula Hyman, 'Immigrant Women and Consumer Protest: The New York City Kosher Meat Boycott of 1902,' *American Jewish History* 70, no. 1 (September 1980): 91–105; Roz Usiskin, 'Winnipeg's Jewish Women of the Left: Radical and Traditional,' in Daniel Stone, ed., *Jewish Life and Times*, vol. 3, *Jewish Radicalism in Winnipeg, 1905–1960* (Winnipeg: Jewish Heritage Centre of Western Canada, 2002), 106–22.

14 Prokop, interview; interview with Alice Maigis and Lil Ilomaki, Toronto, 12 December 1996; interview with Mona Morgan, Peggy Chunn, and Audrey Modzir, Vancouver, 24 July 1998. All interviews by the author.

15 Cameron, *Radicals of the Worst Sort*.

16 Jennifer Guglielmo, 'Italian Women's Proletarian Feminism in the New York City Garment Trades, 1890s–1940s,' in Gabaccia and Iacovetta, *Women, Gender, and Transnational Lives*, 247–98; Donna Gabaccia, *Militants and Migrants: Rural Sicilians Become American Workers* (New Brunswick, NJ: Rutgers University Press, 1988); Iacovetta, *Such Hard-Working People*.

17 *The Canadian Unionist*, 1946–7.

18 Ivan Avakumovic, *The Communist Party in Canada: A History* (Toronto: McClelland and Stewart, 1975); Norman Penner, *Canadian Communism: The Stalin Years and Beyond* (Toronto: Methuen, 1988); William Rodney, *Soldiers of the International: A History of the Communist Party of Canada, 1919–1929* (Toronto: University of Toronto Press, 1968).

19 See Julie Guard, 'Women Worth Watching: Radical Housewives in Cold War Canada,' in Buse, Kinsman, and Steedman, *Whose National Security?*, 73–88.

20 The narrowing of the male left's focus away from the community and onto the labour movement is examined for the United States by George Lipsitz, *Rainbow at Midnight: Labor and Culture in the 1940s* (Urbana and Chicago: University of Illinois Press, 1994). The origins of consumer culture are explored by Gary Cross, *Time and Money: The Making of Consumer Culture* (London: Routledge, 1993).

21 Columba Furio, 'The Cultural Background of the Italian Immigrant Woman and Its Impact on Her Unionization in the New York City Garment Industry, 1880–1919,' in George E. Pozzetta, ed., *Pane e Lavoro: The Italian American Working Class* (Toronto: Multicultural History Society of Ontario, 1980), 95, cited in Guglielmo, 'Italian Women's Proletarian Feminism.'

22 Guglielmo, 'Italian Women's Proletarian Feminism;' José Moya, 'Italians in Buenos Aires' Anarchist Movement: Gender Ideology and Women's Participation, 1890–1910,' in Gabaccia and Iacovetta, *Women, Gender, and Transnational Lives*, 332–67.

23 See, for example, the essays in Gisela Bock and Pat Thane, eds, *Maternity and Gender Policies: Women and the Rise of the European Welfare States, 1880s–1950s* (London: Routledge, 1991); and in Seth Kovan and Sonya Michel, eds, *Mothers of a New World*.

24  Marilyn Lake, 'A Revolution in the Family: The Challenge and Contradictions of Maternal Citizenship in Australia,' in Kovan and Michel, *Mothers of a New World*, 378–95; Jane Lewis, 'Models of Equality for Women: The Case of State Support for Children in Twentieth-Century Britain,' in Bock and Thane, *Maternity and Gender Policies*, 73–92; Pat Thane, 'Visions of Gender in the Making of the British Welfare States: The Case of Women in the British Labour Party and Social Policy, 1906–1945,' in Bock and Thane, *Maternity and Gender Policies*, 93–118.

25  A similar case, in which American Communist women sought to legitimate their political activism by reference to their familial responsibilities is Deborah A. Gerson, 'Is the Family Now Subversive? Familialism against McCarthyism,' in Joanne Meyerowitz, ed., *Not June Cleaver: Women and Gender in Postwar America, 1945–1960* (Philadelphia: Temple University Press, 1994), 151–76. Other examples of working-class American women organizing as housewives and consumers are detailed in Frank, 'Gender, Consumer Organizing, and the Seattle Labor Movement'; Susan Levine, 'Workers' Wives: Gender, Class, and Consumerism in the 1920s United States,' *Gender and History* 3, no. 1 (Spring 1991): 45–64; Paula Pfeffer, 'The Women behind the Union: Halena Wilson, Rosina Tucker, and the Ladies' Auxiliary to the Brotherhood of Sleeping Car Porters,' *Labor History* 36, no. 4 (Fall 1995): 557–78.

26  Caroline Waldron, 'Anarchist Motherhood: Toward the Making of a Revolutionary Proletariat in Illinois Coal Towns,' in Iacovetta and Gabaccia, *Women, Gender, and Transnational Lives*, 217–46.

27  For example, Kealey, *Enlisting Women for the Cause*; Ester Reiter, 'First Class Workers Don't Want Second Class Wages: The Lanark Strike in Dunnville,' in Joy Parr, ed., *A Diversity of Women: Ontario, 1945–1980* (Toronto: University of Toronto Press, 1995), 168–99; Steve Penfold, '"Have You No Manhood In You?": Gender and Class in the Cape Breton Coal Towns, 1920–26,' *Acadiensis* 23, no. 2 (Spring 1994): 21–44; Ventresca, '"Cowering Women, Combative Men?"'

28  Joan Sangster, 'Doing Two Jobs: The Wage-Earning Mother, 1945–70,' in Parr, *A Diversity of Women*, 98–134; Veronica Strong-Boag, 'Canada's Wage-earning Wives and the Construction of the Middle Class, 1945–60,' *Journal of Canadian Studies* 29, no. 3 (Fall 1994): 5–25; Strong-Boag, 'Their Side of the Story: Women's Voices from Ontario Suburbs, 1945–60,' in Parr, *A Diversity of Women*, 46–74.

29  'Demand March on Ottawa to Protest Prices Call from Women's Committee of BC L.P.P., *Ottawa Journal*, 7 February 1947; 'Protesting Housewives,' *Regina Leader Post*, 1 March 1947, RCMP clipping files, NA, RG 146, vol. 3353, pt 2A.

30  'Western Women Find Trip to Ottawa Futile,' *Montreal Standard*, 5 April 1947; 'Protesting Housewives,' *Leader Post*, 1 March 1947; 'Second Prices Delegate Named,' *Regina Leader Post*, 27 March 1947; 'Housewife Envoy Going to Ottawa,' *Winnipeg Free Press*, 27 March 1947, RCMP clipping file, NA, RG 146, vol. 3353, supp. 1, pt 1.

31 'Western Women Determined to See Finance Minister,' *Ottawa Evening Citizen*, 31 March 1947, RCMP clipping file, NA, RG 146, vol. 3353, supp. 1, pt 1.

32 'Women Fail to Have Controls Restored,' *Winnipeg Free Press*, 3 April 1947, RCMP clipping file, NA, RG 146, vol. 3353, supp. 1, pt 1.

33 'Communist Strategy Is Exposed'; 'Programme All Cut and Dried: Winnipeg Central Headquarters for Communist-Led Housewives'; 'Hundreds of Unwary Women Duped: Communists Head Up Housewives' Consumers Group,' *Winnipeg Free Press*, c. April 1947, RCMP clipping files, NA, RG 146, vol. 3353, pt 1 and supp. 1, pt 1.

34 'Communist Strategy Is Exposed.'

35 'Regina Housewives League Plans Picketing Programme,' *Winnipeg Free Press*, May 1947; 'Hoping to Spread Strike of Buyers, Western Women Open Month-Long Campaign against Rising Prices, Sympathy in East,' *Ottawa Citizen*, 10 May 1947; 'Buyers' Strike Started in B.C. by Housewives,' *Montreal Standard*, 10 May 1947; 'Strikes of Buyers Gather Strength,' *Montreal Gazette*, 11 May 1947; 'Housewives to Protest High Prices,' *Ottawa Citizen*, 13 May 1947; RCMP clipping files, NA, RG 146, vol. 3353, pt 1.

36 'Women Attack Prices – With Rolling-Pins,' *Winnipeg Free Press*, 24 June 1947, RCMP clipping file, NA, RG 146, vol. 3353, supp. 1, pt 1.

37 RCMP case file, Housewives and Consumers Association, Saskatoon, Saskatchewan, 23 June 1947, Cst. J.A. MacKenzie, NA, RG 146, vol. 3353, supp. 1, pt 1.

38 Rae Luckock's involvement with the Housewives Consumers Association eventually led to her expulsion from the CCF. See Azoulay, '"Ruthless in a Ladylike Way."'

39 'Housewives Hit Ottawa with Postcard Barrage,' *Globe and Mail*, 23 June 1947; 'Rolling Pin Brigade Opens Local Campaign,' *Ottawa Citizen*, 24 June 1947, RCMP clipping file, NA, RG 146, vol. 3353, supp. 1, vol. 1; Sangster, *Dreams of Equality*, 188.

40 'Women Attack Prices – With Rolling-Pins,' *Winnipeg Free Press*, 24 June 1947, RCMP clipping file, NA, RG 146, vol. 3353, supp. 1, vol. 1.

41 Guglielmo, 'Italian Women's Proletarian Feminism.'

42 'The Greasy Pig,' *Winnipeg Free Press*, 8 July 1947, RCMP clipping file, RG 146, vol. 3353, pt 1A.

43 'The Housewives Go on Strike,' *Albertan*, 12 May 1947; 'Housewives Bent on Rolling Back Prices,' *Ottawa Journal*, 24 June 1947; 'Would Wield Pins on MPs – Ladies Invade Parliament Hill,' *Ottawa Citizen*, 24 June 1947; '"My Wife's Kicking, Too" Abbott Tells Housewives,' *Toronto Daily Star*, 25 June 1947; 'Controls Stay off Abbott Declares,' *Ottawa Evening Citizen*, 25 June 1947; 'Housewives Chase Abbott for Roll-Back in Prices,' *Ottawa Journal*, 25 June 1947; 'Women Wield Rolling-Pins to Help Roll Back Prices,' *Globe and Mail*, 25 June 1947, 12; 'Only His Speed on Foot Saves Him As Irate Housewives Storm Abbott,' *Montreal Gazette*, 25 June 1947, RCMP clipping files, NA, RG 146, vol. 3353, supp. 1, vol. 1.

44  'What a Performance! Housewives Chase Abbott for Roll-Back in Prices,' *Ottawa Journal*, 25 June 1947, RCMP clipping file, NA, RG 146, vol. 3353, supp. 1, vol. 1.
45  Ibid.
46  Ibid.
47  'These Rolling-Pin Women and Their Demands,' *Ottawa Journal*, 25 June 1947; 'Consumers in Trouble,' *Toronto Daily Star*, 12 December 1947; 'Claim Abbott Gave Visitors Frozen Front, Consumers Assert He "Dodged" All Questions,' *Ottawa Citizen*, 13 December 1947, RCMP clipping files, NA, RG 146, vol. 3440, pt 1.
48  'Bacon Hits 90 Cents Toronto Housewives Suggest Buying Strike,' *Toronto Daily Star*, 5 January 1948; 'Buyer's Strike against Increased Prices Advocated,' *Ottawa Citizen*, 6 January 1948, RCMP clipping files, NA, RG 146, vol. 3353, supp. 1, vol. 1.
49  'Will Sign up Million to Make Ottawa Move Symbol 2 Rolling Pins,' *Toronto Daily Star*, 20 January 1948, RCMP clipping files, NA, RG 146, vol. 3440, pt 1; 'Meeting Here of Housewives April Convention Will Discuss Prices,' *Ottawa Citizen*, 10 February 1948, RCMP clipping file, NA, RG 146, vol. 3353, supp. 1, vol. 2; 'Housewives Urge Gov't to Prosecute Bakeries,' *Pacific Tribune*, 19 March 1948; 'Prosecute Big Bakers Housewives Demand; Charge Prices Fixed,' *Canadian Tribune*, 20 March 1948; 'Prices Probe Ignores Housewives Request; Carry Fight to MPs,' *Canadian Tribune*, 27 March 1948, RCMP clipping file, NA, RG 146, vol. 3440, pt 1.
50  RCMP case files, Association of United Ukrainian Canadians, 3 March 1948; 12 April 1948, 5 June 1948, NA, RG 146, vol. 3440, pt 2A; RCMP clipping files, NA RG 146, vol. 3353, pt 1A; supp. 1, pt 2; interviews with Audrey Modzir, Mona Morgan, and Peggy Chunn and with Mary Prokop.
51  'Will Sign up Million to Make Ottawa Move Symbol 2 Rolling Pins,' *Toronto Daily Star*, 20 January 1948, RCMP clipping files, NA, RG 146, vol. 3440, pt 1; RCMP memoranda, NA, RG 146, vol. 3353, pt 2.
52  'Voice of the Bush,' radio broadcast, Timmins, Ontario, 28 April 1948, NA, RG 146, vol. 3353, pt 2; 'Biggest Petition in History Demands King Act on Prices,' *Canadian Tribune*, 17 April 1948.
53  Letter to Prime Minister Mackenzie King from Mrs. Rae Luckock, President, Toronto Housewives Consumers Association, 15 April 1948, NA, RG 146, vol. 3353, pt 2.
54  'Meeting Here of Housewives,' *Ottawa Citizen*, 11 February 1948, RCMP clipping file, NA, RG 146, vol. 3353, supp. 1, pt 2.
55  Don Cameron, 'Loyal Canadians Duped to Aid Red Fifth Column,' *Windsor Daily Star*, 10 March 1948, reprinted in *Halifax Herald*, 13 March 1948, RCMP clipping file, NA, RG 146, vol. 3353, pt 2; 'Some Enlightenment,' *Hamilton Spectator*, 24 January 1948, RCMP clipping file, NA, RG 146, vol. 3440, pt 1.
56  'Is Price Inquiry to Be in Secret?' *Canadian Tribune*, 17 June 1948, 'How the King Gov't Received Price Protest Delegation,' *Westerner*, 1 May 1948; 'But Housewives Take Huge Prices Petition to King's Front Door,' *Westerner*, c. 1948; 'How the King

Gov't Received a Delegation of Electors,' *Canadian Tribune*, 24 April 1948, RCMP clipping file, NA, RG 146, vol. 3353, supp. 1, pt 2.

57 'Cabinet Refuses Housewives' Meet,' *Ottawa Citizen*, 14 April 1948; 'Good Women with a Bad Cause,' *Ottawa Journal*, c. 1948; 'Wives' League Rebuffed as Dupe of Communists; Butter Speculation Bared,' *Montreal Gazette*, 14 April 1948, RCMP clipping file, NA, RG 146, vol. 3353, supp. 1, pt 2.

58 'The Housewives Petition,' *Ottawa Citizen*, c. 1948; 'Abbott, MPs, Weather Turn against "Wives" Consumer League Spend Day in Ottawa with Slight Show of Recognition,' *Montreal Gazette* 16 April 1948; editorial, *Globe and Mail*, c. 17 April 1948, RCMP clipping file, NA, RG 146, vol. 3353, supp. 1, pt 2.

59 'We're Winning – Housewives; They Are, Too, Dealers Say,' *Toronto Daily Star*, c. 12 June 1948, RCMP clipping file, NA, RG 146, vol. 3440, pt 1.

60 'Will "Fellow-Travellers" Control Housewives' Cavalcade to Ottawa?' *Financial Post*, 7 June 1947; 'Are You a Stooge for a Communist?' *Chatelaine*, April 1949.

61 Joy Parr, 'Shopping for a Good Stove: A Parable about Gender, Design, and the Market,' in Parr, *A Diversity of Women*, 75–97; Joy Parr and Gunilla Ekberg, 'Mrs Consumer and Mr Keynes in Postwar Canada and Sweden,' *Gender and History* 8, no. 2 (July 1996): 212–30.

62 'The Housewives' News, vol. 1, no. 11 [1948], RCMP file, NA, RG 146, vol. 3353 pt 3; 'Consumers Claim Drive Will Force Govt. to Action,' *Ottawa Citizen*, c. April 1948, RCMP clipping file, NA, RG 146, vol. 3353, supp. 1, pt 2.

63 'Housewives' Groups Said Propagandists for Reds; Denied Cabinet Hearing,' *Globe and Mail*, 14 April 1948, RCMP clipping file, NA, RG 146, vol. 3353, supp. 1, pt 2; 'Body Rebuffed in Ottawa Not Connected with C.A.C.,' *Montreal Gazette*, c. 1948, RCMP clipping file, NA, RG 146, vol. 3440, pt 2A.

64 'Proposed Program to Be Presented to the Housewives' and Consumers' Federation of Canada Convention, April 15 to 18, 1948, at Ottawa,' RCMP case file, NA, RG 146, vol. 3353, pt 2.

65 Kathryn McPherson, interview with Ann Ross, Winnipeg, 4 August 1988, Manitoba Archives.

66 'Housewives' Group Said Propagandists for Reds; Denied Cabinet Hearing,' ibid.; 'Wives' League Rebuffed As Dupe of Communists,' ibid.

67 Jonah Goldstein, 'Public Interest Groups and Public Policy: The Case of the Consumers' Association of Canada,' *Canadian Journal of Political Science/Revue canadienne de science politique*, 12, no. 1 (March 1979): 137–55.

68 RCMP memorandum for file, The Housewives Consumers' Association, 17 January 1950; RCMP case file, Re: Congress of Canadian Women, British Columbia, 16 June 1951, NA, RG 146, vol. 3353, pt 3; Sangster, *Dreams of Equality*, 189–91.

69 Ellen Carol DuBois and Vicki L. Ruíz, eds, *Unequal Sisters: A Multi-Cultural Reader in U.S. Women's History*, 2d ed. (New York: Routledge, 1994).

# Jell-O Salads, One-Stop Shopping, and Maria the Homemaker: The Gender Politics of Food

FRANCA IACOVETTA AND VALERIE J. KORINEK

## Introduction

Food is about more than recipes, cooking, nutrition, and eating. The practices surrounding its purchase, preparation, and consumption have long been a matter of conflict and contest. Food campaigns have been the site of clashes and accommodations between health professionals and beleaguered mothers told to forsake folk routines to 'scientific' regimes; between food fashion-makers and discerning or ostentatious culinary consumers; and between gatekeepers of receiving societies and immigrants bearing allegedly exotic or offensive cuisine and smells. Forced to consider our own food habits, many might see them as a matter of personal choice, yet such claims overlook the ways in which food tastes and customs are informed, prescribed, or mediated by government, education, social services, multinational food corporations, and mass media. In short, food and its attendant practices are also about power. Food traditions evolve in social and cultural contexts that are shaped by economic conditions and class politics, racial-ethnic relations, and other factors.

Food can also act as a signifier of difference. Historically, 'ethnic' foods have been relegated to the margins of receiving societies, dismissed as unhealthy or inappropriate, or pilloried by food experts in search of new ideas to pick up the palates of bored eaters. Bastardized versions of 'foreign' recipes, with most of the chili peppers or other pungent spices removed, are one aspect of the homogenizing process that comes from adapting ethnic cuisine to mainstream culture. Yet, immigrants have also transformed (albeit unevenly) the cuisine of mainstream cultures even as their own food habits were modified. Though hardly a new phenomenon, the current allure of 'multicultural' dining has brought some immigrant and minority food cultures into the forefront, where, ironically, they have become middle- and upper-middle-class demarcators of status and taste.[1]

Here, we grapple with the complex politics of food through the prism of early post-1945 Canada, a period marked by a mix of social optimism and Cold War hysteria; economic expansion and persistent poverty; heightened domesticity and social and sexual non-conformity.[2] These tensions coincided with another major trend, mass immigration; by 1965, two and one-half million newcomers, many of them women and children, and members of young families, had entered Canada.[3] The Canadian context thus permits us to explore how the dominant gender ideologies of capitalist democracies in the Cold War – including a middle-class model of homemaking and North American–defined standards of food customs and family life – influenced reception work and social service activities among immigrant and refugee women. Did efforts to reshape the culinary and homemaking skills of female newcomers overlap or diverge from the wider campaigns aimed at transforming all Canadian women into efficient shoppers, expert consumers, nutrition-wise cooks, and nurturing wives and mothers? Did Canadian and New Canadian women respond in similar ways to popular postwar campaigns designed to teach women the benefits of modern homemaking, meal planning, and nutritional guides? Notwithstanding the postwar rhetoric of liberal pluralism, these and health and motherhood campaigns also served to isolate Europe's many newcomer women for special attention or blame in ways that not only suggest some important continuities with earlier more aggressive assimilationist campaigns to Canadianize foreigners but that also parallel in certain ways the 'tense and tender relations' that, as Ann Stoler observes, characterized the 'intimate' or 'human' side of the imperial-colonial encounter, particularly as it related to matters of sex, households, and childrearing. In both instances, the complex dynamics and dialectical relations involved cannot be adequately captured by the dichotomy of colonizer and colonized. As Mary Pratt notes, a 'contact' perspective requires careful attention to the ways in which the two subjects, in this case modernizing experts and disadvantaged newcomer mothers, are treated not in terms of their separateness but 'in terms of interlocking understandings and practices, often within radically asymmetrical relations of power.'[4] In tackling such themes and questions, we adopt a comparative approach that probes the varied situations and responses of Canadian- and foreign-born women and of middle- and working-class women from both dominant and immigrant cultures in English Canada. So doing, we hope also to help bridge the continuing gap between what is generally seen as Canadian women's history and the history of immigrant and refugee and racialized women in Canada.[5]

## Canadian 'Affluence' in a World of Hunger

Canadian newspapers and magazines well captured the havoc that war had wreaked on millions of people's health and lives: images of malnourished and disoriented soldiers released from Prisoner of War camps, thin war widows lined up at relief centres, and the bombed-out rubble of London streets, German towns, and Sicilian villages. Overseas Canadian relief worker Ethel Ostry Genkind wrote of the 'destruction' of the European countryside ('miles and miles of it') and the eerie presence of 'sunken-eyed ragged adults and children with outstretched arms, begging hands and rickety bare legs, their chest bones sticking out from thin tattered bits of clothing.' Europe's Displaced Persons (DP) camps contained many war casualties, including the Jewish survivors, whose 'ghastly appearance' set them apart from the decidedly malnourished but healthier Baltic DPs.[6]

As Cold War tensions gripped the globe, stories of half-starved victims seeking asylum could also serve ideological ends. Western commentators portrayed East Europeans refusing repatriation to Soviet-controlled homelands or fleeing Iron Curtain countries as freedom fighters risking lives for a chance at democracy. Many media accounts of these Communist escape narratives[7] highlighted themes of Old World hunger and New World plenty. Even during the late 1940s and early 1950s, when Canadians experienced rations, inflation, and housing shortages, such stories drew attention to the country's relative abundance in food, clothes, appliances, as well as political freedom and jobs.[8] The juxtaposition of Canada's relative abundance and European scarcity also infused postwar articulations of domesticity, which invariably focused on women's primary role as homemaker. In promotional films and pamphlets, women's magazines and advice columns, and health lectures delivered to newcomers, reception activists often promoted a bourgeois and feminine version of postwar Canadian affluence and modernity.[9] A recurring message was that by birth or adoption, women in Canada could enjoy the resources required to meet domestic duties.

Cold War prejudices invited more insidious comparisons between North American and Communist homemakers. U.S. state department materials portrayed the typical 'Mrs America' as a contented and modestly affluent middle-class homemaker who 'cooks the meals, cleans the house, washes, irons, and mends the clothes, cares for the children, and works in her flower garden' – the beneficiary of an economic system that ensured her the skills and resources to raise a healthy family. It even claimed that U.S. capitalism provided plentiful job opportunities and adequate child care for America's wage-earning women. By contrast, the average 'Mrs Soviet Union' faced acute food shortages, the indignity of poorly paid and degrading work, long absences from her children, and line-ups at half-empty stores. Canadian commentators depicted the Soviet women in similar terms.

Describing a recent trip to the Soviet Union, Rev. James F. Drane stressed the disturbing 'spectacles' of women who, removed from their children, toil at heavy, filthy, and dangerous jobs on railway and construction crews and in farm work and machine-making factories. Under communism, he concluded, liberation for women meant misery and the loss of femininity. Such propaganda tools, as Laura Belmonte notes, were not mere cultural by-products of the Cold War but ideological weapons meant to cultivate patriotism and encourage conformity to North American gender ideals.[10]

Canadian propagandists promised immigrant and refugee women a better life. Their promotional materials, including films made by the National Film Board in conjunction with the federal Citizenship Branch, featured enticing images of the modern conveniences and range of choices that helped define Canadian ways. The film *Canadian Notebook* presented the modern store and mail-order catalogue as products of Canadian postwar affluence now within the reach of the New Canadian homemaker. A Maritime rural scene sings the praises of the mail-order catalogue, which brings 'the largest city shopping centres' to the homemaker's 'fingertips.' Greater praise was reserved for the urban department store (a 'meeting place' with a 'wide range of items and variety of styles') and the one-stop, self-serve 'groceteria.' As the following sequence featuring a white, slim, and attractive 'Mrs. Sparks' indicates, depictions of the modern Canadian supermarket emphasized convenience and order, abundance of items, and quality and cleanliness of food. It also delivered messages about the sort of priorities that should preoccupy the Canadian homemaker:

> Mrs. Sparks finds cellophane-wrapped meats in different quantities and grades on the refrigerated shelves. And now for some things for the picnic tonight! Prices, grades, and weights are all clearly marked, and Mrs. Sparks can finish her shopping very quickly. As all her food needs are here, Mrs. Sparks usually buys her whole week's groceries at one time. If she wishes, she can get a few other articles here too: magazines, cigarettes, and candies. When finished, Mrs. Sparks leaves through the cash register aisle, where the cashier totals her bill and gives her an itemized receipt.

Canadians, the narrator concludes, 'find the self-service store well-suited to the faster pace of city life, where a busy housewife has to buy the week's groceries, go to the bank and the hairdresser's and still get home in time to prepare supper.'[11] Another NFB film enthused over that 'newest' trend in postwar merchandising, 'the suburban Shopping Centre, with its "one-stop" buying, and ample parking space for several hundred cars.'[12]

While the Cold War alone cannot explain its renewed popularity as postwar ideology, the homemaker ideal, in that it symbolized the stability and superiority of Western democratic families, took on great political import. That it reflected a misplaced or cultivated nostalgia for a bourgeois ideal that never entirely reflected most people's lives, and a conservative reaction to women's wartime gains, has been well documented.[13] It was also part and parcel of contemporary debates over women's roles engendered by the growing presence of working mothers, daycare lobbies, increasing divorce rates, and other signs of women's changing status in post-1945 society.[14] That many war-weary immigrants and refugees quickly married or remarried and started families does not negate the argument that dominant definitions of family and gender, well encapsulated by the phrase *breadwinner husband and homemaker wife*, privileged middle-class, heterosexual, Christian, and North American ideals.[15] The large presence of immigrant wives and mothers in paid labour did not stop reception workers from encouraging eventual domesticity. Indeed, the greater emphasis now placed on parents' obligations to produce mentally fit as well as socially productive children,[16] made not only working mothers (whether Old or New Canadian), but also stay-at-home immigrant mothers allegedly cut off from mainstream (English) Canadian society, highly vulnerable to professional scrutiny. However, being 'othered' – or marginalized as social problems to be resolved – hardly meant being ignored. Immigrant women, who were part of a wider campaign to reform Canadian women and elevate postwar family life, were isolated for special attention. As women, female immigrants were considered essential to modifying the social habits of family members. As front-line English teachers in Toronto put it, the most effective way to encourage the newcomers' adaptation was to target 'the key person' in the immigrant family, 'the housewife and mother,' and ensure that she was sufficiently exposed to Canadian ways.[17]

The main features of postwar immigration have been well examined elsewhere: economic self-interest, labour shortages, international pressures, and pro-refugee lobbies, prompted Canada to resume, especially after 1950, its historic role as a receiving nation. For Canada, the post-1945 influx was unprecedented; in proportional terms, it parallels the mass migration that markedly changed US society decades earlier.[18] Women, many in their child bearing years, represented about half of the total adult arrivals; among the many British and European adults, their proportions hovered between 47 and 56 per cent. The newcomers' youthful profile (average age was 24.9) was underscored by the many children born before or shortly after their mother's immigration.[19]

Canada's racist restrictions on the admission of 'not-white' peoples were postwar nation-building devices intended to keep Canada (mostly) white. It is thus not surprising that most early postwar newcomers before the 1970s were white Britons, Europeans (led by Italians and Germans), and white Americans, all of whom came in the hundreds of thousands.[20] Canadian officials restricted the number of Jewish refugees largely by bureaucratic means, but Jewish Canadian lobbies helped secure safe passage for tens of thousands of them. Newcomers settled across Canada but Ontario attracted a majority of them. And while countless villages, towns, and cities felt the impact of their presence, Toronto became home to most of them.[21]

Canada's early postwar female newcomers were thus largely 'white ethnics' who shared a British or European heritage but they were not a homogenous group. Among the East European DPs and Jewish survivors, for instance, a number of professional or university educated middle-class women could be found, though plenty of them became homemakers in Canada or found paid work in the lower-skilled industrial and service-sector jobs that also drew humble women from rural, fishing, and working-class backgrounds. While most newcomers were unsympathetic to communism, strong political differences existed among the liberals, social democrats, anti-Communists from Soviet Bloc countries, and those who had lived under fascism and Nazism. As to wartime experiences, Canadian reception workers encountered British and European 'war brides' who had already begun families in wartime; refugee women who had lost kin to war but had formed 'grab bag' families with others in similar circumstances; Jews who had survived Nazi death camps; east and central European women (Protestant and Catholic) forced to work in German-controlled factories or homes following their country's fall to Hitler; wartime rape victims who, as with Mennonite refugee women, claimed the 'illegitimate' children born from the violence as blood children and grandchildren; and Hungarian '56ers.' These women would be joined by a continuing mix of peoples, including West Indians and South Asians,[22] but in the early postwar decades, white newcomers, considered far better suited for Canadian citizenship, garnered the lion's share of attention. Indeed, all this hand-wringing on the part of reception workers reflected the centrality of these immigrants to the remaking of the postwar Canadian nation.[23]

The postwar newcomers quickly faced a barrage of pressures and programs intended to guide and reform them. English teachers, social workers, nurses, and other helping professionals met immigrants at the local level of neighbourhood, school, immigrant aid office, and social agency. They became an increasingly large component of the country's social welfare clientele. In Toronto as elsewhere, settlement houses and social agencies hoped to attract newcomers both to their existing programs (mothers' groups, nursery schools, and teenage social clubs) and to New Canadian classes that, as a Toronto YWCA report put it, 'teach newcomers about shopping, meal planning, health and welfare resources, transportation, social customs, parent-school communication, and about their relationships with children who are better adapted.'[24] Located in a heavily immigrant and working-class west-end neighbourhood, Toronto's Central Neighbourhood House (CNH) offered a representative mix of aims and programs. In the interests of giving help to 'bewildered strangers' and promoting 'good citizenship,' better living conditions, healthier babies, and 'household management' among newcomers, the CNH ran English and sewing classes, field trips, sports, cultural, and social clubs for youths and adults, a nationality club, baby clinic, mothers' group, camp program, and holiday banquets.[25]

These expanding social services, though a continuation of pre-war activity, also reflected Canada's rapidly growing postwar welfare state. With regard to immigrants, reception activists, and social service personnel also adopted some new approaches, including an official endorsement of a modest form of cultural pluralism.[26] First of all, publicly rejecting earlier 'assimilationist' policies, government officials, experts, and volunteers adopted a language of cultural tolerance, including 'integration' as the codeword of reception work, though Canadianization remained popular. Postwar cultural pluralism combined a liberal respect for the newcomers' traditions and sympathy for their plight with an insistence that they embrace Canada and Canadian citizenship – but it did not preclude the cultural chauvinism of middle-class gatekeepers convinced of the superiority of their ways.[27]

Second, postwar reception workers emphasized the multilayered character of integration. While acknowledging that key differences distinguished volunteer immigrants from political refugees who by choice or circumstance were stateless people, all newcomers, they insisted, must learn the lessons of Canadian democracy and 'adapt' their traditions and habits to Canadian patterns. No behaviour was too insignificant for attention: voting, community participation, table manners, and even cocktail party conduct.[28] Certain specific challenges also loomed large. As people from totalitarian regimes, the East European DPs (such as Baltic nationals from Estonia, Latvia, and Lithuania) and later arriving refugees from Iron Curtain countries such as Hungary and Czechoslovakia were considered especially in need of training in democratic citizenship. While valued as anti-Communists, they could also be pathologized as victims of Communism.[29]

Third, ordinary Canadians were encouraged to facilitate immigrant adjustment by extending to them a 'warm' and 'friendly' hand. By volunteering their services to neighbourhood agencies, initiating 'projects for newcomers,' organizing cultural events, or even inviting a New Canadian neighbour to their home, Canadians could help develop in newcomers a sense of belonging-ness and feelings of loyalty to Canada.[30] The corollary was that resentful and disaffected people would undermine the nation, exhaust welfare resources and become vulnerable to Communist propaganda. Beyond the friendly hand of ordinary Canadians was an army of professional experts involved in postwar reception work. In a statement that well captured their views and interests, child welfare administrator David Weiss insisted that social agencies facilitate immigrant adjustment to 'our way of life' and encourage a 'feeling of belonging' by providing 'proper reception and information services,' securing jobs and housing, and otherwise helping newcomers overcome social and cultural barriers to integration. While calling for better hospital and outpatient services, educational facilities, opportunities for religious observance, and recreational venues, Weiss added that up-to-date casework and counselling procedures could handle individual problems.[31]

### Nutritional Experts, Food Fashion-Makers, and Women

Health, and the cultivation of a healthy body politic – literally and figuratively[32] – was linked to postwar nation-building.[33] Feeding thin, hungry newcomers, healing sick refugees, and taking precautions against 'diseased' immigrants was one line of defence. Even more important to national reconstruction was the long-term physical, mental, and moral health of Canada's current and future citizenry. Government and health organizations emphasized nutritional education, stringent health standards, and 'modern' eating regimes. They promoted National Health Week (a wartime initiative) in the hopes of raising public awareness about 'preventive measures' and 'the necessity of early diagnosis and treatment when illness strikes.' Health lobbyists clamoured for greater public funding and education to teach people, particularly mothers, about nutritional 'musts' for people, especially children.[34] Learning 'how to purchase and prepare food' was also considered important to the adjustment of the many immigrants who hailed from countries 'where austerity prevails' or who were otherwise 'deprived' of adequate food and nutrition knowledge.[35]

Food and health campaigns aimed at immigrant women and their families were varied and numerous. Early efforts began in European refugee camps, where Canadian relief workers taught 'Canadian ways' with Canadian magazines, newspapers, school texts, films, and, most popular of all, Eaton's and Simpsons catalogues.[36] The British war brides, whose integration was closely defined in homemaking terms, were the target of better organized culinary campaigns designed to ensure that 'when [they] set up their new homes in the Dominion, they will have a good idea of what's expected of them in the cooking line.'[37] As part of a state-funded and chaperoned scheme to resettle the wives of Canadian servicemen, cooking classes and health lectures for British war brides dominated orientation programs delivered in London; professional dieticians like Canadian Red Cross officer Ruth Adams stressed the importance that Canadians attached 'to well-balanced diets.' 'Time spent in planning meals,' she also advised 'would pay off in saving doctor and dentist bills.' Adams counselled the women 'not to forget their own specialties such as scones and Yorkshire pudding' but 'urged' them 'to get busy and practise on pancakes and Canadian-style salads.' To demonstrate what Canadians 'like to eat,' she brought along 'a real apple pie, tea biscuits, a white cake with fudge icing, several types of salads, [and] the biscuit part of a strawberry shortcake.'[38]

This training continued in Canada. In Ontario, Red Cross staff in North Bay, St Catharines, and elsewhere gave courses in cooking (where women made muffins, tea biscuits, cream sauces, salads, and cakes, and learned to cook vegetables), canning techniques, nutrition, and participated in Department of Health home visits for meal planning and budgeting. One war bride evidently prompted local staff to begin a pastry-making class with her declaration that 'the ambition of every British bride was to make a good lemon pie.'[39] In these records, favourable assessments abound (though other sources, especially oral testimonies, tell more complicated stories).[40] 'The girls,' declared their teachers, gained 'practical experience in actual cooking,' grew familiar with Canadian equipment (including wooden spoons)[41] and enjoyed the chance to socialize, over tea and cookies or cigarettes. Graduates received an appropriately Canadian gift – a set of plastic measuring spoons. Beyond specialized cooking courses, many reception programs for immigrant women included nutrition and food lessons as part of a larger orientation program. English classes in settlement houses, for instance, could became forums for discussing children's food needs and shopping trips.[42]

### *Chatelaine* and Canadian Culinary Ways

For nutrition experts, the first priority was to teach all Canadians, especially mothers, sound nutritional advice and healthy food habits. (They never tired of praising the Canada Food Guide as a simple and flexible teaching tool for raising nutritional awareness.)[43] A good diet, they stressed, improved children's growth rate and physique, resistance to disease, and meant longer lives; a faulty diet established early in life might not show immediate results but could produce far greater damage than a vice such as adult drinking. In dispensing advice, food editors and health experts often prioritized middle-class food customs and efficiency regimes derived from capitalist time-management principles, and emphasized cleanliness. Descriptions of the family meal, especially dinner, invariably assumed (or pictured) a nuclear family, its well-groomed members assembled around an attractively set table in a dining room, happily engaged in conversation while eating mother's nicely presented and healthy meal. Their awareness of the myriad of 'families' inhabiting inner-city flats, boarding houses, and suburban bungalows, did not alter their pitch.

As recent left feminist scholarship demonstrates, women's magazines can shed light on the tensions and contradictions that marked women's lives, including the complex racial-ethnic, gender, and class politics of the early Cold War decades.[44]

An excellent source of Canada's postwar health and homemaking campaigns is the country's premier women's magazine, *Chatelaine*. Although usually dismissed as a bourgeois women's magazine, *Chatelaine* was an affordable, mass-market periodical that by the late 1960s enjoyed the largest circulation of any Canadian magazine in the country. Circulation figures, surveys, and letters to the editor show that its audience came from across Canada and included urban and rural as well as working- and middle-class women and some men and children. The primarily female readership was English-speaking and Anglo-Celtic but included some ethnic Canadian and immigrant women. Certainly, the magazine frequently featured conventional images of the white, middle-class wife and mother, though, significantly, the happy homemaker image was not the only one contained in its pages.[45] Amid the regular departmental material on meal plans, shopping, crafts, and decorating, the magazine tackled provocative issues – consider Dr Marion Hilliard's columns on sexuality and suburban women's anxieties (addressed here before Betty Friedan exposed 'the problem that has no name' in *The Feminine Mystique*).[46] By the late 1950s *Chatelaine* was regularly publishing 'social issue' articles on racism and sexism[47] and on working-class, immigrant, Native, and poor Canadians.[48] Contributions in the 1960s included Christina McCall's 1961 photo essay 'Working Wives Are Here to Stay,' on Gertrude Carpenter, an overworked wife and mother from Toronto's east-end working-class suburb of Scarborough whose profile revealed tremendous resourcefulness and lack of complaint ('It'll come out all right if we keep trying') but underscored a depressingly familiar aspect of working-women's struggle for greater material security, and Ian Adams's 1969 series on poverty, a gritty exposé that defined poverty as a woman's problem and urged women to 'fight back.'[49] The feminist editorials of these years by Doris Anderson, a one-time socialist who became a leading liberal feminist, also helped to distinguish *Chatelaine* from the far less politically overt U.S. women's magazines.[50] All this confirms what cultural studies and feminist scholars exploring the 'polysemic' nature of popular texts like women's magazines suggest about the need to recognize the active role of readers who help create the 'multiple meanings' produced in such texts.[51]

The magazine's food features were largely the creations of the Chatelaine Institute kitchen staff or recipe entries in the annual Family Favourites Contests that had been adjudicated and tested by the Institute staff. Founded in 1930 and modelled after the U.S.-based *Good Housekeeping* Test Kitchen, the Chatelaine Institute was staffed by professional home economists whose white robes and laboratory-style kitchen lent a scientific air to the departmental features. Efficient and economical meal preparation, with a focus on nutrition, was their central message. As female professionals operating in the overlapping worlds of health and fashion, they took their job seriously: taste testings on in-house recipes, inspection visits to factories, and product test runs to determine which items would receive the *Chatelaine* Seal of Approval (again mimicking the *Good Housekeeping* Seal of Approval). Given the critical importance of advertising to the magazine, it is not surprising to find products of corporate sponsors among those accorded the Seal; no doubt, the magazine's business department suggested such products for the Seal, thereby suggesting the power of food corporations to fashion taste through their ability to saturate popular media, including mass market magazines and TV commercials, with their products.[52] The particular gender dynamics that gave Chatelaine Institute nutritionists a degree of autonomy not enjoyed by their counterparts in the United States are also noteworthy. In contrast to the United States, where male editors vetted materials submitted by female writers, *Chatelaine*'s editorial and advertising departments were separate, sundering the usual cozy relationship between editorials and advertising. *Chatelaine*'s male publishers complained about women editors who refused to be dictated to. In the budget features, women food editors who, theoretically, should have been promoting the advertiser's products (many of them processed goods) refused, on the grounds that they were too expensive.[53]

While undergoing some transformations in the two decades under review, *Chatelaine*'s food features remained remarkably consistent. Even amid the changing food fads that appeared, the Canadian way was most commonly represented by images and texts extolling the virtues of affordable abundance. As in the NFB films, recurring images of attractive white WASP women pushing over-flowing grocery carts or posed near well-stocked freezers and store shelves attested to the Canadian homemakers' good fortune. So did recipe and cooking contests. Proud contest winners photographed alongside their prize-winning Jell-O-mould salad, carrot medley, casserole, or dessert parfait promised women readers ease of preparation and family fun. The come-on ads of brand-name food corporations of prepared products, such as canned soups and vegetables, stressed how convenience foods offered maximum return for minimal preparation. By contrast, the advertisers of baking supplies preferred labour-intensive treats to enchant husbands and children. Invariably, their ads drew on women's supposed virtues for self-sacrifice, sending out the message that a mother's proof of her devotion to husband and family was literally in the pudding, or in homemade bread and pies. Indeed, despite the prominence of convenience food corporate advertisers, the majority of recipes in *Chatelaine*'s departmental pages (as opposed to those in name-brand advertisements) involved cooking 'from scratch.' As to economical eating, the magazine increasingly featured frozen foods as a cheaper and healthy alternative to fresh items, though the higher price of frozen goods compared to the tinned variety, and the limited freezer space of the older refrigerators that most fridge-owning Canadian homes had, could put even frozen food beyond the grasp of many struggling families. Not so with canned foods, which were consistently promoted as the cheapest way of attaining the well-balanced meal. Particularly in winter, women were encouraged or cajoled to buy tinned foods instead of more expensive fruit and vegetable imports.

On occasion, the Institute tried to emulate the pages of U.S. women's magazines, where lavish and colourful depictions of weekend brunches or dinner parties regularly appeared. (Most magazine issues were black and white.) But the major bulk of its food features during the 1950s and even more affluent 1960s were aimed at the budget shopper and time-conscious cook. Most commonly featured, particularly during the 1950s, were affordable and healthy meals based on economical cuts of meat, such as hamburg, and usually accompanied by quick potato or rice side dishes, and vegetables. Casseroles were based on the same principle of stretching affordable meats with pasta, rice, or some other starch. Particularly popular with readers was the 'Meals of the Month' page. Designed by the Institute's home economists, this monthlong table of daily menu plans provided the busy, unimaginative, or inexperienced homemaker with ideas for making a variety of nutritious meals on a modest budget. Only infrequently did *Chatelaine*'s food articles acknowledge that many Canadian wives worked outside the home, and some of them offered less than solid advice. 'Seven Dinners on the Double' tantalized working wives with this appealing fantasy: 'You're home at six and dinner's on the table in thirty minutes. Here's how you do it in a small apartment kitchen: work to plan and let your husband help.' The accompanying photo essay depicts a cheerful heterosexual couple, both wearing aprons, preparing food in a tiny kitchen. Some examples from the 1960s highlighted working women who made ends meet by preparing meals the night before or shopping at a well-stocked deli counter. The affordable meals in *Chatelaine*'s sixties repertoire were also slightly more glamorous than their fifties counterparts, though casseroles remained popular. One of the quickest ways of interjecting novelty was to feature 'ethnic' ingredients and food – a process, that as Harvey Levenstein and others have described for the United States, usually meant modifying 'foreign' fare for more timid North American palates. *Chatelaine*'s examples of this homogenizing process include the following 1960 recipe for Easy-to-Make Pizza Pin Wheels: biscuit mix, tomato soup and ketchup, pressed meat, cheese wafers, cheddar cheese, and modest amounts of oregano, green pepper, and onion. Clearly, authenticity was not a hallmark of such recipes.[54]

Still, the magazine's increasing attention to ethnic foods is noteworthy. In the 1960s, the number of ethnic food features published by *Chatelaine* was five times higher than the corresponding 1950s sample.[55] With growing regularity, Institute staff and corporate advertisers were encouraging Canadian women to experiment with 'ethnic' ingredients as a way of injecting more diversity into their family's diet. Ethnic recipes were also presented as new twists on economical eating. The most common ethnic foods featured were European, especially Italian, Chinese, and Spanish. At times, the ubiquitous tuna casserole was replaced by lasagna and

'Meals off the Shelf': One of *Chatelaine's* popular food features was the 'Meals of the Month' page, a month-long table of daily menu plans designed by the magazine's home economists to provide busy, unimaginative, or inexperienced homemakers with ideas for cheap, and nutritious family meals.

even curried chicken dishes, though such nods to cultural experimentation did not preclude food fashion-makers from using ethnic stereotypes or patronizing themes in cute come-on headings. Full-length features like 'South Sea Foods to Enchant Your Natives,' boasted recipes for 'Native Drums Barbecued Chicken, Yams Tahiti, Montezuma Casserole and Muu-Muu Punch.'[56] Such features combined ethnic or exotic food – or *Chatelaine's* version of it – with notions of increased affluence.

Greater attention to ethnic foods – both inside the pages of women's magazines and beyond – also reflected an increasing interest on the part of North Americans in the sort of 'gourmet' cuisine associated with such successful food writers as Julia Child (who sparked interest in French cuisine with the publication of her cookbooks in the early 1960s) as well as a greater degree of culinary experimentation and the internationalization of foods more broadly speaking. Whether dubbed as hippies, radicals, bohemians, or brown-ricers, many middle-class youth were enticed by the alternative tastes of global foods. Their rebellion against the standard 'meat-mashed-potatoes-and-peas' family fare was part of a larger interest in cultural and for some political and sexual experimentation. It suggests the need to pay more attention to what Levenstein aptly referred to as people's growing appreciation of the 'sensuality' of food.[57]

Changes were also taking place in mother's kitchen. A summary of the recipes submitted for *Chatelaine's* 1965 Family Favourites Contest suggests that many Canadian housewives were incorporating ethnic cuisine into the meal plans. 'Chinese food' was 'the most popular dish, followed by Italian'[58] – though such nods towards multicultural eating should not be exaggerated. Even by the end of the 1960s, the 'Canadian way' was best exemplified by the homemaker who had the major burden of food preparation, and the food standard usually meant updated classics like 'hamburgers with class' or 'ten ways with a pound of hamburg,' rather than experimental cuisine.[59]

**From the Point of Nutrition?**

Other sources, including a popular postwar nutritional guide, *Food Customs of New Canadians*,[60] speak more directly to the concerns and practices of health and food experts serving immigrant communities. Produced by an organization of nutritionists and dieticians (Toronto Nutrition Committee [TNC]), the guide appeared in 1959 and was revised and expanded in 1967. A part of a cookbook project launched by the International Institute of Metropolitan Toronto, the city's largest immigrant aid society, the guide's claims to be objective and social scientific, like its rejection of an overtly assimilationist approach, reflects the general approaches of postwar reception activists like those who staffed the Institute.

The TNC's liberal perspective is clearly evident in their counselling of flexibility when assessing immigrant food customs – 'From the viewpoint of nutrition, some food habits may be better than our own, and changes may not be necessary' – but the committee's presumption of expert authority is equally evident. Notwithstanding its constant reference to immigrant groups and New Canadians, the guide's main target is the homemaker whose schooling in Canadian ways was seen as crucial to affecting desired changes in the whole family.

The guide profiled the food customs of fourteen of Toronto's significant ethnic groups,[61] with the British conspicuous by their absence. The data collected (from published texts, military surveys, international agencies, and interviews with immigrants) was organized into categories. For each group, there is a detailed table of food customs both in the Old World setting and in Toronto, with the relevant information broken down into subcategories: food groupings (milk, fruits and vegetables, bread and cereals, meat and fish), meal patterns, and cooking facilities, Vitamin D, fats, sweets, beverages, and condiments. Another category, Food for Special Ages, dealt mainly with prenatal education for mothers, childfeeding patterns, and public health facilities. Conclusions and recommendations were then grouped together under Teaching Suggestions. With two exceptions,[62] the guide used national groupings (Chinese, Portuguese), but was careful to document regional and rural/urban variations in Old World contexts, to highlight patterns in areas of outmigration, and to note changes (for better or worse) in food habits that pertained in Toronto. In most cases, however, stark contrasts are drawn between the more 'primitive' and time-consuming cooking facilities of rural homes, where running water is scarce and women operate charcoal, wood stoves, or clay stoves, and the 'modern' urban homes equipped with gas, electricity, and running water. Although such differences undoubtedly reflected class as much as city residence, only the West Indian entry draws explicit class distinctions.[63] The desire to be precise and comprehensive makes for some very terse summaries, as indicated by the following German-Austrian entry:

> German and Austrian food habits are combined since differences are more regional than national. North Germans like sweet soups and sugar on salads, serve potatoes and vegetables regularly, and drink beer with meals. South-West Germans and Bavarian-Austrians do not eat sweet soups and salads; South-West Germans replace potatoes with noodles and use less vegetable while Bavarian-Austrians use dumplings and fewer vegetables except for sauerkraut. Although South-West Germans replace beer with wine at meals, the Bavarian-Austrians do not.

The guide's claim to neutral assessments of immigrant food customs and liberalism was inexorably mingled with the presumption of scientific, even cultural, authority to define standards for newcomers. Indeed, the guide was designed precisely to inform health and social service personnel 'helping' newcomers 'adapt the familiar food patterns of their homelands to the foods and equipment available in Canada.' The aim was to gradually change the food and eating habits of immigrants so as to bring them in line with Canadian ways and standards. Revising food habits was particularly necessary when immigrant foods were 'markedly different' from Canadian ones, when foods commonly used back home were less plentiful or more expensive in Canada, when food preparation and cooking methods varied 'considerably,' and cooking equipment was 'quite different.' Other sections, notably the teaching suggestions, are blunt about Canadianizing immigrant habits. The overall approach is aptly summarized by their use of a Mark Twain quotation: 'Habit is habit and not to be flung out the window by any man but coaxed downstairs, a step at a time.' The section dealing with the Canada Food Guide offers yet another variant of the theme, Canadian modernity and affordable abundance. The emphasis was on informing newcomers about affordable, nutritious foods they might otherwise miss and their 'proper' preparation. As they might not know about the 'many varieties of raw and processed fruits and vegetables available [in Canada] throughout the year,' newcomers needed 'advice on purchasing these foods, information about preparation and cooking to preserve food value, and suggestions for serving.' Although immigrants could often find 'familiar breads' in local ethnic stores, they needed to know too that 'Canadian bread' (commercially baked white bread) was made from enriched flour, making it an excellent choice 'from the standpoint of nutrients.' As 'home-cooked cereals' and those made from whole grain were also unfamiliar to many immigrants, the guide also encouraged their consumption.

The wisdom encoded in *Food Customs* was meant to be objective, yet the advice involved an act of cultural imperialism: advising conformity to North American health regimes meant deliberately bringing about changes in the daily habits, and social and cultural values, of those being counselled. It might be unfair to equate this guide with the blatantly assimilationist intentions of nineteenth- and early twentieth-century domestic science professionals or residential school staff who taught African-American, Native, and immigrant children to reject their mother's cooking and customary foods in favour of mainstream choices.[64] Still, definitions of health and nutrition can be culturally constructed. Despite its scientific language, the guide reflected a shared normative discourse regarding dominant bourgeois definitions of Canadian 'ways' and 'standards' that were as much about class and capitalist notions of efficiency and budgeting as about nutrition and food. For instance, it held the North American pattern of three meals per day as sacrosanct. 'Canadians,' it said, 'follow a pattern of three meals a day which fits into school and working hours.' That newcomers had to adapt to this industrial pattern was not in dispute.

The main target audience was also clear – women from rural or impoverished regions. Indeed, a major concern was to introduce those accustomed to 'primitive' cooking facilities and time-consuming preparation, to modern resources, as 'guidance in their use' would 'help the homemaker to adjust more easily, produce better meals, and prevent costly waste.' The entry on China is representative. It notes that women operate brick, or, in poorer families, clay ovens, and must constantly stoke with straw, corn, cotton stalks, wood, or charcoal. They also shop daily for food because 'refrigeration is rare' (though it was becoming popular in the cities). In addition, much food is preserved by 'sun-drying' or with sugar or salt. Implicit in these discussions is the same message contained in the NFB films described earlier: women could expect domestic life to improve as they moved from rural Asia, Europe, the Caribbean to modern, urban Canada, provided they learned how to take advantage of the modern conveniences and resources that would smooth their adjustment. Such messages were not inconsistent with those of nationalist boosters or corporate manufacturers encouraging the consumption of the appliances and gadgets of a well-appointed 'modern' kitchen.

The nutrition committee's preoccupation with the shopping habits of immigrant and refugee women also reflected the experts' class and cultural bias. In short, they pathologized this behaviour, seeing it as the consequence of poverty (lack of storage, refrigeration) or rural underdevelopment, and all but ignored its cultural and social significance. In the bakeries, butchers, fish shops, and other specialty stores of Old World towns and villages, women developed important lines of trust and credit with shopkeepers, and maintained critical gossip networks of information and support. For Canadian nutrition experts, however, efficiency concerns predominated: access to clean, well-stocked stores meant shopping less frequently and more efficiently. Such practices were equated with modernity, as suggested by an German-Austrian entry: 'Shopping is done less frequently than before, mostly at neighbourhood stores, but supermarkets are increasing.' Such views also ignored the fact that many thousands of working-class immigrants would live for years in inner-city flats and basement apartments without modern stoves or fridges, and thus rely on daily shopping of perishables. Equally important, the modern supermarket being promoted – large chain stores such as Dominion, Loblaws, and Power – were hardly places where immigrant women well versed in marketplace 'haggling' could practise their craft. Ethnic shops and open markets made greater economic sense than urban or suburban supermarkets. Frequency of contact helped women to forge bonds of trust with local shopkeepers, who often extended credit to families in financial straits.

Harsher professional judgements accompanied discussion of nursing mothers and childfeeding regimes. These evaluations, usually grouped under Food for Special Ages, noted childfeeding practices (breastfeeding or artificial) in each country, availability of specialty foods for children, level of public instruction for mothers, and the state of prenatal health services.[65] Again, immigrant mothers were evaluated in terms of their conformity to 'modern' health regimes. As in the past, postwar nutrition experts showed little respect for the folk traditions and mothering remedies of Europe, Asia, and elsewhere. Rural Chinese women's supposed inadequacies on the childfeeding front, for instance, was attributed to their devotion to folk practices. The entry in *Food Customs* reads:

> No special foods prepared. Mothers increase only their starch intake during pregnancy and, although prenatal health services are improving, the authorities recognize that there is still a need for education of mothers in the kinds of foods required for an adequate pregnancy diet. Following birth of the baby, mother does not eat fruits or vegetables or drink cold water for a month. She eats as much meat, poultry, and eggs as the family can afford. Eggs coloured red are sent to the mother to celebrate the birth.

Women of other countries were depicted as more closely resembling Canadian or North American standards. Of women in Czechoslovakia, the guide observed: 'In rural areas, breast feeding is prevalent although increasing attention is paid to modern methods' (presumably, use of baby formula). In addition, children of working mothers received hot lunches at schools. Even more positive was the assessment for Germany and Austria: 'Infants are mostly breastfed up to 3 or 4 months of age; other foods introduced as in Canada. Nutrition education good; deficiency diseases in children practically non-existent.' Hungarian women were praised for improving their habits upon arrival in Toronto where, evidently, they 'visit the doctor regularly and follow his instructions closely, adding solid foods as directed in the first year.' Highest praise of all went to Dutch women whose childfeeding patterns – which followed a progression from formula feeding to gradual introduction of solid foods – were decidedly modern. In Holland, 'formula feeding is generally accepted' and 'a variety of evaporated milk formulae and canned infant foods,' as well as vitamin supplements, were widely used. Many schoolchildren were served milk at school, and state-subsidized school lunches were made available to 'low income children' to help them meet 'minimal nutritional requirements.'

Amid the details emerge some broad patterns. First, the nutrition experts were careful not to give any group an entirely negative evaluation. They commended most groups for varied diets that combined in-season fruits and vegetables, meat, and fish. Here, Chinese food customs scored well because of the 'economical use of meat, varieties of fish, crisp-tender method of cooking vegetables and consistent use of fruit.' They also acknowledged the fine-honed skills of women from modest rural backgrounds accustomed to stretching economical cuts of meat with starches and vegetables or producing one-dish meals using meat alternatives such as fish. The assessment of the Polish homemaker in Toronto echoed that of most European women under review. She could make 'a small amount of inexpensive meat' go 'a long way in soups and stews,' and she often substituted 'legumes, eggs and fish in all forms' for meat. She had adapted easily to new foods, such as citrus fruits, that had been prohibitively expensive back home, though she did need to learn to cook vegetables for a shorter time and to cook a 'more substantial breakfast.'

Nor did any group receive an entirely positive evaluation; there was always room for improvement, and the experts identified precisely where. Since immigrant children 'become very fond of candy and sweet carbonated beverages,' social service personnel were told to discourage 'the increasing use of sweet fruits' among all newcomers. The TNC also insisted that most immigrant women had to be taught the value of canned or frozen fruits, vegetables, and fruit juices as substitutes for expensive, out-of-season fresh imports.

The guide established a food customs hierarchy of immigrant groups, and it closely resembled Canada's historic racial-ethnic preference ladder. The basis of ranking was the comparative ease with which newcomers made the transition to Canadian foods and customs. Without exception, the most positive evaluations were of Canada's more 'preferred' groups of Europeans: North and West European whites. The 'similarity of foods in the home countries and Canada,' the guide observed of Germans and Austrians, for instance, 'makes adjustment relatively easy.'[66] The most positive evaluation went to the 'Dutch housewife,' who, the TNC declared, 'prizes culinary skill combined with economy and these abilities enable her to make a smooth transition in any adjustment of foods and food customs necessitated by changed environment.' 'Particularly commendable' was 'the generous inclusion of cheese and milk, fruits, a wide variety of vegetables and the limited use of candy and soft drinks.' There was only one main weakness: infrequent use of liver and organ meats.

By contrast, women and families belonging to Canada's 'less preferred' immigrants – Chinese, southern Europeans, and West Indians – appear in the guide as less equipped to adopt modern culinary standards. As we have seen, Chinese hygienic standards needed serious upgrading. Serious adjustments were required of Italians, particularly southern Italians (who regularly use 'strong spices and hot peppers' and 'highly seasoned meats like salami'), before they would better conform to Canadian food ways. This, even though Italians, like other Europeans, earned good marks for a varied diet, use of fresh foods, and a three meals-a-day pattern. Still, serious adjustment problems plagued Italian newcomers, a low-income group, in part, the nutritionists claimed, because they preferred expensive, imported goods, such as olive oil, meats, and cheeses, when cheaper Canadian alternatives (such as corn oil) were available. Hence, the TNC counselled social service personnel to encourage Italian women to forgo familiar items, now dubbed expensive luxury foods, in favour of affordable Canadian products. Alcoholism was not identified as a major problem among the fourteen immigrant groups profiled in *Food Customs* though all of them, save Jews, were described as regular consumers of beer or wine.[67] Still, certain habits, including the Italian tendency to permit children to drink a bit of wine during meals, were frowned upon. Mothers were told to offer a lesser evil – carbonated soft drinks. Regarding drink, however, Caribbean immigrants were singled out; the section on West Indians contains the most references to drink and the only references to drinking patterns outside meal time. 'Alcoholic fruit punch are frequent midafternoon drinks,' it reads, and 'Alcoholic beverages, i.e., beer and rum, widely used.' The absence of comparable information on other groups created a false contrast. Indeed, the guide's assessments of West Indians, especially the rural blacks who dominated Caribbean migration into Canada, are generally more negative. Never acknowledging that probably most were female migrants on temporary work permits, the guide simply describes this group as composed of nutritionally disadvantaged low-income rural families.

**Culinary Pluralism from the Bottom Up?**

Historically, food customs have offered some racial minorities, such as First Nations, African Americans, and urban immigrants, a resource, albeit limited, in resisting the forces of cultural hegemony. Although wary of intruding middle-class professionals, working-class immigrant mothers might more willingly heed the advice of nutrition experts because good health, especially in a child, reflects certain universal qualities.[68] The capacity for choice or resistance greatly differed among Canadian and New Canadian women and, as recently documented for Toronto's postwar inner-city neighbourhoods, low-income women from humble or impoverished rural regions bore the greatest brunt of Canadian professional discourses and front-line practices that singled out immigrant women for special attention or blame. In the late 1950s and 1960s, for example, Portuguese and Italian mothers were branded as too ignorant, isolated, backwards, stubborn, and/or suspicious to access 'modern' health care facilities or to trust the school nurses and visiting homemakers who dispensed advice.[69] Still, neither group should be treated as monolithic categories, and within each group, women displayed a differing willingness and/or capacity to embrace or resist professional interventions. New and Old Canadian women responded in selective and varied ways to external and internal pressures to recast themselves in ways promoted by bourgeois image-makers.

Taking *Chatelaine* and a multiple readings approach to women's responses – one that acknowledges readers' agency and the polysemic nature of popular texts –

permits an evaluation of female responses from across Canada to the postwar homemaker ideal and the food advice of mainstream experts. The admittedly small number of letters received about *Chatelaine*'s food features shows that women were not passive users, or dupes, of the magazine's food and housekeeping material. Canadian housewives, whether rural or urban, Anglo-Celtic or ethnic Canadian, clearly enjoyed consulting recipes even if they did not try to replicate them. Certain food features were popular precisely because women found it helpful. As Mrs C. Flagg of Medicine Hat, Alberta, explained, 'Meals of the Month go up inside my cupboard door – not to be slavishly followed, but for good suggestions.' Complaints were commonplace when the magazine did not run the column; a 'disappointed' Mrs E.H. Donnelly from Windsor, Ontario, liked 'to consult the menu plans' and encouraged their resumption, while Mrs H.M. Pawley of Edmonton reported on the 'many women' who discussed the magazine's 'wonderful' recipes. Such reasoning explains the popularity of the yearly Family Food Favourites contests of the 1950s and 1960s, which showcased countless recipes submitted by readers,[70] and of the highly successful *Chatelaine* cookbooks that the Chatelaine Institute, under director Elaine Collet, began to publish in the mid-sixties.[71] Other features, including 'A Bride's Guide to Cooking,' also took on a life of their own.[72] The many personal jottings that appear on surviving recipe books from this era, such as *The Joys of Jello* or church fundraisers, attest to the frequency with which women experimented with new dishes, tried new ingredients, and returned again and again to family favourites.[73]

But not all *Chatelaine* readers warmed to the magazine's food or housekeeping material. Mrs Ursula McGowan of Smith Falls, Ontario, claimed she enjoyed reading the recipes but tried 'only a few of them.' Significantly, serious critics of the food features tended to be older or working-class women, who included 'A Subscriber' from Harris, Saskatchewan who wrote: 'All the *Chatelaine* seems to contain is recipes of expensive fattening foods.' 'Do come down to earth,' she advised, 'and remember that your readers are Common Canadians (We haven't even plumbing nor electricity and I know many more of your readers haven't.) We are not rich enough for *Chatelaine*'s ideas.' That the Mrs Chatelaine contest – an annual competition to determine the 'best' wife, mother, and homemaker and that each year attracted a large number of applicants – engendered some of the most scathing criticism of the homemaker ideal is also revealing. The letters sent by the self-styled 'Mrs Slob' and her supporters, who declared themselves too unfit, exhausted, opinionated, and financially strapped to meet the lofty standards and smugness of the 'sweet, goody, good' contest winners, capture the frustrations of rural, working-class, and beleaguered middle-class women who rejected what they saw as unrealistic, even oppressive, standards of homemaking.[74]

It is difficult to ascertain racial and ethnic identity from surnames alone, especially of married correspondents, but it is nevertheless clear that many of the letters critical of the Mrs Chatelaine contest and other food and house features were written by women with European surnames or who identified themselves as newcomers. French-Canadian and European surnames (Italian and Dutch) surface among both the winners and regional runners-up of the Mrs Chatelaine contest, and its critics. Some of the latter bore Ukrainian, French-Canadian, and Polish surnames, suggesting that class and income, more than ethnicity, fuelled opposition to the contest. While *Food Customs* assumed that British immigrants easily acclimatized to Canadian cookery habits, some British readers found 'Canadian-style' cuisine, with its emphasis on casseroles, tinned foods, and summer barbecues, strangely foreign.

Refugee and immigrant women also responded selectively to postwar health and homemaking campaigns. Like surviving written sources, oral testimonies, including our sample of twenty-eight taped interviews,[75] reveal patterns that defy easy categorization: immigrant mothers who steadfastly stuck to 'traditional' meals at home and those keen to experiment with Canadian recipes or convenience foods; refugee husbands who pressured wives to stick to familiar meals and those who encouraged wives to incorporate some Canadian foods; and endless permutations of hybrid diets in the households of working- and middle-class immigrants who increasingly combined familiar and Canadian foods and 'ethnic' foods from elsewhere.

Postwar immigrant and refugee narratives contain their own versions of the theme, homeland scarcity and Canadian abundance. Hunger and fears of starvation dominate the war-time stories of early postwar arrivals, including Holocaust survivors. Female survivors recall the smaller rations of food given to women in the camps, and of the courage of Jews and Gentiles who sneaked food into Nazi-created ghettos and camps. When English soldiers arrived to liberate Bergen-Belsen, recalled Amelia S-R., they found 'everyone running to the planted areas to dig beet roots and potatoes out with their hands.' English soldiers helped them to find food, and she and others suffering from typhus and other illnesses were slowly nursed back to health by Red Cross personnel in quarantine hospitals in Sweden. But even there, Amelia added, the fear that they might yet starve never subsided. A Dutch war bride describing the days before Holland's liberation spoke of 'starving under German occupation.' The anti-Soviet DPs had also endured prolonged hunger and inadequate sanitation facilities in the refugee camps, forcing many to take up jobs or begin families in Canada while still suffering from malnourishment and related diseases.[76]

No wonder, then, that many newcomers reacted with astonishment to the comparative abundance of food in Canada. Some, including Dutch newcomer Maria B., marvelled at the stock in Canadian 'self-serve' grocery stores. Many recalled their first taste of new foods, such as 'Canadian-style' bread or cereals, and the joy of eating fresh fruits in scarce supply back home. A German woman, Helga, who arrived with her husband in 1952, swore the apples and oranges 'tasted just like heaven'; they lived on McIntosh apples for months, she added, while her husband, a former electrician, looked for work. A Czech refugee who settled in Hamilton in 1949 recalled her excitement at tasting cornflakes and at once again eating eggs. Financially strapped, she also learned how to bargain shop at the market.[77]

Not everyone enthused over Canadian food, however. Some much preferred their dense dark bread to the light and airy Canadian fare and complained about unappetizing meat. As an East European refugee woman declared 'only the immigrants ... brought good taste in food to Canada.' Whether Baltics from the postwar DP camps, Hungarian 56ers, or Iron Curtain escapees, many refugees expressed their disgust with what they considered Canadian wastefulness, especially in restaurants, where, they noted, people were served an appalling amount of food and an evening's leftovers could have sustained several refugees for weeks at a time.[78] As most volunteer immigrants arrived with little cash or capital, they too could endure a spartan diet – something that worried Canadian nutritionists. Yet, as the example provided by the Portuguese couple who lived for several years on bread and coffee, bean soup, and pigs feet while saving money to start a small family business indicates, the diets were not outrageously unhealthy.[79] Still, illness or injury could cut into a modest food budget, creating yet more pressures for women.

As initial arrival gave way to the pressures of everyday life in Canada, women's concerns shifted to that of maintaining or modifying Old World shopping and food customs in New World contexts. Notwithstanding important differences in the situation of urban and rural dwellers and of middle- and working-class immigrants, the variety of women's responses is striking. The evidence does suggest that some East European refugees who eventually found work in former or alternative professional or white-collar jobs more quickly moved into suburbs and integrated Canadian foods and customs into family meals and holiday celebrations. Nutritionists might have applauded Dagmar Z., a pro-royalist Czech who settled with her husband in suburban Hamilton: she claimed to have maintained a 'traditional Czechoslovakian kitchen' but 'altered it' to be 'more nutritious and healthy,' as she had 'learned' in Canada.[80] But other women put up greater and longer resistance, and shopped in their 'old' city neighbourhoods to get the necessary ingredients. Working-class immigrants such as Italians, Portuguese, and West Indians could largely reproduce their homeland diets precisely because they relied on low-budget food items such as rice and pasta and comparatively little meat – though this kind of cultural continuity, at least early on, was more easily attained in large cities like Toronto, which already had a wide range of ethnic foods, or in smaller cities like Sudbury, which had established Ukrainian, Finnish, and other ethnic businesses.

Women's efforts to negotiate a complex culinary terrain emerges clearly from oral testimonies. Our sample also underscores the importance of individual choice and of differing family and household dynamics. For example, while many mothers experimented with tinned soups, tuna fish sandwiches laden with mayonnaise, hot dogs and hamburgers, and Jell-O in response to their children's persistent requests, others resisted, even for years. An East German refugee woman who liked to supplement her 'mostly German' diet with various foods also recalled the 'tensions' between her and her children over her husband's domineering approach to maintaining 'strict' German standards in food and childrearing.[81] By contrast, Austrian-born Susan M., who married an Italian immigrant she met in Toronto, said she never cooked 'in any particular style' for her family. While proudly insisting that she and her husband were 'international' in tastes and outlook, she believed her daughter identified entirely as a Canadian. Even Helga A., the woman who loved apples and oranges, said that while she had not consciously tried to raise her children 'in a German way,' she had cooked primarily German food and everyone spoke German in her home. Still, over the years more and more Canadian foods had crept into her meal plans. Like many other immigrants, she also saw no contradiction between a continuing commitment to homeland food customs and her strong self-identity as a Canadian. For Nazneed Sadiq, a young and recently married upper-caste Pakistani woman who emigrated with her accountant husband in the early 1960s, learning to cook in her North Toronto apartment building (where everyone else was white) meant experimenting with both 'Indian' and North American foods. The resulting weekly meal pattern: Pakistani food two to three times a week, a lot of salads, and the occasional Canadian-style barbeque.[82] Such experimentation led to many multicultural family diets, of which holiday food customs are perhaps most emblematic: Italian households that combined antipasto and lasagna with turkey for Thanksgiving, Ukrainian mothers who added Canadian cakes and hams to the family favourite, perogies, and so on.[83]

The *Chatelaine* stories dealing with immigrants devoted considerable space to culinary customs or reactions to Canadian patterns of consumption and domestic images. Published in 1957, when the plight and arrival of the Hungarian 56ers had captured the imagination of many Canadians, Jeannine Locke's 'Can the Hungarians Fit In?' about Frank and Katey Meyer illuminates key themes under scrutiny.[84] Like other Iron Curtain 'escape' narratives, Locke's article drew a sympathetic and compelling portrait of the young refugee couple as freedom fighters who fled the Hungarian revolution, spent some harrowing time 'crouched in a ditch' near the Hungarian-Austrian border, and now looked forward to a 'good' life in Canada. The caption that accompanies the cover photograph of an attractive, smiling Katey declares: '[She] resembles that mythical creature, the average young Canadian housewife. In a straight-cut skirt, soft sweater and low-heeled shoes, her brown hair and eyes healthily bright, her skin rosy as a schoolgirl's, she is inconspicuously attractive.' Although she and her engineer husband occupied a small flat in Toronto, Locke added that Katey, 'could fit into any setting from St John's to Saanich.' The domestication of Katey is all the more telling given that she was a professionally educated woman who first worked in Canada as a hospital cleaner and then a bank teller.

Model refugees keen to embrace Canadian ways, the Meyers' adjustment to life in Canada, readers learn, involved exposure to middle-class modes of living, including learning how to shop, eat, and dress 'Canadian-style.' Their middle-class status, it becomes clear, better equipped them to appreciate North American bourgeois standards and indeed, the department store and supermarkets featured in the NFB films described above. Under the provocative subtitle 'Katey Discovers Supermarkets and Limps to Mass in Red Leather Shoes' – Locke describes Katey's first exposure to a modern Canadian household and then grocery store. In Budapest, the couple had shared a three-room apartment with three other family members; they had had no electrical household appliances and endured a 'perpetual chill' due to the scarcity and high cost of fuel. By contrast, their Toronto patrons, a doctor and his large family, had given the couple commodious accommodations: a suite of two rooms, a new refrigerator and stove, and their own bathroom. While living there, Katey discovered the wonders of the Canadian supermarket: one day 'she came home staggering under a load of newly discovered delicacies – sardines, instant coffee, canned soups, ham and chicken legs, and 'so much ice cream that they used it in great scoops even in their coffee.' In a statement that would have pleased Canadian boosters, Katey, wrote Locke, told her husband: 'There is everything you could want to buy in the supermarket ... not like the little shops at home where there was little to buy and what we wanted we could never afford.' Next came department stores. When husband Frank told Katey to buy herself a present, Katey had decided on a pleated nylon slip but on impulse bought high-heeled red leather pumps that cost about $35 (nearly a week's salary for Frank), and then 'limped, painfully but persistently around their rooms in her tall, thin pumps until she was accomplished enough to manoeuvre them, for the first time in public, to Sunday morning mass.' 'Katey's new red shoes,' added Locke, 'were part of their celebration of three most happy events': mail from home; Frank's (and brother Louis') acceptance, with scholarship, into the University of Toronto engineering school; and Katey's bank job.

Canadian nutritionists might have disapproved of Katey's culinary indiscretion (all that ice cream!) but enjoyed the depictions of a Canadian paradise of goods and the Meyers' eagerness to become Canadian consumers. Locke spelled out the stages of their acculturation: learning English, landing a job, one-stop shopping, plans to purchase a suburban home, and their first car. The couple's enthusiasm for all things Canadian was tempered by wistful memories of Hungarian food and gypsy music – which, much to their delight, they rediscovered in a Hungarian restaurant, the Csarda, in downtown Toronto. 'Transported home by the smells and sounds' of Csarda, the Meyers, writes Locke, 'eat goulash and cheese strudel' and 'believe they are back in their favourite restaurant' at the lakeside resort near Budapest where they spent vacations. Although the couple never enjoyed the traditional gypsy music back home (a sign of their class status), Katey is 'amused' to find that the same songs heard here please her very much. So do the Hungarian café's slightly tart desserts that remind her of mother's cooking. Katey has even absorbed North American women's obsession with weight: at home, she yearned for expensive cream-filled eclairs but, here, where she can and, at first, did buy them, '[she] is suddenly calorie conscious.'

The role played by food in the Meyers' tale of escape and redemption is a complex one, at once signifying Canadian abundance, novelty, and satiety, while in the couple's obvious enjoyment of 'traditional' Hungarian cuisine a romanticization of their 'older' ways. As with most public articulations of postwar cultural pluralism, the tension between assimilation and acculturation is never completely resolved, yet its success at weaving a compelling Cold War narrative of a Canadian democratic paradise is suggested by the positive letters the article engendered.[85]

A 1965 article 'The Other Canadians,' in which *Chatelaine* writer Edna Staebler[86] profiled a young Northern Italian couple in Toronto, Alda and Bruno Pilli, and their sons Luigi and Paulo, shared some similar features – for example, a perspective that combined a sympathy for newcomers and voyeurism, most evident in her accounts of clannish Italians and exotic Little Italy; an emphasis on food customs and ethnic cuisine (and introduction to Italian specialties, such as radicchio, 'a bitter-tasting' salad ingredient that is reportedly 'very good for the blood') still foreign to most Canadians; and on physical appearance and domestic virtues, particularly in the description of Alda as a 'sensitive,' 'friendly,' and 'slender and tall' woman 'with the poise of good manners' and a penchant for 'everything to be proper and clean.'[87] But it also differs from the Hungarian piece in several key ways. First, far more attention is given to ethnic shops and markets; significantly, Alda's preference for the European specialty shops in her neighbourhood and daily food shopping is presented as a viable alternative to the one-stop Canadian supermarket model, at least in more self-sufficient ethnic communities. Staebler's description of Alda's shopping skills again serves to introduce readers to yet more 'exotic' Italian specialties that, as in the case of prosciutto and rapini, would by the 1980s become staples of Canadian 'yuppie' cuisine.

> Alda is a compulsive worker ... everything must be spotless. She scrubs walls, sews, cooks, and every day shops for food as she did in Italy. She says, 'I like everything to be fresh.' There are many Italian food stores just around the corner from the Pillis which make Alda feel quite at home. Several have ripe and green olives in barrels of

brine; Italian butcher shops have gutted kids and fleecy black lambs hanging in their windows, with salami and mortadella sausages. At the Violante Grocer, Alda buys fresh anise, rapini, artichokes and oregano. At the Vesuvio Bakery she buys Paulo a cone of spumone or selects fancy Italian cakes with cheese fillings, colored icings, and pistachios. In Johnny Lombardi's Supermarket she enters the door marked *Entrata*, passes spaghetti and espresso coffee-makers, shelves of packaged macaroni. Hanging from bars near the ceiling she sees great provolone cheeses and prosciutto – Italian cured ham that sells for three dollars a pound. At the record bar she hears a hit tune sung by Italy's Luciano Tajoli.

Second, in contrast to the Meyers, who enthusiastically shed their Hungarian skins for more Canadian ones, the Pillis, though evidently striving for the same 'cherished goal – to be Canadian,' had no intentions of abandoning most aspects of their culture, including food. Eating Italian food, made with products bought in local Italian shops, was a daily reality, and Locke detailed Alda's various simple specialties: spaghetti, thin slices of veal, green salad dressed with lemon and olive oil, cauliflower or eggplant or broccoli 'dipped in a batter and fried golden brown.' The meat servings – 'usually thin slices of fried veal or boiled chicken' – reflected pre-migration traditions: little beef was used in Italy because it is 'very tough' and expensive, though in Toronto Alda can afford to feed the family meat more regularly than in Italy. On Sundays, Alda makes pizza from dough and dots it 'with anchovies, olives, and sauce.' No biscuit mix here! With their meal, the Pillis drink Bruno's homemade wine, and when reporting that 'Paulo and Luigi might have a little wine in a glassful of water,' Staebler avoids any explicit judgment. At the same time, Staebler captures the differing ways in which family members are negotiating pressures to conform to Canadian ways; the differing assessments of Canadian cuisine offered by Alda, her husband, and sons reflect generational and uneven differences in acculturation:

- Alda says, 'When Bruno build a little house we have it like [her friend] Marina, beside Canadian family, and learn very fast how speak and do all things Canadian.
- 'Mmmm, Canadian-style cooking,' Luigi rolls his brown eyes. 'Hamburgers, hot dogs, potato chips, Cokes.'
- 'Chewie gum,' Paul adds and rolls his eyes, too
- 'Canada better to live in than Italy,' Bruno says, 'but I still like best how my wife cook – spaghetti, pizza, radichio, lasagne.'
And Alda smiles happily.

The third and most significant difference is that the overall tone of the Pilli piece is negative, highlighting above all the family's difficulties and disappointments but especially Alda's hardships, confusion, and her descent from being a 'fashionable dressmaker' in her Northern Italian hometown ('so pretty, popular, and gay') to 'a pale, unnoticed, hard-working housewife with golden-brown eyes that often are wistful and lonely,' except when husband Bruno, her main source of joy, returns home. Unable to resume her dressmaker occupation ('nobody will pay more than two dollars' for a dress, she says), Alda must rely on her young sons for help with English and things Canadian. The subject of immigrant mothers' retarded integration is underscored by a familiar discussion of the cultural gap between parents and more rapidly Canadianizing children. 'By living among their own countrymen,' writes Staebler, the Pillis 'cling securely to their old ways and language, while their children at school quickly become Canadians.' They do not read Canadian publications, never go out to movies or parties or take holidays (except for one memorable trip to Niagara Falls) but endure 'a monotonous, toiling, self-sacrificing existence' in the hopes of improving their children's life chances – though they socialize a bit with another Northern Italian couple, but always at home.

Domestic images reinforce the Pillis' predicament. Staebler reports on their failure to reduce rental costs despite crowding themselves into two main-floor rooms and renting the rest. Although the house was often crowded, few stayed for any length of time because it is 'old and run down.' Most of their time is spent in a 'narrow, white-walled kitchen with a small refrigerator, a gas stove, and a stainless-steel sink.' The room's only furniture was a 'Formica-topped table and six padded chrome chairs.'[88] The Pillis' small bedroom contained some second-hand furniture and a television that could be viewed from the kitchen. In the cellar were a toilet, a shower, and the laundry tubs at which Alda toils. The monotony of Alda's life is underscored by Staebler's description of daily chores. Staebler stresses the generational divide: 'the tragedy of many immigrants who never can bridge the gap between their old culture and the new while the children for whom they sacrifice adopt with ease ways that are strange to parents and cause conflict as the family grows older if bonds of affection have not been carefully nurtured.' For Staebler, the gap is well illustrated by mother and older son Luigi, a 'quick bright boy' who is 'almost aggressively Canadian' and wants to be just like the other boys at school – though interestingly all of the school friends he names have distinctively Italian names save one – but whose mother, sadly, cannot understand Luigi's desires ('Why he want so much to be Canadian that he no like Italian?')

Interestingly, Staebler had chosen to profile a moderately well-off northern Italian couple – though it does appear that Alda married down, to a transport truck driver who came to Canada on a logging labour contract and later landed work with a unionized plumbing and heating firm – even though the majority of Toronto's, and Canada's, Italians hailed from rural and southern regions and became permanent immigrants. Indeed, they and their northern Italian friends share a certain prejudice against southern Italians, which Staebler appears to accept uncritically. Thus she writes of the southern Italians' greater propensity for clannishness and for clinging to their 'peculiar traditions.' In the end, the Pillis did not remain in Canada; within a year of the article's publication in *Chatelaine* the family had returned to Italy.[89] In this and other ways, the North American middle-class models of homemaking and food customs that significantly shaped reception and social service work among European newcomer women could serve to reduce war-weary, politically oppressed, and/or impoverished peasant mothers into a mass of uncivilized or brutalized women in need of enlightened guidance and improvement. As we have seen, Canadian health and welfare experts frequently discussed the social challenge posed by the mass arrival of European women in terms of introducing modern shopping and cooking regimes, more stringent health standards, and prenatal and childrearing instruction to poorly educated rural women from peripheral Europe. These were women accustomed to conditions of debilitating scarcity and strangers to modern notions of motherhood that required attention to the psychological and emotional well-being of their children. It also applied to the better-off, even bourgeois urban women of Eastern European cities forced by the brutalizing experiences of war, military occupation, and postwar rations to suffer the indignity of meeting familial obligations under crude conditions and thus operate for years in a basic survival mode that left little room for attaining the higher attributes of mothering skills.

**Conclusion**

In adapting ethnic cuisine to mainstream culture, food fashion-makers drew, explicitly or implicitly, on liberal notions of celebrating diversity – a theme that postwar Canadian officialdom encouraged, within limits – but early postwar culinary pluralism also produced uneven and contradictory results: Canadians were encouraged to appreciate immigrant customs while newcomers themselves were often transformed into (or, rather, reduced to) colourful folk figures bearing exotic foods and quaint customs but never accorded an equal status with 'real' Canadians. The emergence in these years of 'multicultural' cookbooks with a 'unity in diversity' theme were financed with some federal government funds because officials considered them 'an excellent medium to further the idea of Canadian unity.'[90] Such texts reflect the contradictory features of postwar cultural pluralism: celebrating ethnic customs and encouraging 'multicultural' cuisines while at the same time perpetuating cute and patronizing stereotypes of immigrants as static folk figures. By stripping immigration of its more threatening aspects, they reduced ethnic diversity to entertainment and novelty.[91]

When postwar Canadian health and welfare experts, food fashion-makers and mass-market magazines promoted a Canadian way of cooking and eating, they prioritized pro-capitalist, middle-class food practices, household regimes, and family values. Approved patterns included careful meal planning, strategic shopping in 'modern' stores, three nutritionally balanced meals per day – all washed down with countless glasses of milk. The bourgeois experts encouraged all Canadian women, and particularly low-income and immigrant mothers, 'to get the most for their food dollar' through planned grocery shopping trips using a seven-day menu plan, taking advantage of grocers' specials, and following the casseroles and roasted-meat diet favoured by Canadians. The Canadian way held centre-stage while ethnic dishes were relegated to the margins as novelty items to entice North American palates (and often bastardized in the process) or as a source of economical meals.

We should be wary of imputing too much influence on the prescriptive literature, however. The different kinds of evidence mined for this paper indicate a range of responses to postwar food and homemaking campaigns. For those eager to embrace all facets of Canadianism, like the Pilli children, eating Canadian was very important. In contrast, the senior Pillis, like many other adult newcomers, expressed their desire to be Canadian but drew the line at Canadian food, while for others, incorporating Canadian food customs meant neither abandoning their previous food culture nor a passive acceptance of 'modern' child-feeding regimes that front-line health and welfare workers tried to impose on them. The differing capacities of both Canadian and New Canadian women to incorporate, ignore, or modify the suggestions of experts should not be overlooked. Indeed, it suggests that the relationship between food experts and newcomers is perhaps best understood as a series of negotiations and encounters that transformed both food cultures, though not equally. Anglo-Canadian experts had the power and position to define 'ethnic' food as un-Canadian, while the *Food Customs* guidebook and other projects for newcomers suggest that nutrition experts and food fashion-makers, like other experts involved in immigrant and refugee reception work, sought to modify, not obliterate the food (and other) cultures of emigrating groups, but liberal intentions did not eliminate cultural chauvinism. In turn, the vast number of postwar immigrants and refugees actually transformed Canadian cuisine even as they incorporated Canadian foods into their own diets. Through *Chatelaine*, some, perhaps many, postwar Anglo-Canadian housewives experimented with their first Italian, Chinese, Indian, and Caribbean dishes. If the recent allure of multicultural dining experiences and conspicuous dining has brought immigrant food cultures into the forefront of North American bourgeois standards of 'taste,' the 1950s and 1960s were more tentative, contested contexts. Still, current food wars – including the recent 'wok wars' in Toronto sparked by an Anglo-Canadian couple who complained about their Chinese neighbours' food smells – remind us

# FEED A FAMILY OF FIVE FOR $22 A WEEK

*Jeanisse family gathers around dinette table for Thursday's dinner. Children, from left, are Rodrigue, Daniel, Susan.*

Before working out a weekly low-cost menu pattern for the Jeanisse family we reviewed Dorothy's grocery-shopping habits. Evidently it had been next to impossible to plan meals ahead and shop regularly because her husband Rod's income was so erratic. When the income was low, Rod would buy a few groceries out of his pocket money on the way home from work. When he was paid for a job, they would shop together at the local plaza, spending more than they could afford.

Now that Dorothy knows exactly what they should spend on food, they will be able to shop regularly. Twice a week they will buy fresh meat, fruits and vegetables — fewer trips would not be wise because their refrigerator has only a small freezer section and

inadequate shelf and crisper space. Twice a month they will stock up on such staples as cereals, sugar, milk powder, canned goods and economical bulk lots of vegetables — potatoes, carrots and turnips — that store well in the cool fruit cellar.

Fortunately, Dorothy does not have to cater to food whims — the family enjoys foods that are necessary to a health-building diet, yet come within the budget category. With Dorothy's co-operation, we drew up a practical plan to provide these foods for less money than before. The plan includes a complete week's menu, and recipes to go with it (the dinner menus shown here start this section of the article); ways to save money in shopping for foods, ways to save money in using foods as well as what foods fill health needs.

MONDAY

WEDNESDAY

TUESDAY

THURSDAY

Aimed at the budget shopper and time-conscious cook, the magazine most commonly featured affordable meals based on economical cuts of meat, such as hamburger, usually accompanied by quick potato or rice dishes and vegetables.

that class and cultural conflict continue.[92] Finally, we leave open for debate two central questions: Are Canadian and New Canadian women of early postwar Canada best viewed as sisters or strangers? Does cultural pluralism, even when practised in positive and affirming ways, always involve a degree of cultural appropriation, an act, literally, of 'eating the other'?[93]

NOTES

1  Our discussion draws on the emerging literatures on food and accompanying practices and issues, such as Stephen Mennell, Anne Murcott and Anneke H. van Otterloo, *The Sociology of Food: Eating, Diet and Culture* (London: Sage, 1992). On social histories of food, see, for the United States, Harvey Levenstein's pioneering works, *Revolution at the Table: The Transformation of the American Diet* (New York: Oxford University Press, 1988) and *Paradox of Plenty: A Social History of Eating in Modern America* (New York: Oxford University Press, 1993) and more recently Donna Gabaccia, *We Are What We Eat: Ethnic Food and the Making of Americans* (Cambridge, MA: Harvard University Press, 1998). A comprehensive survey of the Canadian scene remains to be written, but worthwhile forays into the field are Margaret Visser, *Much Depends on Dinner* (Toronto: McClelland and Stewart, 1986) and *The Rituals of Dinner* (Toronto: HarperCollins, 1991) and Anne Kingston, *The Edible Man: Dave Nichol, President's Choice and the Making of Popular Taste* (Toronto: Macfarlane Walter & Ross, 1994). See also Anne Goldman, '"I Yam What I Yam": Cooking, Culture, and Colonialism,' in Sidonie Smith and Julia Watson, eds, *De/Colonizing the Subject: The Politics of Gender in Women's Autobiography* (Minneapolis: University of Minnesota Press, 1992); Joan Jensen, 'Canning Comes to Mexico: Women and the Agricultural Extension Service 1914-1919,' in *New Mexico Women: Intercultural Perspectives* (Albuquerque: University of New Mexico Press, 1986).

2  For a sample of the emerging social and gender history of post-1945 Canada, see Gary Kinsman, *The Regulation of Desire*, 2d ed. (Montreal: Black Rose Books, 1996); Franca Iacovetta, *Such Hardworking People: Italian Immigrants in Postwar Toronto* (Montreal and Kingston: McGill-Queen's University Press 1992); essays in Joy Parr, ed., *A Diversity of Women: Ontario 1945–80* (Toronto: University of Toronto Press, 1998) and in Gary Kinsman, Dieter K. Buse, and Mercedes Steedman, eds, *Whose National Security? Canadian State Surveillance and the Creation of Enemies* (Toronto: Between the Lines, 2000). Influential U.S. sources include Elaine Tyler May, *Homeward Bound* (New York: Basic Books, 1988), Joanne Meyerowitz, *Not June Cleaver: Women and Gender in Postwar America* (Philadelphia: Temple University Press, 1994); John D'Emilio, *Sexual Politics, Sexual Communities* (Chicago: University of Chicago Press, 1983).

3  The literature on post–Second World War immigration to Canada is extensive, but

useful studies include the relevant chapters in Donald H. Avery, *Reluctant Host: Canada's Response to Immigrant Workers, 1896-1994* (Toronto: McClelland and Stewart, 1995) and in Irving Abella and Harold Troper, *None Is Too Many: Canada and the Jews of Europe 1933–1948* (Toronto: Lester and Orpen Dennys, 1982); and, on the impact of Cold War policy on immigration, Reginald Whitaker, *Double Standard: The Secret History of Canadian Immigration* (Toronto: Lester and Orpen Dennys, 1987).

4 Ann Stoler, 'Tense and Tender Ties: The Politics of Comparison in North American History and (Post) Colonial Studies,' and the roundtable discussion in *Journal of American History* 88, no. 3 (December 2001); Mary Louise Pratt, *Imperial Eyes: Travel Writing and Transculturation* (London: Routledge, 1992).

5 On this topic and on recent efforts at such integration see the discussion in the introduction.

6 Ethel Ostry Genkind, 'Children from Europe,' *Canadian Welfare* 25, nos. 1–2 (April–June 1949); Michael Marrus, *The Unwanted: European Refugees in the Twentieth Century* (New York: Oxford University Press, 1985), 229.

7 For further treatment, see Franca Iacovetta, 'Corrupted Democracy' in Kinsman, Buse, and Steedman, *Whose National Security?*

8 See, for example, 'Outwitted Soviet Police Waded Mountain Snows Czech Girl in Winnipeg,' *Toronto Star*, 23 September 1950 (front page) and Jeannine Locke, 'Can the Hungarians Fit In?' *Chatelaine*, May 1957 (and discussed below).

9 On this theme see also Joy Parr, *Domestic Goods: The Material, the Moral, and the Economic in the Postwar Years* (Toronto: University of Toronto Press, 1999).

10 Laura A. Belmonte, 'Mr and Mrs America: Images of Gender and the Family in Cold War Propaganda,' Berkshire Conference on the History of Women, Chapel Hill, North Carolina, June 1996. Thanks to the author for the copy of her paper. Drane, *Canadian Register*, 19 May 1962, 2.

11 National Film Board Archives (hereafter NFBA), Montreal, file 51-214, *Canadian Notebook*, produced by NFB for Department of Citizenship and Immigration, Information Sheet (April 1953). On the NFB and Cold War, see Reg Whitaker and Gary Marcuse, *Cold War Canada: The Making of a National Insecurity State, 1945–1957* (Toronto: University of Toronto Press, 1994).

12 NFBA, file 57-327, *Women at Work*, produced for Department of Citizenship and Immigration (Gordon Sparling, producer and director) (1958). It highlights white-collar work opportunities for immigrant women (in business, teaching, nursing, social services, and communications) while also promoting a domestic ideal. An early script entitled 'Suggested Treatment for Careers for Women in Canada,' nd) contains the following: 'Most spectacular in merchandising techniques is the self-serve Super Market [capitalized] for handling and selling food. Pre-wrapping, usually in transparent cellophane or polythene, extends to everything including meat, vegetables and fruit.'

13 The vast international literature on the professionalization and medicalization of

'mothercraft' and on 'homemaking' in the pre-1945 period includes valuable Canadian studies such as Cynthia Comacchio, *Nations Are Built of Babies* (Montreal: McGill-Queen's University Press, 1993) and Kathryn Arnup, Andrée Lévesque, and Ruth Pierson eds, *Delivering Motherhood* (London: Routledge, 1990). For studies that deal more explicitly with immigrants and minorities, including First Nations, see J.R. Miller, *Shingwauk's Vision: A History of Native Residential Schools* (Toronto: University of Toronto Press, 1996); Gabaccia, *We Are What We Eat*, and Levenstein, *Paradox of Plenty*. On post-1945 trends, see, for example, Parr, *A Diversity of Women*; Mary Louise Adams, *The Trouble with Normal* (Toronto: University of Toronto Press, 1997); and Mona Gleason, *Normalizing the Ideal* (Toronto: University of Toronto Press, 1999).

14 For Canada, see, for example, Susan Prentice, 'Workers, Mothers, Reds: Toronto's Postwar Daycare Fight,' *Studies in Political Economy* 30 (1989); Veronica Strong-Boag, 'Home Dreams: Canadian Women and the Suburban Experiment,' *Canadian Historical Review* 72, no. 4 (1991); Ruth Roach Pierson, *'They're Still Women After All': The Second World War and Canadian Womanhood* (Toronto: McClelland and Stewart, 1986), Valerie J. Korinek, '"Mrs. Chatelaine" versus "Mrs. Slob": Contestants, Correspondents, and the *Chatelaine* Community in Action, 1961–1969,' *Journal of the Canadian Historical Association*, and the citations in note 13 above.

15 Doug Owram, *Born at the Right Time: A History of the Baby Boom Generation* (Toronto: University of Toronto Press, 1996) chapters 1 to 3; Franca Iacovetta, 'Remaking Their Lives: Women Immigrants, Survivors, and Refugees,' in Parr, *Diversity of Women*; Marlene Epp, *Women without Men: Mennonite Refugees of the Second World War* (Toronto: University of Toronto Press, 2000)

16 Gleason, *Normalizing the Ideal*.

17 City of Toronto Archives (hereafter CTA), Social Planning Collection (SPC), SC 40, box 56, file 9 – c 'Immigrants, Migrants, Ethnic Groups – English Classes – West Toronto, 1954, 1959–1962, 1966,' *Report of the Committee on English Language Instruction*, June 1961.

18 Useful starting points for the U.S. mass migration era are John Bodnar's overview, *The Transplanted: A History of Immigrants in Urban America* (Bloomington: Indiana University Press, 1985) and Donna Gabaccia, *From the Other Side: Women, Gender and Immigrant Life in the U.S., 1820–1990* (Bloomington: Indiana University Press, 1994).

19 Adult means age 18 and over. The median age of immigrants was 24.9; most groups registered a median age of between 23 and 25. The percentages are derived from annual data gathered from the Immigration Branch, *Annual Reports*, 1946–65; on age, residence and other features, see Warren Kalbach, *The Impact of Immigration on Canada's Population* (Ottawa: Dominion Bureau of Statistics, 1970); see my calculations and table in 'Remaking Their Lives.'

20  Not until the 1970s did migration streams from 'not-white' nations reach significant numbers. Government recruitment policies of Caribbean women for domestic service brought only handfuls of these women into Canada before 1965. A modest number of Chinese women arrived by 1965, but their presence was significant: in 1947, Canada rescinded the racist Chinese Immigration Act (1923) (and that had been preceded by the infamous Chinese head taxes dating back to 1895).

21  For details, see Avery, *Reluctant Host*; Abella and Troper, *None Is Too Many.*

22  Iacovetta, 'Remaking Their Lives'; Epp, *Women without Men*; Joyce Hibbert, *The War Brides* (Toronto: PMA Books, 1978); Agnes Calliste, 'Canda's Immigration Policy and Domestics from the Caribbean: The Second Domestic Scheme,' in Jesse Vorst et al., eds, *Race, Class and Gender: Bonds and Barriers* (Toronto: Between the Lines, 1989) and the essays on Caribbean and more recent African women in this volume.

23  On race, racialized women and nation-building – an important theme in recent multi-disciplinary work on immigrant and refugee women and women of colour – see, for example, the essays in the special theme issue, 'Whose Canada Is It?' of *Atlantis*, co-edited by Tania Das Gupta and Franca Iacovetta.

24  Significantly, this statement (a familiar refrain) was made in 1970, suggesting that continuing waves of newcomers posed an ongoing challenge to reception workers. Public Archives of Ontario (hereafter AO), Young Women's Christian Association Collection, MU3027, box 11, Metropolitan Toronto Branch, *Annual Report*, 1970. For similar activities in the 1950s and 1960s see, for example, MU3523, box 7, series A-2, YWCA Committee Minutes, 1885–1966; MU3027, box 11, series B1, *Annual Reports, Toronto*, 1874–1955.

25  CTA, Central Neighbourhood House (CNH Activities), SC (Social Planning Council), vol. 5D, box 1, file 52, manuscript of Marion O. Robinson, *The Heart of the City*, 9–10.

26  In that regard, these years probably mark the origins of Canada's official multiculturalism policy, adopted in 1970. That policy also carried with it a legacy of surveillance of immigrant communities. Both themes are discussed in greater depth in Franca Iacovetta, 'Making New Citizens in Cold War Canada' (in progress).

27  For similar observations, see also Mariana Valverde, 'Building Anti-Delinquent Communities: Morality, Gender, and Generation in the City,' in Parr, *Diversity of Women.*

28  Samuel Edwards, 'Insights of Domesticity,' *Food for Thought*, Special Issue, 'Newcomers to Canada,' (January 1953).

29  For example, see Isobel M. Jordan, 'Canada – Land of Promises?' *Food for Thought* and other contributions to this special theme issue, 'Newcomers to Canada,' of the organ of the Canadian Adult Education Association; numerous speeches by Dr Vladimir Kaye, chief liaison officer, Citizenship Branch, including those in the National Archives (hereafter NA), MG31 D69 vol. 11, 1951; Address Prepared for the Conference of the Executive Council of the Ukrainian Canadian Committee in Winnipeg, 7 November 1951, and others in this file.

30  As the Canadian Association for Adult Education declared, 'We believe that newcomers can make their full contribution to Canadian life only if they are happy and well-adjusted in their new surroundings.' Introduction to *Food for Thought.*

31  David Weiss, executive director, Montreal Jewish Child Bureau, 'Immigrant Meets the Agency,' ibid., 42–5, and reprinted in *Social Casework* (December 1952). On related themes, see Franca Iacovetta, 'The Sexual Politics of Moral Citizenship and Containing Dangerous Foreign Men in Cold War Canada, 1950s–1960s,' *Histoire sociale/Social History* 33, no. 66 (November 2000).

32  Geoffrey S. Smith, 'Containments, "Disease," and Cold War Culture,' in Brian J.C. McKercher and Michael Hennessy, eds, *War in the Twentieth Century: Reflections at Century's End* (Westport, CT: Praeger, 2003); his 'National Security and Personal Isolation: Sex, Gender, and Disease in the Cold War United States,' *International History Review* 14 (May 1992); May, *Homeward Bound*; Whitaker and Marcuse, *Cold War Canada*; Kinsman, Buse, and Steedman, *Whose National Security?*

33  The making of the Canadian nation involved more than the conventional political history or protective tariffs, political deals, and a transcontinental railroad. It involved the official displacement of Aboriginal peoples removed from traditional homelands to make way for white settlers; an immigration policy that was racially selective and sexist, especially where women and families from 'undesirable' (non-white) sources were concerned; and campaigns to shape the morality of the population. Recent work in nation-building draws on the influential postcolonial writings of Edward Said and others, but for the specific Canadian context, see, for example, Mariana Valverde, *The Age of Light, Soap and Water: Moral Reform in English Canada, 1885–1925* (Toronto: McClelland and Stewart, 1991); and Daiva Stasliuis ed., *Unsettling Settler Societies* (Thousand Oaks, CA: Sage, 1995).

34  Charles Heustis had written in response to the Liberal government's decision in May 1948 to commit substantial funds (an annual grant of $30,000 for the next five to ten years) for health education, expansion of hospital and other facilities, and research and training. 'The Nation's Health,' *Toronto Star*, 5 February 1949.

35  Dr Vladimir Kaye, chief liaison officer, Citizenship Branch, concurred, saying that any immigrant 'must go through a change which affects his body and soul – changes of climate, diet, change of culture, change of the whole mode of life,' 'Like Seeks Like,' *Food for Thought*, Special Issue, (January 1953), 'Newcomers to Canada,' 23–5. The theme also emerges in Kaye's speeches.

36  Jean Huggard, 'From Emigrants to Immigrants: Hungarians in a European Camp,' *Canadian Welfare* 33 (February 1958). On women in South Korean refugee camps, for example, see Pierre Berton, 'The Ordeal of Mrs. Tak,' *Maclean's*, 15 June 1951.

37  On this and other examples, Canadian Red Cross, Ontario Division, News Bulletin. Special Issue on the British War Brides (September 1946). Thanks to Frances Swyripa for this source.

38  CRC, Ontario Division *News Bulletin* (Ruth Adams) (September–October 1945). No

doubt strawberries were not easily obtained in postwar London; see also ibid. (May 1946).

39 CRC, Ontario Division, *News Bulletin* (September 1946).

40 For contrasting examples of war-bride experiences, including women's stories of intense loneliness, conflicts with Canadian in-laws, and difficult marriages, see, for example, Iacovetta, 'Remaking Their Lives'; Hibbert, *The War Brides*; and Estella Spergel's collection of oral testimonies (including her own) in her 'British War Brides, World War Two: A Unique Experiment for Unique Immigrants – The Process that Brought Them to Canada' (MA thesis, University of Toronto, 1997). With thanks to Estella for sharing her material.

41 The British measured liquids by weight, North Americans by volume.

42 For examples, consult: YWCA, MU3527, *Annual Reports*, 1941–9; *Annual Report*, 1949 Weston Branch; University Settlement, Social Planning Council, vol 24, N1, box 1, Staff Meeting Minutes 1948–65, 4 June 1957 report.

43 Rather than specifying foods, the Canada Food Guide listed food groupings based on their nutritional value – vegetables, and meat and fish, and so on – and then offered general guidelines for their consumption while allowing for choice and variety. In 1950, a revised guide was issued.

44 This work also contains a critique of Betty Friedan's enduring characterization of women's magazines as strictly bourgeois periodicals that did little more than foster women's second-class status. Joanne Meyerowitz, 'Beyond the Feminine Mystique: A Reassessment of Postwar Mass Culture, 1946–1958,' *Journal of American History* 79, no. 4 (1993): 1455–82; Meyerowitz, *Not June Cleaver*; Valerie Korinek, *Roughing It in the Suburbs: Reading Chatelaine in the Fifties and Sixties* (Toronto: University of Toronto Press, 2000).

45 For further details, see Korinek, *Roughing It in the Suburbs*.

46 To combat depression, Hilliard advised housewives to seek part-time work and to get out into 'another world.' For example, see 'Women's Greatest Enemy Is Fatigue,' *Chatelaine* (January 1954). A recent retrospective of the magazine, *Years of Chatelaine*, notes with regret that the magazine rejected an early excerpt from Friedan's book because they felt the topic was already being addressed in Canada!

47 To take one example (May 1965), the 'social issues' articles included: Mollie Clefton's 'Canada's Seven Most Urgent Social Problems'; Kay Clefton, 'I Am a Common-Law Wife'; 'What They Don't Tell You about Being a Beauty Queen'; a two-parter by Florence Jones and Dorren Mowers, 'How Two Women Fought Race Prejudice: Teaching Freedom in Mississippi' and 'Growing Up Prejudiced in Ontario.' This sort of material did not normally appear in *Ladies Home Journal* or *Good Housekeeping*.

48 In the 1950s and 1960s, the magazine devoted more space to newcomers, the working class, and the urban poor than to rural Canadians. For more details, see Korinek, *Roughing It in the Suburbs*.

49 Christina McCall, 'Working Wives Are Here To Stay' (1961); Ian Adams, 'The Pov-

erty Wall,' (1969) illustrated with a black-and-white photo showing an exhausted woman trudging down an alley, pulling a bundle of groceries as her kids follow behind. In contrast to the usually cheerful images of Canadian abundance and domesticity, this grocery-cart image offered a compelling visual metaphor for the huge burdens imposed on poor mothers forced to feed families on inadequate incomes. For more details on this and other such articles, see Korinek, *Roughing It in the Suburbs.*

50 Doris Anderson, *Rebel Daughter* (Toronto: Key Porter Books, 1996).

51 As in the work of Rolande Barthes, Pierre Bourdieu, John Fiske, and Michel Foucault. For an overview of this rapidly developing field, see 'Cultural Studies: An Introduction,' in Lawrence Grossberg, Cary Nelson, and Paula Treichler, eds, *Cultural Studies* (London: Routledge, 1992).

52 For a useful discussion of the New Left critique of U.S. imperialism in the so-called banana republics and food corporations' advertising schemes, see Levenstein, *Paradox of Plenty,* chapter 12, 'The Politics of Food.'

53 For more details, see Korinek, *Roughing It in the Suburbs.*

54 Marie Holmes, 'Meals off the Shelf' (February 1955); Elaine Collett, '98 Cent January Specials' (January 1960); Seven Dinners on the Double'; and 'Easy-to-Make Pizza Pin Wheels' (1961), all in *Chatelaine.* Levenstein, *Paradox of Plenty;* see also Gabaccia, *We Are What We Eat.*

55 Ethnic cuisine as a theme of food features accounted for 15 per cent of all food articles in the 1960s, and ranked third behind thrift (which was the subject of 26 per cent) and new and improved (which was the subject of 21 per cent). In the 1950s, the theme of ethnic cuisine ranked in eighth spot – at 2.6 per cent of all food articles – behind thrift, traditional values, new and improved, entertainment, special, speed of preparation, and ease of preparation. A comprehensive analysis of this material, based on detailed databases, is available in Korinek 'Roughing It in Suburbia: Reading *Chatelaine* Magazine, 1950–1969' (PhD diss., University of Toronto, 1996, especially appendix).

56 Elaine Collett, 'South Seas Foods To Enchant Your Natives' (May 1963).

57 Levenstein, *Paradox of Plenty,* 218. We also thank the members of the Toronto Labour Studies Group, the faculty at several universities where we delivered this talk (individually or collectively), and other colleagues 'of a certain age' who shared their stories of culinary (and other forms of experimentation) in the 1960s and 1970s!

58 Editors, 'What's New with Us' (March 1965).

59 For example, see Elaine Collett, 'Ten New Ways with a Pound of Hamburg' (September 1961).

60 This and the following references are from the AO, International Institute of Metropolitan Toronto, MU 6410, file: Cookbook Project, booklet: Toronto Nutrition Committee, *Food Customs of New Canadians.* Published with funds from the Ontario Dietic Association.

61 The revised guide profiled Chinese, Czechoslovakian, German and Austrian, Greek,

Hungarian, Italian, Jewish, Dutch, Polish, Portuguese, Spanish, Ukrainian, and West Indian 'food customs.'

62  The entries for Jewish and German-Austrian.

63  Although the guide does not explicitly state it, these class distinctions, in turn, overlapped with racial distinctions between wealthier whites and poorer blacks more likely to emigrate.

64  Miller, *Shingwauk's Vision*; Gabaccia, *We Are What We Eat*; Comacchio, *Nations Are Built of Babies*.

65  Another entry noted the availability and use of vitamin D for mothers and children.

66  As for improvement, it stated: 'If income low the use of more poultry might be encouraged' and 'The cost and relative value' of sugar-coated cereals and milk was explained.

67  For a discussion of drink and ethnic groups in an earlier period, see, for example, Mariana Valverde, *Diseases of the Will* (Cambridge, UK: Cambridge University Press, 1998).

68  For a valuable discussion see Comacchio, *Nations Are Built of Babies*.

69  Franca Iacovetta, 'Recipes for Democracy? Gender, Family and Making Female Citizens in Cold War Canada,' *Canadian Woman Studies* 20, no. 2 (Summer 2000).

70  First launched in 1951, the contest drew so many participants – five thousand entries alone in 1956 – that publication of the results got delayed by months while harried staff made their selections. A victim of its own success, the contest closed for good in 1967.

71  The first *Chatelaine Cookbook* sold 110,000 copies (for $5.50 to $6.95) at a time when any Canadian book reaching sales of ten thousand copies was called a best-seller, and it was later followed by *Chatelaine's Adventures in Cooking* and the *Chatelaine Diet Cookbook*.

72  This feature became a booklet that health and welfare agencies and home economists across the country distributed. The supervisor of Home Economics for Vancouver Island, for example, reported that she had used more than two hundred copies of this guide; after her copies from the magazine ran out, she had the article reprinted. Five years after its original publication she was still handing it out to clients. PAO, Maclean-Hunter Records Series (MHRS) F-4-1-b box 432, Elaine Collett to DHA (Doris Anderson), LMH (Lloyd Hodgkinson), and J. Meredith, 'Western Trip,' (October 1961).

73  One example are the cookbooks of homemaker Margaret Radforth (1911–92), an original resident of the modest, middle-class, planned community of Leaside in Toronto. They included *The Joys of Jello*, 9th ed. (White Plains, NY: General Foods) and her local United Church fundraising cookbooks (in Iacovetta's possession). The popularity of cookbooks and self-help books was also an international phenomenon.

74  For details, see Korinek, 'Mrs. Chatelaine and Mrs. Slob' and *Roughing It in the Suburbs*.

75 The sample is of 28 interviews conducted in the 1970s with immigrant women and couples asked to comment on food customs and with the following national, regional, and ethnoreligious breakdown: European (18), including European Jewry (4), Asian (2), Caribbean (1), and South Asian (mainly from India) (3). This sample was selected from Iacovetta's database of more than 60 interviews with post-1945 immigrants culled from the Oral History Collection, Multicultural History Society of Ontario (hereafter MHSO), Toronto.

76 MHSO sample, interviews with Amelia S-R. and Maria B. Similar reports come from POWs, including Lotta B., a Polish Gentile woman who fought in the Polish Resistance until her arrest during the Warsaw insurrection in 1944. For her, the Germany POW camp meant lack of food, poor sanitary conditions, and total isolation from world events.

77 MHSO sample, interviews with Maria B., Helga A., and Dagmar Z.

78 MHSO sample; the theme also comes up repeatedly in the recordings of reception workers.

79 MHSO sample, interview with Iusa D.

80 MHSO sample, interview with Dagmar Z.

81 MHSO sample, interview with Annemarie H.

82 MHSO sample, interviews with Susan M., Helga A., and Nazneed S.

83 For one example, see Franca Iacovetta, 'From Jellied Salads to Melon and Prosciutto, and Polenta: Italian Foodways and "Cosmopolitan Eating,"' in Jo Marie Powers, ed., *Buon appetito!* (Toronto: Ontario Historical Society, 2000).

84 Jeannine Locke, 'Can the Hungarians Fit In?' (May 1957).

85 All were favourable though for varied reasons. Mrs M. Filwood, Toronto, saw Katey's most attractive asset her apparent willingness to 'iron clothes for the doctor's wife' and carry out other duties 'just out of the sheer enjoyment of helping.' Other readers stressed the émigrés' many accommodations; an 'impressed' Nova Scotian woman declared 'they would make better Canadians than some of us born in Canada if they were given the time and opportunity by us.' A minister involved in a Hungarian resettlement project hoped that readers, 'especially immigrants,' would be 'encouraged' by the couple's 'wonderful successes and achievements.' Mrs M. Filwood, Toronto to Editors, 'Letters to *Chatelaine*,' (July 1957); Letter from a new reader, Halifax, to Editors (August 1957); Rev. G. Simor, SJ, St Elizabeth of Hungary church, Toronto, to Editors (September 1959).

86 Later, she became famous for the *Schmecks* cookbook series featuring Mennonite and Pennsylvania-German cuisine.

87 By contrast, Staebler's portrait of Bruno borders on female oogling: 'When Bruno enters a room,' she writes, 'it is charged with energy. He takes off his jacket, rolls up his shirt sleeves and his marvellous muscles burst forth. So does his laughter and robust lively talk. He is thirty-two, five feet, eight inches tall, thick-set, bronzed and broad-

shouldered, with curly hair, smiling eyes, and a dimple set deep in his chin ... He works hard and loves people. He says, "I want always in my living to be able to hold my head high."' His movie-star good looks were tempered by his commitment to family and fatherhood; he enjoyed 'playing *scopa* and *boccia* [card and lawn-bowling games]' but stayed home at night 'to save money' for a visit to Italy and to buy his family 'a small home.'

88  This is a significant contrast to the maple Canadian furniture that Joy Parr claims in *Domestic Goods* that many postwar Canadians and (at least certain) immigrants preferred.

89  Staebler informed her audience of this fact when years later she published a collection of her articles.

90  For example, see NA, MG31, Citizenship Branch, D69, col 12, file: 1950, Liaison Officer, Dr V. Kaye, Report of Trip to Toronto and Hamilton, 27 September– 2 October 1950.

91  For example, AO, IIMT, file: Cookbook Project, *Special Greetings in Food Christmas 1963* (homemade pamphlet). A more detailed discussion of this theme is in Iacovetta, *Making New Citizens in Cold War Canada* (in progress).

92  See also Marlene Epp's discussion in this volume.

93  The phrase, of course, is borrowed from bell hooks.

PART 4

# *Immigrants, Gender, and Familial Relations*

# Japanese Pioneer Women: Fighting Racism and Rearing the Next Generation

MIDGE AYUKAWA

## Introduction

For years, the social history of certain cultural groups in Canada was ignored. As Franca Iacovetta wrote in 1997: 'little has been written about Asian Canadians as historical actors rather than as objects of scorn.'[1] The few books on Japanese-Canadian history that exist, written by both Japanese Canadians and others, stress victimization, racism, exploitation, and, most prevalent of all, the group's internment and economic destruction during the Second World War.[2] Yet, to fully understand the lives of the Japanese Canadians, it is necessary to understand that they were dynamic actors who made active decisions when dealing with social and political challenges. Furthermore, it is especially necessary to tell the story of the women whose arrival changed the Japanese immigrants from sojourners to settlers.

It is my belief that the immigrant *issei* (first generation) mothers laid the groundwork for success with their efforts to raise the *nisei* (second generation – the Canadian born) as Japanese in both culture and language. The constant admonitions to be proud, to be honest, to always do one's best, to behave properly, not to bring shame to the family or to the Japanese community, appear to have taken root. The mothers' examples of stoicism, patience, and putting on a good face, provided the *nisei* with the resources to pick up the pieces, to rebuild, and to become exemplary Canadians. Like many other immigrant women, the mothers took special pains to acculturate their children to be Japanese in both culture and language.[3]

## A History of Exclusion

Although small in number – Canadians of Japanese descent constitute only about 0.2 per cent of the nation's population – this ethnic group has made significant contributions to Canadian society in the arts, the sciences, and in public service.[4] Behind their contemporary success and adaptation is a formidable history of exclusion that saw Japanese in Canada become one of 'the most despised of minority groups' during the Second World War.[5] As the articles by Enakshi Dua and Lisa Mar in this volume demonstrate for Hindu and Chinese immigrants respectively, Asian newcomers were subject to severe immigration restrictions and Anglo-Canadian hostility during the first part of the century. The first Japanese immigrants to Canada at the beginning of the twentieth century were sojourners who hoped to earn enough capital in a burgeoning labour market to allow them to return to Japan within several years with sufficient funds to rebuild their futures and lead prosperous lives. For many of these adventurers, the fulfillment of such dreams was hampered by a capitalistic stratified labour market on the West Coast. The Japanese immigrants in British Columbia discovered that, like the Chinese who preceded them to Canada, they were hired to replace higher-paid Canadian-born or European workers. In a 1902 Royal Commission inquiry, Richard H. Alexander, the manager of the Hastings Mill in Vancouver stated: 'The Japanese supplies [sic] the want of the proportion of cheap labour that is necessary to compete in the markets of the world.'[6] A policy of hiring cheaper Asian labour led to misunderstanding and agitation among white labourers who resented their uncompetitive positions in the job market.

Escalating resentment against the Asian 'intruders' led to the formation of an Asiatic Exclusion League patterned after similar bodies in the United States. On 7 September 1907, a parade and rally agitating for 'a white man's country,' was held in Vancouver. It degenerated into a violent riot, and the angry mob created havoc in Chinatown and the Japanese section of Vancouver. A 'gentlemen's agreement' between Japan and Canada that quickly followed limited the number of Japanese male immigrant labourers to four hundred. Other Japanese nationals were still permitted to enter Canada, and no restrictions were placed on re-entry after temporary absences or upon wives, children, and parents of Japanese immigrants.[7] After 1908, although the number of Japanese male immigrants declined, the number of female newcomers increased.

Immigration restrictions on Japanese were accompanied by public discrimination and animosity towards those resident in Canada. In the first half of the twentieth century, British Columbia was openly racist towards all Asians. According to Patricia Roy, 'some whites based their antipathy to Asians on real or anticipated economic conflicts; some were inspired by notions of racial differences; most had a number of reasons, both real and irrational, for their hostility and would have had difficulty in ranking their objections.' Roy also noted that British Columbians' 'concept of a "white man's province" reflected the notions of white supremacy.'[8] Peter Ward further observes that there was 'a reservoir of racial animosity

[and] continuing hostility of white British Columbians toward the immigrant from Asia.' In his opinion, 'racism was grounded in the irrational fears and assumptions of whites who lived in the farthest west.' White British Columbians believed that the Asians were unassimilable and that they 'undermine[d] the place of whites in the British Columbian labour market.'[9]

As James C. Scott has argued, those who are dominated resist those who dominate them by a 'hidden transcript.'[10] Japanese immigrants did not meekly accept the institutional racism to which they were subjected because they did not consider themselves inferior; instead, they countered oppressive situations with efforts to retain their cultural identity because 'culture [is] a medium in which power is both constituted and resisted.'[11] Concerned for the welfare of their children, they attempted to 'acculturate' the *nisei* with pride in their heritage so that their offspring would not be intimidated by mainstream society. Thus they taught the *nisei* that the Japanese were morally and intellectually superior to their persecutors. They urged their offspring to outperform their peers both in public school and in the workplace. By enhancing pride and self-image within their ethnic communities, Japanese Canadians were able to resist and subvert a history of exclusion and the resultant obstacles to adaptation.

## Pioneering Women

The hidden transcript required to indoctrinate Canadian-born Japanese was carried out primarily by the immigrant pioneer women, the picture brides. In the years following the exclusionary measures of 1907–8, and as young men reached marriageable age and their dreams of returning to Japan with a nest egg were still unfulfilled, some asked their families back home to find wives for them in Japan. Indeed, hearing stories of the degenerate lives led by these bachelors and concerned about their morality, some parents were already taking the initiative in this endeavour and so women were sent to join the men. According to available statistics, substantial numbers of women arrived between the years 1907 and 1928 (see Table 2). In 1924 the limit of 400 male immigrant Japanese labourers was lowered to 150. Then in 1928 female immigrants were included in the 150 limit and this put an end to the flow of picture brides.

The picture bride system was a practical adaptation of a traditional Japanese custom of the time, where family heads arranged marriages. In Japan the principals would have met briefly before marriage. When the groom was overseas, photographs were exchanged and in Japan, marriage ceremonies and registrations occurred *in absentia*, so that six months later applications could be made for passports. By 1924, there were 6,240 picture brides in Canada.[12] The women were often adventurous souls and many had chosen to emigrate. Picture brides often

TABLE 2
Immigration of Japanese Women, 1900–34

| Year | No. of Female Immigrants | Total No. of Immigrants |
|------|--------------------------|-------------------------|
| 1900 |        | 6      |
| 1901 |        | –      |
| 1902 |        | –      |
| 1903 |        | –      |
| 1904 |        | 354    |
| 1905 |        | 1,911  |
| 1906 |        | 2,142  |
| 1907 | 242    | 7,601  |
| 1908 | 566    | 858    |
| 1909 | 153    | 244    |
| 1910 | 134    | 420    |
| 1911 | 217    | 727    |
| 1912 | 362    | 675    |
| 1913 | 424    | 886    |
| 1914 | 447    | 681    |
| 1915 | 338    | 380    |
| 1916 | 233    | 553    |
| 1917 | 310    | 887    |
| 1918 | 370    | 1,036  |
| 1919 | 530    | 892    |
| 1920 | 389    | 525    |
| 1921 | 338    | 481    |
| 1922 | 300    | 395    |
| 1923 | 197    | 404    |
| 1924 | 233    | 510    |
| 1925 | 269    | 424    |
| 1926 | 214    | 443    |
| 1927 | –      | 511    |
| 1928 | –      | 535    |
| 1929 | –      | 179    |
| 1930 | –      | 217    |
| 1931 | 65     | 174    |
| 1932 | 48     | 119    |
| 1933 | 40     | 106    |
| 1934 | 25     | 125    |
| Total | 6,444 | 25,412 |

*Source*: Statistics of female immigrants are from Rigenda Sumida, 'The Japanese in British Columbia,' MA thesis, University of British Columbia, 1935, 40; statistics of total immigrants are from Ken Adachi, *The Enemy That Never Was* (Toronto: McClelland and Stewart, 1976).

said that they had married *Amerika,* not a particular male. Some had been married previously and were either widowed or divorced. In a society where there was no place for single women, they had chosen to opt for life abroad rather than accept marriage to a widower with many children or become a burden on their families.

The pioneering women soon discovered that life in Canada was not at all what they had envisioned. The early arrivals, like their husbands, expected to be sojourners. The primary reason for going to Canada was to work hard together with their husbands, save money, and return home to greater financial security. To achieve their dreams, nay, to merely survive, they had to do harsh work for long hours both inside and outside their home and still be conscientious wives and homemakers.[13] These women were considerably outnumbered by men. Some women ran boarding houses for their entrepreneurial husbands, catering mainly to other Japanese. Other women worked at lumbering, fishing, or mining camps, where they were responsible for the daily needs of as many as forty men. They washed work clothes under extremely primitive conditions, using wash-boards and heating pails of water, which they had often hauled a great distance, on wood-burning stoves. They also cooked three meals a day of rice, dried fish, and vegetables.[14]

Although the births of children were generally welcomed, it was difficult to find the time to nurture them the way the women wished. In their native villages, they would have enjoyed a strong support system where grandparents or neighbourhood young girls would have been available to take care of the young. In Canada they not only had to struggle on their own but they were also forced to raise their children in a strange and hostile environment. Since the care of youngsters was added to their already heavy burdens, in many cases children were sent to their grandparents in Japan. Extant memoirs tell about lonely childhoods in Japan, awaiting the visits or return of parents, or infrequently, about joyful trips back to the land of their birth.[15] Not all couples were able to send their children away, however; some did not want to for emotional reasons, while others simply could not, either lacking the money or a receptive, willing relative in Japan. Such families realized that their Canadian-born offspring would have to be prepared for the Japanese society they would encounter when they all returned to Japan.

## Educating the *Nisei*

An important part of this preparation for return was Japanese education. Because of educational reforms in Japan in the late nineteenth century, the majority of the picture brides were well educated and arrived in Canada with more formal schooling than their husbands. Therefore they were happy to educate their children in Japanese schools set up in British Columbia by the Japanese Ministry of Education. The first school was established in 1906 in Vancouver, followed by those in Cumberland in 1910 and Steveston in 1911. These early institutions followed the curriculum of primary schools in Japan with teachers provided by the ministry.[16] From about 1915, as the immigrants realized that their dream of returning to Japan was unachievable or ill advised, they began to educate their children in Canadian public schools. Most parents, however, insisted that their children also attend Japanese language schools to learn the language, history, and the culture of Japan as a way to instill in their children pride in their heritage to counter the anti-Asian racism that was rampant around them.

Racism against Asians was a reality that the Japanese immigrants faced daily. The Japanese Canadians, whether naturalized or Canadian-born, did not have full citizenship privileges. In British Columbia, Asians were denied the provincial franchise, and thus also the federal franchise. This legislation automatically closed the door on such professions as pharmacy and law. Without the power of the vote, Asians became the victims of the politicians who blatantly used racism as their platforms for elections. Forced to the balconies of movie theatres, banned from the city swimming pools, many hotels, and restaurants, and constantly called 'dirty Japs,' parents and children alike were upset. Such a climate gave Japanese settlers a strong incentive to counter with measures aimed at securing the self-respect, confidence, and overall mental well-being of their children. B. Singh Bolaria and Peter S. Li refer to racial domination as 'fostering an inferiority complex among the minority members [of a society] to the point where they begin to reject their own heritage in pursuit of white culture and symbols that render a higher social recognition.'[17] To the Japanese pioneers, the potential for 'low self-esteem and other psychological deprivations'[18] in their children would have been intolerable.

Language schools were seen as a primary vehicle for ethnic pride and maintenance and so were established wherever there was a substantial number of Japanese children. The majority of the teachers were women who were well educated themselves. By 1941 there were over fifty Japanese language schools in British Columbia. Although acquisition of language was claimed to be the main goal, the textbooks contained tales of glorified historical and mythical Japanese heroes. According to legend, the islands of Japan were created by gods. These gods were claimed to be still protecting the country and had brought forth the *kamikaze* (the Divine Wind) to defeat the Mongols in 1274 and 1281. Such stories were considered beneficial since they fulfilled the parents' wishes to counter the deleterious effect of racism on their children. Some of these racist notions resided in the very school materials used by Canadian children. In 1921, a nationalistic Japanese citizen who lived in the United States wrote: 'American or European writers of textbooks are not entirely free from the notion that the whole Orient is peopled by inferior or backward races. To offset these unfortunate influences, it is advisable that the Japanese children should be given correct knowledge of Japan and the Japanese. They should know that Japan has had an intensely cultivated civilization of her own, that her people are possessed of moral fibre as strong as that of any other people, that her history is replete with stories of noble deeds and achievements.'[19]

In cases where families did not live near a language school, mothers often undertook their children's Japanese education. One man recalled that as a little boy in the late 1920s, his family lived in Esquimalt which was too far away from the Japanese school in Victoria, and so his mother became his tutor.[20] Mothers also reserved time at home to educate their children in Japanese culture, by entertaining them with Japanese folk tales, for instance. Mrs Imada Ito, whose absent husband was at a lumber camp, struggled on a berry farm in the Fraser Valley while caring for her large family. She wrote in her memoir: 'In my leisure time I read useful or amusing books and told the stories to the children. They enjoyed this so much that after supper they would often say, "Mother, read a story so you can tell it to us and we will do the cleaning up," and the three would clean up for me.'[21] The stories were of samurai heroes and children's folk tales that had strong moral messages emphasizing the nobility of the Japanese race.

While language schools provided a concrete setting for passing on Japanese cultural heritage, homes and communities were equally important in instilling ethnic pride. Here mothers played a primary role in teaching their children duties, roles, and modes of behaviour that were appropriate to their community. Most Japanese families lived in ethnic enclaves, in virtual isolation from members of other races and cultures in Canadian society. Fathers often lived away from home in work camps, and even if the family lived together in company towns, the father was so exhausted after a long hard day of labour that the daily running of the home and the care and supervision of the children were left to the mother. Many *nisei* have remarked that an occasional grunt or an order was their fathers' only acknowledgement of their existence. The isolation from mainstream society that many women at home sometimes felt was offset by a good support system within their own communities, similar to the networks of mutual aid that existed in their native villages. In the case of my own family, our most immediate neighbours were Italians and Czechs, but language barriers and the demands of endless household chores and child care prevented my mother from much social exchange beyond the occasional greeting. She participated primarily in the social network provided by the Japanese community a kilometre away.

In circumstances where women had interaction only with other Japanese, there was little opportunity to learn English, and so while retaining language and customs for themselves, mothers also transmitted them to their children. In their homes, villages, and schools in Japan, women had learned to greet and treat

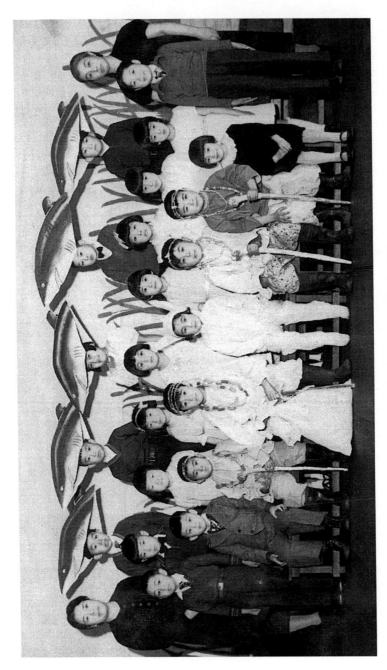

Japanese school play, Grade 2, Alexander Street Japanese School, Vancouver, March 1939.

everyone politely, to be uncomplaining, to not show feelings of pride, happiness, or disappointment. They urged similar behaviour on their children through constantly repeated expressions. The adage, 'the protruding nail will be hammered,' exhorted a person to not draw attention to herself or himself by speaking out about injustices, or even expressing one's opinions in public. This was particularly the case if opinions were contrary to what most of the community believed. The phrase, *makeru ga kachi* (the race is not to the swift) urged youngsters to keep trying. Girls especially were reminded daily to be stoic, to bow, to smile, and to speak polite Japanese. They were told to serve the boys in the family first at meal time, to respect their older brothers, and to care for their younger siblings. This training began at home and was reinforced in the Japanese schools.[22]

The teaching children received at home could, however, sometimes conflict with the ideas presented to them in public schools. For instance, many *nisei* comment on the confusion over the restraint taught at home and their experience at public school where one was supposed to speak out and express one's opinion. There were many differences in 'acceptable' behaviour, that included even simple matters like the proper way to read in front of a class. I recall one instance when my grade six teacher asked the class how one should stand and hold the book when reading aloud. As some Japanese-Canadian students took up the rigid posture of holding the book straight out in front, I felt quite embarrassed, sensing it was wrong. I myself had no idea what was customary until the teacher demonstrated the relaxed stance of the West.

**Education for Employment**

Although the inculcation of Japanese family and social values was deemed important, there was also another very practical need for a good Japanese language education. Language facility was necessary for the *nisei* to find employment in the Japanese-Canadian community, the only place for them where professional and clerical jobs existed. Jorgen Dahlie has noted that 'For the Japanese, facility in two languages became practically an economic imperative,' and 'the urban Nisei found knowledge of Japanese indispensable, since, inevitably, they had little choice but to work in the ethnic community.'[23] Because of the social prejudices in British Columbia, jobs in offices and stores outside the Japanese community were virtually unobtainable.

The first Japanese-Canadian graduate of the University of British Columbia was a female, Chitose Uchida, in 1916. Yet she was unable to obtain any work other than as an English-language teacher for Japanese Canadians. Some *nisei* women went to Japan to attend teachers' college and a few returned to teach at the Japanese language schools in British Columbia. Mothers often went to extraordinary lengths to ensure their daughters' education. One Hiroshima emigrant with an impressive samurai lineage refused to accept the responsibility for the expense of his daughter's education. And so, according to the son, his mother worked as a rag-picker at a salvage company, determined to support her daughter who was attending teachers' college in Japan. While many male high school and university graduates, unable to obtain positions for which they were qualified, laboured at jobs similar to their immigrant fathers, female high school graduates usually could find work only as maids in white households. Thus, many *issei* fathers denied their daughters higher education because of the lack of job opportunities.

Parents often insisted that young women learn a trade such as sewing, citing the unfortunate failure of Miss Uchida to make full use of her university education. In the 1930s young girls were urged to leave school and attend Japanese-run Western-style sewing schools where they learned to draft patterns, make adjustments, and sew men's and women's clothing. There were a number of such schools in both urban and rural areas, with teachers who had learned their craft in Japan. It wasn't long before Japanese Canadians developed a significant presence in this business sector. In Vancouver in 1931, licences for such businesses were held by eighty-one Japanese and there were also thirty-nine dressmaking establishments run solely by women.[24] Sewing was practical since it provided young women with a skill and also guaranteed a good marriage, the ultimate goal for all daughters. *Issei* men who dreamed of owning their own businesses frequently sought English-speaking wives with sewing skills. For instance, Mrs T.F., who grew up on a berry farm in the Fraser Valley, studied sewing; in the late 1930s she married an *issei* and together the couple ran a successful dry-cleaning and dressmaking shop in Vancouver. After the wartime upheaval, they settled in eastern Canada, living first in Montreal and later in Ottawa, where for years Mrs T.F. used her sewing skills to supplement the family income. Her *issei* husband, a skilled carpenter, was handicapped in his trade because of his lack of fluency in English and so her earnings were necessary to support their five children.

In another case, Mrs R.M. left school to study sewing before she graduated from elementary school. She was very beautiful and much admired for her grace in the art of Japanese dancing, yet it was her skill in dressmaking that made her a most desirable mate. In her late teens she reluctantly married an *issei* thirteen years her senior who had been apprenticing at a dry-cleaning and pressing shop. Her romantic relationship with a *nisei* was rejected by her parents as frivolous, especially since the young man was believed to lack the maturity and the economic potential of the older *issei*. She was heartbroken but it would have been unthinkable for a daughter to defy her parents. After marriage, the couple opened a shop in which Mrs R.M. was not only the receptionist, but did all the mending and alterations as well as sewing dresses and other articles for their clientele.

Ironically, while *nisei* women with sewing skills were considered good marriage partners for ambitious *issei* men, many families did not consider *nisei* women suitable wives for *nisei* sons. Their concerns were based on that fact that the *nisei* had absorbed mainstream attitudes and customs in spite of the wishes and efforts of their parents. Stephanie Camelon studied articles written between the years 1938 and 1949 by young *nisei* women, predominantly university students, in *The New Canadian*, an English language biweekly published by *nisei*. She found that the writers expressed a desire to be carefree like their non-Japanese contemporaries and to socialize with young *nisei* men the way other Canadian women appeared to with the opposite sex.[25] It is thus not surprising that young women from Japan were sought after as wives for *nisei* sons, especially eldest sons. Traditionally, the eldest son was the heir and with this privilege came many responsibilities including living with the parents and caring for them later. Japanese pioneer families in Canada feared that *nisei* women might not be as deferential as Japanese women and would be too independent.

The expectation that Japanese wives would be more submissive to authority and culture was not always met, however, as the following case suggests. Mrs H.K. was an educated young woman from Hiroshima whose marriage to a *nisei* from the Comox Valley on Vancouver Island was arranged in the mid-1920s. The couple had little in common and Mrs H.K.'s husband's Japanese was rudimentary. Following the insistence and determination of Mrs. H.K., the couple left the family farm where Mrs H.K. had been forced by her in-laws to work from dawn to dusk. Defying convention and community disapproval, they moved away and lived independently, with Mrs H.K. supplementing the family income by teaching Japanese. Such stories are rare because most young women, in both Japan and Canada, had been trained to accept their lot in life and few dared to disobey their elders.

## Identity and Acculturation

It appears that the indoctrination of the *nisei* to be proud of their heritage and to carry on the old traditions was sometimes thwarted in varying degrees by their exposure to the wider world. The degree of emphasis on Japanese ways also varied. Some *issei* had decided from the very beginning of their days in Canada that they were going to become Canadians and these parents tried to raise their children also as proud Canadians. Although they encouraged Japanese language training for practical reasons, they continued to hope for a better day for their children, where education and job opportunities were not thwarted by racial discrimination. Other parents treasured their Japanese nationality, felt superior to white people, and constantly reminded their children of their proud heritage.

The attitude of the majority of Japanese Canadians was somewhere in between these extremes.

Japanese Canadians also had disparate responses to the acculturating pressures of various Canadian institutions. The influence of Christian churches, as well as that of other Canadians who worked among the Japanese, had different degrees of success in 'Canadianizing' the community. The Japanese who became Christians are often said to have become more Westernized than those who worshipped at the Buddhist temples. As Franca Iacovetta and Valerie Korinek demonstrate in their essay on foodways in this volume, Canadian professionals who attempted to acculturate immigrants to 'Canadian ways' frequently undermined the work of cultural preservation carried on by pioneering mothers. I recall vividly the day my mother returned from a cooking class organized by local social workers intent on improving the diet of Japanese families. That evening she served us mashed potatoes and liver. One of my brothers took one look at the liver and hollered, 'Horse manure!' We children absolutely refused to eat the liver and even my father, who preferred Western food, had difficulty with it. Given the healthiness of most Japanese food, such attempts to 'improve' the diet of the 'poor ignorant Japanese' are rather humorous. The efforts of such earnest social workers usually failed. In fact, the only aspect of their heritage that many of today's Japanese Canadians still retain is food.

Roberto Perin observed that the descendants of Canadian immigrants, 'after several generations, eventually lose touch with the visible expressions of their ancestral culture: its language, its folkways, and even its religion. These cultural signposts are increasingly replaced by Canadian ones.'[26] There is no doubt that this would have happened eventually to the Japanese. However, the destruction of the West Coast Japanese communities in the Second World War precipitated an abrupt change within one generation. When Japan entered the war, Japanese Canadians, even those born in Canada, were considered 'enemy aliens.' Their property was confiscated, and they were forcibly evacuated and relocated away from the West Coast in 1942. After the scattering of the Japanese across Canada, the *issei* not only lost their possessions and their community, but their power, authority, and in some cases, even the respect of the younger generations. Most of them were unable to function in an English-speaking milieu.

Although the *nisei* subconsciously retained many of the values and attitudes taught to them, they all consciously endeavoured to be like their new non-Japanese neighbours so that they would not be thought of as aliens. They also avoided living close together and becoming 'visible,' lest racism rear its ugly head again. The *nisei* had been appalled in the 1930s when the Japanese military began committing atrocities in China. The bombing of Pearl Harbor in the Second World War shocked the entire Japanese-Canadian community and the shame that the *nisei* felt was exacerbated by their uprooting and banishment from the West

Coast. The subsequent defeat and surrender of Japan reinforced their resolve to reject their heritage. The wartime experience was painful, and in response the *nisei* struggled to provide their children with comfortable, middle-class Anglo-Canadian lives, rejecting everything but the food of Japanese culture. The *nisei*, however subconsciously, also encouraged their children to 'marry out' so as to be less noticeable, resulting in a third generation – the *sansei* – that has intermarried at a rate of greater than 90 percent.

## Conclusion

The *nisei*, although they believed they were behaving like '100 percent Canadians,' did in fact draw on the lessons of their youth. Younger siblings of the *nisei*, as well as the *sansei*, were exhorted to study and to excel, because education was viewed as the key to success. The *issei* laid the foundations and provided the tools and inner strength for the *nisei* to succeed. Struggling with racism themselves, and with their own expectations of a return to Japan alongside the expectations of white British Columbians that they acculturate, the 'picture brides' were pivotal in helping their children feel self-confident in an inhospitable environment. The efforts of these pioneer immigrant women were rewarded by the success of subsequent generations. By focusing on these early efforts at preserving culture in a climate of hostility, the social history of Japanese Canadians becomes not only a story of victimization but also an account of ethnic pride and achievement. As studies such as this one demonstrate, immigrant women played central roles in preserving ethnicity within their households but also provided their children with the tools to be successful outside of their ethnic communities.

NOTES

1 Franca Iacovetta, *The Writing of English Canadian Immigrant History*, Canadian Ethnic Group Series 22 (Ottawa: Canadian Historical Association, 1997), 4.

2 See, for instance, Ken Adachi, *The Enemy That Never Was* (Toronto: McClelland and Stewart Limited, 1976); Roy Ito, *Stories of My People: A Japanese Canadian Journal* (Hamilton: Promark Printing, 1994); Rolf Knight and Maya Koizumi, *A Man of Our Times: The Life-History of a Japanese-Canadian Fisherman* (Vancouver: New Star Books, 1976); Catherine Lang, *O-bon in Chimunesu* (Vancouver: Arsenal Pulp Press, 1996); Tomoko Makabe, *Picture Brides: Japanese Women in Canada*, trans. Kathleen Chisato Merken (Toronto: University of Toronto Press, 1995); Keibo Oiwa, ed., *Stone Voices: Wartime Writings of Japanese Canadian Issei* (Montreal: Véhicule Press, 1991); Toyo Takata, *Nikkei Legacy* (Toronto: NC Press, 1983).

3  See, for instance, essays by Apolonja Kojder (Polish), Isabel Kaprielian (Armenian), Dora Nipp (Chinese), and Eleoussa Polyzoi (Greek) in Jean Burnet, ed., *Looking into My Sister's Eyes: An Exploration in Women's History* (Toronto: Multicultural History Society of Ontario, 1986).

4  Midge Michiko Ayukawa and Patricia E. Roy, 'Japanese,' in Paul Robert Magosci, ed., *Encyclopedia of Canada's Peoples* (Toronto: University of Toronto Press, 1999), 842–60.

5  Robert Fulford, 'Canada's People: A Big Book about a Big Country,' *Globe and Mail*, 11 September 1999.

6  Canada, *Royal Commission on Chinese and Japanese Immigration, Report* (Ottawa: King's Printer, 1902; rpt. New York: Arno Press, 1978), 382.

7  Adachi, *The Enemy That Never Was*, 81.

8  Patricia C. Roy, *A White Man's Province: British Columbia Politics and Chinese and Japanese Immigrants, 1858–1914* (Vancouver: UBC Press, 1989), viii–ix.

9  W. Peter Ward, *White Canada Forever*, 2d ed. (Montreal and Kingston: McGill-Queen's University Press, 1978), 167, 169, 10.

10  James C. Scott, *Domination and the Arts of Resistance: Hidden Transcripts* (New Haven: Yale University Press, 1990), xii.

11  Nicholas B. Dirks, Geoff Ely, and Sherry B. Ortner, eds, *Culture/Power/History* (Princeton, NJ: Princeton University Press, 1994), 6.

12  An extended discussion of the picture brides is in my article 'Good Wives and Wise Mothers: Japanese Picture Brides in Early Twentieth-Century British Columbia,' *BC Studies* nos. 105–6 (Spring/Summer 1995): 103–18.

13  Audrey Kobayashi, 'For the Sake of the Children: Japanese/Canadian Workers/Mothers,' in Audrey Kobayashi, ed., *Women, Work, and Place* (Montreal and Kingston: McGill-Queen's University Press, 1994), 45–72.

14  Ayukawa, 'Good Wives and Wise Mothers,' 111.

15  See, for instance: Masuo Matsumiya, *Kaideima Monogatari [Tales of Kaideima]* (Hikoneshi: Sun Rise, 1986); Rigenda Sumida, *Doryoku Hitosuji [A Straightforward Endeavour]* (n.p.: By the author, 1969).

16  Hiroko Noro, 'The Japanese Language Schools in Canada from 1902 to 1941: The Role of Ethnic Language Schools,' working paper. Not all Japanese immigrants planned to return to Japan. A number emigrated dreaming of starting a new life and becoming Canadians. They sent their children to Canadian schools from the outset.

17  B. Singh Bolaria and Peter S. Li, *Racial Oppression in Canada* (Toronto: Garamond Press, 1985), 25.

18  Ibid.

19  K.K. Kawakami, *The Real Japanese Question* (New York: Macmillan, 1921), 148–9.

20  Michiko Midge Ayukawa, 'Creating and Recreating Community: Hiroshima and Canada, 1891–1941' (PhD diss., University of Victoria, 1996), 206.

21 Ibid., 75.

22 There are exceptions to this. In my five years of Japanese school attendance from 1937 to 1941, I had one male teacher who urged students to formulate their own opinions and express them clearly. His final exhortation to us, after Pearl Harbor was bombed and the school was ordered to close, was 'remember you are Canadians and that Canada is where your allegiance lies.'

23 Jorgen Dahlie, 'The Japanese in B.C.: Lost Opporunity? Some Aspects of the Education of Minorities,' *BC Studies* 8 (Winter 1970–71): 3–16.

24 Charles H. Young and Helen R.Y. Reid, *The Japanese Canadians* (Toronto: University of Toronto Press, 1938), 74.

25 Stephanie Jean Marie Camelon, 'Sandwiches or Sushi? Second Generation Japanese Canadian Women and the New Canadian, 1938–1949' (MA thesis, University of Victoria, 1996).

26 Roberto Perin, 'Themes in Immigration History,' in Magocsi, *Encyclopedia*, 1258–67.

# *Odars* and 'Others': Intermarriage and the Retention of Armenian Ethnic Identity

ISABEL KAPRIELIAN-CHURCHILL

## Introduction

Shortly after I took up my professorship in Fresno, California, a student asked me if I was a half-breed or a full-blooded Armenian. A few weeks later a local resident referred to her grandchildren as mongrels. These terms and all that they implied not only disturbed me but complicated my attempts to determine the number of Armenians in various California communities. How, after all, does one define an Armenian in the diaspora, especially one distantly removed from the immigrant generation? I had wrestled with this issue before, when I wrote the history of Armenians in Canada, and at that time found an examination of marriage patterns illuminating. It was particularly so since, as the daughter of foreign-born Armenian immigrants, I myself had married a non-Armenian. Inevitably, I brought a personal dimension to the study of the Armenian experience in Canada: the perspective of a participant. But I was more than a participant for I had also had the opportunity to observe events, people, developments, and relationships over a long period of time. These observations also seeped into the study of Armenians in Canada and formed an integral part of it. Participation, observation, memory, and impression became powerful underpinnings that were linked as part of a history, using the tools and perspectives of the historian. In this essay, I again forge the roles of participant, observer, and historian.

Intermarriage can be a vexing problem especially for foreign-born young people (1.5 generation) and the children of foreign-born parents (second generation). Teenagers growing up in Canadian society but with a different mother tongue and home culture have a dual heritage and may feel torn. The elements of loyalty and betrayal can be charged with intolerable emotion and tension, especially when it involves the choice of a marriage partner. One hears of situations where a family has disowned a son or daughter for not marrying within the group that may be defined in ethnic, racial, or religious terms.

Intermarriage has often been cited as one of the indicators of assimilation into the host society. Endogamy (marrying within one's group) is considered a pertinent index of cultural persistence, and exogamy is viewed as a significant index of the degree of assimilation or loss of ethnic identity. Exogamy is not only a significant *indicator of* the degree of assimilation but it is also an active *contributor to* assimilation. When a Chinese girl, for instance, marries a non-Chinese boy, she is probably already moving away from the Chinese community and its culture. The assimilation process will likely continue and intensify after such marriages, unless deliberate measures are mobilized to combat loss of mother tongue and home culture. On the other hand, if two Chinese marry each other, the chances of retaining mother tongue and home culture are greater, but not necessarily guaranteed.

Using Armenians as the centre of study, this essay will describe the pattern of intermarriage within this ethnic group during the twentieth century. It will examine *attitudes* of Armenians towards intermarriage and will show the impact of those attitudes on Armenian diasporan community life. Finally, the paper will give some suggestions on how the dynamics of identity between home and society might be integrated. The principal issue under discussion in this article will be the resilience or malleability of identity.

**The Armenian Genocide**

In 1915, a terrible catastrophe struck the Armenian people. The events, which lasted from 1915 to 1923, irrevocably changed the course of Armenian history and have become a watershed in the psyche of the Armenian people. One cannot understand the attitude of Armenians to intermarriage without understanding the profound impact of the Genocide. In 1915, under the cloak of war, the Turkish government undertook to annihilate one of its citizen minorities, the Armenians. The Young Turk political party, entrenched in a racist ideology of Turkism, determined to cleanse Turkey of non-Turkish and non-Muslim minorities. The party took control of the army, the Muslim religious hierarchy, and the machinery of state and set up the Secret Organization to implement its policy of extermination. The process of genocide was well planned. First, Armenian soldiers in the Turkish Army were disarmed and either imprisoned or murdered; Armenian leaders were then arrested, imprisoned, and killed. Left without defences and leadership, the civilian population was systematically deported. United States Ambassador Henry Morgenthau denounced this action as another form of massacre. Turkish authorities separated men and boys from the rest of the population and killed them.

Those who escaped this carnage – mostly women, children, and the elderly – were driven on a death march across mountains, over rivers, through deserts. From 1915 to 1923 one and a half million Armenians succumbed to disease, starvation, thirst, exposure, rape, and murder.

The remnants of the survivors – known in the West as 'the starving Armenians' – became refugees dispersed throughout the neighbouring countries in the Middle East, north Africa, Greece, the Caucasus, and the Balkans. An estimated 80 per cent of the 'starving Armenians' were women and children. Armenian men had been imprisoned, conscripted into slave labour gangs, or killed. Those fortunate enough to escape had volunteered in the hurriedly formed Armenian resistance regiments. Survivors experienced a triple-edged agony. They witnessed the destruction of the Armenian nation from its ancient homeland; they lost their family members and property; and they were uprooted from their homes, exiled to foreign lands, and reduced to wretchedness. Each survivor's account of personal trauma is a moving story of tragedy and triumph.[1]

The Genocide left a legacy of broken and scattered families and thousands of widows, widowers, and orphans. It also left a powerful incentive among the survivors to resist extinction and to defy further loss of identity. Armenians have a proud and ancient history as the first nation to adopt Christianity (AD 301) and as a highly creative people in literature, the arts, and architecture. Furthermore, Armenians have a history of survival. Being geographically situated at the crossroads between East and West, North and South, Armenia has for centuries been in the path of warring armies, but has managed to withstand repeated invasions. After each aggression, Armenians restored their churches and homes, rebuilt their farms and businesses, and revived their music, art, and literature. For the remnant survivors of the Genocide, however, the task and responsibility of saving the nation took on enormous proportions, since for the first time in recent history, Armenians had been driven out of their homeland.

Armenian survivors of the Genocide believed they carried the responsibility of rebirth and rehabilitation of the Armenian nation. Furthermore, they recognized the link between marriage and survival. As a community, Armenians have, in principle at least, opposed intermarriage in North America on the grounds that it would lead to the dilution of ethnic purity and eventual extinction. Only within the context of the fear of extinction can we understand the Armenian attitude to intermarriage.

### Armenian Marriage Patterns in the Twentieth Century

My examination of Armenian marriage patterns in North America for the twentieth century reveals, not surprisingly, that: intermarriage rates have risen over the past hundred years; the increase is evident even among the foreign-born, and in relatively new and large Armenian settlements, like Toronto and Montreal; and intermarriage rates will likely continue to rise. The following data are based partly on municipal registers and partly on church records, which admittedly provide an incomplete account because they may not include Armenians marrying in other churches, in civil ceremonies, or in other towns. Nevertheless, using both sets of data yields an adequate picture of trends.

As expected, the vast majority of Armenian immigrants to Canada before 1914 married Armenians. All except one of twelve marriages of Armenians performed in Grace Anglican Church in Brantford, Ontario, from 1905 to 1914, were endogamous.[2] The number of marriages is small, mainly because most of the Armenians in Brantford during the period in question were sojourners, men who had left their villages to work in Canada for a time and return home to their families and farms with badly needed money. The records show that all Armenian marriage partners were foreign-born. As the majority of Armenians were from the region of Keghi in the province of Erzerum, in the Ottoman Empire, most of the marriages were between people from Keghi, and even between people from the same village. This practice was in keeping with an Armenian saying: 'It's good to marry a person from your own region; better from your own town; best from your own street.' This trend is not as evident in the church records of Holy Trinity Armenian Church in Fresno, California. In the pre-1914 period, the rate of endogamy was high, given that most parishioners were newcomers. But settlers had migrated to Fresno from various parts of the Ottoman Empire; marriage patterns reflected not only the recency of arrival but also the disparate geographic origins of the settlers.

Following the Genocide, a massive upheaval of traditional marriage patterns occurred, as survivors, dispersed and impoverished, yet desperate to re-establish family life, were marrying and setting down new roots in different countries of asylum. In Canada, the sojourning men – bachelors and widowers – faced almost insurmountable obstacles in the search for a spouse. Because of the shortage of Armenian women in Canada, the men were obliged to link up with the refugee survivors overseas. But uncompromising immigration regulations all but blocked the resettlement of refugee survivors in Canada. Classifying Armenians as Asians, Canadian immigration authorities placed them under the strict limitations governing the admission of this racial category. In addition, Armenians had to comply with further restraints: a bona fide passport, the sum of $250 at entry, and passage by way of a continuous journey from their country of citizenship.[3] Stateless and poverty-stricken refugees found it almost impossible to comply with these stringent requirements. Between 1918 and 1950, Canadian officials admitted fewer than 1,500 Armenians. Among this group were a number of mail-order brides, young women who came to Canada carrying the picture of a man they knew only through correspondence. Most of these marriages were facilitated by matchmakers, but many women complained that the so-called matchmakers made *arrangements* not *matches*, citing the differences in age, in educational background, and in socioeconomic class.[4]

Not surprisingly, a high degree of endogamy marked the post-Genocide marriages. In southern Ontario and the northern United States between 1924 and 1929, all 40 marriages consecrated by the itinerant Apostolic priest, Rev. Movses der Stepanian, proved to be endogamous.[5] In Brantford, Ontario, Grace Anglican Church registers reveal that of the 68 Armenian marriages consecrated between 1917 and 1931, only two or about 3 per cent were of ethnically mixed couples. Similarly, of 117 Armenian marriages registered in the Fresno, California, county office in 1920, only one was exogamous.[6] Such a low incidence of exogamy during the 1920s is not abnormal given the traumas of the Genocide and the well-founded fear of national extinction, coupled with discrimination against Armenians by the host population and the resistance to marrying 'into the Armenian race.'

During the 1930s and 1940s, a different trend emerged, as second-generation Armenians reached maturity, as Armenian internal political and religious strife alienated many young people, as the Canadianization and Americanization movements through schooling and employment drew Armenian young people into their orbit, and as the Second World War brought Armenians into closer contact with people from other ethnic, racial, regional, and religious groups. Fresno county registers show that in 1930, 10 per cent of the 68 Armenian marriages were exogamous.[7] The figure is almost identical to the 13 per cent found in Fresno's Pilgrim Armenian Congregational Church records for the 31 marriages consecrated in the period from 1930 to 1934. By 1943 the picture changes dramatically. In Fresno county in 1943, 14 of the 49 marriages or 28.5 per cent were exogamous. The rate of intermarriage among Fresno Armenians soared in 1944 to almost 45 per cent.

In St Catharines, Ontario, none of the marriages consecrated in St Gregory's Armenian Apostolic Church in 1946 were exogamous (mostly first- and second-generation Armenians). From 1948 to 1980, however, the rate of exogamy jumped to approximately 59 per cent. By contrast, in Toronto, the marriage registers of Holy Trinity Armenian Church showed that in 1970, 19 per cent of the marriages were exogamous. In Montreal, church registers portrayed a similar trend: from 1958 to 1974 exogamous marriages were in the 24 per cent range.[8] How do we explain these statistics that differ noticeably from the 59 per cent exogamy rates in St Catharines during roughly the same period?

To understand these developments, we need to look at Armenian immigration flows to Canada.[9] After the Second World War, several thousand Displaced Persons were permitted entry into Canada, but Armenians were not among them in appreciable numbers. In other words, the Armenian communities in Canada received no 'new blood' from the 1920s until the situation changed in the late 1950s. During the 1960s, when Canada relaxed its immigration regulations and opened its doors to newcomers, Armenian communities in the Middle East faced war, economic constraints, and persecution. Destabilization drove Armenians out of Greece, Turkey, Egypt, Syria, Lebanon, Iraq, and Iran. In the late 1980s and during the 1990s, Armenian immigrants from the Middle East were joined by compatriots fleeing from violence in Azerbaijan and destitute economic conditions in the Republic of Armenia and other parts of the former Soviet Union. The majority of newcomers settled in Montreal and Toronto. They did not flock to older Armenian settlements like St Catharines and Brantford, Ontario. Before the First World War, Brantford anticipated a prosperous future as a bustling, industrial city. For a number of reasons, Brantford's fortunes declined, the city failed to attract enterprise, immigrants shunned the town, and local young people fled for opportunities elsewhere. The Armenian community withered and only a few Armenian names dot the telephone directory. Only the gravestones in the city cemetery stand as silent monuments to the existence of a once vibrant community.

By contrast, many Armenian settlements in North America, including Toronto, Montreal, and Los Angeles have been nourished and revitalized by successive waves of immigration. Each cohort brought its traditions, expertise, skills, and values and in obvious and subtle ways reshaped and restructured Armenian community life. More to the point of this essay, the successive waves of new immigrants added to the 'critical mass,' which provided a larger pool for choice of spouse. Thus, immigration flows can explain the discrepancies between the exogamy rates in places like St Catharines and Montreal during roughly the same period.

These statistics bear out the findings of others.[10] In his study of Armenian marriage patterns in the United States using Armenian Apostolic Church records, Aharon Aharonian concluded that the older the community and the further removed from the immigrant generation, the more the likelihood of intermarriage. Anny Bakalian confirmed these findings in her analysis of Armenians in New York and Matthew Jendian noted the same trend in his work on Armenian marriage patterns in Fresno. Jendian examined the 59 Armenian marriages in the 1990 Fresno county registers by generation and the parents' place of birth. When both parents were foreign-born, 42 per cent of the marriages were exogamous; when both parents (of Armenian descent) were born in the United States exogamy soared to more than double, to almost 88 per cent.

In reviewing the church files of Holy Trinity in Fresno, I found that in 10 marriages recorded in 1968, 3 non-Armenian men and 4 non-Armenian women married Armenians, yielding a mixed marriage rate of 70 per cent. By striking contrast, the 1982 marriage rolls showed the impact of immigration from the Middle East starting in the 1960s. In 23 marriages listed in the 1982 records, 4 Armenian women and 7 Armenian men took non-Armenian spouses. In other words, 11 or slightly fewer than half the marriages in 1982 were exogamous while 12 marriages or slightly more than 50 per cent were endogamous. Jendian also found a link between marriage patterns and immigration. His analysis of the Fresno registers revealed that 80 per cent of the marriages in 1980 were exogamous but ten years later, exogamy had *declined* to 68 per cent, reflecting the continued flow of immigrants from the Middle East and the availability of potential marriage partners of Armenian descent.

If the Armenian community in North America had remained static and had received no further immigration flows, it might have disintegrated, perhaps even disappeared, like the Armenian communities in Poland and Italy, because the twin forces of intermarriage and assimilation might have submerged Armenian identity altogether. But the regular flow revitalized the communities and provided them with the critical mass necessary to maintain ethnic identity.

### Gender, Family, and Intermarriage

Invariably, the study of intermarriage raises questions about gender. Is there a difference between the rates of intermarriage of boys and girls? If so, what factors contribute to the differential? How do parents treat the intermarriage of their sons as compared to the intermarriage of their daughters? Before the Second World War, most mixed marriages were between Armenian men and non-Armenian women. During and after the war, however, the incidence of female exogamy rose, a clear reflection of the absence of young men away in military service. In Fresno, another factor contributed to exogamy among Armenian women. Three military installations brought marriageable and increasingly autonomous Armenian women into contact with large numbers of eligible non-Armenian men who did not share the same prejudice against Armenians as many local residents. Harold Nelson found that of the 14 exogamous marriages in Fresno County in 1943, 66.6 per cent were of Armenian women to non-Armenian men. In Canada, as well, Armenian women started marrying non-Armenian men in the mid- to late 1940s.

Parents vehemently opposed the intermarriage of their children, regardless of gender, and they often threatened ostracism if their children acted against their wishes. But societal forces became too strong for them to impose such constraints, especially on their sons who enjoyed more freedom than their daughters in moving out into the world. Armenian society, particularly for the immigrant generation, was largely patriarchal. One might argue, then, that parents expected their sons, as potential heads of households, to be able to create an 'Armenian home,' regardless of the ethnic background of their spouse. Therefore, they offered less resistance to their sons' 'aberrant' behaviour. It is also possible that parents held more power over their daughters than over their sons and could be more assertive with the girls. However, as girls began to venture out into Canadian society, attain higher education, and take jobs in the 'Canadian world,' they too began to make their own decisions about marriage partners, even against their parents' will.

Assuming that attendance at Armenian churches and at Armenian day schools are barometric indicators of ethnic heritage retention, I carried out an informal review in Fresno to ascertain whether, in contemporary society, Armenian women or men in mixed marriages brought their families to Armenian churches or sent their children to the Armenian Community School. I hoped to see whether an interviewee's comments about the past were still applicable, given the current rates of intermarriage and the impact of the women's movement: 'In those days [1950s and 1960s], we just followed our husbands. We went where they went. No questions asked.'[11] I asked parishioners on an ad hoc basis whether they thought Armenian men or women in mixed marriages brought their families to church. Without hesitation, interviewees answered that Armenian men in mixed marriages brought their families to church more than did women. I then examined the ratio of mixed marriage families in the membership of three Armenian churches and in the student population of the Armenian Community School in Fresno in 2001. In analyzing the numbers, I found that some Armenian women who had outmarried brought their children, but not their husbands, to church. Out of a membership of 360 people in Pilgrim Armenian Congregational Church, approximately 29 Armenian women and 22 Armenian men who had outmarried brought their spouses and children to church. At First Armenian Presbyterian Church, 47 Armenian men and 28 Armenian women had outmarried and remained part of the total membership of 450. Of 540 church members at Holy Trinity Armenian Apostolic Church, 64 or just over 11 percent had outmarried; among this group were 34 Armenian men and 30 Armenian women. And at the Armenian Community School, out of a student population of 123, 23 were from mixed marriage families. Of the 23 intermarried couples, 12 Armenian women and 11 Armenian men sent their children to Armenian language schools. Although it would require more meticulous research for an accurate comparison of men and women, it would seem, nevertheless, that my findings confirm the perception that men maintain ethnic heritage more than women, at least with respect to church membership and school attendance – but only by a slight margin (114/101). My findings, it would appear, dispel the view of the woman as the mainstay of the mother tongue, the ethnic culture, and the religion. Clearly, forces other than gender are operating in ethnocultural retention.[12]

## Responses to *Odars* (Non-Armenians) as Spouses

Armenian attitudes to mixed marriage couples and families range from acceptance to polite distance to active rejection. No doubt these responses reflect the age of the community, the distance from the immigrant generation, the strength of Armenian organizations and institutions, and the frequency of intermarriage in the community. In many cases, non-Armenians have been totally integrated in the Armenian–North American community. We often hear of non-Armenians who attend Armenian church, engage in Armenian activities, or work for different Armenian organizations, as well as children of mixed marriages who have attended Armenian schools or participated in Armenian youth groups with scarcely any problems.

Far too often, however, non-Armenians have not been treated as welcome additions to the Armenian community. In the past, Armenians denounced inter-marriage as nothing short of 'white massacre' and expressed their fears and anxi-eties in myriad ways. For instance, young women contemplating marriage to non-Armenians were cautioned: '*Odars* will love you when you're young, but when you get old and wrinkled, *odar* men will desert you, but an Armenian man is steadfast.' Or young men were told: 'Armenian women make the best wives!'[13] In her absorbing and meticulous study of the Armenian experience along the U.S. East Coast, Anny Bakalian points out the importance of attitude:

> The marriage of men and women of Armenian descent with non-Armenians (odars) is assumed to be the key to assimilation that will obliterate Armenian presence in the United States – the final straw on the camel's back ... the culprit of all the woes of Armenian-Americans ... the cause of all the changes in the life-style that the immi-grant generation had taken for granted. Armenian-Americans do not realize, as the evidence from the New York survey has shown, that statistically intermarriage is of secondary significance to the passing of generations in the United States and reli-gious affiliation ... A non-Armenian parent decreases the likelihood of participation in the ethnic world; however, *the organized community's reactions are as significant, if not more so. Their attitudes and behavior send the message that odars are not welcome in their midst.*[14] [my emphasis]

Nowhere is Armenian resistance to outmarriage more poignantly symbolized than in the use of the words *odar* (non-Armenian) and *but*, as in: 'My daughter married an *odar, but* he's a good man.' Or 'My son married an *odar, but* she's a nice girl.' Used in this manner, *but* speaks volumes about the Armenian attitude to mixed marriages.

## Vocabulary of the 'Other'

This discussion started with references to labels like 'half-breed' and 'full-blooded,' terms originally used in a derogatory racial sense to refer to American Indians, but now applied to members of the general population, in California, at least. *Yabani*, a word sometimes used by Armenians to describe an uncouth or crude person, derives from the Turkish word for 'foreigner.' For Armenians, *yabani* has much the same connotation as *goy*, the Yiddish word used for a non-Jew, or the Greek word, *barbaroi*, from which we derive the English word 'barbarian' – the outsider, someone unlike us, the uncivilized, the foreigner. For many immigrants and their children, 'foreigner' conjures up distressing childhood memories of intolerance and contempt. Anglo-Americans and Anglo-Canadians scorned those who were not descended of British stock, even if they were born in North America, with epithets such as, 'those foreigners, they all reek of garlic and eat weird food.' Or, 'those foreigners, why don't they speak English?' Or, 'those foreigners, they take jobs away from us.'

Words like *half-breed, shiksa, odar,* and *foreigner* can have different meanings and implications in different times and places. In reading literature from the region of Keghi in the province of Erzerum (present-day Turkey), where my father was born, I was struck by an intriguing distinction between the words *yergiratsi* and *odar*. All Armenians from Keghi were *yergiratsi*, or countrymen, while all Armenians from outside Keghi were *odar*. Armenians from Kessab (Syria) still use this distinction between Kessabtsis and *odars*. All non-Kessabtsis, even other Armenians, are *odars*.

When Armenian settlers arrived in North America at the turn of the century, they continued to identify themselves according to their home regions. The bonds of kith and kin and the attachment to village and region persisted, and expanded to generate far-flung networks of *yergiratsis*. This network, in turn, led to a proliferation of village, town, and city compatriotic associations, which helped to transmit the bonds of kith and kin to subsequent generations. As a result, Canadian-born and American-born children frequently identified themselves as Erzerumtsis, Vanetsis, or Kharpertsis depending on where their parents or grandparents were born – Erzerum, Van, or Kharpert. In California, people still ask (in English), 'What *tsi* are you?' – Where do your parents or grandparents come from? While Armenians may identify themselves in their own communities by their old country family region, in the larger North American context, they identify themselves as Armenians or *Hyes* and all others as non-Armenians or *odars*.

In the early years of Armenian settlement in North America, when Armenian immigrants referred to the host Anglo-Saxons as *odars*, they attached no stigma to the word, for they considered the Anglo-Saxon society modern and progressive. In the *Armeno-American Letter-Writer*, the author repeatedly and respectfully refers to Americans as genteel, cultured, and civilized people.[15] Conversely, new immigrants – often impoverished and semi-literate – felt inferior, backwards, and unsophisticated. These feelings were reinforced as widespread intolerance towards immigrants, particularly those from eastern Europe and Asia, pervaded North American society. Spurred by nativism, the United States Congress passed exclusionary immigration acts throughout the 1920s which, for almost forty years, curtailed the entry of Armenians to the United States. Gripped by similar nativist sentiments, the Canadian Parliament also enacted immigration regulations that restricted Armenians from entering the dominion for the first half of the twentieth century.

Bigotry and racism plagued Armenians already living in the United States and Canada, especially in areas where they were numerous, notably in places like Fresno, California, or Boston, Massachusetts.[16] Armenians were restricted from joining certain clubs and organizations, excluded from living in certain areas, even after such discriminatory land covenants were declared illegal, and constrained in their professional education and their professional practice.[17] In response to prejudice and ostracism, Armenians either repudiated their ethnic heritage and melted into mainstream North America, or turned inward and became 'ethnoverted,' to coin a term. Where prejudice swelled to ugly, anti-Armenian hostility, the distinction between Armenian and non-Armenian, between *Hye* and *odar*, became charged with animosity; and the word *odar* soon carried a pejorative twist. Today, attitudes towards Armenians have improved, especially in older settlements, and *odar* has lost its derisive connotations, but the past has not been totally forgotten.

### Mixed Marriage Families and the Retention of Ethnic Identity

Armenians form a numerically small ethnic group in North America. Given the forces of assimilation, they cannot afford to lose anyone if, as a community, they have any hope of retaining their ethnocultural identity. Relying on immigration to enhance the numbers and bolster Armenian community life is both unrealistic and precarious because immigration is subject to conditions and regulations beyond the control of the Armenian North American community. Nor can Armenians depend on natural birth increase, since their fertility rate is relatively low, probably averaging about two children per woman of childbearing age. (Under current demographic conditions, an average of 2.1 children per woman is required for population replacement.)

In my view, mixed marriage families are one of the greatest, but unrecognized, unappreciated, and underused assets of the Armenian community in the diaspora.

If, for example, an Armenian couple has two children, the population remains static, but if a mixed marriage couple has two children who identify as Armenians, that is, if one Armenian parent has two children, the population is effectively doubled. Armenians can increase their numbers, enlarge their critical mass, and improve their chances of survival if the spouse and children of mixed marriages feel comfortable in the Armenian orbit. Consider, for example, an informant whose non-Armenian mother was rejected by the Armenian community. With little choice, the father and the family, which eventually numbered six children, withdrew from all things Armenian. Today, all six children are married with families of their own, but not one feels or thinks Armenian. In other words, an entire family of twenty-one people – many carrying an Armenian surname – are lost to the Armenian collectivity because the community rejected one non-Armenian parent. If Armenians persist in such intolerance, they run the risk of someone saying, as an informant told me without intended irony: 'My grandfather used to be an Armenian.'

Assuming that Armenians take their ethnocultural survival seriously, and make a conscious decision to cope with it, then what is to be done? Responses to this question can be quite different. On the one hand, some have argued that for Armenians – or any other ethnic or racial group – to pursue its continued identity in North America is selfish, self-serving, and segregationist. Others have complained that Armenians who marry outside the ethnic group are selfish individualists who are acting against the best interests of the Armenian collectivity. For the community to seek, at some cost and effort, to bring their spouses and families into the fold would put undue pressure and demands on limited community resources, they contend.

Obviously, many Armenians would argue that the most effective method of dealing with intermarriage is to avoid it altogether. My own view is that a conscious, well-planned, and determined effort should be made both in the home and the community to welcome intermarried families as a meaningful and respected part of Armenian North American life. As a beginning, the role of identifiers in influencing attitudes and outlook should not be underestimated. Perhaps Armenians should consider changing their descriptors to define the spouse and offspring not as *odars*, half-Armenians, non-Armenians, or new Armenians, but rather, just simply as Armenians. Such inclusiveness need not deny other loyalties or ethnic identities because in societies like Canada and the United States, one has the freedom to make multiple accommodations.

Community outreach programs should encourage mixed marriage families to share in Armenian community life. Participation engenders commitment; commitment engenders loyalty. If language is a barrier to participation, then other means should be found to attract non-Armenians, such as the use of both Armenian and English at meetings and services, or the establishment of new groups – social or religious ones – using only English. Furthermore, perhaps we should reconsider whether linguistic expertise is the only or principal definition of being Armenian. Certain individuals might be drawn in more effectively by an appreciation of Armenian music, art and architecture, or literature in translation, by church attendance, by political involvement, or by a better knowledge of Armenian history.

For many, however, identity revolves around language. If knowing the language is important, then more Armenian language classes should be established for non-Armenian speakers. Few facilities exist where non-Armenian speakers can learn to speak the language. I know several newlyweds who, with hope and dedication, attended Armenian night-school classes to learn to read, but gave up in frustration because although they learned the alphabet and could read the exercises, they could not understand the words. Properly designed Armenian conversation courses for second-language learners should be organized and adapted to the age and level of the learner.

Clearly, the most functional place to learn the language is in the home. Recently, at a dinner at the Armenian Community Centre in Toronto, I spoke in Armenian with a young woman sitting beside me. As she was conversing in Eastern Armenian, I asked her whether she was from Armenia or Iran. She smiled and told me she was Dutch and credited her husband for teaching her to speak Armenian. She felt totally comfortable in the community centre, participated in a women's group, and sent her children to Armenian school and the Armenian church. At the same time, she had not forsaken her Dutch heritage and willingly passed it on to her children, whose lives were thus enriched by a multicultural and multilinguistic exposure, a fitting experience in a country like Canada. The challenge of ethnic retention is best focused on the children. Ethnic culture, ethnic identity, and ethnic loyalty are best absorbed in childhood. The warmth and love of grandparents, for example, can establish a lasting link between a child and his/her Armenian ancestry, something I have witnessed in the lives of my students.

Armenian schools, whether they are Saturday, Sunday, or full-day schools should encourage the admission of mixed marriage children and indeed, the community should find means to facilitate sending such children to Armenian school. Schools are powerful mechanisms that can offset intermarriage transmissional decline. In Canada, research has shown that if, in a mixed francophone marriage, one parent speaks French to the child and the child attends a French-language school, then the results of intergenerational transfer are as potent as if both parents spoke French to the child. Under the same conditions, the Armenian language would fare equally well. Also, Armenian as a second language (ASL) classes can be designed for children using the same methodology as English as a second language (ESL) courses, including the creation of appropriate computer programs.

For a group to retain its ethnic identity, the host society laws and structures need to be conducive to heritage retention. It is well known that heritage languages have a better chance of survival in Montreal than in Toronto, in part because the Quebec government provides public funding for allophone (non-French, non-English) schools. As a colleague commented, 'Compared to Montreal, Toronto is a graveyard for heritage languages.' As evidence of this, the 1996 census showed that among ethnic origin Armenians, the mother tongue is retained 83.4 per cent in Montreal and only 79.5 per cent in Toronto. Home language as a percentage of mother tongue is also higher in Montreal (78.6 per cent) than in Toronto (68.3 per cent).[18] It is evident that schools are part of the institutional completeness that sociologist Raymond Breton put forward as a means of coping with assimilation. In addition, the involvement of mixed marriage offspring in specifically Armenian activities could be increased through programs such as camps, guides and scouts, dance ensembles, youth groups, and youth travel to Armenia. Courses in Armenian language and on Armenian subjects at the high school, college, and university levels should also be institutionalized and reinforced.

The more young people learn about Armenian history and culture, the greater will be their appreciation of their unique heritage. The more they strengthen friendships with each other, the more intimate will be their ties with the Armenian collectivity. Some of the most memorable comments I heard during my first year at Fresno State University were student responses explaining why they were taking my courses in Armenian history. They wanted to find out about their Armenian heritage and they wanted to learn what their parents had not taught them. Some felt they had been 'shortchanged. I'm missing my roots. I want to make up for my loss.'

## Choosing One's Ethnic Identity

The names we are given at birth and the names we choose to use are powerful identifiers. I can recall how, as a child, I would wince every time I had to give my surname. And I never used my Armenian given name at school. So in effect, I had two names: Zabel Kaprielian in the home and in the Armenian community and Isabel Kaprielian in Canadian society. When I married Stacy Churchill, the change in reactions was dramatic. When people asked for my surname, I would often say Churchill, to which they replied, 'Oh, like the [former British] prime minister [Winston Churchill]?' But it never suited me to use only my husband's name and so I use both. A colleague, who is of Rumanian descent and married to an 'Anglo,' could not understand why I would choose to use my father's name when I had such a prestigious name like Churchill. In a way, she had a point, for a name can make a difference: doors open for Churchill far more readily than for Kaprielian. But I would feel untrue to myself if I dropped my name of descent. Not only that, I am not ashamed about my ethnic background. I talk about *madzoon*, *lavash*, *dolma*, and *beorag*, and take great joy in serving these dishes to my non-Armenian friends.[19]

Not only names, but location of residence and participation in organizational life can also reflect our choice of identity. In cities that have attracted large numbers of newcomers, we see the emergence of barrios and neighbourhoods with a concentration of immigrant ethnics. Armenians in Fresno, Los Angeles, Montreal, and Hamilton, Italians in Toronto, Chinese in San Francisco and Vancouver, Hmong in Fresno, and Chicanos all over California and Texas gravitate to their ethnic enclaves, their urban villages. Here they live next to, upstairs, or downstairs from others of their group. They shop at ethnic stores, eat ethnic foods, listen to ethnic music, frequent ethnic churches, and celebrate ethnic festivals. Invariably, they transfer their values and their culture to their children and grandchildren.

In spite of these physical, religious, cultural, and emotional bonds, every ethnic or racial group, especially those not sustained by new waves of immigration, has experienced major changes in group dynamics, as well as an enormous loss of descent group identity and solidarity in North America.[20] Marriage patterns reveal the extent of structural assimilation among both European and non-European groups. The 1990 U.S. census showed that of married persons between the ages of twenty-five and thirty-four, born in the United States, the rate of outmarriage is as follows: 81 per cent among Poles, 73 per cent among Italians, 35 per cent among Chicanos, and over 50 per cent among Asians.[21] The children of these marriages, in turn, reflect the changing demographics. While those in North American society today having a single heritage are declining, those with multiethnic, multiracial, multicultural, and multireligious backgrounds are multiplying. A *Los Angeles Times* analysis of birth certificates found that one in six births in California in 1998 was to parents of mixed race or ethnicity, up from one in seven in 1989. In California, multiracial births run third behind white and Chicano births.[22] Recognizing these developments and responding to continued pressure, the U.S. Census Bureau included a multiple race classification in the 2000 census. For its part, Canada has recognized multiple heritages since the 1991 census.

In an article in the *Toronto Star* entitled 'Roots in Two Races,' children of mixed racial marriages are described as 'the diversity within the diversity,' those 'who blur the distinctions between Toronto's 100 languages and 169 countries of origin,' 'a growing part of our population,' 'our future.' The article then quotes from several children of biracial marriages whose comments were as varied as the respondents themselves: 'The first thing that comes to my mind is Jewish,' says a young man whose mother is Thai and father a Polish Jew. 'I don't think skin colour is enough to identify race, and terms like half-breed and mulatto have an implication of insult in my mind,' remarks another interviewee. 'I'm half Chinese, half Portuguese but all Canadian.'[23] My sojourn in Fresno has highlighted this trend. In Toronto, I could usually determine a person's ethnic and racial origin by his or her appearance, surname, or accent. To do so in Fresno is impossible because of the greater degree of intermarriage over a longer period of time. A blond, blue-eyed student with the name O'Brien, could be part African American, part Finnish, and part Scotch-Irish.

## Conclusion

Identity can be malleable for both the individual and the community of descent. Momentous shifts in the world will have profound and widespread ramifications. If ethno/racial/religious communities wish to survive in such a 'new' world, they must make conscious, prudent, and practical decisions, since they do have the power to exercise some control over their future. One of the repercussions of societal transformation will be on marriage patterns, as it seems evident that intermarriage can only increase. Like other groups, the Armenian community in the diaspora faces major decisions that bring exogamy into the larger dynamic. For Armenians, mixed marriages and the children of mixed marriages represent a valuable asset, which they can afford neither to alienate nor to ignore. Armenians need to undertake the mission to create outreach programs necessary to draw them into the group every bit as much as they need mechanisms to keep those already in 'the warm embrace of the community.' A re-evaluation of goals, priorities, and strategies is fundamental if Armenians envisage any hope of surviving as an ethnic collectivity in a fast-changing world.

Armenians derive a measure of assurance that their language, culture, and identity has survived over a period of almost three millennia. Their historic neighbours, the Lydians and Circassians, have vanished, as have the Ostrogoths and Visigoths. Yet a small nation like the Armenians has managed to survive, despite conquest and genocide. But contemporary society is brutally taking its toll on small nations, either through military defeat, assimilation, or the powerful impact of the Internet. If the Armenian language, the principal vehicle of Armenian culture, is not to be among the five thousand or more languages destined for extinction by the end of this century, if Armenian culture is not to be reduced to an academic pursuit, fit only for museums and archives, and if Armenian identity is not to disappear in what Jared Diamond calls 'the tragic loss of diversity,' then Armenians must take strong measures to assure their continued survival.[24]

NOTES

1 See, for example, Kerop Bedoukian, *The Urchin: An Armenian's Escape* (London: J. Murray, 1978) and David Kherdian, *The Road from Home: The Story of an Armenian Girl* (New York: Greenwillow Books, 1979).

2 Most Armenians belong to the Armenian Apostolic Church, which is an autocephalic church with the Mother See in Echmiadzin, Armenia. Armenian newcomers to Canada often joined the Anglican Church until they built their own church edifices. Their relationship with the Anglican Church reflects the theological closeness between the Anglican and the Armenian Apostolic Churches.

3 For an account of Armenian entry into Canada during the post-Genocide period, see Isabel Kaprielian, 'Armenian Refugees and Their Entry into Canada: 1919–1930,' *Canadian Historical Review* 71, no. 1 (Spring 1990): 80–108.

4 For an account of picture brides, see Isabel Kaprielian, 'Armenian Refugee Women: The Picture Brides, 1920–30,' *Journal of American Ethnic History* 12, no. 3 (Spring 1993): 3–29.

5 Father Der Stepanian's records are in the Armenian Apostolic Church Prelacy Archives, Montreal.

6 Harold Nelson, 'Intermarriage among Fresno Armenians,' *Sociologus* 4, no. 2 (June 1954): 42–59.

7 Matthew Jendian, 'The Farming Community and Marriage Patterns of Armenians in Fresno County,' paper presented at the symposium, *Armenians in the Raisin Industry: 1890–1990* held at California State University at Fresno, Fresno, California, 1997.

8 The author wishes to thank historian Edward Melkonian for giving her access to his findings on marriage records at St Gregory the Illuminator and Soorp Hagop [St. James] Apostolic churches in Montreal.

9 These flows were more or less similar in the United States, except that considerably more Displaced Persons settled in the United States after the Second World War than in Canada.

10 Aharon G. Aharonian, *Intermarriage and the Armenian-American Community* (Shrewsbury, MA: By the author, 1983); Anny Bakalian, *Armenian-Americans: From Being to Feeling Armenian* (New Brunswick, NJ: Transaction Publishers, 1994); Nelson, 'Intermarriage'; Jendian, 'Marriage Patterns.'

11 Oral interview by the author, name withheld, Fresno, 2001.

12 Mr Set Atamian provided information for the Armenian Community School; Mrs Lucille Gahvejian for Holy Trinity; Mrs Donna Robinson for Pilgrim Armenian Congregtional Church; and for First Armenian Presbyterian Church, Mr Phil Tavlian.

13 Oral interview by the author, Toronto.

14 Bakalian, *Armenian-Americans*, 393–4.

15  Haroutiune Chakmakjian, *Armeno-American Letter-Writer* (Boston: Hairenik Press, 1914).

16  See Robert Mirak, *Torn Between Two Lands: Armenians in America, 1890 to World War I* (Cambridge, MA: Harvard University Press, 1983).

17  The 1948 Supreme Court case of *Shelley v. Kraemer* outlawed restrictive land covenants in the United States. Similar restrictive land covenants existed in Canada. See J.C. Weaver, 'From Land Assembly to Social Maturity: The Suburban Life of Westdale (Hamilton), Ontario, 1911–1951,' *Histoire sociale/Social History* 2 (1978): 421.

18  Armenian population by ethnic origin, Mother Tongue and Home Language, for Canada, Provinces, Territories and Census Metropolitan Areas, 1996 Census – 20% Sample Data. Special tabulation provided by Department of Canadian Heritage.

19  *Madzoon* is yogurt; *lavash* is thin unleavened bread; *dolma* is rice or meat wrapped in grape leaves; and *beorag* is cheese or meat wrapped in phyllo pastry.

20  This excludes Hispanics, especially in the U.S. southwest where their numbers have increased partly through immigration. Indeed, some commentators arguably believe that Hispanics now outrank African Americans as the largest minority in the United States, basing their conclusions on the results of the 2000 census.

21  Cited in David Hollinger, *Postethnic America: Beyond Multiculturalism* (New York: Basic Books, 2000), 204–5. Hollinger is citing from Neil J. Smelser and Jeffrey C. Alexander, eds, *Diversity and Its Discontents: Cultural Conflict and Common Ground in Contemporary American Society* (Princeton, NJ: Princeton University Press, 1999), 85–128.

22  *Los Angeles Times*, 13 March 2001.

23  *Toronto Star*, 11 March 2000.

24  Jared Diamond, 'Deaths of Languages,' *Natural History* 4 (2001): 30–8.

# Sisterhood versus Discrimination: Being a Black African Francophone Immigrant Woman in Montreal and Toronto

GERTRUDE MIANDA

## Introduction

This article examines the situation of immigrant women of African origin who live in Toronto and Montreal. In particular, it focuses on these women's experiences of gender relations in the Canadian context, both within and beyond the domestic sphere. From this perspective, the paper also explores the rapport between these women and other women who do not belong to the African community.

African immigrant women are part of the new wave of migration to Canada that began in the 1970s. Indeed, the new wave of migration is characterized by the arrival of increasing numbers of people from Third World countries and by a larger percentage of women.[1] In 1996, 55.4 per cent of immigrants to Canada came from Asia and the Pacific, 16.1 per cent came from Africa and the Near East, and 8.2 per cent came from South and Central America, in contrast to 17.7 per cent from Europe and the United Kingdom and 2.6 per cent from the United States.[2] In total, Canada received 196,998 immigrants and 28,315 refugees during this same year.[3]

Canada proclaims itself to be a multicultural country. Given that it is traditionally recognized as one of the Western countries that welcomes a large number of immigrants, it is not surprising that people born abroad account for 17 per cent of Canada's population.[4] A good number of these newcomers arrive in Canada with customs and religions that differ from the Judeo-Christian traditions associated with Canadian culture. The new immigrants include increasing numbers of people referred to as 'visible minorities,' estimated to account for 9 per cent of Canada's population in 1991. It is predicted that visible minorities will account for 20 per cent of Canada's population by 2016.[5] By 1996, visible minorities already accounted for 3.2 million people. Half of these individuals resided in Ontario and British Columbia.[6] The size of the black population in Canada is estimated to be one-half million, with blacks of African origin representing 15 per cent of this number.[7] African immigrants are included in the category of 'visible minorities' even though black Africans first arrived in Canada as early as the seventeenth century.[8] In the twentieth century, African blacks began to emigrate to Canada after the Second World War.[9] The number of African immigrants reached a high of 8.7 per cent of total immigrants in 2000.[10] Although the rates from Africa tended to decrease after 1992, they remained relatively constant between 1993 and 1996, as indicated in Table 3.

Like most permanent migrants, Africans who establish themselves in Canada wish to maintain their ethnic identity.[11] Certain observers note, however, that maintaining cultural traits that are dissimilar to a host country's dominant culture appears to impede the new arrivals' integration because they provoke intolerant reactions and rejection by the mainstream population.[12] Polls indicate that Canadians fear increasing immigration, which they view as a menace to the national white culture. One Canadian in three opposes immigration, to preserve the national white culture. This opposition results from a false perception that immigrants do not respect certain basic principles of Canadian society, such as separation of church and state, and gender equality.[13] The immigrants generally considered culturally different come from Third World countries; the obstacles to integration for such immigrants are greater than for immigrants of European origin.[14]

In this exploratory study, I examine black French-speaking African immigrant women's experiences and perceptions of gender relations in the Canadian context. Because Ontario and Quebec received the majority of African immigrants since 1987 (see Table 3), I have chosen to focus on the cities Toronto and Montreal. An analysis of Citizenship and Immigration statistics reveals that there are more men than women of African origin in Canada. The same observation can be made with respect to the gender distribution of Africans in the City of Toronto and the Province of Quebec. For instance, in Toronto between the years 1961 and 1991, there were 36,830 male (53.8 per cent) compared to 31,655 female (46.2 per cent) African immigrants.[15] Similarly, in the province of Quebec overall, between the years 1987 and 1996, the proportion of female African immigrants was consistently below 50 per cent; in 1996 it was 46.8 per cent.[16] Furthermore, the number of women fluctuated from year to year, while the number of men per year remained relatively constant.

African immigrants were admitted to Canada in one of the following categories: family class, refugees, independents, or other. The number of women in the family class category was generally higher than in any other category. The number of African men admitted as refugees has been consistently higher than the

TABLE 3
African Immigrants to Canada, Ontario, and Quebec, as a % of Total Immigrants and
Refugees, 1970–2000

| Year | Africans to Canada | Africans to Canada (%) | Africans to Ontario | Africans to Ontario (%) | Africans to Quebec | Africans to Quebec (%) |
|------|------|------|------|------|------|------|
| 1970 | 2,863 | 1.9 | – | – | – | – |
| 1971 | 2,841 | 2.3 | – | – | – | – |
| 1972 | 8,308 | 6.8 | – | – | – | – |
| 1973 | 8,307 | 4.5 | 3,983 | 3.9 | 1,331 | 5.1 |
| 1974 | 10,450 | 4.8 | 5,313 | 4.4 | 2,139 | 6.4 |
| 1975 | 9,867 | 5.3 | 5,086 | 5.2 | 1,730 | 6.2 |
| 1976 | 7,752 | 5.2 | 3,792 | 5.3 | 1,635 | 5.6 |
| 1977 | 6,372 | 5.5 | 3,129 | 5.5 | 1,210 | 6.3 |
| 1978 | 4,261 | 4.9 | 2,099 | 5.0 | 859 | 6.0 |
| 1979 | 3,958 | 3.5 | 1,915 | 3.7 | 805 | 4.1 |
| 1980 | 4,330 | 3.0 | 2,020 | 3.2 | 891 | 4.0 |
| 1981 | 4,887 | 3.8 | 2,126 | 3.8 | 1,056 | 5.0 |
| 1982 | 4,510 | 3.7 | 1,833 | 3.4 | 1,188 | 5.6 |
| 1983 | 3,659 | 4.1 | 1,391 | 3.5 | 1,085 | 6.6 |
| 1984 | 3,552 | 4.0 | 1,513 | 3.6 | 860 | 5.9 |
| 1985 | 3,545 | 3.9 | 1,447 | 3.5 | 984 | 6.6 |
| 1986 | 4,770 | 5.1 | 2,300 | 4.6 | 1,166 | 6.0 |
| 1987 | 8,501 | 5.6 | 4,668 | 5.5 | 2,163 | 8.1 |
| 1988 | 9,380 | 5.8 | 5,051 | 5.7 | 2,411 | 9.3 |
| 1989 | 12,199 | 6.3 | 6,538 | 6.0 | 3,273 | 9.5 |
| 1990 | 13,442 | 6.3 | 6,773 | 5.7 | 4,360 | 11.0 |
| 1991 | 16,087 | 7.0 | 7,961 | 6.7 | 5,663 | 11.0 |
| 1992 | 19,636 | 7.8 | 11,929 | 8.5 | 5,071 | 10.5 |
| 1993 | 16,918 | 6.6 | 9,955 | 7.2 | 4,329 | 9.6 |
| 1994 | 13,706 | 6.1 | 7,377 | 6.0 | 2,939 | 10.5 |
| 1995 | 14,631 | 6.9 | 8,490 | 7.0 | 3,564 | 12.0 |
| 1996 | 14,859 | 6.7 | 7,993 | 6.4 | 4,400 | 14.8 |
| 1997 | 14,525 | 6.7 | – | – | – | – |
| 1998 | 12,675 | 7.3 | – | – | – | – |
| 1999 | 15,678 | 8.3 | – | – | – | – |
| 2000 | 19,750 | 8.7 | – | – | – | – |

Source: The 1995 Canadian Global Almanac (1956–72) 66; Citizenship and Immigration
Canada, Statistics: Permanent residents by country of last residence (Total Africa), 19
(1996); Citizenship and Immigration Canada, Facts and Figures, 1997–2000,
www.cic.gc.ca.

number of women refugees, despite the fact that the number of refugee women and children across the world are higher than the number of refugee men.[17] The twenty women who are the subjects of this study were categorized in the family class when they came to Canada. After coming to join their husbands or to study, each decided to stay on to live in Canada.

For this study, I selected ten African women residing in Montreal and ten residing in Toronto. The women's countries of origin included Benin, Burundi, Cameroon, the Congo (Congo-Brazzaville), the Democratic Republic of the Congo (former Zaire), Ivory Coast, and Senegal. Each woman had lived as a married woman in Africa for at least five years before coming to Canada. It seemed to me that this was a sufficient time period to permit these women to compare their experiences in Canada vis-à-vis in their countries of origin. The women identified themselves as Catholic, Protestant, or Muslim. At the time they were interviewed, all had jobs that were inferior to their qualification levels. In Africa, all these women had had occupations, including that of secretary, teacher, clothes designer, or merchant, that accorded with their qualifications. With the exception of one who was still studying before she came to Canada, all were economically independent. Research shows that, whether living in urban or rural milieus, African women are generally homemakers who work long hours to maintain their families, sometimes even to the detriment of their health.[18]

In her comprehensive review of the literature on immigrant women in Canada, Micheline Labelle reports that studies focus on the functional integration of women of several ethnic communities and on the diversity of problems they encounter, such as discrimination on the basis of sex and race. She observes that the studies also deal, whether in a veiled or explicit manner, with the politics of immigration and women's participation in institutional life.[19] However, there is very little literature that reports specifically on the situation of immigrants of African origin, and there is even less on the situation of African immigrant women. One of the earliest studies examining the situation of African immigrants in Toronto, by A.B.K. Kasozi, documents their experiences of racial discrimination in the labour market.[20] Another report, by Musisi and Turrittin, focusing specifically on African immigrant and refugee women, presents detailed data on these women's labour market experiences.[21] Emphasizing both the gender and racial discrimination of which African women are victims, their study also examines gender issues in relation to experiences in Canada. For this reason, Musisi and Turrittin's study can be described as a continuation of earlier work on immigrant women.

While not neglecting these issues, my research concentrates specifically on gender relations, focusing on francophone African women's experiences and their views on how African women are perceived in Canada. Even though I used a guideline questionnaire, the interviews were very open, giving each woman the opportunity to tell her own story about being in Canada. This method seemed most appropriate for this type of research because it gave my informants the opportunity to speak about their daily experience of gender relations.

Given that the social relations of gender are complex and vary according to a woman's spatial and temporal situation as well as her socioeconomic, political, and cultural context, certain factors about my informants' relationships with their husbands/partners appeared more salient in the Canadian context than in Africa. For these women, issues relating to the husband's authority, the division of domestic responsibilities, the wife's salaried work, as well as her management of her income and household decision-making, were most important. Thus, gender equality for these African women can be understood as equality or autonomy with respect to these factors. This is the analysis I present first of all.

A second aspect of my exploratory study, no less important, is how African women think their relationships with their husbands/partner are perceived by Canadians; conversely, it examines how African women perceive Canadian women's relationships with their husbands/partners. In the context of the cosmopolitan multicultural milieus found in Montreal and Toronto, where social service agents are often asked to work with immigrant women of different cultures, knowledge of African women's points of view can be especially important. Not only can such knowledge facilitate intercultural exchange, but it can also allow social agents to understand African women's adherence or resistance to certain values relating to gender equality as understood in Canadian society. In effect, intervening in a multicultural milieu requires knowledge about diverse cultures.[22]

Being a black francophone African immigrant woman myself, I sometimes became very conscious of the fact that I shared similar experiences with these women: most of what they had to say regarding their daily lives resonated with my own experience. Realizing that they could identify with their informants, certain feminists have underlined the importance of interaction between researcher and respondent.[23] In my case, because of this social interaction, the tone of the interviews became friendlier, verging on confidentiality. My experience as an immigrant woman, and still more as an attentive listener, contributed to the rapport necessary for the interview process, though it did not hide the reality of the multiplicity of women's experiences according to their class, race, and ethnic identity.[24] The interviews took place in the privacy of the women's homes, mostly as we sat in their kitchens.

For a better understanding of the lives and perceptions of African women immigrants with respect to the social relations of gender, it is appropriate to begin by retracing the itinerary of their settlement in Canada, and in Toronto and Montreal in particular. This will permit us to grasp a further issue – how African immigrant women experience their conjugal relations in the Canadian context – and, finally, to clarify their view of Canadian values with respect to gender relations by examining their relationships with other Canadian women.

## The Itinerary of African Immigrant Women

Five of the ten women in Toronto with whom I spoke entered Canada through Quebec. Each had come to join a husband who preceded her when he came to study.[25] The wife's arrival in Quebec was part of the couple's plan to get a high-level diploma, especially for the husband, so that they could return to their country of origin and attain a decent socioeconomic position. Until very recently, possession of a university-level diploma guaranteed a prestigious socioeconomic position in Africa, despite the politically arbitrary and often ethnic nature of upward mobility. However, persistent political instability and the constant deterioration of the material conditions of existence have constrained African students and their families to remain in Canada as immigrants.

In more than one respect, then, Africans who came to Canada first as students find themselves in the same situation as conventional immigrants. As radical studies emphasize, immigrants are attracted to the West to sell their labour power, moving to the West in the hope of ameliorating their economic situation.[26] Momentarily setting aside the question of the mobility of capital, even if the phenomenon of international immigration can be explained by the idyllic image the North projects toward the South via the media, among other channels, this idyllic image does not prevent the immigrant, once here, from very quickly becoming disillusioned.[27] African women experience this harsh reality through their spouses initially who, despite their Canadian diplomas, spend years waiting for jobs to correspond to their qualifications. For want of something better to do, the spouse often ends up accepting a low-level position in order to survive with dignity. The situation is even more dramatic for those who did not get their diploma in Canada. For two woman who arrived in Canada via Quebec, leaving that province turned out to be a promising route:

> My husband lost a contract that he had in Montreal because he didn't speak English. As he didn't find work, he preferred that we move to Toronto. At least, one could learn English. Who knows if one day ...

> We left Montreal because my husband wanted to. There was no longer any work, so my husband decided that we should come to Toronto to find work. He had good contacts and at the end of two weeks he found a modest job. It is not the best, but it is better than nothing.

Life in Toronto or Montreal does not necessarily offer more valuable prospects for these African women in comparison to an economic position that would confer a certain prestigious social status in their country of origin. For want of a career, they have their own autonomous sources of revenue as petty merchants – from a small sewing business to hairdressing. Through such entrepreneurial activity, these African women feel that they have a respectable socioeconomic status that assures them a certain dignity.

> In coming here, I lost status. I worked. I was secretary to the director. What I earn here is what I can offer my children for their studies. Still, I sometimes find it necessary to ask myself what I lost; these children will never have the education that I would have liked to give them ... One has to fear for one's own children. Since I am no longer working here as a secretary, I must work in the factories – mentally it is very difficult. I have sacrificed my status for my children's sake.

> I worked as a public health physiotherapist. At the moment, I am not working as a physiotherapist; I work as an assistant in physiotherapy. But in fact, the work I do is more like that of a receptionist while I wait for equivalence. I didn't study statistics. When they evaluated my diploma, they found that I had not done statistics so, for them, my diploma is not complete. They don't want us to be here. They don't want people who have studied elsewhere, so it is really a problem to have equivalence.

Despite a level of education that permits them access to employment that corresponds more or less to their qualifications in their countries of origin, these African women did not find jobs easily. Given the demand that one have Canadian experience, they had to go through a long process of adaptation, accepting the first job offered in order to survive. However, taking up the cycle of studies again in the hope of integrating into the labour market seemed to be a way of perfecting their qualifications. But the fact of being a woman, and a black one at that, was felt as a difficulty that they had to overcome on a daily basis. As Bannerji and Schecter clearly emphasize, black women constitute the most disadvantaged group in the Canadian labour market.[28] Three of the women I interviewed agreed:

> In my work – I was a legal secretary – they thought that because I was a black African woman I did not know, I knew, nothing. Typically, when people telephone, they never think of me as a black women – never, never. And then, well, they are more or less satisfied with the first interview. But when they arrive they are surprised. And then afterward I see a change in their attitude. Appreciation comes with time, with the discovery of the individual. But before that, when they see that they are dealing with a black person, it is negative. After, they realize that I do my work, am polite,

am correct and efficient, and little by little the appreciation comes. But before they get to know you, you are nothing. You must prove yourself and you must do more than others.

My employers know that I work here as an assistant receptionist but, in fact, they know that I have the same skills as they do. They know that it is not statistics that prevents a person from being a good physiotherapist. But the thing is that one is in a system that discriminates. In fact, I have two bosses – a woman and a man. In the woman's case, she has more experience with people; she has more respect for others. However, in the man's case, he tries to exert control over me. Maybe this is because he is a man, but I am not able to ignore it. And today, I have earned [their] respect, but I had to fight hard for that. Me, I do not do this to be difficult. I can't stand it when someone believes that I am not as good because I am black. I am African.

There is always this astonished reaction, 'Oh, you did that, you solved this problem.' It is as if they assume you are not capable. However, they are not going to change their conception. You know, [respect] is never granted; it is never won. It is a continual struggle.

These African women feel that they are victims of racial discrimination. Integration into the work world proves to be a perpetual struggle, an eternal daily re-beginning, until they are able to convince their colleagues of their ability by the quality of their work. For these black women, being confronted by the constant questioning of their competence, in an employment context that is already precarious, is a supplementary factor of stress that accentuates the sentiment of humiliation. Being obligated to work hard in poorly paid jobs, even when one has better qualifications, seems to be African immigrant women's lot.[29] Conscious of this loss of their status and of being, at the same time, in a situation in which they no longer benefit from familial support, they must assume heavier domestic responsibilities.

## The Paradox of Gender Relations

As a basis to discuss conjugality among immigrant African women in Canada, it is useful to briefly outline family dynamics in the African context. In Africa, the family is generally not limited to the narrow unit of father, mother, and biological children. In addition, the family does not usually live alone. Moreover, certain members of the family, the husband as much as the wife, share responsibility for daily household tasks with others. Even if one admits, given current economic realities, that the family is shrinking into a nuclear family especially in urban milieus,[30] the fact remains that it still includes some members of the extended family.

No matter whether the kinship system is matrilineal or patrilineal, in African families the man is always considered the 'chief' or head of the domestic unit. The father represents family authority and is for this reason exempt from certain domestic tasks. A division of labour very strongly segregated by sex has existed for a long time in Africa;[31] certain household tasks are specifically conferred to women, such as responsibility for domestic work, which is shared among a family's daughters. Although women are overburdened with work in Africa because the mother usually has a career or other economic occupation, they do not carry the heavy responsibility for domestic work alone.[32] In the urban milieu, families that are financially able can hire help, usually a man, to take responsibility for domestic tasks and maintain the household. When both a man and a woman are hired as household help, one observes the sexual division of labour being reproduced at their level, with the woman being responsible for cooking African meals, caring for children, and so on.

For African women living far from the African context, family composition is atomized, frequently being reduced to the married couple and their children, that is, the nuclear family. When this happens, African immigrant women generally experience the birth of a new kind of conjugality, very much more intimate than that which they experienced in Africa. This form of conjugality seems to be increasingly widespread in Africa, especially in urban areas.[33] However, in terms of gender relations, this change does not carry with it a more equitable division of labour between the husband/wife. Nor does it result in a questioning of the father's authority, which may even be somewhat reinforced.[34] While this new conjugality allows a progressively closer affective tie between the couple, this tie takes root in a certain tension, whereby the lack of extended family means that domestic labour is not shared with other women to the extent it was in Africa.

For the African women interviewed for this study, however, the experience of being black and immigrant in a context marked by discrimination, humiliation, and a certain loss of dignity, is made considerably heavier by domestic tasks. To the extent to which domestic obligations encumber women culturally, the lack of help means that African immigrant women are often confronted with too much work to do. For those who work away from home, the hurdles to mount are different from the ones they knew in Africa:

Each morning I drop the children at daycare. We leave home at 7:15 am. We wait in front of the daycare until the doors open. At 7:25 they open, but I have to wait until 7:30 because there isn't any insurance in case something happens before then. Then I leave the baby first; afterward I say good-bye to the older one. You have to sign in each time you enter – it's an 'in and out' routine. I leave the older one at school and then I go to work, usually getting there about 8:00 or 8:05. After work, I have to do the housework. Meals must be prepared. But I am organized because I prepare most of the meals during the weekend. I store them in plastic containers. I always do these tasks alone. My husband has never helped with domestic work. There is no sharing of tasks. Whether or not my husband is there, he must rest. The only thing that he is willing to do is cleaning on Saturday.

My husband never does housework. That is not his role. The help that we had at home does not exist here. Here wives demand that husbands help with the housework but, you know, marriage is like a business. In a household, each person has his role. In any enterprise there is a director. The chief, the captain, is the man; the wife is the guardian of values. She is the one who gets things done. I cannot ask him to do housework. If he wants to help, that's different. Here, the context is different. He can help if he wants, but that's not his role. It's very hard for me to be torn like this, that's for sure, running after time, but I know that I will find a way out.

Some women accept doing all domestic responsibilities alone out of respect for gender roles. Despite social conditions that differ from those in Africa, women give a functional interpretation to gender roles and acknowledge the husband's authority, which spares him of housework; women accommodate to the double workload in order to preserve cultural values. Others, in contrast, experience the fact of doing all the housework alone in addition to having work outside the home as a heavy burden. Such women are not able to avoid certain conjugal conflicts; sometimes they are even the victims of gossip in their circle of African friends or compatriots. In Africa, where marriage necessitates relationships with relatives, a wife essentially adjusts her behaviour in relation to the presence of others. In Canada, the social network between African immigrants substitutes for kinship relations in Africa and plays more or less the same role as the latter. The disparagement of friends can therefore affect a couple's behaviour, especially in public, influencing husband and wife to appear to conform to cultural norms governing spousal behaviour. Couples in which the husband participates in some domestic work manipulate the game of appearance in order to maintain the couple's social status in the community:

When we married, we had to make sacrifices. That which a wife is able to put up with or accept, a husband can't deal with. And me, I decided that I could no longer put up with being married, for example, and having sole responsibility for the children. I found that the pain of pretending to be married was not worth it if it is to do everything all alone. If it's just for appearances, that has no sense. In that case, I don't know who I appear to give pleasure to; it isn't me, in any case.

In Africa, everything would have been different because the emotional and social context would have been different. I would have been surrounded by family. I would have had emotional support that would have permitted me to get along all right in my husband's absence. I would not have suffered in the same way. It would have minimized, for example, the fact that my husband was not involved in household tasks. I would have had another source of emotional support despite his absence; I would have had a source of practical support in dealing with the children. I would have had help. I would have had a *nounou*. I would have had someone to do the cleaning for me, or to do the cooking. I would not have had all that weigh on my shoulders today. To be sure, I would have had other problems but, with respect to the practical organization of the day, I would not have had that. To leave home at 6 a.m. in the morning to leave the children at school, to leave work at 6 p.m. to pick up the children. No sooner arrive than to give them their bath, prepare supper, do homework, put them to bed ... There are ever so many things to do that I can't do them all alone. I need my husband's help. He helps from time to time, but not always. Often enough I must grumble too. You know, men are not used to changing their habits easily. If me, the wife, doesn't push, that's it. Perhaps he wouldn't want to learn; he wouldn't understand. I would find myself doing everything all by myself.

The problem is different in Africa because the support of other family members is there. One doesn't feel the responsibilities in the same way and staying married doesn't interfere, despite everything.

Tension occurs when housework is shared. For some women, the price of getting it done requires persistent requests while not necessarily questioning the husband's authority or role. Because African wives in Canada are overburdened by work and they do not have the help they had in Africa, they have to solicit their husband's support, especially when there are no older children in the family. For some women, a dispute may arise about the roles in marriage or a situation of latent conflict may occur:

An African woman believes in marriage and in the importance of staying married no matter what happens. I see them around me. There are many African women who are convinced that being unhappy is an integral part of marriage. Sadness, unhappiness because of taking care of all the domestic responsibilities – it takes that to make her marriage succeed, even if it is too hard. To be married is important for a woman. I am speaking about African women who live in Canada, not in Africa ... What I find difficult here is the stress that one must live with on top of supporting a husband who doesn't help you and who reserves the right to beat you. I find that intolerable. You know what I find difficult? It's to have so many things to do and to have to do them alone, although I am married. This being the case, I said to myself, I don't need a husband who doesn't help me and who adds to my problems. No, I decided that I don't need more stress. Me, I stopped putting up with it; I stopped making an effort. That was my downfall. I changed because I thought that I deserved better than that.

In Africa, a woman's fate is still tied to marriage and procreation, which currently confers a more honourable social status to married than to single women.[35] Similarly, the sexual division of labour confers a heavier domestic responsibility on the wife while recognizing the husband's authority.[36] In short, marriage confers certain rights to the husband over the wife, such as correction, for example. However, the wife can rebel in situations in which her husband mistreats her. Similarly, the arbitrary exercise of the husband's authority is not permitted.[37]

In addition to the loss of family support for domestic work, life in Canada also shapes a woman's relationship with her husband. While the change brought about the rearrangement of the relative share of domestic work for certain women, for others it gave rise to strife and a rupture of the dream of marriage. As the following remarks show, however, there is not complete adherence to the idea of gender equality in the division of household tasks, or to what is perceived as the Canadian concept of marriage:

> The conception of marriage is different here. Sex doesn't belong only in marriage. Already, even here, one can see that in Quebec and in Toronto it is very different. In Quebec, women are very independent. They are too feminist; sometimes there is even a little exaggeration. But even so, women have fought to get their rights. What I noticed in Quebec is that a woman can live her sexuality in an expanded manner without having to marry. I haven't noticed the same sexual liberty in Ontario that I noticed in Quebec. Also, perhaps it is because in Ontario one has the impression that everyone comes from elsewhere except from here. Given that there are too many immigrants, there is an important cultural influence, [so] one does not see the *pure laine*.

The idea of separating procreation from marriage is not explicit in this statement, but it is implied in the following phrase: 'to live her sexuality in an expanded manner without having to marry.' This indicates a certain distance from the African concept of marriage, which is unthinkable without children.[38] Paradoxically, nothing supports the conclusion that there is total acceptance of the Canadian model of gender relations. This informant does, however, make statements that recognize the struggle and demands of Canadian women.

### Here, But Always from Somewhere Else

Sisterhood is based on the fact that women constitute a category because they have common interests in opposition to men.[39] With respect to marriage, the sexual division of labour in the domestic sphere is a common site for the exploitation of women, and is perhaps one of the points that unites women.[40] Because of a strict sexual division of labour within their culture and because they must work excessively hard in the Canadian context in order to survive, African immigrant women bear a double workload. Canadian-born women also know this reality well, despite the fact that men are gradually becoming more involved in certain tasks. Paradoxically, this same reality does not seem to unite African immigrant women and white women. Here are some of their comments:

> Women here are not bound up with African women. Certainly, we are all women, but there is the skin barrier. In one way or another, a white woman always believes she is better than you. There is nothing more to say. There is no true solidarity, even if they sometimes experience the same problems that we do. For example, if I look around me, my white Ontario women friends here, they don't have any more help at home than I do. That depends, a man will do what he feels like doing. For example, he will shovel snow, perhaps because doing this doesn't bother him. On the other hand, he won't necessarily do the dishes all the time. In this sense, some husbands don't do anything. In contrast to this, one can also find African men who do everything for their wives. Despite this, women here always consider us as obedient, exploited women. A woman who repeatedly makes the error of accepting anything from a man, a woman too good who lets herself be a man's slave – there is always that cliché that is there.

> Me, I don't like to discuss things with women from here. I don't talk with feminists. I don't even argue anymore; it's not worth it. They have their notion. For them, we are African women; therefore we are exploited, obedient. You see, even in the course to learn the English language, the lady who gives us the course always used that kind of language – African women do this, they do that. It is necessary to let the men help with the work at home, change the baby's diaper, do the dishes. In fact, there are some things that I find normal and that I cannot understand. It's normal that my husband makes decisions, that he manages the money. I was raised like that; I didn't see my older sisters ask their husbands to do the dishes. You see, with all the racism that one encounters here, already my husband can't find work easily. He feels humiliated, and if, on top of that, I force him to do housework, you see what that ends up like. That's why my friends are African; I don't count on finding friends among the women here.

> You know our culture – cooking, the woman always does it. Whether you work or not, you have to do housework and laundry, ironing. My daughter it very helpful – she does the ironing. This morning, she mowed the lawn. In fact, she helps her father because he is the one who always mows the lawn. Here, there is a sharing of

tasks. I appreciate that. The other day I was visiting a Québécois friend. I found her husband scrubbing and cleaning the toilets. My husband has never touched a toilet-cleaning brush. He would not do it. But if I asked him to do it, he could do it. However, he would do it all wrong. He would splash water everywhere. But I must not complain; there are many things that he didn't used to do that he has started to do already.

When we came here, my husband was already able to do certain household tasks. He could even do the shopping. I have really appreciated that. In the kitchen, he doesn't know anything. Thus, I cannot let him do things there. After all, even if I have lived in Montreal for [eighteen years] now, deep inside I am still an African.

In evaluating African husbands on their lack of participation in household tasks, among other things, white Canadian women seem to regard African immigrant women condescendingly. Cultural differences get in the way of sisterhood between women, no matter what their race. Feminist theorist bell hooks invites us to take cultural codes into account so that women can build bridges of solidarity between one another.[41]

Rather than simply denying the gender inequalities of their own culture, African immigrant women are very conscious of them and they talk about them:

Here, a woman's life isn't tied to marriage even though it is in Africa. You have more respect if you're married. Even in the Afro-Canadian milieu here, when you're not married, you're not respected.

A wife has to be obedient. She must marry to live with a man. She must be there for her husband; she must assume her responsibilities in the household. A young unmarried woman is viewed badly because she isn't married. In Africa, feminine identity is defined by marriage. Here, one is a woman because one is a human being. You have to recognise that the women here have striven for that; they really fought. In this regard, I envy them even though I don't always agree with them about certain things.

The Québécois find that we, Africans, we work a lot. In fact, they already know that it is the women who do everything in Africa. But they do not understand why we endure all that from our men. We have told them that our culture is like that.

Above all, I think we must respect our culture. We must not confuse ourselves by what we find here as soon as we arrive. As soon as one comes here, you know, people tell you that there is 911, that women are protected here. A husband does not have the right to hit you. If he hits you, you can call 911. But I said that you have to think before you call 911. At home in Africa we solve the problem in a different way. Why not try first to solve the problem in the family or with friends with whom one can confide, even if this is a country with laws? We have to guard our culture so that it will not disappear. And then, the husband must know that his wife is not his dog, that she has a right to live, to be happy.

African women's discourse about women's status is paradoxical. On the one hand, they discuss women's disobedience as a cultural reality. On the other hand, they are conscious of gender inequality, while not daring to contest it openly. To the extent that they recognize that white women have won their place in society as human beings with the same rights as men, they admit, consequently, the discomfort of their own situation. For some of them, cultural attachment seems to be a powerful normative force able to neutralize any possible dispute.

Furthermore, the relationship with white women is tarnished by a colonial history that established a power relationship of white women's dominance over black women. Despite the fact that Canada is not viewed as a participant in the colonization of their country in Africa, the racial link is nevertheless incorporated into it. The haughty look that white women use when they glimpse African immigrant women is revealed in this logic. Racism, more than sisterhood, then, characterizes the relationship between white Canadian women and black women immigrants from Africa. Because white women don't experience racial discrimination, they tend to prioritize patriarchy.

Yet even the same skin colour does not imply sisterhood. The black community in Canada is not homogeneous, but rather is characterized by cultural diversity, including blacks from the Caribbean and Bermuda, the African continent, Central America, the United Kingdom, the United States, and other regions.[42] According to the African immigrant women interviewed, relationships between them and black women from the islands (the Caribbean) are also characterized by a certain type of distrust:

> Black women from the islands socialize easily with white women. They imitate white women easily and believe we are obedient women. Skin colour is simply the only thing we have in common.

We are not like black women from the islands. Culturally, we are very different. I went around with a group of Afro-Canadians a little. I stopped because I felt that we didn't have the same problems. We are not alike. In this society, that is to say, in Canada, there are blacks from the islands, blacks from Africa, whites, Indians, etc. What strikes me is that the communities don't mix. We become acquainted without ever mixing. A Jamaican, when she speaks about an African woman, it's as if she's disgusted. For her, African women love marriage. Most Jamaican women that I know are not married. They don't understand how African women can drag along after men who sometimes make them suffer. Likewise, they view us as submissive women.

Cultural differences in gender relationships seem to stand in the way of the development of solidarity between black African immigrant women and white women, as well as between black women of other cultures. In this context, sisterhood does not appear to transcend racial and cultural barriers. Thérèse Pujolle believes that being African means having to affirm your dignity in relation to the other on an indefinite basis.[43] It is evident from their statements that African immigrant women experience this reality as much in their daily lives as at work.

I have had very good Québécois friends for eighteen years now. But at work it is a different thing. Now, you must do more than others because you are a black woman. You have to struggle if you want to keep your job.

Competent or not competent, you must always do more than the Québécois. And they always demand twice as much from you. For them, a black woman is a person who is incompetent – who does not know either how to speak or write French. There are too many prejudices against African women. And the racism that I have experienced, I situate it at the level of prejudice.

In this country, if you are a black woman, you must struggle to survive. I came here with a degree from my country as a teacher. But I had to retrain at a CEGEP. Diplomas from our countries, they don't recognize. They say that our African diplomas are worthless. You have to prove that you are capable even in French; here, because you are an African woman, your French isn't good.

## Conclusion

This exploratory study demonstrates how immigration can challenge cultural gender norms in ways that have both positive and negative effects. To the extent that conjugal relations in Canada are increasingly characterized by expectations of shared household responsibilities between men and women, African women are drawn to also expect such a reorientation of gender roles within their families. The pressure for men to co-operate in domestic labour becomes greater when women are without an extended family of women with whom to share those tasks, something they were accustomed to in their country of origin. Yet, discord results when new forms of conjugality in Canada run counter to traditional patterns of male authority that shaped family life in Africa. Discord also occurs when white Canadians discriminate against African immigrants based in part on stereotypical notions of gender relations amongst the latter.

Racism is a central factor in understanding the situation of sub-Saharan African immigrant women in the labour market and in daily life in Canada, where racism remains omnipresent. While white Canadian women and black African immigrant women share some similar experiences in terms of their conjugal relations and domestic roles, racial discrimination towards African women overrides any sisterhood that patriarchy might induce. The fact of being black, combined with the stereotypes that white Canadian women associate with and use to look at African women, undermine the basis of a real sisterhood. It follows from this that African immigrant women easily make common cause among themselves and with men of their community who, like themselves, are victims of the same racial discrimination.

NOTES

This paper is a revised version of 'Etre une immigrante noire africaine francophone à Toronto,' published in *Reflets* 4, no. 1 (1998): 34–52. I am grateful to my institution, Glendon College, York University, which granted me funds to conduct this research, and to Jane Turrittin, who kindly and patiently did the translation. She updated and added to that data originally presented in N.B. Musisi and J. Turrittin, *African Women and the Metropolitan Toronto Labour Market in the 1990s: Migrating to a Multicultural Society in a Recession* (Toronto: n.p., 1995). Available at www.ceris.metropolis.ca.

1  M. Labelle, 'Femmes et immigration au Canada: Bilan et perspective,' *Études ethniques au Canada* 22, no. 1 (1990): 67–82; A.B. Simmons, '"New Wave" Immigrants: Origins and Characteristics,' in Shiva S. Halli, Frank Trovato, and Leo Driedger, eds, *Ethnic Demography: Canadian Immigrant, Racial and Cultural Variations* (Ottawa: Carleton University Press, 1990), 141–59.

2  *Faits et chiffres 1996. Aperçu de l'immigration* (Ottawa: Citizenship and Immigration Canada, 1997).

3  Ibid., 7.

4  Ibid. In effect, since the 1980s the rate of growth of Canada's population has increased constantly. Only Australia has a larger number of immigrants.

5  Ibid., 11.

6  P.E. Okeke et al., eds, 'Black Women and Economic Autonomy in Edmonton, Alberta,' Report submitted by the Black Women Working Group (Ottawa: Status of Women Canada, 2000), 4.

7  Ibid.

8  J.C. Naidoo, 'Africans,' *The Canadian Encyclopedia* (Edmonton: Hurtig Publishers, 1985).

 9  A.B.K. Kasozi, *The Integration of Black African Immigrants in Canadian Society: A Case Study of Toronto, CMA, 1986* (Toronto: Canadian African Newcomer Aid Centre of Toronto, 1988); Musisi and Turrittin, *African Women,* 34.

10  See www.cic.gc.ca.

11  J.W. Berry, R. Kalin, and D.M. Taylor, *Attitudes à l'égard du multiculturalisme et des groupes ethniques au Canada* (Ottawa: Ministry of State for Multiculturalism, 1976), 8.

12  J. Langlois, P. Laplante, and J. Levy, *Le Québec de demain et les communautés culturelles* (Montreal: Editions du Méridien, 1990), 18.

13  D. Helly, *Le Québec face à la pluralité culturelle, 1977–1984: Un bilan documentaire des politiques* (Quebec: Les Presses de l'Université Laval, 1996), 66.

14  J-P. Rogel, *Le Défi de l'immigration* (Quebec: Institute québécois de recherche sur culture, 1989), 9.

15  Statistics Canada, 1991 Census. Immigrants and Non-permanent Residents by Selected Places of Birth and Sex, Showing Period of Immigration for Immigrants to Canada, Provinces, Territories and Census Metropolitan Areas.

16  Citizenship and Immigration Canada, Statistics: Country of Last Permanent Residence by Province or Territory or Intended Destination.

17  M. Boyd, 'Canada's Refugee Flows: Gender Inequality,' *Canadian Social Trends* (Spring 1994): 8.

18  C. Berthoud, 'Ces femmes oubliées,' *Le monde diplomatique: Manière de voir* 51 (2000): 85–87.

19  Labelle, 'Femmes et immigration au Canada,' 67–82.

20  A.B.K. Kasozi, *The Integration of Black African Immigrants*; A.B.K. Kasozi, 'Adjustment of Black African Immigrants to Canadian Society, 1980-1992' (unpublished paper, 1992).

21  Musisi and Turrittin, *African Women.*

22  E. Cohen, 'L'approche interculturelle dans le processus d'aide,' *Revue française de service social* 171 (1993): 7–19; S. Bellfort, 'Au carrefour de plusieurs vérités: une réflexion sur la pratique en milieu scolaire pluriculturel,' *Intervention* 96 (1993): 36–46.

23  A. Oakley, 'Interviewing Women: A Contradiction in Terms,' in Helen Roberts, ed., *Doing Feminist Research* (London: Routledge and Kegan Paul, 1981), 30–61; C. Ramazanoglu, 'Improving on Sociology: The Problems of Taking a Feminist Standpoint,' *Sociology* 23, no. 3 (1989): 427–42; M.L. Devault, 'Talking and Listening from Women's Standpoint: Feminist Strategies for Interviewing and Analysis,' *Social Problems* 37, no. 1 (1990): 96–113; P. Cotterill, 'Interviewing Women: Issues of Friendship, Vulnerability and Power,' *Women's Studies International Forum* 5, no. 6 (1992): 29–42.

24  See C. Ramazanoglu, *Feminism and the Contradictions of Oppression* (London: Routledge, 1986).

25  Despite this general tendency, certain African women now come to Canada first and their husbands join them after they have settled.

26  G. Lavigne, *Les ethniques et la ville* (Montreal: Les Editions du Préambule, Collection Science et théorie, 1987).

27  N. Samin, 'Mondialisation et migrations: l'axe Sud-Nord,' *Les migrations internationales* (Lausanne, CH: Payot, 1995).

28  H. Bannerji, ed., *Returning the Gaze: Essays on Racism, Feminism and Politics* (Toronto: Sister Vision, 1993); T. Schecter, *Race, Class, Women and the State: The Case of Domestic Labour* (Montreal: Black Rose Books, 1998).

29  This fact is clearly indicated in Musisi and Turrittin, *African Women.*

30  L.V. Thomas and R. Luneau, *La terre africaine et ses religions* (Paris: L'Harmattan, 1995), 271–2.

31  A.P. Van Eetvelde, *L'homme et sa vision du monde dans la société traditionnelle negro-africaine* (Louvain-La-Neuve, BE: Bruylant-Academia, S.A., 1998), 140–2.

32  Berthoud, 'Ces femmes oubliées,' 85–7.

33  Thomas and Luneau, *La terre africaine.*

34  Ibid., 274.

35  Van Eetvelde, *L'homme et sa vision du monde*; M. Lecarme, 'Le "fatigue" des femmes, le "travail" de la mère en milieu populaire dakaroise,' in *Femmes plurielles: les représentations des femmes – discours, normes et conduites* (Paris: Editions de la Maison des sciences de l'homme, 1999), 261. See also J.M. Ela, 'Fécondité, structure sociales et fonctions dynamiques de l'imaginaire en Afrique noire,' *La Sociologie des populations* (Montreal: Les Presses de l'Université de Montréal, 1995), 189–215; Lecarme, 'Le "fatigue" des femmes,' 259–62.

36  Lecarme, 'Le "fatigue" des femmes,' 263–69.

37  Van Eetvelde, *L'homme et sa vision du monde*, 134–40.

38  Ela, 'Fécondité, structure sociales,' 195–200.

39  L. Juteau, *L'ethnicité et ses frontières* (Montreal: Les Presses de l'Université de Montréal, 1999), 109–14. See also S.J. Ship, 'Au delà de la soidarité,' *Revue québécoise de science politique* 19 (1991): 5–36.

40  C. Delphy, *L'ennemi principal: 1'économie politique du patriarcat* (Paris: Editions Syllepse, 1998); C. Guillaumin, *Sexe, race et politique du pouvoir* (Paris: Coté-femmes, 1992), 20–49.

41  b. hooks, 'Sisterhood: Political Solidarity between Women,' in Janet A. Kourany, James P. Sterba, and Rosemarie Tong, eds, *Feminist Philosophies: Problems, Theories and Applications*, 2d ed. (London: Pluto Press/Prentice-Hall, 1999), 495.

42  Okeke, 'Black Women,' 4.

43  T. Pujolle, *L'Afrique noire* (Paris: Dominos/Flammarion, 1994), 30.

PART 5

# *Symbols and Representations*

# Propaganda and Identity Construction: Media Representation in Canada of Finnish and Finnish-Canadian Women during the Winter War of 1939–1940

VARPU LINDSTRÖM

## Introduction

Small ethnic groups in Canada have rarely been at the centre of media attention. If they have found their activities described in major Canadian dailies, the news has usually been negative or sensational in nature. During the Depression, the Finns, like many other European immigrants in Canada, grew accustomed to bad press about their community. The media reported on arrests of radical labour leaders, trials of Finnish strikers, demonstrators, communists, newspaper editors, and deportation cases – and they did so in ways that demonized left immigrant workers as 'dangerous foreigners.'[1] Such lopsided coverage hardly increased Canadians' understanding of ethnic communities nor did it provide useful information about the countries of origin.

Wars inevitably call into question the loyalty of citizens and place immigrants under special scrutiny. Many of those deemed to be a threat to the government's war efforts – pacifists, left-wing radicals, and enemy nationals – had their civil liberties curtailed.[2] If, in addition, they belonged to so-called visible minority groups, as Midge Ayukawa observes in this volume, they became 'objects of scorn.'[3] Considering this background, one might well imagine how stunned were Finns in Canada by the overwhelmingly favourable coverage by the Canadian media of Finland and Finnish Canadians during the Winter War, which raged from 30 November 1939 until 13 March 1940. Triggered by a Soviet invasion into Finland and characterized by truly ferocious fighting, the Winter War that pitted Finns against Russians captured the imagination of the media. Almost instantly, the Canadian media was 'drenched with sympathy' for the small nation of Finland. Newspapers depicted the war as a battle between David and Goliath, the underdog and the bully, the small 'gallant and heroic' nation of lawabiding and civilized people against the 'barbarous,' 'greedy,' Communist Russians.[4]

During the more than one hundred days of intense press coverage of the Winter War, the media also discovered the 'Finnish woman' and, indeed, actively promoted various constructions of this female ethnic subject. This photo essay explores the media manipulation of the 'Finnish woman' and how it served a variety of different propaganda agendas. Such manipulation was a complex and multilayered process: the Finnish woman's race and the many gendered roles she played made her a malleable role model, an ideal sister to heterosexual Anglo-Canadian women – at least during a particular historical moment.

An understanding of the Canadian media's glorification of these female strangers requires us to look briefly at the events during the first year of the Second World War. When Canada declared war on Germany on 10 September 1939, the initial flurry of wartime activity, recruitment, patriotic speeches, and the creation of new enemy aliens in the country, captured the lion's share of media attention. But as these early dramatic events soon gave way to what became known as the 'phony war' (when little happened on the European battle front), the lack of action in Europe meant few exciting stories for war correspondents. According to Canadian military historian J.L. Granatstein, early wartime activity had 'stagnated, degenerating to a battle of leaflets and loudspeakers across the Rhine.'[5] All this changed, however, when the Soviet Union attacked Finland on 30 November 1939. Suddenly the world became witness to an active theatre of war replete with heroes and enemies, bombed-out cities, suffering civilians, and soldiers ambushed and frozen in the battle between 'mighty Russia and the tiny nation of Finns.' The Winter War became front-page news as Finns fought against Canada's ideological enemy – Communist Russia – for democracy and independence. Canadian war correspondents were dispatched to the Arctic front. Day after day, bold headlines trumpeted the message of the small heroic nation's dogged determination to defend its borders. The media reported stunning successes of the Finnish Army against formidable odds: 'Finns Drive Russians from Petsamo, Soviet "Parachute Army" Wiped Out; Russians' Losses Soar as Retreat Continues Along Three Sectors; Russians Lose 100,000 Men and 300 Tanks; Finns Smash Invader on Four Fronts, Annihilate Flower of Russian Army.' Characteristic of the media coverage of the Winter War was the following depiction: 'Pitted against Finn supermen Russians flounder hopelessly in deep drifts of arctic forest.'[6] Inspired Canadians flocked to volunteer to fight the Russians alongside the 'Finn supermen.' An influential committee, headed by Senator Arthur Meighen, recruited the volunteers and raised funds for the Finnish war effort. Canadian military leader Col. Hunter announced that two thousand Canadian volunteers were ready to leave for Finland on 14 March 1940.[7]

And then, almost as suddenly, came the announcement that an armistice was declared on 13 March 1940. Canadians were perplexed. What they had read in the newspapers or heard on the radio had not prepared them for an armistice, let alone for the heavy territorial losses suffered by Finland. Furthermore, as the hostilities ceased, the fate of the Finns soon became yesterday's news. In the spring and summer of 1940, the media attention shifted to the new and disturbing developments in Europe as Hitler's successful *Blitzkrieg* began conquering one democratic country after another. On 22 June 1941, Hitler attacked the Soviet Union and four days later, Finland, alongside Germany, followed suit. Intent on reclaiming its lost territory, Finland was now a co-belligerent of Germany, which in turn, prompted the Canadian government, on 7 December 1941, to declare Finland an enemy of Canada. Finns in Canada thus became enemy aliens. Thereafter, if the Finns received any press coverage at all, they were depicted as tired, reluctant soldiers fighting on the wrong side. The 'barbaric' Russians had now become valuable allies. As this brief summary suggests, the window of opportunity for this study is small indeed. The positive media coverage began during late summer 1939, as war clouds gathered over Europe, followed by a groundswell of coverage during the Winter War, which then waned soon after the Armistice was declared.

These changing contexts shaped in fundamental ways the portrayal of Finnish people, including women, in Canada and their changing status as sisters or strangers. During the summer of 1939 the government of Finland provided the North American press with photos designed to depict a nation of civilized, healthy, athletic, and beautiful people. Initially, this propaganda was part of an advertising campaign to entice Canadians to travel to the summer Olympics to be hosted by Helsinki in 1940. By the fall, the focus shifted to describing a small, brave nation in need of support, and Finnish state propaganda emphasized the role of women in nation-building, their crucial role in preparing Finland's defences, and later their role in Finland's war effort.[8]

Canada recognized the potential need to recruit women to bolster its own war effort. The intense attention given to the activities of the Finnish women at the beginning of the war foreshadowed the later wartime propaganda in Canada intended to recruit women *en masse*. Finnish sisters were deemed suitable heroines and role models for Canadian women. After all, they were fighting on the 'right' side against Canada's – and democracy's – ideological enemy, the Communist Soviet Union. Stories of Finnish women served as positive examples of how women became critical contributors to the war effort while still maintaining their 'womanhood.'[9] At the same time, the Finnish-Canadian community, which numbered more than 41,000 in 1941, quickly seized on the opportunities offered by this exceptional period of the glorification of everything Finnish. Community members, especially those belonging to nationalist and religious organizations, plotted how best they could get their own message across. They wanted the media to cover their assurances of their continuing loyalty to Canada while raising funds in aid of the Finnish war effort. More significantly, the Winter War presented an unparalleled opportunity for Finnish Canadians to have their voices heard across Canada. Finnish-Canadian women were willing participants in the community's propaganda efforts and in the creation of an idealized 'Finnish woman.' It also offers a dramatic illustration of how 'ethnic nationalism' can be gendered, a theme that Frances Sywripa also addresses in this volume.

The representation of the Finnish woman during this period of crisis had many and seemingly contradictory layers. The mythical Finnish woman who appeared on the pages of the major Toronto and Montreal English-language newspapers was at once objectified as a beautiful woman, an aggressive soldier, a sacrificing 'traditional' mother and wife, a strong peasant or construction worker, and an emancipated and independent woman. She was a victim and an initiator, supportive and demanding, weak and powerful. In other words, she represented the underlying ferment of Canadian women's changing roles in society, the simmering challenges to their sexual identities and the increasing dissatisfaction with the unequal economic and political power of women. The many different constructs of Finnish women co-existed in harmony and went uncontested on the pages of Canada's leading newspapers.

Why, one might ask, were the Finnish women deemed suitable role models? One reason may be that they were distant and strange enough not to pose any immediate threat. So little was known about Finland that fact and fiction about its women could safely mingle. Indeed, erroneous and often sensationalist reports went without protest. Another reason may be that a Eurocentric and often racist press found Finnish women eminently acceptable. They were white and belonged to the northern race; in fact, the press never tired of pointing out just how 'fair' or 'blonde' they were. They were also Protestant, Western in habits, and relatively well educated. In other words, mainstream Anglo-Canadian women could conceivably identify with their newly found Finnish heroines who stood beside – not behind – their men. Drawing on the coverage and especially images of Finnish women to appear in several English-Canadian newspapers during the period under review, the following sections examine the seven complex images of Finnish women that emerged in the Canadian media. These were the traditional woman, the beautiful blonde, the worker, the emancipated woman, the woman in the Lotta Svärd auxiliary, the soldier, and the immigrant woman as fundraiser.

**The Traditional Woman**

The national costume of Finnish women became an important propaganda weapon and a symbol of traditional peasant way of life. National costumes caught the attention of the reader and many of the captions that accompanied the numerous photos had a didactic quality to them. Identifying images of Finnish peasant women at work, for example, were captions that informed the Canadian public that notwithstanding the 'peculiar' costumes worn by Finnish women they really were just like Canadian women. In reality, women in Finland never wore national costumes, except on very special holidays or when performing traditional folk dances or songs on stage. Indeed, most women never owned the colourful ceremonial outfit, which was made of wool, cotton, intricate lace, and worn with heavy bronze or silver jewelry. Although hardly an outfit suitable for daily routines, press photographs released by the Finnish government suggested otherwise. They frequently portrayed women in these costumes. Four photographs published in the *Toronto Star* on 5 December 1939 are emblematic. The first photograph shows a young woman in national costume weaving; the second one has ten women in national costumes surrounding on old bearded man who looks like a traditional rune singer of Finnish mythological songs. The third image portrays a Sami woman and the text draws attention to her costume: 'Lapland girls have their own peculiar dress.' The fourth is a picture of a stout peasant woman baking, with the explanation: 'Peasant women maintain the old-fashioned way of cooking.' In stark contrast to these peaceful, though exotic, photographs of women in their most traditional roles is the bold caption: 'Women of Finland Stand Beside Their Men' and 'They Live and Fight in Traditional Style.'[10]

Finland also sent photographs meant to depict the 'typical' Finnish women, and some of them also contain images of women wearing a national costume – including one of a young Finnish mother holding her impeccably dressed plump child. The caption reads: 'Typical of the hardy, vigorous and purposeful character of the Finns is this peasant mother and child.'[11] Similarly, the *Montreal Standard* carried a large photograph of two young maidens, dressed in the national costume who were described as 'typical of Finland.'[12]

## The Beautiful Blonde

The construction of the beautiful, mythical, healthy, and, again, exotic Finnish woman took many forms. One of the first such stories that dwelt on this theme in the Canadian press appeared on 10 November 1939, when Birgit Kansanen, 'a pretty Finnish student studying at the University of Toronto' was interviewed for the *Toronto Star*. This 'student' had in fact been supervisor of nursing for the Red Cross in northern Lapland. Her life, which was hardly typical of Finnish women, was described in exciting and daring terms. Her skiing trips through the wilderness and forests of Lapland to reach remote communities are depicted as heroic. Far above the Arctic Circle, in the darkness of the northern winter, she was pulled in sleighs by reindeer and sheltered from blizzards by her St Bernard dog. Far

## WOMEN IN FINLAND STAND BESIDE THEIR MEN
## THEY LIVE AND FIGHT IN TRADITIONAL STYLE

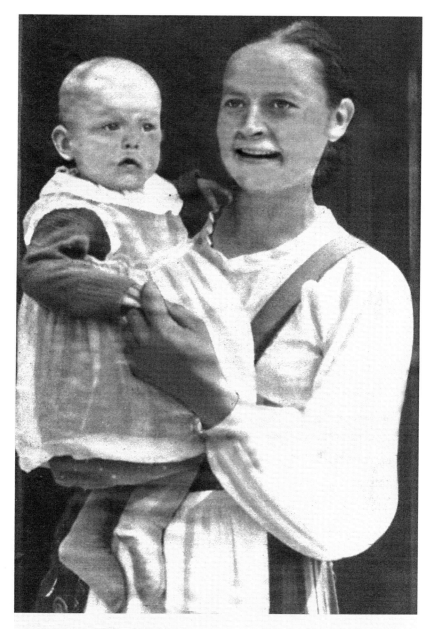

**TYPICAL OF THE HARDY,** vigorous and purposeful character of the Finns is this peasant mother and child.

# FINNISH GIRLS ARE FAIR

**TYPICAL OF FINLAND** are these happy country girls with their long fair hair, broad foreheads and strong white teeth.

from being a passive female subject, Kansanen assisted the media by providing details of her lonely and brave struggles against the elements. At one point, she described being 'caught in a snowstorm without [matches] and I slept beside my St. Bernard dog all night to keep from freezing.' Kansanen's story is exceptional indeed. Most Finnish women would have only seen reindeers in a zoo and few would have travelled alone in a blizzard through the vast wilder-

**TUULIKI PAANEN** above is Finland's leading screen star.

ness. This dramatic story was accompanied by a photograph of smiling Birgit Kansanen.[13]

On 9 December 1939, the *Montreal Standard* published in its weekly magazine several pages of photographs of Finland depicting Finnish cultural heroes, Finnish architecture, and the Finnish landscape. Included is also a special section on 'Finland's Women.' One of its captions, referring to a photograph of two blonde girls leaning against a log cabin, tells the reader that 'Finnish Girls Are Fair.' It then elaborates further: 'Typical of Finland are these happy country girls with their long fair hair, broad foreheads, and strong white teeth.' Another page is dominated by a smiling, saluting Tuulikki Paananen. The caption, while misspelling her name, refers to her as 'Finland's leading screen star.' The popular photograph of Paananen, who spent the war years in Hollywood, was featured again on 30 December 1939 in the *Toronto Star Weekly*. This time her photograph filled the entire page.[14] Needless to say, not all Finnish women were fair, strong, or healthy, and only the exceptional few ever became Hollywood stars.

**ABOVE** are Finnish women street cleaners. Their conscientious scrubbing of pavements and sidewalks and the feminine thoroughness they bring to such jobs in other walks of life have given Finland the reputation of the cleanest country in Europe. Right: A sturdy girl worker in a paper-board factory

## The Worker

In stark contrast to the smiling beauties in national costumes are the strong women engaged in heavy manual labour. A factory worker included in a special *Star Weekly* photo coverage entitled 'Finland Resists Threat to Her Independence,' was described as 'a sturdy girl worker in a paper-board factory.' The woman in the picture, looking directly into the camera, is wearing loose overalls with rolled-up shirt sleeves, and she is carrying a heavy load of paper boards. A picture on the same page shows five stout, elderly women crouching with brushes over a cobblestone street. Described as Finnish women street cleaners, the caption told readers that 'their conscientious scrubbing of pavements ... and the feminine thoroughness they bring to such jobs in other walks of life have given Finland the reputation of the cleanest country in Europe.' For many readers it undoubtedly required quite a stretch of imagination to associate these stout, elderly street scrubbers with 'feminine' attributes, though they might well have got the message that in Finland women could perform all kinds of heavy labour.[15]

The large number of women in heavy industries was partially due to Finland's legislation of compulsory labour laws for all healthy Finns, eighteen to fifty-five years of age, that was enacted in October 1939 in anticipation of the war. Once the war started, the war industries were in desperate need of workers. Indeed, during the war more than half the people working in Finland's war industries were women.[16] Some parallels were drawn with the British women's war effort as young girls and women were organized to do a variety of jobs 'behind the lines.' Two photographs show 'a group of girls making window blinds for blackouts at night.' The women 'aided by a lone man' are 'adept with tools.' Another photograph is of a roomful of women busily at work preparing bandages. The caption states: 'Standing By – Women in Finland were as resolute as their men in demanding independence.'[17] Canada, too, anticipated the need to recruit housewives into war industries. Many immigrant women who were originally recruited into the low-paying domestic service sector found new employment opportunities in war industries. Finnish-Canadian domestics were quick to follow the example set by women in their homeland and changed their aprons to overalls and their small paycheques to 'men's wages.'[18]

The stories and photo images of Finnish women workers happily doing 'men's work' while maintaining their 'femininity' helped set the stage for the later strong recruitment of Canadian women into the war industries. For this purpose the federal government established the Women's Voluntary Service Division in 1941. As the labour shortage became critical in Canada, the Women's Division of the Selective Service agency carried out a national registration in 1942 of all women aged twenty to twenty-four.[19]

**The Emancipated Woman**

Finnish government propaganda wished to create the image of a modern, emancipated woman who could stand next to the traditional woman. Educational material proudly proclaimed the positive, even enviable, position of women in Finland. And some Canadian newspapers, as the following excerpt shows, quoted it at length:

> In Finland women take their places alongside their menfolk in every walk and profession from the highest to the lowest. Granted the vote in 1906 when their sisters in

# Women Behind Finland's Lines

STANDING BY—Women of Finland were as resolute as their men in demanding independence. These women have been at work preparing bandages.

other countries were only just beginning to think about such things they have carried on from there and one of their number, a domestic servant named Miina Sillanpää was elected one of the first women deputies and worked her way to a cabinet post.[20]

First-wave feminist and suffrage leader Nellie McClung joined the chorus of praises of the emancipated Finnish woman, pointing out, for instance, that they had received the right to vote eleven years before their Canadian sisters. McClung became interested in Finnish women through her own Finnish domestic servant; the protagonist in her novel *Painted Fires* was a stubborn and independent Finnish maid. In a lengthy article about the war in Finland, McClung reinforced this image of emancipated Finnish women, and also described women's independent role in the Lotta Svärd 'women's unit of defense.' But she also declared that Finnish women were 'just like ourselves,' and, as supporting evidence, noted that 'Finnish women have many societies, including the YWCA and the National Council of Women, both affiliated with the international bodies.'[21]

In short, Canadian press coverage gave the impression that Finnish women enjoyed equality with Finnish men. In reality, of course, they earned much less than men, were less likely to find themselves in leadership positions, and have yet today to reach equal pay or equal representation in the parliament.

## Women's Auxiliary: The Lotta Svärd

Many references in articles, interviews, and photographs were made to the Lotta Svärd organization and its uniformed women soldiers. The main impression gleaned from the newspaper coverage is of an organization for all Finnish women, that its members were 'conscripted' and that they served both as an auxiliary and as a fighting force. The press carried an unusual image of elderly, stern, and important-looking Finnish women in grey military uniforms seated in a meeting, holding documents in their hands, while a large portrait of Marshall Mannerheim hangs behind them, thus presenting an authoritative and respectful image of the women in Finland's Lotta Svärd. One of the women is identified as Fanni Luukkonen, the head of the 100,000-member organization. These were not young women looking for adventure but mature women with serious wartime business on their hands.

Finnish women were portrayed as most eager and willing participants in the activities of the Lotta Svärd. Under the title 'Women Rush to Serve,' for example, the *Toronto Star Weekly* told readers the following:

Stenographers whose jobs were wiped out by the war have rushed into Red Cross canteen work in Finland's splendid auxiliary, the Lotta Svärd. Finnish women are

Fanni Luukkonen, head of the Lotta Svard organization of over 100,000 women, whose members will step into vital jobs in wartime

**SHE WATCHES AND WHEN RAIDERS COME THE FINNS ARE READY**

—Associated Press Wirephoto

Essential to Finland's weak air | from her vantage point among the | forewarned, are at their stations
defences are the services of this | trees she sights raiding planes, she | and with good marksmanship bring
girl (LOWER). From her observa- | signals the defences and the air- | down enemy craft.
tion post she scans the skies. When | raid alarms are sounded. Gunners,

now serving 10 to 15 hours a day for the country's freedom. This is little Finland, unflinching and undaunted before the mighty Soviet Goliath which threatens its life.[22]

The text accompanying four pictures of quintessentially 'traditional'-looking Finnish women in national costumes declares that 'Women of Finland Stand Beside Their Men,' and then offers the following examples:

Household Crafts such as the weaving this girl is doing have been forsaken for more active service now that Finland is at war. Girls and women have been trained in the part they must play in defence of their homeland. Like the women of Britain, they are now engaged in air raid precaution and army auxiliary work.[23]

Yet, the Lotta Svärd organization was far from an inclusive female organization. On the contrary, it was a political auxiliary organization for conservative Finnish women. It had strict screening procedures and only admitted as its members right-wing, mainly middle-class 'Christian and moral' women. The organization was founded immediately after Finland's civil war in 1919, which had pitted 'red' Finns against the conservative 'white' Finns. It originated as an auxiliary force to the conservative government's Civil Guard by women who had participated on the side of the 'White Guard' against the 'Red Guard.' When the Winter War broke out, the Lotta Svärd had an elaborate network of what they called 'reputable women' ready to serve in auxiliary roles. Decidedly anti-Communist, the organization did not allow left-wing Finnish women to join, and only after the Second World War did it agree to co-operate with women from Social Democratic organizations. It was thus seriously misleading to suggest that 'all' Finnish women flocked to join the Lotta Svärd, but an impressive number did. During the Winter War, about 90,000 Lottas were mobilized. About 25,000 of them worked within the war zone, where they served in the field kitchens (11,000), took care of supplies (3,500), stood on guard in some 650 air defence locations (3,000), provided medical services (2,500), and clerical services (2,000). An additional 6,100 nurses worked through the Red Cross in the field hospitals. The example of a well-organized, uniformed, female defence unit engaged in important auxiliary work in aid of Finland's war effort, could serve as an appropriate model for Canadian women.

**The Soldier**

Some articles and photographs give the impression that Finnish women were not only serving behind the lines or in auxiliary roles but were an integral part of the army, fighting as soldiers on the battlefield. Photographs depict uniformed 'female members of Finland's army on an observation post high in a tree.' Another uniformed woman peers through her binoculars: 'She watches and when raiders come the Finns are ready.' The caption assures the reader that 'Essential to Finland's weak air defences are the services of this girl.'[24]

Finnish women were also described as fierce gun-carrying soldiers. A bizarre article, which went uncontested, gives an image of a fully mobilized army of women. A section of the article, based on an interview with Mary Lehtonen of Toronto, sports the subheading, 'Women Better Fighters.' It deserves to be quoted at length:

'Wait until the Russian soldiers come face to face with a regiment of determined Finnish women soldiers,' advised Mary Lehtonen today. This 19-year old girl has just returned from a two-month visit to the homeland and claims, from what she saw of the war preparations, that the women of Finland are more daring than men. 'I saw whole regiments of women digging trenches along the Russian-Finland border. They

# Draft Women To Fight Reds

One of Finnish women who have been drafted for army service as ski-troops receiving one of her first skiing lessons under military instructors near Helsinki recently. The Finns have reported many successful attacks by their silently gliding ski troops in surprise attacks on the invading Russians.

worked side-by-side with the men and are trained to shoulder a gun if necessary. If that does happen, the Russians had better look out,' said Ms Lehtonen grimly. 'Our men are good fighters but our women are better' ... 'From past experience in war,' Ms Lehtonen continued, 'we know that our enemies are more afraid of the women than men.'[25]

The Winter War became famous for the Finnish ski troops which swiftly ambushed the enemy during the exceptionally cold and snowy winter. Canadians were told that women were part of the ski troops. A headline above a uniformed woman on skis says 'Draft Women to Fight Reds.' The *Globe and Mail* identifies her as '[o]ne of [the] Finnish women who has been drafted for army service as ski-troops.' The article continues, 'The Finns have reported many successful attacks by their silently gliding ski troops in surprise attacks on the invading Russians.'[26] A Finnish-Canadian woman, Aili Laatunen, declared, 'I think it is the sacred duty of every man and woman to fight for his country when that country is attacked.'[27] Despite media reports to the contrary, Finnish women did not carry arms or join the army as soldiers during the Winter War. Only at the end of the Second World War in 1944 did the Ministry of Defence actually train 145 women to carry arms.[28] Thus, the articles in Canadian newspapers that suggested that Finnish women fought as soldiers were sensationalist fiction misrepresenting the activities of the Lotta Svärd.

During the Winter War, hundreds of Finnish-Canadian men volunteered to go to Finland where they joined the 'American Legion.' Some Finnish-Canadian women, eager to heed Finland's call for help, also travelled to Finland. Their departures were covered with great fanfare. The women were depicted as hoping to join the famous Lotta Svärd organization. For example: 'Mrs. Lenki Dankar [*sic*] is attractive, blonde and Finnish. She hopes to leave Toronto in a few days for her nativeland to serve in the front line trenches.' The emphasis on the woman's looks, combined with the 'fact' that she was going to serve in the 'front line trenches,' fortified the tantalizing image of beautiful, blonde, Finnish female warriors.[29]

Another headline declared that Mrs Salonen, 'Would sell her furniture to fight again for Finland: Twice decorated by homeland Toronto woman is anxious to return.'[30] Although 'heroic and attractive' women in battle intrigued the press and offered impressions of role reversals, they were fictitious. Only eleven Finnish-Canadian women left with the volunteers to serve in some capacity during the Winter War. Three of them were accepted into the Lotta Svärd auxiliary where they worked as cooks and nurses. All three had been members of the organization before emigrating to Canada. Other emigrant women were rejected and bitterly concluded, 'We weren't good enough.' There were no follow-up articles on the women's experience in Finland, leaving the reader with the false impression that

## FINNISH FIGHTERS SUPPORTED BY TORONTO KIN

While the Finnish army defends its land, relatives in Toronto are working hard to raise money and supply necessities through the Canadian Red Cross. Here are a few members of the "Finnish War Aid Auxiliary" busily knitting and sewing at the Church of All Nations while they think of their beloved homeland. LEFT to RIGHT, Miss Signe Miettinen, 1938 Finnish beauty contest winner; Mrs. William Kojola, auxiliary treasurer; Mrs. J. Heiskanen, convener of supplies, and Mrs. M. D. Sulonen, captain of Huron St. hall group.

## FOR THEIR BELOVED ANCESTRAL FINLAND THESE CANADIAN GIRLS SING

Finnish-Canadian women were 'flocking' to serve in the front line trenches of the Winter War.[31]

## The Fundraiser

Throughout the settlement history of Finnish Canadians, women carried the main responsibility for raising funds.[32] The fundraising activity intensified just prior to the Winter War. The community issued carefully worded, short news releases designed to solicit funds for Finland while at the same time calming any fears of disloyalty to Canada, such as the following: 'Following a mass meeting of Finnish people at the Church of All Nations, at which an expression of loyalty to the Canadian government was passed unanimously, an organizing meeting of captains was held.' The article continued to cover all bases by describing how women planned to 'do handwork during the winter for the Red Cross of Finland, should the need arise, and to assist enlisted Finnish men in the Canadian army and Canadian soldiers in general.'[33] Finns soon discovered what kind of stories would make it into the media. They included interviews with worried Finnish-Canadian women with family in Finland but also pictures of Finnish-Canadian women in their national costumes. In fact, just scanning the newspapers one gets the impression that Finnish-Canadian women routinely wore this outfit. The community learned that young and beautiful women were the ones most likely to be photographed by reporters. Since the object was to raise money it was important to get photographs into the press that would draw attention to their printed message. For example, a photograph of four Finnish-Canadian women in national costumes, knitting and sewing, has the caption: 'Finnish fighters supported by Toronto kin.' The text below the photograph stated the community's fundraising message: 'While the Finnish army defends its land, relatives in Toronto are working hard to raise money and supply necessities through the Canadian Red Cross. Here are a few members of the "Finnish War Aid Auxiliary" busily knitting and sewing at the Church of All Nations while they think of their beloved homeland.'[34] The women are then identified by name and their position in the auxiliary, except for Signe Miettinen who is identified as a '1938 Finnish beauty contest winner.' During the following months the smiling photograph of Signe Miettinen in her national costume was published many times in different poses as the photographers focused their lenses on the 'beauty queen.' The treasurer of the Finland Aid organization in Toronto, Elsie Kojola, who still sixty years later values her collection of newspaper clippings of the period, explained in an interview how the Finland Aid organization appointed press secretaries and staged photo opportunities in order to get their fundraising message across: 'We discovered that beautiful, young women in national costumes worked the best.'[35] Finnish-Canadian women were consciously part of image-building for the 'Finnish Woman.' The need to raise funds was paramount in their minds and the end justified the means. Thus, images of smiling costumed women proliferated the papers. The *Toronto Star* carried two more photographs of Finnish women in Toronto 'who donned national costumes.' The women, once again, are sewing. An adjacent picture shows piles of money scattered on the table. Smiling Mrs Lina [*sic*] Aho is donating the funds to a Red Cross Nurse 'for their campaign to give help to their homeland.' Another two women packing clothes for shipment to Finland were featured the following day.[36] Images of the smiling women in traditional costumes continued to be printed regularly throughout, and even for a few months after, the Winter War.

Another image which worked well for fundraising purposes was to show women and children who were victims of war. A long-sustained fundraising campaign called 'Help for Heroic Finland' in the *Montreal Star*, featured a photograph of a sad and tired looking elderly woman. Her image was designed to evoke the sympathies of Montrealers who may have been able to identify with the plight of this one woman, who reminded people of their mothers and grandmothers. The photograph and the accompanying article brought the human tragedy of Finland to the homes of Montreal:

> The tragedy that is Finland seems to peer out of the face of this elderly Finnish woman as she sits in a shelter ... the face is sorrowful, but there is determination and strength written on it, as it is written all over the little Republic which is fighting for its life against overwhelming odds ... Take one more glance at the pitiful, almost beseeching, face of the destitute Finnish woman pictured above, and resolve to send a donation NOW.[37]

## Conclusion

In exploring the gendered nature of the iconography of Canadian newspapers' coverage of Finnish women in Canada during Finland's Winter War against Russia, this essay explores a little studied topic, namely the role that the media played in rallying readers to the cause of war by drawing on gendered and ethnic images of foreign women who, though not despised, were not normally seen in heroic terms. At the same time, racialized notions of beauty also mattered, and Finnish women conveniently fit with exotic – but not too exotic – notions of 'white goddesses.' Revealed here are the changing and mutable cultural and political meanings that were applied to a normally marginal group of immigrant women in Canada.

The media coverage of the Finnish women must be evaluated in its exceptional

FAR FROM HOME—Thoughts of Canadian Finns are with their people far away. Mrs. Sonja Skuggevik and Miss Paula Wide donned national costume for celebrations

FOR WAR WORK—Mrs. Lina Aho and a Red Cross nurse display some of the $600 raised by local Finns in their campaign to give help to their homeland

# Help For Heroic Finland

The tragedy that is Finland's seems to peer out of the face of this elderly Finnish woman as she sits in a shelter in the Swedish border town of Haparanda, where she and hundreds of women and children found refuge in their flight from Soviet bombing attacks. The face is sorrowful, but there is determination and strength written on it, as it is written all over the little Republic which is fighting for its life against overwhelming odds.

GALLANT Finland's urgent call for aid is finding a generous response in the hearts of the good people of Montreal.

The usually tranquil Finnish consular office has galvanized into busy life. A steady stream of well-wishers offering material or financial help attests to the sympathy for the plight of the Finnish people.

Norwegians, Swedes, Danes, Jews, Hungarians, English, French, and even German names are on the list of callers. Consuls of other countries, too, have rallied to the call.

News today from many parts of the civilized world brings out in bold relief the anxiety of all decent peoples to stem the tide of barbaric plunderers and the forces of primitive savagery.

France is sending military aid. Finnish volunteers are arriving in their native land from the Western Hemisphere. Supplies and money are going from the United States.

While the response has been magnificent, there is still urgent need of further funds. All lovers of human liberty will want to lighten the road of despair now being travelled by the sorely pressed Finnish people.

Take one more glance at the pitiful, almost beseeching, face of the destitute Finnish woman pictured above, and resolve to send a donation NOW wartime context. For a few months the insatiable desire of the Canadian media to glorify the events in Finland pre-empted their critical observation skills. So distorted was the media coverage that most Canadians, and Finnish Canadians in particular, were stunned to learn that these heroes in fact lost the Winter War and ultimately, in 1940, had to make severe concessions to the Soviet Union. The headlines had described one Finnish victory after another and declared the near annihilation of the Russian army as David was defeating Goliath. Russian women and children also suffered but received no sympathy from the Canadians. Russian soldiers were brutally slaughtered by the thousands and many, unable to move with their heavy equipment, froze in the bitterly cold winter. Their slaughter was not necessarily heroic. Similarly, the images of women were designed, largely by the propaganda agencies of Finland, to create a multilayered super woman, attractive to all readers. She was at once sensual and exotic, beautiful and healthy, traditional yet modern and emancipated.

This glorification of Finland benefited, even if only briefly, the Finnish Canadians who supported Finland's war effort. For decades, the Finns had been marginalized and shunned by the media, attracting attention only when they did something that offended Canadian sensibilities. Now, suddenly, they could do no wrong. For a few months the Finnish Canadians, while distraught over the events in their homeland, basked in their hero status and tried to use it to their best advantage. Nationalistic community leaders painted a false picture of a united Finnish-Canadian community whose political differences had all but disappeared. The community learned to use its women, frequently described as 'girls,' to promote its nationalistic message and to aid in its fundraising. No one tried to correct or contradict the one-sided messages and often erroneous depictions of the role of Finnish women during the Winter War that had been constructed by the various propaganda agencies, the newspapers, and the Finnish-Canadian community.

The goodwill and attention towards Finland and its women was fleeting. National costumes from enemy nations soon fell out of favour. As the heroes turned into enemies, their community was silenced. No more feminine street cleaners or smiling beauty queens from Finland adorned the newspapers. Stories of Finnish women were replaced by information and intense propaganda about Canadian women's war efforts and the exotic Finnish woman vanished from the press. The mythical 'Finnish Woman' had served her purpose. Her stories and images had sold newspapers, she had created goodwill and sympathy toward Finland's war effort, she had shown that women could be unified in the support of their homeland, she had provided examples of unusual working situations, her dedication in women's auxiliary work had served as a model, and she was also depicted as a soldier standing 'beside the men.'

The stranger became a familiar sister, a role model with whom Anglo-Canadian women could identify. Like them, she was battling cold climates, she was Protestant and white, educated, and her country needed her. This made her a well-suited warm-up act to the publicity campaigns that recruited Canadian housewives into war industries and later into the Canadian army, navy, and air force. For a fleeting moment in history the stranger had a familiar face. She was a Finnish sister peering out of Canada's major daily newspapers.

NOTES

1 See, for example, Carmela Patrias, 'Relief Strike: Immigrant Workers and the Great Depression in Crowland, Ontario, 1930–1935,' and Ian Radforth, 'Finnish Radicalism and Labour Activism in the Northern Ontario Woods,' in Franca Iacovetta et al., eds, *A Nation of Immigrants: Women, Workers, and Communities in Canadian History, 1840s–1960s* (Toronto: University of Toronto Press, 1998), 293–316, 322–58.

2 See, for example, Franca Iacovetta, Roberto Perin, and Angelo Principe, *Enemies Within: Italians and Other Internees in Canada and Abroad* (Toronto: University of Toronto Press, 2000); Frances Swyripa and John Heard Thompson, eds, *Loyalties in Conflict: Ukrainians in Canada during the Great War* (Edmonton: Canadian Institute of Ukrainian Studies, 1983); Norman Hillmer, Bohdan Kordan, and Lubomyr Luciuk, eds, *On Guard for Thee: War, Ethnicity and the Canadian State, 1939–1945* (Ottawa: Canadian Committee for the History of the Second World War, 1988).

3 See also Ken Adachi, *The Enemy That Never Was: A History of Japanese Canadians* (Toronto: McClelland and Stewart, 1976); Ann Gomer Sunahara, *The Politics of Racism: The Uprooting of Japanese Canadians during the Second World War* (Toronto: Lorimer 1981); Barry Broadfoot, *Years of Sorrow, Years of Shame: The Story of Japanese Canadians in World War II* (Toronto: Double Day Canada, 1972); Patricia Roy, J.L. Granatstein, Masuko Ino, and Hiroko Takamura, eds, *Mutual Hostages: Canadians and Japanese during the Second World War* (Toronto: University of Toronto Press, 1990).

4 For information on the wartime experience of Finnish Canadians, see Varpu Lindström, *From Heroes to Enemies: Finns in Canada, 1937–1947* (Beaverton, ON: Aspasia Books, 2000).

5 J.L. Granatstein and J.M. Hitsman, *Broken Promises: A History of Conscription in Canada* (Toronto: Oxford University Press, 1977), 135.

6 *Toronto Daily Star,* 2 December 1939; *Globe and Mail,* 25 December 1939; *Toronto Daily Star,* 30 December 1939; 2 January 1940, and 8 January 1940.

7 Ministry of Foreign Affairs Archives, Finland, package 2, Finnish Consulate General of Montreal archives, *Toronto Daily Star,* 8 March 1940; *Toronto Telegram,* 11 March 1940.

8   For example, see multipage photo essays in the *Star Weekly*, 18 November 1939 and the *Montreal Standard*, 9 December 1939.

9   On the recruitment and image of Canadian women in the armed forces, see Ruth Roach Pierson, '*They're Still Women After All*': *The Second World War and Canadian Womanhood* (Toronto: McClelland and Stewart, 1986). On women and sexuality during the war, see Marilyn Lake, 'Female Desires: The Meaning of World War II,' in Joan Wallach Scott, ed., *Feminism in History* (Toronto: Oxford University Press, 1996), 429–49.

10   *Toronto Star*, 5 December 1939.

11   *Star Weekly*, 16 December 1939.

12   *Montreal Standard*, 9 December 1939.

13   *Toronto Star*, 10 November 1939.

14   *Montreal Standard*, 9 December 1939; *Star Weekly*, 30 December 1939.

15   *Star Weekly*, 30 December 1939.

16   Lea Tuiremo, *Sota ja Nainen* (*War and Woman*), Snellman Institute Series B/31 (Kuopio, Finland, 1992), 28.

17   *Montreal Star*, 29 December 1939; *Toronto Star*, 1 December 1939.

18   Interview with Aune Jokinen, Sault Ste Marie, 1998. See also Lindström, *From Heroes to Enemies*, 155–6.

19   On recruitment of Canadian women into war industries, see Pierson '*They're Still Women After All*.'

20   *Montreal Standard*, 9 December 1939.

21   Nellie McClung, 'Finns Fight for Freedom against Russian Invasion: Finland Is Crowned with Immortality as Russia Attempts to Blot Out Her Independent Little Neighbor.' Unidentified newspaper clipping, 20 January 1940.

22   *Star Weekly*, 4 December 1939.

23   *Toronto Star*, 5 December 1939.

24   *Montreal Standard*, 9 December 1939; *Toronto Star*, 17 January 1940.

25   *Toronto Star*, 30 November 1939.

26   *Globe and Mail*, 1 January 1940.

27   *Toronto Star*, 8 January 1940.

28   Tuiremo, *Sota ja Nainen*, 30–4; for a comprehensive treatment of this organization see V. Lukkarinen, *Suomen Lotat* (Finland's Lottas) (Jyväskylä, Finland, 1986).

29   *Toronto Star*, 2 January 1940.

30   *Toronto Star*, 1 January 1940.

31   University of Turku Archives SSK no. 81, letters from Anni Korsberg to Finland Society, Vaasa, 19 January 1941; Lempi Tiinus to A. Suomal. Kotiuttamisosasto, Viljakala, 6 November 1940; Laura Virta to Päämajan Vapaaehtoistoimisto, Järvenpää, 28 October 1940; Aili Viita to Päämajanvapaaehtoistoimisto, 14 November 1940; Interview with Helmi Huttunen, Astoria, Oregon, 1992. For further information of Finnish-

Canadian women in the Winter War of Finland see, Varpu Lindström, *From Heroes to Enemies*, 98–9.

32  For a history of Finnish immigrant women in Canada, see Varpu Lindström-Best, *Defiant Sisters: A Social History of Finnish Immigrant Women in Canada, 1890–1930* (Toronto: Multicultural History Society of Ontario, 1988).

33  *Toronto Star*, 10 November 1939.

34  *Toronto Star*, 6 December 1939.

35  Interview with Elsie Kojola, Toronto, 1998 and her private collection of newspaper clippings in author's possession.

36  *Toronto Star*, 4 January 1940.

37  *Montreal Star*, newspaper clipping, n.d., in Kojola collection.

# The Semiotics of Zwieback:
# Feast and Famine in the Narratives of
# Mennonite Refugee Women

MARLENE EPP

## Introduction

Nearly fifty years ago, a prominent American sociologist of the Mennonites wrote a popular booklet about Mennonite beliefs and customs. In a section devoted to culinary practices, he noted the reputation of Mennonite women for good cooking, suggested that 'they eat well' and as evidence of it, noted their lack of concern for waistlines.[1] Images of contented, indeed jolly, robust Mennonite women whipping up huge batches of borscht, pie, and buns come to mind. Slim Mennonite women who are not especially inclined towards cooking, or those who well remember homeland experiences of famine, may chafe at such stereotyping of both their gender and their ethnicity. Yet the linkages between food and ethnicity cannot be denied. Anthropologists Peter Farb and George Armelagos once said: 'The surest way of discovering a family's ethnic origin is to look into its kitchen.'[2] The 1999 legal dispute between neighbouring Toronto households over the smoke and fumes produced by a Chinese-Canadian family's wok-cooking quickly became, in the media anyway, a clash of ethnicities. At the same time, Canadians point proudly to their multicultural palates, evidenced in the popularity of Thai, Indian, and Portuguese (for instance) restaurants and food stores, not to mention the expanding 'ethnic' sections of grocery store chains. Donna Gabaccia's fascinating *We Are What We Eat* effectively demonstrates the manner in which American eating habits represent an amalgam of eclectic ethnicities. One might posit from this that food is the primary site for ethnic fusion and where multiculturalism has the potential to thrive.

When we apply gender analysis to the construct of eating and ethnicity, the roles and self-identity of immigrant women become an important focus for discussion.

Franca Iacovetta and Valerie Korinek, in their essay in this volume, demonstrate how 'ethnic' foods and eating habits became a site of contestation between post–Second World War immigrants and certain 'gatekeeping' institutions of Canadian culture. As much as it connotes ethnicity, food also signifies gender. That woman are customarily linked with food and cooking is evident in the sociological stereotyping of Mennonite women remarked upon earlier. Vivid images – generated both 'inside' and 'outside' of ethnic groups – frequently highlight and stereotype the Italian grandmother's skill with pasta and sausage, the Jewish mother's reputation as latke-maker, and the Ukrainian Baba's deftness with perogies.

In times of both famine and feast, the consumption of food and communication about food hold meaning particularly applicable to gender. Especially for mothers, whose most fundamental relationship with their children is that of providing physical sustenance, self-identity is intrinsically linked with their ability to fulfill that role. The preparation of food and its distribution within the household is historically an activity over which women have had an important measure of control; 'women's ability to prepare and serve food gives them direct influence over others, both material and magical.'[3] When that domain is threatened by food shortage or by the complete displacement of the household, women are accordingly disempowered by the loss of that domain.

Women have been the primary conveyors of ethnic culinary traditions, passing their knowledge through generations of daughters. As immigrants, women assume the responsibility of maintaining food customs often in a social environment that is inhospitable to such ethnic persistence, as Iacovetta and Korinek demonstrate. In the kitchen, they are 'strangers' more than 'sisters' to some other Canadian women. Indeed, women's roles in immigrant communities have often been evaluated in terms of their contribution to 'ethnic cohesion.' At the same time, however, the kitchen is quite often the setting in which particular traditions are transformed through the introduction of 'outside' cultures to the act of food preparation. For instance, while many historians have emphasized the isolationism of Mennonite settlements in southern Ukraine in the nineteenth century, it was largely through the influence of hired Ukrainian kitchen help that Mennonite women learned to include borscht, coarse dark bread, pickled cucumbers, and cabbage in their diet.[4] For this ethnoreligious group, women were the primary conduits of foodways that became the signature characteristics of their culture. The relationship between food and culture is singularly important for immigrant women for whom preparing, serving, and eating meals is often the site at which the old and new worlds meet.

Anthropologists and ethnographers have long proposed the centrality of food in understanding particular social groups and relationships within those groups. For instance, in the introduction to their reader on food and culture, anthropologists Carol Counihan and Penny Van Esterik underline the magnitude of food's influence: 'Food touches everything. Food is the foundation of every economy. It is a central pawn in political strategies of states and households. Food marks social differences, boundaries, bonds, and contradictions. Eating is an endlessly evolving enactment of gender, family, and community relationships.'[5] And while food is an immediate and material reality – needed for sustenance and pleasure – it also communicates meaning and represents signification. It is 'both itself and more than itself.'[6] The way in which food and eating functions symbolically in communication and experience is at the core of semiotics, the philosophical study of signs and symbols. Or as Hilde Bruch has noted, food is 'endowed with complex values and elaborate ideologies, religious beliefs, and prestige systems.'[7]

Historians have been less prominent in studies of food and eating amongst particular groups. But recent work by American feminist ethnic historians Gabaccia and Hasia Diner, as well as the presence of 'food' panels at historical conferences, suggests a growing interest in food and eating as historical subject. In the past confined mainly to the realm of material culture, the study of food has become multidimensional as it draws on theories of discourse and semiotics, for instance. The historical study of food is thus important in and of itself, as a central feature in a social group's daily existence. Yet it is also much more. Insofar as multiple levels of meaning can be derived from the usage of food and discourse about eating, much can be learned about, in this case, the social relationships, gender roles, and self-identity of women within immigrant communities.

Discourse about food, both concrete and metaphorical, is manifest especially in the memory sources and 'subjective documents'[8] of immigrants: diaries, written memoirs, autobiography, letters, oral interviews, for instance. Memory sources, especially those created after significant passage of time, may be considered overly subjective by the process of remembering, but this should not suggest that substantial objective information is absent as a result. As memory theorists James Fentress and Chris Wickham observe, memory is often 'selective, distorted and inaccurate,' yet 'it is not necessarily any of these; it can be extremely exact.'[9] A comparison of the memory sources of Mennonite immigrant women demonstrates a remarkable consistency in factual detail as well as commonality in impressions and reflections. Individual narratives offer much in the way of anecdotal and qualitative evidence arising from personal experience, while 'reading' such sources collectively illuminates patterns of meaning and myth.

Literary theorist Evelyn Hinz observes that the current tendency to call autobiography 'life-writing' 'locates such literature in the physiological facts of existence, of which eating is the central component.'[10] Food may be especially important in life-writing because it functions as a means of recall. For individuals going through traumatic events such as starvation, political repression, war and displacement, activities as basic as cooking and eating can bring relief, sometimes even humour, to personal narratives that otherwise seem to be an endless spiral of disaster. Emotions of fear, pain, sadness, and despair elicited by events in an immigrant woman's life do not disappear, but can be veiled behind detailed descriptions of 'what we ate that day.'

This paper will focus on Mennonite women refugees whose experience of eating ranges from famine to feast through the process of uprooting and immigration to Canada after the Second World War. Examining issues of food, gender, and ethnicity is particularly interesting in the context of the refugee sojourn in which individuals frequently experience dramatically shifting environments of famine and feast, and in which long-held food identities are challenged and modified to meet the exigencies of particular situations.

## Mennonites under Stalin

The Mennonites are an ethnoreligious group with origins in the sixteenth century Reformation in Germany, Switzerland, and the Netherlands who established autonomous settlements near the banks of the Dnieper River in Ukraine beginning in the late eighteenth century. Their distinctive religious beliefs included voluntary adult baptism into the church, pacifism and non-participation in military service, mutual aid as an expression of Christian love, and the exercise of discipline towards members within their communities as a way of maintaining a pure church. Many of their cultural forms have their origins in a Dutch ancestry, yet Mennonites in Russia were identified as ethnic German colonists within the Russian empire. A small minority in a large empire, Mennonites nevertheless carved out a thriving economic and cultural niche for themselves in imperial Russia. A 'golden age' of prosperity and a flourishing Russian Mennonite culture began its disintegration with the Bolshevik Revolution and the First World War. Mennonite communities were targeted with varying degrees of repressive measures because of their material wealth, their German culture, their Christian religious beliefs, and their resistance to communism. During the 1920s, civil war, famine, the emigration of 25,000 Mennonites to North and South America, followed by collectivization (transfer of private property to collective ownership) and de-kulakization (the arrest and exile of property owners and perceived subversives) had depleted the male leadership strength and deeply challenged the self-identity of the Mennonites. The decade of the 1930s, which witnessed famine in Ukraine, along with several waves of arrests, deportations, and executions, broke the spirit of Mennonite communities further. Families were wrenched apart, as fathers, brothers, and sons, in particular, disappeared in the purges of Stalin, which climaxed in 1937–8. By the time the German army occupied Ukraine during the Second World War (1941–3), the demography of Mennonite villages was decidedly that of women, children, and the elderly. Estimates suggest that 50 per cent and more of Mennonite families were without a male head of household.

When the German forces retreated westward from Ukraine in the fall of 1943, they took with them approximately 300,000 German colonists, of which about 35,000 were Mennonite. Of the roughly 23,000 Mennonites who made it to western Europe and escaped repatriation to the Soviet Union, 8,000 immigrated to Canada in the great postwar migration.[11] The latter migrant group was numerically imbalanced in terms of gender – a female-male ratio of slightly greater than two-to-one existed amongst adult immigrants in 1948 – and consisted of fragmented families, many of whom were female-headed. They were integrated into a Canadian Mennonite population that, while sharing a cultural-religious heritage and familial connections with the postwar refugees, could not identify with the two decades of deprivation and trauma that shaped the psyche and behaviour of the newcomers. And although their postmigration lives gradually settled into socioeconomic stability and prosperity, the self-identity of Mennonite refugee women and the manner in which they negotiated their lives in a new country continued to be shaped by their pre-migration life experiences. Indeed, for all Canadian refugee women, the homeland is much more than a starting point or background, but represents a crucial aspect of identity for individuals who have a sense of 'being simultaneously "home away from home" or "here and there."'[12]

**Deprivation: The Famine**

While culinary memories from Russia were of a simple but hearty diet, rich in fat, those who lived through famines in the early 1920s and 1930s and wartime shortages in Europe also knew severe deprivation firsthand. The contradictions between a cultural heritage that included a rich mixture of food traditions from the Netherlands, Prussia, and Ukraine and the lived experience of near-starvation became part of the historical self-identity of Mennonite immigrants to Canada. Just as the years of prosperity and self-sufficiency are often described with reference to bountiful tables, community feasts, and the daily tasks of growing, harvesting, and preserving foodstuffs, the years of hardship similarly are conveyed in a narrative that centres on the existential details of physical sustenance. The deep emotional pain of watching family members die of starvation and for women especially, the inability to feed one's children, remain a subtext beneath the concrete descriptions of scarcity.

The famine in Ukraine in the early 1920s followed an already tumultuous period after the First World War when Mennonite property-owners were plundered by anarchist terrorists and almost every family experienced rapes and murders; in some cases, entire families were massacred. Civil war between the Bolshevik army and Tsarist loyalists fought in southern Ukraine brought further turmoil and in its wake, left typhus and other diseases that claimed hundreds of lives. In an Anne Frank-like memoir, Anna Baerg wrote her diary on the backs of evaporated milk can labels included in relief packages sent to Russia by American Mennonites. In March 1922 Baerg, age twenty-five, wrote, 'I have heard that some people have even eaten their own children,' then went on to describe her own family's somewhat less desperate situation:

> Although we haven't actually starved, we are hardly ever full. Today at lunch, for example, there was buttermilk and water, thickly cooked wheat with a sauce made from milk, oil, and onions, and a small piece of bread. Bread, by the way, isn't made according to the old recipe anymore – half of it consists of clay. And last time we added old, brewed *Prips* grounds [roasted wheat used as a coffee substitute] to the dough. Not long ago we would have pushed the concoction away in disdain. Now we don't even ask how it tastes just as long as it's edible.[13]

Historian John B. Toews further describes the kind of foodstuffs that people resorted to: 'As the famine intensified late in 1921, anything edible was included in the menu – dried pumpkins or beets, chaff, dried weeds, ground-up corncobs, the remains of processed linseed, dogs, cats, gophers, and such carcasses as were available.'[14] It was the hardships of these years that prompted a mass exodus from Russia and saw some 25,000 Mennonites migrate to Canada and South America.

Those who were unable or unwilling to leave in the twenties faced more food hardship a decade later. In 1932–3 several million peasants, mostly Ukrainian, starved to death in a famine generally acknowledged as man-made when Stalin's government seized with force the 1932 crop and produce.[15] Although individuals did not have enough food to meet delivery quotas placed on them, many were accused of withholding foodstuffs from the collective and were subject to warnings and possible imprisonment. The fears of retribution for unmet production brought stress to families already on the brink of starvation.

Recollections of this time include stories of eating acacia flowers, tree bark, sawdust, cornstalks, thistles, and sweeping out granaries and silos to salvage whatever kernels of corn or grain might be left behind. Desperation even drove some people to pick kernels of grain from dried cow's manure and 'to eat the fetid carcasses of dogs, cats, and mice.'[16] Severe malnutrition was accompanied by diseases such as typhus, smallpox, pneumonia, diptheria, and malaria, all of which contributed to a high death rate and decreasing birth rate. Mennonite families may have experienced lesser losses than occurred in the Ukrainian population, mainly because of care packages and money sent by relatives in North America.

Reading letters sent abroad gives one a sense of how the lack of food and creative ways of devising edible foodstuffs preoccupied the thoughts and activities of women and their families.

In the letters of Susan Toews to her brother Gerhard in Canada in the early 1930s, her concerns revolve mainly around issues of survival, what they are eating, and their doubts for the future.[17] Mariechen Peters relates the food hardships in a 1931 letter to her sister in Canada: 'Very few remain in Gnadenheim (Molotschna) who have bread. They live on gruel, and there isn't enough of that. They don't have many potatoes. Sister Sara only had ½ pud [pound] corn flour left for the children. She and Peter were eating gruel.'[18] Similarly, Maria Bargen wrote to her children in Canada in 1932: 'It seems so hard to live through the experiences here. We have had no bread at all for 2 months. We have had no flour in the house and very little hope for any in the future. There are only 5 months until the harvest, and then perhaps we can get some potatoes.'[19] Many such letters were published in German-language Mennonite newspapers in Canada during the early 1930s, generating sympathy among North American Mennonites but also creating a disparity in historical experience that would shape familial relationships for decades to come.

During periods of deprivation, the Mennonite diet also evolved to include foods that, under normal conditions, would not have been part of their culinary traditions. One individual wrote that beets normally used to feed livestock were consumed as a delicacy.[20] Mushrooms were a common part of the Russian peasant diet, mainly as a substitute for meat and dairy on those days where religious observance prohibited such foods. Mennonites generally did not adopt this affinity, perhaps because they didn't have a similar practice of religious fasting, or because their preference for a hearty meat-and-potatoes diet made mushrooms seem insubstantial. But under conditions of exile in Siberia and also during the refugee flight, Mennonites too, it appears, gathered mushrooms for survival.[21] For instance, Tina Dyck Wiebe recalled that living in an orphanage in Siberia, dinner would always consist of a bowl of soup made from mushrooms and that she and her sister would gather mushrooms to eat because they were so hungry.[22] And recalling his boyhood years as a refugee, one man said that at a time when he should have been learning 'reading, writing and arithmetic,' he instead was learning how to 'beg for food and find edible berries, leaves and mushrooms in their natural setting.'[23] The necessity of eating foods not normally part of their diet contributed to a long-term cultural transformation that saw Mennonites absorb Ukrainian and Russian ethnic traditions.

Bread, a mainstay of the Russian Mennonite diet, became particularly scarce, and women devised ways of baking even a semblance of the fluffy white or heavy rye bread that was symbolic of better times. Sorghum, a grain hitherto disdained, was added liberally because its sticky consistency allowed a small amount of wheat flour to go a long way. The amount of bread available to each person also corresponded to increasing scarcity. Susan Toews, in a letter to her family in Canada in 1931, observed that as conditions worsened, the morsel of bread became smaller: 'The piece of bread does not become larger, but quite the opposite. If there is no more [bread], and many don't have any, what will happen?'[24]

Starvation affected everyone – men, women, and children – but its impact also had particular gendered meanings. On the one hand, Paul Fieldhouse, a specialist in food and nutrition states: 'It has long been recognized as a home-truth that when food is scarce women often do without, to the detriment of their health and strength, in order to ensure that their children receive adequate nourishment.'[25] And indeed, the memoirs of Mennonite immigrants abound with stories of mothers who sacrificially gave the last morsel of bread to their children. Yet other authors exploring the relationship between gender and famine have raised the question of women's greater resiliency to food deprivation. For instance, some analyses of the mid-nineteenth century Irish famine found that overall the mortality rates for adult women were lower than for adult men. Explanations for this have been partly physiological, that is, women's superior capacity to store body fat and their lesser caloric intake needs. Other sociological explanations have focused on women's functions as household managers, providers of 'affection and consolation,' and caregivers, roles that become more crucial and are therefore safeguarded during times of deprivation.[26]

There is no specific statistical evidence from sources regarding the starvation of Soviet Mennonites that would allow one to test such a theory about gender. Yet a letter from a Soviet Mennonite woman to her parents in Canada suggests that fathers may indeed have been more prone to death by starvation than mothers: Helene Janzen wrote, 'almost daily, a grave was sealed over the father of a family who had gone *home*. [Her husband said], Again and again the family father in the coffin, mostly a victim of hunger, with the mother bent over, her children around her.'[27] Another possible factor in women's greater resiliency may have to do with maternal desires for self-preservation, as many women cited the need to care for and protect their children as their main, sometimes only, reason to live. Conversely, the high mortality rates of men in the Soviet concentration camps, separated from their families and with little hope for reunion, may reflect in part an increased level of despair produced by the loss of loved ones.

The severe deprivation of the early 1930s lessened later in the decade and further during the German military occupation of Ukraine during the Second World War. However, a new form of food hardship, that of the refugee sojourn and general wartime scarcity, made food once again central in the narratives of Soviet Mennonites. The so-called great trek of Mennonites from the Soviet

Union, led by retreating German forces, began in September 1943. As the Soviet Army advanced from the east, Mennonite villagers had barely a day or two warning to vacate their homes. Not surprisingly, preparations centred on food. Animals were butchered and the meat packed in lard for preservation. Fruit was dried and bagged. And most importantly, zwieback (two-layered white buns) were roasted and dried in abundance.

Most families had begun the trek with an ample supply of food but as weeks lengthened into months of travel, supplies ran out and the refugees had to scavenge for meals. Mary Krueger, age ten at the time, remembered when her family's food supply was completely gone. One evening her mother gave each of the three children a spoonful of syrup with a little sugar on top, their last meal.[28] Children were sent ahead into villages to beg door-to-door or into farmers' fields to search for grain or root vegetables left after the harvest. Cows, brought along for their precious milk supply, were butchered.

Only sometimes along the trek did the refugees stop long enough to cook a meal, which might consist of some cooked potatoes, or a pot of soup, hastily prepared when a hole was dug in the ground, a fire lit, and some stones put in. Camp fires had to be doused when air raids threatened, sometimes before the meal was prepared. More often than not, the daily fare consisted of bread and water.

The escape westward changed from a trek to a flight in the latter months of the war as the Red Army advanced on the eastern edges of German-occupied territory. This time Mennonite refugees, along with millions of other displaced civilians, found themselves in even more desperate circumstances, trying to obtain limited places on trains, trucks, and wagons and, in the midst of hurried and chaotic travel, trying to find enough to eat. This time, flight occurred in the midst of a particularly hard winter and one woman recalled that her limited supply of bread froze so hard she was unable to cut it.[29] Katie Friesen describes her flight with her schoolmates and teachers. She was awakened at four in the morning of 19 January 1945 with orders to evacuate; the Russians were very close. 'Before leaving we took time to carry all the textbooks into the basement, just in case we would return. We wrote messages on the chalkboards, played one last song on the piano, bade farewell to our classrooms and then assembled in the schoolyard with tears streaming down our cheeks.' In the days that followed, the girls and their teachers travelled by wagon, bicycle, foot, and finally by train, barely stopping to eat or sleep. On more than one occasion they had to abandon a hastily cooked pot of unpeeled potatoes. During a three-day stretch by train, they were lucky to receive one piece of bread per day; to quench their thirst, they ate handfuls of snow when the train stopped long enough for them to disembark.[30]

Over 10,000 Mennonite refugees made it to the West where, once Allied relief supplies began to flow at war's end, they saw a beginning to the end of a long

Women gather each morning to prepare vegetables and peel potatoes for noonday camp meal, ca. 1947, Gronau, Germany.

period – for some a lifetime – of inadequate nourishment. Many others, caught in the Russian zone of occupied Germany and Poland, existed in what Eve Kolinsky has called a 'culture of physical survival' in which German nationals and displaced persons alike 'lived close to starvation levels.'[31] Military rations being far below what was needed for subsistence, two women in the Russian zone swept out the floor of a granary into a bag and brought it home, washed the grain, dried it, ground it, and made a kind of porridge soup from it.[32]

During the periods of 'famine' described above, access to food became foremost as an activity and as a value in the lives of women and their families. Agatha Schmidt, a young refugee widow who fled the Soviet Union with her mother and two sisters, said: 'When you are hungry you forever think about food, it is like an obsession.'[33] Abraham Maslow, in applying his famed hierarchy of human needs to food usage, said: 'For the man who is extremely and dangerously hungry, no other interests exists, but food. He dreams food, he remembers food, he thinks food; he emotes only about food, he perceives only food, and he only wants food.'[34] An interview project with Vietnamese-Chinese 'boat people' who settled in Montreal in the early 1980s offers supportive evidence: the foremost response to the question 'What happened during the flight?' related to the lack of drinking water and food. It rated higher, remarkably, than concerns about suicides, deaths, rapes, piracy, and so on.[35] Myrna Goldenberg has similarly observed the 'preoccupation with hunger and obtaining food' in the memoirs of Auschwitz survivors.[36] Food did indeed become an obsession and procuring it by whatever means was paramount.

Descriptions of food and eating during conditions of shortage also serve to illustrate the breakdown of regular social relations and behaviour within the Mennonite community. The lack of regular meals particularly on the trek and flight reinforced the sense of normalcy breaking down, of life turning to chaos. The regularity of eating is a fundamental rite that maintains the structure of daily life even when there is disruption in other aspects of a routine. During times of famine, the entire day could become a preoccupation with scrounging for and preparing something edible for one's family, while on the refugee flight there was sometimes little opportunity to eat at all. The hurried movement westward was almost constant and cooking fires frequently had to be doused when approaching Soviet tanks or aircraft could be heard. Insecurity about the future was heightened when even the patterned ritual of meal preparation and eating was destabilized.

Another important impact that food shortage had on social relations was to challenge ideas about family. Anne Murcott has written that the idea of the 'proper' meal has much to do with the idea of 'proper' family life.[37] So that the lack of adequate food and thus 'good' meals as part of daily routine during the 1930s and throughout the war years coincided with the breakdown of family life, and may in fact have reinforced the idea that social/moral life was disintegrating amongst Soviet Mennonites. The breakdown of eating routines and the shortage of food also had the effect of broadening the idea of family. With the losses of numerous individuals – mainly male – from Mennonite villages throughout the 1930s, the structure of families altered to meet the exigencies of the situation. Women, children, and the elderly were all that remained in most families and, as a result, living units composed of individuals with extended family or village relationships became common. Especially during the refugee flight, individuals rallied together to share limited resources – food, shelter, transportation – as well as the emotional support needed to confront fearful situations. Judith Tydor Baumel, in her study of the Holocaust, observes that the act of group food-sharing was one of the most powerful ways to create and reinforce communal bonds and mutual assistance.[38] For Mennonites, the sharing of meagre food portions solidified the bonds of village, family, and 'grab bag' households in a way that never happened when individual households and families had plenty of their own. Yet evidence also exists that hunger induced covetous behaviour and that a 'survival of the fittest' attitude sometimes prevailed.

The sharing of food extended beyond the Mennonite group, and this too, could have a significant affect on how 'outsiders' were viewed. Relations with Soviet Ukrainians, Germans, and later Canadians, were often shaped in the context of accessing food. Generosity or stinginess on the part of non-Mennonites in a situation of extreme need could have a significant effect on attitudes towards 'strangers' and 'others.' In her description of the benevolence that Ukrainian villagers showed towards her and her sister during the refugee trek, Susanna Toews writes of the 'kind' Russians who were 'good to us' – sharing their food and in one instance, offering such luxuries as apples. Because Susanna was malnourished, her sister scouted a Ukrainian village for eggs and 'in a few hours had collected 150 eggs. Not one woman refused her request. These Russians were very good to us.'[39] She contrasted this with some of the German military – ostensibly their liberators and protectors – who stole valuable foodstuffs from both the refugees and Ukrainian peasants along the way. The interaction also represented a socioeconomic reversal, since prior to the Revolution, Mennonite colonists had by and large been much wealthier than the indigenous population. The benevolence of Ukrainians towards their banished neighbours was humbling for Mennonites who had often looked down upon the former.

## Food as Sign and Symbol

Food deprivation had particular social affects, but in the context of immigrant narratives and memoirs, it had semiotic significance as well. When scarcity was particularly acute, certain foods became symbolic of survival and indeed life itself. Two of these, potatoes and zwieback, were mainstays of the Mennonite diet and became even more so when other foods were unavailable. Potatoes, along with other root vegetables, became an important part of the Mennonite diet in West Prussia in the 1800s and were grown in great abundance in south Russia. As Norma Jost Voth has observed, 'In the Mennonite home ... potato was king, always a staple part of the everyday diet as well as Sunday's traditional menu ... Sometimes potatoes were served twice a day.' By contrast, the Ukrainian custom of cooking or baking cereals as a porridge, was disdained as a poor substitute.[40]

Potatoes became symbolic of both survival and starvation. As a means to survival, potatoes were often the last remaining food in a diet of deprivation: the lowest common denominator, if you will. As Anne Penner Klassen recalled in the spring of 1940: 'It was becoming more and more difficult to get bread. After I had been standing in the bread lines for several days without getting any, I bought 110 pounds of potatoes for 54 rubles.'[41] Potatoes, it appears, were the last resort as the centrepiece of a meal, bread being much more preferable. She goes on to describe the struggle to meet nutritional needs, before her garden would produce vegetables: 'I bought another 80 pounds of potatoes for 34 rubles because that is what we lived on at this time. Although the vegetables in the garden were coming up nicely, it would be quite some time before we could use any of them. We supplemented out diet with sorrel which we picked in the wild, and occasionally we could buy skim milk or some very thin soup. Many people were suffering from hunger, and we didn't always know what we would eat for our next meal.'[42] Mennonites exiled to Siberia similarly recall that the only thing that allowed for physical survival was when the truck or train would occasionally stop by a potato field long enough for refugees to dig a few of the vegetables, build a fire, and cook them.[43] And when the war ended, one refugee woman in Germany recalled that potatoes again became the centre of her family's diet, when, given the scarcity of bread, local farmers gave them sacks full in exchange for help with the harvest.[44] Yet another woman recalled that her mother was careful about measuring out their supply of potatoes, but other families who were not as careful, came begging for potato peels.[45]

Yet, while the lowly potato kept people alive, it was also a fearful sign that starvation was not far away. Because even though potatoes were the preferred staple food of Russian Mennonites, when eaten alone and incessantly, they were a sign of poverty. This Mennonite perception was akin to that of some Jewish immigrant families in America, for whom potatoes were the staple of poverty.[46]

If the potato became a symbol of survival against starvation, then roasted zwieback was first of all a sign of migration and preparedness against hunger. Zwieback (literally two-buns, a smaller one stacked atop a larger one) was not unique to Mennonite fare, but was a central feature on their tables already in the Netherlands and Prussia. It also became the main staple of the immigrant and refugee family's diet while en route. In preparation for departure, first in the nineteenth century, and then in the 1920s, and 1940s, Mennonite women baked thousands of zwieback and roasted them for the journey. When roasted properly, thoroughly dried out, and cooled, they can last for up to several months without turning rancid. Such is the typical description of one man who recalled his family's journey to Canada in 1923: 'Mother roasted buns in the oven in order to dry them out so they would not go mouldy on the trip. When they were roasted, they kept for months. Many a little youngster was raised as a baby with a portion of dry bun soaked in coffee, sprinkled with sugar, wrapped in cloth as a soother.'[47]

Zwieback are prominent in stories in which predominant emotions are loss and sadness: leaving homes, saying good-bye to loved ones sent into exile, and preparing packages for those in prison. But zwieback was also about looking to the future. To the extent that rituals 'permit the expression of sentiments which can not always be put into words and can thus act as a unifying social force,' the roasting and packing in sacks of zwieback became a ritual of hope and movement forward.[48] Or as Norma Jost Voth remarks, 'Baskets filled with toasted buns have been a blessing on long treks and journeys, partially sustaining the wanderers in their search for new homes.'[49]

The life-giving potential of this modest breadstuff is epitomized in Tina Dyck Wiebe's description of her mother's death in exile in Siberia. The family was severely malnourished and suffering from scurvy when a package of food arrived from relatives:

At last the sleigh came with a package. How much joy! But Mother was hardly able to smile as Father opened it. He soaked a roasted *Zwieback*, and tried to feed her. But she only looked at it with big eyes as she sank down in her pillow. She whispered with her lips: 'I don't need it anymore.' It was barely audible. 'No, No! You cannot die!' Father cried out in despair. 'Don't leave me alone with the children!' But Mother never opened her eyes again.[50]

Because of its biblical significance – manna in the desert, 'give us this day our daily bread,' the 'staff of life' – bread carries symbolic connotations of being life-giving. The central Christian symbol of the Eucharist – for Mennonites the communion meal – whereby Christ's body (his life) is received in the eating of the bread, reinforces this connection between bread and life. Thus, when those in need of food receive bread, it is more than just something to satisfy hungry stomachs or meet nutritional requirements. It carries the hope that there may in fact be survival and hope. In Northern and Western societies, it is the basic means of subsistence.

Thus, numerous anecdotes or references to bread occur in stories that are about more than just giving bread, but about giving life. Anny Penner Klassen Goerzen relates the story of how one day in 1939, her mother, brother and sister-in-law were arrested by the Soviet secret police. As the prisoners were loaded up, soldiers guarded the house and prevented the remaining family members from going outside. 'Since they had no bread in the house, and Margareta [Anny's sister] was the one who always bought it, she climbed out of the bedroom window and ran to the store to buy bread. When she got back, the "prisoners" were already on the truck, so she quickly ran and threw the bread to them. Margareta was ten at the time.'[51] Not only was this a story of a girl's extreme bravery, but the bread was symbolic of the family ties that were so important and were a gift of what was most fundamental to survival.

**Abundance: The Feast**

For those Mennonite refugees who made it to the western zones of the postwar occupation, and for those who later immigrated to Canada, the previous two decades of deprivation were replaced by a time of abundance: the feast. In personal narratives, a border crossing to the West, the arrival at a refugee camp, or the trip to Canada are frequently marked with reference to the foods encountered, most of which offered a stark contrast to the immediate past. In her memoir of the flight from the Soviet Union, Susanna Toews makes frequent references to the food they received and ate at various points of the journey. When they finally crossed the border into Holland, she says, 'we were served such food as we hadn't seen for a long time – milk, cheese, sausage, white bread and butter.'[52] Katie Siemens too cited white bread and butter as her first memory of Holland. Siemens, with her mother and sister had spent a year in Poland, then a year in Germany, and then in order to escape repatriation, had heard about the possibility of crossing the border to Holland where they would be safe.[53] White bread, a symbol of prestige and plenty,[54] marked a departure from hardship, when any morsel of dark, rough bread was devoured eagerly.

The preparation of some traditional Russian Mennonite foods in Mennonite agency-run refugee camps was a welcome treat after the deprivation of the trek and earlier; it also provided a symbol of ethnic identity for people who were in doubt about their national and religious affiliations. Along with Low German, it was a badge of Mennonitism. Justine Thiessen Warkentin recalled her arrival at the Mennonite Central Committee refugee camp in Berlin: 'There on the table was a green bean soup and a plate full of bread. We could eat as much as we wanted. We could not imagine that something like this existed.'[55] At Christmas at the Berlin camp, peppernuts – a small spice cookie – were baked during the night, much to the delight of Mennonite children awakening the next morning.[56] Elizabeth Klassen, recalling time spent at a Mennonite Central Committee refugee centre in the Netherlands, remembered that 'on festive occasions our cooks arranged for the use of the baker's ovens [in a nearby village]. They would come back with piles and piles of *Zwieback* to everyone's delight.'[57]

If potatoes were symbolic during times of shortage, of scarcity and survival, then after the war they were eaten in abundance. In the west zone of occupied Germany, Agnes Dyck and her family lived on an estate. Earlier residents had planted potatoes and when the Dycks arrived they were given forty sacks of potatoes. They had enough to feed the rabbits, pigs, and themselves. 'From potatoes you can make lots of things. We had some milk everyday. We cooked some milk soup with grated potatoes in there which tasted great. We had cooked potatoes, and fried potatoes and soup and what not all.'[58] In her mind, potatoes were abundance, even though they were so exactly because, in the immediate aftermath of war, many other food items were expensive or unavailable. One family, unable to subsist on the portions of bread and potatoes allowed by their refugee ration cards, went to a 'rich farmer' who sold them a 'hundred weight [50 kg] of potatoes for five marks.' They were 'so happy, for we could now eat until we had had enough.' This same family earlier bemoaned the fact that potatoes were all that they received even though the German woman that took them in had 'three hams and two sides of bacon in the pantry and many cans of meat and fruit in her basement.'[59]

As zwieback and potatoes could be signs of scarcity, sugar was symbolic of prosperity and abundance. Sugar, which was dear and often scarce, offered caloric energy but its sweetness was also a metaphor for better times. Susan Toews wrote the following to her brother in Canada in the fall of 1929: 'One is happy for a dreamless night, for life has become very bitter. Some time ago we got some syrup from the store in order to sweeten our lives a little. We can only imagine sugar. Enough of all this bitterness ...'[60]

The possibility of consuming sugar, physically and also metaphorically, was realized for many refugees upon immigrating to Canada. Indeed, the sweetness of oranges eaten on the overseas journey is highlighted in many narratives, though rough seas often meant that food could hardly be kept down at all. Edna Schroeder Thiessen described the Jell-O and fruit desserts she received on her transatlantic journey in 1949, saying, 'It was like being at a wedding every day!'[61] And Agnes Pauls recalled that when her sickly young son was asked by a medical officer in a refugee camp, 'And what do you want in Canada?' the boy replied, 'I want to eat myself full of chocolate.'[62] If refugee camps in Europe offered a rescue from starvation, then Canada, at least ideas about it, represented the epitome of abundance. In this, Mennonite notions bore little difference from those of other immigrants. In her study of Lithuanian DPs, Milda Danys quotes a woman who received letters in Europe from a friend who had migrated earlier. The girl had offered the amazing information that in Canada they poured the cooking fat outside on the ground: 'We couldn't understand why people didn't gather at those puddles of fat – we didn't have enough to fry a pancake.'[63]

Again, white bread spread thickly with butter, tall glasses of milk, and sausage are often mentioned as precious memories of arrival in Canada. One sixteen-year-old girl was enthralled with the plentiful food available during the train trip from Halifax to Alberta: 'We had never tasted such white soft bread or drank such cold rich milk before,' she said.[64] The consumption of foods traditional to their diets, but that hadn't been available for a long time, provided new immigrants a comforting connection with a past culture and offered an important sense of belonging to the newcomers. The absorption of postwar refugees into Canadian Mennonite communities, even while beset with clashes based on disparate experience, also presented the opportunity of reproducing, in a new national setting, the 'golden year' of Russian Mennonite culinary culture. As Paul Fieldhouse has observed: 'Immigrants use familiar foods as a means of feeling secure and not losing their identity in a foreign land.'[65] Young women, however, who had grown up during the years of deprivation, felt inadequate when their abilities to 'cook Mennonite' were found wanting.[66] At the same time, unfamiliar foods were a reminder to newcomers of their immigrant identity and were symbolic of the strangeness of Canada, alongside its abundance. When Anny Penner Klassen and her family arrived in Winnipeg in 1948, they were met by groups of Mennonites who gave them bags of fruit that included oranges and bananas. 'We were not familiar with bananas and oranges, so we did not take a fancy to them immediately. However, we soon learned to enjoy and appreciate these fruits.'[67] Particularly for children and teenagers, new and unfamiliar foods offered a sense of wonderment. Mary Krueger says, 'I remember seeing ice cream in a store and wanting it but I didn't know what it was called.'[68]

Food acculturation occurred especially in the context of the workplace. A primary source of income for many immigrant Mennonite families of the 1920s and also for postwar refugees, were the wages earned by women working in domestic service in cities like Winnipeg, Saskatoon, and Vancouver. These women became the conveyors of urban manners and foods from other ethnic traditions, such as 'kosher,' English, Scottish, and Icelandic. They in turn introduced 'Mennonite' foods to their employers, so that cooking and eating became a form of cultural exchange.[69] The abundance of new foods also presented particular challenges for cooks who had known only scarcity. Stefania Niesiobędzka, a Polish woman employed as a cook's helper in Hamilton after the Second World War, was terrified by the amount of learning she had to do in her new job, given that 'during the war, there was seldom more to cook than a few potatoes.'[70] As well, class differences meant that in some isolated cases, maltreatment of domestic servants included an inadequate diet. For instance, some girls received only vegetables while their employers ate meat; one young woman sneaked dry cereal between meals to supplement her inadequate diet, but didn't dare take any bread or milk, fearing her employer's retribution.[71] Thus, Mennonite girls whose families had survived famine in Russia, experienced want even in a land of plenty.

As most Mennonite refugees settled into postwar lives of economic stability and prosperity, memories of their pre-migration years of hardship and scarcity persisted but provoked varying responses. One response is a fixation on good eating and lots of it. Paul Fieldhouse notes that excessive food consumption is sometimes a response to insecurity over food supply based on experience of scarcity: 'Parents who have lived through hard times, when food was scarce or rationed, are determined that their offspring will not be similarly deprived, and so overfeed and force food on them.'[72] He further says that hoarding behaviour often reflects anxiety about security of the future food supply, especially if that individual or group has experienced shortage or famine. Evidence for this comes particularly from the post–Second World War Mennonite refugee family into which I married some fifteen years ago. I was struck immediately and continually since my first introduction to their dinner table, by the excessive nature of some of their meals – custard-based tortes for breakfast, for instance – and by the perpetual talk about meals both past and future, which seemed to eclipse all other topics. Although materially prosperous in many other ways, they seem to measure wealth by the amount of food available, and behave not unlike the Bemba people of Zambia about whom it is said: 'The village echoes all day with shouts from hut to hut about what is to be eaten at the next meal, what was eaten at the previous meal, and what is in prospect for the future.'[73]

Another, sometimes co-existent, response to abundance was an attitude that viewed food as never to be taken for granted, since hunger might be just around the corner once again. Fifty years after migrating to Canada, Agnes Pauls says she still marvels at 'the rows of rich fruit, the abundance of food, and my ability to buy as much as I want' at the grocery store.[74] One Mennonite woman employed as a domestic after immigrating to Canada remarked that her upbringing of deprivation had taught her never to leave any food over or wasted, so that if she baked a cake and it didn't turn out, she would eat the whole thing and then bake another; she was caught between her desire to please her employers and her belief in frugality.[75] The outlook in many Mennonite immigrant households was like that of the Palestinian refugee described by psychologist Mary Roberson; one of the principal ways in which the woman continued to be influenced by her refugee experience was in her appreciation of food: 'She cannot bear to throw food away.'[76]

## Food and Religiosity

Aside from functioning materially and figuratively as an focal point during feast and famine, food served to both heighten faith amongst the Mennonites and also acted as a substitute for customary religious observances. For a people whose notions of religious piety included a denial of the flesh, an obsession with physicality that persistent hunger produced could have been problematic. At the same time, for a religious people stripped of all the rituals and institutions traditionally associated with the expression of their faith, food may in fact have begun to serve in a sacramental sense. Following the Communist Revolution, religious institutions and practice were increasingly restrained and repressed. During successive waves of arrest and exile in the 1920s and 1930s, ministers were among the first to be seized from Mennonite communities; and by 1935 all Mennonite churches in the Soviet Union were closed. When families could no longer worship together, sharing a mealtime prayer and breaking bread may have served symbolically to affirm their belief that their lives were in the hands of a protecting higher power. That they continued to have a minimum to eat helped to confirm the existence of God as 'bread of life' even in the midst of the worst despair. Preferences for particular foods or forms of preparation also acted as a badge of ethnic identity, along with their Low German dialect, that offered a sense of group belonging, in the absence of historic religious rituals.

Where food figures most prominently in a religious sense is in stories of providential rescue when all sources of hope seem lost. Such anecdotes occur especially in narratives of the Ukrainian famine and during the refugee flight out of the Soviet Union. For instance, Agatha Schmidt remembers an incident from the time of severe famine in 1932–3:

> That our family ever lived through this time is truly a miracle. One time I remember mother baked a 'korshik' [flatbread] which she divided into four equal parts. After we had each eaten our portion she said: 'Children, that was the last flour. We have no food left for tomorrow.' Then she took us into the living room where we all knelt down while she prayed with us. That evening a knock came at the door. Then the figure of a woman thoroughly shrouded to conceal her identity, came in, set a freshly-baked loaf on the table and disappeared into the darkness once more. We had no opportunity even to thank her, and to this day we have never discovered the identity of our benefactor who took risks to help us.[77]

In a similar account, Peter Epp describes the experience of his wife, who, alone with five children and expecting the sixth, fled Poland ahead of the Soviets in the winter of 1945. In her haste to leave, she had left behind her bag of provisions and had only one loaf of bread with her. He continues, 'But God was always there!

When her hope had all but vanished, my wife found a kettle with warm boiled potatoes on an abandoned farm.'[78] Agatha Schmidt also tells the story of her cousin, a young man who hid in a haystack for over a week to escape deportation to Siberia as the German Army advanced into Ukraine in 1941. In this account, a hen came into the stack and laid an egg each day as 'an answer to prayer and a life-saver for the fugitive.'[79]

Given its metaphoric meaning as life-giving and a source of salvation, bread is the foodstuff cited most often in stories of unexpected fortune. Walter Loewen, who was a child at the time, describes an incident on the trek:

> In time we arrived at a town with a sugar manufacturing plant. Mother walked up to the German manager and asked for some food. He insulted her, calling her a beggar woman and chased her away. Mother cried. Then we met a Russian lady who gave us a bread. This was not an ordinary bread, but a shiny, artfully braided and decorated bread, a work of art! It was obviously produced with much love and respect! With thankful hearts we admired the bread before we ate it, for this woman had given us more than just a bread! May God bless her for it.[80]

Images of food also offer a means for individuals to focus their memories of loss. All of the postwar Mennonite refugees had stories of family members – usually husbands and fathers – who had been arrested and disappeared. Most families received no confirmations of death in these cases but were left with only particular anecdotes as symbols to reify loved ones who were dead and yet not dead. Anny Penner Klassen Goerzen related the following story that was forever linked to the departure of her husband. On the day her husband Johann was taken in 1938 she had cooked his favourite *Wareneki* (a Mennonite version of perogies) with cottage cheese inside; later the two had visited the garden and seen the first cucumber that was growing but she had told him to let it grow longer before picking it. That night the GPU (Soviet secret police) arrived and arrested her husband. 'That day I couldn't eat the leftover *Wareneki*. I could not get myself to eat that first cucumber either, for it drove me to tears. After that, whenever I made *Wareneki*, I always thought of that last evening. And every year when the first cucumber was ready for picking I was reminded of that evening, and I couldn't hold back my tears.'[81] In this case, food items – the *Wareneki* and the cucumber – gave Anny concrete memories of her husband, whom she had married only three years before his arrest and about whom her recollections may well have been rather dim. Focus on the prosaic and everyday – food – offered a point of reference for narrating significant, but extremely painful, life events.

Procuring food in times of deprivation also became a moral and ethical question for Mennonites, whose religious framework included an entrenched sense of right and wrong, and strong feelings of guilt over actions perceived as sinful.

Many families recounted stories of stealing produce from farmers' fields during the refugee trek, actions that were taken for sheer survival but that nevertheless prompted reflection over behaviour otherwise considered sinful or immoral. One woman who spent her childhood years as a refugee recalled taking potatoes and carrots from farmers' fields: 'We talked about stealing one time too. Over there we sometimes took things that didn't belong to us because we were hungry. We were starving. We decided that's something that God will forgive.'[82] That Mennonites in Canada already believed the postwar immigrants to be in need of 'religious rehabilitation,' only heightened the sense among refugees that they were morally accountable for deeds they committed in an effort to procure food.

The linkage between food and ethical questions may have been heightened for those who had experienced the extreme suspicion levelled against workers on the Soviet collective farms during the early 1930s. During this era, women and men could often be accused of withholding foodstuffs (they had very little to eat themselves) and be arrested and their children orphaned. The dilemmas presented were exacerbated when officials offered to overlook the 'stolen goods' in a woman's possession in exchange for sexual favours.[83] The exchange of food for sex became more common for Mennonite women refugees living in the Soviet zone of occupation after war ended. One woman who was assigned to do housework for Soviet officers, said she initially submitted to the sexual propositions of one officer in order to gain protection from molestation by others: 'It was better ... if you had a friend, then the others would leave you alone.' As food became increasingly scarce, however, her motivation for submitting to his sexual demands became the desperate need to feed her three young children. In later years she categorized her actions as sinful – especially when confronted by a Canadian Mennonite minister – yet felt justified in her choices because of her maternal responsibility.[84]

## Food and Motherhood

The need to provide nourishment for their children in a context when resources were at their most scarce drew mothers, perhaps more than anyone else, into grey ethical areas. One man illustrated this by telling the story of his mother's deceit towards Communist officials who came to search their house for flour or grain in 1933. His father stated that they had nothing but a small container of sorghum and since he had a reputation for being truthful, the officials believed him. When the family managed to survive the winter, the mother quizzed the father as to why he had never asked how she could cook sorghum the way she did. She then admitted that she had hidden 30 kilograms of flour and each day she had mixed in a little with the sorghum to make it stick together. To explain her deception to the authorities while her husband told the truth, she said, 'I had to save my children ... my truth is my children.'[85] In another case, a widowed mother of three hid a small piece of meat in a bucket of dirty floor-washing water and smuggled it out of the home where she did housework after the war.[86] In such cases, the moral imperative to keep children alive surpassed a dogmatic separation between truthfulness and dishonesty.

A mother's inability to provide nutritional sustenance for her children was publicly displayed when children resorted to begging for food. And despite their family's hunger, women sometimes disallowed this course of action. Agatha Schmidt recalls going begging with an aunt and, though she anticipated her mother's disapproval, she returned home with a bag of beans, some flour, a few eggs and butter. Her mother would not accept the food: 'We had not yet sunk so low as to resort to begging, she said.'[87]

The inability to counter hunger in their households had a direct impact on the self-identity of mothers and others, sometimes elder sisters or grandmothers, who became effective heads of their families: 'When they cannot feed their families, heads of households can no longer fulfill their traditional responsibilities; their self-respect and the esteem of others may be rapidly eroded.'[88] Peter P. Janzen relates the following incident from his childhood of hardship in the Soviet Union: 'I remember very well one occasion when we hadn't had bread for a number of weeks. Mother traded something for one slice of bread. She divided the slice into two pieces, one for my sister and one for me. "Mother, my sister's piece is a little bigger than mine," I complained. Mother cried out, "Children, I wish I could give you enough to eat!" I was so embarrassed. She had no bread for herself and had little else than potatoes and salt in the house.'[89] When women could no longer provide adequate nourishment, their primary role as caregiver was undermined and an important sense of gender identity called into question.

## Conclusion

Many immigrants to Canada cannot be considered 'voluntary' migrants, having fled their homes reluctantly and under the duress of war, political oppression, or natural disaster. The stereotypical nineteenth-century immigrant who sought adventure and new social and economic opportunities in Canada is not reflective of the many refugees fleeing intolerable circumstances especially during the latter decades of the twentieth century, as papers in this volume by Gertrude Mianda and Paula Draper demonstrate. This paper has described one such refugee movement, atypical also because of its numerical gender imbalance of women over men. One way of understanding the trauma experienced by refugee migrants is through material symbols that are both realistic descriptors of experience but also semiotic indicators of that experience. In this study, food functions in multiple ways to organize the immigration narratives of Mennonite refugee women.

Mennonite refugee women arriving in Canada after the Second World War came with a history of food deprivation that would shape their attitudes towards food and eating even after they had feasted for decades in the land of plenty. If eating is used as a metaphor to define their pre- and postmigration lives, their life experience could easily be divided into images of famine and feast. Deprivation symbolically encompassed all the hardship, loss, and trauma that Mennonite women and their families had experienced throughout the 1930s and during the war, while abundance signified arrival, settlement, and acculturation. Because the preparation and distribution of food is traditionally such a gendered function, the activity of cooking and eating during times of both feast and famine present challenges and opportunities of especial significance to women. Furthermore, the extremes of food availability also reinforced, modified, or completely contested commonly held notions about ethnicity. At a concrete level then, food – or the lack thereof – is a central motif in the immigrant accounts of Mennonite refugee women. But at another level, images and recollections of food and eating also serve to organize memories and create narrative devices that offer individuals a familiar way in which to describe the unfamiliar and insecure terrain of uprooting and settlement.

NOTES

1 John A. Hostetler, *Mennonite Life* (Scottdale, PA: Herald Press, 1954), 15–16. See also my column on Hostetler's booklets: 'Research Findings from Mennonite History: Shrinking Waistlines and Changing Perceptions,' *Mennonite Reporter* 18 (6 June 1988) 7.

2 Peter Farb and George Armelagos, *Consuming Passions: The Anthropology of Eating* (Boston: Houghton Mifflin, 1980), 6.

3 Carole Counihan and Penny Van Esterik, 'Introduction,' in *Food and Culture: A Reader* (New York: Routledge, 1997), 3.

4 Norma Jost Voth, *Mennonite Foods and Folkways from South Russia*, vol. 1 (Intercourse, PA: Good Books, 1990), 26.

5 Counihan and Van Esterik, *Food and Culture*, 1.

6 Phyllis Passariello, 'Anomalies, Analogies, and Sacred Profanities: Mary Douglas on Food and Culture, 1957–1989,' *Food and Foodways* 4, no. 1 (1990): 53.

7 Quoted in Marta Dvorak, 'The Ethno-Semiotics of Food: A.M. Klein's *Second Scroll* as Recipe for Multiculturalism,' *Mosaic* 29, no. 3 (September 1996): 16.

8 The descriptor 'subjective documents' is used by Virginian Yans-McLaughlin for personal data such as 'autobiographies, life histories, letters, oral narratives, interviews, and court records.' See 'Metaphors of Self in History: Subjectivity, Oral Narrative, and Immigration Studies,' in Virginian Yans-McLaughlin, ed., *Immigration Reconsidered: History, Sociology, and Politics* (New York: Oxford University Press, 1990), 254.

9  James Fentress and Chris Wickham, *Social Memory* (Cambridge, MA: Blackwell, 1992), 2.

10  Evelyn J. Hinz, 'Introduction,' *Mosaic* 24, nos. 3–4 (Summer-Fall 1991): vii.

11  For an analysis of this migrant group of Mennonites see my book, *Women without Men: Mennonite Refugees of the Second World War* (Toronto: University of Toronto Press, 2000).

12  Steven Vertovec and Robin Cohen, 'Introduction,' in Vertovec and Cohen, eds, *Migration, Diasporas and Transnationalism* (Cheltenham, UK: E. Elgar, 1999), xviii.

13  1 March 1922. *Diary of Anna Baerg, 1916–1924*, trans. and ed. Gerald Peters (Winnipeg: CMBC Publications, 1985), 89. *Prips* is a coffee substitute made from roasted grain.

14  John B. Toews, *Czars, Soviets and Mennonites* (Newton, KS: Faithland Life Press, 1982), 112.

15  See James E. Mace, 'Soviet Man-Made Famine in Ukraine,' in Samuel Totten et al., eds, *Century of Genocide: Eyewitness Accounts and Critical Views* (New York: Garland Publishing, 1997): 78–90. He suggests that 5 to 7 million people in Ukraine were victims of the famine.

16  For a brief description of some of the foods eaten, see for instance Colin P. Neufeldt, 'Through the Fires of Hell: The Dekulakization and Collectivization of the Soviet Mennonite Community, 1928–1933,' *Journal of Mennonite Studies* 16 (1998): 28–9.

17  John B. Toews, trans. and ed., *Letters from Susan: A Woman's View of the Russian Mennonite Experience, 1928–1941* (Newton, KS: Bethel College, 1988).

18  Mariechen Peters, 'Dearly Beloved,' in Sarah Dyck, trans. and ed., *The Silence Echoes: Memoirs of Trauma and Tears* (Kitchener, ON: Pandora Press, 1997), 59.

19  Maria Martens Bargen to her children, 2 February 1932. In Peter F. Bargen, ed. and Anne Bargen, trans., *From Russia with Tears: Letters from Home and Exile, 1930–1938* (Calgary: By the authors, 1991), 352.

20  Neufeldt, 'Through the Fires of Hell,' 28.

21  Voth, *Mennonite Foods and Folkways*, 29.

22  Tina Dyck Wiebe, 'Memories Written by My Life,' in *The Silence Echoes*, 83–4.

23  Erwin Strempler, 'Uprooted, But Not Without Opportunity to Go On,' *Der Bote*, no. 38 (13 October 1993): 22–3.

24  Toews, *Letters from Susan*, 96.

25  Paul Fieldhouse, *Food and Nutrition: Customs and Culture*, 2d (London: Chapman and Hall, 1995), 116.

26  Some of these arguments are summarized in Margaret Kelleher, 'Woman As Famine Victim: The Figure of Woman in Irish Famine Narratives,' in Ronit Lentin, ed., *Gender and Catastrophe* (London: Zed Books, 1997), 241–54.

27  Helene Janzen, 'Dear Uncle and Aunt,' in *The Silence Echoes*, 225.

28  Mary Krueger, 'An Unforgettable Childhood Experience,' *EMMC Recorder* 26, no. 2 (February 1989): 7.

29  Elisabeth Wiens, *Schicksalsjahr 1945: Erlebnisse nach Tagebuchnotizen* (Niagara-on-the-Lake: By the author, 1993).

30  Katie Friesen, *Into the Unknown* (Steinbach, MB: By the author, 1986), chapter 5.

31  Eve Kolinsky, *Women in Contemporary Germany: Life, Work and Politics*, rev. ed. (Providence, RI: Berg, 1993), 26–8.

32  Interview #28. During the years 1992 to 1994 I conducted taped interviews with Mennonites who immigrated to Canada and Paraguay after the Second World War. To respect the requested anonymity of individuals who shared their stories with me, I use first name pseudonyms and refer to interviews by number.

33  Agatha Loewen Schmidt, *Gnadenfeld, Molotschna, 1835–1943* (Kitchener, ON: By the author, 1989), 81.

34  Quoted in Fieldhouse, *Food and Nutrition*, 21.

35  Lawrence Lam, *From Being Uprooted to Surviving: Resettlement of Vietnamese-Chinese 'Boat People' in Montreal, 1980–1990* (Toronto: York Lanes Press, 1996), 86.

36  Ibid., 335.

37  Anne Murcott, *The Sociology of Food and Eating: Essays on the Sociological Sifnificance of Food* (Aldershot, UK: Gower, 1984), 102.

38  Judith Tydor Baumel, *Double Jeopardy: Gender and the Holocaust* (London: Vallentine Mitchell, 1998), 79.

39  Susanna Toews, *Trek to Freedom: The Escape of Two Sisters from South Russia during World War II*, trans. Helen Megli (Winkler, MB: Heritage Valley Publications, 1976), 30–1.

40  Voth, *Mennonite Foods and Folkways*, 29.

41  Anny Penner Klassen Goerzen, *Anny: Sheltered in the Arms of God – A True Story of Survival in Russia* (Fort St James, BC: By the author, 1988), 187.

42  Ibid., 188.

43  Schmidt, *Gnadenfeld*, 72.

44  Goerzen, *Anny*, 209.

45  Interview no. 28.

46  Donna R. Gabaccia, *We Are What We Eat: Ethnic Food and the Making of Americans* (Cambridge, MA: Harvard University Press, 1998), 46–7.

47  Myrtle V. Ebert, *Wir Sind Frei! We Are Free! A Mennonite Experience: From the Ukraine to Canada* (Scarborough, ON: Lochleven Publishers, 1995), 29.

48  Fieldhouse, *Food and Nutrition*, 100.

49  Voth, *Mennonite Foods and Folkways*, 55.

50  Tina Wiebe, nee Dyck, 'Memories Written by My Life,' in *The Silence Echoes*, 82–3.

51  Goerzen, *Anny*, 166.

52  Susanna Toews, *Trek to Freedom*, 40.

53 Interview no. 8.

54 Farb and Armelagos, *Consuming Passions*, 110.

55 Harry Loewen, ed., *Road to Freedom: Mennonites Escape the Land of Suffering* (Kitchener, ON: Pandora Press, 2000), 147.

56 Voth, *Mennonite Foods and Folkways*, 33.

57 Elizabeth Klassen, 'My Experiences and My Flight from Russia' (unpublished manuscript, 1946), iii.

58 Interview no. 13.

59 Klassen, My Experiences and My Flight from Russia,' 23–4.

60 John B. Toews, ed. and trans., *Letters from Susan: A Woman's View of the Russian Mennonite Experience (1928–1941)* (Newton, KS: Bethel College, 1988), 62–3.

61 Edna Schroeder Thiessen and Angela Showalter, *A Life Displaced: A Mennonite Woman's Flight from War-Torn Poland* (Kitchener, ON: Pandora Press, 2000), 153.

62 Loewen, *Road to Freedom*, 72.

63 Antanas Kenstavicius, quoted in Milda Danys, *DP: Lithuanian Immigration to Canada after the Second World War* (Toronto: Multicultural History Society of Ontario, 1986), 135.

64 Debbie Kirkpatrick, 'The Story of Mrs. Suse Rempel and Her Family,' research paper, Mennonite Heritage Centre, Winnipeg, 1979, 44.

65 Fieldhouse, *Food and Nutrition*, 192.

66 See Pamela E. Klassen, *Going by the Moon and the Stars: Stories of Two Russian Mennonite Women* (Waterloo, ON: Wilfrid Laurier University Press, 1994), 91.

67 Goerzen, *Anny*, 217.

68 Mary Krueger, 'An Unforgettable Childhood Experience, Part II,' *EMMC Recorder*, 4.

69 See, for instance, Frieda Esau Klippenstein, '"Doing What We Could": Mennonite Domestic Servants in Winnipeg, 1920s to 1950s,' *Journal of Mennonite Studies* 7 (1989): 145–66; Marlene Epp, 'The Mennonite Girls' Homes of Winnipeg: A Home Away from Home,' *Journal of Mennonite Studies* 6 (1988): 100–14.

70 Stefania Niesiobędzka, 'A Polish Displaced Person's Memories,' *Polyphony* 8, nos. 1–2 (1986): 96.

71 Epp, 'Mennonite Girls' Homes,' 110.

72 Fieldhouse, *Food and Nutrition*, 22, 192.

73 Farb and Armelagos, *Consuming Passions*, 7.

74 Loewen, *Road to Freedom*, 74.

75 Epp, 'Mennonite Girls' Homes,' 109.

76 Mary K. Roberson, 'Birth, Transformation, and Death of Refugee Identity: Women and Girls of the Intifada,' in Ellen Cole, Oliva Espin, and Esther Rothblum, eds, *Refugee Women and Their Mental Health: Shattered Societies, Shattered Lives* (New York: Haworth Press, 1992), 40.

77 Schmidt, *Gnadenfeld*, 47.

78  Peter Epp, 'Memories of Difficult Years,' *Der Bote* no. 38 (13 October 1993): 24–5.

79  Schmidt, *Gnadenfeld*, 31.

80  Ibid., 75.

81  Goerzen, *Anny*, 153.

82  Interview no. 28.

83  See, for instance, the story: 'Vanya, the Terrible,' in *The Silence Echoes*, 101–2.

84  Interview no. 28.

85  Interview no. 20.

86  Interview no. 28.

87  Schmidt, *Gnadenfeld*, 47.

88  Sara Millman and Robert W. Kates, 'Toward Understanding Hunger,' in Lucile F. Newman, ed., *Hunger in History: Food Shortage, Poverty, and Deprivation* (Cambridge, MA: Blackwell, 1990), 18.

89  Peter P. Janzen, 'A Mother's Example,' *Mennonite Reporter*, 19 April 1993, B4.

# The Mother of God Wears a Maple Leaf: History, Gender, and Ethnic Identity in Sacred Space

FRANCES SWYRIPA

## Introduction

Since the mid-1990s worshippers in Holy Cross Ukrainian Catholic church in northeast Edmonton have prayed before an icon called 'Our Lady of Canada,' in which the Mother of God wears a mantle embroidered in gold, red-veined maple leaves. Traditionally, Christ's instruments of torture (the spear, the vinegar-soaked sponge on a rod, the crown of thorns, the cross) appear in the upper corners of such icons. But here a red-robed angel on the left and a blue-robed angel on the right each hold a golden globe: one features a map of Canada, the other a red maple leaf.[1] The Mother of God in this instance is both indisputably female and indisputably holy or spiritual in function. Yet her image has been co-opted independently of her sex to serve a purely secular political function, telling everyone that although this is a Ukrainian parish, its members are also good Canadians.

The ambiguous relationship of gender to the interplay among religion, ethnicity, and collective memory or identity in the sacred space of ethnic communities in Western Canada is complicated. It is reflected best in the ways in which ethnic churches access and manipulate often very different images and symbols in the interests of group-specific agenda that ultimately address the parameters of belonging within Canadian society. First, the mobilization of history and expressions of secular consciousness in the Prairie region's (im)migrant churches reveal that many ethnic groups identify simultaneously as diasporas, in communion with the homeland, and as Canadians with roots in the local community. Second, religion is shown to act not only as a crucial element of ethnic identity but also as a measure of ethnic power and legitimacy that privileges certain groups over others. Gender is irrelevant to the creation and articulation of collective memory and group agenda in that the images chosen draw freely on male and female historical figures that tie the local ethnic community to its counterparts worldwide. Thus, sex and attributes of femininity or masculinity clearly matter less than individuals' significance, as first national symbols in the homeland and then as ethnic symbols in Canada, to the messages the keepers of these sacred spaces wish to communicate. When it comes to collective memory and group agenda constructed around a congregation's own past or Prairie regional experience, however, men and male imagery are valued more. The marginalization or exclusion of flesh-and-blood women, in contrast to the politicized symbolism ascribed to their sisters from the distant past, serves as a reminder that sacred space is not a bastion of female equality but reflects the male privilege that has historically prevailed in both Christian churches and secular Western society. Much more difficult to evaluate is whether either the presence or absence of women in churches' visual imagery, or the use of specifically female and male images (especially when they also embody gendered qualities of excellence and example), positively or negatively affects female worshippers.

### Edmonton As a Case Study

Whenever religion is important to defining the nation or the state, it helps to inform a sense of peoplehood. In such circumstances, faith tends to merge with national or political identity, and sacred space, through its visual images and rituals, becomes a crucial meeting place where the two interact. To cultivate and reinforce people's sense of belonging to a secular community, churches turn to history; at the same time they accept custodianship of the 'imagined' past around which that sense of belonging is constructed. Moreover, by providing the setting for and participating in the rites of state occasions or landmark moments in the life of the nation, churches themselves become active partners in making history and inventing tradition. (E)migration challenges the power and status that national or quasi-national religious institutions enjoy. The impact is particularly acute when they are transplanted from mature communities marked by a high degree of cultural, 'racial,' and/or religious cohesiveness and a strong historical consciousness to a more fluid environment, initially without entrenched interests and shared memory. In the new setting, they must often negotiate for position, influence, and the right to belong. Just as often they must readjust their self-image and learn to function, at least in dealings with the surrounding society, as minority ethnic organizations.

There are several reasons for choosing Edmonton as the site for examining how Canadian ethnic groups and their churches use sacred space as politicized and gendered places to deal with the demotion of (e)migration and to promote new secular identities grounded in both the homeland and the Canadian experience. The city has been a multiethnic reality since its founding as a fur trade post in 1795, and during the settlement era that began a century later it attracted a wide variety of peoples who came in significant numbers at more or less the same time. As part of a coalescing frontier society, 'non-establishment' groups could potentially assert themselves and their institutions as important participants in community and/or nation-building. In important respects, the Edmonton context (frontier, multi-ethnic) also transformed both the French Roman Catholic and the English Anglican churches from national into ethnic institutions, forced to behave differently than they had in their home settings. The two denominations founded missions when Edmonton was still a fort, but neither could presume upon a privileged pre-(im)migration status to secure similar dominance either then or in the settlement period that followed. In fact, without any rules or consensus automatically elevating one church over the other, especially with respect to secular community ritual, they had to jockey for position in a political contest that (perhaps inevitably) the Anglican Church with its British establishment connections won.

Two of the six churches whose sacred space and visual imagery form the basis of this case study originated in the fur trade era and represent Canada's 'charter peoples.' The older, St Joachim's Roman Catholic parish was named a mission by the archbishop of St Boniface in 1854, sixteen years after two itinerant priests first visited Edmonton. By the time the present building was consecrated in 1899, the focus of St Joachim's had moved from its Native/Metis roots to identify with Edmonton's fledgling French community, assuming an ethnic identity it retains today.[2] All Saints Anglican had its beginnings in 1875 with the arrival of English-born Reverend (later Canon) William Newton, supported by the Society for the Propagation of the Gospel in England. The present cathedral, the fourth church, opened in 1956.[3] The origins of two other churches are tied to the early settlement period and attest to the impact of the large East European (Slavic) peasant immigration to the Edmonton area beginning in the 1890s. The first St Josaphat's Ukrainian Catholic church was built in 1904; noted prairie church architect the Reverend Philip Ruh designed the current structure, completed between 1939 and 1947. Served by the Ukrainian Order of St Basil the Great since its inception, St Josaphat's became the cathedral church of the eastern-rite Edmonton Ukrainian Catholic eparchy in 1948.[4] Both St Josaphat's and St Joachim's are registered Alberta Historic Sites. In 1911 Father Paweł Kulawy initiated discussions with Bishop Legal of St Albert to create a separate Roman Catholic Polish parish in the city; he celebrated the first mass in Holy Rosary church on New Year's Day, 1913. The present building was erected between 1953 and 1956.[5] The two remaining churches portray the ethnic character of more contemporary Edmonton. Consecrated in 1987, St Emeric's Roman Catholic church ministers to a Hungarian parish, formed in 1958 around individuals arriving in the aftermath of the 1956 anti-

Communist uprising in Hungary.[6] Lastly, in 1993 the old downtown Sacred Heart church was designated the 'official parish for the Catholic First Nations Peoples of Edmonton and surrounding communities.'[7]

None of these churches, as physical spaces incorporating an array of objects and images, has remained static over time. The secular statements they make at the beginning of the twenty-first century can thus embrace the worldview and priorities of successive generations. In terms of the material things that give them form, these various perspectives are unevenly represented and often sit uneasily with one another. It is also not unusual for inertia or loyalty to tradition to obstruct change, so that the continued presence of certain objects and images perpetuates points of view that members as a whole no longer support. In other instances, the messages projected illustrate accommodation by current congregations with the multilayered legacies of their predecessors. Yet the sacred space of each of these six places of worship nurtures and celebrates a peculiar sense of place and belonging, or ethnic identity, that is constructed around some combination and interpretation of the following: Canadian national or state symbols, the homeland heritage, and the Edmonton group's historical evolution as part of a community. At different moments the imagery employed is unabashedly secular and nationalistic, appropriates and politicizes the religious, and elevates the worldly to sacred. It also vacillates between being conscious of and indifferent to sex and gender. Sometimes female and male figures are mobilized equally, in which case neither functions in a gendered fashion, while at other times men are privileged, reflecting and reinforcing gender stereotypes that disadvantage women.

**Canadian Consciousness**

The ways in which the sacred space of the six churches expresses the ethnic group's attachment to the Canadian nation and state – identifying with its formal symbols and landmark events – illustrates the ambiguous role of gender. It does not, for example, enter into a decision to hang the Maple Leaf flag. All Saints is unusual for an Anglican church in that it currently has *no* flags in the interior, although this was not always the case, and the issue is a recurring and controversial one.[8] However, three of the ethnic Catholic churches – the exceptions are Sacred Heart and Holy Rosary – announce their loyalty to Canada by standing the country's national flag near the altar. St Josaphat's also displays the Alberta flag (and uses the Alberta rose, with the Ukrainian sunflower, as a motif on the ceiling above the iconostasis).[9] But as a site of remembering and honouring Canadian landmark events, sacred space becomes inevitably, if inadvertently, gendered. The memorabilia dedicated to a parish's military past, for example, reinforce women's traditional exclusion from spheres considered integral to nation-building. Not only are the targets of commemoration overwhelmingly men (war is, or was, a male activity), but sacred space also collaborates in privileging this male theatre of activity and its heroes around ideals such as patriotism, freedom, and sacrifice. The sacrifice of its men in turn binds the parish to the nation and to the ideals for which they fought and died. Yet there are great differences among these six churches with respect to the visible symbols tying them to Canada and its wars, as historical exclusion from or inclusion in Canadian nation-building coloured ethnic-group collective memory and identity. The differences also demonstrate that if their maleness benefited some men, ethnicity disempowered others. In essence, the sacred space of these Edmonton churches mirrors the secular dominance of the British element in late nineteenth- and early twentieth-century Canadian society, at the same time as it reinforces and reflects the marginality of Natives, the French, and East European immigrants.

All Saints Anglican, long referred to as 'the English church,' attests to a lengthy, intimate, and proud association with Canada's (para)military institutions and their activities.[10] Besides the articles and furnishings given in memory of parishioners lost in war, or in thanks for their safe return, are a handful of brass and marble wall plaques that form a permanent part of the nave. Some are personal, remembering dead husbands, brothers, fathers, and sons. In others, a community pays homage to its men's courage and sacrifice. The Canadian Mounted Rifles, for example, eulogize 'a brave and gallant comrade' killed trying to save a wounded fellow officer in the Boer War. On a far grander scale, sixty-eight names in gilt lettering engraved in marble remember 'the men of this congregation who gave up their lives in the Great War 1914–1918.' This plaque substitutes for what was envisaged, in plans for the present church, as a 'Soldiers' Corner,' and replaces the original honour roll burned in the 1919 fire that destroyed the existing church.[11] Surprisingly, despite discussions in the 1960s, there is no memorial to parishioners who fought in the Second World War.[12] Nor, although the Royal Canadian Navy flag was once hung, are there any military banners or standards, or reminders of their one-time presence, formally tying All Saints to the local representative institutions of 'official Canada.' But the Griesbach Memorial Window, commemorating two members of this prominent Edmonton family (and by name only their wives), more than compensates. Major General William Antribus Griesbach (CB, CMG, DSO, VD) founded the 49th Battalion, Edmonton Regiment, 1915; Lieutenant Colonel Arthur Henry Griesbach was the first enlisted member of the North-West Mounted Police, 1873.[13] Not only are the military credentials of these two individuals impeccable, opening All Saints to the grand narrative of Canadian history, but they also establish a special relationship between the parish and the police force whose heroic trek west and image of manly courage and integrity are so much part of regional Prairie identity. In fact, the cathedral functioned as the home church of the RCMP in the area, and in 1974 it hosted the force's local centennial service.

The five Catholic churches contain no evidence of such mainstreaming.[14] The absence of Canadian military memorabilia with its associated nation-building implications at St Emeric's is easily explained. Hungarians did not come to Edmonton in significant numbers until 1956, and the parish is even more recent, putting Canada's two great wars outside their experience. French-Canadian support of both the First and the Second World Wars, as British 'imperialist' ventures, was lukewarm, even outside Quebec. The nationalist St Jean Baptiste Society had existed at St Joachim's since 1894, its mixed political-cultural and religious program proclaiming solidarity with all French Canada.[15] Natives were disfranchised and confined largely to reserves, although some served in 1939–45 especially. A sign that symbols of Sacred Heart's mainstream past do not belong to its Native present, the parish's wartime honour roll hangs in the vestibule outside the place of worship itself. Ukrainians and Poles, as former subjects of the Austro-Hungarian empire, faced widespread prejudice as well as enemy-alien status (if unnaturalized) during World War I, which excluded them from military service. That neither St Josaphat's nor Holy Rosary possesses, or chooses to display, a memorial from the Second World War is more intriguing. By then both Ukrainian and Polish ethnic groups had almost half a century of Canadian and Edmonton roots behind them, and both communities anxiously encouraged wartime service as proof of patriotism. Perhaps, despite the best exhortations of their leaders, Ukrainians and Poles in these two pioneer parishes did not volunteer in satisfactory numbers. Perhaps imperfect integration into Canadian fellowship left them detached from the honour rolls generated by the thousands for community groups across Canada. Or perhaps they rejected their sacred space as a suitable place for such secular, Canadian statements.[16] The bottom line is that in all five non-Anglo churches the special gendered (male) nature of the sacred space cultivated at All Saints by virtue of its Canadian military memorials is missing. But far from saying that non-British women enjoy an equality with their men denied to British women, its absence indicates how the priorities and impositions of ethnic-group membership have reduced non-British men to the status of women, outside the great enterprises of nation-building.

### Homeland Heritage

The unique position of All Saints is further underlined by how these six churches express their homeland ties and identity. While the Anglican imagery is largely genderless, and indeed divorced from actual historical figures, the five Catholic churches draw on both the men and the women in their nations' pasts and use them independently of any gendered associations. Also, All Saints has historically enjoyed a comfortable symmetry between 'Canadian' and 'homeland,' in which expressions of Britishness and British ties were understood by the parish (and others) to be synonymous with Canadian. For both the soldiers commemorated within the nave and their descendants, there was no conflict between old and new homelands, in whose joint names these parishioners volunteered for service and made the supreme sacrifice. The Boer War plaque, for example, represents unity with imperial aims and adventures, and will have counterparts in Australia and New Zealand as well as Britain itself. More significantly, drawing on its historically privileged position as the 'establishment' church, All Saints has been the host of choice for state or semi-official ceremonial occasions, emphasizing the British tie and putting it at the centre of Edmonton's corporate ritualistic life. Most recently, its dean deemed the cathedral the 'natural' venue for a memorial service for Diana, Princess of Wales, although in the mid-1980s, he had deemed it unsuitable for commemorating the Battle of the Atlantic and controversially cancelled its annual May service. These two contradictory positions suggest at least a partial shift away from a politicized British identity. Yet there are crucial differences between an Anglican parish distancing itself from secular homeland nationalism, and the accompanying historical baggage, and ethnic churches to whom this is not a mainstream issue.

For overseas immigrant ethnics in three of the Catholic churches, sacred space is a legitimate site in which to express ongoing, often ideologically coloured, identification with a homeland and people that are *not* synonymous (and are often in tension) with 'Canadian.' The more these Polish, Ukrainian, and Hungarian congregations see themselves as diasporas in continuity with the homeland and its history, the more the visual images they evoke are predicated upon and exploit sources external to Canada. National flags become especially powerful tools if forbidden or repressed in the homeland because they symbolize a vision of the nation, and thus an opposition or counter movement, anathema to the ruling regime. But while it can be daring, even dangerous, to brandish such symbols in political protest at home, emigrants in a country like Canada can use them freely – to assert solidarity with 'captive' compatriots in the homeland and in defiance of their oppressors. Before the fall of the Iron Curtain, the congregations of St Josaphat's and St Emeric's adamantly opposed the Communist regimes in Ukraine and Hungary. The outlawed blue-and-yellow Ukrainian nationalist flag (and now the flag of post-Soviet independent Ukraine) in the one, and the red-white-and-green flag of Hungary bearing the traditional coat of arms, plus the flag of the Hungarian Scouts (banned under Communism), in the other, once made strong political statements and still appeal emotionally. At Holy Rosary, the red-and-white Polish national flag is flown on the anniversary of the 3 May 1791 constitution, when there is a special service attended by Polish veterans.

The extent to which these three ethnic groups, as religious communities, dwell mentally outside Canada in a world inhabited by the heroes and villains of Eastern Europe is best illustrated by the painting of the Last Judgment in St Josaphat's cathedral. The work of Julian Bucmaniuk, who immigrated to Canada as a displaced person after the Second World War, its heaven and hell were peopled with famous figures from recent Ukrainian history as well as local individuals (men and women) whom Bucmaniuk admired or disliked. Hitler, Stalin, and Lenin were clearly recognizable burning with the damned. The parishioners who joined them included one of Bucmaniuk's former students, a woman who helped finish painting the iconostasis after the artist's death. Conspicuous among the saved were Metropolitan Andrei Sheptytsky, head of the Greek Catholic Church in Galicia from 1900 to 1944; and Josyf Cardinal Slipyj, who survived almost twenty years in the Gulag to become titular head of the Ukrainian Catholic Church in the free world.

Significantly, much of the politicized homeland imagery in the sacred space of the three East European churches is religious in nature or blurs the line between religious and secular. That this is so underscores the highly politicized nature of the religious past in each of Ukraine, Poland, and Hungary, as well as the importance of religion to the identity of the secular nation and/or state in those countries. In the Edmonton context, it also illustrates how the peculiarities of their respective national, pre-immigration pasts cut across common Catholicism in Canada. National churches in the homeland, in other words, have become distinctive ethnic institutions in emigration, where symbols and images regarded as normal and familiar in the sacred space of one are alien or incongruous in the others. Moreover, these symbols and images are simultaneously often gender-specific, in that they draw freely on both male and female historical figures, yet innocent of gender, in that it is their national function or service to the nation, rather than their sex or any feminine/masculine attributes, that determines their presence. Individual saints, for example, might have been revered and canonized for holy virtues tied to stereotypically 'female' or 'male' behaviour and traits. But the reasons why they appear in these particular ethnic churches are as much political and nationalistic (that is, ethnic-specific) as they are spiritual, and certainly more than they reflect qualities identified with gender.[17]

Three large portraits dominate the interior of St Emeric's. One is of St Emeric himself, son of St Stephen, the eleventh-century king who united and Christianized the Magyars to found the Hungarian nation. One is of 'Our Lady of Hungary' (Stephen dedicated his nation to Mary on his deathbed) – crowned, dressed in red and blue, and holding her son. And one is of St Margaret of Hungary (1242–70), given to God before her birth by her parents, Bela IV and Marie Laskaris, in gratitude for Hungary's liberation from the Tatars; known for her kindness and severe penance, Margaret refused to marry the king of Bohemia.[18] The Ukrainian cathedral honours its own array of national-religious figures, beginning with its patron saint, the monk and bishop St Josaphat of Polotsk. Martyred for his faith following the Union of Brest in 1596, which carved the Ukrainian world into Catholic and Orthodox spheres, he was canonized in 1867. There are also millennium mosaics of SS Olha and Volodymyr, the convert princess and her grandson, who, as ruler, Christianized Kievan Rus' in 988. The pair are present in a painting as well, together with early monks SS Antonii Pechersky and Teodosii Pechersky, politicized against a background of tridents, the Ukrainian national emblem banned in the Soviet Union.[19] Holy Rosary, too, ties itself to the religious underpinnings of secular Poland. The stained-glass window in the south transept is dedicated to the millennium of the baptism of Poland, 966 to 1966. The individuals on the windows in the choir loft include St Casimir, son of Casimir IV of Poland and supporter of the poor, named patron saint of his country in 1602; St Stanisław Kostka, eleventh-century bishop of Cracow and martyr, murdered by Bolesław II for criticizing his private conduct, and canonized as a symbol of Poland's unity; St John of Kanti, a fifteenth-century priest revered in his native Poland, especially for his generosity to Cracow's poor; and St Cecilia, patron of musicians and popular Polish saint.[20] Holy Rosary also possesses a relic of St Stanisław, a gift from Karol Cardinal Wojtyła in 1970, following his visit to the parish well before election as pontiff made him a celebrity far beyond the Polish community.[21] At All Saints Anglican, the homeland associations are less nationalistic, largely invisible, depersonalized, and ungendered. There are no English kings or queens, no English saints or martyrs (except vicariously in a small cross of St George, patron saint of England, on the Griesbach Memorial Window).[22]

The mobilization of homeland imagery differs profoundly at Sacred Heart and St Joachim's. Most importantly, it shows Natives and Franco-Albertans behaving as ethnic communities whose historical roots and memory lie not outside but inside Canada. This domestication of the concept of 'homeland' is reflected in their saints. St Joachim's, for example, has a stained-glass window of St Anne – wife of St Joachim, mother of Mary, patron saint of Canada and Quebec, and historically the protectress of Canadian voyageurs and fur traders. In 1844 the pioneer Oblates named their mission northwest of Edmonton Lac-Ste-Anne, and the annual pilgrimage to the lake's shores on her feast day still lures thousands of Natives.[23] Both St Joachim's and Sacred Heart, as Oblate parishes, contain icons of St Eugene de Mazenod, the French founder of the Missionary Oblates of Mary Immaculate, who have served Western Canada, and its Native Christian converts, since the fur trade. But St Eugene has a special bond with Sacred Heart: one of his miracles (he was canonized in 1995) occurred in northern Alberta, curing a young Native boy of tuberculosis.[24] Although Polish Holy Rosary is also an Oblate parish, and has been since its creation, the order's founder is not honoured with an image.[25] At Sacred Heart the spot St Eugene now occupies was once held by Louis Riel, the Metis leader in the Red River uprising of 1869–70 and the Northwest Rebellion of 1885, but his picture was removed and destroyed after a Native elder decided that the eyes were bad medicine.[26] In a chapel to the left of the altar, saint-hood and Canadian Native history merge more canonically, showing that Native saints can act like their East European counterparts as national figures blind to gender. It contains a statue of the Iroquois virgin and ascetic, Kateri Tekakwitha, venerated in New France after her death in 1680, and beatified in 1980, without proven miracles, as part of Pope John Paul II's campaign to give indigenous peoples their own saints.[27] While Sacred Heart has images of only the two saints, St Joachim's depicts several on its stained-glass windows, some acknowledging the non-French immigrants the pioneer parish served: St Patrick (Irish), SS Anthony of Padua and Stanisław Kostka (Polish), St Basil the Great (Ukrainian). The last window, presented by the 'Galician Night School Girls,'[28] and featuring the founder of the monastic order that supplied Canada (and Edmonton) with its first permanent Ukrainian priests, makes the local multicultural connection explicit.

The interior of St Joachim's also maintains links with France: a stained-glass image of St François de Sales; the names of French-born pioneer priests – Grouard, Lemarchand, and Leduc.[29] The more actively recognized psychological homeland is Quebec, although the connection is made outside not inside the church. In 1934 the parish erected a cross to Jacques Cartier, father of Quebec and 'discoverer' of Canada, to mark the four-hundredth anniversary of his voyage up the St Lawrence River. Overall, however, St Joachim's is curiously rootless. Ironically, given that St Joseph's was formed in 1910 as an English-speaking parish to counter the French-ness of St Joachim's, the Roman Catholic cathedral is much more visually assertive in the appropriation of the notion of Quebec as homeland. But elevation to cathedral status in 1922 (which confirmed Anglo ascendancy in local affairs) forced the church to look beyond itself for historical legitimacy and embrace, now as the diocese (and later archdiocese), heritage and ethnic associations it had once, as a parish, fled. Four windows in the present cathedral celebrate Quebec, its sons and daughters, and its missionary record in western Canada. One features 'Blessed Mother d'Youville,' who in 1737 founded the Sisters of Charity or Grey Nuns in New France. A century later they entered the Native mission field in the West, coming to present-day Alberta (Lac-Ste-Anne) in 1859; in 1895 they opened the General Hospital as part of the French Catholic complex coalescing around St Joachim's. Two windows remember local figures: Father Albert Lacombe, Quebec-born missionary to the Natives, above the church he built in nearby St Albert in 1861; and French-born Bishop Vital Grandin, above the 1872 cathedral, again in St Albert. In the fourth window a male Native convert in a blue blanket and red undergarment stands above a teepee camp outside a stockaded fort.[30]

The Canadian homeland evoked in Sacred Heart is at once broader and narrower than that claimed in St Joachim's (or St Joseph's). As the church interior was redone to show parishioners' Native heritage, it embraced a historical past that was both Canadawide (Kateri Tekakwitha) and regional (Louis Riel). Not only did Riel draw in the Metis, but at one point the homeland is implicitly equated, as in Metis mythology more generally, with pre-1870 Red River, from which collective memory says they were exiled.[31] Paralleling this evocation of a Canadian homeland is the Canadianization of the biblical story via First Nations history and symbols, making faith potentially more personal but also highly politicized. On the wall above St Eugene, a teepee, an igloo, a longhouse, a canoe, and a kayak are sketched in a landscape of mountains, forest, and river; superimposed over them, two enjoined hands imitate Michelangelo's God creating Adam. A statue of a Native Christ – dark-skinned, a brown robe over his shirtdress, an eagle feather in his hand – sits on the adjacent side altar. Behind him a vivid wall painting, dominated by a huge teepee and immense blue sky above with a distant mountain range on the horizon, collapses the Bible into a few images and key events using stylized Native figures. At the top is the Ghost Buffalo or Creator. Below to the left, a circle holds Mary, her infant son, and three teepees representing the Three Wise Men. Next, along a downwardly spiralling ribbon, an outline of the Rocky Mountains holds the silhouette of a small male figure leading an ox as it pulls a Red River cart – symbolizing both the exodus of the Metis from Red River after the events of 1869–70 and the Flight into Egypt. At the bottom of the ribbon a crucified Christ hangs on the cross, a bowed figure kneels at its foot, the mountains behind are dark and foreboding. A soaring orange eagle above Christ's head heralds the Resurrection.

The remaining instances of Nativizing Christ's life lack the same Canadian political pointedness, although they are more consciously gendered. In the chapel dedicated to Kateri Tekakwitha, the wall paintings by Barbara Marquis include three grey-haired women based on parish members (fellow painter, Sheldon Meek, had objected to female figures in the chapel).[32] Finally, the Stations of the Cross, which atypically circle the nave clockwise, following nature, eschew images of Roman soldiers and the Holy Land in favour of reference points that strike personal and emotional chords with Canadian Natives. For example, the First Fall (#3) captures Native connectedness to nature (even the latter is falling); at the Second Fall (#7), the Northern Lights blaze across the sky; and the Tomb (#14) is a raised Indian bier. Yet if more cultural and spiritual than political as Canadian images, the Stations of the Cross still convey a very strong political message. It is also one that intentionally transcends Canada to express unity with aboriginal peoples and their suffering worldwide. At the eighth station, the Women, an open white palm print on the face of a full moon rising over the mountains represents the thousands of Disappeared in Latin America; the four figures kneeling in front of an outstretched hand are the mothers and wives who grieve for them.

## The Local Community

While Sacred Heart fully embraces its secular as well as its spiritual Canadian Native past, the only references to a specifically Edmonton or Alberta identity are the incongruous military honour roll in the vestibule and, for worshippers who know their miracles, the icon of St Eugene. This feeling of dislocation from the larger community is natural given First Nations marginalization from mainstream society, past and present. The sacred space of the other five churches does tie parish and ethnic groups to their local secular roots. Despite the dominance of the British symbolized by the military memorabilia in All Saints, however, no correlation exists between high rank in Canada's ethnic hierarchy and the creation or assertion of local identity stemming from a sense of participation and therefore entitlement as community builders. Rather, the important point is that sacred space is one of the few 'public' spaces non-charter peoples control, allowing them to present an uncontested alternative version of history and their place in it. That both Polish Holy Rosary and Ukrainian St Josaphat's have deliberately used their churches to make group claims as Edmontonians and Albertans, while English All Saints and French St Joachim's have not, testifies both to this imbalance of opportunity and to East Europeans' particular hunger for recognition and inclusion. In constructing their local credentials, Poles and Ukrainians (and to a lesser extent, Hungarians) appeal to a series of disparate historical legacies, ingeniously synthesizing old and new worlds, their people and mainstream Canada, themselves and other Albertans and Edmontonians. St Joachim's and All Saints have done little by way of a calculated statement linking their ethnic congregations with the pioneer French and English contribution to early Edmonton, or using it as a vehicle of validation, perhaps because they feel no need to do so. That contribution, and the Anglo-French pre-eminence it automatically affirms, are clear without special prodding or massaging by their descendants.

In this local secular sphere, when maleness or femaleness is not irrelevant or subsumed under the ethnic message, the imagery (like traditional history itself) is almost exclusively male. Seldom acknowledged as individual and independent actors, flesh-and-blood women, when they do appear, appear passively – named on donor plaques or memorial windows and gifts to the parish – as appendages of their husbands, more rarely on their own, otherwise unseen. They are not even present as nuns. A noticeable exception, especially considering the absence of any recognition of the pioneer labours of the Sisters Servants of Mary Immaculate, is the presence in St Josaphat's of the standard of the Ukrainian Catholic Women's

League alongside that of the Ukrainian Catholic Brotherhood. All Saints alone directly acknowledges women's contribution, but only to the church not to the larger Edmonton community, in personal memorials to a handful of parish workers, and in a generic stained-glass window dedicated 'To the glory of God and with deep thankfulness for the service of the faithful women.'[33] Male parishioners are not singled out for generic recognition, that is, thanked collectively for their labours simply because they are men. Instead, individuals are named and acknowledged personally, with or without underlining their role in the larger community. Also, excluding priests and parish functionaries, they are not identified with (beyond financial contribution) or confined to parish activities. In some instances, men and male activities become privileged through what the parish, and the ethnic group, value as crucial to their collective priorities and identity. In other instances, such is the overriding significance attached to both priorities and identity that neither maleness nor femaleness matters as much as the message about the ethnic group that the visual imagery is intended to make.

In keeping with the pattern of Hungarian immigration to Edmonton, long past the city's formative years, evidence of identification by either the parish or local Hungarians with the surrounding society is sparse at St Emeric's. The Hungarian homeland and its struggles clearly eclipse any sense of Canadianness or attachment to Edmonton and its history. Yet Edmonton and Hungary *are* brought together – albeit only by subordinating the city's Hungarian diaspora to its compatriots overseas, to whom they are bound through shared patriotic ideals extolling the Hungarian nation. The link is made in a monument, topped by the Crown of St Stephen, that stands outside the church/hall complex and broadly commemorates those who lived and died for their country and liberty between 896 and 1956. The English text reads: 'This memorial honours the heroes who sacrificed their lives for the freedom and basic human rights of their compatriots during the Hungarian freedom fight in 1956, erected by those Edmonton citizens of Hungarian origin.' The Hungarian text, a stirring patriotic verse by the poet Petöfi, is more generic and omits the Edmonton reference.[34] Not only is the sex of these heroes irrelevant, but the priority of place and honour accorded their sacrifice in the name of Hungary also opens up their ranks to men and women equally.

In contrast, at the English and French 'mainstream' churches, the gendered imagery denoting the local roots and identity of the parish and its members is decidedly male. Claims to Edmonton history, and to the city's French and English ethnic communities, are in any case muted. Only two items in St Joachim's deliberately forge a link between past and present; both are inward-looking and neither forms part of the permanent fabric of the church interior. Four photographs on the rear wall depict the 1859, 1886, 1899, and present churches, while a painted banner of the current building links it to its 1838 and Oblate roots. But despite the parish's origins in the fur trade and nearby Native communities, neither is commemorated anywhere in its visual imagery. Yet St Joachim's settlement-era credentials have inadvertently been preserved, in the names of the donors of the stained-glass windows installed soon after the present church was built – names like Lessard, Gariepy, and Larue, representing the French secular elite in pioneer Edmonton. Like the stained-glass saints acknowledging St Joachim's contemporary immigrant parishioners, united by their common Catholicism, these men reinforce an identity and sphere of activity increasingly outside Edmonton's crystallizing Anglo-Protestant ethos. The latter's influence is illustrated, without fanfare, at All Saints. If any one impression of local roots and identity emerges here, it is of Anglicans' prominence in the early history of Edmonton, as major players in a small intertwined spiritual, socioeconomic, political, and military circle at the apex of Edmonton society. The stained-glass memorial windows are a veritable who's who of prominent Edmontonians, from the military Griesbachs and Henry Allen Gray, first Anglican bishop and juvenile court judge, to Richard Secord, affluent merchant, and Ernest Sheldon, professor of mathematics at the University of Alberta. Romanticized and nostalgic, but specific to nowhere, the secular images below the traditional biblical scenes also celebrate the frontier: an early model car, a log cabin in the bush, stereotypical Victorians (top hat, fur muff), a Prairie street with false-fronted buildings, a lake and canoe.

Both Holy Rosary and St Josaphat's identify self-consciously, and politically, with Canada and the local community as well as with the old Polish and Ukrainian homelands. Within their sacred space itself, the Poles are less assertive in their Canadianness and claims for the ethnic group based on an appeal to history, but overall their message is the more overtly secular and all-encompassing. While Polish symbols proper dominate in Holy Rosary, the congregation's local roots are acknowledged in a bronze plaque near the main door commemorating the pioneer priest and founder of the parish, Paweł Kulawy. The text, however, makes no mainstream claims on behalf of Polish Edmontonians, and in fact, through Kulawy's death in Auschwitz, ties Polish pioneers in Canada to the wartime martyrdom of Poles in the homeland.[35] But outside the church, the Polish community has marshalled an array of symbols to effect a three-way link among Poland, Canada, and themselves. A cement monument with the words 'Polonia semper fidelis' (Poland always faithful) and the numbers 100 and 1000 across the front features a Maltese cross, mosaics of the Alberta coat of arms and the crowned Polish eagle against a red maple leaf, and three bronze plaques. One, the stylized Canadian Centennial maple leaf, attributes the monument project to the Holy Rosary Men's Club; the other two (in English and in Polish) read: 'In honour of the Polish pioneers of Alberta on the occasion of the Polish millennium of Christianity and Canadian Centennial.'[36] An almost mind-boggling amalgam of Polish imperial and religious history, Canadian nation-building, and the local (Alberta) Polish pioneer experience, the monument offers this complex legacy to Poles of both sexes.

St Josaphat's claim on behalf of its Ukrainian pioneers occurs solely within sacred space. Moreover, it celebrates only the achievements of the Ukrainian Catholic church, specifically the Basilian Fathers since 1902; the Sisters Servants who accompanied the missionaries to Canada, and worked alongside them, remain unsung. In major respects, the interior of St Josaphat's functions as a historical record of Basilian activity and Ukrainian Catholicism in east central Alberta, and despite its strong Ukrainian character, the visual imagery proclaims that this is a Canadian institution proud of its past and sure of its place. On the walls of the nave and lower arms of both transepts large likenesses of important Basilians and other clerics unite Ukraine, Canada, Alberta, and Edmonton. In addition to Metropolitan Sheptytsky, who visited his emigrant flock in 1910, are the first two bishops of the Canadian church; the first bishop of the Edmonton eparchy; the first missionary; the priest who began regular pastoral work in Edmonton and laid the base for St Josaphat's; his contemporary and the order's superior in Galicia; two former Canadian heads, one holding the Basilian Rules with a 'Canadianized' crest, the other in office when the idea for the present church took shape; and the pioneer missionary who served as second priest of St Josaphat's.[37] While these figures speak primarily of the Basilians' own history and identity, two silhouettes on the ceiling to the right and left of the iconostasis reach outward. One, a collapsed skyline of rural Alberta where the first Basilians founded their mission, moves from the original chapel at Beaverlake to the imposing Basilian monastery and first SS Peter and Paul church in nearby Mundare. The second, a collapsed Edmonton skyline, is more ambitious in its presumptions: beginning with St Josaphat's cathedral, it moves through the downtown core to end with St Joachim's and the Legislature Building. Both cryptic and bold, the implication of shared legitimacy shows how Ukrainians understand sacred space as a place to assert their sense of partnership in the Canadian community to which they belong and which they helped build.

### Conclusion

The female imagery in the sacred space of these prairie ethnic churches often has little to do with women as such. The images are there because the persons concerned – saints, queens, and princesses who lived their lives in another time and place, far from early-twenty-first-century Edmonton – symbolize the aspirations of their people or nation. Saintliness alone was not enough to secure their presence, or the Native Kateri Tekakwitha would be in Ukrainian St Josaphat's, Ukrainian St Olha in Hungarian St Emeric's, and Hungarian St Margaret in Native

Sacred Heart. Even the Mother of God, or the Virgin Mary, has been appropriated and nationalized. Although fewer in number, these politicized figures perform the same function as their male counterparts in the same space. When the imagery moves from the overarching narrative of their people or nation to the local experience and collective memory of the ethnic group itself, however, gender becomes significant. Women and female images are either absent (military memorabilia), recalled but invisible (collection plates, pews, and other gifts bought in their name), or subordinated to men and male images (handmaidens to the parish but not priests or captains of business). More positively, women are sometimes included by implication (generic pioneer memorials). How these six churches use the past to construct their secular identity around a sense of community, then, is simultaneously free of gender bias, giving priority to the nation or ethnic group, and gendered in a way that privileges men and male activities. Overall, they are more comfortable with women and female imagery in their sacred space when it is passive and remote than when it is close and familiar.

In that they look to, or are expected to look to, these images and symbols as role models, contemporary female worshippers receive a mixed message. On the one hand, national saints encourage them to identify strongly as Native, Ukrainian, Hungarian, French, Polish, or English, with explicit or implicit instructions to serve the cause of their people or nation. On the other hand, the virtues celebrated in these women, as both holy figures and secular symbols, encourage behaviour and values that are stereotypical for their sex: motherhood, sexual purity, dedicated service, piety, helpfulness, retiring modesty. These values are reinforced by the ways in which contemporary female worshippers' own predecessors in the parish are treated or commemorated. As participants in and co-builders of the religious and ethnic communities represented in the sacred space of these six Edmonton churches, women remain junior partners slotted into roles that reinforce their difference.

NOTES

I would like to acknowledge the owners and patrons of La Trattoria Tacconi in Cortona, Italy, especially Angiolo and Graziella, who not only fed me but also let me scribble away in one corner while their regular cluster of pensioners played cards in another. They will all be relieved to know that yes, at last, it is finished.

1   The iconographer was André Prevost. For a discussion of the role of the Mother of God in the iconography of Ukrainian-Canadian women's organizations, see Frances Swyripa, *Wedded to the Cause: Ukrainian-Canadian Women and Ethnic Identity, 1891–1991* (Toronto: University of Toronto Press, 1993), 131–7.

2  Fieldwork at St Joachim's (9928 – 110 Street) was conducted at various times between November 1997 and May 2000, initially with Sister Edna who was both welcoming and knowledgeable. See also the six-page 'Historical Overview of the St. Joachim Parish' (photocopy, 22 August 1992) produced for visitors to the church; the official jubilee history, France Levasseur-Ouimet, *Saint-Joachim, la première paroisse catholique d'Edmonton, 1899–1999* (Edmonton: the author, 1999), published on the occasion of the 160th anniversary of a Roman Catholic presence in Edmonton and the centenary of the present church; and the related video, Le Comité des Fêtes du Centenaire, *Saint Joachim: Première paroisse catholique d'Edmonton* (Edmonton: Patenaude Communications, 1999).

3  All Saints (11039 – 103 Street) was visited in September 1997 and again in May 2001; on the first occasion, conversations with the Reverend Harold Munn, dean, and Dr Gust Olson, warden, were most helpful. Other sources included Lewis G. Thomas, 'Establishing an Anglican Presence,' in Bob Hesketh and Frances Swyripa, eds, *Edmonton: The Life of a City* (Edmonton: NeWest Press, 1995), 21–30; the church's own anniversary booklets, *Cathedral Church of All Saints, 1875–1935*, and Jean Monckton, *All Saints Anglican Cathedral, 1875–1975*; the brochure, 'A Walking Tour of the Edmonton Cathedral of All Saints' (n.d.); and especially the Records of the Anglican Diocese of Edmonton, Ed.15/All Saints and Acc.95.31, Provincial Archives of Alberta, Edmonton, AB.

4  St Josaphat's (10825 – 97 Street) was visited specifically for the project in September 1997 and again in May 2000. Additional information came from Orest Kupranets, osbm, *Katedra sv. Iosafata v. Edmontoni* (Edmonton: Ukrainska katolytska eparkhiia Edmontonu, 1979); the visitor pamphlet (n.d.), *St. Josaphat's Ukrainian Catholic Cathedral*, prepared by the 'Dobra volia' (Goodwill) cathedral branch of the Ukrainian Catholic Women's League of Canada; Mykhailo Khomiak, ed., *Iuliian Butsmaniuk* (Edmonton: Kanadske naukove tovarystvo im. Shevchenka, oseredok na Zakhidniu Kanadu, 1982); and Bucmaniuk's archives in the Ukrainian Canadian Archives and Museum of Alberta, Edmonton, AB.

5  Holy Rosary (11485 – 106 Street) was first visited in September 1997, accompanied by Fr Stanisław Kowal, and again in May 2000. See also John Huculak, *History of the Holy Rosary Parish in Edmonton, 1913–1988* (Edmonton: Holy Rosary Parish, 1988); the Polish-language summary by Teofil Szendzielarz, omi, *Dom Ojca na Zachodzie*, forms Part III.

6  St Emeric's (12960 – 112 Street) was visited formally in September 1997, together with the Reverend Joseph Occhio and Gabor Botar, and informally several times since.

7  Fieldwork was undertaken at Sacred Heart (10821 – 96 Street) in September 1997 and May 2000; on those and other occasions the Reverend James Holland was most forthcoming about the meaning of the objects and symbols in the sanctuary. See also the brochure, *Sacred Heart Church of the First Peoples* (n.d.), which explains the symbolism of the official logo, the 'Circle of Love.'

8  The flag issue in All Saints over the decades, from the Union Jack to the standards of First Troop Boy Scouts and Beaver Lodge IODE, can be followed in the Records of the Anglican Diocese of Edmonton, Ed.15, esp. files 52–54, 56–58, 78, 80, 106–109, 116, 117a. Currently, the Canadian and Anglican Church of Canada flags fly outside the church.

9  The UCWL pamphlet, *St. Josaphat's Ukrainian Catholic Cathedral,* ascribes only religious significance to the rose (St Josaphat's 'crest,' symbolizing the Mother of God) and the sunflower (symbolizing humility and obedience and the Christian's duty always to face Christ just as the sunflower always faces the sun).

10  Thomas, 'Establishing an Anglican Presence,' 28. Without providing evidence, Thomas claims that 'nominal Anglicans probably predominated among arrivals from the United Kingdom, their ecclesiastical allegiance as much cultural as doctrinal.' He also argues that in pre-1914 Edmonton the '"English church" did act as a rallying point and a comforting support for those who saw themselves as inheritors of an English, or perhaps more properly, a British tradition.'

11  On the loss of both the honour roll and battalion colours, see the comments by Rector Goulding, *Edmonton Parish Magazine,* January 1920, Records of the Anglican Diocese of Edmonton, Ed.15, file 117a; on the proposed Soldiers' Corner, see the fundraising pamphlets (especially 'c,' blueprint/Plate B) published by the Building Fund Committee in the 1950s, files 106–9.

12  The dean broached a 'memorial for those who had lost their lives in the Second World War' just after Remembrance Day in 1961; see ibid., file 57, vestry minutes, 14 November 1961.

13  William Griesbach offered to dedicate a stained-glass window to his parents in 1933 and Arthur's widow agreed in 1950 on behalf of her husband; initiatives to add that Arthur was the first enlisted member of the North-West Mounted Police were begun in 1973. See ibid., files 52 and 54, vestry minutes, 13 November 1933, 13 November 1950. Also Acc.95.31, box 1, letter, George McClellan, Office of the Ombudsman, 25 October 1973; letter, Randall Ivany, Dean, to Peter Lougheed, Premier, 15 March 1972; and vestry minutes, 11 February 1974.

14  In contrast, St Joseph's Roman Catholic cathedral – intended as an 'English-speaking' parish when it was formed in 1910 – has two rolls of honour: one in the vestibule and a second off to its side flanked by the Canadian and Vatican flags.

15  Levasseur-Ouimet, *Saint-Joachim,* 57–60, 101–2, 123–31, 175–91; the centenary history of the parish identifies sixty-two parishioners who served in the Second World War (178) but also notes that the local newspaper, *La Survivance,* encouraged Franco-Albertans to vote no to conscription in 1942 (177); no names of volunteers, or total numbers, are provided for the Great War.

16  On Ukrainians' wartime experience, see John Herd Thompson and Frances Swyripa, eds, *Loyalties in Conflict: Ukrainians in Canada and the Great War* (Edmonton: Cana-

dian Institute of Ukrainian Studies, 1983); Gordon Panchuk, ed., *Memorial Souvenir Book 1: Ukrainian Branches, Royal Canadian Legion* (Montreal: Ukrainian Canadian Veterans Association, 1986). During both world wars the fate of their homeland (a resurrected Polish state in 1918, its security in 1939) and Polish Canadians' own agenda dovetailed with Canadian and allied interests. Viktor Turek, *Poles in Manitoba* (Toronto: Canadian Polish Congress, 1967), 139–40, acknowledges as much, while deploring Poles' enemy-alien status in the Great War until Ottawa recognized the 'absurdity' of the situation. William Makowski, *History and Integration of Poles in Canada* (Niagara Peninsula: Canadian Polish Congress, 1967), 179–84, ignores the enemy-alien issue altogether.

17 Other ethnic Catholic churches in Edmonton reinforce this point: Our Lady of Fatima (Portuguese), Our Lady of Guadalupe (Latin American), Our Lady Queen of Poland (Polish), Queen of Martyrs (Vietnamese – in 1988 John Paul II canonized 117 Christian martyrs from Vietnam, a move opposed by its Communist rulers), and Santa Maria Goretti (Italian, after the peasant girl killed in 1902 defending her purity and canonized in 1950; dedication program, 21 December 1958, and *La Voce Italiana*, 3 July 1966, Provincial Archives of Alberta, Acc.83.311). On the political implications of the canonization of the Vietnamese martyrs and Maria Goretti, in particular the controversy surrounding the latter after the publication of Bruno Guerri's *Povera Santa, Povero Assassino* (1985), see Kenneth Woodward, *Making Saints: How the Catholic Church Determines Who Becomes a Saint, Who Doesn't, and Why* (New York: Touchstone, 1990), 115, 122–4, 152, 222.

18 See, for example, Michael Freze, *Patron Saints* (Huntingdon, IN: Our Sunday Visitor, 1992), 24, 76, 201–2; and Donald Attwater, *The Penguin Dictionary of Saints*, 2nd ed. (Harmondsworth: Penguin, 1983), 223, 304–5.

19 See Attwater, *Penguin Dictionary of Saints*, 47–8, 312–13.

20 See, for example, Freze, *Patron Saints*, 27–8, 30; and Attwater, *Penguin Dictionary of Saints*, 38, 77, 81, 191.

21 Huculak, *History of Holy Rosary Parish*, 36.

22 Indicative of All Saints mindset are objects like a silver chalice rededicated to service in the cathedral after '300 years of use in an unknown English church,' and a Children's Processional Cross 'made from nails from Coventry Cathedral ... blitzed in 1941'; see Records of the Anglican Diocese of Edmonton, Ed.15, file 111.

23 The shrine at Ste-Anne-de-Beaupré in Quebec, for whom Lac-Ste-Anne was named, has attracted pilgrims seeking its miraculous cures since 1658. On St Anne in the Canadian fur trade during the 1700s, see the 'Patron Saints Index: Anne' at www.catholic-forum.com/saints; the Oblate version of the Alberta mission as a healing site and place of pilgrimage beginning in 1889 is found in EO Drouin, omi, *Lac Ste-Anne Sakahigan* (Edmonton: Editions de l'Érmitage, 1973), 52–63.

24 Alfred Hubenig, *Living in the Spirit's Fire: St Eugene de Mazenod, Founder of the Mis-*

*sionary Oblates of Mary Immaculate* (Toronto: Novalis, 1995), was published at the time of Eugene's canonization; his two Canadian miracles are reported in the Order of Service, Mass of Thanksgiving, St Joseph's Basilica, Edmonton, 16 February 1996; the case of the Native boy, David Courteoreille, in de Mazenod's cause was presented 8 December 1937 by Ferdinand Thiry, omi, postular general.

25  Yet the seventy-fifth jubilee history of Holy Rosary contains, seemingly within the context of the parish's legacy, brief pieces on the Oblates of Mary Immaculate, the Indians of Canada, and the fur trade origins of the diocese of St Albert; Huculak, *History of Holy Rosary Parish*, 109–14.

26  After removal of the picture, Fr Holland insists, parish life revived; conversation, 16 September 1997. The priest would also like to commission what he termed a 'proper icon' of Riel from the commercial firm, Bridge Building Images of Vermont, which specializes in such religious items.

27  The parish possesses an icon of Kateri Tekakwitha, not yet installed, painted by Robert Lentz for Bridge Building Images; one of two choices sold by the company, whose iconographic offerings include Mohandas Gandhi and John Donne, it features a turtle (Kateri was from the Turtle clan) with an evergreen on its back and a flying eagle above (symbolizing God). On Kateri Tekakwitha herself, see Ferdinand Holböck, *New Saints and Blesseds of the Catholic Church, 1979–83*, vol. 1, trans. Michael J. Miller (San Francisco: Ignatius Press, 2001), 45–7; the popular hagiographies, Lillian Fisher, *Kateri Tekakwitha: The Lily of the Mohawks* (Boston: Pauline Books and Media, 1996), and Margaret Bunson, *Kateri Tekakwitha: Mystic of the Wilderness* (Huntingdon, IN: Our Sunday Visitor, 1992); K. Koppedrayer, 'The Making of the First Iroquois Virgin: Early Jesuit Biographies of the Blessed Kateri Tekakwitha,' *Ethnohistory* 40, no. 2 (1993): 277–306; Allan Greer, 'Colonial Saints: Gender, Race and Hagiography in New France,' *William and Mary Quarterly* 57, no. 2 (2000): 323–48; and 'Patron Saints Index: Kateri Tekakwitha' at www.catholic-forum.com/saints, which is particularly good on visual portrayals.

28  The school was run by the Sisters Faithful Companions of Jesus for Ukrainian immigrant girls working in the city. When the Ukrainian Sisters Servants of Mary Immaculate arrived in Edmonton in 1902, they initially lived in the attic of old St Joachim's, located just west of the present building.

29  See Gaston Carrière, *Dictionnaire biographique des Oblats de Marie-Immaculée au Canada*, vol. 2 (Ottawa: Éditions de l'Université d'Ottawa, 1977), 116–7 (Emile Grouard), 288–9 (Hippolyte Leduc), 309 (Alphonse Lemarchand).

30  See Mary Pauline Fitts, Grey Nuns of the Sacred Heart (GNSH), *Hands to the Needy: Blessed Marguerite d'Youville, Apostle to the Poor* (Yardley, PA: Grey Nuns of the Sacred Heart, 2000); Thérèse Castonguay, *A Leap in Faith: The Grey Nun Ministries in Western and Northern Canada*, vol. 1 (Edmonton: Grey Nuns of Alberta, 1999), esp. 179–216; and Carrière, *Dictionnaire biographique des Oblats de Marie-Immaculée au Canada*, vol. 2, 106–7 (Vital-Justin Grandin), 219–21 (Albert Lacombe).

31  This sense of identity is the underlying assumption of Gerhard Ens, *From Homeland to Hinterland: The Changing Worlds of the Red River Metis in the Nineteenth Century* (Toronto: University of Toronto Press, 1996).

32  The others depict the story of the loaves and fishes (in which Christ wears a ground-length eagle headdress) and the fishermen casting their nets on the other side from a West Coast canoe; Meek's objection to women in the chapel comes from Fr Holland. The Stations of the Cross, painted in 1992, are by Meek, although he and Barbara Marquis shared the work.

33  The dedication on a stained-glass window at nearby Christ Church Anglican, also a pioneer parish, 'in grateful recognition of the service and devotion of the women of this parish since its founding,' is similarly generic and non-commital.

34  Thanks to Anna Könye for translating the Hungarian text. A second monument outside the St Emeric complex is a bronze relief of Cardinal Mindzenty, 'The Spiritual Leader of Hungary.'

35  See also Carrière, *Dictionnaire biographique des Oblats de Marie-Immaculée au Canada*, 2: 209–10.

36  The monument was designed by Mr Strzelski and Mrs Mirska did the mosaics (Huculak, *History of Holy Rosary Parish*, 35).

37  They are identified in Kupranets, *Katedra sv. Iosafata v. Edmontoni*, 184–5.

# PART 6

# *History and Memory*

# Camp Naivelt and the Daughters of the Jewish Left

ESTER REITER

## Introduction

On 6 August 2000, Camp Naivelt (New World), located in El Dorado Park on the outskirts of Brampton, Ontario, celebrated its seventy-fifth anniversary. The children's camp, Kinderland (Children's Land), closed its doors in 1962, but Naivelt, the sister community where the adults had cottages, remains. With the memory fresh in my mind of my own Camp Kinderland reunion in New York in May 1999, I participated in the planning for this Canadian event. I attended Camp Kinderland in Poughkeepsie, New York, from 1949 to 1956 at the height of the Cold War. Although political events in the United States, such as the execution of Ethel and Julius Rosenberg, who were convicted as Communist spies, were deeply felt in the Canadian Jewish left, such events were experienced differently at the Ontario Camp Kinderland and Camp Naivelt, as anti-Communist fervour was less pronounced in Canada than in the United States. I was twelve when the Rosenbergs were executed in 1953 and my friends whose parents were Communists were terrified that their parents would be taken away from them, just as the Rosenbergs had been taken from their two young boys. Indeed, fellow American campers told stories of being followed by the FBI and hounded to reveal where their parents were hiding.[1]

The camps in New York State, Ontario, and Quebec were pieces of a mosaic. They were part of a wider network of political and cultural organizations that provided credit, health care, and cemetery plots.[2] This network included clubs where members met for political and cultural activities, such as a chorus, a mandolin orchestra, a Yiddish *shule* (school) where the children were taught the language and culture, a dance troupe, and sports leagues. The motto for the camps in the early years was '*fun kemp tsu shule, fun shule tsu kemp*' (from camp to school, from school to camp). The '*zumer heym*' (summer home) was a continuation and extension of the political, cultural, and educational activities that went on all winter long in the city. Camp was a place where children played and their parents relaxed in a community where Yiddishkait, radical politics, socialist values and visions mixed comfortably with the pleasures of being in the country. Naivelt was a working-class camp created by workers, and it taught socialist values to the next generation.

This paper will consider the role of women of the *Yiddishe Arbeiter Froyen Farein* (Jewish Women's Labour League) in the establishment and maintenance of this left-wing Jewish camp, and the children's summer experience at it. Most of the literature on cottages and camping focuses on a more affluent group that could afford the luxury of a summer home or of sending their children away for the summer. Naivelt was designed by and for people with very little money, and it was organized by women. Although the leadership after its inception reverted to the men, women are credited with maintaining the community. For the children who attended the camp, those summers were a powerful experience, and a sense of identity was forged that remained central over the years. Sherri Bergman, a camper from the late 1950s to the early 1970s, described Camp Naivelt/Camp Kinderland as 'my home, my heart, my security. With all the times that I moved and all the places I moved to, Camp was always there. It was my grounding place.'[3]

## Seeing Red: A Gendered Glimpse

The children's camp, first located at Long Branch, Ontario, on the outskirts of Toronto, was organized in 1925 by a group of progressive Jewish women from the *Yiddishe Arbeiter Froyen Farein*. The activities of these socialist women have been for the most part ignored, or treated as an 'embarrassment' in many books on the history of the Jews in Canada. Like many of my parents' generation who arrived in the new world in the early twentieth century, the experiences of bloody pogroms in Eastern Europe and the contemptuous treatment meted out to 'greenhorns' in the new world, taught these women that to be a Jew with dignity and with hope meant also to be a socialist and a Communist. They were people who dreamed (in Yiddish) of a better world for Jews, and for all the world's downtrodden as well. Many had been radicalized in the old country in the dying days of the czarist empire. The socialists or social democrats were convinced that a '*nayer frayer velt*' – a new freer world – was not just an idle dream and so they worked hard to build this new society in their lifetime. Breaking away from what they experienced as the confining yoke of orthodoxy, radical Jews articulated an equal role for women that flowed quite comfortably from how secular life was lived.

For many men and women who became part of this community, the lure was cultural as well as political. The left offered an environment in which one could get an education through lectures, discussions, and reading books. For those living in cramped quarters struggling to make a living, the progressive movement offered a place to learn, grow intellectually, and be treated with respect. It offered an outlook that rejected the materialist capitalist values so dominant in the new world and promised a life focused on the mind and the spirit. Becky Lapedes, one of the founders and first managers of the children's camp, said she became radicalized through the influence of her older sister who was already a radical in Russia. The sister would go to the forest near her town where speakers from the bigger cities would lecture. When the family came to Canada prior to the First World War, this sister joined the socialist *Arbeiter Ring* (Workman's Circle) and took Becky along to banquets, lectures, and picket lines. Becky enjoyed it all.

Although radical ideas took hold with young women as well as young men, a girl faced particular, gendered challenges in living the life of an intellectual and a revolutionary. Becky's family was poor in Canada, and she did not get much of a formal education because her father kept her home from school every afternoon to take care of the second-hand store while he looked for goods to buy. Her father believed 'a boy you had to send [to school] but a girl ... you don't have to worry. She'll get married, she'll make her way.'[4] When her sister died in childbirth, Becky lost contact with the socialists for a while, until she befriended a young woman named Ethel Roder, who was a kindred spirit: 'Ethel was so much like me. She didn't care about clothes. I didn't know it then, but she was mingling with the Russian Jewish intelligentsia.'[5] Becky's involvement with the left intensified in her teenage years and her political activities often led to dealings with the police. One of her friends, Lil Himmelfarb (Ilomaki), otherwise known as 'Red Lil,' had the distinction of being arrested no fewer than ten times from 1928 to 1934, when she was between the ages of sixteen and twenty-two.[6]

After the Bolshevik Revolution in 1917, the socialist ranks divided over attitudes to the Soviet Union. The revolution was particularly attractive to left-wing Jews who saw Jewish culture flourish in the Soviet Union in the early 1920s. Despite the Bolshevik opposition to Zionism or any form of nationalism, there was a deliberate attempt in the early years of the revolution to eradicate Great Russian chauvinism and grant all small nations and national minorities equality. A power struggle took place in the *Arbeiter Ring* in North America between those who supported the Bolshevik Revolution and those who remained social democrats.

In Canada, the women were the first to leave the *Arbeiter Ring* to formally create their own organization, the *Yiddishe Arbeiter Froyen Farein* – the Jewish Women's Labour League – in 1923. In 1926, the left-wing men broke away to organize the Labour League. The Jewish Women's Labour League had a vision of an alternative society and of solving a practical problem – how to keep their children off the streets during the summer. They felt a responsibility to engage in social activism as women, as Jews and as Communists. People were poor, many of the women as well as the men were working, and there was nowhere to leave the children, so they decided to organize a camp. At the time, the Jewish Women's Labour League was a group of only thirty women, most of them married and with families to look after. As Becky Lapedes, the secretary manager, noted, '[I]t was very idealistic, but it certainly wasn't practical.' They rented a furnished cottage in Long Branch, Ontario, and operated the camp on supplies donated from their own homes: pots, silverware, an ice box, and whatever else was needed. All the *Farein* members committed themselves to two-week work shifts at the camp without pay. They even paid for their own food and charged from $3.50 to 4.00 a week per child according to age.[7] The cottage was filled to capacity with eleven children, but one night a man showed up with his five children because his wife was giving birth to another baby. 'We took care of them somehow,' Becky recalled.[8]

After the first year, an appeal went out to the left-wing Jewish community describing the camp. The women radicals presented their project as 'women's work' but with the goal of contributing to social transformation. They did not see the charity offered by some of the institutions an appropriate alternative for what they wanted for their children. Their article, published in the Yiddish newspaper *Der Kamf* (*The Struggle*), graphically described why the women undertook such a difficult task; it also provided a taste of the polemical and militant language characteristic of the pro-Bolshevik left at this time:

> With little experience and even less financial resources or, to put it more accurately, completely without any means, we, the Jewish Woman's Labour League have undertaken the project of a summer camp. No one believed that it was possible, neither our foes, nor our friends who called us dreamers of beautiful fantasies. They didn't believe we could survive for more than one week, and how could we survive without a cent in the treasury and with expenses of $100 a week? We faced unheard-of obstacles, but our courage kept us moving ahead. We borrowed from one place, and paid in the second, and despite the obstacles, we managed to pull through the enormous difficulties of those first few weeks.
>
> And now, with the season over, we can say with full understanding, that we managed to carry this undertaking through successfully. The camp served 50 children over the summer, ages ranging from 3 to 15. All of them were happy and satisfied. They had all the conveniences – food, games, etc. We also organized a reading circle, concerts, lectures, and other events from the workers' children's world. And so the children were never bored, and also learned something.
>
> Next summer, we hope to expand this undertaking. If possible, we would like to

have our own place, if our sympathizers respond to our appeal. We are especially appealing to all working women with the call to join us in our labour league; the larger our organization, the more successful our work will be. We will explore all avenues in order to create a summer home for workers' children so that they don't have to go to the rich charity institutions who with one hand take the skin from our bodies, and with the other throw us a bone and humiliate. But we, class conscious working women, must not and will not take their charity offerings, we throw them back: we will not kiss the whip that lashes us; we will not send our children to them, where they will be trained to be faithful and obedient slaves of capitalism and exploitation. We must raise our children in a free atmosphere. They must know who are their friends and who are their foes. Creating a summer home for children must be the work of the women workers.[9]

In 1926, the women expanded the camp. They rented a farm in Rouge Hills north of Toronto that had a stream running through it and bought tents and beds; but the farmhouse was too small and because they charged so little, they ended up with a deficit. They solved this problem by organizing an out door banquet and making an appeal for funds to pay off the deficit. As happened often, they also looked to New York for expertise in running a camp. The entire camp continued to run on the volunteer labour of the women who did what needed to be done, including cooking outdoors on cookers heated with coal oil; but they faced many challenges. For instance, there were no garbage services so the men would bring a clean garbage container when they came to help out on weekends, and take away the full one when they left. There was no running water and no electricity; a small house served as the office and the dining room. The children lived in tents put up in a circle around the field and went down to the river to wash. The women were able to hire a handyman to do the heavy work, which included carrying water from the spring up the hill. Becky Lapedes recalled, 'Ethel Temkin and I were papering the kitchen. How we did it I'll never know because I'm not very handy, but we did it. So I was supposed to be the manager. So how am I going to tell somebody to go and clean the toilets? So I did it myself. I used to clean them twice a week with soda. I cleaned the walls, the toilet, the floor.'[10] One wonders if the contradictions between being a Communist and ordering someone else to clean the toilets would have even been noticed if there had been a man in charge. Given the traditional division of labour in the home, one suspects not, as Communist men, like most other men, had wives who 'naturally' cooked and cleaned for them.

Alongside the difficulties, the experience of running a camp presented new opportunities for Becky Lapedes and her friend Ethel Temkin, such as learning to hitchhike. If they ran short of anything, the women would have to go into town to get needed supplies; but there was no car and no driver during the week. The town was about three miles away and while Becky and Ethel were walking, cars would stop and offer them a lift. Becky describes one incident when she and Ethel were hitchhiking. A car came along and stopped for them, but there were two men in it and the women usually avoided getting into a car with more than one man. However, there had been few cars on the road because it was under construction. In Becky's words: 'I look at Ethel and Ethel looks at me. The way we were dressed. We had a suit, a man's suit with a tie with a cap and I say, "we have to go. We can't help it." We got into the car and the man says, "I bet you two girls are Bolsheviks. I bet you have your party cards in your rucksacks." I was always the spokesman. I said, "What of it? This is a free country, what if I do have my party card."' The driver started telling them about the divide between rich and poor, and how 20 percent live at the expense of 80 percent of the people, and how the rich build the nicest schools which most children can't attend. It turned out one of the men was a labour lawyer.[11] Perhaps Becky and Ethel's unconventional dress (knickers and caps) and their unconventional activity (hitchhiking) marked them as political radicals. If a woman had the courage to break the gendered rules of proper womanly behaviour, it might be expected that she also held a strong ideological opposition to all of bourgeois society.

The political activism of women such as Becky and Ethel forces one to reconsider how we define feminism. These women would have reacted to the term *feminist* as an insult, because to them feminism meant formal bourgeois equality, rather than the total transformation of society that they sought. As we have seen, however, the activities of some of these women involved a personal freedom quite uncommon at the time. We often make analytical distinctions between 'class' and 'gender,' but in real life these categories cannot be treated separately. Jewish women from this community for the most part accepted a notion of a class-conscious worker that appeared to be gender-neutral, but in effect was modelled on the lives of men. As class-conscious women, they accepted as natural their responsibilities as wives and mothers, yet because of their political beliefs and their personal histories in Eastern Europe they engaged in practices that could extend the boundaries of gender considerably.

In 1928, after the fourth year of the camp, the women decided to ask the male-run Labour League to take over because it had become simply too much of an undertaking. Despite their fears of being reduced to a 'women's auxiliary,' they felt they had no alternative because the Labour League was larger and had more resources.[12] The fourth season was conducted as a co-operative effort of the *Farein* and the Labour League but after that the women gave over full control of the camp to the Labour League. In photographs of the early leadership of the Labour League, Becky Lapedes, as secretary, stands out as the only woman. Nevertheless, the involvement of the women continued. Becky said, 'We helped them just like they helped us.'[13]

## Memories of Early Campers

The adult community Camp Naivelt came to be known as the 'Roite Kolonia,' the Red Colony. The children's camp, Kindervelt (called Kinderland after 1936), flourished from the late 1920s until the l950s. The memories of four of the early campers – Bessie Grossman, Lil Robinson, Shirley Fistell, and Al Soren – include experiences that were unique to a left-wing camp. All four were the Canadian-born children of immigrant parents who came to Canada already radicalized, and as such, Yiddish was their *mame loshn* (mother tongue). Although Yiddish was spoken in the camp, and skits and performances often were in Yiddish, it's the camp songs in English that are remembered best. The politics and the serious intentions of the adults to raise children who would understand class struggle were woven into the play of children just being children. Sometimes the political was the play and the play was political.

Lil Robinson recalled the neighbouring upper-crust camp for Jewish children called Winnibago. Camp Naivelt children used to walk by that camp on hikes, red flags flying, deliberately bursting into revolutionary songs, voices raised as loud as possible as they passed by. The *Arbeiter Ring* camp was also nearby and so the two camps had volleyball games together. Lil recalled, 'One time the group who went to cheer on the team sang, in Yiddish, "*a Grus tzu Yungvelt* (Greetings to Youth World). We should be united forever against all foes of the workers." Their adults had apoplexy. They were social democrats. What do you want?'[14]

In the 1920s, most of the camp counsellors were *shule* (school) teachers during the winter. Summer camp was a twenty-four-hour opportunity to teach socialist principles in Yiddish in the context of a 'fresh air'country camping experience: '*fun kemp in shul, fun shul in kemp*' (from camp in school, from school in camp). Along with happy memories of campfires stories, and songs such as 'That Harlem Goat Was Feeling Fine,' campers remember that political events were quite central, and these had no borders. All four of the early campers recalled Sacco and Vanzetti, the two Italian anarchists who were executed in Boston for a murder they didn't commit. When Sacco and Vanzetti were killed in August 1927, it was like a day of mourning in the camp.[15] Lil Robinson recalled, 'We were so sad. We all felt these things very, very keenly.'[16] The children would prepare plays and skits with their counsellors, and that too was a route to a political education. Shirley Fistell recalled a skit that the children put on about the Scottsboro boys in the early 1930s, a case about eight young black men accused of rape. After a worldwide campaign and several trials, four of the boys were freed, but the others languished in prison for many years. Shirley was supposed to play one of the prostitutes who had made the accusation of rape but who later recanted her story saying she was lying. Depicting a prostitute was not considered appropriate for a young girl, so she was called a 'flapper' in the skit. Lil recalled the excitement when some of the marchers from the On to Ottawa Trek – the march to publicize the plight of the unemployed – stayed at the camp during 1935, its last year at Rouge Hills. 'I remember my mother helped in serving food. I remember seeing them in their shirts and their caps,' she said.[17]

The children were taught to be socialist Jewish children, but for the four campers who spent so much of their life in the movement, this was such a given that it hardly entered into the conversation as a distinct subject when they reminisced about their experiences. It became an integral part of the overall camping experience. The parents were 'progressive' Jews and the parameters of the children's world were their parents' politics. The political lessons came from the adult world, but the children made them their own, along with the energy and mischief and pointlessness of just playing and being who they were as children.

**El Dorado Park**

When the ten-year lease for the Rouge Hills site expired, the Labour League found a hundred acres in what had been an amusement park owned by the Canadian National Railways, just outside of Brampton and bordering the Credit River. A sign at the gate read 'no Jews or dogs allowed,' and so a left-wing Ukrainian friend handled the purchase. Again the camp leaders called upon the Jewish community to contribute financially, although in 1935 most were still quite poor. To raise money for the purchase, people bought shares in the camp for $5 each. Through lots of hard work and the generous sharing of time and money, Camp Naivelt was built. The camp officially opened on 28 June 1936. The children's Camp Kindervelt became Camp Kinderland after 1936 when it moved to its new location. When the United Jewish People's Order emerged from the Labour League in 1940, Naivelt and Kinderland became part of this new, larger organization.

In the early years of Camp Kinderland, the children slept together in tents. Some of the women worked as 'Camp Mothers' and lived in family tents or cottages while their children attended the camp. A camp director was hired for Kinderland and eventually the 'Ritz' – communal showers, a dining room, and a 'hospital' cabin for the nurse and campers who became sick – was built. By the late 1940s, the tents were replaced by twelve cabins. At its peak, in the 1940s and 1950s, Camp Kinderland served more than three hundred children each summer. The parents could rent a tiny little shack on King's Row, stay in their own cottages if they could afford it, or pitch a tent so that they too could enjoy the surroundings and visit with their children. If they couldn't afford to rent a cottage and didn't have a tent, they could always sleep on the floor of the dance hall.

For the children of working-class immigrants, being in such beautiful surroundings provided cherished memories. Many Jewish immigrants were confined to the physical ugliness of the city in crowded, unpleasant living quarters and unhealthy, cramped workplaces. Although few missed the bitter poverty of the old country, some could still remember the beauty of the forests and fields they left behind and they felt the loss. For these immigrants and their children, the beauty of the countryside liberated them from the oppressive and exploitative conditions in which they lived and under which they worked.

Rita Bergman, recalling her first year in Naivelt in 1936 when she was eleven years old, was delighted with her first view of the hills and the river and remembered the wonderful feeling it gave her. 'I absolutely loved camp,' she said.[18] When Rita was a teenager and started working, her parents bought a cottage at the camp. The cottage was actually a garage bought at a department store that they put up under a big tree on the second hill. Her father then finished the inside and made a kitchen and a bedroom. The family of four – including her mother, father, and sister Honey – all slept in two three-quarter beds in the bedroom. Rita recalls bringing her friends out to the cottage when she was fifteen. 'Imagine bringing friends to sleep in this little cottage! I brought a friend, but another one showed up without a place to sleep so that night, four of us slept in that three-quarter bed – Honey, myself, and my two girlfriends.'[19] Rita and her dad would come out by train for the weekends, while her mother, who did not work for pay, remained in the camp all week with her younger sister.

A number of young people met their future partners at the camp. Mollie Myers, one of the oldest cottage owners still to be found at Naivelt during the summer, described how she met her Hymie. Mollie, who remains a committed Communist, reveals how serious political activities did not preclude the courtship games of young men and women. Born in the Ukraine, Mollie immigrated to Winnipeg when she was sixteen where she became a member of the 'Kultur Centre' of the Labour Temple. When she arrived in Toronto in 1939, she immediately visited the office of the Labour League and got a job as a waitress at Camp Naivelt. One day, a group of men arrived and asked to be served. It was past the lunch hour, but Mrs Shprager, the cook, reluctantly agreed to get food ready. The ringleader of the group ordered *kratz borscht*, and Mollie did not know what that was and so went to the kitchen to ask. The staff burst out laughing, and the cook explained that it is a dish marinated in the '*milch* of a herring' and that she was to tell them it was not on the menu. Mollie became angry and refused to continue serving the men, but Mrs Shprager explained that these men were 'unattached' and were trying to impress her, so she should ignore them. Mollie eventually married the leader of the gang, Hymie, and they pitched their own tent in Camp Naivelt. Mollie has a long history at Naivelt. 'In that cottage we raised two children and three grandchildren. I still spend the summers there with wonderful memories of lasting friendships, political discussions, joys, sorrows, and I think of my grandchildren enjoying the beautiful surroundings.'[20]

Some of the fond memories are tempered with a realization that for the mothers, the beauty of the country was coupled with having to deal with the primitive conditions. Sandy (Fine) Traub's parents bought their cottage in 1950. They packed up their daughters, rented a U-Haul, and asked some relatives to take the family out to camp. Sandy remembers that her sister, Marsha, was only a few months old. Naivelt was new and exciting for Sandy: 'I didn't know anyone who had a summer cottage.' For her mother, it was not quite the same. When Helen Fine saw the cottage, she cried. It was dark inside, and there was no running water, just a tank outside the cottage that they filled every day with cold water from a tap near the cottage. They were one of the lucky families, since the outhouse was attached to the back of the cottage. The ice man from Brampton delivered ice for the ice box, the Kosher butcher bought meat from the city, a Jewish bakery and a milk truck provided the other basic food requirements. Sandy Fine remembers that her father worked in the city during the week and came to camp on the weekends, like many other men, although sometimes he would also get a lift to come on Wednesdays. Sandy loved it, but of course didn't realize how much work her mother had to do. Helen, however, learned to love it as well: 'It was hard but we were all happy. We were a whole community. People that we know used to sing and we'd have fires, big fires, a lot.' Helen recalled that it was even more crowded next door – one small cottage that housed two families, one with five children and the other with two children. 'People *wanted* to come out here,' she said, 'and they didn't mind the kind of circumstances, only to be out here. Everybody was anxious to come out here!'[21]

### Gender and Power

After the male-run Labour League took over Naivelt and Kindervelt in 1929, women remained responsible for the day-to-day operations of the camp. One of the contradictions in describing political perspectives is the role these camp women played as formal decision-makers within both Naivelt and the United Jewish People's Order (UJPO) power structure. A woman like Mollie Myers, for example, was politically active, outspoken, and an unflagging peace activist, even into her nineties. She would never accept a view of herself as subservient or traditional or limited in the decision-making process because of her gender. Mary Winer, on the other hand, saw things quite differently. Mary was quite clear about who wielded power in the UJPO and who did the work of running the camp. According to Mary, the women not only were the first to organize the camp, but they continued to run everything. When asked about who was on the camp executive, she replied, 'The Order [United Jewish People's Order] was the men, because they were the bosses … they collected the money … but women did the work.'

Mary Winer was born in Lodz, Poland, and arrived in Montreal in 1920 at the age of seventeen. She worked in the camp canteen for many years from the 1930s on so that her children could attend the camp. Interviewed in 1994, Mary expressed her reactions to the difficult red-baiting years, and her continuing commitment to political activity. She recalled the 'big propaganda' against the camp. Like many of her generation, her reaction to the bitterness of red baiting, and the mistaken assumption that everyone in the camp was a card-carrying Communist was to deny that there was any Communist connection at all. She said, 'In the papers, in the Jewish papers, in the English paper – 'it's a bunch of Communists' – we did a good thing for the kids and they called us Communists.'[22] She recalled a headline in the Jewish paper that said something like, 'In the Communist Camp They Run Around Naked!' Mary said, 'You know why? We [the women] started to wear shorts.' In an era of widespread distrust of left-wing thinkers, unconventional behaviour was considered evidence of 'subversive' political views.

Mary, like Mollie, was free to be as active as she liked and has a long record to prove it. Her husband looked after the children while she did strike support work or attended demonstrations. As an elderly woman, she described one of her last political actions: 'I marched [for peace] here, in Toronto. Four generations we marched. A reporter came over to me and asked me "Oh, you're four generations marching. Since when are you marching?" "Since I understood that I am against war." And that's what they wrote in the paper and it was on the television too. I went to all demonstrations. All of them. And if I could I would go now too.' For this older generation, gender equality was defined in a very public way. When it came to the organization of the UJPO, the leadership was male. But the women's political involvement is evidence that they were never subservient to the men. A division of labour that left them in charge at home or responsible for the camp's day-to-day maintenance did not signify to them their oppression as women, and this was not their perception of themselves.

Like the first group of campers in the 1920s, the children who grew up in Kinderland in later years recalled memories that linked the personal with the political. Camp was the place to take the big steps through adolescence – the first secret kiss, dances at the Rec Hall, and summer romances that evaporated instantly after Labour Day. Later, when these young women had to work for pay, the camp was the place to bring a new city boyfriend and experience it anew through his eyes. Many of the activities had a political twist to them as well. The game 'Steal the Flag' was called CLDL after the Canadian Labour Defence League, which defended worker rights. Later in the 1930s, the camp held ceremonies honouring those who went off to fight in the Spanish Civil War in the Mackenzie-Papineau Battalion. During the Second World War, the children played at being partisans in the woods. Each Sunday, the children dressed in white for 'Sunday Salutes,' and greeted visiting dignitaries. In the early 1940s, they included the Soviet-Jewish intellectuals, actor Shloime Mikhoels and poet Itzik Feffer, who were later murdered by Stalin when he turned against the Jews in a rampage of Soviet anti-Semitism in the 1950s. And living in a socialist community in Kinderland was translated into 'sharing.' After the parents' visiting day, the counsellors would confiscate all the food – salamis, chocolate bars, etc. – to be shared equally among all the children.

Many of the activities continued to be carried on in Yiddish, the language a number of the children spoke at home. They did recitations, created plays and spectacles, and sang Yiddish songs, including the camp's theme song. Most campers recall the memorable Saturday night concerts. For instance, Ben Shek vividly recalls one concert where they dramatized the true story of an orphan and how he, along with his two brothers, survived the war in Belgium. The Chojnacki brothers actually became campers at Naivelt when they arrived in Canada.[23]

A number of factors – the red baiting of the 1950s, the disillusionment with Communism following the revelations of what had happened to Jews in the Stalin period, the emergence of a more affluent generation that wanted a different kind of camping experience – all contributed to some difficult years for Naivelt. The overnight camp closed in 1962 and the day camp in 1971. Faced with growing debt, the camp committee sold off the southern portion of the property, which became a conservation area, Eldorado Park. The town of Brampton acquired the pool, dance hall, and swings. Many felt pessimistic about the continued survival of the camp as the cottagers aged, and some of the new people did not participate in the community. The difficulties that the camp still faces are not unconnected to the success of the founders, the immigrant generation. Their political beliefs and sympathies were coupled with personal efforts to provide the 'best' for their children.

I am part of that next generation, and the contradictions are glaring. My friends and I are the first generation to be born in the New World, and we were to live different lives than those of our mothers. We were taught to love Yiddishkait, and to care about social justice, but this did not extend into the kitchen where we were not expected to burden ourselves, girls included. Our mothers did all the work. Above all, we were to devote ourselves to making up for the deprivations that they had suffered as children. We were to play the piano, take dancing lessons, learn Yiddish in left-wing secular Jewish schools, and get a good education. For a girl, this meant getting a university degree in order to become a teacher or social worker and marry a doctor or a lawyer – a dentist would do, and

From a Maiseh for the New World: little girls playing at Camp Naivelt, 1992.

possibly an accountant. We were to live at home until we got married, work at our professions as our husbands became established, and then devote ourselves to wifehood and motherhood when the children came along. The sacrifices and hard work of our mothers would then be made worthwhile by the kind of lives we, the daughters, would lead.[24]

Naivelt did survive. It remains rustic, green, and even more wooded than when it was first purchased, even though it is now surrounded by the city of Brampton. In recent years the camp has been 'discovered' by a new generation of people with young families who have come to love the connection with a Yiddishkait with which they can identify, and to respect the history in the camp. The concerns with social justice, equality, and antiracism remain central in a community where children are free to explore, and everyone can laugh, cry, think, argue and enjoy themselves. For many, it is still 'unzer zumer heym.' The seventy-fifth anniversary souvenir book included a contribution by nine-year-old Amil Bain-Shaul. Amil's mother is from Trinidad and Tobago, and his father is a Jewish trade union activist. Amil describes how he likes to swim, play with friends, and hike with his dad. He also enjoys the campfires at night. Amil embodies what has been best about Naivelt for four generations: 'I like to learn about Jewish culture, like Jewish dances and songs. I can learn about my friends' cultures at Camp Naivelt. I can teach my friends about Yiddish culture and who I am.'

**Conclusion**

There is much to be learned about the wider cultural, recreational, and literary dimensions of the lives of Canadian Jewish women on the left. This essay represents a preliminary contribution towards writing that history, as well as a step towards writing a history of childhood and rustic camp culture on the left by centring on the collective memories of Camp Naivelt female founders and child campers. The collection of Jewish women who established Camp Naivelt and Camp Kinderland were nurturing both ethnic and political loyalties amongst their children, while resisting a class and ethnically based paternalism that would have seen their children's lives and values shaped by Anglo-Saxon charitable institutions. Their gender roles within their homes and in relation to the men in their organizations were shaped by societal norms for the era; they performed all the 'housekeeping' labour for their families and also in the upkeep of the camp. As often occurs in the development of organizations and institutions, men took over the formal leadership and power structures once the camp was established and successful. Yet for daughters of the Jewish left, gender and politics were not easily separated. Their deep commitment to certain leftist political ideals prompted them to act in ways unconventional for other women, and caused them to cross gender boundaries in their class-conscious activism, even if the social equality they called for in the workplace did not necessarily extend into their own homes. Camp Naivelt was thus a setting in which the fluid interaction of gender, ethnicity, and class shaped a whole generation of Jewish children, girls and boys.

NOTES

1 At Kinderland's seventy-fifth reunion in 1990, I met the fellow who told me about this. He and his younger sister never told their mother about what was happening to them, because they felt their mother was upset enough about her husband and they didn't want to worry her.

2 Cemetery plots were a concern in a period when mortality rates, particularly for the

poor, were high, and a proper burial was important. Many *landsmanschaften* (societies derived from the same town or city) collectively organized burial plots.

3  Sherri Bergman, 'My Home, My Heart,' in *Unzer Zumer Haim* (Toronto: United Jewish People's Order, 2000).

4  Cheryl Tallan, the daughter of Becky Lapedes and her second husband, Sam, recorded her mother in a series of interviews in 1984. The interviews are not only a priceless family memento of an extraordinary woman, but also provide insight into women of her era. One must be careful, however, to note that Becky Lapedes was an unusually capable woman who made her place among the men from sheer strength of character and intelligence. She was much admired and loved. Becky died in 1993.

5  Ibid.

6  Ester Reiter, 'My Neighbour, Red Lil,' *Outlook* (August 1996).

7  Becky Lapedes, 'A Camp Is Born,' *Souvenir Book for the 20th Jubilee of the Camps in Brampton, 1956.*

8  Cheryl Tallan's interview with her mother Becky Lapedes, 1984.

9  The Press Committee, 'Report from the Workers' Children's Camp in Toronto,' *Der Kampf.* Ruth Frager brought this article to my attention and Lil (Himmelfarb) Ilomaki assisted in the translation.

10  Cheryl Tallan's interview with her mother Becky Lapedes, 1984.

11  Ibid.

12  Ibid.

13  Ibid.

14  The hostility between the *Arbeiter Ring* and those who left to form the Labour League was enormous. In the United States, I recall the children from the *Arbeiter Ring* camp calling out to us, 'Commies, go back to Russia,' while we responded with the equally uncivil, 'Fascists.' Interview by the author with Lil Robinson, Spring 2000.

15  Interview by the author with Al Soren, Spring 2000.

16  Interview by the author with Lil Robinson, Spring 2000.

17  The On-to-Ottawa Trek was a march of the unemployed to speak to Premier Bennett about the terrible conditions and slave wages in the work camps for the unemployed. It began in Vancouver, and when the RCMP forcibly halted the march in Regina, the Workers Unity League in Toronto decided to organize a march to Ottawa to complete the trek.

18  Interview by Michelle Cohen with Rita Bergman, August 1994.

19  Ibid.

20  Mollie Myers, *Unzer Zumer Haim* (Toronto: United Jewish People's Order, 2000).

21  Interview by Michelle Cohen with Helen and Izzy Fine, August 1994.

22  In Morris Biderman's book, *A life on the Jewish Left: An Immigrant's Experience* (Toronto: Onward Publishing, 2000), he estimates that perhaps only 5 per cent of the people in the UJPO were actually party members, although the leadership was Com-

munist. The camp attracted an even broader group of people. Biderman, as former president, left the Order in 1959 to form a new organization, the New Jewish Fraternal Order.

23  The Chojnacki brothers were not the only war orphans at the camp. I met one other child survivor who describes the camp, and what that meant to him.

24  I am not making generalizations about all the daughters in the left. Families come in all varieties. However, I know that my experience is not unique.

# Experience and Identity: Black Immigrant Nurses to Canada, 1950–1980

KAREN FLYNN

## Introduction

Scholarship on Caribbean migration has dealt primarily with the economic factors that precipitated migration. A common argument is that conditions of economic uncertainty in the Caribbean region in the post–Second World War era prompted people to migrate in search of a better life. For those able and willing to move, immigration served as a means to economic and social mobility.[1] Studies on contemporary migration to Canada focus on how the Canadian state encourages migration when there is a demand for labour and on how immigrants are funnelled into menial and unskilled work. Included in these analyses is an examination of the racialization of labour markets with emphasis on where immigrants are incorporated within the political economy.[2] Studies of Caribbean domestic workers have shown how the state maintained racial *and* gender inequality.[3] Scholars such as Agnes Calliste have explored how 'professional' women, such as nurses, need to be included in our discussions of the immigration process. Her research on the role of the state bureaucracy in influencing the subordination of Caribbean nurses provides an initial framework for thinking about a professional group of female migrants that has largely been ignored in scholarship on immigration. Thus, Calliste provides an invaluable analysis of the state's racist, sexist and classist exclusionary policies used to curtail the migration of Caribbean nurses.

Using oral interviews, this paper seeks to move beyond a preoccupation with immigration polices and labour recruitment to examine how Caribbean immigrant nurses explained, interpreted, and understood their experiences. I will focus on how Caribbean nurses' lives were structured by a number of factors: their workplace, the hospital; the role of their professional colleagues in frustrating the migration process; and racism in both nursing and broader society. The goal of this paper is to break down the image of black migrant nurses as a homogenous category, by focusing on a group of middle-class, black nurses across age, time of migration, experience, skills and location of training.[4] In doing so, I consider how race, nation, gender, and professionalism worked together to shape the interpretations black immigrant nurses placed on their experiences.

Oral history provides a useful way to recover silenced voices and has long been a tool used by feminist social scientists to place in the historical records those who have been marginalized. Despite its centrality in feminist history, oral history as a methodology needs to be interrogated especially in relation to memory: what and how people remember as well as the context in which memories emerge. Furthermore, questions about interpretation and explanation are considerations to be addressed when using oral history. While paying attention to the deficiencies in oral history, Franca Iacovetta reminds us that in acknowledging such limitations, it 'hardly justifies dismissing [oral history], anymore than the fragmented and biased character of preserved written records should prompt us to abandon the archives.'[5] Thus, I use oral history critically, while being mindful of the importance of language, the cultural and ideological influences that shape the nurses' recollections, and issues surrounding subjectivity.

## Caribbean Nurses and Immigration Officials

Following the Second World War, improved state funding for health services combined with the growth of new areas of work for women, led to an acute nursing shortage. Attempts to increase nursing enrollment through direct recruitment of young women, particularly from rural areas, to reduce the turnover rate, to entice unemployed nurses to re-enter the workforce, and to increase immigration (and reduce emigration) were the key strategies employed to alleviate the nursing shortage. White nurses primarily from Britain, and to a lesser extent, Greece, Germany and Scandinavia, were encouraged to find employment in Canada. There was such a dire need for nurses that immigration officials and hospital representatives travelled to various countries on recruitment schemes to convince trained nurses of the benefits of working in Canada.

Despite this nursing shortage, government policies ensured that immigration from the Caribbean was negligible. The 1952 Immigration Act, for example, allowed the minister of immigration 'wide-sweeping discretion to prohibit or limit the admission of people on the basis of ethnicity, nationality, geographic origin, peculiarity of customs, unsuitability of climate or inability to become assimilated.'[6] Despite the fact that with this Act, the category 'race,' was changed to ethnicity,[7] the goal of the policy was to ensure that Canada maintained its British character. Which meant that with respect to Caribbean migration, the federal Cabinet decided that it would admit an insignificant number of Caribbean migrants of '"exceptional merit," on humanitarian grounds with government discretion.'[8] Included in this group of Caribbean migrants of 'exceptional merit' were professional and skilled workers such as nurses.[9] In 1944, the Canadian Nurses Association (CNA) passed a resolution that 'reaffirmed its policy to support the principle that there be no discrimination in the selection of students for enrollment into the schools of nursing.'[10] The CNA also assured immigration officials that no provincial registered nursing associations would reject registration of Caribbean nurses.[11]

In spite of the CNA's assurance, immigration officials frequently blocked the migration of Caribbean nurses. The case of Beatrice Adassa Massop is one illustration of how immigration officials used their discretionary powers. The Registered Nursing Association of Ontario (RNAO) had already approved Massop's qualifications and she had secured employment at Mt Sinai Hospital, but Massop was denied entry by immigration officials.[12] It took fourteen months before Massop, with the assistance of Canadian activist Donald Moore and the Negro Citizenship Association, to convince immigration officials that she was indeed 'worthy' of immigrating to Canada.[13] Massop, upon appeal, was granted entry into Canada and she immigrated in December 1953. Although none of the nurses in this study recalled difficulties with immigration officials, Massop's experience is not unique. Other Caribbean immigrant nurses also secured employment as well as their Canadian registration but were refused entry by the state, at times without any apparent rationale.

The few black nurses that entered Canada prior to 1962 did so because of demands by hospital administrators, lobby efforts by black activists, and new antidiscrimination protocols adopted by the Canadian nursing elite. These various organizations played a role in forcing the state to rethink its position on the immigration of Caribbean nurses. This did not mean, however, that Canada readily opened its gates to Third World immigrants; there were restrictions placed on the number of black people and nurses who could migrate to Canada. At the same time, the professional status and the demand for this labour pool placed black nurses in a more 'desirable' position vis-à-vis the state than other Caribbean workers.

### Caribbean Nurses and Nursing Authorities

The reasons that prompted Caribbean nurses to migrate to Canada varied as much as the nurses themselves. Canadian hospital personnel in Britain on a recruitment drive recruited two of the nurses who made this decision because, according to one of the nurses, 'it seemed like the right thing to do.' While Caribbean regions were experiencing high unemployment, the majority of nurses in this study made no reference to the lack of job opportunities in the Caribbean as the impetus behind their decision to migrate. Inez Mackenzie immigrated to Canada from Jamaica in 1960 because her partner, who was attending school in Canada, encouraged Mackenzie to join him in Canada. According to Mackenzie, 'things were serious between us' to the point that they were discussing marriage. While her partner pursued his studies at Ryerson Polytechnic Institute in Toronto, she found employment at the Oshawa General Hospital. Eventually they married. Nurses who were single and had no family responsibilities sometimes viewed migration as a form of adventure. Monica Mitchell was working at the University Hospital in Kingston, Jamaica when her roommate approached her one day and said, 'Monica, we have to start to travel. I just went to the Canadian High Commission, and I've gotten us the applications.' Mitchell thought it was a great idea, filled out the forms, and six months later, they immigrated to Canada. According to Mitchell, 'the world was our oyster and we were having a great time.' While a few recalled hearing of the nursing shortage and did migrate because of the wage opportunities, other nurses were encouraged to immigrate because they had family members who were already established in Canada. In the case of Caribbean nurses interviewed for this study, economic uncertainty did not determine their decision to migrate nor was migration driven by the single goal of earning a better salary.

Regardless of the nurses' own sense of agency around their migration decisions, prospective migrants had to deal with a powerful Canadian immigration bureaucracy. While Linda Carty's conclusion that 'through its immigration laws the state regulates the selection and rejection of prospective domestic workers as immigrants'[14] certainly held true for nurses as well, the latter were sometimes cast in a more positive light than domestic workers. For example, Calliste points out that Caribbean nurses were expected by government officials in Canada to act as 'ambassadors for their race' and to assist white Canadians in familiarizing themselves with blacks. Referring to the migration of Caribbean nurses, Calliste maintains that 'these workers were expected to contribute appreciably to the social, economic, or cultural life in Canada, and to help in making blacks acceptable to the Canadian population.'[15] Such attitudes on the part of some immigration officials may help explain why a disproportionate number of nurses in this study maintained that they were dealt with in a timely manner. They considered the expediency with which Immigration Canada dealt with their applications to be a direct result of Canada's nursing shortage and the fact that they were skilled, educated professionals.

By contrast, when the nurses interviewed for this study did experience difficulty it was usually with nursing organizations, especially the nurses' associations charged with adjudicating professional qualifications. Many immigrant nurses who settled in Ontario complained that the provincial nursing association and later the College of Nurses could not decipher foreign-trained qualifications. Therefore, it was the nursing bodies responsible for accreditation, as opposed to the state, which often proved pivotal in determining how Caribbean nurses were placed within nursing.

Calliste argues that Caribbean immigrant nurses were required to have nursing qualifications over and above those required of white nurses in order to be eligible for landed immigrant status. She asserts that graduate Caribbean nurses – which would include four of the nurses in this study – were required to complete a three-month obstetrics course, be eligible for registration with the registered nurses association, as well as have guaranteed employment with a hospital that was aware of their racial origin.[16] Calliste's research focused primarily on Caribbean immigrant nurses as opposed to British-trained Caribbean nurses, making it difficult to make assumptions about how their qualifications were assessed given that British trained nurses were preferred over non-European immigrants. Whatever the case, there is some discrepancy in terms of how Caribbean immigrant nurses' qualifications in this study were assessed.

The process of having their qualifications assessed placed immigrant nurses in one of four sets of experiences. First, there were registered nurses (RNs) who were graduates of a three-year program either in the Caribbean or Britain, and who met the provincial licensing standards. For example, Orphelia Bennett immigrated to Canada in 1955 from Jamaica. Bennett trained at the University of the West Indies as a general nurse. She also obtained a midwifery certificate and her qualifications were accepted without upgrading. Likewise, Vera Cudjoe trained in Britain, later returned to Trinidad, and subsequently immigrated to Canada in 1960; because she had midwifery training, she was also granted her RN status without having to upgrade or take additional courses. When June Heaven immigrated to British Columbia from Jamaica in 1967 she did not need additional courses to obtain her registration. But there were definite differences in terms of how provincial nurses associations adjudicated immigrant nurses' credentials. When, for example, Heaven went to Ontario seven months later, she had to take a three-month obstetrics course to obtain her registration. Both Mitchell and Mackenzie had to upgrade in order to obtain their registration even though, like Cudjoe and Bennett, they too had midwifery training. Some of the nurses did not take a formal obstetrics course but read the necessary materials and then wrote the exams.

The nurses in the second group who obtained their RN status upon arrival were the exception, in comparison to their other Caribbean counterparts who had to upgrade by taking additional courses and writing the RN examination. Because the British system defined obstetrical, and sometimes pediatric, training as separate qualifications not included in the regular RN stream, there were some who lacked this crucial component necessary for Canadian licensure. Practitioners who did not undertake separate midwifery or pediatric training at home had to write an exam (or complete a special course) within three to six months of their arrival in Canada; they were then granted RN status. Calliste is generally correct in that Caribbean nurses did have to take a three-month obstetrics course in order to be eligible for registration and obtain their landed immigrant status. With respect to racial origin, either the nurses did not remember or were not asked, or the automatic assumption by the nurses association was that since they were from the Caribbean they were black. Most of the nurses interviewed for this project did not recall being asked about their racial origin prior to migration. Others said no; still, some maintained that given the time period, it would not have been unusual if they were asked about their racial origin, and as a result it would not have been etched in their memory as extraordinary.

A third group refused to undertake extra training or examinations, or failed in their efforts, and thus remained in a subsidiary category of nurse-worker. For example, Mryna Blackman was a registered mental nurse (RMN) in Britain who immigrated to Canada in 1971. Blackman felt that she should have been granted her RN status without having to upgrade. And so she refused to upgrade and chose to work instead as a registered nursing assistant (RNA) because she felt that her additional Canadian training would still be limited or unsatisfying compared to her training in England.

Finally, there were specific groups of immigrant nurses whose qualifications were not accepted at all and who would have had to complete a full RN or RNA program or work in non-professional categories of nursing work, for instance, as nurses' aides or health care aides. For example, Britain's state enrolled nurses (SENs) were similar to nursing assistants in Canada. When Elaine Mcleod immigrated in 1969, she was told by the College of Nurses that she did not have enough pediatric background and needed a further twenty-one hours in training to be considered a Registered Nursing Assistant. Mcleod then inquired at the school where the course was being offered, and was told by the administrators that she had to go through the entire program even though the College of Nurses stated that she needed only twenty-one hours. Even though it was the nursing school and not the college who told Mcleod she had to repeat the program, she blamed the College of Nurses because it was the body responsible for adjudicating immigrant nurses' qualifications. In making reference to the College of Nurses,

Mcleod contended, 'they didn't think it was up to their standard having done two years [in England] when theirs [in Canada] is just a 10 month program.' Similarly, Brenda Lewis, an RN in Trinidad with training in psychiatry, immigrated to Canada in 1970 and was told by the College of Nurses that she had to redo the entire program. Lewis worked as a nurses' aide while attending Ryerson at nights. It remains unclear as to why Lewis's qualifications did not at least enable her to work as an RNA, rather than as a nurses' aide.

Although most of the nurses who worked as RNAs or nursing assistants did eventually upgrade, many remained convinced that the process of credential evaluation disadvantaged them. Thus, while black activists like Donald Moore continued to criticize the process whereby the Canadian state impeded the immigration of Caribbean nurses, for many practitioners it was their professional colleagues in Canada, not state officials, who frustrated the migration process.

## Deskilling and Working in Canadian Hospitals

Nurses who migrated from the Caribbean or Britain to Canada entered a health care system that was undergoing dramatic change. During the period following the Second World War there emerged in hospitals a two-tier system of nurse-managers (RNs) and nurse-workers in hospital wards. Furthermore, the introduction of subsidiary workers (RNAs) in nursing meant that the personal care tasks that were once the domain of RNs were now given over to these new groups of workers.[17] These changes constituted deskilling, the process whereby certain skills once central to a job are no longer utilized. Deskilling in nursing was accomplished through the introduction of technology, the fragmentation of tasks, and the introduction of subsidiary workers. Because many Caribbean immigrant nurses had to work in subsidiary areas where their substantial experience and training was underutilized, for black and immigrant nurses the process of deskilling was further intensified by race and migration.

One group who experienced deskilling were those nurses whose credentials were not recognized and as a result were concentrated in subordinate positions and were responsible for tasks for which they were overqualified. Immigrant nurses that worked as assistants, health care aides, and nursing assistants, according to Evelyn Nakanno Glenn, 'constituted the hands that performed routine work that were directed by others.'[18] Caribbean nurses who required upgrading were often concentrated in these subordinate positions. The autonomy Caribbean SENs and other specialized nurses were accustomed to in England and the Caribbean was replaced in Canada with repetitive and monotonous duties subject to the authority of white nurse-managers. Lewis, who had previously worked as an RN in Trinidad, after migration worked as a nurses' aide in a nursing home, a shift that she considered demoralizing. Making reference to her responsibilities as an RN in Trinidad, she said: 'As an RN, you had more responsibilities and being in charge. Here [I] was doing baths, changing patients, really back breaking work ... I wasn't used to that sort of thing, being under somebody and having to do this kind of work. And then you were working with people who never had any skills at all in regards to nursing. They just hire them because they needed somebody.' For Lewis, the menial and unskilled tasks of her job were inappropriate to the qualifications she earned in Trinidad. Mcleod's experience on the ward was similar in that she classified her responsibilities as 'non-educational tasks,' that is, tasks that had no theoretical support.

Immigrant nurses who were granted RN status in Canada experienced deskilling in different ways. RNs took on more leadership and administrative roles, they performed patient care duties, which the nursing leadership felt was an indication of professionalism. Conversely, British-trained RNs felt that the fragmentation of work actually deskilled the job of caring. For example, Cudjoe pointed out that patient care was the essence of 'real' skill, something that Canadian nurses lacked. In making reference to patient care in England, Cudjoe commented: 'The job of nursing a patient was different in England. We spent time with the patient and that meant a lot psychologically. It was very good medicine. We knew that to be true.' For nurses such as Cudjoe, patient care that she considered central to the occupation was being replaced with more administrative duties.

Just as some Caribbean nurses experienced deskilling in terms of their position in the nursing hierarchy, and others criticized the way Canadians 'do nursing,' practising midwives were further deskilled due to the lack of recognition for midwifery generally in Canada. Writing about midwifery in the nineteenth and twentieth centuries, Diane Dodd asserts that the medicalization of childbirth with an emphasis on 'physician-controlled and eventually hospital birthing' was part of male practitioners' dominance over the midwifery role.[19] Doctors' hegemony over the birthing process continued well into the twentieth century with practising midwives virtually eliminated in most provinces. By contrast, midwives continued to play a central role in the Caribbean and Britain. In fact, many RNs in those countries went on to do extensive obstetrical nursing training and to license as midwives. Caribbean and British-trained midwives viewed Canadian nurses as lacking in autonomy particularly around childbirth, and argued vehemently that managing childbirth ought to be within nurses' domain.

The experience of British-trained Nancy Ward who immigrated to Canada in the 1970s illustrates the contradictory positions licensed midwives faced. Ward had difficulty finding employment because, according to the Ontario College of Nurses, she lacked 'Canadian experience.' Ward recalled that 'when I came here, they said I needed Canadian experience. Every hospital you went to it was Canadian experience. I went back to the College of Nurses; they said they would send me to a place. It was a thousand miles away, away from Toronto.' Ward refused to relocate because of family commitments. A trained midwife, she drew on her own experience as a pregnant mother to illustrate how limited general nurses' training in Canada was, but also to show the power of the doctors in obstetrics. Ward who in 2001 was working at Baycrest Hospital in Toronto remembered: 'When I was pregnant, no one told me anything. I didn't tell them that I was a nurse. I didn't go to the doctor until I was six months. I knew I was having a good pregnancy, no complications. I had the child and still no one told me what to do. If I were a new mother, I wouldn't know what to do.' Ward further explained the difference between the doctor's role in childbirth in England and Canada: 'Over here, most of the doctors do the delivery. I took that to mean that the nurses really had nothing to do in terms of examining the baby. In England when you do midwifery, you have to know everything about labour. The nurse is there, even if it's a student nurse [she] examines you. You were told everything about the pregnancy and what to look for. You don't have to be a midwife to know that.'

According to Ward, student nurses in Britain were expected to check for abnormalities once a pregnant patient entered the hospital, a procedure that nurses did not perform in Canada. Getting acquainted and accustomed to the Canadian system would have been a challenge for Ward had she not been employed in a hospital with a number of white British-trained nurses. Still, Ward recalled, the nurses at the hospital where she worked found it hard to stay practised in some of the procedures that they were taught in England. She pointed out that 'when I came here, some of the girls would say, you can tell us some of the things we forgot.'

Lilli Johnson had an extensive career in England and Scotland as a midwife before immigrating to Canada in 1960. Johnson concurred with Ward regarding the gendered division of labour in Canada, but captured how patriarchy defined the relationship between doctors and nurses. 'They give you no responsibility. The doctor has to order to everything. Although it seems to be getting better, it seems all [the doctors] want is a handmaiden. There are so many British-trained nurses who have their midwifery training, but none of them are accredited for it here.' Johnson's experience working in Canada and the United States, especially her assessment of the role of doctors in both countries, ultimately influenced the choice she made when seeking employment. Johnson decided to never work on the obstetrics floor once in Canada. She commented:

> There was no way I could supervise anyone in the first stage in labour and see that she is ready for delivery, and tell her to wait for the anesthetist and the doctor. We didn't have all that before and we didn't have women sticking up their feet in pedals and we went ahead and delivered the baby, whether you are practising midwife or

not. We were the ones who taught the doctors in England how to deliver to babies. The business of doctors of delivering babies is a North American concept.

Similarly, Eileen Jacobson, another trained midwife who worked on the pediatrics floor, criticized the role of Canadian doctors and claimed their monopoly over certain procedures undermined the role of nurses. Mackenzie, who worked at the University of the West Indies Hospital in Jamaica before immigrating to Canada, also expressed criticism about the respective roles of nurses and doctors. Mackenzie maintained that, in Jamaica, 'the doctor would leave you to make a bit more decisions. If a patient has a headache, we give the patient the medication, and tell the doctor when they come. [In Canada] they take away a lot of the responsibility that you used to carry. I don't know if it's because they have more doctors. You have to go to them for everything.'

These examples reveal how Caribbean nurses' experience of deskilling varied depending on time of migration, and how skills and experience were being assessed at the time. The almost non-existent practice of midwifery in Canada further deskilled those who had midwifery training. Over all, the nurses used their performance, skill, and experience of the British system, which in their perception was superior, to challenge the Canadian system. In response to what some nurses perceived as an unfair system, Caribbean immigrant nurses emphasized their own sense of professionalism. Maintaining that they were good nurses who were better than white Canadian nurses helped to shape their identity as immigrant nurses working within a different system, and also offset the racism within that system.

### Racism within Nursing

In examining power relations in health care, it is generally accepted that a system of social stratification exists between doctors and nurses that shapes the roles of both groups. The argument is that the power accorded doctors results in an unequal relationship between them and nurses whereby the latter occupy a subordinate position in a male-dominated profession.[20] Inherent sexism arising from gender inequality is evident in that the medical profession is male-dominated; nursing is female-dominated. While scholars acknowledge how patriarchy defines and influences the relationship between nurses and doctors, gender remains the primary lens through which feminists examine power relationships in health care. Much less attention is paid to how racism shapes the experiences of black nurses. How black nurses experienced and dealt with racism and the day-to-day realities of nursing depended on the period in which they immigrated and the extent to which racism was politicized in Canadian society. Whether the nurses immigrated directly from the Caribbean or from Britain also played a role in their interpretations of racism. Furthermore, transformations in the structure of the occupation continued to be a major factor influencing black nurses' experiences, which sometime obscured the reality of racism.

In contrast to the overt racism against blacks in Britain generally, nurses interviewed for this study who came to Canada in the 1950s and 1960s recalled that they did not face much racism in Canada. If an incident occurred that could be construed as racist, it only appeared to have racial overtones in the context of today's society. These early migrants pointed out that they were accepted and treated well because of the nursing shortage and because racism was tempered due to the small population of blacks in Canada. Mitchell, for example, pointed out that 'I have often said to people that when I came to Canada the first time, I was comfortable. I never heard all this black and white thing, and my feeling is that my group did not represent a threat to white people. Now I think my group is a threat.'

Cudjoe expressed similar sentiments: 'The issue of racism was not evident and apparent at that time as it is now. There were so few of us here that they [meaning whites] had not begun to panic, to feel afraid or intimidated by our presence. On the other hand, in the hospital we were a minority, and we were just concerned about doing our work. They seemed to want us more than anything else.'

Heaven, who was mentioned earlier, recounted how she was exoticized because there were few or no blacks in these remote areas. Heaven maintained that 'in BC I was a novelty. A lot of people had never seen anyone black where I was in Trail. Some days it was fun, some days it was annoying.' For Heaven and her friend, having fun meant observing the stares and reactions of people who were unable to hide their curiosity. At the same time, the ongoing questions about their identity, coupled with the feeling of being constantly on display, irritated the two women. They eventually left for Toronto. These immigrant nurses were more concerned with their general survival in terms of being in a new country than focusing on racism.

Mackenzie suggested that she did not experience any racism at the Oshawa General Hospital primarily because she did not have a clear understanding of what it meant to be identified as black until she immigrated to Canada. Describing her experiences around 'race,' and thinking about being black at her first place of employment, Mackenzie said: 'It was 1960, and at the time there were not too many black nurses, and it was okay. You know, I realized that I was new, that the colour of my skin was new, they were very polite. It was so very funny how children did not see too many black nurses. I remember this little three-year-old looked at me and says, "oh you are burnt," and I just smiled and I said, "poor little thing, you have never seen a black nurse."'

Theorist Stuart Hall has observed that until he left Jamaica in the 1950s, he had never heard anyone call themselves or refer to anyone else as 'black.' In the Caribbean, there were many different ways of identifying people ranging from different shades of brown, quality of hair, the quality of family one came from, and even the street a person lived on. Hall says that it was not until the 1970s, 'for the first time that black people recognized themselves as blacks. It was the most profound cultural revolution in the Caribbean, much greater than they have ever had.'[21] For those nurses who immigrated to Britain and then to Canada, the cultural revolution to which Hall alludes would have not been part of their experience; they would have missed this process of identification as black that was taking place in the Caribbean. It also explains why these nurses did not attach too much significance to racial status, or their identity as blacks until later because, for the most part, they were just learning how to be black.

Even if incidents or certain actions were not construed as racist at the time, in retrospect these nurses were able to find some defining moments in their careers when they wondered about particular acts of injustice. In thinking about whether she had ever experienced racism, Cudjoe said: 'I was not aware of racism at that time, but in hindsight, I think there was because there were times when people were being unfair and you didn't know why. You never thought it was because of me being black. You were more concerned with the actual victimization of what's being done to you and trying to work it out and resolve it rather than point at somebody else and call them a racist.'

Tensions, especially between white and black nurses, which could be interpreted today as having racial undertones, were explained using other non-racial explanations. On many occasions, nurses would point to personality, education, or position in the nursing hierarchy as reasons for tensions as opposed to racism. For other nurses, conflicts emerged on the wards between black nurses who had more experience and education than their white counterparts. Black nurses felt that despite having the education and training, white personnel were still granted more authority even if they had less education. Black RNs found that white nursing assistants, for example, attempted to assume RN responsibilities when black nurses were in charge. Mackenzie found that this happened quite frequently throughout her career. She recalled: 'You will find some of those nursing assistants want to act like RNs, especially the white ones. When the doctors come, they are there with the charts, and they can't write on the chart, they have the doctor write the chart. I have worked with a nursing assistant where the doctor was having a hard time realizing that she is not the RN.' Though Mackenzie later acknowledged that race was a factor in these relationships, she only realized the significance of these assistants' actions much later on. That racism did not figure prominently in these women's memories illustrates the changing nature and meaning of racism within specific contexts. At the same time, black nurses were not always concerned with issues of racism because it was not a major issue of contention at the time. Others were, as Cudjoe pointed out, 'just concerned with doing our work.'

While racism may not have been recognizable to the nurses who immigrated during the 1950s and 1960s, those who immigrated in the 1970s and 1980s were more cognizant of the ways in which race structured social relations in the hospitals. These nurses recognized the power imbalance between white and non-white nurses, and the types of work or wards where black nurses predominated. These nurses recognized that racism influenced white nurses' perceptions of Caribbean nurses. Carmencita Gomez, who immigrated to Canada during the late 1970s, felt that black nurses who spoke out or asked questions that offended the head nurse or supervisor were more likely to be penalized than their white counterparts. Gomez recalled working on a floor where the nurse manager made a decision to remove nurses from other areas of the ward to care for a sick child who came from a wealthy family. Gomez questioned her decision in light of the fact that other patients would be left unattended. Perturbed that Gomez questioned her decision, the nurse manager asked Gomez to leave because she did not want to be told how to run her ward. Gomez was subsequently placed on another ward and forbidden to return to the floor for a year. Although Gomez realized that she was being penalized for questioning the head nurse, she appreciated the move because it allowed her to work independently even if it meant being isolated from her peers. According to Gomez, 'I was not allowed to go upstairs where all the other nurses were; there were just two of us downstairs.' Gomez also felt some satisfaction from being outspoken because the nurse manager did address her concern regarding the lack of nurses on the ward that evening. Gomez pointed out that 'despite the fact that she put me down, whatever I said, she knew it was [the truth] and at least there was extra coverage and that [child] wasn't getting just two nurses and the rest of the ward was suffering.' Despite being ostracized, Gomez focused on the issue of patient care, the independence she gained working with fewer nurses, and the freedom of not having to interact with the head nurse, rather than on racism.

Gomez's experience was not an isolated incident but captured an important dimension of those nurses who immigrated in later decades. Tania Das Gupta's research in the 1990s noted the way in which black nurses were racialized within nursing.[22] Racialization is the process whereby certain meanings are attached to the presence of black nurses in nursing that influences not only how they are viewed but also their interactions with their white counterparts. According to Das Gupta, the idea that blacks constitute a problem is a phenomenon that is endemic to nursing; the perceptions of outspoken black nurses and the reaction of white supervisors and administrators demonstrates an attempt to keep black nurses in a defined place. Das Gupta points out that incidents such as that experienced by Gomez are indicative of 'what can happen in a racist and sexist culture where black women workers with high levels of skill and leadership qualities challenge the status quo. Individuals who have much to gain from the status quo, i.e., those with relative power, White in most instances, struggle to put black women back in their "ascribed" place.'[23] Although none of the nurses in this paper were fired for speaking out, they were acquainted with, or knew of, nurses who were fired, or demoted, or were themselves reprimanded in some ways for questioning their superiors. For example, Dorothy Jones, who immigrated to Canada from Britain in 1971, describes one particular nurse who spoke out against racism and other inequities that took place on the ward: 'This one girl in particular, she would stand up for her rights and you always find when you stand up for your rights, you're a troublemaker. She was branded a troublemaker because she was able to stand up to them. And of course, they didn't like this girl at all, but you know she didn't care.' Jones pointed out that even though other black nurses agreed with this nurse and the steps she pursued to ensure that she was taken seriously, the majority of the nurses, both black and white, neglected to publicly support her for fear they would lose their jobs.

Racism also manifested itself with respect to the number of patients black nurses were assigned. A number of nurses noted that they always had the heavier and more difficult patients, while white nurses had lighter patients. Janet Barrett, who immigrated from Jamaica in 1968, attended night school in Canada and obtained her nursing diploma in 1974. Barrett explained a typical scenario in relation to patient care: 'If you were a black nurse and you're working a twelve hour shift and you have this patient from 7:30 a.m., but there was somebody that wasn't black coming in, a Canadian (white) that was coming on at 3:30 p.m., instead of leaving you with that patient, what they would do is take away your light patients from you at 3:30 p.m. and give it to that person.' Having worked with patients for the entire day, Barrett refused to change her lighter patients for heavier ones. According to Barrett, 'I was known at work to stand up for myself. If it's a new staff they would say to her, "If you upset her, you will hear about it. And if she's right, she ain't going to change."' For the most part, black nurses in this study developed other methods of dealing with inequities within nursing, such as being silent in the face of adversity. Other relied on their friends, community, and religious networks to provide a space free from the racism experienced at work.

Some nurses pointed out that obtaining holiday vacations was another contentious issue that surfaced repeatedly. Regardless of holiday policies that ensured that nurses only work one of the statutory holidays, black nurses would be scheduled to work on both Christmas Day and New Year's Eve. As one nurse described it, 'These were the subtleties of racism.' Racist incidents on the wards were rarely dealt with in ways that would bring about change, and as result, the problems continued. If and when the issue was raised, Jones said 'somehow it always got resolved, but without blaming the white ones.' While black nurses were penalized for challenging their white superiors, these same superiors ignored or downplayed the racial harassment meted out towards black nurses.

The gendered and ideological premise on which nursing was constructed contributed to the difficulties in discussing and naming racism in the occupation. Nurses interviewed for this study never explicitly discussed the racism at the hands of white nurses. However, the majority of nurses could relate to instances of racism on the part of patients. The idea that black hands were touching their white bodies disturbed many patients. These patients would request, sometimes subtly and other times more blatantly, if there were 'other' nurses (read white) available. Mackenzie, who initially maintained that she did not experience any racism working at Oshawa General Hospital, was able to identify acts of racism from patients in later years. Mackenzie remembered elderly patients who would say, 'Take your black hands off of me.' To which Mackenzie responded 'Who is going to bathe you? You can't even wash your face, so I'm going to bathe you whether you like it or not. This black nurse is going to look after you, so you better get accustomed to it.' Having been given 'their rights,' the majority of patients, according to Mackenzie, often refused to comment further. Acts of racism from patients or white nurses towards black nurses were rarely dealt with in any systematic way, which for black nurses contributed to the ongoing problems within the occupation. If, for example, a patient refused to be examined by a white nurse, often the patient's request would be granted.

Although the racism faced in the workplace took many forms, one of the most common complaints was with respect to discrimination in housing. After repeatedly being turned down by property mangers who refused to lease their apartments to blacks, one nurse placed the following advertisement in the newspaper: 'coloured couple require apartment...' Bennett, the first immigrant in this study, pointed out that the ongoing racism she faced when attempting to rent a room compelled her to purchase her own home, which she used to entertain other Caribbean immigrants. She recalled: 'After being [in Canada] for two years, I bought a house. You think they had apartments then? You had to rent out rooms. And when you come they would slam the door in your face because you are black. And when you call, they say "yes," but when you came they said it was gone. And even if they had a kitchen, you have to use a hot plate in the bedroom.'

In 1962, the *Canadian Nurse* decided to investigate racism within the profession after a nurse won a discrimination suit against a Montreal hotel, acknowledging that 'discrimination occurred more frequently than is generally recognized.'[24]

The three Caribbean nurses interviewed by the magazine were described as 'well established, competent nurses.'[25] Two of the women had extensive education and held leadership positions. They did, however, admit that discrimination existed 'to some degree in their social environment.' The three women were able to identify racism and individual acts of discrimination outside of their workplace. For example, Miss Nichols, one of nurses interviewed, pointed out that 'relations among white and coloured persons in Canada are bad ... and will not improve as long as the both races continue to deny the existence of prejudice and discrimination.'[26] The *Canadian Nurse* reported that, when asked about racism within the occupation, the women 'agree that there is little or no discrimination in their profession.'[27] The failure of these women to acknowledge that racism existed among nurses may have reflected their positions. These women exemplified the epitome of professionalism in terms of education and status within nursing and were most likely among only a few black nurses working in the hospitals.

## Conclusion

Despite the fact that Caribbean nurses experienced frustration and sometimes racism dealing with immigration agents, with landlords and neighbours, with co-workers and supervisors, none of the nurses expressed any regrets over migrating to Canada. By focusing on their identities as professional women with concrete skills needed in the Canadian health care system, and as professionals trained in what they perceived as a superior British system, they were able to overcome some of the difficulties they faced. Nurses who immigrated during the 1950s and 1960s were less likely to acknowledge racism as a fundamental feature of their experience even when they realized that only one, or a few, black nurses worked in the hospital. To a certain extent, these nurses were exoticized and were rarely seen as a threat because they were so few in numbers. Interviews with black nurses who immigrated to Canada in the 1970s through 1980s reveals a range of experiences with racism in the workplace and community. Yet these nurses did not always acquiesce to the difficulties they faced but rather developed forms of resistance that enabled them to work and live in environments not always hospitable to their presence.

In her historiographical treatment of Canadian immigration history, Franca Iacovetta noted that certain racialized groups, such as the Chinese and Japanese, were for too long understood primarily as targets or victims of racism, while their own perspectives and strategies, mental maps, and family and community lives were largely ignored.[28] Caribbean women in Canada have similarly often been treated, by historians and social scientists, as one-dimensional female subjects – the labour recruits of a racist rich-world country and economically self-serving immigration policy. While fully agreeing with this premise, this essay suggests that a great deal of work still needs to be done in recovering the complex lives of Caribbean women immigrants in Canada, in writing a Canadian feminist labour history of black nurses, and in multiracial and gendered relations in the workplace. This study has aimed to create a multidimensional portrait of Caribbean women immigrants that acknowledges the range and diversity of their social experiences both in the workplace and community.

NOTES

Financial assistance from the Hannah Institute of Medicine is gratefully acknowledged.

1 Frances Henry, *The Caribbean Diaspora in Toronto: Learning to Live with Racism* (Toronto: University of Toronto Press, 1994).

2 See, for example, B. Singh Bolaria and Peter S. Li, *Racial Oppression in Canada* (Toronto: Garamond Press, 1985); Linda Carty, 'African Canadian Women and the State: Labour Only Please,' in Peggy Bristow et al., '*We're Rooted Here and They Can't Pull Us Up:' Essays in African Canadian Women's History* (Toronto: University of Toronto Press, 1994); Dionne Brand, 'A Working Paper on Black Women in Toronto: Gender, Race and Class,' in Himani Bannerji, ed., *Returning the Gaze: Essays on Racism, Feminism and Politics* (Toronto: Sister Vision Press, 1993).

3 Makeda Silvera, *Silenced*, 2d ed. (Toronto: Sister Vision Press, 1989); Agnes Calliste, 'Canada's Immigration Policy and Domestics from the Caribbean: The Second Domestic Scheme,' in Jesse Vorst et al., eds, *Race, Class, Gender: Bonds and Barriers*, rev. ed. (Toronto: Garamond Press in co-operation with the Society for Socialist Studies, 1991); Patricia Daenzer, *Regulating Class Privilege: Immigrant Servants in Canada, 1940s–1990s* (Toronto: Canadian Scholars' Press, 1993).

4 Three of the women were interviewed in 1993 for this paper. The remaining interviews took place during 1995–2000. The interviewees were identified using a snowball method and occasional referrals.

5 Franca Iacovetta, 'Manly Militants, Cohesive Communities, and Defiant Domestics: Writing about Immigrants in Canadian Historical Scholarship,' *Labour/Le Travail* 36 (Fall 1995): 227.

6 Lisa Marie Jakubowski, *Immigration and the Legalization of Racism* (Halifax: Fernwood Publishing, 1997), 17.

7 Ibid.

8 Agnes Calliste, '"Women of 'Exceptional Merit'": Immigration of Caribbean Nurses to Canada,' *Canadian Journal of Women and the Law* 6, no. 1 (1993): 91.

9 Ibid.

10  Kathryn McPherson, *Bedside Matters: The Transformation of Canadian Nursing, 1900–1990* (Toronto: Oxford University Press, 1996), 213.

11  Calliste, 'Women of Exceptional Merit,' 93.

12  Donald Moore, *Don Moore: An Autobiography* (Toronto: Williams-Wallace Publishers, 1985), 139–50.

13  Ibid.

14  Carty, 'African Canadian Women and the State,' 212.

15  Calliste, 'Women of Exceptional Merit,' 91.

16  Ibid., 88.

17  McPherson, *Bedside Matters,* 205.

18  Evelyn Nakano Glenn, 'From Servitude to Service Work: Historical Continuities in the Racial Division of Paid Reproductive Labour,' in Vicki L. Ruíz and Ellen Carol Dubois, eds, *Unequal Sisters: A Multi-cultural Reader in U.S. Women's History,* 2nd ed. (New York: Routledge, 1994), 427.

19  Dionne Dodd and Helen MacMurchy, 'Popular Midwifery and Maternity Services for Canadian Pioneer Women,' in Dianne Dodd and Deborah Gorman, eds, *Caring and Curing: Historical Perspectives on Women and Healing in Canada* (Ottawa: University of Ottawa Press, 1994), 135.

20  See, for example, Pat Armstrong, Jacqueline Choiniere, and Elaine Day, *Vital Signs: Nursing in Transition* (Toronto: Garamond Press, 1993); Barbara Keddy et al., 'Nurses' Work World: Scientific or Womanly Ministering,' *Resources for Feminist Research* 7, no. 3 (1987): 99–102; McPherson, *Bedside Matters.*

21  Stuart Hall, 'Old and New Identities,' in Les Back and John Solomos, eds, *Theories of Race and Racism: A Reader* (New York: Routledge, 2000), 150.

22  Tania Das Gupta, *Racism and Paid Work* (Toronto: Garamond Press, 1996); Agnes Calliste, 'Anti-Racism Organizing and Resistance in Nursing: African-Canadian Women,' *Canadian Review of Sociology and Anthropology* 3, no. 33 (1996): 360–90.

23  Das Gupta, 'Racism in Nursing,' 87.

24  'Do Canadians Agree on Racial Equality,' *Canadian Nurse* 62, no. 4 (April 1962): 49.

25  Ibid.

26  Ibid.

27  Ibid.

28  Iacovetta, 'Manly Militants.'

# Surviving Their Survival: Women, Memory, and the Holocaust

PAULA J. DRAPER

## Introduction

What does it mean to be a survivor of the Holocaust?[1] This is the question that has informed my research over the years, as I've listened to hundreds of Canadian survivors recount their life stories. As a scholar collecting, on both audio and video tapes, the stories of individuals who experienced the Holocaust, and as a Holocaust educator who has presented these stories to numerous audiences, I have learned that this particular history is not static, and that its implications continue to resonate in the lives of those who lived through it. For understanding and presenting history includes exploring and explaining how people live their personal and collective histories today.[2]

In the past decade or so, practitioners and theorists of oral history have increasingly been asking the question, 'How do people remember?' This question arose from the recognition that when people tell of their past lives, in some cases decades after the actual events, their accounts are filtered through a complex memory process that is created through an interplay of who they were then and who they are now.[3] Understanding history then becomes not only learning 'what really happened' but also gaining a sense of how past events continue to influence and shape the lives of individuals and groups who were in the midst of those events. Especially for those who experienced a history of great trauma such as Holocaust survivors, the past is often lived very much in the present. Henry Greenspan warns that by 'celebrating survivors' ongoing lives, we tend to ignore their ongoing deaths,' yet by looking only at the tragedy and trauma, 'we miss the vitality of their ongoing lives.'[4]

The individuals whom I have interviewed were born in almost every country in Europe. When the Holocaust overtook them, some were infants, many were children and teenagers, and some were parents with children of their own. Most were concentration camp survivors. Others hid, passed on false papers, fought in resistance groups, or moved from place to place, one step ahead of death. Those whose stories I was able to hear did escape death, but their personal histories did not end with their Liberation.[5] They came to Canada, had families, achieved financial security, and became reasonably content with their new lives.

Yet the Holocaust continued to shape who they were and are, both in terms of the actual impact of family losses and psychological trauma on their developing identities, and how their memories of the past were constructed and fitted into their sense of the present. Despite their remarkable accomplishments, and living what many describe as a so-called normal life, there is much to be seen behind the façade. As Brana Gurewitsch remarks about Holocaust testimonies, there are no 'happy endings'; because most survivors 'still live in their identities, their memories are part of their post-Holocaust identities, informing their lives on a day-to-day basis.'[6]

One man I interviewed stated that survivors are great actors, never really able to be themselves around those who did not share their experiences.[7] For others, the trauma of the Holocaust continues to diminish their ability to live full lives. For instance, Vera Glaser was not yet fifteen when she was liberated in 1945. Born in Prague, Czechoslovakia, she had managed to live through terms at the Theresienstadt, Auschwitz-Birkenau, and Bergen-Belsen concentration camps.[8] Interviewed forty-six years later in Montreal, she was asked how her experiences had affected her. Vera responded, 'I'm not afraid of dying. I'm afraid of living.'[9] Her comments demonstrate the 'permanent irresolution'[10] between the events of the present and the shadows of the past that shape the daily lives and thoughts of survivors. Those who endured to see Liberation, yet live every day with their memories of the horrors of the Holocaust, are in many ways still trying to survive their survival.[11]

While my larger research project explores the stories of both male and female survivors, this paper will focus on women's stories. Most studies of the Holocaust have not attempted to discern how men and women may have experienced those events differently. Indeed, the argument has repeatedly been made that a gendered analysis of the Holocaust 'meant doing an injustice to the larger issue: the annihilation of both men and women as *Jews*.'[12] Or, as Dalia Ofer and Lenore J. Weitzman have observed, many fear 'that a focus on gender could diminish the importance of the Holocaust as a singular cataclysmic event and thereby add to the banalization and trivialization of the Holocaust.'[13] Another difficulty in reaching a gender conceptualization of the Holocaust, according to Judith Tydor Baumel, has to do with 'an overwhelming tendency to focus upon the death process which made little distinction between men and women, while shunting any discussion of the survival process.'[14] More recently, however, scholars have argued that gender identity was one of the variables that shaped an individual's experience of the Holocaust. And that the testimonies of women survivors illuminate ways in which gender shapes a woman's reflections on her past. As Sara Horowitz recently put it, 'Jewish women survivors experienced, and reflect back upon, the war both as Jews and as women.'[15]

Even so, women survivors of the Holocaust do not themselves often interpret and reflect upon dimensions of their stories that are gendered. Their postwar lives mesh into the narratives of immigrants and refugees, with the appropriate gendered roles. By examining various themes in the recollections of survivors, this paper will raise questions and offer some speculation regarding the gendered nature of Holocaust memories, but will stop short of a conclusive thesis on that point. The discussion that follows examines the theme of survival in the life stories of female Holocaust survivors with a focus on topics of escaping death, psychological health, relationships with family and community, attitudes towards faith and religious observance, adjustment to life in Canada, and struggles with bereavement.

## Psychological Impact

Most of those women and men interviewed for this study arrived in Canada as children, teenagers, and young adults in the early postwar years. Psychological trauma, manifested in nightmares, depression, and somatic illness, was especially pronounced in those early years.[16] Elizabeth De Jong survived the medical experiments conducted on Dutch women in Auschwitz. When she returned to her home in the Netherlands, she was haunted by dreams about family members who had died. 'In the night I dreamed always that my mother was there, and in the day time she wasn't ... I didn't believe she was dead, and I saw her go, that was the crazy thing.' She also spent three months in the hospital for undiagnosed stomach pain, likely a somatic manifestation of her emotional pain. Elizabeth's dreams continue to plague her and she has been under psychiatric care since the war. She laments, 'For me, they won the war anyway. Mentally, I'm never normal again.'[17] Similarly, Sue Kohn was still frustrated in 1981 by the 'noise in her head.' Her nightmares began in 1940 when she was a child in a Polish ghetto and her mother would try waking her as she screamed in her sleep. Seeking help from a neurologist, Sue's mother was told, 'What do you expect? She's frightened, every day she's frightened.'[18]

For children in their formative years, the Holocaust challenged development of their personalities. Returning to her home in Hungary from Auschwitz, one survivor realized she was 'a completely changed person. From an outgoing, lively, friendly child,' she said she had become 'gloomy, terribly depressed, lonely and introvert[ed].'[19] In Toronto, the Jewish Family and Child Service became legal guardian of the orphans who arrived as wards of the Jewish community in Canada. The case files are filled with tragic stories of survivors who succumbed to their psychic wounds. 'Helen' was twenty-three in 1953 when she suffered a complete mental breakdown. An account of her behaviour says she walked around naked and refused to speak. 'She had bizarre delusions regarding her own body,' the social worker wrote, 'and stated that she was dead, and that she had been killed by Hitler. She made an attempt to strangle herself. She responded to auditory hallucinations.' Helen was given electric shock treatment and was eventually diagnosed as a schizophrenic. She was institutionalized and spent only fourteen months of the next twenty years out of the hospital. Agency social workers visited her, prevented the government from deporting her, and tried unsuccessfully to find her a home.[20] Her 'liberation' from the Nazis had left her imprisoned by psychological trauma and a permanent ward of the state.

For some survivors, especially children, the full psychological impact of their experiences was not felt until many years later. Susanne Reich was fourteen when she emerged from the camps. She struggled to keep her memories buried for a long time, and, in fact, thought that perhaps her youth had protected her. She said, '[My youth] was my advantage and disadvantage at the same time, because I did not understand what was happening, and that probably helped me [and maintained] my sanity. But, at the same time, the understanding had to come some time.' Susanne's understanding did come, in 1961, when the publicity of the Eichmann trial led her to seek psychiatric help.[21] 'Even though I did not die in Auschwitz,' she said, 'I died later.'[22]

There were individuals who sought relief in death. Suicides were not uncommon just after the war. To overcome the loss of everything that gave a person identity, to be alone, with no one – neither family nor community – who knew you before, was a tremendous burden. To this day, suicide has remained an option for those who feel they can no longer live with their survival.

While some survivors dealt with their trauma by suppressing their memories and not talking about their experiences, others avoided seeking assistance because of the stigma, held by many Europeans, towards psychological therapy. There was also the fear that once the wounds of the past were opened, no one would know how to heal them. Many survivors made a few visits to psychiatrists when applying for restitution, but long-term therapy was seldom sought, nor was it often successful.[23] Renata Zajdman was advised to attempt ongoing therapy after filing her claim for restitution in 1963. Her family doctor, however, advised against it, saying, 'Don't do it, they'll destroy you. They'll rip you apart and they won't be able to put you back together.'[24] Indeed, psychiatry was not yet equipped to aid this group, and long-term therapy has seldom been a successful remedy.

The psychological effects of the Holocaust changed as the survivors aged, though certain elements have remained or been exacerbated by the aging process. Some former partisan fighters keep licensed guns in their homes for self-defence, maintaining a sense of power distinct from the powerlessness of their past. Some who came as refugees before the war never purchase real estate, choosing to rent their homes and thus be ready to move at a moment's notice. Eleanor Simkevitz survived in hiding in Belgium. Now she leaves every door open inside her house, even the bathroom. 'I have phobias,' she explained. 'You'll never get me. I cannot stand closed doors. I have to have a valid passport. I have to be able to find all my belongings ... everything has to be in its place. I have to be able to find everything in the dark. We were hiding, we were blacked out, we couldn't turn on any lights so if we had to run, we had to go and find whatever we needed ... in the dark.'[25] Similar phobias – fear of showers and hoarding of food, for instance – are being documented today in the Jewish Homes for the Aged and by children who are aware of their parents' paranoia. For instance, one man was said to have four deadbolts on his door which he rises to check throughout the night.

Other ongoing effects include anger towards parents who died in the Holocaust and whose children felt abandoned. Martha Shemtov is still tortured by the anger she feels towards her mother for abandoning her through her death, and at her father, who survived, for letting her believe her stepmother was her mother until she was sixteen.[26] A Romanian survivor fights the hatred that sometimes over-comes her: 'If I were to hate all my life, I think Hitler will have even hurt me to the end of my days. If I permit hate to really stay and destroy the joy that I have in life, then he has succeeded. But you do hate. You put them together in a block and when the pictures come on, you feel violent against everyone of them who speaks German. And there was a long time when I went on the street and I saw a uniform and I broke out in sweat. Anytime that anybody would appear like a German.'[27] For most survivors, their struggle is against a general sense of unhappiness and a constant feeling of loss. As Valerie Good remarks, 'I try sometimes to smile, to be happy about certain things, but I can never be really ... like I see people laugh and be very joyful, I can never be like that.'[28] For some who survived, the physical and mental trauma of the Holocaust continues to manifest itself in a variety of psycho-logical ailments and somatic illnesses.

## Reconstituting Families

The most important step towards recovering a semblance of joy was to create life. And so survivors married, had children, and reconstituted families as quickly as they could in order to recapture their losses. Often the sole survivors of large extended families, couples sought to create ties among groups of survivors. As the next generation was born without relatives, so other survivors became their 'aunts' and 'uncles,' other children their 'cousins.'

Marriage brought hope for the future, but it was bittersweet. Valerie Good's husband Mendel said the happiest day of his life was his wedding day 'because finally my life started to be normal. And yet it was totally tempered with tragedy, because there are [only] two people standing there ... how can we be totally happy?'[29] Many survivors married soon after their Liberation, motivated by the simple need to bond with another person who had some connection to their past. As Abram Schwemer expressed it, 'You look always for somebody that you know. After the war, you look for somebody, because you want somebody ... anybody. I said to [my wife] Fela, it's no use, you've got nobody, I haven't got nobody, so let's get married.'[30] Shared losses and trauma that nobody else could possibly understand, drew couples together and created marriages with unique dynamics. And if psychological therapy was considered taboo or was unsuccessful, loved ones could sometimes play the same role. Larry and Esther Brandt met when they arrived in Winnipeg in 1947 on the Orphan Scheme and married in 1951.[31] At the age of twenty-seven, with two small children, Esther suffered a nervous breakdown and began a long period of therapy for her depression. Yet she remains sceptical of the results of this professional help. Rather, she said, 'I think the best psychiatrist was Larry, because he was able to understand what I was going through and he was able to help me to become strong, because I just couldn't do it.'[32]

Bearing children was a means for survivors to re-establish their murdered families. The child of one survivor, who carries the name of murdered relatives, said he often felt 'that I am eighty-five people.'[33] Yet having children also triggered tremendous fears. Could their babies be deformed as a result of the torture their parents had endured? Could children deprived of their own childhoods be good parents? One of the women who had been raped by liberating Soviet soldiers was told by doctors in Germany that she would never be able to have a child. After two dangerous deliveries, she did have her children, but she then had terrible dreams that her own children were being tortured. She would hover by their rooms at night, watching them sleep.[34] Helene Kravitz was eleven years old when she was liberated in Belgium. She lamented the fact that she had no role models to teach her mothering skills. In Helene's words: 'I remember thinking very often how I wish I had a mother to be able to show me. I felt I wasn't a good mother, but I didn't know how to be a mother.'[35]

Many survivors became overprotective and fearful for their children, hoping to shield them from knowledge of their suffering and also from experiences that might cause pain. Most only began to lift the veil on their past when their children became teenagers. Bertha Weisz said she could never find the right time. 'I didn't want to hurt my children because I felt it's not their fault, they had nothing to do with it.'[36] Yet survivors believed that their past did affect the way they raised the second generation, and that they did pass on their fears and anguish to their offspring. As well, some felt they didn't have the capacity for expressing love that was needed for parenting. Rosa Rubin said, 'I always felt that I missed something in life ... the love and affection of a mother. And in turn, was never to this day, not able to really show this to my children and my grandchildren. I love them all but I can't express myself or show it to them. And this is the cross that I bear since the war.'[37] Other parents focused on creating close family ties, and took extraordinary efforts to pass on a certain kind of legacy to their children. For instance, Kitty Salsberg, an orphan of the Holocaust, filled her home with foster children in addition to her biological children. She didn't realize the frightening effect she had on her teenagers when she left them an 'ethical will' every time she went out of town. She had no value system handed down from her parents, so she wanted to be sure she passed her own values on to her children.[38]

For the most part, children of survivors are very proud of their parents. Judith Leitner's father Bernard has spent every day of the last fifteen years caring for his wife, who has Alzheimer's disease. They survived the war together, hiding in Belgium, and then raised their two orphaned nieces with their own children. Judith said of her father, 'Here was a quiet, unassuming man who had committed such wonderful, amazing acts of bravery. This taught us a lot about being humble. We all grew up in a household that was full of joy, humour, laughter, optimism and looking towards the future. Take care of the things that matter the most to you. Through his life he showed us this.'[39]

When survivors lost their own children through disease, accident, or suicide, the tragedy of loss was replicated and sharpened. Sara Dickerman named her first child after her murdered mother, but the baby died at four weeks old. 'It was very hard,' she remembered. 'I told myself I don't want to live anymore. I remember I used to say, there is no God anymore. How could you do this to me. I went through hell in my life ... please God, you took away my parents, my brothers and sisters, and now the best thing in my life.'[40] Similarly, Lucy Rapuch recorded, 'We went through a lot of heartache here, we lost a son here, our first-born was killed by a car, and that again made me wonder, why did I survive? Sometimes I'm still thinking that I survived to suffer. But as the years went by, you got used to it, time heals everything.'[41]

It is possible that women's capacity to bear children and become mothers made their memories and experience of survival gendered in particular ways. Lawrence Langer observes that some women survivors were unable to celebrate the birth of their own children because they had 'tainted memories' of pregnant women and mothers with children who were murdered in concentration camps.[42] The process of reconstituting families in Canada was especially important for women who, in the context of home-based rituals, were often viewed as the primary conveyors of Jewish culture through the generations. The challenge of maintaining the 'primacy of the Jewish family' when almost all other connective tissue was broken, was a task taken up mainly by women.

## Faith and Religion

As with the family, Jewish women traditionally carried special responsibility for preserving their culture through religious observance in the home. Religious belief and individual faith were also severely challenged by the near annihilation of the Jewish people. Ethnicity and religious identity are intertwined in the Jewish community, so that even if individuals were not observant, the experience of the Holocaust compelled most survivors to question and re-evaluate their faith and beliefs.[43] The responses varied. For some individuals, whether questioners or believers prior to the war, their experiences led to a complete rejection of traditional Jewish beliefs in God. Nate Leipciger, as a thirteen-year-old in camp 'was very angry with God.' He could never understand why, if God was 'forgiving and good,' 'pious and religious people [were] the first ones to go to the gas chamber.' 'What did my mother do that she deserved to, to go through this. What did I do?' he asked. For Nate, 'there was no answer.'[44] Some survivors rejected their Jewish identity and faith and chose to convert, often to protect their children from what they had suffered. One woman said she could not set foot in a synagogue because it would invoke painful memories of her lost childhood. When she contemplated recording her story, she insisted she could not be identified by her married name because she was fearful that her children would be persecuted if their Jewish roots were uncovered. Much to her astonishment, her children reacted with pride to the revelation that they were half-Jewish, a fact they insisted on broadcasting to their friends.[45]

Other survivors, however, attest to a strengthening of Jewish religious belief and practice as a consequence of their experiences. Myra Guttman, for instance, discovered a new faith after the war, which she ascribed to the 'miracle' of survival. In her words: 'We came out of it, and we came out as human beings. You form families, you continue a beautiful life. I think it's a miracle that we survived.'[46]

Even when their religious faith weakened, or was lost altogether, most survivors maintained an unwavering sense of their Jewish identity. Yet the early postwar years were a time when some Jews, often from very observant backgrounds, decided to go into a kind of spiritual hiding. One woman escaped Vienna on a *Kindertransport* when she was twelve and was sent to live with a Christian family in a small English town. Although raised as an observant Jew, she loved the nuns at the convent school she attended. She recalled, 'I felt good being Christian because I was accepted.' She later married a Christian and raised a family who knew nothing of her past or her identity.[47] Another form of hidden Jews were those who never denied their ethnicity, yet chose to live their lives detached from community and religion. A Czech couple who had survived three years in Theresienstadt with their baby son, determined that after the war there were only two choices, 'either you go to Israel ... or you try to forget your past and let the children assimilate so they will never have to suffer again. Maybe it's wrong, maybe now I would do it differently, but in 1946 that's how I felt.'[48]

The greatest challenge to religious identity faced those Jewish children who were hidden and protected by Christian families. For them, memories of their Jewish identity were laced with ignorance and fear, while their experiences of Christianity consisted of safety and comfort. Some of these hidden children did not learn about Judaism until they were adults. Renata Zajdman came out of Poland 'terrified of synagogues. I was never a religious Jew. I was brought up as a Catholic, and thank God I was not a deep thinker or I'd probably be a nun in a monastery. A lot of my friends were.' She says she still has 'unfinished business with God.'[49]

Eve Bergstein's experience was different. She was ten years old after the war when her uncle found her and had to drag her away from the Polish couple that had saved her. It was only after he placed her in a Jewish orphanage in France that she came to realize the importance of regaining her Jewish identity. Eve came to feel that by continuing in her Jewish heritage, she could 'avenge the deaths' of her family members: 'How important that I continue what they couldn't. So I became a very strong Jew.'[50] Some 'hidden Jews' were brought back to their Jewish roots only many years later. After her British husband died in 1984, the child who found refuge in England began to long for her childhood Shabbat meals and the warm feelings associated with those rituals. She finally decided to tell her children, who at first didn't believe her, but many of her friends said, 'We knew all along you were Jewish. It's no big deal.'[51]

There were different forms to assert one's Jewish ethnic and/or religious identity. For some it was religious observance, for others ethnic rituals, and for others, passing on their heritage to their children in a variety of ways. For many survivors, this meant obtaining a Jewish education for their children, even for those who had lost their faith in God. One of the many survivors who arrived in Canada in the 1950s and 1960s from Hungary, Romania, and Czechoslovakia recounted how she tried to join one of the larger Toronto synagogues in 1965. A divorced single mother, she was anxious that her only child attend Hebrew school. The synagogue demanded a flat fee of $800 and when she asked if she could pay in monthly installments, she was refused. The humiliation of her treatment kept her away from the organized Jewish community.

When Mania and Moishe Kay married in Bergen-Belsen Displaced Persons' Camp, their first purchase was a pair of Shabbat candlesticks. Mania explained, 'From that time we decided that we are going to be kosher and Jewish, that if we gonna have children they should know, they should have their background.' She recalled that her commitment to her Jewish faith 'hesitated' while she was in Auschwitz-Birkenau. But later she decided, 'If you are born with a belief, it's not easy to shake it. So I believe.'[52]

Although some survivors continue to question their faith, others find it strengthened. Perhaps most representative is an outlook that places an emphasis on human values and behaviour over and above religious beliefs. As Lucy Rapuch testified, 'I stopped believing in God, where was He when we needed him most? I come from a very religious home, and I'm not religious at all because I think that religion is not important. Important is what you are inside, if you are a good person or a bad person and that's what matters most.'[53]

### Adjustment to Canada

Upon immigrating to Canada, along with masses of other refugees and displaced persons after the war, survivors faced another stage in the process of dealing with a painful past. This was adjusting to a postwar society in the midst of economic boom and trying to establish social normalcy after the disruption of the Second World War.[54] Even while individuals sought to reconstitute family life as part of personal and cultural survival, they were also conforming, however subconsciously and unintentionally, to postwar Canadian ideals 'that everybody ought to live within the confines of a private single-family household and that men and women performed gender-specific roles.' As well, the tendency to repress and not talk about the trauma of the Holocaust may have been reinforced by a host of authorities and experts who viewed the newcomers as 'dysfunctional.'[55]

For those survivors who chose to hide their Jewish identity, absorption into the Canadian mosaic was easiest, despite the generally negative attitudes directed towards all newcomers. Anti-Semitism was still a strong factor in Canadian life and a painful reminder of what they had hoped to leave behind in Europe.[56] Survivors were often met with attitudes of ignorance and suspicion, even on the part of Canadian Jews with whom they had so hoped to create a new community. Indeed, there was a widely held assumption that those who survived must have collaborated in some way, or must have 'done something' questionable in order to cheat death. Renata Zajdman explained that she began to avoid the Jews in Montreal: 'I was afraid that they look at me in suspicion that since I'm a refugee I probably did something bad,' cause usually when you tell them that you're a survivor, they look at you, what did you do, how did you survive, so that was a horrible feeling, that guilt ... My generation of Canadian-born Jews, they wouldn't even look at us! The called us "muckies" – you come from muck.'[57]

Few Canadians, Jew or non-Jew, seemed willing to hear survivors' stories. Either they were preoccupied with their own wartime experiences, or didn't want to process the idea of such tremendous suffering, or sometimes because they didn't believe the stories at all. Henry Greenspan observes that not only was there a lack of response to the stories of survivors, but there was also 'an active process of suppression and stigmatization.'[58] Renata, who is a frequent public speaker, says that she still finds it difficult to deal with her own generation of Canadian Jews who have only a kind of voyeuristic curiosity. She remarks that some people are more interested in seeing a number tattooed on her arm to prove the truth of her account. In Renata's eyes, 'We suffered [and] there was no empathy at all.'[59] Ellen Tissenbaum was a hidden child from the Netherlands. She too began to push her memories back because, 'If I started talking, people would say, stop making up those stories. It's not true.'[60] Because of these reactions, many survivors chose to bury their pasts and not tell anyone about their experiences.

Survivors looked to family as the last connection to an old life and the comfort of shared memory. Anita Ekstein was just fourteen when she came to Toronto with her aunt, Sala Stern, whose husband and children had perished. Anita recalled how her aunt wanted to talk but her own sister, who had come to the United States before the war, would not listen. '[Aunt Sala] wanted to pour her heart out to her ... She never got over the fact that her sister didn't understand what she went through and that she lost her children and [her sister] is telling her about coupons for butter.' Anita felt talking about the Holocaust was taboo, that it was too soon, or 'survivors didn't want to talk about it or they figured nobody cared so why bother.' But Anita, who had been hidden with Poles in Ukraine during the war, heard the stories from the other camp survivors who visited, and from her aunt as well. It was Anita who was silent. She said, 'Some survivors made you feel ... you were a kid, what do you know, you were hidden. When I knew what my aunt went through, she lost her children and the hell she went through ... how could I possibly talk to her ... about what I felt.'[61] Anita quickly integrated, made friends with Canadians, and lost her accent. No one asked what had happened to her. She was simply an orphan from Europe. Yet there was another aspect to these early years. Survivors themselves found the retelling too painful, preferring to bury the memories in the hope they would fade. Yet memory continued to inform their lives, always near the surface. It was only at the first Gathering of Child Survivors in New York City in 1991 that Anita realized the depth of the impact the Holocaust had had on her life. And how being denied a voice had crippled her.

### Mourning the Losses

Much of the ongoing psychological trauma and obstacles to adjustment, as well as difficulties reconstituting family life has to do with the burden of bereavement. Every Holocaust survivor and refugee lost family members, murdered by the Nazis or their collaborators. Only a few know the exact fate of their loved ones and only a handful have a grave to visit. The absence of memorial sites and the impossibility of a normative grieving process has had a profound and lasting effect on survivors. Ellen Tissenbaum has never found anyone who can verify the fate of her parents and so continues to scan photos of the Holocaust, in books and on television, searching for images of them. With no concrete evidence of death, survivors maintain faint hopes that their loved ones might still be alive. When Esther Brandt visits Israel she scans faces in the crowds, looking for a woman in her nineties who might be her lost mother.[62]

Attendance at yearly Yizkor services and Yom HaShoah, and the erection of memorials in Jewish cemeteries are examples of rituals that have created a forum for public mourning.[63] Mania Kay explains why the grief has never left: 'When we say the Yizkor prayer in the shul, I don't look into the siddur, I see like a movie in front of my eyes, I see the people, I see the places and I see everything what happened, and that's my Yizkor prayer.'[64] Some survivors have found tangible ways to commemorate those who perished in the Holocaust. Ilse Steinhart and her husband were German Jewish refugees. When Ilse erected a double tombstone after her husband's death in 1991, she had the names of their murdered parents and siblings inscribed on the back. On summer weekends she takes her grandchildren to visit the grave and tells them stories of their lost family.[65] For many survivors the grieving process was delayed until immediate family members died years later in Canada. When Renata Zajdman's husband died suddenly in 1983, she was overwhelmed. 'I couldn't cope with death,' she said. 'I never saw death, I saw only murder. I didn't know how to act, I didn't know how to take it. I never knew what grieving is. Never had a chance.'[66]

Faced with the deaths of their spouses, survivors found the walls they had so carefully built over the decades crumble around them. One woman fell apart and had to seek therapy when her husband died. She realized she 'was mourning for my parents too, because I never really even mourned for them. It was a double whammy.' Her psychiatrist suggested that she enlarge her parents' passport photos and put them in her bedroom. Which she did, though it took about five years for the intense pain of mourning to subside.[67] Some survivors describe the other extreme, a complete lack of affect. Not even the funerals of their friends touched them. Eugenia Pernal was a nurse in the Warsaw Ghetto and says she became 'immune' to death. It took a long time for her to feel and cry again.[68] Kitty Salsberg did cry 'when somebody else had a nice funeral, and I thought that my father would be lying in a ditch like a dog. The indignity of it bothered me. But I also grieve with pride, by living and surviving and having as many children as I could ... To have their issue survive and continue ... I live every day in honour of them.'[69]

## Conclusion

The lessons of the Holocaust do not lie solely in the need to understand the past so as not to repeat it. They lie also in the courageous lives of the survivors who have struggled so hard to overcome, to rebuild, and to bring new life into the world. The life histories of women who survived the Holocaust did not end when they were liberated from the Nazis and their collaborators. Their anguish and survival were ongoing, as they attempted to create new lives, new families, indeed new identities, in Canada. Yet the burden of memory keeps them forever strangers.

NOTES

1 The term *Holocaust* (*Shoah* in Hebrew) originally meant a sacrifice totally burnt by fire. It was adopted in the 1950s to describe the mass extermination of Jews during the Second World War. See Israel Gutman, ed., *Encyclopedia of the Holocaust* (New York: Macmillan, 1990), 681.

2 The past two decades have seen a marked increase in the awareness, study, and teaching of the Holocaust. Holocaust survivors have been at the forefront of many of these activities, speaking about their experiences to school groups and coming forward to have their life stories recorded in a variety of large and small oral history projects. Some of these testimony collections are cited in this paper, along with private interviews completed with the author. This paper is part of a larger research project focusing on the postwar experiences of Canadian Holocaust survivors.

3 Of particular interest for Holocaust scholars interested in memory history are: Henry Greenspan, *On Listening to Holocaust Survivors: Recounting and Life History* (Westport, CT: Praeger, 1998); Aaron Haas, *The Aftermath: Living with the Holocaust* (Cambridge: Cambridge University Press, 1995); Lawrence Langer, *Holocaust Testimonies: The Ruins of Memory* (New Haven: Yale University Press, 1991).

4 Greenspan, *On Listening to Holocaust Survivors*, 169.

5 Liberation is the term used by survivors to describe the moment they regained their freedom by the arrival of Allied soldiers.

6 Brana Gurewitsch, ed., *Mothers, Sisters, Resisters: Oral Histories of Women Who Survived the Holocaust* (Tuscaloosa: University of Alabama Press, 1998), 314.

7 Author's interview with Mendel Good, 13 January 1994, Toronto. Unless otherwise indicated, the interviews were conducted by the author.

8 Camp survivors experienced years of forced labour and abuse, often in more than one camp. There were transit camps, where entire families were housed in preparation for deportation to the 'east.' One of these was Theresienstadt, a unique camp in Czechoslovakia that the Nazis used as a model to hide their crimes. Bergen-Belsen was a con-

centration camp in Germany. Most of the Jews liberated there in 1945 had come on forced 'death marches' from camps in the east. Auschwitz-Birkenau in Poland was both a death camp, where gas chambers murdered over a million Jews, as well as a complex of forced labour camps.

 9  Interview with Vera Glaser, Canadian Jewish Congress Archives/Montreal (hereafter CJC), Montreal, 29 October 1981. Interviewer: Josh Freed.

10  See Henry Greenspan, 'Imagining Survivors: Testimony and the Rise of Holocaust Consciousness,' in Hilene Franzbaum, ed., *The Americanization of the Holocaust* (Baltimore: Johns Hopkins University Press, 1999), 48.

11  In Calgary, as I packed up my tape recorder, Bronia Cyngiser surprised me with her comment. After several hours discussing her life after the war, Bronia joked, 'I survived the survival!' Interview with Bronia Cyngiser, Calgary, 17 October 1993.

12  Judith Tydor Baumel, *Double Jeopardy: Gender and the Holocaust* (London: Vallentine Mitchell, 1998), xii.

13  'Introduction: The Role of Gender in the Holocaust,' in Lenore J. Weitzman and Dalia Ofer, eds, *Women in the Holocaust* (New Haven, CT: Yale University Press, 1998), 12.

14  Baumel, *Double Jeopardy*, 26.

15  Sara R. Horowitz, 'Women in Holocaust Literature: Engendering Trauma Memory,' in Ofer and Weitzman, *Women in the Holocaust*, 365.

16  Much of the literature on Holocaust survivors and their descendants regards their psychological responses to trauma. See Morton Weinfeld and John Sigal, *Trauma and Rebirth: Intergenerational Effects of the Holocaust* (Westport, CT: Praeger, 1989); Robert Krell and Marc Sherman, eds, *Medical and Psychological Effects of Concentration Camps on Holocaust Survivors* (Jerusalem: Transaction Publishers/Institute on the Holocaust and Genocide, 1997); Leo Etinger and Robert Krell, *Psychological and Medical Effects of Concentration Camps and Related Persecutions on Survivors of the Holocaust: A Research Bibliography* (Vancouver: University of British Columbia Press, 1985).

17  Interview with Elizabeth De Jong, Holocaust Education and Memorial Centre/Toronto (hereafter HC) Toronto, 2 September 1987. Interviewer: Marion Seftel.

18  Interview with Sue Kohn, CJC/Montreal, Halifax, 7 August 1981. Interviewer: Josh Freed.

19  Interview with Clara Forrai, CJC/Montreal, Vancouver, 11 January 1982. Interviewer: Josh Freed.

20  Jewish Family and Child Services Toronto (JFCS) case file 13019.

21  For almost two decades after the end of World War II little was said or written about the Holocaust. In May 1960, Adolf Eichmann – one of the chief architects of the murder of European Jewry – was kidnapped in Argentina and brought to Israel to stand trial. This trial, held in Jerusalem in 1961–2, detailed the Nazi crimes against the Jewish peo-

ple and was highly publicized. Many survivors cite this as a turning point in their struggle to come to terms with their past. The trial and execution of Eichmann also began a new awareness and interest in the genocide of the Jews that persists to this day.

22 Interview with Susanne Reich, CJC/Montreal, Montreal, 22 October 1981. Interviewer: Josh Freed.

23 Beginning in the 1950s payments of restitution were made by the German government to victims of Nazi oppression. Proof of physical or psychological damage was sometimes a requirement for payment. Many Canadian survivors met briefly with psychiatrists in order make their claims.

24 Interview with Renata Zajdman, Toronto, 13 November 1993.

25 Interview with Eleanor Simkevitz, CJC/Montreal, Montreal, 1981. Interviewer: Josh Freed.

26 Interview with Martha Shemtov, HC/Toronto, 23 March 1993. Interviewer: Janice Karlinsky.

27 Interview, name restricted, Saskatoon, 1 November 1993.

28 Interview with Valerie Good, Toronto, 13 January 1994.

29 Interview with Mendel Good, Toronto, 13 January 1994.

30 Abram Schwemer, interview by Survivors of the Shoah Visual History Foundation (hereafter SF), Winnipeg, 27 August 1996. Interviewer: Evita Smordin.

31 On 18 September 1947 the first of a group of 1,116 child survivors of the Holocaust entered Canada as wards of the Jewish community. They were placed in Jewish homes across Canada, and local Jewish social service agencies became their guardians.

32 Interview with Esther Brandt, Vancouver, 26 October 1993.

33 Rabbi Charles Grysman and Meyer Grysman, SF, Winnipeg, 7 July 1997. Interviewer: Francesca David.

34 Interview with FK, Toronto, 23 November 1993.

35 Helene Kravitz, SF, Montreal, 19 January 1997. Interviewer: Marilyn Krelenbaum.

36 Bertha Weisz, SF, Guelph, Ontario, 27 May 1997. Interviewer: Linda Davidson.

37 Rosa Rubin, SF, Montreal, 19 January 1997. Interviewer: Marilyn Krelenbaum.

38 Kitty created a list of moral rules for her children to follow. Interview with Kitty Salsberg, Toronto, 12 June 1998.

39 Bernard Leitner, SF, London, Ontario, 6 February 1995. Interviewer: Richard Bassett.

40 Sarah Dickerman, SF, Montreal, 24 February 1997. Interviewer: Sylvia Aikens.

41 Lucy Rapuch, HC/Toronto, 4 November 1988. Interviewer: Cheryl Wetstein.

42 Lawrence L. Langer, 'Gendered Suffering? Women in Holocaust Testimonies,' in Ofer and Weitzman, *Women in the Holocaust*, 354–5. Note that pregnant women and women with young children were, without exception, murdered immediately after their arrival at the death camps.

43 For information on Holocaust survivors and faith see Reeve Robert Brenner, *The Faith and Doubt of Holocaust Survivors* (New York: Jason Aronson, 1997).

44  Interview with Nathan Leipciger, CJC/Montreal, Toronto, 23 November 1981.

45  Telephone conversation with BG, November 1987.

46  Interview with Myra Guttman, CJC/Montreal, Montreal 22 October 1981. Interviewer: Josh Freed.

47  Interview, name restricted, Vancouver, 27 October 1993.

48  Interview, name restricted, Saskatoon, 31 October 1993.

49  Interview with Renata Zajdman.

50  Eve Bergstein, SF, Waterloo, Ontario, 5 September 1995. Interviewer: Judy Schwartz.

51  Interview, name restricted, Vancouver.

52  Interview with Mania Kay, Kitchener-Waterloo, Ontario, 26 December 1993.

53  Interview with Lucy Rapuch.

54  For more on the early years of survivors in Canada, see Paula J. Draper, 'Canadian Holocaust Survivors: From Liberation to Rebirth,' *Canadian Jewish Studies* 4–5, Special issue on New Perspectives on Canada, The Holocaust and Survivors (1996–7): 39–62; Franklin Bialystok, *Delayed Impact: The Holocaust and the Canadian Jewish Community* (Montreal and Kingston: McGill-Queen's University Press, 2000).

55  Franca Iacovetta, 'Remaking Their Lives: Women Immigrants, Survivors, and Refugees,' in Joy Parr, ed., *A Diversity of Women: Ontario, 1945–1980* (Toronto: University of Toronto Press, 1995), 135–67.

56  On anti-Semitism in Canada during the war years, see Irving Abella and Harold Troper, *None Is Too Many: Canada and the Jews of Europe* (Toronto: University of Toronto Press, 1983). For the postwar years, see Bialystok, *Delayed Impact*; Alan Davies, ed., *Anti-Semitism in Canada: History and Interpretation* (Waterloo, ON: Wilfrid Laurier University Press, 1992).

57  Interview with Renata Zajdman.

58  Greenspan, 'Imagining Survivors,'50.

59  Ibid.

60  Ellen Tissenbaum, SF, Montreal, 22 January 1997. Interviewer: Rachel Alkallay.

61  Interview with Anita Ekstein, Toronto, 15 April 1994.

62  Interview with Esther Brandt.

63  The Yizkor service on the high holiday of Yom Kippur is a memorial service for relatives who have died. Yom HaShoah is the annual community commemoration for the victims of the Holocaust.

64  Mania Kay (Audio) Kitchener.

65  Interview with Ilse Steinhart, Holocaust Remembrance Committee/Toronto n.d.

66  Interview with Renata Zajdman.

67  Interview, name restricted, Vancouver.

68  Interview with Eugenia Pernal, Toronto, 15 April 1994.

69  Kitty Salsberg (Audio) Toronto.

# Contributors

**Midge Ayukawa**, a former chemist, obtained her PhD in history from the University of Victoria in 1997, specializing in Japanese-Canadian pioneer history. She has published a number of articles on Japanese picture brides and community history, and is co-author of 'The Japanese' in *The Encyclopedia of Canada's Peoples*, ed. Paul Robert Magocsi (University of Toronto Press, 1999).

**Marilyn Barber** is an associate professor of history at Carleton University, Ottawa. Her research is in the fields of Canadian immigration and ethnic history, and women's history. She has published *Immigrant Domestic Servants in Canada* (Canadian Historical Association Booklet, 1991).

**Paula J. Draper** is an historian and educator who has published widely on the topic of memory history, Canada and the Holocaust. She is the historical consultant for the Toronto Holocaust Education and Memorial Centre, and was lead interviewer trainer for the Shoah Foundation. Dr Draper is presently researching the postwar experiences of Canadian Holocaust survivors.

**Enakshi Dua** is an associate professor in the School of Women's Studies at York University. She teaches anti-racist feminist theory, postcolonial studies, development studies, and globalization. She is the co-editor of *Scratching the Surface: Canadian Anti-Racist Feminist Thought* (Women's Press, 1999).

**Marlene Epp** is an associate professor of history at Conrad Grebel University College at the University of Waterloo. Her teaching and research are in the areas of women's history, immigration and ethnicity, and peace history. She is author of

*Women without Men: Mennonite Refugees of the Second World War* (University of Toronto Press, 2000).

**Karen Flynn** is an assistant professor in the Women's Studies Program at St Cloud State University, Minnesota. Her research interests include women, work, family, health, racism, feminism, and postcolonial theory. She writes a regular column for the community newspaper *Share*.

**Julie Guard** is an associate professor in the Economics Department at the University of Manitoba, where she teaches labour studies and coordinates the Labour and Workplace Studies Program. She is also a political activist and unionist. Her articles on gender, ethnicity, and working-class identity have been published in *Labour/Le Travail* and the *Journal of Women's History*.

**Franca Iacovetta** is a professor of history at the University of Toronto and co-editor of the Studies in Gender and History series at the University of Toronto Press. She is a feminist historian of women and immigrant workers and of immigration-refugee reception and moral regulation in post-1945 Canada. Her recent works include *On the Case: Explorations in Social History* (University of Toronto Press, 1998), edited with Wendy Mitchinson; *Women, Gender, and Transnational Lives: Italian Workers of the World* (University of Toronto Press, 2002), edited with Donna Gabaccia; and a book manuscript currently entitled *Cold War Citizens*.

**Isabel Kaprielian-Churchill** is professor of Armenian and immigration history, Department of History, California State University, Fresno, California. Her primary areas of teaching and writing include the Armenian diaspora, ethnic and immigration studies, genocide and refugee studies, and the history of children and the family. Her book, *Like Our Mountains: A History of Armenians in Canada* is forthcoming from McGill-Queen's University Press.

**Valerie J. Korinek** is an associate professor in the Department of History, University of Saskatchewan. A cultural and gender historian, she is currently working on a book entitled *Prairie Fairies: The History of Gay and Lesbian Communities in Western Canada, 1945–1980*. She is the author of *Roughing It in the Suburbs: Reading 'Chatelaine' Magazine in the Fifties and Sixties* (University of Toronto Press, 2000).

**Varpu Lindström** is a professor of history and women's studies at York University. Her research is on Canadian immigration and ethnic studies. Her publications include *Defiant Sisters: A Social History of Finnish Immigrant Women*, 3rd ed. (Aspasia Books, 2003, originally published by the Multicultural History Society of Ontario in 1988 under the name of Lindström-Best) and *From Heroes to Enemies: Finns in Canada, 1937–1947* (Aspasia Books, 2000).

**Lisa R. Mar** is an assistant professor in the Department of History and in the Asian American Studies Program at the University of Maryland at College Park. Her research explores the history of immigration, race, and ethnicity in Canada and the United States. She is currently working on a book about Chinese-Canadian leaders and citizenship politics in Vancouver from the 1920s to the 1960s.

**Lorna R. McLean** is an assistant professor in the Faculty of Education at the University of Ottawa. Her teaching and research are in the areas of history, education, citizenship, gender, immigration, and ethnicity. She is co-editor, with Sharon Anne Cook and Kate O'Rourke, of *Framing Our Past: Canadian Women's History in the Twentieth Century* (McGill-Queen's University Press, 2001).

**Gertrude Mianda** is an associate professor in the Departments of Sociology and Women's Studies at Glendon College, York University. Her research interests include gender, development, and globalization; colonialism and gender in Belgian Congo; and francophone African immigrant women in Canada.

**Cecilia Morgan** is an associate professor in the Department of Theory and Policy Studies, Ontario Institute for Studies in Education / University of Toronto. She teaches and researches in the areas of gender and women's history, cultural history, and the histories of colonialism, imperialism, and nationalism. Her most recent publication is, with Colin M. Coates, *Heroines and History: Representations of Madeleine de Verchères and Laura Secord* (University of Toronto Press, 2002).

**Adele Perry** is an associate professor of history and Tier II Canada Research Chair in Western Canadian Social History at the University of Manitoba. Her book *On the Edge of Empire: Gender, Race, and the Making of British Columbia* (University of Toronto Press, 2001) won the Clio prize for the best book on British Columbia history and co-won the American Historical Association–Pacific Branch prize.

**Ester Reiter** is an associate professor of social science and women's studies at Atkinson College, York University. Ester has been researching, writing about, and participating in the secular Jewish left in Toronto. She has recently become a member of the Camp Naivelt community.

**Frances Swyripa** is an associate professor of history at the University of Alberta in Edmonton. Her teaching and research are in the areas of women's history, immigration and ethnicity, and the Prairie West. She is the author of *Wedded to the Cause: Ukrainian-Canadian Women and Ethnic Identity, 1891–1991* (University of Toronto Press, 1993).

**Barrington Walker** is an assistant professor of history at Queen's University. His research and teaching are in the areas of Black Canadian history, race and race relations, and immigration history.

# Credits

*Chatelaine*: 'Meals Off the Shelf,' February 1955; 'Feed a Family of Five,' January 1961.

**Ester Reiter:** Camp Naivelt, collection of the author.

**Mennonite Central Committee Photography Collection,** Archives of the Mennonite Church, Goshen, Indiana: Mennonite women preparing meal.

**Midge Ayukawa:** Japanese school play.

*Montreal Standard*: 'Finnish Girls Are Fair,' 9 December 1939; Fanni Luukkonen, 9 December 1939.

*Montreal Star*: 'Women Behind Finland's Lines,' 29 December 1939; 'Help for Heroic Finland,' n.d.

*Toronto Star*: 'Women in Finland Stand ...,' 5 December 1939; 'She Watches ...,' 17 January 1940; 'Draft Women to Fight Reds,' 8 January 1940; 'Finnish Fighters Supported by Toronto Kin,' 6 December 1939; 'For Their Beloved Ancestral Finland ...,' 6 December 1939; 'Far from Home,' 4 January 1940; 'For War Work,' 4 January 1940.

*Toronto Star Weekly*: 'Typical of the hardy ...,' 16 December 1939; Tuuliki Paanen, 30 December 1939; Finnish women street cleaners, 30 December 1939.

IES IN GENDER AND HISTORY

General Editors: Franca Iacovetta and Karen Dubinsky